Toyota Tercel Automotive Repair Manual

by Larry Warren and John H Haynes

Member of the Guild of Motoring Writers

Models covered:

All Toyota Tercel sedan and liftback models
1987 through 1994
Does not include four-wheel drive or station wagon models

(2A2 - 92085)
(2106)

ABCDE
FGHIJ
KL

Haynes Publishing Group
Sparkford Nr Yeovil
Somerset BA22 7JJ England

Haynes North America, Inc
861 Lawrence Drive
Newbury Park
California 91320 USA

Acknowledgements
We are grateful to the Toyota Motor Corporation for their assistance with technical information and certain illustrations. Technical writers who contributed to this project include Rob Maddox, Mike Stubblefield and Mark Ryan.

© **Haynes North America, Inc. 1995**

With permission from J.H. Haynes & Co. Ltd.

A book in the Haynes Automotive Repair Manual Series

Printed in the U.S.A.

ISBN 1 56392 106 5

Library of Congress Catalog Card Number 95-75234

Contents

Haynes mechanic, author and photographer with 1990 Toyota Tercel

About this manual

Its purpose

The purpose of this manual is to help you get the best value from your vehicle. It can do so in several ways. It can help you decide what work must be done, even if you choose to have it done by a dealer service department or a repair shop; it provides information and procedures for routine maintenance and servicing; and it offers diagnostic and repair procedures to follow when trouble occurs.

We hope you use the manual to tackle the work yourself. For many simpler jobs, doing it yourself may be quicker than arranging an appointment to get the vehicle into a shop and making the trips to leave it and pick it up. More importantly, a lot of money can be saved by avoiding the expense the shop must pass on to you to cover its labor and overhead costs. An added benefit is the sense of satisfaction and accomplishment that you feel after doing the job yourself.

Using the manual

The manual is divided into Chapters. Each Chapter is divided into numbered Sections, which are headed in bold type between horizontal lines. Each Section consists of consecutively numbered paragraphs.

At the beginning of each numbered Section you will be referred to any illustrations which apply to the procedures in that Section. The reference numbers used in illustration captions pinpoint the pertinent Section and the Step within that Section. That is, illustration 3.2 means the illustration refers to Section 3 and Step (or paragraph) 2 within that Section.

Procedures, once described in the text, are not normally repeated. When it's necessary to refer to another Chapter, the reference will be given as Chapter and Section number. Cross references given without use of the word "Chapter" apply to Sections and/or paragraphs in the same Chapter. For example, "see Section 8" means in the same Chapter.

References to the left or right side of the vehicle assume you are sitting in the driver's seat, facing forward.

Even though we have prepared this manual with extreme care, neither the publisher nor the author can accept responsibility for any errors in, or omissions from, the information given.

NOTE

A **Note** provides information necessary to properly complete a procedure or information which will make the procedure easier to understand.

CAUTION

A **Caution** provides a special procedure or special steps which must be taken while completing the procedure where the Caution is found. Not heeding a Caution can result in damage to the assembly being worked on.

WARNING

A **Warning** provides a special procedure or special steps which must be taken while completing the procedure where the Warning is found. Not heeding a Warning can result in personal injury.

Introduction to the Toyota Tercel

Toyota Tercel models are available in two-and four-door sedan and liftback body styles.

The transversely mounted inline four-cylinder engines used in these models are equipped with both carbureted and electronic fuel injection.

The engine drives the front wheels through either a four- or five-speed manual or a three-speed automatic transaxle via independent driveaxles.

Independent suspension, featuring coil spring/strut damper units, is used on the front wheels while a beam axle and coil spring/strut dampers are used at the rear. The rack and pinion steering unit is mounted behind the engine with power-assist available as an option.

The brakes are disc at the front and drums at the rear, with power assist standard. An Anti-lock Brake System (ABS) became available on later models.

Vehicle identification numbers

Modifications are a continuing and unpublicized process in vehicle manufacturing. Since spare parts manuals and lists are compiled on a numerical basis, the individual vehicle numbers are essential to correctly identify the component required.

Vehicle Identification Number (VIN)

This very important identification number is stamped on the firewall in the engine compartment and on a plate attached to the dashboard inside the windshield on the driver's side of the vehicle **(see illustration)**. The VIN also appears on the Vehicle Certificate of Title and Registration. It contains information such as where and when the vehicle was manufactured, the model year and the body style.

Manufacturer's Certification Regulation label

The manufacturer's Certification Regulation label is attached to the driver's side door end or post **(see illustration)**. The plate contains the name of the manufacturer, the month and year of production, the Gross Vehicle Weight Rating (GVWR), the Gross Axle Weight Rating (GAWR) and the certification statement.

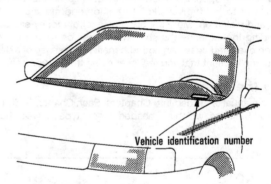

Vehicle identification number

The Vehicle Identification Number (VIN) is visible through the driver's side of the windshield

Engine number

The engine code number can be found on a pad on the front (radiator) side of the cylinder block **(see illustration)**.

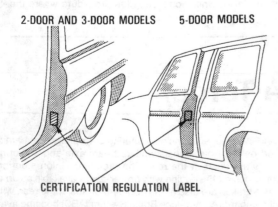

2-DOOR AND 3-DOOR MODELS   5-DOOR MODELS

CERTIFICATION REGULATION LABEL

Location of the Certification Regulation labels

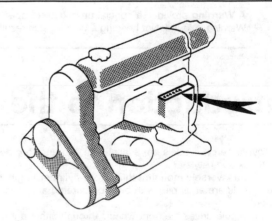

Location of the engine identification number

Buying parts

Replacement parts are available from many sources, which generally fall into one of two categories - authorized dealer parts departments and independent retail auto parts stores. Our advice concerning these parts is as follows:

Retail auto parts stores: Good auto parts stores will stock frequently needed components which wear out relatively fast, such as clutch components, exhaust systems, brake parts, tune-up parts, etc. These stores often supply new or reconditioned parts on an exchange basis, which can save a considerable amount of money. Discount auto parts stores are often very good places to buy materials and parts needed for general vehicle maintenance such as oil, grease, filters, spark plugs, belts, touch-up paint, bulbs, etc. They also usually sell tools and general accessories, have convenient hours, charge lower prices and can often be found not far from home.

Authorized dealer parts department: This is the best source for parts which are unique to the vehicle and not generally available elsewhere (such as major engine parts, transmission parts, trim pieces, etc.).

Warranty information: If the vehicle is still covered under warranty, be sure that any replacement parts purchased - regardless of the source - do not invalidate the warranty!

To be sure of obtaining the correct parts, have engine and chassis numbers available and, if possible, take the old parts along for positive identification.

Maintenance techniques, tools and working facilities

Maintenance techniques

There are a number of techniques involved in maintenance and repair that will be referred to throughout this manual. Application of these techniques will enable the home mechanic to be more efficient, better organized and capable of performing the various tasks properly, which will ensure that the repair job is thorough and complete.

Fasteners

Fasteners are nuts, bolts, studs and screws used to hold two or more parts together. There are a few things to keep in mind when working with fasteners. Almost all of them use a locking device of some type, either a lockwasher, locknut, locking tab or thread adhesive. All threaded fasteners should be clean and straight, with undamaged threads and undamaged corners on the hex head where the wrench fits. Develop the habit of replacing all damaged nuts and bolts with new ones. Special locknuts with nylon or fiber inserts can only be used once. If they are removed, they lose their locking ability and must be replaced with new ones.

Rusted nuts and bolts should be treated with a penetrating fluid to ease removal and prevent breakage. Some mechanics use turpentine in a spout-type oil can, which works quite well. After applying the rust penetrant, let it work for a few minutes before trying to loosen the nut or bolt. Badly rusted fasteners may have to be chiseled or sawed off or removed with a special nut breaker, available at tool stores.

If a bolt or stud breaks off in an assembly, it can be drilled and removed with a special tool commonly available for this purpose. Most automotive machine shops can perform this task, as well as other repair procedures, such as the repair of threaded holes that have been stripped out.

Flat washers and lockwashers, when removed from an assembly, should always be replaced exactly as removed. Replace any damaged washers with new ones. Never use a lockwasher on any soft metal surface (such as aluminum), thin sheet metal or plastic.

Fastener sizes

For a number of reasons, automobile manufacturers are making wider and wider use of metric fasteners. Therefore, it is important to be able to tell the difference between standard (sometimes called U.S. or SAE) and metric hardware, since they cannot be interchanged.

All bolts, whether standard or metric, are sized according to diameter, thread pitch and length. For example, a standard 1/2 - 13 x 1 bolt is 1/2 inch in diameter, has 13 threads per inch and is 1 inch long. An M12 - 1.75 x 25 metric bolt is 12 mm in diameter, has a thread pitch of 1.75 mm (the distance between threads) and is 25 mm long. The two bolts are nearly identical, and easily confused, but they are not interchangeable.

In addition to the differences in diameter, thread pitch and length, metric and standard bolts can also be distinguished by examining the bolt heads. To begin with, the distance across the flats on a standard bolt head is measured in inches, while the same dimension on a metric bolt is sized in millimeters (the same is true for nuts). As a result, a standard wrench should not be used on a metric bolt and a metric wrench should not be used on a standard bolt. Also, most standard bolts have slashes radiating out from the center of the head to denote the grade or strength of the bolt, which is an indication of the amount of torque that can be applied to it. The greater the number of slashes, the greater the strength of the bolt. Grades 0 through 5 are commonly used on automobiles. Metric bolts have a property class (grade) number, rather than a slash, molded into their heads to indicate bolt strength. In this case, the higher the number, the stronger the bolt. Property class numbers 8.8, 9.8 and 10.9 are commonly used on automobiles.

Strength markings can also be used to distinguish standard hex nuts from metric hex nuts. Many standard nuts have dots stamped into one side, while metric nuts are marked with a number. The greater the number of dots, or the higher the number, the greater the strength of the nut.

Metric studs are also marked on their ends according to property class (grade). Larger studs are numbered (the same as metric bolts), while smaller studs carry a geometric code to denote grade.

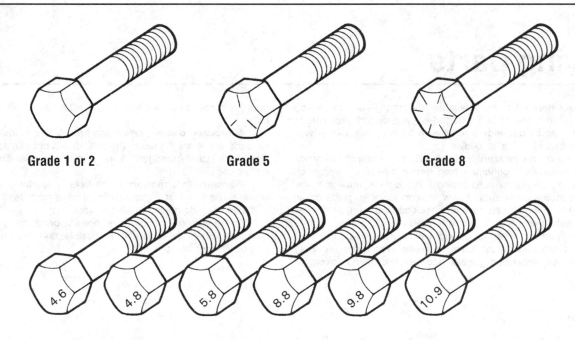

Bolt strength markings (top - standard/SAE/USS; bottom - metric)

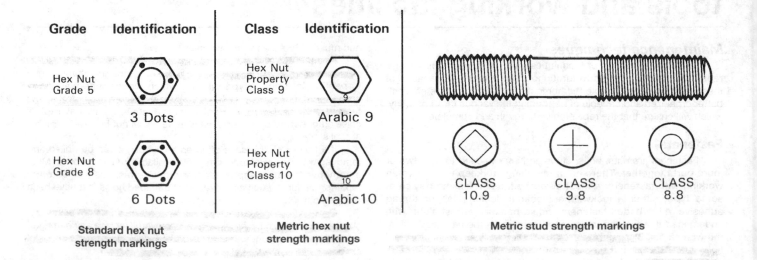

Standard hex nut strength markings

Metric hex nut strength markings

Metric stud strength markings

It should be noted that many fasteners, especially Grades 0 through 2, have no distinguishing marks on them. When such is the case, the only way to determine whether it is standard or metric is to measure the thread pitch or compare it to a known fastener of the same size.

Standard fasteners are often referred to as SAE, as opposed to metric. However, it should be noted that SAE technically refers to a non-metric fine thread fastener only. Coarse thread non-metric fasteners are referred to as USS sizes.

Since fasteners of the same size (both standard and metric) may have different strength ratings, be sure to reinstall any bolts, studs or nuts removed from your vehicle in their original locations. Also, when replacing a fastener with a new one, make sure that the new one has a strength rating equal to or greater than the original.

Tightening sequences and procedures

Most threaded fasteners should be tightened to a specific torque value (torque is the twisting force applied to a threaded component such as a nut or bolt). Overtightening the fastener can weaken it and cause it to break, while undertightening can cause it to eventually come loose. Bolts, screws and studs, depending on the material they are made of and their thread diameters, have specific torque values, many of which are noted in the Specifications at the beginning of each Chapter. Be sure to follow the torque recommendations closely. For fasteners not assigned a specific torque, a general torque value chart is presented here as a guide. These torque values are for dry (unlubricated) fasteners threaded into steel or cast iron (not aluminum). As was previously mentioned, the size and grade of a fastener determine the amount of torque that can safely be applied to it. The

Metric thread sizes	Ft-lbs	Nm
M-6	6 to 9	9 to 12
M-8	14 to 21	19 to 28
M-10	28 to 40	38 to 54
M-12	50 to 71	68 to 96
M-14	80 to 140	109 to 154

Pipe thread sizes		
1/8	5 to 8	7 to 10
1/4	12 to 18	17 to 24
3/8	22 to 33	30 to 44
1/2	25 to 35	34 to 47

U.S. thread sizes		
1/4 - 20	6 to 9	9 to 12
5/16 - 18	12 to 18	17 to 24
5/16 - 24	14 to 20	19 to 27
3/8 - 16	22 to 32	30 to 43
3/8 - 24	27 to 38	37 to 51
7/16 - 14	40 to 55	55 to 74
7/16 - 20	40 to 60	55 to 81
1/2 - 13	55 to 80	75 to 108

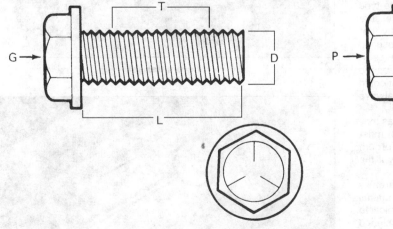

Standard (SAE and USS) bolt dimensions/grade marks

G   Grade marks (bolt length)
L   Length (in inches)
T   Thread pitch (number of threads per inch)
D   Nominal diameter (in inches)

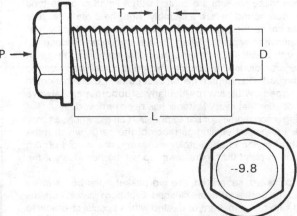

Metric bolt dimensions/grade marks

P   Property class (bolt strength)
L   Length (in millimeters)
T   Thread pitch (distance between threads in millimeters)
D   Diameter

figures listed here are approximate for Grade 2 and Grade 3 fasteners. Higher grades can tolerate higher torque values.

Fasteners laid out in a pattern, such as cylinder head bolts, oil pan bolts, differential cover bolts, etc., must be loosened or tightened in sequence to avoid warping the component. This sequence will normally be shown in the appropriate Chapter. If a specific pattern is not given, the following procedures can be used to prevent warping.

Initially, the bolts or nuts should be assembled finger-tight only. Next, they should be tightened one full turn each, in a criss-cross or diagonal pattern. After each one has been tightened one full turn, return to the first one and tighten them all one-half turn, following the same pattern. Finally, tighten each of them one-quarter turn at a time until each fastener has been tightened to the proper torque. To loosen and remove the fasteners, the procedure would be reversed.

Component disassembly

Component disassembly should be done with care and purpose to help ensure that the parts go back together properly. Always keep track of the sequence in which parts are removed. Make note of special characteristics or marks on parts that can be installed more than one way, such as a grooved thrust washer on a shaft. It is a good idea to lay the disassembled parts out on a clean surface in the order that they were removed. It may also be helpful to make sketches or take instant photos of components before removal.

When removing fasteners from a component, keep track of their locations. Sometimes threading a bolt back in a part, or putting the washers and nut back on a stud, can prevent mix-ups later. If nuts and bolts cannot be returned to their original locations, they should be kept in a compartmented box or a series of small boxes. A cupcake or muffin tin is ideal for this purpose, since each cavity can hold the bolts and nuts from a particular area (i.e. oil pan bolts, valve cover bolts, engine mount bolts, etc.). A pan of this type is especially helpful when working on assemblies with very small parts, such as the carburetor, alternator, valve train or interior dash and trim pieces. The cavities can be marked with paint or tape to identify the contents.

Whenever wiring looms, harnesses or connectors are separated, it is a good idea to identify the two halves with numbered pieces of masking tape so they can be easily reconnected.

Gasket sealing surfaces

Throughout any vehicle, gaskets are used to seal the mating surfaces between two parts and keep lubricants, fluids, vacuum or pressure contained in an assembly.

Many times these gaskets are coated with a liquid or paste-type gasket sealing compound before assembly. Age, heat and pressure can sometimes cause the two parts to stick together so tightly that they are very difficult to separate. Often, the assembly can be loosened by striking it with a soft-face hammer near the mating surfaces. A regular hammer can be used if a block of wood is placed between the hammer and the part. Do not hammer on cast parts or parts that could be easily damaged. With any particularly stubborn part, always recheck to make sure that every fastener has been removed.

Avoid using a screwdriver or bar to pry apart an assembly, as they can easily mar the gasket sealing surfaces of the parts, which must remain smooth. If prying is absolutely necessary, use an old broom handle, but keep in mind that extra clean up will be necessary if the wood splinters.

After the parts are separated, the old gasket must be carefully scraped off and the gasket surfaces cleaned. Stubborn gasket material can be soaked with rust penetrant or treated with a special chemical to soften it so it can be easily scraped off. A scraper can be fashioned from a piece of copper tubing by flattening and sharpening one end. Copper is recommended because it is usually softer than the surfaces to be scraped, which reduces the chance of gouging the part. Some gaskets can be removed with a wire brush, but regardless of the method used, the mating surfaces must be left clean and smooth. If for some reason the gasket surface is gouged, then a gasket sealer thick enough to fill scratches will have to be used during reassembly of the components. For most applications, a non-drying (or semi-drying) gasket sealer should be used.

Hose removal tips

Warning: *If the vehicle is equipped with air conditioning, do not disconnect any of the A/C hoses without first having the system depressurized by a dealer service department or a service station.*

Hose removal precautions closely parallel gasket removal precautions. Avoid scratching or gouging the surface that the hose mates against or the connection may leak. This is especially true for radiator hoses. Because of various chemical reactions, the rubber in hoses can bond itself to the metal spigot that the hose fits over. To remove a hose, first loosen the hose clamps that secure it to the spigot. Then, with slip-joint pliers, grab the hose at the clamp and rotate it around the spigot. Work it back and forth until it is completely free, then pull it off. Silicone or other lubricants will ease removal if they can be applied between the hose and the outside of the spigot. Apply the same lubricant to the inside of the hose and the outside of the spigot to simplify installation.

As a last resort (and if the hose is to be replaced with a new one anyway), the rubber can be slit with a knife and the hose peeled from the spigot. If this must be done, be careful that the metal connection is not damaged.

If a hose clamp is broken or damaged, do not reuse it. Wire-type clamps usually weaken with age, so it is a good idea to replace them with screw-type clamps whenever a hose is removed.

Tools

A selection of good tools is a basic requirement for anyone who plans to maintain and repair his or her own vehicle. For the owner who has few tools, the initial investment might seem high, but when compared to the spiraling costs of professional auto maintenance and repair, it is a wise one.

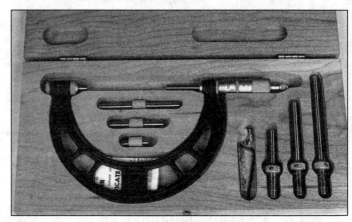

Micrometer set

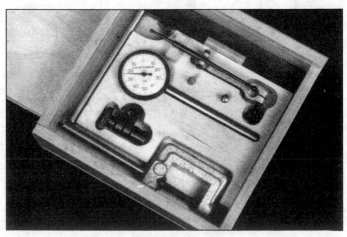

Dial indicator set

Dial caliper

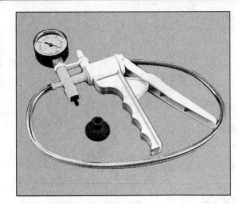

Hand-operated vacuum pump

Timing light

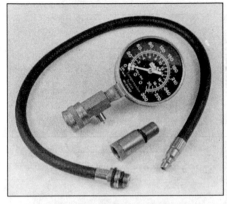

Compression gauge with spark plug hole adapter

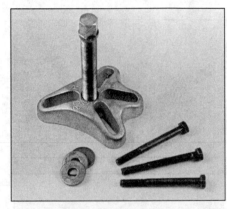

Damper/steering wheel puller

General purpose puller

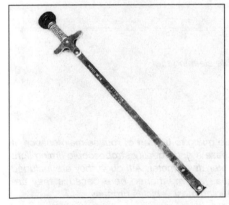

Hydraulic lifter removal tool

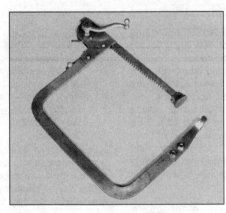

Valve spring compressor

Valve spring compressor

Ridge reamer

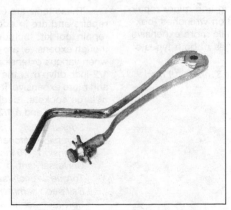

Piston ring groove cleaning tool

Ring removal/installation tool

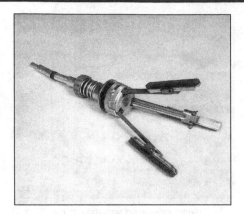

Ring compressor

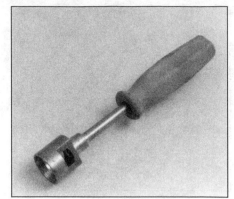

Brake hold-down spring tool

Brake cylinder hone

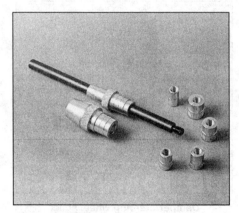

Clutch plate alignment tool

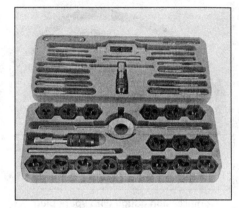

Tap and die set

To help the owner decide which tools are needed to perform the tasks detailed in this manual, the following tool lists are offered: *Maintenance and minor repair, Repair/overhaul* and *Special.*

The newcomer to practical mechanics should start off with the *maintenance and minor repair* tool kit, which is adequate for the simpler jobs performed on a vehicle. Then, as confidence and experience grow, the owner can tackle more difficult tasks, buying additional tools as they are needed. Eventually the basic kit will be expanded into the *repair and overhaul* tool set. Over a period of time, the experienced do-it-yourselfer will assemble a tool set complete enough for most repair and overhaul procedures and will add tools from the special category when it is felt that the expense is justified by the frequency of use.

Maintenance and minor repair tool kit

The tools in this list should be considered the minimum required for performance of routine maintenance, servicing and minor repair work. We recommend the purchase of combination wrenches (box-end and open-end combined in one wrench). While more expensive than open end wrenches, they offer the advantages of both types of wrench.

> *Combination wrench set (1/4-inch to 1 inch or 6 mm to 19 mm)*
> *Adjustable wrench, 8 inch*
> *Spark plug wrench with rubber insert*
> *Spark plug gap adjusting tool*
> *Feeler gauge set*
> *Brake bleeder wrench*
> *Standard screwdriver (5/16-inch x 6 inch)*
> *Phillips screwdriver (No. 2 x 6 inch)*
> *Combination pliers - 6 inch*
> *Hacksaw and assortment of blades*
> *Tire pressure gauge*
> *Grease gun*

> *Oil can*
> *Fine emery cloth*
> *Wire brush*
> *Battery post and cable cleaning tool*
> *Oil filter wrench*
> *Funnel (medium size)*
> *Safety goggles*
> *Jackstands (2)*
> *Drain pan*

Note: *If basic tune-ups are going to be part of routine maintenance, it will be necessary to purchase a good quality stroboscopic timing light and combination tachometer/dwell meter. Although they are included in the list of special tools, it is mentioned here because they are absolutely necessary for tuning most vehicles properly.*

Repair and overhaul tool set

These tools are essential for anyone who plans to perform major repairs and are in addition to those in the maintenance and minor repair tool kit. Included is a comprehensive set of sockets which, though expensive, are invaluable because of their versatility, especially when various extensions and drives are available. We recommend the 1/2-inch drive over the 3/8-inch drive. Although the larger drive is bulky and more expensive, it has the capacity of accepting a very wide range of large sockets. Ideally, however, the mechanic should have a 3/8-inch drive set and a 1/2-inch drive set.

> *Socket set(s)*
> *Reversible ratchet*
> *Extension - 10 inch*
> *Universal joint*
> *Torque wrench (same size drive as sockets)*
> *Ball peen hammer - 8 ounce*
> *Soft-face hammer (plastic/rubber)*
> *Standard screwdriver (1/4-inch x 6 inch)*

Standard screwdriver (stubby - 5/16-inch)
Phillips screwdriver (No. 3 x 8 inch)
Phillips screwdriver (stubby - No. 2)
Pliers - vise grip
Pliers - lineman's
Pliers - needle nose
Pliers - snap-ring (internal and external)
Cold chisel - 1/2-inch
Scribe
Scraper (made from flattened copper tubing)
Centerpunch
Pin punches (1/16, 1/8, 3/16-inch)
Steel rule/straightedge - 12 inch
Allen wrench set (1/8 to 3/8-inch or 4 mm to 10 mm)
A selection of files
Wire brush (large)
Jackstands (second set)
Jack (scissor or hydraulic type)

Note: *Another tool which is often useful is an electric drill with a chuck capacity of 3/8-inch and a set of good quality drill bits.*

Special tools

The tools in this list include those which are not used regularly, are expensive to buy, or which need to be used in accordance with their manufacturer's instructions. Unless these tools will be used frequently, it is not very economical to purchase many of them. A consideration would be to split the cost and use between yourself and a friend or friends. In addition, most of these tools can be obtained from a tool rental shop on a temporary basis.

This list primarily contains only those tools and instruments widely available to the public, and not those special tools produced by the vehicle manufacturer for distribution to dealer service departments. Occasionally, references to the manufacturer's special tools are included in the text of this manual. Generally, an alternative method of doing the job without the special tool is offered. However, sometimes there is no alternative to their use. Where this is the case, and the tool cannot be purchased or borrowed, the work should be turned over to the dealer service department or an automotive repair shop.

Valve spring compressor
Piston ring groove cleaning tool
Piston ring compressor
Piston ring installation tool
Cylinder compression gauge
Cylinder ridge reamer
Cylinder surfacing hone
Cylinder bore gauge
Micrometers and/or dial calipers
Hydraulic lifter removal tool
Balljoint separator
Universal-type puller
Impact screwdriver
Dial indicator set
Stroboscopic timing light (inductive pick-up)
Hand operated vacuum/pressure pump
Tachometer/dwell meter
Universal electrical multimeter
Cable hoist
Brake spring removal and installation tools
Floor jack

Buying tools

For the do-it-yourselfer who is just starting to get involved in vehicle maintenance and repair, there are a number of options available when purchasing tools. If maintenance and minor repair is the extent of the work to be done, the purchase of individual tools is satisfactory. If, on the other hand, extensive work is planned, it would be a good idea to purchase a modest tool set from one of the large retail chain stores. A set can usually be bought at a substantial savings over the individual tool prices, and they often come with a tool box. As additional tools are needed, add-on sets, individual tools and a larger tool box can be purchased to expand the tool selection. Building a tool set gradually allows the cost of the tools to be spread over a longer period of time and gives the mechanic the freedom to choose only those tools that will actually be used.

Tool stores will often be the only source of some of the special tools that are needed, but regardless of where tools are bought, try to avoid cheap ones, especially when buying screwdrivers and sockets, because they won't last very long. The expense involved in replacing cheap tools will eventually be greater than the initial cost of quality tools.

Care and maintenance of tools

Good tools are expensive, so it makes sense to treat them with respect. Keep them clean and in usable condition and store them properly when not in use. Always wipe off any dirt, grease or metal chips before putting them away. Never leave tools lying around in the work area. Upon completion of a job, always check closely under the hood for tools that may have been left there so they won't get lost during a test drive.

Some tools, such as screwdrivers, pliers, wrenches and sockets, can be hung on a panel mounted on the garage or workshop wall, while others should be kept in a tool box or tray. Measuring instruments, gauges, meters, etc. must be carefully stored where they cannot be damaged by weather or impact from other tools.

When tools are used with care and stored properly, they will last a very long time. Even with the best of care, though, tools will wear out if used frequently. When a tool is damaged or worn out, replace it. Subsequent jobs will be safer and more enjoyable if you do.

Working facilities

Not to be overlooked when discussing tools is the workshop. If anything more than routine maintenance is to be carried out, some sort of suitable work area is essential.

It is understood, and appreciated, that many home mechanics do not have a good workshop or garage available, and end up removing an engine or doing major repairs outside. It is recommended, however, that the overhaul or repair be completed under the cover of a roof.

A clean, flat workbench or table of comfortable working height is an absolute necessity. The workbench should be equipped with a vise that has a jaw opening of at least four inches.

As mentioned previously, some clean, dry storage space is also required for tools, as well as the lubricants, fluids, cleaning solvents, etc. which soon become necessary.

Sometimes waste oil and fluids, drained from the engine or cooling system during normal maintenance or repairs, present a disposal problem. To avoid pouring them on the ground or into a sewage system, pour the used fluids into large containers, seal them with caps and take them to an authorized disposal site or recycling center. Plastic jugs, such as old antifreeze containers, are ideal for this purpose.

Always keep a supply of old newspapers and clean rags available. Old towels are excellent for mopping up spills. Many mechanics use rolls of paper towels for most work because they are readily available and disposable. To help keep the area under the vehicle clean, a large cardboard box can be cut open and flattened to protect the garage or shop floor.

Whenever working over a painted surface, such as when leaning over a fender to service something under the hood, always cover it with an old blanket or bedspread to protect the finish. Vinyl covered pads, made especially for this purpose, are available at auto parts stores.

Jacking and towing

Jacking

Warning: *The jack supplied with the vehicle should only be used for changing a tire or placing jackstands under the frame. Never work under the vehicle or start the engine while this jack is being used as the only means of support.*

The vehicle should be on level ground. Place the shift lever in Park, if you have an automatic, or Reverse if you have a manual transaxle. Block the wheel diagonally opposite the wheel being changed. Set the parking brake.

Remove the spare tire and jack from stowage. Remove the wheel cover and trim ring (if so equipped) with the tapered end of the lug nut wrench by inserting and twisting the handle and then prying against the back of the wheel cover. On aluminum wheels, tap the back side of the wheel hub cover after removing the wheel (do not attempt to pull off the wheel hub cover by hand). Loosen, but do not remove, the lug nuts (one-half turn is sufficient).

Place the scissors-type jack under the side of the vehicle and adjust the jack height until it fits between the notches in the vertical rocker panel flange nearest the wheel to be changed. There is a front and rear jacking point on each side of the vehicle **(see illustration)**.

Turn the jack handle clockwise until the tire clears the ground. Remove the lug nuts and pull the wheel off. Replace it with the spare.

Install the lug nuts with the beveled edges facing in. Tighten them snugly. Don't attempt to tighten them completely until the vehicle is lowered or it could slip off the jack. Turn the jack handle counter-clockwise to lower the vehicle. Remove the jack and tighten the lug nuts in a diagonal pattern.

Install the cover (and trim ring, if used) and be sure it's snapped into place all the way around.

Stow the tire, jack and wrench. Unblock the wheels.

Towing

As a general rule, the vehicle should be towed with the front (drive) wheels off the ground. If they can't be raised, place them on a dolly. The ignition key must be in the ACC position, since the steering lock mechanism isn't strong enough to hold the front wheels straight while towing.

On 1990 and earlier models, vehicles equipped with an automatic transaxle can be towed from the front only with all four wheels on the ground, provided that speeds don't exceed 30 mph and the distance is

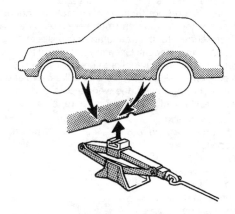

The jack fits over the rocker panel flange, between the two notches (there are two jacking points on each side of the vehicle)

not over 50 miles. Before towing, check the transmission fluid level (see Chapter 1). If the level is below the HOT line on the dipstick, add fluid or use a towing dolly.

When towing a vehicle equipped with a manual transaxle with all four wheels on the ground, be sure to place the shift lever in neutral and release the parking brake.

Equipment specifically designed for towing should be used. It should be attached to the main structural members of the vehicle, not the bumpers or brackets.

Safety is a major consideration when towing and all applicable state and local laws must be obeyed. A safety chain system must be used at all times.

On 1991 and later models, the manufacturer does not recommend towing except with a towing dolly under the front wheels. In an emergency the vehicle can be towed a short distance with a cable or chain attached to one of the towing eyelets located under the front or rear bumpers following the precautions above. The driver must remain in the vehicle to operate the steering and brakes (remember that power steering and power brakes will not work with the engine off).

Booster battery (jump) starting

Observe these precautions when using a booster battery to start a vehicle:

a) *Before connecting the booster battery, make sure the ignition switch is in the Off position.*
b) *Turn off the lights, heater and other electrical loads.*
c) *Your eyes should be shielded. Safety goggles are a good idea.*
d) *Make sure the booster battery is the same voltage as the dead one In the vehicle.*
e) *The two vehicles MUST NOT TOUCH each other!*
f) *Make sure the transaxle is in Neutral (manual) or Park (automatic).*
g) *If the booster battery is not a maintenance-free type, remove the vent caps and lay a cloth over the vent holes.*

Connect the red jumper cable to the positive (+) terminals of each battery **(see illustration)**.

Connect one end of the black jumper cable to the negative (-) terminal of the booster battery. The other end of this cable should be connected to a good ground on the vehicle to be started, such as a bolt or bracket on the body.

Start the engine using the booster battery, then, with the engine running at idle speed, disconnect the jumper cables in the reverse order of connection.

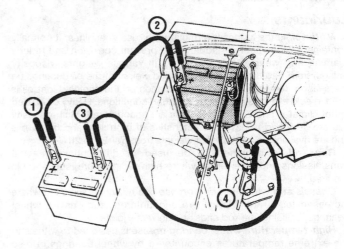

Make the booster battery cable connections in the numerical order shown (note that the negative cable of the booster battery is NOT attached to the negative terminal of the dead battery)

Stereo anti-theft system precaution

Stereo systems displaying "ANTI-THEFT SYSTEM" on the cassette tape slot cover have a built-in theft deterrent system designed to render the stereo inoperative should the stereo be stolen. If the power source to the stereo is cut, the anti-theft system will activate. Even if the power source is immediately reconnected, the stereo will not function. If your vehicle is equipped with this anti-theft system, do not disconnect the cable from the negative terminal of the battery, remove the stereo or disconnect related components unless you have the individual ID (code) number for the stereo.

If you discover that the system is inoperative after disconnecting and reconnecting the power source, enter the ID number. If the wrong number is entered, "Err" will appear on the display. You may make up to nine errors - a tenth error will activate the system and "HELP" will appear on the display. If this occurs, contact your local Toyota dealer service department.

Automotive chemicals and lubricants

A number of automotive chemicals and lubricants are available for use during vehicle maintenance and repair. They include a wide variety of products ranging from cleaning solvents and degreasers to lubricants and protective sprays for rubber, plastic and vinyl.

Cleaners

Carburetor cleaner and choke cleaner is a strong solvent for gum, varnish and carbon. Most carburetor cleaners leave a dry-type lubricant film which will not harden or gum up. Because of this film it is not recommended for use on electrical components.

Brake system cleaner is used to remove grease and brake fluid from the brake system, where clean surfaces are absolutely necessary. It leaves no residue and often eliminates brake squeal caused by contaminants.

Electrical cleaner removes oxidation, corrosion and carbon deposits from electrical contacts, restoring full current flow. It can also be used to clean spark plugs, carburetor jets, voltage regulators and other parts where an oil-free surface is desired.

Demoisturants remove water and moisture from electrical components such as alternators, voltage regulators, electrical connectors and fuse blocks. They are non-conductive, non-corrosive and non-flammable.

Degreasers are heavy-duty solvents used to remove grease from the outside of the engine and from chassis components. They can be sprayed or brushed on and, depending on the type, are rinsed off either with water or solvent.

Lubricants

Motor oil is the lubricant formulated for use in engines. It normally contains a wide variety of additives to prevent corrosion and reduce foaming and wear. Motor oil comes in various weights (viscosity ratings) from 5 to 80. The recommended weight of the oil depends on the season, temperature and the demands on the engine. Light oil is used in cold climates and under light load conditions. Heavy oil is used in hot climates and where high loads are encountered. Multi-viscosity oils are designed to have characteristics of both light and heavy oils and are available in a number of weights from 5W-20 to 20W-50.

Gear oil is designed to be used in differentials, manual transmissions and other areas where high-temperature lubrication is required.

Chassis and wheel bearing grease is a heavy grease used where increased loads and friction are encountered, such as for wheel bearings, balljoints, tie-rod ends and universal joints.

High-temperature wheel bearing grease is designed to withstand the extreme temperatures encountered by wheel bearings in disc brake equipped vehicles. It usually contains molybdenum disulfide (moly), which is a dry-type lubricant.

White grease is a heavy grease for metal-to-metal applications where water is a problem. White grease stays soft under both low and high temperatures (usually from -100 to +190-degrees F), and will not wash off or dilute in the presence of water.

Assembly lube is a special extreme pressure lubricant, usually containing moly, used to lubricate high-load parts (such as main and rod bearings and cam lobes) for initial start-up of a new engine. The assembly lube lubricates the parts without being squeezed out or washed away until the engine oiling system begins to function.

Silicone lubricants are used to protect rubber, plastic, vinyl and nylon parts.

Graphite lubricants are used where oils cannot be used due to contamination problems, such as in locks. The dry graphite will lubricate metal parts while remaining uncontaminated by dirt, water, oil or acids. It is electrically conductive and will not foul electrical contacts in locks such as the ignition switch.

Moly penetrants loosen and lubricate frozen, rusted and corroded fasteners and prevent future rusting or freezing.

Heat-sink grease is a special electrically non-conductive grease that is used for mounting electronic ignition modules where it is essential that heat is transferred away from the module.

Sealants

RTV sealant is one of the most widely used gasket compounds. Made from silicone, RTV is air curing, it seals, bonds, waterproofs, fills surface irregularities, remains flexible, doesn't shrink, is relatively easy to remove, and is used as a supplementary sealer with almost all low and medium temperature gaskets.

Anaerobic sealant is much like RTV in that it can be used either to seal gaskets or to form gaskets by itself. It remains flexible, is solvent resistant and fills surface imperfections. The difference between an anaerobic sealant and an RTV-type sealant is in the curing. RTV cures when exposed to air, while an anaerobic sealant cures only in the absence of air. This means that an anaerobic sealant cures only after the assembly of parts, sealing them together.

Thread and pipe sealant is used for sealing hydraulic and pneumatic fittings and vacuum lines. It is usually made from a Teflon compound, and comes in a spray, a paint-on liquid and as a wrap-around tape.

Chemicals

Anti-seize compound prevents seizing, galling, cold welding, rust and corrosion in fasteners. High-temperature ant-seize, usually made with copper and graphite lubricants, is used for exhaust system and exhaust manifold bolts.

Anaerobic locking compounds are used to keep fasteners from vibrating or working loose and cure only after installation, in the absence of air. Medium strength locking compound is used for small nuts, bolts and screws that may be removed later. High-strength locking compound is for large nuts, bolts and studs which aren't removed on a regular basis.

Oil additives range from viscosity index improvers to chemical treatments that claim to reduce internal engine friction. It should be noted that most oil manufacturers caution against using additives with their oils.

Gas additives perform several functions, depending on their chemical makeup. They usually contain solvents that help dissolve gum and varnish that build up on carburetor, fuel injection and intake parts. They also serve to break down carbon deposits that form on the inside surfaces of the combustion chambers. Some additives contain upper cylinder lubricants for valves and piston rings, and others contain chemicals to remove condensation from the gas tank.

Miscellaneous

Brake fluid is specially formulated hydraulic fluid that can withstand the heat and pressure encountered in brake systems. Care must be taken so this fluid does not come in contact with painted surfaces or plastics. An opened container should always be resealed to prevent contamination by water or dirt.

Weatherstrip adhesive is used to bond weatherstripping around doors, windows and trunk lids. It is sometimes used to attach trim pieces.

Undercoating is a petroleum-based, tar-like substance that is designed to protect metal surfaces on the underside of the vehicle from corrosion. It also acts as a sound-deadening agent by insulating the bottom of the vehicle.

Waxes and polishes are used to help protect painted and plated surfaces from the weather. Different types of paint may require the use of different types of wax and polish. Some polishes utilize a chemical or abrasive cleaner to help remove the top layer of oxidized (dull) paint on older vehicles. In recent years many non-wax polishes that contain a wide variety of chemicals such as polymers and silicones have been introduced. These non-wax polishes are usually easier to apply and last longer than conventional waxes and polishes.

Conversion factors

Length (distance)
	X		=		X		=	
Inches (in)	X	25.4	=	Millimetres (mm)	X	0.0394	=	Inches (in)
Feet (ft)	X	0.305	=	Metres (m)	X	3.281	=	Feet (ft)
Miles	X	1.609	=	Kilometres (km)	X	0.621	=	Miles

Volume (capacity)
Cubic inches (cu in; in^3)	X	16.387	=	Cubic centimetres (cc; cm^3)	X	0.061	=	Cubic inches (cu in; in^3)
Imperial pints (Imp pt)	X	0.568	=	Litres (l)	X	1.76	=	Imperial pints (Imp pt)
Imperial quarts (Imp qt)	X	1.137	=	Litres (l)	X	0.88	=	Imperial quarts (Imp qt)
Imperial quarts (Imp qt)	X	1.201	=	US quarts (US qt)	X	0.833	=	Imperial quarts (Imp qt)
US quarts (US qt)	X	0.946	=	Litres (l)	X	1.057	=	US quarts (US qt)
Imperial gallons (Imp gal)	X	4.546	=	Litres (l)	X	0.22	=	Imperial gallons (Imp gal)
Imperial gallons (Imp gal)	X	1.201	=	US gallons (US gal)	X	0.833	=	Imperial gallons (Imp gal)
US gallons (US gal)	X	3.785	=	Litres (l)	X	0.264	=	US gallons (US gal)

Mass (weight)
Ounces (oz)	X	28.35	=	Grams (g)	X	0.035		Ounces (oz)
Pounds (lb)	X	0.454	=	Kilograms (kg)	X	2.205	=	Pounds (lb)

Force
Ounces-force (ozf; oz)	X	0.278	=	Newtons (N)	X	3.6	=	Ounces-force (ozf; oz)
Pounds-force (lbf; lb)	X	4.448	=	Newtons (N)	X	0.225	=	Pounds-force (lbf; lb)
Newtons (N)	X	0.1	=	Kilograms-force (kgf; kg)	X	9.81	=	Newtons (N)

Pressure
Pounds-force per square inch (psi; lbf/in^2; lb/in^2)	X	0.070	=	Kilograms-force per square centimetre (kgf/cm^2; kg/cm^2)	X	14.223	=	Pounds-force per square inch (psi; lbf/in^2; lb/in^2)
Pounds-force per square inch (psi; lbf/in^2; lb/in^2)	X	0.068	=	Atmospheres (atm)	X	14.696	=	Pounds-force per square inch (psi; lbf/in^2; lb/in^2)
Pounds-force per square inch (psi; lbf/in^2; lb/in^2)	X	0.069	=	Bars	X	14.5	=	Pounds-force per square inch (psi; lbf/in^2; lb/in^2)
Pounds-force per square inch (psi; lbf/in^2; lb/in^2)	X	6.895	=	Kilopascals (kPa)	X	0.145	=	Pounds-force per square inch (psi; lbf/in^2; lb/in^2)
Kilopascals (kPa)	X	0.01	=	Kilograms-force per square centimetre (kgf/cm^2; kg/cm^2)	X	98.1	=	Kilopascals (kPa)

Torque (moment of force)
Pounds-force inches (lbf in; lb in)	X	1.152	=	Kilograms-force centimetre (kgf cm; kg cm)	X	0.868	=	Pounds-force inches (lbf in; lb in)
Pounds-force inches (lbf in; lb in)	X	0.113	=	Newton metres (Nm)	X	8.85	=	Pounds-force inches (lbf in; lb in)
Pounds-force inches (lbf in; lb in)	X	0.083	=	Pounds-force feet (lbf ft; lb ft)	X	12	=	Pounds-force inches (lbf in; lb in)
Pounds-force feet (lbf ft; lb ft)	X	0.138	=	Kilograms-force metres (kgf m; kg m)	X	7.233	=	Pounds-force feet (lbf ft; lb ft)
Pounds-force feet (lbf ft; lb ft)	X	1.356	=	Newton metres (Nm)	X	0.738	=	Pounds-force feet (lbf ft; lb ft)
Newton metres (Nm)	X	0.102	=	Kilograms-force metres (kgf m; kg m)	X	9.804	=	Newton metres (Nm)

Power
Horsepower (hp)	X	745.7	=	Watts (W)	X	0.0013	=	Horsepower (hp)

Velocity (speed)
Miles per hour (miles/hr; mph)	X	1.609	=	Kilometres per hour (km/hr; kph)	X	0.621	=	Miles per hour (miles/hr; mph)

Fuel consumption*
Miles per gallon, Imperial (mpg)	X	0.354	=	Kilometres per litre (km/l)	X	2.825	=	Miles per gallon, Imperial (mpg)
Miles per gallon, US (mpg)	X	0.425	=	Kilometres per litre (km/l)	X	2.352	=	Miles per gallon, US (mpg)

Temperature
Degrees Fahrenheit = (°C x 1.8) + 32   Degrees Celsius (Degrees Centigrade; °C) = (°F - 32) x 0.56

*It is common practice to convert from miles per gallon (mpg) to litres/100 kilometres (l/100km), where mpg (Imperial) x l/100 km = 282 and mpg (US) x l/100 km = 235

Safety first

Regardless of how enthusiastic you may be about getting on with the job at hand, take the time to ensure that your safety is not jeopardized. A moment's lack of attention can result in an accident, as can failure to observe certain simple safety precautions. The possibility of an accident will always exist, and the following points should not be considered a comprehensive list of all dangers. Rather, they are intended to make you aware of the risks and to encourage a safety conscious approach to all work you carry out on your vehicle.

Essential DOs and DON'Ts

DON'T rely on a jack when working under the vehicle. Always use approved jackstands to support the weight of the vehicle and place them under the recommended lift or support points.

DON'T attempt to loosen extremely tight fasteners (i.e. wheel lug nuts) while the vehicle is on a jack - it may fall.

DON'T start the engine without first making sure that the transmission is in Neutral (or Park where applicable) and the parking brake is set.

DON'T remove the radiator cap from a hot cooling system - let it cool or cover it with a cloth and release the pressure gradually.

DON'T attempt to drain the engine oil until you are sure it has cooled to the point that it will not burn you.

DON'T touch any part of the engine or exhaust system until it has cooled sufficiently to avoid burns.

DON'T siphon toxic liquids such as gasoline, antifreeze and brake fluid by mouth, or allow them to remain on your skin.

DON'T inhale brake lining dust - it is potentially hazardous (see *Asbestos* below).

DON'T allow spilled oil or grease to remain on the floor - wipe it up before someone slips on it.

DON'T use loose fitting wrenches or other tools which may slip and cause injury.

DON'T push on wrenches when loosening or tightening nuts or bolts. Always try to pull the wrench toward you. If the situation calls for pushing the wrench away, push with an open hand to avoid scraped knuckles if the wrench should slip.

DON'T attempt to lift a heavy component alone - get someone to help you.

DON'T rush or take unsafe shortcuts to finish a job.

DON'T allow children or animals in or around the vehicle while you are working on it.

DO wear eye protection when using power tools such as a drill, sander, bench grinder, etc. and when working under a vehicle.

DO keep loose clothing and long hair well out of the way of moving parts.

DO make sure that any hoist used has a safe working load rating adequate for the job.

DO get someone to check on you periodically when working alone on a vehicle.

DO carry out work in a logical sequence and make sure that everything is correctly assembled and tightened.

DO keep chemicals and fluids tightly capped and out of the reach of children and pets.

DO remember that your vehicle's safety affects that of yourself and others. If in doubt on any point, get professional advice.

Asbestos

Certain friction, insulating, sealing, and other products - such as brake linings, brake bands, clutch linings, torque converters, gaskets, etc. - contain asbestos. Extreme care must be taken to avoid inhalation of dust from such products, since it is hazardous to health. If in doubt, assume that they do contain asbestos.

Fire

Remember at all times that gasoline is highly flammable. Never smoke or have any kind of open flame around when working on a vehicle. But the risk does not end there. A spark caused by an electrical short circuit, by two metal surfaces contacting each other, or even by static electricity built up in your body under certain conditions, can ignite gasoline vapors, which in a confined space are highly explosive. Do not, under any circumstances, use gasoline for cleaning parts. Use an approved safety solvent.

Always disconnect the battery ground (-) cable at the battery before working on any part of the fuel system or electrical system. Never risk spilling fuel on a hot engine or exhaust component. It is strongly recommended that a fire extinguisher suitable for use on fuel and electrical fires be kept handy in the garage or workshop at all times. Never try to extinguish a fuel or electrical fire with water.

Fumes

Certain fumes are highly toxic and can quickly cause unconsciousness and even death if inhaled to any extent. Gasoline vapor falls into this category, as do the vapors from some cleaning solvents. Any draining or pouring of such volatile fluids should be done in a well ventilated area.

When using cleaning fluids and solvents, read the instructions on the container carefully. Never use materials from unmarked containers.

Never run the engine in an enclosed space, such as a garage. Exhaust fumes contain carbon monoxide, which is extremely poisonous. If you need to run the engine, always do so in the open air, or at least have the rear of the vehicle outside the work area.

If you are fortunate enough to have the use of an inspection pit, never drain or pour gasoline and never run the engine while the vehicle is over the pit. The fumes, being heavier than air, will concentrate in the pit with possibly lethal results.

The battery

Never create a spark or allow a bare light bulb near a battery. They normally give off a certain amount of hydrogen gas, which is highly explosive.

Always disconnect the battery ground (-) cable at the battery before working on the fuel or electrical systems.

If possible, loosen the filler caps or cover when charging the battery from an external source (this does not apply to sealed or maintenance-free batteries). Do not charge at an excessive rate or the battery may burst.

Take care when adding water to a non maintenance-free battery and when carrying a battery. The electrolyte, even when diluted, is very corrosive and should not be allowed to contact clothing or skin.

Always wear eye protection when cleaning the battery to prevent the caustic deposits from entering your eyes.

Household current

When using an electric power tool, inspection light, etc., which operates on household current, always make sure that the tool is correctly connected to its plug and that, where necessary, it is properly grounded. Do not use such items in damp conditions and, again, do not create a spark or apply excessive heat in the vicinity of fuel or fuel vapor.

Secondary ignition system voltage

A severe electric shock can result from touching certain parts of the ignition system (such as the spark plug wires) when the engine is running or being cranked, particularly if components are damp or the insulation is defective. In the case of an electronic ignition system, the secondary system voltage is much higher and could prove fatal.

Troubleshooting

Contents

This section provides an easy reference guide to the more common problems which may occur during the operation of your vehicle. These problems and their possible causes are grouped under headings denoting various components or systems, such as Engine, Cooling system, etc. They also refer you to the chapter and/or section which deals with the problem.

Remember that successful troubleshooting is not a mysterious black art practiced only by professional mechanics. It is simply the result of the right knowledge combined with an intelligent, systematic approach to the problem. Always work by a process of elimination, starting with the simplest solution and working through to the most complex - and never overlook the obvious. Anyone can run the gas tank dry or leave the lights on overnight, so don't assume that you are exempt from such oversights.

Finally, always establish a clear idea of why a problem has occurred and take steps to ensure that it doesn't happen again. If the electrical system fails because of a poor connection, check the other connections in the system to make sure that they don't fail as well. If a particular fuse continues to blow, find out why - don't just replace one fuse after another. Remember, failure of a small component can often be indicative of potential failure or incorrect functioning of a more important component or system.

Engine

1   Engine will not rotate when attempting to start

1   Battery terminal connections loose or corroded (Chapter 1).
2   Battery discharged or faulty (Chapter 1).
3   Automatic transaxle not completely engaged in Park (Chapter 7) or clutch pedal not completely depressed (Chapter 8).
4   Broken, loose or disconnected wiring in the starting circuit (Chapters 5 and 12).
5   Starter motor pinion jammed in flywheel ring gear (Chapter 5).
6   Starter solenoid faulty (Chapter 5).
7   Starter motor faulty (Chapter 5).
8   Ignition switch faulty (Chapter 12).
9   Starter pinion or flywheel teeth worn or broken (Chapter 5).

2   Engine rotates but will not start

1   Fuel tank empty.
2   Battery discharged (engine rotates slowly) (Chapter 5).
3   Battery terminal connections loose or corroded (Chapter 1).
4   Leaking fuel injector(s), faulty fuel pump, pressure regulator, etc. (Chapter 4).
5   Broken or stripped timing belt (Chapter 2).
6   Ignition components damp or damaged (Chapter 5).
7   Worn, faulty or incorrectly gapped spark plugs (Chapter 1).
8   Broken, loose or disconnected wiring in the starting circuit (Chapter 5).
9   Loose distributor is changing ignition timing (Chapter 5).
10   Broken, loose or disconnected wires at the ignition coil or faulty coil (Chapter 5).

3   Engine hard to start when cold

1   Battery discharged or low (Chapter 1).
2   Malfunctioning fuel system (Chapter 4).
3   Faulty coolant temperature sensor or intake air temperature sensor (Chapter 6).
4   Injector(s) leaking (Chapter 4).
5   Carburetor or choke problem (Chapter 4).
6   Faulty ignition system (Chapter 5).

4   Engine hard to start when hot

1   Air filter clogged (Chapter 1).
2   Fuel not reaching the carburetor or fuel injection system (Chapter 4).
3   Corroded battery connections, especially ground (Chapter 1).
4   Faulty coolant temperature sensor or intake air temperature sensor (Chapter 6).
5   Carburetor or choke problem (Chapter 4).

5   Starter motor noisy or excessively rough in engagement

1   Pinion or flywheel gear teeth worn or broken (Chapter 5).
2   Starter motor mounting bolts loose or missing (Chapter 5).

6   Engine starts but stops immediately

1   Loose or faulty electrical connections at distributor, coil or alternator (Chapter 5).
2   Insufficient fuel reaching the carburetor or fuel injector(s) (Chapters 1 and 4).
3   Vacuum leak at the gasket between the intake manifold/plenum and throttle body or carburetor (Chapters 1 and 4).
4   Idle speed incorrect (Chapter 1).

7   Oil puddle under engine

1   Oil pan gasket and/or oil pan drain bolt washer leaking (Chapter 2).
2   Oil pressure sending unit leaking (Chapter 2).
3   Cylinder head covers leaking (Chapter 2).
4   Engine oil seals leaking (Chapter 2).
5   Oil pump housing leaking (Chapter 2).

8   Engine lopes while idling or idles erratically

1   Vacuum leakage (Chapters 2 and 4).
2   Leaking EGR valve (Chapter 6).
3   Air filter clogged (Chapter 1).
4   Fuel pump not delivering sufficient fuel to the carburetor or fuel injection system (Chapter 4).
5   Leaking head gasket (Chapter 2).
6   Timing belt and/or pulleys worn (Chapter 2).
7   Camshaft lobes worn (Chapter 2).

9   Engine misses at idle speed

1   Spark plugs worn or not gapped properly (Chapter 1).
2   Faulty spark plug wires (Chapter 1).
3   Vacuum leaks (Chapter 1).
4   Incorrect ignition timing (Chapter 1).
5   Uneven or low compression (Chapter 2).
6   Problem with the carburetor or fuel injection system (Chapter 4).

10   Engine misses throughout driving speed range

1   Fuel filter clogged and/or impurities in the fuel system (Chapter 1).
2   Low fuel output at the carburetor or injector(s) (Chapter 4).

3   Faulty or incorrectly gapped spark plugs (Chapter 1).
4   Incorrect ignition timing (Chapter 5).
5   Cracked distributor cap, disconnected distributor wires or damaged distributor components (Chapters 1 and 5).
6   Leaking spark plug wires (Chapters 1 or 5).
7   Faulty emission system components (Chapter 6).
8   Low or uneven cylinder compression pressures (Chapter 2).
9   Weak or faulty ignition system (Chapter 5).
10   Vacuum leak in fuel injection system, intake manifold, air control valve or vacuum hoses (Chapter 4).

11   Engine stumbles on acceleration

1   Spark plugs fouled (Chapter 1).
2   Problem with fuel injection system or carburetor (Chapter 4).
3   Fuel filter clogged (Chapters 1 and 4).
4   Incorrect ignition timing (Chapter 5).
5   Intake manifold air leak (Chapters 2 and 4).
6   Problem with the emissions control system (Chapter 6).

12   Engine surges while holding accelerator steady

1   Intake air leak (Chapter 4).
2   Fuel pump or fuel pressure regulator faulty (Chapter 4).
3   Problem with carburetor or fuel injection system (Chapter 4).
4   Problem with the emissions control system (Chapter 6).

13   Engine stalls

1   Idle speed incorrect (Chapter 1).
2   Fuel filter clogged and/or water and impurities in the fuel system (Chapters 1 and 4).
3   Distributor components damp or damaged (Chapter 5).
4   Faulty emissions system components (Chapter 6).
5   Faulty or incorrectly gapped spark plugs (Chapter 1).
6   Faulty spark plug wires (Chapter 1).
7   Vacuum leak in the carburetor or fuel injection system, intake manifold or vacuum hoses (Chapters 2 and 4).
8   Valve clearances incorrectly set (Chapter 1).

14   Engine lacks power

1   Incorrect ignition timing (Chapter 5).
2   Excessive play in distributor shaft (Chapter 5).
3   Worn rotor, distributor cap, spark plug wires or faulty coil (Chapters 1 and 5).
4   Faulty or incorrectly gapped spark plugs (Chapter 1).
5   Problem with the carburetor or fuel injection system (Chapter 4).
6   Plugged air filter (Chapter 1).
7   Brakes binding (Chapter 9).
8   Automatic transaxle fluid level incorrect (Chapter 1).
9   Clutch slipping (Chapter 8).
10   Fuel filter clogged and/or impurities in the fuel system (Chapters 1 and 4).
11   Emission control system not functioning properly (Chapter 6).
12   Low or uneven cylinder compression pressures (Chapter 2).
13   Obstructed exhaust system (Chapter 4).

15   Engine backfires

1   Emission control system not functioning properly (Chapter 6).
2   Ignition timing incorrect (Chapter 5).

3   Faulty secondary ignition system (cracked spark plug insulator, faulty plug wires, distributor cap and/or rotor) (Chapters 1 and 5).
4   Problem with the carburetor or fuel injection system (Chapter 4).
5   Vacuum leak at fuel injector(s), intake manifold, air control valve or vacuum hoses (Chapters 2 and 4).
6   Valve clearances incorrectly set and/or valves sticking (Chapter 1).

16   Pinging or knocking engine sounds during acceleration or uphill

1   Incorrect grade of fuel.
2   Ignition timing incorrect (Chapter 5).
3   Carburetor or fuel injection system faulty (Chapter 4).
4   Improper or damaged spark plugs or wires (Chapter 1).
5   Worn or damaged distributor components (Chapter 5).
6   EGR valve not functioning (Chapter 6).
7   Vacuum leak (Chapters 2 and 4).

17   Engine runs with oil pressure light on

1   Low oil level (Chapter 1).
2   Idle rpm below specification (Chapter 1).
3   Short in wiring circuit (Chapter 12).
4   Faulty oil pressure sender (Chapter 2).
5   Worn engine bearings and/or oil pump (Chapter 2).

18   Engine diesels (continues to run) after switching off

1   Idle speed too high (Chapter 1).
2   Excessive engine operating temperature (Chapter 3).
3   Ignition timing in need of adjustment (Chapter 5).

Engine electrical system

19   Battery will not hold a charge

1   Alternator drivebelt defective or not adjusted properly (Chapter 1).
2   Battery electrolyte level low (Chapter 1).
3   Battery terminals loose or corroded (Chapter 1).
4   Alternator not charging properly (Chapter 5).
5   Loose, broken or faulty wiring in the charging circuit (Chapter 5).
6   Short in vehicle wiring (Chapter 12).
7   Internally defective battery (Chapters 1 and 5).

20   Alternator light fails to go out

1   Faulty alternator or charging circuit (Chapter 5).
2   Alternator drivebelt defective or out of adjustment (Chapter 1).
3   Alternator voltage regulator inoperative (Chapter 5).

21   Alternator light fails to come on when key is turned on

1   Warning light bulb defective (Chapter 12).
2   Fault in the printed circuit, dash wiring or bulb holder (Chapter 12).

Fuel system

22 Excessive fuel consumption

1 Dirty or clogged air filter element (Chapter 1).
2 Incorrectly set ignition timing (Chapter 5).
3 Emissions system not functioning properly (Chapter 6).
4 Carburetor or fuel injection system not functioning properly (Chapter 4).
5 Low tire pressure or incorrect tire size (Chapter 1).

23 Fuel leakage and/or fuel odor

1 Leaking fuel feed or return line (Chapters 1 and 4).
2 Tank overfilled.
3 Evaporative canister filter clogged (Chapters 1 and 6).
4 Problem with carburetor or fuel injection system (Chapter 4).

Cooling system

24 Overheating

1 Insufficient coolant in system (Chapter 1).
2 Water pump drivebelt defective or out of adjustment (Chapter 1).
3 Radiator core blocked or grille restricted (Chapter 3).
4 Thermostat faulty (Chapter 3).
5 Electric coolant fan inoperative or blades broken (Chapter 3).
6 Radiator cap not maintaining proper pressure (Chapter 3).
7 Ignition timing incorrect (Chapter 5).

25 Overcooling

1 Faulty thermostat (Chapter 3).
2 Inaccurate temperature gauge sending unit (Chapter 3).

26 External coolant leakage

1 Deteriorated/damaged hoses; loose clamps (Chapters 1 and 3).
2 Water pump defective (Chapter 3).
3 Leakage from radiator core or coolant reservoir bottle (Chapter 3).
4 Engine drain or water jacket core plugs leaking (Chapter 2).

27 Internal coolant leakage

1 Leaking cylinder head gasket (Chapter 2).
2 Cracked cylinder bore or cylinder head (Chapter 2).

28 Coolant loss

1 Too much coolant in system (Chapter 1).
2 Coolant boiling away because of overheating (Chapter 3).
3 Internal or external leakage (Chapter 3).
4 Faulty radiator cap (Chapter 3).

29 Poor coolant circulation

1 Inoperative water pump (Chapter 3).

2 Restriction in cooling system (Chapters 1 and 3).
3 Water pump drivebelt defective/out of adjustment (Chapter 1).
4 Thermostat sticking (Chapter 3).

Clutch

30 Pedal travels to floor - no pressure or very little resistance

1 Master or release cylinder faulty (Chapter 8).
2 Hose/pipe burst or leaking (Chapter 8).
3 Connections leaking (Chapter 8).
4 No fluid in reservoir (Chapter 8).
5 If fluid level in reservoir rises as pedal is depressed, master cylinder center valve seal is faulty (Chapter 8).
6 If there is fluid on dust seal at master cylinder, piston primary seal is leaking (Chapter 8).
7 Broken release bearing or fork (Chapter 8).

31 Fluid in area of master cylinder dust cover and on pedal

Rear seal failure in master cylinder (Chapter 8).

32 Fluid on release cylinder

Release cylinder plunger seal faulty (Chapter 8).

33 Pedal feels spongy when depressed

Air in system (Chapter 8).

34 Unable to select gears

1 Faulty transaxle (Chapter 7).
2 Faulty clutch disc or pressure plate (Chapter 8).
3 Faulty release lever or release bearing (Chapter 8).
4 Faulty shift lever assembly or control cables (Chapter 8).

35 Clutch slips (engine speed increases with no increase in vehicle speed)

1 Clutch plate worn (Chapter 8).
2 Clutch plate is oil soaked by leaking rear main seal (Chapter 8).
3 Clutch plate not seated (Chapter 8).
4 Warped pressure plate or flywheel (Chapter 8).
5 Weak diaphragm springs (Chapter 8).
6 Clutch plate overheated. Allow to cool.

36 Grabbing (chattering) as clutch is engaged

1 Oil on clutch plate lining, burned or glazed facings (Chapter 8).
2 Worn or loose engine or transaxle mounts (Chapters 2 and 7).
3 Worn splines on clutch plate hub (Chapter 8).
4 Warped pressure plate or flywheel (Chapter 8).
5 Burned or smeared resin on flywheel or pressure plate (Chapter 8).

37 Transaxle rattling (clicking)

1   Release lever loose (Chapter 8).
2   Clutch plate damper spring failure (Chapter 8).
3   Low engine idle speed (Chapter 1).

38 Noise in clutch area

1   Fork shaft improperly installed (Chapter 8).
2   Faulty bearing (Chapter 8).

39 Clutch pedal stays on floor

1   Clutch master cylinder piston binding in bore (Chapter 8).
2   Broken release bearing or fork (Chapter 8).

40 High pedal effort

1   Piston binding in bore (Chapter 8).
2   Pressure plate faulty (Chapter 8).
3   Incorrect size master or release cylinder (Chapter 8).

Manual transaxle

41 Knocking noise at low speeds

1   Worn driveaxle constant velocity (CV) joints (Chapter 8).
2   Worn side gear shaft counterbore in differential case (Chapter 7A).*

42 Noise most pronounced when turning

Differential gear noise (Chapter 7A).*

43 Clunk on acceleration or deceleration

1   Loose engine or transaxle mounts (Chapters 2 and 7A).
2   Worn differential pinion shaft in case.*
3   Worn side gear shaft counterbore in differential case (Chapter 7A).*
4   Worn or damaged driveaxle inboard CV joints (Chapter 8).

44 Clicking noise in turns

Worn or damaged outboard CV joint (Chapter 8).

45 Vibration

1   Rough wheel bearing (Chapters 1 and 10).
2   Damaged driveaxle (Chapter 8).
3   Out of round tires (Chapter 1).
4   Tire out of balance (Chapters 1 and 10).
5   Worn CV joint (Chapter 8).

46 Noisy in neutral with engine running

1   Damaged input gear bearing (Chapter 7A).*
2   Damaged clutch release bearing (Chapter 8).

47 Noisy in one particular gear

1   Damaged or worn constant mesh gears (Chapter 7A).*
2   Damaged or worn synchronizers (Chapter 7A).*
3   Bent reverse fork (Chapter 7A).*
4   Damaged fourth speed gear or output gear (Chapter 7A).*
5   Worn or damaged reverse idler gear or idler bushing (Chapter 7A).*

48 Noisy in all gears

1   Insufficient lubricant (Chapter 7A).
2   Damaged or worn bearings (Chapter 7A).*
3   Worn or damaged input gear shaft and/or output gear shaft (Chapter 7A).*

49 Slips out of gear

1   Worn or improperly adjusted linkage (Chapter 7A).
2   Transaxle loose on engine (Chapter 7A).
3   Shift linkage does not work freely, binds (Chapter 7A).
4   Input gear bearing retainer broken or loose (Chapter 7A).*
5   Dirt between clutch cover and engine housing (Chapter 7A).
6   Worn shift fork (Chapter 7A).*

50 Leaks lubricant

1   Side gear shaft seals worn (Chapter 7).
2   Excessive amount of lubricant in transaxle (Chapters 1 and 7A).
3   Loose or broken input gear shaft bearing retainer (Chapter 7A).*
4   Input gear bearing retainer O-ring and/or lip seal damaged (Chapter 7A).*

51 Locked in gear

Lock pin or interlock pin missing (Chapter 7A).*

Although the corrective action necessary to remedy the symptoms described is beyond the scope of this manual, the above information should be helpful in isolating the cause of the condition so that the owner can communicate clearly with a professional mechanic.

Automatic transaxle

Note: *Due to the complexity of the automatic transaxle, it is difficult for the home mechanic to properly diagnose and service this component. For problems other than the following, the vehicle should be taken to a dealer or transaxle shop.*

52 Fluid leakage

1   Automatic transaxle fluid is a deep red color. Fluid leaks should not be confused with engine oil, which can easily be blown onto the transaxle by air flow.

2   To pinpoint a leak, first remove all built-up dirt and grime from the transaxle housing with degreasing agents and/or steam cleaning. Then drive the vehicle at low speeds so air flow will not blow the leak far from its source. Raise the vehicle and determine where the leak is coming from. Common areas of leakage are:

a) *Pan (Chapters 1 and 7)*
b) *Dipstick tube (Chapters 1 and 7)*
c) *Transaxle oil lines (Chapter 7)*
d) *Speed sensor (Chapter 7)*
e) *Driveaxle oil seals (Chapter 7).*

53 Transaxle fluid brown or has a burned smell

Transaxle fluid overheated (Chapter 1).

54 General shift mechanism problems

1   Chapter 7, Part B, deals with checking and adjusting the shift linkage on automatic transaxles. Common problems which may be attributed to poorly adjusted linkage are:

a) *Engine starting in gears other than Park or Neutral.*
b) *Indicator on shifter pointing to a gear other than the one actually being used.*
c) *Vehicle moves when in Park.*
2   Refer to Chapter 7B for the shift linkage adjustment procedure.

55 Transaxle will not downshift with accelerator pedal pressed to the floor

Throttle valve cable out of adjustment (Chapter 7B).

56 Engine will start in gears other than Park or Neutral

Neutral start switch malfunctioning (Chapter 7B).

57 Transaxle slips, shifts roughly, is noisy or has no drive in forward or reverse gears

There are many probable causes for the above problems, but the home mechanic should be concerned with only one possibility - fluid level. Before taking the vehicle to a repair shop, check the level and condition of the fluid as described in Chapter 1. Correct the fluid level as necessary or change the fluid and filter if needed. If the problem persists, have a professional diagnose the cause.

Driveaxles

58 Clicking noise in turns

Worn or damaged outboard CV joint (Chapter 8).

59 Shudder or vibration during acceleration

1   Excessive toe-in (Chapter 10).
2   Incorrect spring heights (Chapter 10).
3   Worn or damaged inboard or outboard CV joints (Chapter 8).
4   Sticking inboard CV joint assembly (Chapter 8).

60 Vibration at highway speeds

1   Out of balance front wheels and/or tires (Chapters 1 and 10).
2   Out of round front tires (Chapters 1 and 10).
3   Worn CV joint(s) (Chapter 8).

Brakes

Note: *Before assuming that a brake problem exists, make sure that:*
a) *The tires are in good condition and properly inflated (Chapter 1).*
b) *The front end alignment is correct (Chapter 10).*
c) *The vehicle is not loaded with weight in an unequal manner.*

61 Vehicle pulls to one side during braking

1   Incorrect tire pressures (Chapter 1).
2   Front end out of alignment (have the front end aligned).
3   Front, or rear, tire sizes not matched to one another.
4   Restricted brake lines or hoses (Chapter 9).
5   Malfunctioning drum brake or caliper assembly (Chapter 9).
6   Loose suspension parts (Chapter 10).
7   Loose calipers (Chapter 9).
8   Excessive wear of brake shoe or pad material or disc/drum on one side.

62 Noise (high-pitched squeal when the brakes are applied)

Front and/or rear disc brake pads worn out. The noise comes from the wear sensor rubbing against the disc (does not apply to all vehicles). Replace pads with new ones immediately (Chapter 9).

63 Brake roughness or chatter (pedal pulsates)

1   Excessive lateral runout (Chapter 9).
2   Uneven pad wear (Chapter 9).
3   Defective disc (Chapter 9).

64 Excessive brake pedal effort required to stop vehicle

1   Malfunctioning power brake booster (Chapter 9).
2   Partial system failure (Chapter 9).
3   Excessively worn pads or shoes (Chapter 9).
4   Piston in caliper or wheel cylinder stuck or sluggish (Chapter 9).
5   Brake pads or shoes contaminated with oil or grease (Chapter 9).
6   Brake disc grooved and/or glazed (Chapter 1).
7   New pads or shoes installed and not yet seated. It will take a while for the new material to seat against the disc or drum.

65 Excessive brake pedal travel

1   Partial brake system failure (Chapter 9).
2   Insufficient fluid in master cylinder (Chapters 1 and 9).
3   Air trapped in system (Chapters 1 and 9).

66 Dragging brakes

1   Incorrect adjustment of brake light switch (Chapter 9).
2   Master cylinder pistons not returning correctly (Chapter 9).
3   Restricted brakes lines or hoses (Chapters 1 and 9).
4   Incorrect parking brake adjustment (Chapter 9).

67 Grabbing or uneven braking action

1 Malfunction of proportioning valve (Chapter 9).
2 Malfunction of power brake booster unit (Chapter 9).
3 Binding brake pedal mechanism (Chapter 9).

68 Brake pedal feels spongy when depressed

1 Air in hydraulic lines (Chapter 9).
2 Master cylinder mounting bolts loose (Chapter 9).
3 Master cylinder defective (Chapter 9).

69 Brake pedal travels to the floor with little resistance

1 Little or no fluid in the master cylinder reservoir caused by leaking caliper piston(s) (Chapter 9).
2 Loose, damaged or disconnected brake lines (Chapter 9).

70 Parking brake does not hold

Parking brake linkage improperly adjusted (Chapters 1 and 9).

Suspension and steering systems

Note: *Before attempting to diagnose the suspension and steering systems, perform the following preliminary checks:*

a) *Tires for wrong pressure and uneven wear.*
b) *Steering universal joints from the column to the rack and pinion for loose connectors or wear.*
c) *Front and rear suspension and the rack and pinion assembly for loose or damaged parts.*
d) *Out-of-round or out-of-balance tires, bent rims and loose and/or rough wheel bearings.*

71 Vehicle pulls to one side

1 Mismatched or uneven tires (Chapter 10).
2 Broken or sagging springs (Chapter 10).
3 Wheel alignment out-of-specifications (Chapter 10).
4 Front brake dragging (Chapter 9).

72 Abnormal or excessive tire wear

1 Wheel alignment out-of-specifications (Chapter 10).
2 Sagging or broken springs (Chapter 10).
3 Tire out-of-balance (Chapter 10).
4 Worn strut damper (Chapter 10).
5 Overloaded vehicle.
6 Tires not rotated regularly.

73 Wheel makes a thumping noise

1 Blister or bump on tire (Chapter 10).
2 Improper strut damper action (Chapter 10).

74 Shimmy, shake or vibration

1 Tire or wheel out-of-balance or out-of-round (Chapter 10).

2 Loose or worn wheel bearings (Chapters 1, 8 and 10).
3 Worn tie-rod ends (Chapter 10).
4 Worn lower balljoints (Chapters 1 and 10).
5 Excessive wheel runout (Chapter 10).
6 Blister or bump on tire (Chapter 10).

75 Hard steering

1 Lack of lubrication at balljoints, tie-rod ends and rack and pinion assembly (Chapter 10).
2 Front wheel alignment out-of-specifications (Chapter 10).
3 Low tire pressure(s) (Chapters 1 and 10).

76 Poor returnability of steering to center

1 Lack of lubrication at balljoints and tie-rod ends (Chapter 10).
2 Binding in balljoints (Chapter 10).
3 Binding in steering column (Chapter 10).
4 Lack of lubricant in steering gear assembly (Chapter 10).
5 Front wheel alignment out-of-specifications (Chapter 10).

77 Abnormal noise at the front end

1 Lack of lubrication at balljoints and tie-rod ends (Chapters 1 and 10).
2 Damaged strut mounting (Chapter 10).
3 Worn control arm bushings or tie-rod ends (Chapter 10).
4 Loose stabilizer bar (Chapter 10).
5 Loose wheel nuts (Chapters 1 and 10).
6 Loose suspension bolts (Chapter 10).

78 Wander or poor steering stability

1 Mismatched or uneven tires (Chapter 10).
2 Lack of lubrication at balljoints and tie-rod ends (Chapters 1 and 10).
3 Worn strut assemblies (Chapter 10).
4 Loose stabilizer bar (Chapter 10).
5 Broken or sagging springs (Chapter 10).
6 Wheels out of alignment (Chapter 10).

79 Erratic steering when braking

1 Wheel bearings worn (Chapter 10).
2 Broken or sagging springs (Chapter 10).
3 Leaking wheel cylinder or caliper (Chapter 10).
4 Warped rotors or drums (Chapter 10).

80 Excessive pitching and/or rolling around corners or during braking

1 Loose stabilizer bar (Chapter 10).
2 Worn strut dampers or mountings (Chapter 10).
3 Broken or sagging springs (Chapter 10).
4 Overloaded vehicle.

81 Suspension bottoms

1 Overloaded vehicle.

2   Worn strut dampers (Chapter 10).
3   Incorrect, broken or sagging springs (Chapter 10).

82   Cupped tires

1   Front wheel or rear wheel alignment out-of-specifications (Chapter 10).
2   Worn strut dampers (Chapter 10).
3   Wheel bearings worn (Chapter 10).
4   Excessive tire or wheel runout (Chapter 10).
5   Worn balljoints (Chapter 10).

83   Excessive tire wear on outside edge

1   Inflation pressures incorrect (Chapter 1).
2   Excessive speed in turns.
3   Front end alignment incorrect (excessive toe-in). Have professionally aligned.
4   Suspension arm bent or twisted (Chapter 10).

84   Excessive tire wear on inside edge

1   Inflation pressures incorrect (Chapter 1).

2   Front end alignment incorrect (toe-out). Have professionally aligned.
3   Loose or damaged steering components (Chapter 10).

85   Tire tread worn in one place

1   Tires out-of-balance.
2   Damaged or buckled wheel. Inspect and replace if necessary.
3   Defective tire (Chapter 1).

86   Excessive play or looseness in steering system

1   Wheel bearing(s) worn (Chapter 10).
2   Tie-rod end loose (Chapter 10).
3   Steering gear loose (Chapter 10).
4   Worn or loose steering intermediate shaft (Chapter 10).

87   Rattling or clicking noise in rack and pinion

1   Steering gear loose (Chapter 10).
2   Steering gear defective.

Chapter 1
Tune-up and routine maintenance

Contents

Specifications

Recommended lubricants and fluids

Engine oil	API grade SG, SH, or SG/CD or SH/CD multigrade and fuel efficient oil
Viscosity	See accompanying chart

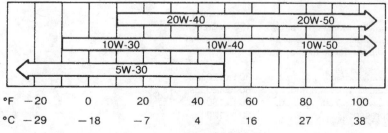

Recommended engine oil viscosity

TEMPERATURE RANGE ANTICIPATED BEFORE NEXT OIL CHANGE

Recommended lubricants and fluids (continued)

Fuel	Unleaded gasoline, 87 octane or higher
Automatic transaxle	
Fluid	DEXRON II automatic transmission fluid
Differential lubricant	DEXRON II automatic transmission fluid
Manual transaxle lubricant	API GL-5 75W-90 gear oil
Brake fluid	DOT 3 brake fluid
Clutch fluid	DOT 3 brake fluid
Power steering system	DEXRON II automatic transmission fluid
Wheel bearings	NLGI no. 2 lithium-base grease

Capacities*

Engine oil (including filter)	3.4 qts
Coolant	5 qts
Transaxle	
Automatic (drain and refill)	2.6 qts
Differential	1.5 qts
Manual	2.5 qts

All capacities approximate. Add as necessary to bring up to appropriate level.

Ignition system

Spark plug type and gap	
Type	NGK BPR5EY11 or equivalent
Gap	0.043 inch
Spark plug wire resistance	10,000 to 25,000 ohms
Engine firing order	1-3-4-2

Idle speed adjustment

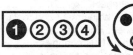

Carbureted engine

Carbureted model	
Curb idle speed setting	
Manual transaxle	800 rpm
Automatic transaxle	900 rpm
Fast idle speed setting	
Manual transaxle	3000 rpm
Automatic transaxle	2800 rpm
Fuel injected model	
Idle speed setting	
Manual transaxle	750 rpm
Automatic transaxle	800 rpm

Fuel-injected engine

2106-1-specs HAYNES

The blackened terminal shown on the distributor cap indicates the Number One spark plug wire position

Cylinder location and distributor rotation

Throttle Positioner (TP) setting (carbureted models only)

TP at first step	1100 rpm
TP at second step	1800 to 2200 rpm

Valve clearances (engine hot)

Intake valve	0.008 inch
Exhaust valve	0.008 inch

Cooling system

Thermostat rating	
Starts to open	190-degrees F
Fully open	212-degrees F
Accessory drivebelt tension (with Burroughs or Nippondenso tension gauge)	
Used belt	
Alternator	80 to 120 lbs
Power steering pump	80 to 120 lbs
Air conditioning compressor	90 to 130 lbs
Power steering and air conditioning compressor	80 to 120 lbs
New belt	
Alternator	140 to 180 lbs
Power steering pump	135 to 185 lbs
Air conditioning compressor	150 to 180 lbs
Power steering and air conditioning compressor	140 to 180 lbs

Clutch pedal

Freeplay	3/16 to 5/8 inch
Height	
1990 and earlier models	
EZ model..	6-3/16 to 6-3/4 inches
All others	6-1/8 to 6-1/2 inches
1991 and later models	
Four-speed	5-3/4 to 6 inches
Five speed...	5-1/2 to 5-7/8 inches

Brakes

Disc brake pad lining thickness (minimum)...	1/16 inch
Drum brake shoe lining thickness (minimum)........................	1/16 inch
Parking brake adjustment...	4 to 7 clicks

Suspension and steering

Steering wheel freeplay limit..	1-3/16 inch
Balljoint allowable movement	0 inch

Torque specifications

	Ft-lbs (unless otherwise indicated)
Automatic transaxle	
Pan bolts	48 in-lbs
Filter bolts...	84 in-lbs
Drain plugs	36
Manual transaxle drain and filler plugs.............................	29
Spark plugs...	13
Seat bolts/nuts	27
Wheel lug nuts	76

1

1   Introduction

This chapter is designed to help the home mechanic maintain the Toyota Tercel for peak performance, economy, safety and long life.

On the following pages is a master maintenance schedule, followed by sections dealing specifically with each item on the schedule. Visual checks, adjustments, component replacement and other helpful items are included. Refer to the accompanying illustrations of the engine compartment and the underside of the vehicle for the location of various components.

Servicing your Tercel in accordance with the mileage/time maintenance schedule and the following Sections will provide it with a planned maintenance program that should result in a long and reliable service life. This is a comprehensive plan, so maintaining some items but not others at the specified service intervals will not produce the same results.

As you service your Tercel, you will discover that many of the procedures can - and should - be grouped together because of the nature of the particular procedure you're performing or because of the close proximity of two otherwise unrelated components to one another.

For example, if the vehicle is raised for any reason, you should inspect the exhaust, suspension, steering and fuel systems while you're under the vehicle. When you're rotating the tires, it makes good sense to check the brakes and wheel bearings since the wheels are already removed.

Finally, let's suppose you have to borrow or rent a torque wrench. Even if you only need to tighten the spark plugs, you might as well check the torque of as many critical fasteners as time allows.

The first step of this maintenance program is to prepare yourself before the actual work begins. Read through all sections pertinent to the procedures you're planning to do, then make a list of and gather together all the parts and tools you will need to do the job. If it looks as if you might run into problems during a particular segment of some procedure, seek advice from your local parts man or dealer service department.

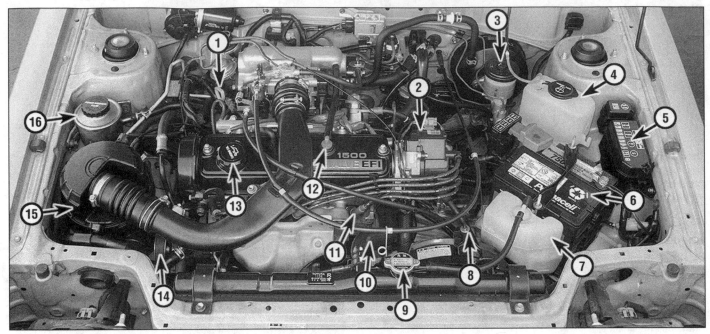

Engine compartment components (1990 model shown)

1	Engine oil dipstick (Section 4)	7	Coolant reservoir (Section 4)	12	PCV valve (Section 35)
2	Distributor (Section 26)	8	Automatic transaxle dipstick	13	Oil filler cap (Section 4)
3	Brake fluid reservoir (Section 4)		(Section 7)	14	Drivebelt (Section 12)
4	Windshield washer fluid reservoir	9	Radiator cap (Section 14)	15	Air cleaner assembly (Section 17)
	(Section 4)	10	Upper radiator hose (Section 14)	16	Power steering fluid reservoir
5	Fuse block (Chapter 12)	11	Spark plugs (Section 25)		(Section 6)
6	Battery (Section 11)				

Engine compartment components (1993 model shown)

1	Engine oil dipstick (Section 4)	7	Windshield washer fluid reservoir	11	PCV valve (Section 35)
2	Distributor (Section 26)		(Section 4)	12	Oil filler cap (Section 4)
3	Brake fluid reservoir (Section 4)	8	Battery (Section 11)	13	Spark plugs (Section 25)
4	Clutch fluid reservoir (Section 4)	9	Upper radiator hose (Section 14)	14	Drivebelt (Section 12)
5	Air cleaner assembly (Section 17)	10	Radiator cap (Section 14)	15	Coolant reservoir (Section 4)
6	Fuse block (Chapter 12)				

Engine compartment underside components (1990 model shown, others similar)

1	Engine oil pan drain plug (Section 8)	5	Automatic transaxle drain plug(Section 32)
2	Front disc brake (Section 16)	6	Exhaust system (Section 31)
3	Driveaxle boot (Section 22)	7	Steering gear boot (Section 21)
4	Automatic transaxle differential drain plug (Section 32)	8	Brake hose (Section 16)

Typical rear underside components (1990 model shown, others similar)

1	Muffler (Section 31)	5	Gas tank (Section 18)
2	Suspension strut and spring (Section 21)	6	Gas tank filler hose (Section 18)
3	Exhaust system (Section 31)	7	Rear brake assembly (Section 16)
4	Exhaust system hanger (Section 31)		

2 Toyota Tercel Maintenance schedule

The maintenance intervals in this manual are provided with the assumption that you, not the dealer, will be doing the work. These are the minimum maintenance intervals recommended by the factory for Tercels that are driven daily. If you wish to keep your vehicle in peak condition at all times, you may wish to perform some of these procedures even more often. Because frequent maintenance enhances the efficiency, performance and resale value of your car, we encourage you to do so. If you drive in dusty areas, tow a trailer, idle or drive at low speeds for extended periods or drive for short distances (less than four miles) in below freezing temperatures, shorter intervals are also recommended.

When your vehicle is new, it should be serviced by a factory authorized dealer service department to protect the factory warranty. In many cases, the initial maintenance check is done at no cost to the owner.

Every 250 miles or weekly, whichever comes first

Check the engine oil level (Section 4)
Check the engine coolant level (Section 4)
Check the windshield washer fluid level (Section 4)
Check the brake fluid level (Section 4)
Check the tires and tire pressures (Section 5)

Every 3000 miles or 3 months, whichever comes first

All items listed above plus:
Check the power steering fluid level (Section 6)
Check the automatic transaxle fluid level (Section 7)
Change the engine oil and oil filter (Section 8)

Every 7500 miles or 6 months, whichever comes first

Inspect and replace if necessary the windshield
   wiper blades (Section 9)
Check the clutch pedal for proper freeplay (Section 10)
Check and service the battery (Section 11)
Check and adjust if necessary the engine
   drivebelts (Section 12)
Inspect and replace if necessary all underhood
   hoses (Section 13)
Check the cooling system (Section 14)
Rotate the tires (Section 15)

Every 15,000 miles or 12 months, whichever comes first

All items listed above plus:
Inspect the brake system (Section 16)*
Replace the air filter (Section 17)

Inspect the fuel system (Section 18)
Check the manual transaxle lubricant level (Section 20)
Inspect the suspension and steering components
   (Section 21)*
Check the driveaxle boots (Section 22)
Change the power steering fluid (Section 6)

Every 30,000 miles or 24 months, whichever comes first

All items listed above plus:
Check and adjust if necessary, the valve clearances
   (Section 23)
Replace the fuel filter (Section 24)
Check and replace if necessary the spark
   plugs (Section 25)
Inspect and replace if necessary the spark plug
   wires, distributor cap and rotor (Section 26)
Service the cooling system (drain, flush and
   refill) (Section 27)
   Check and adjust if necessary, the throttle positioner
   (carbureted models only) (Section 28)
   Check and adjust if necessary, the engine idle speed
   (Section 29)
Inspect the evaporative emissions control system
   (Section 30)
Inspect the exhaust system (Section 31)
Change the automatic transaxle fluid and filter and
   differential lubricant (Section 32) **
Change the manual transaxle lubricant (Section 33)**
Check, repack and adjust the rear wheel bearings
   (Section 34)
Check and replace if necessary the PCV valve (Section 35)

Every 60,000 miles or 48 months, whichever comes first

Replace the timing belt (Chapter 2A)

* This item is affected by "severe" operating conditions as described below. If your vehicle is operated under "severe" conditions, perform all maintenance indicated with an asterisk (*) at 3000 mile/3 month intervals. Severe conditions are indicated if you mainly operate your vehicle under one or more of the following conditions:

   Operating in dusty areas
   Towing a trailer
   Idling for extended periods and/or low speed operation
   Operating when outside temperatures remain below
   freezing and when most trips are less than 4 miles

** If operated under one or more of the following conditions, change the, manual or automatic transaxle fluid and differential lubricant every 15,000 miles:

   In heavy city traffic where the outside temperature
   regularly reaches 90-degrees F (32-degrees C) or higher
   In hilly or mountainous terrain
   Frequent trailer pulling

3 Tune-up general information

The term tune-up is used in this manual to represent a combination of individual operations rather than one specific procedure.

If, from the time the vehicle is new, the routine maintenance schedule is followed closely and frequent checks are made of fluid levels and high wear items, as suggested throughout this manual, the engine will be kept in relatively good running condition and the need for additional work will be minimized.

More likely than not, however, there will be times when the engine is running poorly due to lack of regular maintenance. This is even more likely if a used vehicle, which has not received regular and frequent maintenance checks, is purchased. In such cases, an engine tune-up will be needed outside of the regular routine maintenance intervals.

The first step in any tune-up or engine diagnosis to help correct a poor running engine would be a cylinder compression check. A check of the engine compression (Chapter 2 Part B) will give valuable information regarding the overall performance of many internal components and should be used as a basis for tune-up and repair procedures. If, for instance, a compression check indicates serious internal engine wear, a conventional tune-up will not help the running condition of the engine and would be a waste of time and money.

The following series of operations are those most often needed to bring a generally poor running engine back into a proper state of tune.

Minor tune-up

Clean, inspect and test the battery (Section 11)
Check all engine related fluids (Section 4)
Check and adjust the drivebelts (Section 12)
Replace the spark plugs (Section 25)
Inspect the distributor cap and rotor (Section 26)
Inspect the spark plug and coil wires (Section 26)
Check and adjust the idle speed (Section 29)
Check the air filter (Section 17)
Check the cooling system (Section 14)
Check all underhood hoses (Section 13)

Major tune-up

All items listed under Minor tune-up, plus . . .
Check the ignition system (Section 26)
Check the charging system (Chapter 5)
Check the fuel system (Section 18)
Replace the air filter (Section 17)
Replace the distributor cap and rotor (Section 26)
Replace the spark plug wires (Section 26)

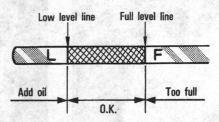

4.4 The oil level should be at or near the F mark - if it isn't, add enough oil to bring the level to near the F mark (it takes one full quart to raise the level from the L to the F mark)

4 Fluid level checks (every 250 miles or weekly)

1   Fluids are an essential part of the lubrication, cooling, brake, clutch and other systems. Because these fluids gradually become depleted and/or contaminated during normal operation of the vehicle, they must be periodically replenished. See *Recommended lubricants and fluids and Capacities* at the beginning of this Chapter before adding fluid to any of the following components. **Note:** *The vehicle must be on level ground before fluid levels can be checked.*

Engine oil

Refer to illustrations 4.2, 4.4 and 4.6

2   The engine oil level is checked with a dipstick located at the front side of the engine **(see illustration)**. The dipstick extends through a metal tube from which it protrudes down into the engine oil pan.

3   The oil level should be checked before the vehicle has been driven, or about 15 minutes after the engine has been shut off. If the oil is checked immediately after driving the vehicle, some of the oil will remain in the upper engine components, producing an inaccurate reading on the dipstick.

4   Pull the dipstick from the tube and wipe all the oil from the end with a clean rag or paper towel. Insert the clean dipstick all the way back into its metal tube and pull it out again. Observe the oil at the end of the dipstick. At its highest point, the level should be between the L and F marks **(see illustration)**.

5   It takes one quart of oil to raise the level from the L mark to the F mark on the dipstick. Do not allow the level to drop below the L mark or oil starvation may cause engine damage. Conversely, overfilling the engine (adding oil above the F mark) may cause oil fouled spark plugs, oil leaks or oil seal failures.

6   Remove the threaded cap from the valve cover to add oil **(see illustration)**. Use a funnel to prevent spills. After adding the oil, install the filler cap hand tight. Start the engine and look carefully for any small leaks around the oil filter or drain plug. Stop the engine and

4.2 The engine oil dipstick (arrow) is located on the right side of the engine on the back side of the engine

4.6 The threaded oil filler cap is located on the valve cover - always make sure the area around the opening is clean before unscrewing the cap to prevent dirt from contaminating the engine

4.8 The coolant reservoir is located next to the battery - make sure the level is between Low and Full marks on the reservoir

4.14a The windshield washer fluid reservoir tank is located on the left side of the engine compartment on earlier models - fluid can be added after flipping up the cap

4.14b On later models, the windshield washer fluid reservoir tank is located in the left front corner of the engine compartment - keep the level near the upper mark on the neck

check the oil level again after it has had sufficient time to drain from the upper block and cylinder head galleys.

7   Checking the oil level is an important preventive maintenance step. A continually dropping oil level indicates oil leakage through damaged seals, from loose connections, or past worn rings or valve guides. If the oil looks milky in color or has water droplets in it, a cylinder head gasket may be blown. The engine should be checked immediately. The condition of the oil should also be checked. Each time you check the oil level, slide your thumb and index finger up the dipstick before wiping off the oil. If you see small dirt or metal particles clinging to the dipstick, the oil should be changed (Section 8).

Engine coolant

Refer to illustration 4.8
Warning: *Do not allow antifreeze to come in contact with your skin or painted surfaces of the vehicle. Flush contaminated areas immediately with plenty of water. Don't store new coolant or leave old coolant lying around where it's accessible to children or pets – they're attracted by its sweet smell. Ingestion of even a small amount of coolant can be fatal! Wipe up garage floor and drip pan spills immediately. Keep antifreeze containers covered and repair cooling system leaks as soon as they're noticed.*

8   All vehicles covered by this manual are equipped with a pressurized coolant recovery system. A white coolant reservoir located in the left (early models) or right (later models) front corner of the engine compartment is connected by a hose to the base of the coolant filler cap **(see illustration)**. If the coolant heats up during engine operation, coolant can escape through a pressurized filler cap, then through a connecting hose into the reservoir. As the engine cools, the coolant is automatically drawn back into the cooling system to maintain the correct level.

9   The coolant level should be checked regularly. It must be between the Full and Low lines on the tank. The level will vary with the temperature of the engine. When the engine is cold, the coolant level should be at or slightly above the Low mark on the tank. Once the engine has warmed up, the level should be at or near the Full mark. If it isn't, allow the fluid in the tank to cool, then remove the cap from the reservoir and add coolant to bring the level up to the Full line. Use only ethylene/glycol type coolant and water in the mixture ratio recommended by your owner's manual. Do not use supplemental inhibitor additives. If only a small amount of coolant is required to bring the system up to the proper level, water can be used. However, repeated additions of water will dilute the recommended antifreeze and water solution. In order to maintain the proper ratio of antifreeze and water, it is advisable to top up the coolant level with the correct mixture. Refer to your owner's manual for the recommended ratio.

10   If the coolant level drops within a short time after replenishment, there may be a leak in the system. Inspect the radiator, hoses, engine coolant filler cap, drain plugs, air bleeder plugs and water pump. If no leak is evident, have the radiator cap pressure tested by your dealer. **Warning:** *Never remove the radiator cap or the coolant recovery reservoir cap when the engine is running or has just been shut down, because the cooling system is hot. Escaping steam and scalding liquid could cause serious injury.*

11   If it is necessary to open the radiator cap, wait until the system has cooled completely, then wrap a thick cloth around the cap and turn it to the first stop. If any steam escapes, wait until the system has cooled further, then remove the cap.

12   When checking the coolant level, always note its condition. It should be relatively clear. If it is brown or rust colored, the system should be drained, flushed and refilled. Even if the coolant appears to be normal, the corrosion inhibitors wear out with use, so it must be replaced at the specified intervals.

13   Do not allow antifreeze to come in contact with your skin or painted surfaces of the vehicle. Flush contacted areas immediately with plenty of water.

Windshield washer fluid

Refer to illustrations 4.14a and 4.14b

14   Fluid for the windshield washer system is stored in a plastic reservoir which is located on the left (driver's) side of the engine compartment **(see illustrations)**. In milder climates, plain water can be used to top up the reservoir, but the reservoir should be kept no more than two-thirds full to allow for expansion should the water freeze. In

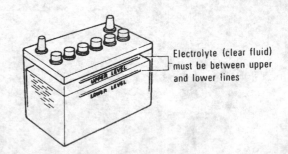

4.15 On non-sealed batteries, keep the electrolyte level of all the cells in the battery between the Upper and Lower levels - use only distilled water to replenish a cell and never overfill it or electrolyte may squirt out of the battery during periods of heavy charging

4.16 The clutch cylinder is mounted on the firewall - the fluid level should be kept near the top of the reservoir

4.17 The brake fluid level should be kept between the MIN and MAX marks on the translucent plastic reservoir - lift up the cap to add fluid

colder climates, the use of a specially designed windshield washer fluid, available at your dealer and any auto parts store, will help lower the freezing point of the fluid. Mix the solution with water in accordance with the manufacturer's directions on the container. Do not use regular antifreeze. It will damage the vehicle's paint.

Battery electrolyte

Refer to illustration 4.15

15   On models not equipped with a sealed battery, check the electrolyte level of all six battery cells. It must be between the upper and lower levels **(see illustration)**. If the level is low, unscrew the filler/vent cap and add distilled water. Install and securely retighten the cap. **Caution:** *Overfilling the cells may cause electrolyte to spill over during periods of heavy charging, causing corrosion or damage.*

Brake and clutch fluid

Refer to illustrations 4.16 and 4.17

16   The brake master cylinder is mounted on the front of the power booster unit in the engine compartment. The clutch cylinder used on manual transaxles is located next to the master cylinder **(see illustration)**.

17   To check either the fluid level of the brake master cylinder or clutch reservoir, simply look at the MAX and MIN marks on the reservoir **(see illustration)**. To check the fluid level of the clutch master cylinder reservoir, note whether the fluid level is even with the maximum level line. The level should be within the specified distance from the maximum fill line for both reservoirs.

18   If the level is low for either reservoir, wipe the top of the reservoir cover with a clean rag to prevent contamination of the brake or clutch system before lifting the cover.

19   Add only the specified brake fluid to the brake or clutch reservoir (refer to *Recommended lubricants and fluids* at the front of this chapter or to your owner's manual). Mixing different types of brake fluid can damage the system. Fill the brake master cylinder reservoir only to the dotted line - this brings the fluid to the correct level when you put the cover back on. **Warning:** *Use caution when filling either reservoir- brake fluid can harm your eyes and damage painted surfaces. Do not use brake fluid that has been opened for more than one year or has been left open. Brake fluid absorbs moisture from the air. Excess moisture can cause a dangerous loss of braking.*

20   While the reservoir cap is removed, inspect the master cylinder reservoir for contamination. If deposits, dirt particles or water droplets are present, the system should be drained and refilled (see Chapter 8 for clutch reservoir or Chapter 9 for brake reservoir).

21   After filling the reservoir to the proper level, make sure the lid is properly seated to prevent fluid leakage and/or system pressure loss.

22   The brake fluid in the master cylinder will drop slightly as the

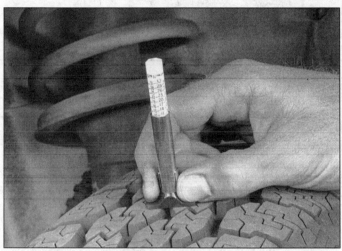

5.2 A tire tread depth indicator should be used to monitor tire wear - they are available at auto parts stores and service stations and cost very little

brake pads at each wheel wear down during normal operation. If the master cylinder requires repeated replenishing to keep it at the proper level, this is an indication of leakage in the brake system, which should be corrected immediately. Check all brake lines and connections, along with the wheel cylinders and booster (see Section 16 for more information).

23   If, upon checking the master cylinder fluid level, you discover one or both reservoirs empty or nearly empty, the brake system should be bled (see Chapter 9).

5   Tire and tire pressure checks (every 250 miles or weekly)

Refer to illustrations 5.2, 5.3, 5.4a, 5.4b and 5.8

1   Periodic inspection of the tires may spare you from the inconvenience of being stranded with a flat tire. It can also provide you with vital information regarding possible problems in the steering and suspension systems before major damage occurs.

2   Normal tread wear can be monitored with a simple, inexpensive device known as a tread depth indicator **(see illustration)**. When the tread depth reaches the specified minimum, replace the tire(s).

Condition	Probable cause	Corrective action	Condition	Probable cause	Corrective action
Shoulder wear	• Underinflation (both sides wear) • Incorrect wheel camber (one side wear) • Hard cornering • Lack of rotation	• Measure and adjust pressure. • Repair or replace axle and suspension parts. • Reduce speed. • Rotate tires.	Feathered edge Toe wear	• Incorrect toe	• Adjust toe-in.
Center wear	• Overinflation • Lack of rotation	• Measure and adjust pressure. • Rotate tires.	Uneven wear	• Incorrect camber or caster • Malfunctioning suspension • Unbalanced wheel • Out-of-round brake drum • Lack of rotation	• Repair or replace axle and suspension parts. • Repair or replace suspension parts. • Balance or replace. • Turn or replace. • Rotate tires.

5.3 This chart will help you determine the condition of your tires, the probable cause(s) of abnormal wear and the corrective action necessary

3   Note any abnormal tread wear (see illustration). Tread pattern irregularities such as cupping, flat spots and more wear on one side than the other are indications of front end alignment and/or balance problems. If any of these conditions are noted, take the vehicle to a tire shop or service station to correct the problem.

4   Look closely for cuts, punctures and embedded nails or tacks. Sometimes a tire will hold its air pressure for a short time or leak down very slowly even after a nail has embedded itself into the tread. If a slow leak persists, check the valve stem core to make sure it is tight (see illustration). Examine the tread for an object that may have embedded itself into the tire or for a "plug" that may have begun to leak (radial tire punctures are repaired with a plug that is installed in a puncture). If a puncture is suspected, it can be easily verified by spraying a solution of soapy water onto the puncture area (see illustration). The soapy solution will bubble if there is a leak. Unless the puncture is inordinately large, a tire shop or gas station can usually repair the punctured tire.

5   Carefully inspect the inner sidewall of each tire for evidence of brake fluid leakage. If you see any, inspect the brakes immediately.

6   Correct tire air pressure adds miles to the lifespan of the tires, improves mileage and enhances overall ride quality. Tire pressure cannot be accurately estimated by looking at a tire, particularly if it is a radial. A tire pressure gauge is therefore essential. Keep an accurate gauge in the glovebox. The pressure gauges fitted to the nozzles of air hoses at gas stations are often inaccurate.

7   Always check tire pressure when the tires are cold. "Cold," in this

5.4a If a tire loses air on a steady basis, check the valve core first to make sure it's snug (special inexpensive wrenches are commonly available at auto parts stores)

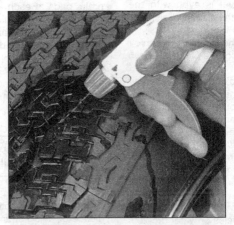

5.4b If the valve core is tight, raise the corner of the vehicle with the low tire and spray a soapy water solution onto the tread as the tire is turned slowly - slow leaks will cause small bubbles to appear

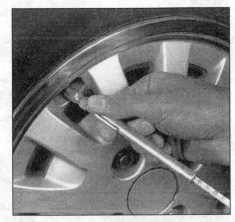

5.8 To extend the life of your tires, check the air pressure at least once a week with an accurate gauge (don't forget the spare!)

6.6 On earlier models the power steering fluid is checked with a dipstick which is part of the cap - the fluid level varies with temperature, so the fluid can be checked hot or cold

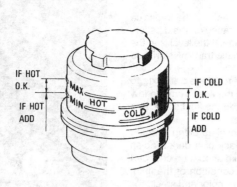

6.7 On later models, the power steering fluid reservoir is translucent so the fluid level can be checked without removing the cap

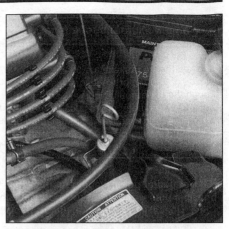

7.4a The automatic transaxle dipstick is located in a tube which extends forward from the transaxle toward the radiator

case, means the vehicle has not been driven over a mile in the three hours preceding a tire pressure check. A pressure rise of four to eight pounds is not uncommon once the tires are warm.

8   Unscrew the valve cap protruding from the wheel or hubcap and push the gauge firmly onto the valve **(see illustration)**. Note the reading on the gauge and compare this figure to the recommended tire pressure shown on the tire placard on the left door. Be sure to reinstall the valve cap to keep dirt and moisture out of the valve stem mechanism. Check all four tires and, if necessary, add enough air to bring them up to the recommended pressure levels.

9   Don't forget to keep the spare tire inflated to the specified pressure (consult your owner's manual). Note that the air pressure specified for the compact spare is significantly higher than the pressure of the regular tires.

6   Power steering fluid level check (every 3000 miles or 3 months)

All models

1   Unlike manual steering, the power steering system relies on fluid which may, over a period of time, require replenishing.

2   The fluid reservoir for the power steering pump is located on the inner fender panel near the front of the engine.

3   For the check, the front wheels should be pointed straight ahead and the engine should be off.

1990 and earlier models

Refer to illustration 6.6

4   Use a clean rag to wipe off the reservoir cap and the area around the cap. This will help prevent any foreign matter from entering the reservoir during the check.

5   Twist off the cap and check the temperature of the fluid at the end of the dipstick with your finger.

6   Wipe off the fluid with a clean rag, reinsert it, then withdraw it and read the fluid level. The level should be at the HOT mark if the fluid was hot to the touch. It should be at the COLD mark if the fluid was cool to the touch. Note that the marks (HOT and COLD) are on opposite sides of the dipstick **(see illustration)**. At no time should the fluid level drop below the upper mark for each heat range.

1991 and later models

Refer to illustration 6.7

7   On these models the reservoir is translucent plastic and the fluid level can be checked visually **(see illustration)**.

All models

8   If additional fluid is required, pour the specified type directly into the reservoir, using a funnel to prevent spills.

9   If the reservoir requires frequent fluid additions, all power steering hoses, hose connections, the power steering pump and the rack and pinion assembly should be carefully checked for leaks.

7   Automatic transaxle fluid level check (every 3000 miles or 3 months)

Refer to illustrations 7.4a and 7.4b

1   The level of the automatic transaxle fluid should be carefully maintained. Low fluid level can lead to slipping or loss of drive, while overfilling can cause foaming, loss of fluid and transaxle damage.

2   The transaxle fluid level should only be checked when the transaxle is hot (at its normal operating temperature). If the vehicle has just been driven over 10 miles (15 miles in a frigid climate), and the fluid temperature is 160 to 175-degrees F, the transaxle is hot. **Caution:** *If the vehicle has just been driven for a long time at high speed or in city traffic in hot weather, or if it has been pulling a trailer, an accurate fluid level reading cannot be obtained. Allow the fluid to cool down for about 30 minutes.*

3   If the vehicle has not just been driven, park the vehicle on level ground, set the parking brake and start the engine. While the engine is idling, depress the brake pedal and move the selector lever through all the gear ranges, beginning and ending in Park.

4   With the engine still idling, remove the dipstick from its tube **(see illustration)**. Check the level of the fluid on the dipstick **(see illustration)** and note its condition.

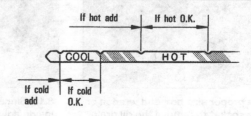

7.4b If the automatic transaxle fluid is cold, the level should be between the two lower notches; if it's at operating temperature, the level should be between the two upper notches

5   Wipe the fluid from the dipstick with a clean rag and reinsert it back into the filler tube until the cap seats.

6   Pull the dipstick out again and note the fluid level. If the transaxle is cold, the level should be in the COLD or COOL range on the dipstick. If it is hot, the fluid level should be in the HOT range. If the level is at the low side of either range, add the specified automatic transmission fluid through the dipstick tube with a funnel.

7   Add just enough of the recommended fluid to fill the transaxle to the proper level. It takes about one pint to raise the level from the low mark to the high mark when the fluid is hot, so add the fluid a little at a time and keep checking the level until it is correct.

8   The condition of the fluid should also be checked along with the level. If the fluid at the end of the dipstick is black or a dark reddish brown color, or if it emits a burned smell, the fluid should be changed (see Section 32). If you are in doubt about the condition of the fluid, purchase some new fluid and compare the two for color and smell.

8   Engine oil and oil filter change (every 3000 miles or 3 months)

Refer to illustrations 8.2, 8.7, 8.13, and 8.15

1   Frequent oil changes are the best preventive maintenance the home mechanic can give the engine, because aging oil becomes diluted and contaminated, which leads to premature engine wear.

2   Make sure that you have all the necessary tools before you begin this procedure **(see illustration)**. You should also have plenty of rags or newspapers handy for mopping up any spills.

3   Access to the underside of the vehicle is greatly improved if the vehicle can be lifted on a hoist, driven onto ramps or supported by jackstands. **Warning:** *Do not work under a vehicle which is supported only by a bumper, hydraulic or scissors-type jack.*

4   If this is your first oil change, get under the vehicle and familiarize yourself with the location of the oil drain plug. The engine and exhaust components will be warm during the actual work, so try to anticipate any potential problems before the engine and accessories are hot.

5   Park the vehicle on a level spot. Start the engine and allow it to reach its normal operating temperature (the needle on the temperature gauge should be at least above the bottom mark). Warm oil and sludge will flow out more easily. Turn off the engine when it's warmed up. Remove the filler cap in the rear cam cover.

6   Raise the vehicle and support it on jackstands. **Warning:** *To avoid personal injury, never get beneath the vehicle when it is supported by*

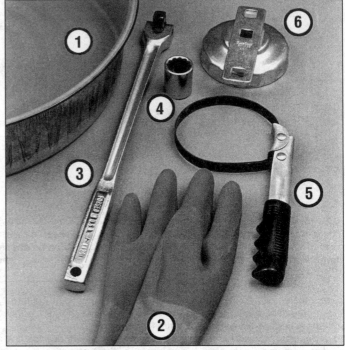

8.2 These tools are required when changing the engine oil and filter

1   **Drain pan -** *It should be fairly shallow in depth, but wide in order to prevent spills*

2   **Rubber gloves -** *When removing the drain plug and filter, it is inevitable that you will get oil on your hands (the gloves will prevent burns)*

3   **Breaker bar-** *Sometimes the oil drain plug is pretty tight and a long breaker bar is needed to loosen it*

4   **Socket –** *To be used with the breaker bar or a ratchet (must be the correct size to fit the drain plug)*

5   **Filter wrench -** *This is a metal band-type wrench, which requires clearance around the filter to be effective*

6   **Filter wrench -** *This type fits on the bottom of the filter and can be turned with a ratchet or beaker bar (different size wrenches are available for different types of filters)*

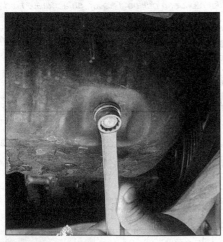

8.7 Use a proper size box-end wrench or six-point socket to remove the oil drain plug and avoid rounding it off

8.13 Since the oil filter is mounted in the upside down position, pack rags around it before removal it to minimize the mess - since it's usually on very tight, you'll need a special wrench for removal - DO NOT use the wrench to tighten the new filter

8.15 Lubricate the oil filter gasket with clean engine oil before installing the filter on the engine

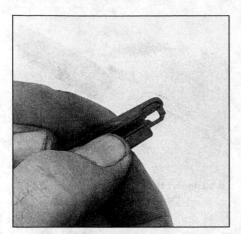

9.5a To remove the old wiper blade element, pull the top end of the element down until you can see the replacement hole in the frame . . .

9.5b . . . then pull the element tab out of the hole (note the relationship to the frame) and slide the element from the frame

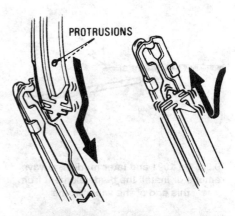

9.7 To install a new element, insert the end of the blade with the small protrusions into the replacement hole and work the rubber along the slot in the blade frame - once all the rubber is in the frame slot, allow it to expand and fill in the end

only by a jack. The jack provided with your vehicle is designed solely for raising the vehicle to remove and replace the wheels. Always use jackstands to support the vehicle when it becomes necessary to place your body underneath the vehicle.

7   Being careful not to touch the hot exhaust components, place the drain pan under the drain plug in the bottom of the pan and remove the plug **(see illustration).** You may want to wear gloves while unscrewing the plug the final few turns if the engine is really hot.

8   Allow the old oil to drain into the pan. It may be necessary to move the pan farther under the engine as the oil flow slows to a trickle. Inspect the old oil for the presence of metal shavings and chips.

9   After all the oil has drained, wipe off the drain plug with a clean rag. Even minute metal particles clinging to the plug would immediately contaminate the new oil.

10   Clean the area around the drain plug opening, reinstall the plug and tighten it securely, but do not strip the threads.

11   Move the drain pan into position under the oil filter.

12   Remove all tools, rags, etc. from under the vehicle, being careful not to spill the oil in the drain pan, then lower the vehicle.

13   Loosen the oil filter **(see illustration)** by turning it counterclockwise with the filter wrench. Any standard filter wrench should work. Once the filter is loose, use your hands to unscrew it from the block. Just as the filter is detached from the block, immediately tilt the open end up to prevent the oil inside the filter from spilling out. **Warning:** *The engine exhaust manifold may still be hot, so be careful.*

14   With a clean rag, wipe off the mounting surface on the block. If a residue of old oil is allowed to remain, it will smoke when the block is heated up. It will also prevent the new filter from seating properly. Also make sure that the none of the old gasket remains stuck to the mounting surface. It can be removed with a scraper if necessary.

15   Compare the old filter with the new one to make sure they are the same type. Smear some engine oil on the rubber gasket of the new filter and screw it into place **(see illustration).** Because overtightening the filter will damage the gasket, do not use a filter wrench to tighten the filter. Tighten it by hand until the gasket contacts the seating surface. Then seat the filter by giving it an additional 3/4-turn.

16   Add new oil to the engine through the oil filler cap in the valve cover. Use a spout or funnel to prevent oil from spilling onto the top of the engine. Pour three quarts of fresh oil into the engine. Wait a few minutes to allow the oil to drain into the pan, then check the level on the oil dipstick (see Section 4 if necessary). If the oil level is at or near the F mark, install the filler cap hand tight, start the engine and allow the new oil to circulate.

17   Allow the engine to run for about a minute. While the engine is

running, look under the vehicle and check for leaks at the oil pan drain plug and around the oil filter. If either is leaking, stop the engine and tighten the plug or filter slightly.

18   Wait a few minutes to allow the oil to trickle down into the pan, then recheck the level on the dipstick and, if necessary, add enough oil to bring the level to the F mark.

19   During the first few trips after an oil change, make it a point to check frequently for leaks and proper oil level.

20   The old oil drained from the engine cannot be reused in its present state and should be discarded. Oil reclamation centers, auto repair shops and gas stations will normally accept the oil, which can be refined and used again. After the oil has cooled, it can be drained into a suitable container (capped plastic jugs, topped bottles, milk cartons, etc.) for transport to one of these disposal sites.

9   Windshield wiper blade inspection and replacement (every 6000 miles or 6 months)

Refer to illustrations 9.5a, 9.5b, 9.7, 9.9a, 9.9b and 9.10

1   The windshield wiper and blade assembly should be inspected periodically for damage, loose components and cracked or worn blade elements.

2   Road film can build up on the wiper blades and affect their efficiency, so they should be washed regularly with a mild detergent solution.

3   The action of the wiping mechanism can loosen bolts, nuts and fasteners, so they should be checked and tightened, as necessary, at the same time the wiper blades are checked.

4   If the wiper blade elements are cracked, worn or warped, or no longer clean adequately, they should be replaced with new ones.

1990 and earlier models

5   Lift the arm assembly away from the glass for clearance and pull the top end of the rubber blade element in **(see illustrations)** until the rubber blade is free of the end slot and you can see the replacement hole.

6   Remove the rubber blade from the frame and discard it.

7   To install a new rubber wiper element, insert the end with the small protrusions **(see illustration)** into the replacement hole and work the rubber along the slot in the blade frame.

8   Once all the rubber is in the frame slot, allow it to expand and fill in the end.

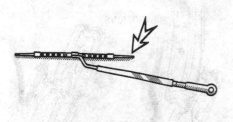

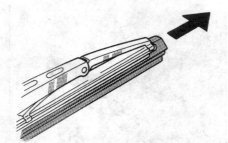

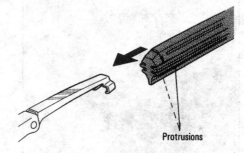

9.9a On 1991 and later models, always remove or install the blade element from this end of the wiper frame

9.9b After detaching the end of the element, slide it out of the end of the frame

9.10 Insert the end of the element with the protrusions in first

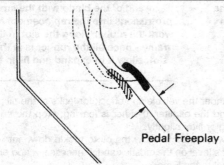
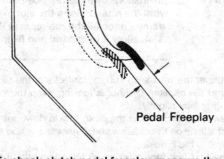

10.1 To check clutch pedal freeplay, measure the distance between the natural resting place of the pedal and the point at which you encounter resistance

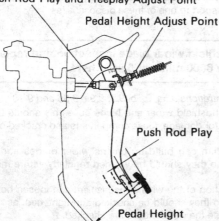

10.2 The clutch pedal pushrod play, pedal height and freeplay adjustments are made by loosening the locknut and turning the threaded adjuster

1991 and later models

9   Detach the blade insert element and pull it out of the right end of the wiper frame **(see illustrations)**.

10   Insert the new element end with the small protrusions into the right side of the wiper frame **(see illustration)**. Slide the element fully into place, then seat the protrusions in the end of the frames to secure it.

10   Clutch pedal freeplay check and adjustment (every 6000 miles or 6 months)

Refer to illustrations 10.1 and 10.2

1   Press down lightly on the clutch pedal and, with a small steel ruler, measure the distance that it moves freely before the clutch resistance is felt **(see illustration)**. The freeplay should be within the specified limits. If it isn't, it must be adjusted.

2   Loosen the locknut on the pedal end of the clutch pushrod **(see illustration)**.

3   Turn the pushrod until pedal freeplay and pushrod freeplay are correct.

4   Tighten the locknut.

5   After adjusting the pedal freeplay, check the pedal height.

6   If pedal height is incorrect, loosen the locknut and turn the stopper bolt until the height is correct. Tighten the locknut.

11   Battery check, maintenance and charging (every 6000 miles or 6 months)

Refer to illustrations 11.1, 11.6a, 11.6b, 11.7a and 11.7b

Warning: *Certain precautions must be followed when checking and servicing the battery. Hydrogen gas, which is highly flammable, is always present in the battery cells, so keep lighted tobacco and all other open flames and sparks away from the battery. The electrolyte inside the battery is actually dilute sulfuric acid, which will cause injury if splashed on your skin or in your eyes. It will also ruin clothes and painted surfaces. When removing the battery cables, always detach the negative cable first and hook it up last!*

1   A routine preventive maintenance program for the battery in your vehicle is the only way to ensure quick and reliable starts. But before performing any battery maintenance, make sure that you have the proper equipment necessary to work safely around the battery **(see illustration)**.

2   There are also several precautions that should be taken whenever battery maintenance is performed. Before servicing the battery, always turn the engine and all accessories off and disconnect the cable from the negative terminal of the battery.

3   The battery produces hydrogen gas, which is both flammable and explosive. Never create a spark, smoke or light a match around the battery. Always charge the battery in a ventilated area.

4   Electrolyte contains poisonous and corrosive sulfuric acid. Do not allow it to get in your eyes, on your skin on your clothes. Never ingest it. Wear protective safety glasses when working near the battery. Keep children away from the battery.

5   Note the external condition of the battery. If the positive terminal and cable clamp on your vehicle's battery is equipped with a rubber protector, make sure that it's not torn or damaged. It should

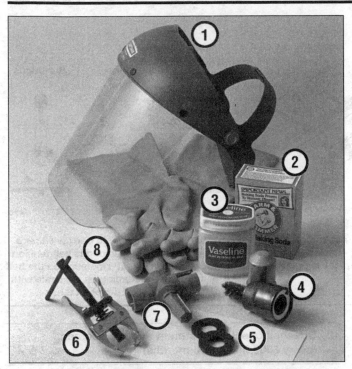

11.1 Tools and materials required for battery maintenance

1   *Face shield/safety goggles* - *When removing corrosion with a brush, the acidic particles can easily fly up into your eyes*

2   *Baking soda* - *A solution of baking soda and water can be used to neutralize corrosion*

3   *Petroleum jelly* - *A layer of this on the battery posts will help prevent corrosion*

4   *Battery post/cable cleaner* - *This wire brush cleaning tool will remove all traces of corrosion from the battery posts and cable clamps*

5   *Treated felt washers* - *Placing one of these on each post, directly under the cable clamps, will help prevent corrosion*

6   *Puller* - *Sometimes the cable clamps are very difficult to pull off the posts, even after the nut/bolt has been completely loosened. This tool pulls the clamp straight up and off the post without damage*

7   *Battery post/cable cleaner* - *Here is another cleaning tool which is a slightly different version of number 4 above, but it does the same thing*

8   *Rubber gloves* - *Another safety item to consider when servicing the battery; remember that's acid inside the battery*

completely cover the terminal. Look for any corroded or loose connections, cracks in the case or cover or loose hold-down clamps. Also check the entire length of each cable for cracks and frayed conductors.

6   If corrosion, which looks like white, fluffy deposits **(see illustration)** is evident, particularly around the terminals, the battery should be removed for cleaning. Loosen the cable clamp bolts with a wrench, being careful to remove the ground cable first, and slide them off the terminals **(see illustration)**. Then disconnect the hold-down clamp bolt and nut, remove the clamp and lift the battery from the engine compartment.

7   Clean the cable clamps thoroughly with a battery brush or a terminal cleaner and a solution of warm water and baking soda **(see illustration)**. Wash the terminals and the top of the battery case with the same solution but make sure that the solution doesn't get into the battery When cleaning the cables, terminals and battery top, wear safety goggles and rubber gloves to prevent any solution from coming in contact with your eyes or hands. Wear old clothes too - even diluted, sulfuric acid splashed onto clothes will burn holes in them. If the

1

11.6a Battery terminal corrosion usually appears as light, fluffy powder

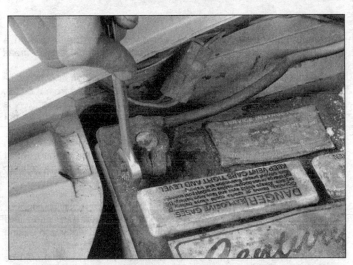

11.6b Removing a cable from the battery post with a wrench - sometimes a special battery pliers is required for this procedure if corrosion has caused deterioration of the nut hex (always remove the ground cable first and hook it up last!)

11.7a When cleaning the cable clamps, all corrosion must be removed (the inside of the clamp is tapered to match the taper on the post, so don't remove too much material)

11.7b Regardless of the type of tool used to clean the battery posts, a clean, shiny surface should be the result

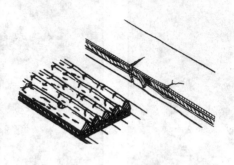

12.3 Check the multi-ribbed belt for signs of wear like these – if the belt looks worn, replace it

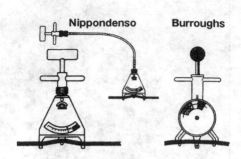

12.4 If you are able to borrow either a Nippondenso or Burroughs belt tension gauge, this is how it's installed on the belt - compare the reading on the scale with the specified drivebelt tension

terminals have been extensively corroded, clean them up with a terminal cleaner **(see illustration)**. Thoroughly wash all cleaned areas with plain water.
8   Make sure that the battery tray is in good condition and the hold-down clamp bolt or nut is tight. If the battery is removed from the tray, make sure no parts remain in the bottom of the tray when the battery is reinstalled. When reinstalling the hold-down clamp bolt or nut, do not overtighten it.
9   Information on removing and installing the battery can be found in Chapter 5. Information on jump starting can be found at the front of this manual. For more detailed battery checking procedures, refer to the *Haynes Automotive Electrical Manual*.

Cleaning

10   Corrosion on the hold-down components, battery case and surrounding areas can be removed with a solution of water and baking soda. Thoroughly rinse all cleaned areas with plain water.
11   Any metal parts of the vehicle damaged by corrosion should be covered with a zinc-based primer, then painted.

Charging

Warning: *When batteries are being charged, hydrogen gas, which is very explosive and flammable, is produced. Do not smoke or allow open flames near a charging or a recently charged battery. Wear eye protection when near the battery during charging. Also, make sure the charger is unplugged before connecting or disconnecting the battery from the charger.*
12   Slow-rate charging is the best way to restore a battery that's discharged to the point where it will not start the engine. It's also a good way to maintain the battery charge in a vehicle that's only driven a few miles between starts. Maintaining the battery charge is particularly important in the winter when the battery must work harder to start the engine and electrical accessories that drain the battery are in greater use.
13   It's best to use a one or two-amp battery charger (sometimes called a "trickle" charger). They are the safest and put the least strain on the battery. They are also the least expensive. For a faster charge, you can use a higher amperage charger, but don't use one rated more than 1/10th the amp/hour rating of the battery. Rapid boost charges that claim to restore the power of the battery in one to two hours are hardest on the battery and can damage batteries not in good condition. This type of charging should only be used in emergency situations.
14   The average time necessary to charge a battery should be listed in the instructions that come with the charger. As a general rule, a trickle charger will charge a battery in 12 to 16 hours.

12 Drivebelt check, adjustment and replacement (every 6000 miles or 6 months)

Refer to illustrations 12.3, 12.4, 12.5, 12.6 and 12.10

Check

1   The alternator, power steering pump and air conditioning compressor drivebelts, also referred to as simply "fan" belts, are located at the right end of the engine. The good condition and proper adjustment of the alternator belt is critical to the operation of the engine. Because of their composition and the high stresses to which they are subjected, drivebelts stretch and deteriorate as they get older. They must therefore be periodically inspected.
2   The number of belts used on a particular vehicle depends on the accessories installed. One belt transmits power from the crankshaft to the alternator and air conditioning. If the vehicle is equipped with power steering, the pump is driven by it's own belt.
3   With the engine off, open the hood and locate the drivebelts at the left end of the engine. With a flashlight, check each belt for separation of the adhesive rubber on both sides of the core, core separation from the belt side, a severed core, separation of the ribs from the adhesive rubber, cracking or separation of the ribs, and torn or worn ribs or cracks in the inner ridges of the ribs **(see illustration)**. Also check for fraying and glazing, which gives the belt a shiny appearance. Both sides of the belt should be inspected, which means you will have to twist the belt to check the underside. Use your fingers to feel the belt where you can't see it. If any of the above conditions are evident, replace the belt (go to Step 8).
4   To check the tension of each belt in accordance with factory specifications, install either a Nippondenso or Burroughs belt tension gauge on the belt **(see illustration)**. Measure the tension in accordance with the manufacturer's instructions and compare your measurement to the specified drivebelt tension for either a used or new belt. **Note:** *A "used" belt is defined as any belt which has been operated more than five minutes on the engine; a "new" belt is one that has been used for less than five minutes.*
5   If you don't have either of the above tools, and cannot borrow one, the following rule of thumb method is recommended: Push firmly on the belt with your thumb at a distance halfway between the pulleys and note how far the belt can be pushed (deflected). Measure this deflection with a ruler **(see illustration)**. The belt should deflect 1/4-inch if the distance from pulley center to pulley center is between 7 and 11 inches; the belt should deflect 1/2-inch if the distance from pulley center to pulley center is between 12 and 16 inches.

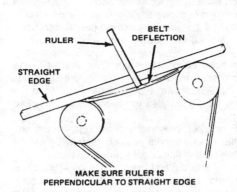

12.5 Measuring drivebelt deflection with a straightedge and ruler

12.6 After loosening the pivot bolt and nut (A), a socket with an extension can be used to turn the adjusting bolt (B)

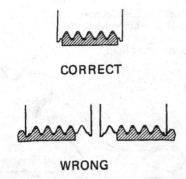

12.10 When installing a multi-ribbed belt, make sure that it is centered - it must not overlap either edge of the pulley

Adjustment

6   If the alternator/air conditioner compressor belt must be adjusted, loosen the alternator pivot bolt located on the front left corner of the block. Loosen the locking bolt and turn the adjusting bolt **(see illustration)**. Measure the belt tension in accordance with one of the above methods. Repeat this step until the air conditioning compressor drivebelt is adjusted.

7   Adjust the power steering pump belt by loosening adjustment bolt that secures the pump to the slotted bracket and pivot the pump (away from the engine to tighten the belt, toward it to loosen it). Repeat the procedure until the drivebelt tension is correct and tighten the bolt.

Replacement

8   To replace a belt, follow the above procedures for drivebelt adjustment but slip the belt off the crankshaft pulley and remove it. If you are replacing the power steering pump belt, you will have to remove the air conditioning compressor belt first because of the way they are arranged on the crankshaft pulley. Because of this and because belts tend to wear out more or less together, it is a good idea to replace both belts at the same time. Mark each belt and its appropriate pulley groove so the replacement belts can be installed in their proper positions.

9   Take the old belts to the parts store in order to make a direct comparison for length, width and design.

10   After replacing the drivebelt, make sure that it fits properly in the ribbed grooves in the pulleys **(see illustration)**. It is essential that the belt be properly centered.

11   Adjust the belt(s) in accordance with the procedure outlined above.

13   Underhood hose check and replacement (every 6000 miles or 6 months)

Caution: *Replacement of air conditioning hoses must be left to a dealer service department or air conditioning shop that has the equipment to depressurize the system safely. Never remove air conditioning components or hoses until the system has been depressurized.*

General

1   High temperatures in the engine compartment can cause the deterioration of the rubber and plastic hoses used for engine, accessory and emission systems operation. Periodic inspection should be made for cracks, loose clamps, material hardening and leaks.

2   Information specific to the cooling system hoses can be found in Section 14.

3   Some, but not all, hoses are secured to the fittings with clamps.

Where clamps are used, check to be sure they haven't lost their tension, allowing the hose to leak. If clamps aren't used, make sure the hose has not expanded and/or hardened where it slips over the fitting, allowing it to leak.

Vacuum hoses

4   It's quite common for vacuum hoses, especially those in the emissions system, to be color coded or identified by colored stripes molded into them. Various systems require hoses with different wall thickness, collapse resistance and temperature resistance. When replacing hoses, be sure the new ones are made of the same material.

5   Often the only effective way to check a hose is to remove it completely from the vehicle. If more than one hose is removed, be sure to label the hoses and fittings to ensure correct installation.

6   When checking vacuum hoses, be sure to include any plastic T-fittings in the check. Inspect the fittings for cracks and the hose where it fits over the fitting for distortion, which could cause leakage.

7   A small piece of vacuum hose (1/4-inch inside diameter) can be used as a stethoscope to detect vacuum leaks. Hold one end of the hose to your ear and probe around vacuum hoses and fittings, listening for the "hissing" sound characteristic of a vacuum leak. **Warning:** *When probing with the vacuum hose stethoscope, be very careful not to come into contact with moving engine components such as the drivebelts, cooling fan, etc.*

Fuel hose

Warning: *There are certain precautions which must be taken when inspecting or servicing fuel system components. Work in a well ventilated area and do not allow open flames (cigarettes, appliance pilot lights, etc.) or bare light bulbs near the work area. Mop up any spills immediately and do not store fuel soaked rags where they could ignite.*

8   Check all rubber fuel lines for deterioration and chafing. Check especially for cracks in areas where the hose bends and just before fittings, such as where a hose attaches to the fuel filter.

9   High quality fuel line, usually identified by the word Fluoro-elastomer printed on the hose, should be used for fuel line replacement. Never, under any circumstances, use unreinforced vacuum line, clear plastic tubing or water hose for fuel lines.

10   Spring-type clamps are commonly used on fuel lines. These clamps often lose their tension over a period of time, and can be "sprung" during removal. Replace all spring-type clamps with screw clamps whenever a hose is replaced.

Metal lines

11   Sections of metal line are often used for fuel line between the fuel pump and fuel injection unit. Check carefully to be sure the line has not been bent or crimped and that cracks have not started in the line.

12   If a section of metal fuel line must be replaced, only seamless

ALWAYS CHECK hose for chafed or burned areas that may cause an untimely and costly failure.

SOFT hose indicates inside deterioration. This deterioration can contaminate the cooling system and cause particles to clog the radiator.

HARDENED hose can fail at any time. Tightening hose clamps will not seal the connection or stop leaks.

SWOLLEN hose or oil soaked ends indicate danger and possible failure from oil or grease contamination. Squeeze the hose to locate cracks and breaks that cause leaks.

14.4 Hoses, like drivebelts, have a habit of failing at the worst possible time - to prevent the inconvenience of a blown radiator or heater hose, inspect them carefully as shown here

steel tubing should be used, since copper and aluminum tubing don't have the strength necessary to withstand normal engine vibration.

13   Check the metal brake lines where they enter the master cylinder and brake proportioning unit (if used) for cracks in the lines or loose fittings. Any sign of brake fluid leakage calls for an immediate thorough inspection of the brake system.

14   Cooling system check (every 6000 miles or 6 months)

Refer to illustration 14.4

1   Many major engine failures can be attributed to a faulty cooling system. If the vehicle is equipped with an automatic transaxle, the cooling system also cools the transaxle fluid and thus plays an important role in prolonging transaxle life.

2   The cooling system should be checked with the engine cold. Do this before the vehicle is driven for the day or after the engine has been shut off for at least three hours.

3   Remove the radiator cap by turning it to the left until it reaches a stop. If you hear a hissing sound (indicating there is still pressure in the system), wait until it stops. Now press down on the cap with the palm of your hand and continue turning to the left until the cap can be removed. Thoroughly clean the cap, inside and out, with clean water. Also clean the filler neck on the radiator. All traces of corrosion should be removed. The coolant inside the radiator should be relatively transparent. If it's rust colored, the system should be drained and refilled (see Section 27). If the coolant level isn't up to the top, add additional antifreeze/coolant mixture (see Section 4).

4   Carefully check the large upper and lower radiator hoses along with the smaller diameter heater hoses which run from the engine to

the firewall. Inspect each hose along its entire length, replacing any hose which is cracked, swollen or shows signs of deterioration. Cracks may become more apparent if the hose is squeezed **(see illustration)**. Regardless of condition, it's a good idea to replace hoses with new ones every two years.

5   Make sure that all hose connections are tight. A leak in the cooling system will usually show up as white or rust colored deposits on the areas adjoining the leak. If wire-type clamps are used at the ends of the hoses, it may be a good idea to replace them with more secure screw-type clamps.

6   Use compressed air or a soft brush to remove bugs, leaves, etc. from the front of the radiator or air conditioning condenser. Be careful not to damage the delicate cooling fins or cut yourself on them.

7   Every other inspection, or at the first indication of cooling system problems, have the cap and system pressure tested. If you don't have a pressure tester, most gas stations and repair shops will do this for a minimal charge.

15   Tire rotation (every 6000 miles or 6 months)

Refer to illustration 15.2

1   The tires should be rotated at the specified intervals and whenever uneven wear is noticed. Since the vehicle will be raised and the tires removed anyway, check the brakes (see Section 16) at this time.

2   Radial tires must be rotated in a specific pattern **(see illustration)**.

3   Refer to the information in *Jacking and towing* at the front of this manual for the proper procedures to follow when raising the vehicle and changing a tire. If the brakes are to be checked, do not apply the parking brake as stated. Make sure the tires are blocked to prevent the vehicle from rolling.

4   Preferably, the entire vehicle should be raised at the same time. This can be done on a hoist or by jacking up each corner and then lowering the vehicle onto jackstands placed under the frame rails. Always use four jackstands and make sure the vehicle is firmly supported.

5   After rotation, check and adjust the tire pressures as necessary and be sure to check the lug nut tightness.

6   For further information on the wheels and tires, refer to Chapter 10.

16   Brake check (every 15,000 miles or 12 months)

Note: *For detailed photographs of the brake system, refer to Chapter 9.*

1   In addition to the specified intervals, the brakes should be inspected every time the wheels are removed or whenever a defect is suspected. Any of the following symptoms could indicate a potential brake system defect: The vehicle pulls to one side when the brake pedal is depressed; the brakes make squealing or dragging noises when applied; brake travel is excessive; the pedal pulsates; brake fluid leaks, usually onto the inside of the tire or wheel.

2   The disc brake pads have built-in wear indicators which should make a high pitched squealing or scraping noise when they are worn to the replacement point. When you hear this noise, replace the pads immediately or expensive damage to the discs can result.

3   Loosen the wheel lug nuts.

4   Raise the vehicle and place it securely on jackstands.

5   Remove the wheels (see *Jacking and towing* at the front of this book, or your owner's manual, if necessary).

Disc brakes

Refer to illustration 16.6

6   There are two pads - an outer and an inner - in each caliper. The pads are visible through small inspection holes in each caliper **(see illustration)** .

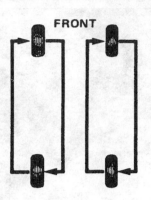

15.2 The recommended tire rotation pattern for these vehicles

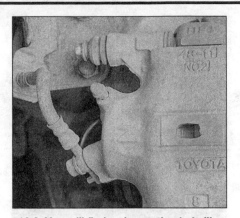

16.6 You will find an inspection hole like this in each caliper - placing a steel ruler across the hole should enable you to determine the thickness of remaining pad material for both inner and outer pads

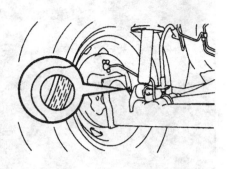

16.12 A quick check of the remaining drum brake shoe lining material can be made by removing the rubber plug in the backing plate and looking through the inspection hole

7   Check the pad thickness by looking at each end of the caliper and through the inspection hole in the caliper body. If the lining material is less than the thickness listed in this Chapter's Specifications, replace the pads. **Note:** *Keep in mind that the lining material is riveted or bonded to a metal backing plate and the metal portion is not included in this measurement.*

8   If it is difficult to determine the exact thickness of the remaining pad material by the above method, or if you are at all concerned about the condition of the pads, remove the caliper(s), then remove the pads from the calipers for further inspection (refer to Chapter 9).

9   Once the pads are removed from the calipers, clean them with brake cleaner and remeasure them with a small steel pocket ruler or a vernier caliper.

10   Measure the disc thickness with a micrometer to make sure that it still has service life remaining. If any disc is thinner than the specified minimum thickness, replace it (refer to Chapter 9). Even if the disc has service life remaining, check its condition. Look for scoring, gouging and burned spots. If these conditions exist, remove the disc and have it resurfaced (see Chapter 9).

11   Before installing the wheels, check all brake lines and hoses for damage, wear, deformation, cracks, corrosion, leakage, bends and twists, particularly in the vicinity of the rubber hoses at the calipers. Check the clamps for tightness and the connections for leakage. Make sure that all hoses and lines are clear of sharp edges, moving parts and the exhaust system. If any of the above conditions are noted, repair, reroute or replace the lines and/or fittings as necessary (see Chapter 9).

Rear drum brakes

Refer to illustrations 16.12, 16.15 and 16.17

12   To check the brake shoe lining thickness without removing the brake drums, remove the rubber plug from the backing plate and use a flashlight to inspect the linings **(see illustration)**. For a more thorough brake inspection, follow the procedure below.

13   Refer to Section 34 and remove the rear brake drums.

14   **Warning:** *Brake dust produced by lining wear and deposited on brake components contains asbestos, which is hazardous to your health. DO NOT blow it out with compressed air and DO NOT inhale it! DO NOT use gasoline or solvents to remove the dust. Brake system cleaner should be used to flush the dust into a drain pan. After the brake components are wiped clean with a damp rag, dispose of the contaminated rag(s) and solvent in a covered and labeled container. Try to use non-asbestos replacement parts whenever possible.*

15   Note the thickness of the lining material on the rear brake shoes **(see illustration)** and look for signs of contamination by brake fluid and grease. If the lining material is within 1/16-inch of the recessed rivets or metal shoes, replace the brake shoes with new ones. The shoes should also be replaced if they are cracked, glazed (shiny lining

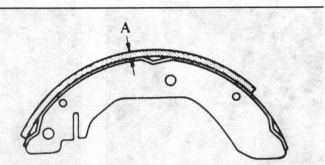

16.15 If the lining is bonded to the brake shoe, measure the lining thickness from the outer surface to the metal shoe, as shown here; if the lining is riveted to the shoe, measure from the lining outer surface to the rivet head

16.17 Carefully peel back the wheel cylinder boot and check for leaking fluid indicating that the cylinder must be replaced or rebuilt

surfaces) or contaminated with brake fluid or grease. See Chapter 9 for the replacement procedure.

16   Check the shoe return and hold-down springs and the adjusting mechanism to make sure they're installed correctly and in good condition. Deteriorated or distorted springs, if not replaced, could allow the linings to drag and wear prematurely.

17   Check the wheel cylinders for leakage by carefully peeling back the rubber boots **(see illustration)**. If brake fluid is noted behind the

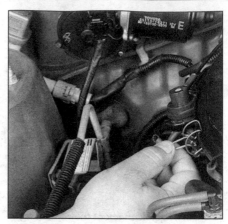

17.2a Lift up on the four clips to detach them, then remove the wingnut and lift the cover off

17.2b Raise the air cleaner cover and lift the element out of the housing

17.3a Detach the clips and separate the cover from the air cleaner housing (early model)

17.3b Lift the element out of the housing

17.3c On later models, detach the four clips and pull the cover up

17.3d Hold the cover up out of the way and lift the element out

boots, the wheel cylinders must be replaced (see Chapter 9).

18   Check the drums for cracks, score marks, deep scratches and hard spots, which will appear as small discolored areas. If imperfections cannot be removed with emery cloth, the drums must be resurfaced by an automotive machine shop (see Chapter 9 for more detailed information).

19   Refer to Chapter 9 and install the brake drums.

20   Install the wheels and snug the wheel lug nuts finger tight.

21   Remove the jackstands and lower the vehicle.

22   Tighten the wheel lug nuts to the torque listed in this Chapter's Specifications.

Brake booster check

23   Sit in the driver's seat and perform the following sequence of tests.

24   With the engine stopped, depress the brake pedal several times- the travel distance should not change.

25   With the brake fully depressed, start the engine - the pedal should move down a little when the engine starts.

26   Depress the brake, stop the engine and hold the pedal in for about 30 seconds - the pedal should neither sink nor rise.

27   Restart the engine, run it for about a minute and turn it off. Then firmly depress the brake several times - the pedal travel should decrease with each application.

28   If your brakes do not operate as described above when the preceding tests are performed, the brake booster is either in need of repair or has failed. Refer to Chapter 9 for the removal procedure.

Parking brake

29   Slowly pull up on the parking brake and count the number of clicks you hear until the handle is up as far as it will go. The adjustment is correct if you hear the specified number of clicks. If you hear more or fewer clicks, it's time to adjust the parking brake (refer to Chapter 9).

30   An alternative method of checking the parking brake is to park the vehicle on a steep hill with the parking brake set and the transaxle in Neutral. If the parking brake cannot prevent the vehicle from rolling, it is in need of adjustment (see Chapter 9).

17   Air filter replacement (every 15,000 miles or 12 months)

Refer to illustrations 17.2a, 17.2b, 17.3a, 17.3b, 17.3c and 17.3d

1   On carburetor-equipped models, the filter is located inside a housing on top of the engine.

2   Release the spring clips, remove the wingnut and detach the cover, then lift the element out **(see illustrations)**.

3   On fuel-injected models, the air filter is located inside a housing at the right (passenger) side of the engine compartment. To remove the air filter, release the four spring clips that keep the two halves of the air cleaner housing together, then lift the cover up and remove the air filter element **(see illustrations)**.

4   Inspect the outer surface of the filter element. If it is dirty, replace it. If it is only moderately dusty, it can be reused by blowing it clean

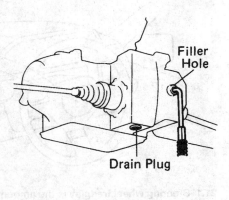

19.3 Use a pump to fill the differential

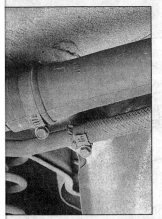

... filler and breather hoses for
... nd make sure the clamps
are tight

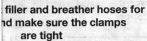

5   Wipe out the inside of the air cleaner housing.
6   Place the new filter into the air cleaner housing, making sure it
seats properly.
7   Installation of the cover is the reverse of removal.

18   Fuel system check (every 15,000 miles or 12 months)

Refer to illustrations 18.2 and 18.5
Warning: *Certain precautions should be observed when inspecting or servicing the fuel system components. Work in a well ventilated area and do not allow open flames (cigarettes, appliance pilot lights, etc.) near the work area. Mop up spills immediately and do not store fuel soaked rags where they could ignite. It is a good idea to keep a dry chemical (Class B) fire extinguisher near the work area any time the fuel system is being serviced.*

1   If you smell gasoline while driving or after the vehicle has been sitting in the sun, inspect the fuel system immediately.
2   Remove the gas filler cap and inspect if for damage and corrosion. The gasket should have an unbroken sealing imprint. If the gasket is damaged or corroded, remove it and install a new one **(see illustration)**.
3   Inspect the fuel feed and return lines for cracks. Make sure that the threaded flare-nut type connectors which secure the metal fuel lines to the fuel injection system and the banjo bolts which secure the banjo fittings to the in-line fuel filter are tight.
4   Since some components of the fuel system - the fuel tank and part of the fuel feed and return lines, for example - are underneath the vehicle, they can be inspected more easily with the vehicle raised on a hoist. If that's not possible, raise the vehicle and support it securely on jackstands.
5   With the vehicle raised and safely supported, inspect the gas tank and filler neck for punctures, cracks and other damage. The connection between the filler neck and the tank is particularly critical. Sometimes a rubber filler neck will leak because of loose clamps or deteriorated rubber **(see illustration)**. These are problems a home mechanic can usually rectify. **Warning:** *Do not, under any circumstances, try to repair a fuel tank (except rubber components). A welding torch or any open flame can easily cause fuel vapors inside the tank to explode.*
6   Carefully check all rubber hoses and metal lines leading away from the fuel tank. Check for loose connections, deteriorated hoses,

crimped lines and other damage. Carefully inspect the lines from the tank to the fuel injection system. Repair or replace damaged sections as necessary (see Chapter 4).

19   Automatic transaxle differential lubricant level check (every 15,000 miles or 12 months)

Refer to illustration 19.3
1   The automatic transaxle differential has a separate lubricant supply with a check/fill plug which must be removed to check the level. If the vehicle is raised to gain access to the plug, be sure to support it safely on jackstands - DO NOT crawl under the vehicle when it's supported only by the jack.
2   Remove the check/fill plug from the front of the differential.
3   Use your little finger as a dipstick to make sure the lubricant level is even with the bottom of the plug hole. If not, use a syringe or a gear oil pump to add the recommended lubricant (see this Chapter's Specifications) until it just starts to run out of the opening **(see illustration)**.
4   Install the plug and tighten it securely.

20   Manual transaxle lubricant level check (every 15,000 miles or 12 months)

Refer to illustration 20.1
1   The manual transaxle does not have a dipstick. To check the fluid level, raise the vehicle and support it securely on jackstands. On the

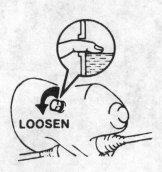

20.1 Use your finger as a dipstick to check the manual transaxle lubricant level

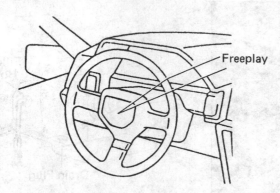

21.1 Steering wheel freeplay is the amount of travel between an initial steering input and the point at which the front wheels begin to turn (indicated by a slight resistance)

lower front side of the transaxle housing, you will see a plug **(see illustration)**. Remove it. If the lubricant level is correct, it should be up to the lower edge of the hole.

2   If the transaxle needs more lubricant (if the level is not up to the hole), use a syringe or a gear oil pump to add more. Stop filling the transaxle when the lubricant begins to run out the hole.

3   Install the plug and tighten it securely. Drive the vehicle a short distance, then check for leaks.

21   Steering and suspension check (every 15,000 miles or 12 months)

Refer to illustrations 21.1, 21.7 and 21.8
Note: *For detailed illustrations of the steering and suspension components, refer to Chapter 10.*

With the wheels on the ground

1   With the vehicle stopped and the front wheels pointed straight ahead, rock the steering wheel gently back and forth. If freeplay **(see illustration)** is excessive , a front wheel bearing, main shaft yoke, intermediate shaft yoke, lower arm balljoint or steering system joint is worn or the steering gear is out of adjustment or broken. Refer to Chapter 10 for the appropriate repair procedure.

2   Other symptoms, such as excessive vehicle body movement over rough roads, swaying (leaning) around corners and binding as the

21.7 To check a balljoint for wear, raise the vehicle, and support it on jackstands, place a 7-inch thick block of wood under the tire, block the wheel with chocks and lower the jack until there is about half a load on the coil spring - then move the lower arm up and down with a prybar to make sure there is no play in the balljoint (if there is, replace it)

steering wheel is turned, may indicate faulty steering and/or suspension components.

3   Check the shock absorbers by pushing down and releasing the vehicle several times at each corner. If the vehicle does not come back to a level position within one or two bounces, the shocks/struts are worn and must be replaced. When bouncing the vehicle up and down, listen for squeaks and noises from the suspension components. Additional information on suspension components can be found in Chapter 10.

Under the vehicle

4   Raise the vehicle with a floor jack and support it securely on jackstands. See *Jacking and towing* at the front of this book for the proper jacking points.

5   Check the tires for irregular wear patterns and proper inflation. See Section 5 in this Chapter for information regarding tire wear and Chapter 10 for the wheel bearing replacement procedures.

6   Inspect the universal joint between the steering shaft and the steering gear housing. Check the steering gear housing for grease leakage or oozing. Make sure that the dust seals and boots are not damaged and that the boot clamps are not loose. Check the steering

21.8 Push on the balljoint boot to check for damage

22.2 Flex the driveaxle boots by hand to check for cracks and/or leaking grease

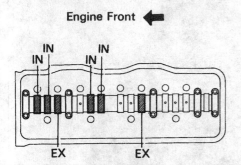

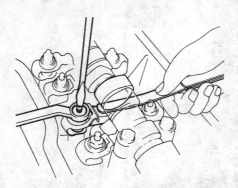

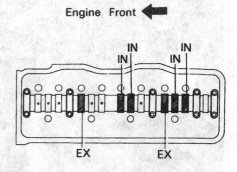

23.5 When the no. 1 piston is at TDC on the compression stroke, the valve clearances for the indicated valves can be measured

23.6 Measure the clearance for each valve with a feeler gauge of the specified thickness - if the clearance is correct, you should feel a slight drag on the gauge as you pull it out

23.8 Rotate the crankshaft 360-degrees, then measure and adjust the indicated valves

linkage for looseness or damage. Check the tie-rod ends for excessive play. Look for loose bolts, broken or disconnected parts and deteriorated rubber bushings on all suspension and steering components. While an assistant turns the steering wheel from side to side, check the steering components for free movement, chafing and binding. If the steering components do not seem to be reacting with the movement of the steering wheel, try to determine where the slack is located.

7   Check the balljoints for wear by placing a 7-inch thick wooden block under each tire. Lower the jack until there is about half a load on the coil spring. Make sure that the front wheels are in a straight forward position and block the wheel with chocks. Move each lower arm up and down with a pry bar **(see illustration)** to ensure that its balljoint has no play. If any balljoint does have play, replace it. See Chapter 10 for the front balljoint replacement procedure.

8   Inspect the balljoint boots for damage and leaking grease **(see illustration)**. Replace the balljoints with new ones if they are damaged (see Chapter 10).

22 Driveaxle boot check (every 15,000 miles or 12 months)

Refer to illustration 22.2

1   The driveaxle boots are very important because they prevent dirt, water and foreign material from entering and damaging the constant velocity (CV) joints. Oil and grease can cause the boot material to deteriorate prematurely, so it's a good idea to wash the boots with soap and water.

2   Inspect the boots for tears and cracks as well as loose clamps **(see illustration)**. If there is any evidence of cracks or leaking lubricant, they must be replaced as described in Chapter 8.

23 Valve clearance check and adjustment (every 30,000 miles or 24 months)

Refer to illustrations 23.5, 23.6 and 23.8

1   Disconnect the negative cable from the battery. **Caution:** *If the stereo in your vehicle is equipped with an anti-theft system, make sure you have the correct activation code before disconnecting the battery.*

2   Disconnect the cruise control cable, air cleaner duct or other components which will interfere with valve cover removal.

3   Remove the valve cover (refer to Chapter 2).

4   Refer to Chapter 2 and position the number 1 piston at TDC on the compression stroke. The number one cylinder rocker arms (closest to the timing belt end of the engine) should be loose and the camshaft lobes facing away from the rocker arms.

5   With the crankshaft in this position, the indicated valves can be checked and adjusted **(see illustration)**.

6   Measure the clearances of the indicated valves with a feeler gauge of the specified thickness as shown **(see illustration)**. To adjust the clearance, loosen the locknut, turn the adjusting screw counterclockwise and insert the appropriate size feeler gauge between the rocker arm and the camshaft. Carefully tighten the adjusting screw until you can feel a slight drag on the feeler gauge as you withdraw it from between the rocker arm and camshaft.

7   Hold the adjusting screw with a screwdriver (to keep it from turning) and tighten the locknut. Recheck the clearance to make sure it hasn't changed.

8   Turn the crankshaft one complete revolution and realign the timing marks. Measure the remaining valves **(see illustration)**.

9   Repeat this procedure until all the valves which are out of clearance have been corrected.

10   Installation of the valve cover, air cleaner duct, etc. is the reverse of removal.

24 Fuel filter replacement (every 30,000 miles or 24 months)

Refer to illustrations 24.2, 24.11a and 24.11b

1   Disconnect the negative battery cable.

Carburetor-equipped engines

2   The translucent plastic fuel filter is located in a spring clip, below

24.2 The fuel filter is clipped to a bracket below the brake master cylinder

1

24.11a Using a backup wrench, remove the banjo bolt at the top and . . .

24.11b . . . loosen the fitting at the bottom of the filter

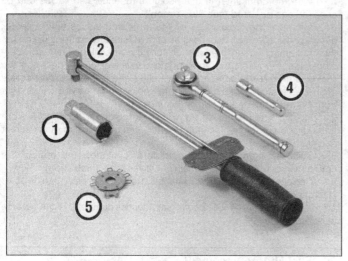

25.1 Tools required for changing spark plugs

1   **Spark plug socket** - *This will have special padding inside to protect the spark plug porcelain insulator*
2   **Torque wrench** - *Although not mandatory, use of this tool is the best way to ensure that the plugs are tightened properly*
3   **Ratchet** - *Standard hand tool to fit the plug socket*
4   **Extension** - *Depending on model and accessories, you may need special extensions and universal joints to reach one or more of the plugs*
5   **Spark plug gap gauge** - *This gauge for checking the gap comes in a variety of styles. Make sure the gap for your engine is included*

the brake master cylinder **(see illustration)**.
3   For easier access, pull the filter out of the clip so both fittings can be reached.
4   Release the hose clamps at the filter fittings and slide them back up the hoses.
5   Disconnect the hose and remove the filter.
6   Push the hoses onto the new filter and position the clamps approximately 1/4-inch back from the ends.
7   Press the filter into the spring clip. Check to make sure its held securely and the hoses aren't kinked.
8   Start the engine and check for leaks.

Fuel-injected engines

9   The canister filter mounted in a bracket on the firewall near the brake master cylinder.
10   Remove any components that would interfere with access to the top of the filter.
11   Using a backup wrench to steady the filter, remove the threaded banjo bolt at the top and loosen the fitting at the bottom of the fuel filter (use a flare-nut wrench if possible **(see illustrations)**.
12   Remove both bracket bolts from the firewall and remove the old filter and the filter support bracket assembly.
13   Note that the inlet and outlet pipes are clearly labeled on their respective ends of the filter and that the flanged end of the filter faces down. Make sure the new filter is installed so that it's facing the proper direction as noted above. When correctly installed, the filter should be installed so that the outlet pipe faces up and the inlet pipe faces down.
14   Using the new crush washers provided by the filter manufacturer, install the inlet and outlet fittings and tighten them securely.
15   The remainder of installation is the reverse of the removal procedure.

25 Spark plug check and replacement (every 30,000 miles or 24 months)

Refer to illustrations 25.1, 25.4a, 25.4b, 25.6, 25.8a, 25.8b and 25.10
1   Spark plug replacement requires a spark plug socket which fits onto a ratchet wrench. This socket is lined with a rubber grommet to protect the porcelain insulator of the spark plug and to hold the plug while you insert it into the spark plug hole. You will also need a wire-type feeler gauge to check and adjust the spark plug gap and a torque wrench to tighten the new plugs to the specified torque **(see illustration)**.
2   If you are replacing the plugs, purchase the new plugs, adjust them to the proper gap and then replace each plug one at a time. **Note:** *When buying new spark plugs, it's essential that you obtain the correct plugs for your specific vehicle. This information can be found in the Specifications Section at the beginning of this Chapter, on the Vehicle Emissions Control Information (VECI) label located on the underside of the hood or in the owner's manual. If these sources specify different plugs, purchase the spark plug type specified on the VECI label because that information is provided specifically for your engine.*
3   Inspect each of the new plugs for defects. If there are any signs of cracks in the porcelain insulator of a plug, don't use it.
4   Check the electrode gaps of the new plugs. Check the gap by inserting the wire gauge of the proper thickness between the

25.4a Spark plug manufacturers recommend using a wire-type gauge when checking the gap - if the wire does not slide between the electrodes with a slight drag, adjustment is required

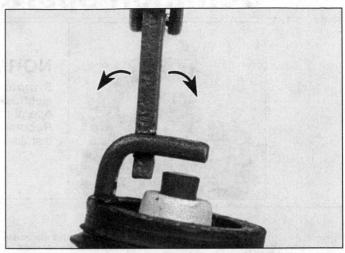

25.4b To change the gap, bend the side electrode only, as indicated by the arrows, and be very careful not to crack or chip the porcelain insulator surrounding the center electrode

1

25.6 When removing the spark plug wires, pull only on the boot and use a twisting/pulling motion - a tool like this one is helpful

25.8a Use a socket wrench with a long extension to unscrew the spark plug

25.8b Lift the spark plug out of the cylinder head

electrodes at the tip of the plug **(see illustration)**. The gap between the electrodes should be identical to that listed in this Chapter's Specifications or on the VECI label. If the gap is incorrect, use the notched adjuster on the feeler gauge body to bend the curved side electrode slightly **(see illustration)**.

5   If the side electrode is not exactly over the center electrode, use the notched adjuster to align them. **Caution:** *If the gap of a new plug must be adjusted, bend only the base of the ground electrode – do not touch the tip.*

Removal

6   To prevent the possibility of mixing up spark plug wires, work on one spark plug at a time. Remove the wire and boot from one spark plug. Grasp the boot - not the cable - as shown, give it a half twisting motion and pull straight up **(see illustration)**.

7   If compressed air is available, blow any dirt or foreign material away from the spark plug area before proceeding (a common bicycle pump will also work).

8   Remove the spark plug **(see illustrations)**.

9   Whether you are replacing the plugs at this time or intend to reuse the old plugs, compare each old spark plug with those shown in the accompanying photos to determine the overall running condition of the engine.

Installation

10   Prior to installation, it's a good idea to lubricate the spark plug threads. A drop of oil from the engine dipstick is a convenient way to do this. It's often difficult to insert spark plugs into their holes without cross-threading them. To avoid this possibility, fit a short piece of

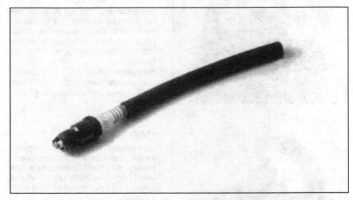

25.10 A length of 3/8-inch ID rubber hose will save time and prevent damaged threads when installing the spark plugs

Common spark plug conditions

NORMAL

Symptoms: Brown to grayish-tan color and slight electrode wear. Correct heat range for engine and operating conditions.

Recommendation: When new spark plugs are installed, replace with plugs of the same heat range.

WORN

Symptoms: Rounded electrodes with a small amount of deposits on the firing end. Normal color. Causes hard starting in damp or cold weather and poor fuel economy.

Recommendation: Plugs have been left in the engine too long. Replace with new plugs of the same heat range. Follow the recommended maintenance schedule.

CARBON DEPOSITS

Symptoms: Dry sooty deposits indicate a rich mixture or weak ignition. Causes misfiring, hard starting and hesitation.

Recommendation: Make sure the plug has the correct heat range. Check for a clogged air filter or problem in the fuel system or engine management system. Also check for ignition system problems.

ASH DEPOSITS

Symptoms: Light brown deposits encrusted on the side or center electrodes or both. Derived from oil and/or fuel additives. Excessive amounts may mask the spark, causing misfiring and hesitation during acceleration.

Recommendation: If excessive deposits accumulate over a short time or low mileage, install new valve guide seals to prevent seepage of oil into the combustion chambers. Also try changing gasoline brands.

OIL DEPOSITS

Symptoms: Oily coating caused by poor oil control. Oil is leaking past worn valve guides or piston rings into the combustion chamber. Causes hard starting, misfiring and hesitation.

Recommendation: Correct the mechanical condition with necessary repairs and install new plugs.

GAP BRIDGING

Symptoms: Combustion deposits lodge between the electrodes. Heavy deposits accumulate and bridge the electrode gap. The plug ceases to fire, resulting in a dead cylinder.

Recommendation: Locate the faulty plug and remove the deposits from between the electrodes.

TOO HOT

Symptoms: Blistered, white insulator, eroded electrode and absence of deposits. Results in shortened plug life.

Recommendation: Check for the correct plug heat range, over-advanced ignition timing, lean fuel mixture, intake manifold vacuum leaks, sticking valves and insufficient engine cooling.

PREIGNITION

Symptoms: Melted electrodes. Insulators are white, but may be dirty due to misfiring or flying debris in the combustion chamber. Can lead to engine damage.

Recommendation: Check for the correct plug heat range, over-advanced ignition timing, lean fuel mixture, insufficient engine cooling and lack of lubrication.

HIGH SPEED GLAZING

Symptoms: Insulator has yellowish, glazed appearance. Indicates that combustion chamber temperatures have risen suddenly during hard acceleration. Normal deposits melt to form a conductive coating. Causes misfiring at high speeds.

Recommendation: Install new plugs. Consider using a colder plug if driving habits warrant.

DETONATION

Symptoms: Insulators may be cracked or chipped. Improper gap setting techniques can also result in a fractured insulator tip. Can lead to piston damage.

Recommendation: Make sure the fuel anti-knock values meet engine requirements. Use care when setting the gaps on new plugs. Avoid lugging the engine.

MECHANICAL DAMAGE

Symptoms: May be caused by a foreign object in the combustion chamber or the piston striking an incorrect reach (too long) plug. Causes a dead cylinder and could result in piston damage.

Recommendation: Repair the mechanical damage. Remove the foreign object from the engine and/or install the correct reach plug.

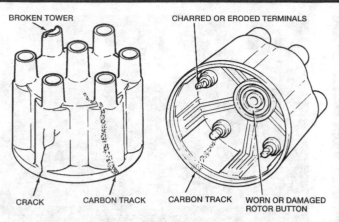

BROKEN TOWER

CHARRED OR ERODED TERMINALS

CRACK

CARBON TRACK

CARBON TRACK

WORN OR DAMAGED ROTOR BUTTON

26.11a Shown here are some of the common defects to look for when inspecting the distributor cap (if in doubt about its condition, install a new one)

26.11b The contacts on this high-mileage distributor cap are burned and it should be replaced with a new one

3/16-inch ID rubber hose over the end of the spark plug **(see illustration)**. The flexible hose acts as a universal joint to help align the plug with the plug hole. Should the plug begin to cross-thread, the hose will slip on the spark plug, preventing thread damage. Tighten the plug to the torque listed in this Chapter's Specifications.

11   Attach the plug wire to the new spark plug, again using a twisting motion on the boot until it is firmly seated on the end of the spark plug.

12   Follow the above procedure for the remaining spark plugs, replacing them one at a time to prevent mixing up the spark plug wires.

26   Spark plug wire, distributor cap and rotor check and replacement (every 30,000 miles or 24 months)

Refer to illustrations 26.11a, 26.11b, 26.12 and 26.13

1   The spark plug wires should be checked whenever new spark plugs are installed.

2   Begin this procedure by making a visual check of the spark plug wires while the engine is running. In a darkened garage (make sure there is ventilation) start the engine and observe each plug wire. Be careful not to come into contact with any moving engine parts. If there is a break in the wire, you will see arcing or a small spark at the damaged area. If arcing is noticed, make a note to obtain new wires, then allow the engine to cool and check the distributor cap and rotor.

3   The spark plug wires should be inspected one at a time to prevent mixing up the order, which is essential for proper engine operation. Each original plug wire should be numbered to help identify its

location. If the number is illegible, a piece of tape can be marked with the correct number and wrapped around the plug wire.

4   Disconnect the plug wire from the spark plug. A removal tool can be used for this purpose or you can grasp the rubber boot, twist the boot half a turn and pull the boot free. Do not pull on the wire itself.

5   Check inside the boot for corrosion, which will look like a white crusty powder.

6   Push the wire and boot back onto the end of the spark plug. It should fit tightly onto the end of the plug. If it doesn't, remove the wire and use pliers to carefully crimp the metal connector inside the wire boot until the fit is snug.

7   Using a clean rag, wipe the entire length of the wire to remove built-up dirt and grease. Once the wire is clean, check for burns, cracks and other damage. Do not bend the wire sharply, because the conductor might break.

8   Disconnect the wire from the distributor. Again, pull only on the rubber boot. Check for corrosion and a tight fit. Replace the wire in the distributor.

9   Inspect the remaining spark plug wires, making sure that each one is securely fastened at the distributor and spark plug when the check is complete.

10   If new spark plug wires are required, purchase a set for your specific engine model. Pre-cut wire sets with the boots already installed are available. Remove and replace the wires one at a time to avoid mix-ups in the firing order.

11   Detach the distributor cap by removing the two cap retaining bolts. Look inside it for cracks, carbon tracks and worn, burned or loose contacts **(see illustrations)**.

12   Pull the rotor off the distributor shaft and examine it for cracks and carbon tracks **(see illustration)**. Replace the cap and rotor if any damage or defects are noted.

13   It is common practice to install a new cap and rotor whenever new spark plug wires are installed, but if you wish to continue using the

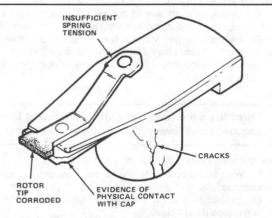

INSUFFICIENT SPRING TENSION

CRACKS

ROTOR TIP CORRODED

EVIDENCE OF PHYSICAL CONTACT WITH CAP

26.12 The ignition rotor should be checked for wear and corrosion as indicated here (if in doubt about its condition, buy a new one)

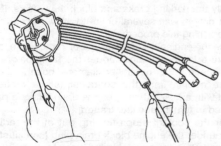

26.13 Measure the resistance value of the distributor cap and the spark plug wires - if it exceeds the specified maximum value, replace either the cap, or the wires, or both

27.4 On most models you will have to remove a cover for access to the radiator drain fitting located at the bottom of the radiator - before opening the valve, push a short section of 3/8-inch ID hose onto the plastic fitting to prevent the coolant from splashing

27.5 After draining the radiator, be sure to fully drain the cooling system by remove the block drain plug located on the side of the engine block (exhaust manifold removed for clarity)

old cap, check the resistance between the spark plug wires and the cap first **(see illustration)**. If the indicated resistance is more than the maximum value listed in this Chapter's Specifications, replace the cap and/or wires.

14   When installing a new cap, remove the wires from the old cap one at a time and attach them to the new cap in the exact same location – do not simultaneously remove all the wires from the old cap or firing order mix-ups may occur.

27   Cooling system servicing (draining, flushing and refilling) (every 30,000 miles or 24 months)

Warning: *Do not allow engine coolant (antifreeze) to come in contact with your skin or painted surfaces of the vehicle. Rinse off spills immediately with plenty of water. Antifreeze is highly toxic if ingested. Never leave antifreeze laying around in an open container or in puddles on the floor; children and pets are attracted by it's sweet smell and may drink it. Check with local authorities about disposing of used antifreeze. Many communities have collection centers which will see that antifreeze is disposed of safely.*

1   Periodically, the cooling system should be drained, flushed and refilled to replenish the antifreeze mixture and prevent formation of rust and corrosion, which can impair the performance of the cooling system and cause engine damage. When the cooling system is serviced, all hoses and the radiator cap should be checked and replaced if necessary.

Draining

Refer to illustrations 27.4 and 27.5

2   Apply the parking brake and block the wheels. If the vehicle has just been driven, wait several hours to allow the engine to cool down before beginning this procedure.

3   Once the engine is completely cool, remove the radiator cap.

4   Move a large container under the radiator drain to catch the coolant. Attach a 3/8-inch inner diameter hose to the drain fitting to direct the coolant into the container (some models are already equipped with a hose), then open the drain fitting (a pair of pliers may be required to turn it) **(see illustration)**.

5   After the coolant stops flowing out of the radiator, move the container under the engine block drain plug **(see illustration)**. Loosen the plug and allow the coolant in the block to drain.

6   While the coolant is draining, check the condition of the radiator hoses, heater hoses and clamps (refer to Section 13 if necessary).

7   Replace any damaged clamps or hoses (see Chapter 3).

Flushing

8   Once the system is completely drained, flush the radiator with fresh water from a garden hose until water runs clear at the drain. The flushing action of the water will remove sediments from the radiator but will not remove rust and scale from the engine and cooling tube surfaces.

9   These deposits can be removed by the chemical action of a cleaner. Follow the procedure outlined in the manufacturer's instructions. If the radiator is severely corroded, damaged or leaking, it should be removed (see Chapter 3) and taken to a radiator repair shop.

10   Remove the overflow hose from the coolant recovery reservoir. Drain the reservoir and flush it with clean water, then reconnect the hose.

Refilling

11   Close and tighten the radiator drain. Install and tighten the block drain plug.

12   Place the heater temperature control in the maximum heat position.

13   Slowly add new coolant (a 50/50 mixture of water and antifreeze) to the radiator until it's full. Add coolant to the reservoir up to the lower mark.

14   Leave the radiator cap off and run the engine in a well-ventilated area until the thermostat opens (coolant will begin flowing through the radiator and the upper radiator hose will become hot).

15   Turn the engine off and let it cool. Add more coolant mixture to bring the level back up to the lip on the radiator filler neck.

16   Squeeze the upper radiator hose to expel air, then add more coolant mixture if necessary. Replace the radiator cap.

17   Start the engine, allow it to reach normal operating temperature and check for leaks.

28   Throttle positioner check and adjustment (carbureted engines only) (every 30,000 miles or 24 months)

Refer to illustrations 28.2, 28.3, 28.4 and 28.6

1   Connect a tachometer to the engine according to the manufacturers instructions.

2   Disconnect the vacuum hose from throttle positioner diaphragm A and plug it **(see illustration)**.

3   Disconnect and plug the throttle positioner vacuum hose connection at the EGR valve **(see illustration)**.

4   Place the throttle positioner on it's first step, check the speed and compare it to the Specifications Section at the beginning of this

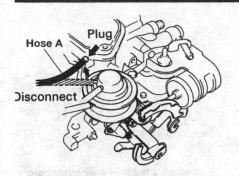

28.2 Disconnect and plug the diaphragm A hose

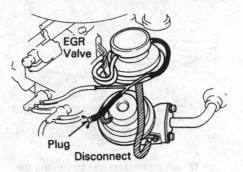

28.3 Disconnect the hose from the EGR valve and plug it

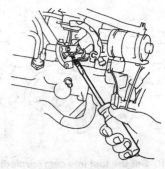

28.4 Turn this screw to adjust the throttle positioner idle speed

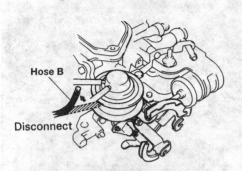

28.6 Pull the hose off the throttle positioner diaphragm B and plug it

29.6 Make sure that fuel squirts out of the accelerator nozzle inside the carburetor opening when the throttle valve is opened

29.7 Turn the screw on the side of the carburetor to adjust the curb idle speed

Chapter. Turn the adjusting screw, if necessary, to obtain the correct speed **(see illustration)**. **Note:** *Make adjustments with the engine cooling fan off.*

5   Reconnect the vacuum hose to diaphragm B. If the idle speed changes from that specified, readjust it.

6   Disconnect the vacuum hose from diaphragm B and plug the hose **(see illustration)**.

7   Move the throttle positioner to the second step and check the rpm reading. Compare this figure to that listed in the Specifications Section at the beginning of this Chapter. If necessary, turn the adjusting screw to obtain the correct speed.

8   After adjustment, reconnect the hoses and turn off the engine.

29   Engine idle speed check and adjustment (every 30,000 miles or 24 months)

1   Engine idle speed is the speed at which the engine operates when no accelerator pedal pressure is applied, as when stopped at a traffic light. This speed is critical to the performance of the engine itself, as well as many engine subsystems.

2   Set the parking brake firmly and block the wheels to prevent the vehicle from rolling. Put the transaxle in Neutral. Unplug the engine fan electrical connector(s). If the fan(s) should come on during the idle adjustment procedure, idle speed is affected.

3   Connect a hand held tachometer. **Caution:** *Don't allow the tachometer to touch ground or damage to the igniter and/or the ignition coil may occur.* **Note:** *Some tachometers may not be compatible with this ignition system. It is recommended that you consult the manufacturer.*

4   Start the engine and allow it to reach normal operating temperature.

5   Check, and adjust if necessary, the ignition timing (see Chapter 5).

29.8 Disconnect the hose from the EGR valve and plug it

Carbureted engines

Refer to illustrations 29.6, 29.7, 29.8, 29.10 and 29.12

Curb idle

6   Open the throttle valve to make sure fuel sprays out of the accelerator nozzle **(see illustration)**. Start the engine and check the engine curb idle speed on the tachometer and compare it to those listed in the Specifications Section at the beginning of this Chapter or the Vehicle Emission Control Information label in the engine compartment. If there is a difference between the Specifications Section and the VECI label, always assume that the information on the label is correct.

7   If the curb idle speed is too low or too high, use a screwdriver to turn the idle speed adjusting screw until the specified curb idle speed is obtained **(see illustration)**.

Fast idle

8   Turn off the engine, disconnect and plug the vacuum hose leading from the EGR valve **(see illustration)**.

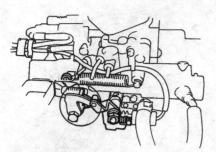

29.10 Set the fast idle cam (circled) by holding the throttle body open slightly, then releasing it

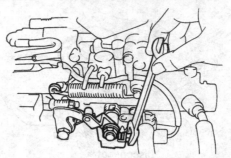

29.12 Adjust the fast idle by turning the fast idle screw with a small wrench

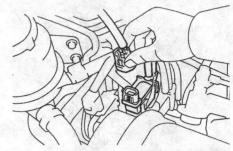

29.14 Unplug the VCV connector before adjusting the idle speed on fuel-injected models

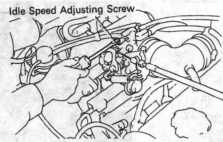

29.17 Pry out the rubber plug and use a screwdriver to turn the adjusting screw on the throttle body - note that the idle speed is quite sensitive to even the slightest turn of this screw

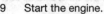

9   Start the engine.
10   Set the fast idle adjusting cam by holding the throttle valve open slightly, then release it **(see illustration)**.
11   Check the engine fast idle speed on the tachometer and compare it to those listed in the Specifications Section at the beginning of this Chapter or the Vehicle Emission Control Information label in the engine compartment. If there is a difference between the Specifications Section and the VECI label, always assume that the information on the label is correct.
12   If the fast idle speed is too low or too high, use a small wrench to turn the fast idle speed adjusting nut **(see illustration)** until the specified fast idle speed is obtained.
13   Turn off the engine, disconnect the tachometer and reconnect any components which were disconnected.

Fuel-injected engines

Refer to illustrations 29.14 and 29.17
14   Unplug the idle-up VCV connector **(see illustration)**.
15   Start the engine and allow it to run at 2500 rpm for two minutes.
16   Check the engine idle speed on the tachometer and compare it to those listed in the Specifications Section at the beginning of this Chapter or the Vehicle Emission Control Information label in the engine compartment. If there is a difference between the Specifications Section and the VECI label, always assume that the information on the label is correct.
17   If the idle speed is too low or too high, turn the idle speed adjusting screw **(see illustration)** until the specified idle speed is obtained.
18   Turn off the engine, disconnect the tachometer and reconnect any components which were disconnected.

**30   Evaporative emissions control system check
(every 30,000 miles or 24 months)**

Refer to illustration 30.2
1   The function of the evaporative emissions control system is to

30.2 Check the evaporative canister for damage and the hose connections (arrows) for cracks and damage

draw fuel vapors from the gas tank and fuel system, store them in a charcoal canister and then burn them during normal engine operation.
2   The most common symptom of a fault in the evaporative emissions system is a strong fuel odor in the engine compartment. If a fuel odor is detected, inspect the charcoal canister, located at the front of the engine compartment. Check the canister and all hoses for damage and deterioration **(see illustration)**.
3   The evaporative emissions control system is explained in more detail in Chapter 6.

**31   Exhaust system check
(every 30,000 miles or 24 months)**

1   With the engine cold (at least three hours after the vehicle has been driven), check the complete exhaust system from its starting point at the engine to the end of the tailpipe. This should be done on a hoist where unrestricted access is available.
2   Check the pipes and connections for evidence of leaks, severe corrosion or damage. Make sure that all brackets and hangers are in good condition and tight.
3   At the same time, inspect the underside of the body for holes, corrosion, open seams, etc. which may allow exhaust gases to enter the passenger compartment. Seal all body openings with silicone or body putty.
4   Rattles and other noises can often be traced to the exhaust system, especially the mounts and hangers. Try to move the pipes, muffler and catalytic converter. If the components can come in contact with the body or suspension parts, secure the exhaust system with new mounts.
5   Check the running condition of the engine by inspecting inside the end of the tailpipe. The exhaust deposits here are an indication of engine state-of-tune. If the pipe is black and sooty or coated with white deposits, the engine is in need of a tune-up, including a thorough fuel system inspection.

32.7 Use an Allen wrench to remove the transaxle drain plug

32.8a After loosening the front bolts, remove the rear transaxle pan bolts and . . .

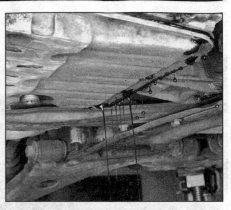

32.8b . . . allow the remaining fluid to drain out

32.9 Remove the filter bolts and lower the filter (be careful, there will be some residual fluid) - note that here one of the pan magnets is stuck to the filter (arrow), be sure to clean any magnets and return them to the pan

32.11 Noting their locations, remove any magnets and wash them and the pan in solvent before reinstalling them

32 Automatic transaxle/differential fluid and filter change (every 30,000 miles or 24 months)

Refer to illustrations 32.7, 32.8a, 32.8b, 32.9, 32.11, 32.13a and 32.13b

1   At the specified time intervals, the automatic transaxle and differential fluid should be drained and replaced.
2   Before beginning work, purchase the specified transmission fluid (see *Recommended fluids and lubricants* at the front of this chapter).
3   Other tools necessary for this job include jackstands to support the vehicle in a raised position, a 10 mm Allen wrench, a drain pan capable of holding at least four quarts, newspapers and clean rags.
4   The fluid should be drained immediately after the vehicle has been driven. Hot fluid is more effective than cold fluid at removing built up sediment. **Warning:** *Fluid temperature can exceed 350-degrees F in a hot transaxle. Wear protective gloves.*
5   After the vehicle has been driven to warm up the fluid, raise it and place it on jackstands for access to the transaxle and differential drain plugs.
6   Move the necessary equipment under the vehicle, being careful not to touch any of the hot exhaust components.
7   Place the drain pan under the drain plug in the transaxle pan and remove the drain plug with the Allen wrench **(see illustration)**. Be sure the drain pan is in position, as fluid will come out with some force. Once the fluid is drained, reinstall the drain plug securely.
8   Remove the front transaxle pan bolts, then loosen the rear bolts and carefully pry the pan loose with a screwdriver and allow the remaining fluid to drain **(see illustrations)**. Once the fluid had drained, remove the bolts and lower the pan.

32.13a Use an Allen wrench to remove the differential drain plug

9   Remove the filter retaining bolts, disconnect the clip (some models) and lower the filter from the transaxle **(see illustration)**. Be careful when lowering the filter as it contains residual fluid.
10   Place the new filter in position, connect the clip (if equipped) and install the bolts. Tighten the bolts to the torque listed in the Specifications Section at the beginning of this Chapter.
11   Carefully clean the gasket surfaces of the fluid pan, removing all traces of old gasket material. Noting their location, remove the magnets, wash the pan in clean solvent and dry it with compressed air. Be sure to clean and reinstall any magnets **(see illustration)**.
12   Install a new gasket, place the fluid pan in position and install the bolts in their original positions. Tighten the bolts to the torque listed in this Chapter's Specifications.
13   Locate the differential drain plug. Place the drain pan underneath

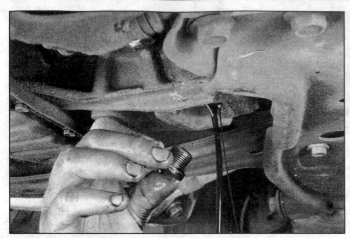

32.13b Be careful when removing the plug because the fluid usually comes out with some force

the plug, remove it with the Allen wrench and drain the fluid **(see illustrations)**. When the differential fluid has drained, reinstall the plug securely.

14   Referring to Section 19, add new fluid to the differential until it begins to run out of the filler hole (see *Recommended lubricants and fluids* at the beginning of this Chapter for the specified fluid type and capacity). **Caution:** *Do not overfill. The automatic transaxle and the differential are separate units.*

15   Lower the vehicle.

16   With the engine off, add new fluid to the transaxle through the dipstick tube (see *Recommended fluids and lubricants* for the recommended fluid type and capacity). Use a funnel to prevent spills. It is best to add a little fluid at a time, continually checking the level with the dipstick (see Section 7). Allow the fluid time to drain into the pan.

17   Start the engine and shift the selector into all positions from P through L, then shift into P and apply the parking brake.

18   With the engine idling, check the fluid level. Add fluid up to the Cool level on the dipstick.

---

33   Manual transaxle lubricant change (every 30,000 miles or 24 months)

---

1   Remove the drain plug(s) and drain the fluid.

2   Reinstall the drain plug(s) securely.

3   Add new fluid until it begins to run out of the filler hole (Section 20). See *Recommended lubricants and fluids* for the specified lubricant type.

---

34   Rear wheel bearing check, repack and adjustment (ever 30,000 or 24 months)

Check

Refer to illustration 34.1

1   In most cases the rear wheel bearings will not need servicing until the brake shoes are changed. However, the bearings should be checked whenever the rear of the vehicle is raised for any reason. Several items, including a torque wrench and special grease, are required for this procedure **(see illustration)**.

2   With the vehicle securely supported on jackstands, spin each wheel and check for noise, rolling resistance and freeplay.

3   Grasp the top of each tire with one hand and the bottom with the other. Move the wheel in-and-out on the spindle. If there's any noticeable movement, the bearings should be checked and then repacked with grease or replaced if necessary.

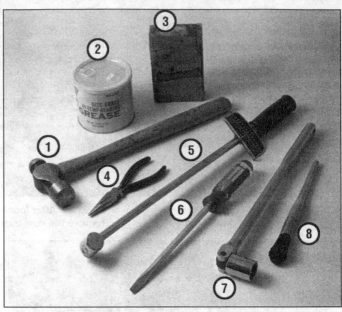

34.1 Tools and materials needed for front wheel bearing maintenance

1   **Hammer** - *A common hammer will do just fine*

2   **Grease** - *High-temperature grease that is formulated for front wheel bearings should be used*

3   **Wood block** - *If you have a scrap piece of 2x4, it can be used to drive the new seal into the hub*

4   **Needle-nose pliers** - *Used to straighten and remove the cotter pin in the spindle*

5   **Torque wrench** - *This is very important in this procedure; if the bearing is too tight, the wheel won't turn freely - if it's too loose, the wheel will "wobble" on the spindle. Either way, it could mean extensive damage*

6   **Screwdriver** - *Used to remove the seal from the hub (a long screwdriver is preferred)*

7   **Socket/breaker bar** - *Needed to loosen the nut on the spindle if it's extremely tight*

8   **Brush** - *Together with some clean solvent, this will be used to remove old grease from the hub and spindle*

Repack

Refer to illustrations 34.6, 34.7, 34.8, 34.9, 34.10, 34.14 and 34.15

4   Remove the wheel.

5   Pry the dust cap out of the hub using a screwdriver or hammer and chisel.

6   Straighten the bent ends of the cotter pin, then pull the cotter pin out of the nut lock **(see illustration)**. Discard the cotter pin and use a

34.6 Use wire cutters to pull the cotter pin out

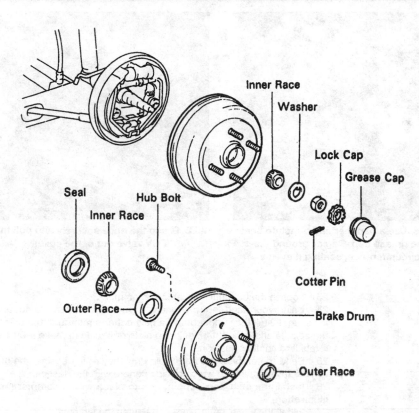

34.7 Typical rear hub and bearing components

34.8 Pull the drum/hub out slightly and push it back in to unseat the outer bearing

34.9 Hold the bearing in place with your thumb so in won't fall out as you remove the drum/hub

new one during reassembly.

7   Remove the nut lock cap, nut and washer from the end of the spindle (see illustration).

8   Pull the hub/disc assembly out slightly, then push it back into its original position (see illustration). This should force the outer bearing off the spindle enough so it can be removed.

9   Pull the hub/disc assembly off the spindle (see illustration). If it does not come off easily, back off the adjuster as described in the drum brake shoe replacement procedure in Chapter 9.

10   Use a screwdriver to pry the seal out of the rear of the hub (see illustration). As this is done, note how the seal is installed.

11   Remove the inner wheel bearing from the hub.

12   Use solvent to remove all traces of the old grease from the

bearings, hub and spindle. A small brush may prove helpful; however make sure no bristles from the brush embed themselves inside the bearing rollers. Allow the parts to air dry.

13   Carefully inspect the bearings for cracks, heat discoloration, worn rollers, etc. Check the bearing races inside the hub for wear and damage. If the bearing races are defective, the hubs should be taken to a machine shop with the facilities to remove the old races and press new ones in. Note that the bearings and races come as matched sets and old bearings should never be installed on new races.

14   Use high-temperature front wheel bearing grease to pack the bearings. Work the grease completely into the bearings, forcing it between the rollers, cone and cage from the back side (see illustration).

34.10 Use a large screwdriver to pry the grease seal out of the rear of the hub

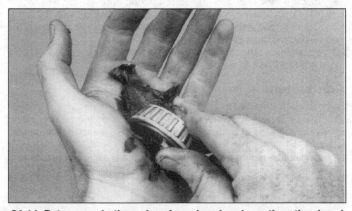

34.14 Put grease in the palm of one hand and use the other hand to force the large-diameter-end edge of each bearing onto the rollers (you should see grease come out the other end) - work all the way around the bearing edge, completely packing the bearing with grease

34.15 Apply a thin coat of grease to the spindle

34.26 Use a hammer and punch to seat the grease cap - tap all around the circumference, seating it evenly

35.2 Grasp the hose securely and pull the PCV valve out of the cover

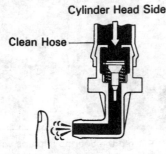

Cylinder Head Side

Clean Hose

35.4 To check the PVC valve, first attach a clean section of hose to the cylinder head side of the valve and blow through it - air should pass through easily - then blow through the intake manifold side of the valve and verify that air passes through with difficulty

15 Apply a thin coat of grease to the spindle at the outer bearing seat, inner bearing seat, shoulder and seal seat **(see illustration)**.
16 Put a small quantity of grease inboard of each bearing race inside the hub. Using your finger, form a dam at these points to provide extra grease availability and to keep thinned grease from flowing out of the bearing.
17 Place the grease-packed inner bearing into the rear of the hub and put a little more grease outboard of the bearing.
18 Place a new seal over the inner bearing and tap the seal evenly into place with a hammer and blunt punch until it's flush with the hub.
19 Carefully place the hub assembly onto the spindle and push the grease-packed outer bearing into position.
20 Install the washer and spindle nut. Tighten the nut only slightly (no more than 12 ft-lbs of torque).

Adjustment

Refer to illustration 34.26
21 Spin the hub in a forward direction to seat the bearings and remove any grease or burrs which could cause excessive bearing play later.
22 Check to see that the tightness of the nut is still approximately 12 ft-lbs.

23 Loosen the nut until it's just loose, no more.
24 Using your hand (not a wrench of any kind), tighten the nut until it's snug. Install the lock cap and a new cotter pin through the hole in the spindle and lock. If the lock cap slots don't line up, take it off and rotate it to another position.
25 Bend the ends of the cotter pin until they're flat against the nut. Cut off any extra length which could interfere with the dust cap.
26 Install the dust cap, tapping it into place with a hammer **(see illustration)**.
27 Install the wheel on the hub and tighten the lug nuts.
28 Grasp the top and bottom of the tire and check the bearings in the manner described earlier in this Section.
29 Lower the vehicle.

35 Positive Crankcase Ventilation (PCV) valve and hose check and replacement(every 30,000 miles or 24 months)

Refer to illustrations 35.2 and 35.4
1 The PCV valve and hose is located in the valve cover.
2 Pull the PCV valve from the cover **(see illustration)**.
3 With the engine idling at normal operating temperature, place your finger over the end of the valve. If there's no vacuum at the valve, check for a plugged hose or valve. Replace any plugged or deteriorated hoses.
4 Turn off the engine. Remove the PCV valve from the hose. Connect a clean piece of hose and blow through the valve from the valve cover (cylinder head) end. If air will not pass through the valve in this direction, replace it with a new one **(see illustration)**.
5 When purchasing a replacement PCV valve, make sure it's for your particular vehicle and engine size. Compare the old valve with the new one to make sure they're the same.

36 Seat fastener check (every 30,000 miles or 24 months)

1 Tighten the front seat mounting bolts to the torque listed in this Chapter's Specifications.

Chapter 2 Part A
Engines

Contents

Specifications

General

Engine type (all years)	SOHC four-cylinder, three valves per cylinder
3E	Carbureted
3E-E	Fuel-injected
Cylinder numbers (drivebelt end-to-transaxle end)	1-2-3-4
Firing order	1-3-4-2

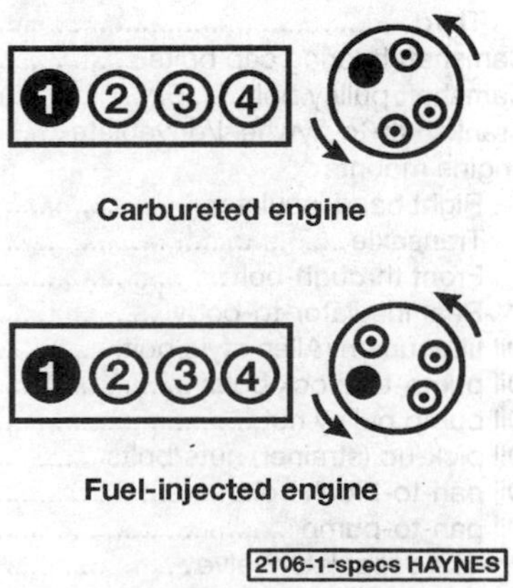

Warpage limits

Cylinder head-to-block surface	0.002 inch
Intake and exhaust manifolds	
1989 and earlier	
Intake manifold	0.008 inch
Exhaust manifold	0.012 inch
1990 on	
Intake manifold	0.002 inch
Exhaust manifold	0.008 inch

Timing belt

Idler pulley spring tension	
1989 and earlier	18.3 ft-lbs @ 2.157 inches
1990 on	11.3 ft-lbs @ 2.028 inches
Idler pulley spring free length	
1989 and earlier	1.528 inches
1990 on	1.512 inches

Carbureted engine

Fuel-injected engine

2106-1-specs HAYNES

The blackened terminal shown on the distributor cap indicates the Number One spark plug wire position

Cylinder location and distributor rotation

Camshaft

Thrust clearance (endplay)

    Standard .... 0.0031 to 0.0071 inch

    Service limit... 0.098 inch

Journal diameter (all journals) .... 1.0622 to 1.0628 inches

Bearing oil clearance

    Standard .... 0.0015 to 0.0029 inch

    Service limit... 0.0039 inch

Runout limit (all) .... 0.016 inch

Lobe height (all years)

    Standard

        Intake

            Main .... 1.3917 to 1.3957 inches

            Sub .... 1.3744 to 1.3783 inches

        Exhaust .... 1.4106 to 1.4116 inches

    Service limit

        Intake

            Main .... 1.3839 inches

            Sub .... 1.3665 inches

        Exhaust .... 1.4028 inches

Oil pump

Pressure (at normal operating temperature)

    Idle.. 4.3 lbs (minimum)

    3000 rpm .... 36 to 71 lbs

Driven rotor-to-pump body

    Standard .... 0.0039 to 0.0063 inch

    Service limit... 0.0079 inch

Drive rotor-to-case side clearance

    Standard.. 0.0012 to 0.0035 inch

    Service limit... 0.0039 inch

Rotor tip clearance

    Standard.. 0.0024 to 0.0059 inch

    Service limit... 0.0079 inch

Torque specifications   **Ft-lbs** (unless otherwise indicated)

Intake manifold bolts .... 168 in-lbs

Exhaust manifold-to-block bolts 38

Exhaust manifold-to-exhaust pipe 46

Crankshaft pulley-to-crankshaft bolt.. 112

Flywheel/driveplate bolts... 65

Idler pulley bolts

    Number 1 .... 156 in-lbs

    Number 2 20

Cylinder head bolts (in sequence - see Section 12)

    First 22

    Second 36

    Third .... turn an additional 90-degrees

Camshaft bearing cap bolts .... 120 in-lbs

Camshaft pulley bolt.. 37

Crankshaft-to-flywheel/driveplate 65

Engine mounts

    Right hand insulator 43

    Transaxle 35

    Front through-bolt 47

    Rear insulator-to-body 58

Oil filter union (Allen style bolt) 18

Oil pump-to-block bolts .... 65 in-lbs

Oil pump pulley nut.. 27

Oil pick-up (strainer) nuts/bolts .... 84 in-lbs

Oil pan-to-block bolts.. 74 in-lbs

Oil pan-to-pump .... 74 in-lbs

Pressure regulator valve 22

Rear main oil seal retainer bolts .... 65 in-lbs

Rear end plate .... 84 in-lbs

Valve cover nuts .... 61 in-lbs

1   General information

This Part of Chapter 2 is devoted to in-vehicle repair procedures for all engines. All information concerning engine removal and installation and engine block and cylinder head overhaul can be found in Part B of this Chapter.

The following repair procedures are based on the assumption that the engine is installed in the vehicle. If the engine has been removed from the vehicle and mounted on a stand, many of the steps outlined in this Part of Chapter 2 will not apply.

The Specifications included in this Part of Chapter 2 apply only to the procedures contained in this Part. Part B of Chapter 2 contains the Specifications necessary for cylinder head and engine block rebuilding.

2   Repair operations possible with the engine in the vehicle

Warning: *Some later models are equipped with airbags. The airbag is armed and can deploy (inflate) any time the battery is connected. To prevent accidental deployment (and possible injury), disconnect the negative battery cable whenever working near airbag components. After the battery is disconnected, wait at least 90 seconds before beginning work (the system has a back-up capacitor that must fully discharge). See chapter 12 for more information.*

Many major repair operations can be accomplished without removing the engine from the vehicle.

Clean the engine compartment and the exterior of the engine with some type of degreaser before any work is done. It will make the job easier and help keep dirt out of the internal areas of the engine.

Depending on the components involved, it may be helpful to remove the hood to improve access to the engine as repairs are performed (refer to Chapter 11 if necessary). Cover the fenders to prevent damage to the paint. Special pads are available, but an old bedspread or blanket will also work.

If vacuum, exhaust, oil or coolant leaks develop, indicating a need for gasket or seal replacement, the repairs can generally be made with the engine in the vehicle. The intake and exhaust manifold gaskets, oil pan gasket, crankshaft oil seals and cylinder head gasket are all accessible with the engine in place.

Exterior engine components, such as the intake and exhaust manifolds, the oil pan, the oil pump, the water pump, the starter motor, the alternator, the distributor and the fuel system components can be removed for repair with the engine in place.

Since the cylinder head can be removed without pulling the engine, camshaft and valve component servicing can also be accomplished with the engine in the vehicle. Replacement of the timing belt and pulleys is also possible with the engine in the vehicle.

In extreme cases caused by a lack of necessary equipment, repair or replacement of piston rings, pistons, connecting rods and rod bearings is possible with the engine in the vehicle. However, this practice is not recommended because of the cleaning and preparation work that must be done to the components involved.

3   Top Dead Center (TDC) for number one piston - locating

Refer to illustration 3.8
Note: *The following procedure is based on the assumption that the distributor is correctly installed. If you are trying to locate TDC to install the distributor correctly, piston position must be determined by feeling for compression at the number one spark plug hole, then aligning the ignition timing marks as described in step 8.*

1   Top Dead Center (TDC) is the highest point in the cylinder that each piston reaches as it travels up-and-down when the crankshaft turns. Each piston reaches TDC on the compression stroke and again on the exhaust stroke, but TDC generally refers to piston position on the compression stroke.

2   Positioning the number one piston at TDC is an essential part of many procedures, such as camshaft and timing belt/pulley removal and distributor removal.

3   Before beginning this procedure, be sure to place the transmission in Neutral and apply the parking brake or block the rear wheels. Also, disable the ignition system by disconnecting the primary (low voltage) electrical connectors at the distributor) (see Chapter 5). Remove the spark plugs (see Chapter 1).

4   In order to bring any piston to TDC, the crankshaft must be turned using one of the methods outlined below. When looking at the front of the engine (timing belt end), normal crankshaft rotation is clockwise.

   a) *The preferred method is to turn the crankshaft with a socket and ratchet attached to the bolt threaded into the front of the crankshaft.*

   b) *A remote starter switch, which may save some time, can also be used. Follow the instructions included with the switch. Once the piston is close to TDC, use a socket and ratchet as described in the previous paragraph.*

   c) *If an assistant is available to turn the ignition switch to the Start position in short bursts, you can get the piston close to TDC without a remote starter switch. Make sure your assistant is out of the vehicle, away from the ignition switch, then use a socket and ratchet as described in Paragraph a) to complete the procedure.*

5   Note the position of the terminal for the number one spark plug wire on the distributor cap. If the terminal isn't marked, follow the plug wire from the number one cylinder spark plug to the cap.

6   Use a felt-tip pen or chalk to make a mark on the distributor body directly under the number one terminal.

7   Detach the cap from the distributor and set it aside (see Chapter 1 if necessary).

8   Turn the crankshaft (see Step 4) until the notch in the crankshaft pulley is aligned with the 0 on the timing plate (located at the front of the engine) **(see illustration)**.

9   Look at the distributor rotor - it should be pointing directly at the mark you made on the distributor body.

10   If the rotor is 180-degrees off, the number one piston is at TDC on the exhaust stroke.

11   To get the piston to TDC on the compression stroke, turn the crankshaft one complete revolution (360-degrees) clockwise. The rotor should now be pointing at the mark on the distributor. When the rotor is pointing at the number one spark plug wire terminal in the distributor cap and the ignition timing marks are aligned, the number one piston is at TDC on the compression stroke. **Note:** *If it's impossible to align the ignition timing marks when the rotor is pointing at the mark on the*

3.8 Align the crankshaft pulley notch (arrow) with the 0 (zero) on the timing plate

2A

4.2a Carbureted models require the removal of the following
items for valve cover removal:

1   Air intake duct
2   PCV (positive crankcase ventilation) hose
3   Throttle Valve (TV) cable (automatic transaxle only)
4   Accelerator cable

distributor body, the timing belt may have jumped the teeth on the
pulleys or may have been installed incorrectly.

12   After the number one piston has been positioned at TDC on the
compression stroke, TDC for any of the remaining pistons can be
located by turning the crankshaft and following the firing order. Mark
the remaining spark plug wire terminals on the distributor body just like
you did for the number one terminal, then number the marks to
correspond with the cylinder numbers. As you turn the crankshaft, the
rotor will also turn. When it's pointing directly at one of the marks on
the distributor, the piston for that particular cylinder is at TDC on the
compression stroke.

---

4   Valve cover - removal and installation

Refer to illustrations 4.2a, 4.2b, 4.4 and 4.7

1   Disconnect the battery cable from the negative battery terminal.
Caution: *If the stereo in your vehicle is equipped with an anti-theft
system, make sure you have the correct activation code before disconnecting the battery.*
2   On carbureted models, detach the air intake breather duct, PCV
hose, throttle cable (automatic transaxle only) and accelerator cable
from the valve cover **(see illustrations)**.
3   Detach the spark plug wires from the clips on the valve cover.
4   Remove the acorn-type cap nuts and sealing washers **(see**

4.4 Remove the acorn style nuts and sealing washers (arrow) at
each hold-down stud

4.2b If you're removing the valve cover on a fuel-injected model,
detach the following from the cover:

1   PCV (positive crankcase ventilation) hose
2   Accelerator cable

illustration), then detach the cover and gasket from the head. If the
cover is stuck to the head, bump the end with a block of wood and a
hammer to jar it loose. If that doesn't work, try to slip a flexible putty
knife between the head and cover to break the seal. **Caution:** *Don't pry
at the cover or housing-to-head joint or damage to the sealing surfaces
may occur, leading to oil leaks after the cover is reinstalled.*
5   Remove the gasket from the valve cover.
6   The mating surfaces of the valve cover and cylinder head must be
clean when the cover is installed. Use a gasket scraper to remove all
traces of sealant and old gasket material, then clean the mating
surfaces with lacquer thinner or acetone. If there's residue or oil on the
mating surfaces when the cover is installed, oil leaks may develop.
7   Apply a thin, uniform layer of RTV sealant to the gasket-to-seal
joint areas **(see illustration)**.
8   Position a new gasket on the valve cover, then install the valve
cover, sealing washers and nuts.
9   Tighten the nuts to the torque listed in this Chapter's Specifications. The remainder of installation is the reverse of removal.

---

5   Intake manifold - removal and installation

Refer to illustrations 5.3, 5.6 and 5.7

1   If you're working on a fuel-injected model, relieve the fuel system
pressure (see Section 2). Disconnect the cable from the negative
battery terminal. **Caution:** *If the stereo in your vehicle is equipped with
an anti-theft system, make sure you have the correct activation code
before disconnecting the battery.*
2   Drain the cooling system (see Chapter 1).
3   Label and detach all wire harnesses, control cables, coolant and
vacuum hoses connected to the intake manifold **(see illustration)**.
4   Remove the fuel rail and injectors (see Chapter 4).

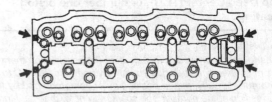

4.7 Apply RTV sealant to the four points indicated by the arrows
before installing the valve cover

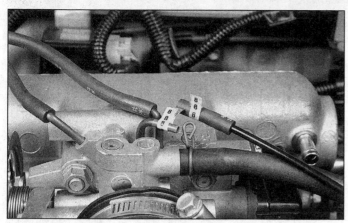

5.3 The various hoses should be marked to ensure correct reinstallation

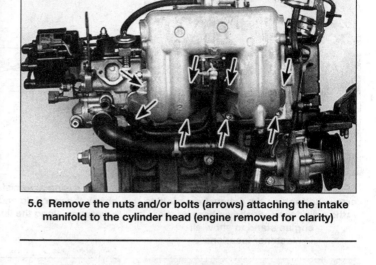

5.6 Remove the nuts and/or bolts (arrows) attaching the intake manifold to the cylinder head (engine removed for clarity)

5   Unbolt and remove the brace underneath the intake manifold (at the timing belt end of the manifold).

6   Remove the mounting nuts/bolts, then detach the manifold from the engine (see illustrations).

7   Use a scraper to remove all traces of old gasket material and sealant from the manifold and cylinder head, then clean the mating surfaces with lacquer thinner or acetone. If the gasket was leaking, check for warpage with a straightedge and a feeler gauge (see illustration), using the specification at the beginning of this Chapter. have the manifold resurfaced if necessary.

8   Install a new gasket, then position the manifold on the head and install the nuts/bolts.

9   Tighten the nuts/bolts in three or four equal steps to the torque listed in this Chapter's Specifications. Work from the center out towards the ends to avoid warping the manifold.

10   Install the remaining parts in the reverse order of removal. Refill the cooling system (see Chapter 1).

11   Before starting the engine, check the throttle linkage for smooth operation.

12   Run the engine and check for coolant and vacuum leaks.

13   Road test the vehicle and check for proper operation of all accessories, including the cruise control system.

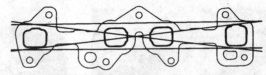

5.7 Using a precision straightedge, check the manifold and head surfaces for warpage along the lines indicated here

1   Disconnect the cable from the negative battery terminal. **Caution:** *If the stereo in your vehicle is equipped with an anti-theft system, make sure you have the correct activation code before disconnecting the battery.*

2   Remove the oxygen sensor (see Chapter 6).

3   Remove the heat insulator from the manifold (see illustration).

4   Block the rear wheels and set the parking brake.

5   Support the front of the vehicle securely on jackstands (see Chapter 1).

6   Remove the engine splash shields (see Chapter 11).

7   Apply penetrating oil to the exhaust manifold-to-head and manifold-to-exhaust pipe mounting nuts/bolts.

8   From beneath the vehicle, disconnect the exhaust pipe from the exhaust manifold (see illustration).

9   Unbolt the exhaust pipe brace at the engine mount (see illustration).

6   Exhaust manifold - removal and installation

Refer to illustrations 6.3, 6.8, 6.9, 6.10 and 6.11

Warning: *The engine must be completely cool before beginning this procedure.*

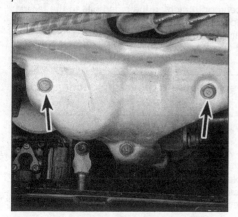

6.3 Remove the exhaust manifold heat insulator bolts (arrows)

6.8 Remove the two nuts (arrows) attaching the exhaust pipe to the exhaust manifold

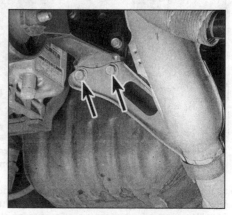

6.9 Unbolt the support bracket at the engine mount (arrows)

2A

6.10 Remove the nuts and/or bolts (arrows) attaching the exhaust manifold to the cylinder head, shown here on the engine stand to show all fastener locations

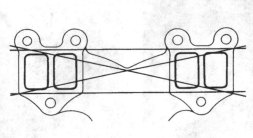

6.11 Using a precision straightedge, check the manifold and head surfaces for warpage along the lines indicated here

7.7 Unbolt the single bolt (arrow) and remove the vacuum switching valve from the engine mount

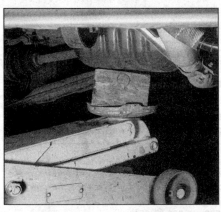

7.9 Using a block of wood on a floor jack, support the weight of the engine to remove pressure from the mount

7.14 Remove the four bolts (arrows) and the outer drive belt pulley

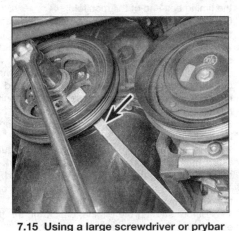

7.15 Using a large screwdriver or prybar (arrow) placed through the pulley and wedged against the block as shown, loosen and remove the center bolt with a socket and breaker bar

7.16 It may be necessary to use some leverage and pry evenly on both sides of the pulley to remove it

10   Remove the manifold-to-head nuts/bolts and detach the manifold, gaskets and inner heat shield **(see illustration)**.
11   Use a scraper to remove all traces of old gasket material and carbon deposits from the manifold and cylinder head mating surfaces. If the gasket was leaking, have the manifold checked for warpage with a straightedge **(see illustration)**, using the specification at the

beginning of this Chapter. Have the manifold resurfaced if necessary. **Caution:** *When scraping, be very careful not to gouge or scratch the soft aluminum of the cylinder head.*
12   Position the new exhaust manifold gaskets over the cylinder head studs.
13   Install the manifold and thread the mounting nuts/bolts into place.
14   Working from the center out, tighten the nuts/bolts to the torque listed in this Chapter's Specifications in three or four equal steps.
15   Reinstall the remaining parts in the reverse order of removal.
16   Run the engine and check for exhaust leaks.

---

7   Timing belt and sprockets - removal, inspection and installation

Removal

Refer to illustrations 7.7, 7.9, 7.14, 7.15, 7.16, 7.17, 7.18, 7.19a, 7.19b, 7.19c, 7.20, 7.21, 7.24 and 7.25

1   Disconnect the cable from the negative battery terminal. **Caution:** *If the stereo in your vehicle is equipped with an anti-theft system, make sure you have the correct activation code before disconnecting the battery.*
2   Block the rear wheels and set the parking brake.
3   Loosen the lug nuts on the right front wheel and raise the vehicle. Support the front of the vehicle securely on jackstands.

7.17 Remove the timing cover bolts (arrows) (engine removed for clarity)

7.19a An assembled view of the timing belt and sprocket locations

7.18 If you intend to re-use the timing belt, mark the direction of rotation on the belt (arrow)

7.19b Align the crankshaft sprocket groove with the zero mark

1   *Alignment marks at Top Dead Center (TDC)*
2   *Timing belt guide*

7.19c With the engine set at TDC compression for cylinder number 1, the "3E" and the dowel pin should be in the 12 o'clock position (arrows). If you look through the hole you should see a dimple stamped in the camshaft bearing cap, indicating proper alignment

2A

4   Remove the right (passenger's) side engine splash shield.
5   Remove the valve cover (see Section 4).
6   Remove the drivebelts (see Chapter 1).
7   Remove the vacuum switching valve **(see illustration)**.
8   On 3E-E (fuel-injected models) remove the air cleaner element and housing (see Chapter 4).
9   Support the engine with a floor jack and a wood block **(see illustration)**. **Warning:** *DO NOT support the engine to the point where the vehicle comes off the jackstands. Just raise the engine up enough to unload the weight from the mounts.*
10   Remove the right engine mount through-bolt (see Section 17).
11   Remove the right side engine mount insulator (see Section 17).
12   Remove the alternator and bracket (see Chapter 5).
13   Bring the engine to TDC on the number one cylinder (see Section 3). Check to be sure the rocker arms on the number one cylinder are loose. If they aren't, rotate the crankshaft 360-degrees (one complete revolution), clockwise.
14   Remove the outer pulley **(see illustration)**. **Note:** *This may not be necessary but it allows for easier access to the main pulley center bolt.*
15   To proceed with timing belt removal, keep the damper/pulley from turning with a screwdriver or prybar wedged between the damper and engine block. **Caution:** *DON'T allow the prybar to bottom against the oil pan.* Remove the bolt **(see illustration)**.
16   Remove the damper/pulley. If necessary, pry it off with two large

screwdrivers **(see illustration)** or use a bolt-type puller that bears on the hub of the damper. **Caution:** *DON'T use a jaw-type gear puller on the outer edge of the damper because it will damage the damper.*
17   Remove the timing belt covers and gaskets **(see illustration)**.
18   If you plan to reuse the timing belt, paint an arrow on the belt indicating direction of rotation **(see illustration)**.
19   Mark, or make note of, the positions of the timing alignment

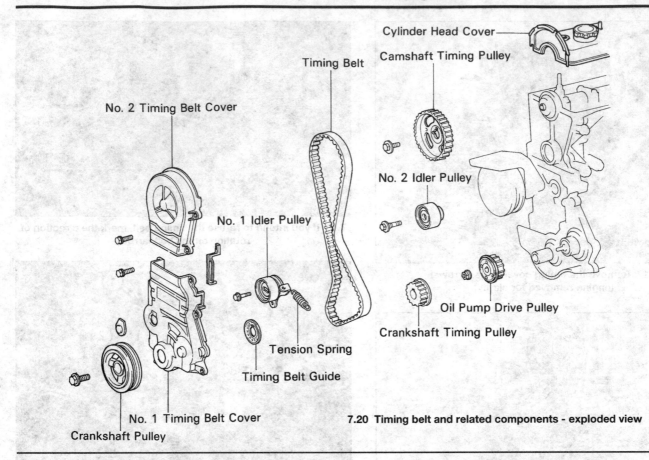

7.20 Timing belt and related components - exploded view

marks **(see illustrations)**.

20   Slide the timing belt guide **(see illustration)** off the end of the crankshaft.

21   Remove the tension spring by disconnecting one end with needle-nose pliers **(see illustration)**.

22   Loosen the idler pulley bolt and push the pulley as far left as it will go to allow timing belt removal **(see illustration 7.21)**.

23   Slip the timing belt off the sprockets.

24   If the crankshaft sprocket is worn or damaged, or if you need to get at the crankshaft front oil seal, remove the sprocket by sliding it off the crankshaft **(see illustration)**.

25   If the camshaft sprocket is worn or damaged, remove the valve cover (see Section 4), hold the camshaft with a large wrench and remove the bolt, then detach the sprocket **(see illustration)**.

Inspection

Refer to illustrations 7.26, 7.27, 28a and 7.28b

Caution: *Do not bend, twist or turn the timing belt inside out. Do not allow it to come in contact with oil, coolant or fuel. Do not utilize timing belt tension to keep the camshaft or crankshaft from turning when installing the sprocket bolt. Do not turn the crankshaft or camshaft more than a few degrees (necessary for tooth alignment) while the*

7.21 Loosen the set bolt for the timing belt tensioner pulley, then unhook the spring to release tension on the belt

1   Timing belt tensioner set bolt
2   Tension spring

7.24 The sprocket should slide off the crankshaft quite easily

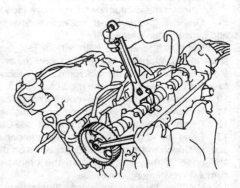

7.25 Remove the valve cover and hold the camshaft with a large wrench on the raised hex as the sprocket bolt is loosened - DO NOT use the timing belt tension to keep the sprocket from turning!

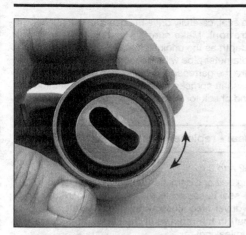

7.26 Check the idler pulley bearing for smooth operation

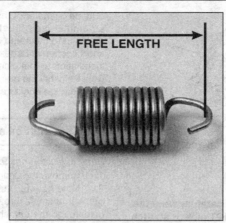

7.27 Measure the free length of the tension spring and compare it to the Specifications

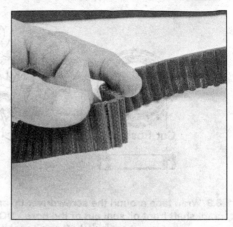

7.28a Check the timing belt for cracked and/or missing teeth

timing belt is removed.

26   Remove the idler pulleys. Roll the bearing and "feel" the bearings for smooth operation and check for excessive play **(see illustration)**. Replace the bearing if either condition is found.

27   Inspect the spring for damage and compare the free length to the Specifications **(see illustration)** at the beginning of this Chapter.

28   If the belt teeth are cracked or pulled off **(see illustrations)**, the distributor, water pump, oil pump or camshaft may have seized. **Caution:** *If the timing belt broke during engine operation, the belt may have been contaminated or over-tightened.*

29   If there is noticeable wear or cracks in the belt, check to see if there are nicks or burrs on the sprockets.

30   If there is wear or damage on only one side of the belt, check the belt guide and the alignment of all sprockets.

31   Replace the timing belt with a new one if obvious wear or damage is noted or if it is the least bit questionable. Correct any problems which contributed to belt failure prior to belt installation. **Note:** *Professionals recommend replacing the belt whenever it is removed, since belt failure can lead to expensive engine damage.*

Installation

32   Remove all dirt and oil from the timing belt area at the front of the engine.

33   If they were removed, install the idler pulleys and tension spring. The lower (no. 1) idler should be pulled back against spring tension as far as possible and the bolt temporarily tightened.

34   If they were removed, install the camshaft and crankshaft sprockets. Recheck the camshaft and crankshaft timing marks to be sure they are properly aligned (see Step 19).

35   Install the timing belt on the crankshaft, oil pump and idler pulleys. If the original belt is being reinstalled make sure the arrow is pointed in the correct direction (clockwise).

36   Slip the belt guide onto the crankshaft with the cupped side facing out.

37   Slip the timing belt over the camshaft sprocket. Keep tension on the side nearest the front of the vehicle. If the original belt is being reinstalled, align the marks made during removal.

38   Loosen the lower (no. 1) idler pulley bolt 1/2-turn, allowing the spring to apply pressure to the idler pulley.

39   Slowly turn the crankshaft clockwise two complete revolutions (720-degrees) by hand. **Caution:** *If you feel resistance while rotating the engine by hand, do not use force. The valves may be contacting the pistons due to incorrect valve timing.*

40   Tighten the idler pulley mounting bolt to the torque listed in this Chapter's Specifications.

41   Install the timing belt guide **(see illustration 7.19b)**.

42   Recheck the timing marks **(see illustration 7.19a)**. If the marks are not aligned exactly as shown, repeat the belt installation

procedure. **Caution:** *DO NOT start the engine until you're absolutely certain that the timing belt is installed correctly. Serious and costly engine damage could occur if the belt is installed wrong.*

43   Reinstall the remaining parts in the reverse order of removal.

44   Run the engine and check for proper operation.

8   Crankshaft front oil seal - replacement

Refer to illustrations 8.3 and 8.5

1   Remove the timing belt (see Section 7).

2   Remove the crankshaft timing belt sprocket **(see illustration 7.24)**.

3   Note how far the seal is seated in the bore, then carefully pry it out of the oil pump housing with a screwdriver or seal removal tool **(see illustration)**. **Caution:** *Don't scratch the housing bore or damage the crankshaft in the process. If the crankshaft is damaged, the new seal will end up leaking.* **Note:** *For more information on seal removal*

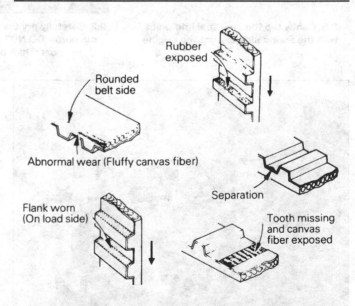

7.28b If the belt is cracked or worn, check the pulleys for nicks and burrs. Wear on one side of the belt indicates pulley misalignment problems

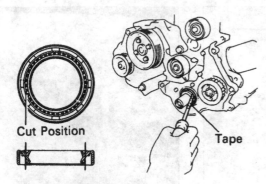

8.3 Wrap tape around the screwdriver tip and carefully work the crankshaft front oil seal out of the bore - DO NOT nick or scratch the crankshaft or oil seal bore!

with the oil pump housing removed from the engine see Section 14 of this Chapter.

4   Clean the bore in the housing and coat the outer edge of the new seal with engine oil or multi-purpose grease. Also lubricate the seal lip.

5   Using a socket with an outside diameter slightly smaller than the outside diameter of the seal, carefully drive the new seal into place with a hammer **(see illustration)**. Make sure it's installed squarely and driven in to the same depth as the original. If a socket isn't available, a short section of large diameter pipe will also work. Check the seal after installation to make sure the garter spring didn't pop out of place.

6   Reinstall the crankshaft sprocket and timing belt (see Section 7).

7   Run the engine and check for oil leaks at the front seal.

9   Camshaft oil seal - replacement

Refer to illustrations 9.2 and 9.4

1   Remove the timing belt and camshaft sprocket (see Section 7).

2   Note how far the seal is seated in the bore, then carefully pry it out with a small screwdriver **(see illustration)**. Don't scratch the bore or damage the camshaft in the process (if the camshaft is damaged, the new seal will end up leaking).

3   Clean the bore and coat the outer edge of the new seal with engine oil or multi-purpose grease. Also lubricate the seal lip.

4   Using a socket with an outside diameter slightly smaller than the outside diameter of the seal **(see illustration)**, carefully drive the new seal into place with a hammer. Make sure it's installed squarely and driven in to the same depth as the original. If a socket isn't available, a short section of pipe will also work.

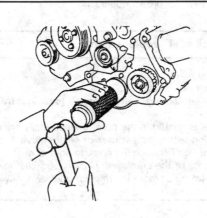

8.5 Gently tap the new seal into place with the spring side toward the engine

9.2 Carefully pry the camshaft seal out of the bore - DO NOT nick or scratch the camshaft or seal bore

9.4 Gently tap the new seal into place with the spring side toward the engine

10.4 Position the dial indicator as shown, pry the camshaft back-and-forth with a screwdriver and note the endplay

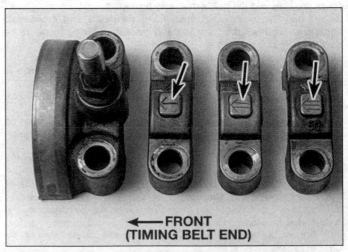

10.5 The bearing caps should have engraved arrows in the cap (arrows) indicating position and direction. If not, be sure to mark the caps before removal

10.6 Camshaft bearing cap LOOSENING sequence

10.8a Pry the rocker arm spring while lifting, as shown, and remove the spring with the rocker arm

5   Reinstall the camshaft sprocket and timing belt (see Section 7).
6   Run the engine and check for oil leaks at the camshaft seal.

10 Camshaft, rocker arms and lash adjusters - removal, inspection and installation

Removal

Refer to illustrations 10.4, 10.5, 10.6, 10.8a and 10.8b
1   Detach the cable from the negative terminal of the battery. **Caution:** *If the stereo in your vehicle is equipped with an anti-theft system, make sure you have the correct activation code before disconnecting the battery.*
2   Remove the valve cover (see Section 4).
3   Remove the timing belt and the camshaft sprocket (see Section 7).
4   Use a dial indicator to check camshaft endplay **(see illustration)**. Mount the dial indicator so the gauge tip can be placed at the end of the camshaft. Move the camshaft all the way to the rear and zero the dial indicator. Next, use a screwdriver to pry it all the way forward. If the endplay, the total amount of movement, exceeds the limit listed in this Chapter's Specifications, replace the camshaft and/or cylinder head.
5   The camshaft bearing caps **(see illustration)** have arrows

engraved in the top of each cap (except the front bearing cap). The number of lines on each arrow indicate the position of the bearing caps. **Caution:** *Keep the caps in order. They must go back in the same location they were removed from.* Number these caps, if there are no identification marks.
6   Loosen the camshaft bearing caps, 1/4-turn at a time, following the proper sequence **(see illustration)** until they are all loose enough to remove.
7   Remove the bearing caps and camshaft.
8   Remove the rocker arm(s) and rocker arm spring(s) by lifting the top of the rocker arm spring, as shown, while prying the spring back with a screwdriver **(see illustration)**, then remove the spring and rocker arm together. **Caution:** *The rocker arm spring (see illustration) is a non-reusable part. They lose their tension after prying them off during rocker arm removal. Toyota recommends replacement any time they are removed.* **Caution:** *Keep the rocker arms in order. They must be reassembled with the same camshaft lobe that they were removed from.*

Inspection

Refer to illustrations 10.9a, 10.9b, 10.9c, 10.9d, 10.10a, 10.10b, 10.10c, 10.11a and 10.11b
9   Visually examine the camshaft journals, rocker arms, pivot points and metal-to-metal contact areas. Check for score marks, pitting and evidence of overheating (blue, discolored areas) **(see illustrations)**. If wear is excessive or damage is evident, the component will have to be

2A

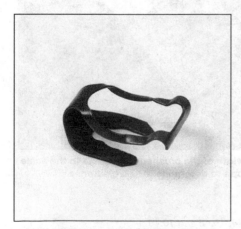

10.8b The rocker arm springs lose their tension and are NOT reusable - replace them any time they are removed from the rocker arm

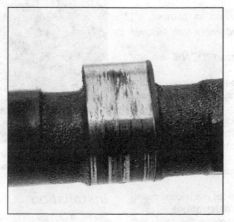

10.9a Check the cam lobes, journals and seal surfaces for pitting, wear and score marks - if scoring is excessive, as is the case here, replace the camshaft

10.9b Check the rocker arms at the pivot point and valve stem contact area (arrows) for excessive wear and damage

10.9c Inspect the rocker arm surface that contacts the camshaft (arrow)

10.9d Check the pivots in the cylinder head for smoothness and signs of possible overheating

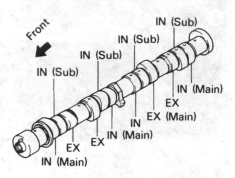

10.10a Intake and exhaust lobe locations for each cylinder

10.10b Measure each journal diameter with a micrometer (if any journal measures less than the specified limit, replace the camshaft)

10.10c Measure the lobe heights - if any lobe height is less than the minimum listed in this Chapter's Specifications, replace that camshaft

10.11a Lay a strip of Plastigage (arrow) on each camshaft journal

replaced. **Note:** *When replacing the cylinder head, install new rocker arm pivots* **(see illustration 10.9d)**. *They must be driven in with a hammer and brass drift.*

10   Using a micrometer, measure camshaft journal diameter and lobe height **(see illustrations)**, and compare it to the Specifications. If the lobe height is less than the minimum allowable, the camshaft is worn and must be replaced.

11   Check the oil clearance for each camshaft journal as follows:

a) *Clean the bearing caps and the camshaft journals with lacquer thinner or acetone.*

b) *Carefully lay the camshaft in place in the head. DON'T use any lubrication.*

c) *Lay a strip of Plastigage on each journal* **(see illustration)**.

d) *Install the bearing caps with the arrows pointing toward the front (timing belt end) of the engine.*

e) *Tighten the bolts in sequence* (use the sequence opposite the one shown in **illustration 10.6**) *to the torque listed in this Chapter's Specifications in 1/4-turn increments.* **Caution:** *Don't turn the camshaft while the Plastigage is in place.*

f) *Remove the bolts, in the proper sequence, and detach the bearing caps*

g) *Compare the width of the crushed Plastigage (at it's widest point) to the scale on the Plastigage envelope* **(see illustration)**.

h) *If the clearance is greater than specified, replace the camshaft and/or cylinder head.*

12   Scrape off the Plastigage with your fingernail or the edge of a credit card - don't scratch or nick the journals or bearing caps.

10.11b Compare the width of the crushed Plastigage to the scale on the envelope to determine the oil clearance

Installation

Refer to illustrations 10.14, 10.15 and 10.16

13   Installation is basically the reverse of the removal procedure.

14   Install the rocker arm(s) and rocker arm spring(s) together. **Caution:** *The spring must be installed* **under** *the rocker arm pivot* **(see illustration)**.

10.14 When installing the rocker arm spring, make certain that the bottom of the clip goes under the pivot (arrow)

10.15 Apply camshaft installation lube to the cam lobes and journals before installing the camshaft in the engine

10.16 If in doubt, the slotted end of the camshaft goes to the rear (transaxle end) of the engine

2A

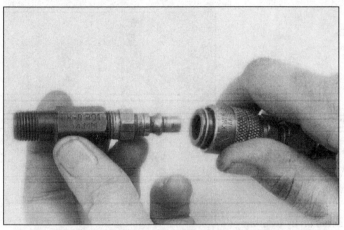

11.4a This is what the air hose adapter that threads into the spark plug hole looks like - they're commonly available from auto parts stores

11.4b Once threaded into the cylinder head the air line can easily be connected with the quick release coupler

15   Apply camshaft installation lube to the camshaft lobes and journals **(see illustration)**. Also apply the same lubricant to the rocker arm contact surfaces.

16   Install the camshaft. **Note:** *The slotted end of the camshaft* **(see illustration)** *is the rear (transaxle end). The distributor is driven by the camshaft when inserted in this slot.*

17   Install the bearing cap bolts and tighten them, in sequence (use the sequence opposite the one shown in **illustration 10.6**), to the torque listed in this Chapter's Specifications.

18   The remainder of installation is the reverse of removal.

---

11   Valve springs, retainers and seals - replacement

Refer to illustrations 11.4a, 11.4b, 11.9, 11.10, 11.15a, 11.15b and 11.17

Note: *Broken valve springs and leaking/worn out valve stem seals can be replaced without removing the cylinder head. Two special tools and a compressed air source are normally required to perform this operation, so read through this Section carefully and rent or buy the tools before beginning the job. If compressed air isn't available, a length of nylon rope can be used to keep the valves from falling into the cylinder during this procedure.*

1   Refer to Section 10 and remove the camshaft and rocker arms. **Note:** *It is only necessary to remove the rocker arm springs and rocker arms of the cylinders where the valve guide seal is being replaced.*

Remember the rocker arm springs are not reusable and must be replaced.

2   Remove the spark plug from the cylinder which has the defective component. If all of the valve stem seals are being replaced, all of the spark plugs should be removed.

3   Turn the crankshaft until the piston in the affected cylinder is at Top Dead Center (TDC) on the compression stroke (see Section 3). If you're replacing all of the valve stem seals, begin with cylinder number one and work on the valves for one cylinder at a time. Move from cylinder-to-cylinder following the firing order sequence (see the Specifications).

4   Thread an adapter into the spark plug hole **(see illustrations)** and connect an air hose from a compressed air source to it. Most auto parts stores can supply the air hose adapter. **Note:** *Many cylinder compression gauges utilize a screw-in fitting that may work with your air hose quick-disconnect fitting.*

5   Apply compressed air to the cylinder. **Warning:** *The piston may be forced down by compressed air, causing the crankshaft to turn suddenly. If the wrench used when positioning the number one piston at TDC is still attached to the bolt in the crankshaft nose, it could cause damage or injury when the crankshaft moves.*

6   The valves should be held in place by the air pressure. If the valve faces or seats are in poor condition, leaks may prevent air pressure from retaining the valves - refer to the alternative procedure below.

7   If you don't have access to compressed air, an alternative method can be used. Position the piston at a point approximately 45-degrees before TDC on the compression stroke, then feed a long piece of nylon

11.9 Compress the valve spring(s) and remove the two keepers (arrow) with needle-nose pliers or a magnet

11.10 Remove the valve stem seal(s)

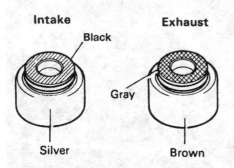

Intake   **Exhaust**

Black

Gray

Silver   Brown

11.15a If using factory supplied valve stem oil seals the colors determine which seal is used for intake and exhaust valves. Aftermarket seals will normally be all the same color and may be used in either location (unless specified by the seal manufacturer)

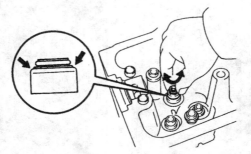

11.15b Place the new seals on by twisting the seal, while pushing them down to their seated position - never use a driver (or socket) to tap them into place (the seal may be damaged)

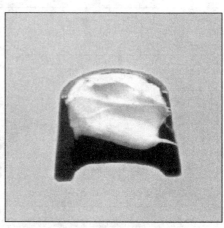

11.17 Apply a small dab of grease to each keeper before installation to hold them in place on the valve stem until the spring is released

rope through the spark plug hole until it fills the combustion chamber. Be sure to leave the end of the rope hanging out of the engine so it can be removed easily.

8   Use a large ratchet and socket to rotate the crankshaft in the normal direction of rotation (clockwise, viewed from the front) until slight resistance is felt.

9   Stuff shop rags into the cylinder head areas, above and below the valves, to prevent parts and tools from falling into the engine, then use a valve spring compressor to compress the spring **(see illustration)**. Remove the keepers with small needle-nose pliers or a magnet.

10   Remove the spring retainer, valve spring and shim(s) then remove the stem oil seal with pliers **(see illustration)**. **Note:** *If air pressure fails to hold the valve in the closed position during this operation, the valve face and/or seat is probably damaged. If so, the cylinder head will have to be removed for additional repair operations.*

11   Wrap a rubber band or tape around the top of the valve stem so the valve won't fall into the combustion chamber, then release the air pressure. **Note:** *If a rope was used instead of air pressure, turn the crankshaft slightly in the direction opposite normal rotation.*

12   Inspect the valve stem for damage. Rotate the valve in the guide and check the end for eccentric movement, which would indicate that the valve is bent.

13   Move the valve up-and-down in the guide and make sure it doesn't bind. If the valve stem binds, either the valve is bent or the guide is damaged. In either case, the head will have to be removed for

repair.

14   Reapply air pressure to the cylinder to retain the valve in the closed position, then remove the tape or rubber band from the valve stem. If a rope was used instead of air pressure, rotate the crankshaft in the normal direction of rotation until slight resistance is felt.

15   Lubricate the valve stem with engine oil and install the new oil seals **(see illustrations)**. Carefully push down on the areas indicated. **Caution:** *DON'T use a socket to drive the seal into place - it may damage the seal. Rotate and push the oil seal onto the valve stem guide by hand. Check that it is firmly installed.* **Note:** *The valve seals that come in the gasket kit from Toyota are color coded. Intake seals are silver and black, and exhaust seals are brown and gray. Seals found in aftermarket gasket kits may all be the same color and can be used on either valve stem.*

16   Install the spring in position over the valve. **Caution:** *Make sure the valve spring shim(s) or hardened washer is in place before the spring is installed. Never place a valve spring directly on the cylinder head without the shim. Damage from a spring sitting directly on the soft aluminum cylinder head will require replacement of the cylinder head or possibly cause engine damage.*

17   Install the valve spring retainer. Compress the valve spring **(see illustration 11.9)** and carefully position the keepers in the groove. Apply a small dab of grease to the inside of each keeper to hold it in place if necessary **(see illustration)**.

18   Remove the pressure from the spring tool and make sure the

12.12 If the head is stuck, pry only at the overhang, not between the mating surfaces

12.15 Remove all traces of old gasket material - the cylinder head and block mating surfaces must be perfectly clean to ensure a good gasket seal

keepers are seated.

19 Disconnect the air hose and remove the adapter from the spark plug hole. If a rope was used in place of air pressure, pull it out of the cylinder.

20 The procedure is the same for all valve stems seals, both intake and exhaust.

21 Refer to Section 10 and install the camshaft.

22 The rest of the installation is the reverse of the removal procedure.

23 Start and run the engine, then check for oil leaks and unusual sounds coming from the valve cover area.

12 Cylinder head - removal and installation

Note: *The engine must be completely cool before beginning this procedure.*

Removal

Refer to illustration 12.12

1 Relieve the fuel system pressure (see Section 2), then disconnect the cable from the negative battery terminal. **Caution:** *If the stereo in your vehicle is equipped with an anti-theft system, make sure you have the correct activation code before disconnecting the battery.*

2 Drain the coolant from the engine block and radiator (see Chapter 1).

3 Drain the engine oil and remove the oil filter (see Chapter 1).

4 Remove the carburetor or fuel rail and injectors, depending on which fuel system is on the vehicle (see Chapter 4).

5 Remove the intake manifold (see Section 5).

6 Remove the exhaust manifold (see Section 6).

7 Remove the timing belt (see Section 7).

8 Remove the alternator and distributor (see Chapter 5).

9 Unbolt the power steering pump (see Chapter 10) and set it aside without disconnecting the hoses.

10 Check the cylinder head. Label and remove any remaining items, such as coolant fittings, tubes, cables, hoses or wires that would interfere with removal. At this point the head should be ready for removal.

11 Using a breaker bar and the appropriate socket, loosen the cylinder head bolts in 1/4-turn increments until they can be removed by hand. Loosen the bolts in a pattern *opposite* that of the tightening sequence **(see illustration 12.24a)** to avoid warping or cracking the head.

12 Lift the cylinder head off the engine block. If it's stuck, very carefully pry up at the transaxle end, beyond the gasket surface, at a casting protrusion **(see illustration).**

13 Remove all external components from the head to allow for thorough cleaning and inspection. **Note:** *See Chapter 2, Part B, for cylinder head servicing procedures.*

Installation

Refer to illustrations 12.15, 12.18, 12.21, 12.24a, 12.24b and 12.24c

14 The mating surfaces of the cylinder head and block must be perfectly clean when the head is installed.

15 Use a gasket scraper to remove all traces of carbon and old gasket material **(see illustration)**, then clean the mating surfaces with lacquer thinner or acetone. If there's oil on the mating surfaces when the head is installed, the gasket may not seal correctly and leaks could develop. When working on the block, stuff the cylinders with clean shop rags to keep out debris. Use a vacuum cleaner to remove material that falls into the cylinders.

16 Check the block and head mating surfaces for nicks, deep scratches and other damage. If damage is slight, it can be removed with a file; if it's excessive, machining may be the only alternative.

17 Use a tap of the correct size to chase the threads in the head bolt holes, then clean the holes with compressed air - make sure that nothing remains in the holes. **Warning:** *Wear eye protection when using compressed air!*

18 Mount each bolt in a vise and run a die down the threads to remove corrosion and restore the threads **(see illustration)**. Dirt, corrosion, sealant and damaged threads will affect torque readings.

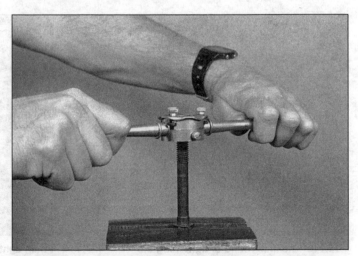

12.18 A die should be used to remove sealant and corrosion from the head bolt threads prior to installation

2A

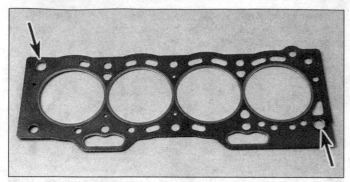

12.21 **When placing the head gasket on the block, place the appropriate holes (arrows) over the alignment dowels on the block deck surface**

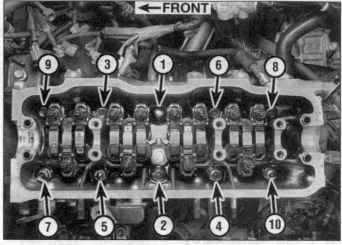

12.24a **Cylinder head bolt TIGHTENING sequence**

19   Check the cylinder head for warpage (see Chapter 2B). Check head gasket, intake and exhaust manifold surfaces.
20   Install the components that were removed from the head.
21   Position the new cylinder head gasket over the dowel pins in the block **(see illustration)**.
22   Carefully set the head on the block without disturbing the gasket.
23   Before installing the head bolts, apply a small amount of clean engine oil to the threads and hardened washer.
24   Install the bolts in their original locations and tighten them finger tight. Then tighten the bolts following the procedure (torque-angle method) described below:

   a) *Using the proper sequence* **(see illustration)**, *tighten the bolts to 22 ft-lbs.*
   b) *Next, in sequence, tighten the bolts to 36 ft-lbs.*
   c) *Finally, in sequence, tighten all bolts an additional 90-degrees (1/4-turn).* **Note:** *Gauges that connect to your torque wrench and measure angles are available at most auto parts stores. Another method is to make a small paint mark* **(see illustrations)** *on each head bolt after the first two tightening steps have been reached, indicating the beginning position before the bolt is turned, then turn each an additional 1/4-turn (90-degrees) by noting the position of the paint mark.*

25   The remaining installation steps are the reverse of removal.
26   Check and adjust the valves as necessary (see Chapter 1).
27   Refill the cooling system, install a new oil filter and add oil to the engine (see Chapter 1).
28   Run the engine and check for leaks. Set the ignition timing (see Chapter 5) and road test the vehicle.

13 Oil pan - removal and installation

Refer to illustrations 13.7, 13.11a and 13.11b

1   Disconnect the cable from the negative battery terminal. **Caution:** *If the stereo in your vehicle is equipped with an anti-theft system, make sure you have the correct activation code before disconnecting the battery.*
2   Set the parking brake and block the rear wheels.
3   Raise the front of the vehicle and support it securely on jackstands (see Chapter 1).
4   Remove the splash shields under the engine (see Chapter 1).
5   Drain the engine oil and remove the oil filter (see Chapter 1). Remove the oil dipstick and tube.
6   Disconnect the front exhaust pipe from the engine (see Section 6) and remove the clamp behind the engine to allow the pipe to hang down.
7   Remove the nuts and bolts and separate the oil pan from the engine block **(see illustration)**. If it's stuck, pry it loose very carefully with a small screwdriver or putty knife. Don't damage the mating surfaces of the pan and block or oil leaks could develop.
8   Use a scraper to remove all traces of old gasket material and sealant from the block and oil pan. Clean the mating surfaces with lacquer thinner or acetone. **Caution:** *Be careful not to scratch or gouge*

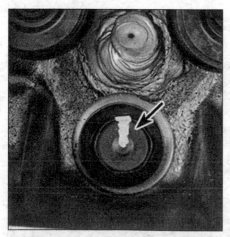

12.24b **The final round of tightening the head bolts is where the torque-angle method is used. Make a mark on each head bolt (arrow) . . .**

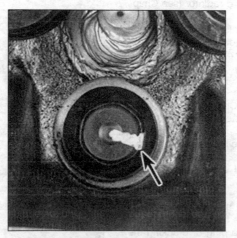

12.24c **. . . then tighten each head bolt (in sequence) the required 90-degrees (arrow), as indicated by the mark moving 1/4 turn, to achieve the final torque**

13.7 **Remove the oil pan bolts (arrows)**

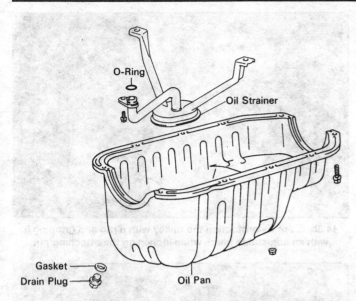

13.11a Exploded view of oil pan and oil pick-up screen assembly

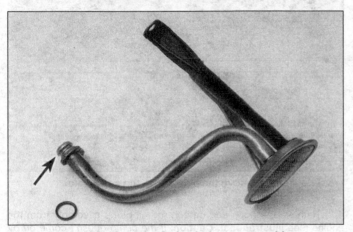

13.13 Replace the O-ring before reassembly

the gasket surface of the block or oil pan. A leak could develop after the repairs have been completed.

9   Make sure the threaded bolt holes in the block are clean.

10   Check the oil pan flange for distortion, particularly around the bolt holes. If necessary, place the pan on a block of wood and use a hammer to flatten and restore the gasket surface.

11   Remove the oil strainer/pick-up tube assembly **(see illustrations)**.

Installation

Refer to illustrations 13.13 and 13.14

12   Clean the strainer assembly thoroughly, inspecting for cracks and/or a blocked strainer.

13   Install the strainer/pick-up tube assembly, using a new O-ring **(see illustration)**. Tighten the fasteners to the torque listed in this Chapter's Specifications.

14   Apply a 5 mm wide bead of RTV sealant around the oil pan flange **(see illustration)**. **Note:** *The oil pan must be installed within 15 minutes once the sealant has been applied.*

15   Carefully position the oil pan on the engine block and install the nuts and bolts. Working from the center out, tighten the fasteners in three or four steps to the torque listed in this Chapter's Specifications.

16   The remainder of installation is the reverse of removal. Be sure to install a new oil filter and add oil (see Chapter 1).

17   Run the engine and check for oil pressure and leaks.

13.11b Remove the three bolts (arrows) and remove the strainer

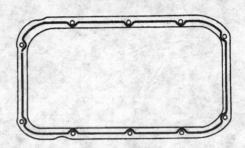

13.14 Apply a bead of sealant to the oil pan flange

14.2 Unscrew the oil pressure relief valve (arrow) from the block

14   Oil pump - removal, inspection and installation

Removal

Refer to illustrations 14.2, 14.3a, 14.3b, 14.4a, 14.4b, 14.5, 14.6, 14.7a and 14.7b

1   Remove the oil pan and pick-up tube/strainer assembly (see Section 13).

2   Remove the oil pressure relief valve **(see illustration)**.

2A

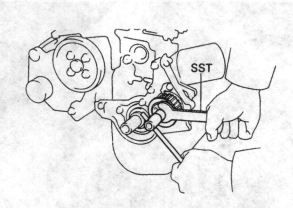

14.3a Removal of the oil pump drive pulley can be done by using either a spanner type wrench . . .

14.3b . . . or by protecting the pulley with a rag and gripping it with an adjustable pliers while loosening the attaching nut

14.4a Remove the oil pump bolts (arrows)

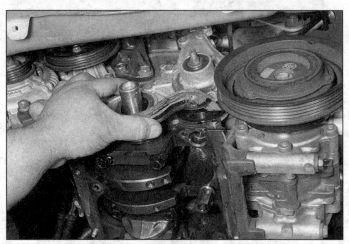

14.4b Remove the pump from the engine block

3   Remove the timing belt, lower idler pulley and tension spring and crankshaft sprocket (see Section 7). **Note:** *Loosen the oil pump drive gear nut before removal of the timing belt. If the belt is already removed, use either a pin spanner type holding tool* **(see illustration)** *or wrap the sprocket with a rag or towel, carefully hold it with large adjustable pliers and break the nut loose* **(see illustration).** *Check the sprocket for any damage to the teeth after removal.*

4   Remove the bolts and detach the oil pump assembly from the engine **(see illustrations). Caution:** *If the pump doesn't come off by hand, tap it gently with a soft-faced hammer. The back of the pump is open, so be extremely careful not to drop the pump or the pump gears while removing the assembly from the engine block.*
5   Remove the O-ring **(see illustration).**
6   Remove the oil pump drive and driven gears from the pump body **(see illustration). Caution:** *Be very careful with these parts. Close tolerances are critical in creating the correct oil pressure. Any nicks or*

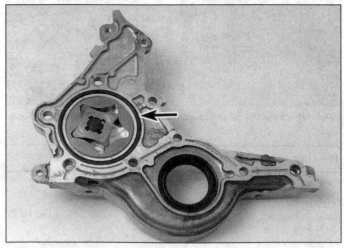

14.5 Turn the pump over to expose the gears and sealing areas, then remove the O-ring (arrow)

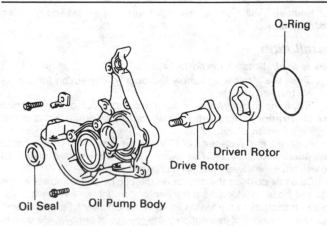

14.6 Oil pump components - exploded view

14.7a Support the pump on two wood blocks and drive the crankshaft oil seal out from behind, using a small punch and hammer

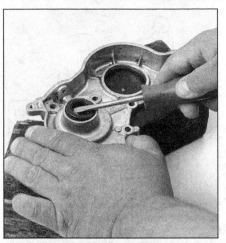

14.7b It is difficult to access the seal from the back side of the pump housing (without damaging the housing surface), so pry the oil pump seal out from the front side with a small screwdriver

14.8 Clean all components, including the block surface (arrow) which acts as the rear pump housing cover once the assembly is bolted back on the block

2A

other damage will require replacement of the complete pump assembly.

7   Drive the crankshaft oil seal out from the rear of the housing **(see illustration)** and then pry out the oil pump shaft seal from the front of the housing **(see illustration)**. **Caution:** *Be certain the aluminum housing is properly supported so it is not damaged during seal removal.* **Note:** *For information on removing the crankshaft oil seal, without removal of the oil pump housing, see Section 8 of this Chapter.*

Inspection

Refer to illustrations 14.8, 14.9, 14.10a, 14.10b and 14.10c

8   Clean all components including the block surfaces **(see illustration)**, with solvent, then inspect all surfaces for excessive wear and/or damage.

9   Disassemble the relief valve by removing the snap-ring **(see illustration)** and separating the parts. **Note:** *Snap-ring pliers are inexpensive, and can be found at local auto parts stores.* Check the oil pressure relief valve piston sliding surface and valve spring. If either the spring or the valve is damaged, they must be replaced as a set. If no damage is found reassemble the relief valve parts, coating the parts with oil, and reinstall it in the cylinder block.

10   Check the oil pump component clearances with feeler gauges **(see illustrations)** and compare the results to the specifications at the beginning of this Chapter.

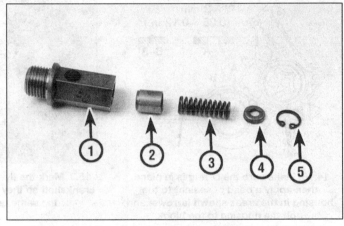

14.9 Remove the snap-ring to disassemble the oil pressure relief valve

1	Pressure relief valve body	3	Spring
2	Piston	4	Retainer
		5	Snap-ring

14.10a Measure the driven rotor-to-case clearance . . .

14.10b . . . and the rotor tip clearance . . .

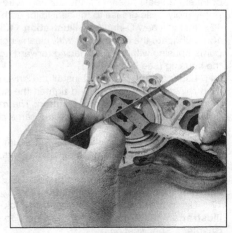

14.10c . . . and the clearance between the gears and the housing mating surfaces

14.11a Supporting the housing on wooden blocks, gently drive a new oil pump seal into place . . .

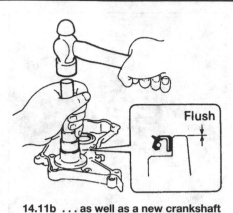

14.11b . . . as well as a new crankshaft seal by using a socket, or piece of pipe, that is just slightly smaller than the outside diameter of the seal - the seal should be driven in flush with the casting surface

14.13 When reinstalling the oil pump gears in the housing be sure the marks (arrows) both go the same direction, into the housing

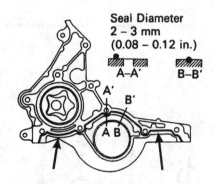

14.16 Make sure the O-ring is in place, then apply a bead of sealant to the housing in the areas shown (arrows) and bolt the housing to the block

15.3 Mark the flywheel/driveplate to the crankshaft so they can be reassembled in the same relative positions

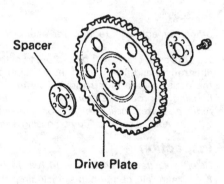

15.5 On models with driveplates, note the positions of the spacer plates (arrow)

Installation

Refer to illustrations 14.11a, 14.11b, 14.13 and 14.16

11   For the oil pump seal and the crankshaft seal, use a socket large enough to contact only the outer edge of the seal, and a carefully drive a new seal into place **(see illustration)**. Install the oil pump and crankshaft seals flush with the casting **(see illustration)** as shown. Apply moly-base grease to the seal lip of both seals before assembly.

12   Install a new O-ring **(see illustration 14.5)**.

13   Lubricate the driven rotor with clean engine oil and place it in the pump housing with the mark facing forward (towards the closed end of the housing **(see illustration)**.

14   Lubricate the shaft and install the drive rotor in the pump body, then reinstall the sprocket and tighten the nut to the torque listed in this Chapter's Specifications. **Caution:** *The marks on the pump gears* **(see illustration 14.13)** *must face the same direction - into the pump housing.*

15   Pack the pump cavities with petroleum jelly. This will prime the pump and enable it to develop suction as soon as the engine is cranked over.

16   Apply a bead of sealant to the oil pump body **(see illustration)**, and attach the pump assembly to the block.

17   Using a new O-ring, install the oil pick-up tube assembly **(see illustration 13.13)**. Tighten the fasteners to the torque listed in this Chapter's Specifications.

18   Reinstall the remaining parts in the reverse order of removal.

19   Install a new oil filter and engine oil (see Chapter 1).

20   Start the engine and check for oil pressure and leaks.

21   Recheck the engine oil level.

15 Flywheel/driveplate - removal and installation

Refer to illustrations 15.3 and 15.5

1   Raise the vehicle and support it securely on jackstands (see Chapter 1), then remove the transaxle (see Chapter 7). If it's leaking, now would be a very good time to replace the front pump seal/O-ring (automatic transaxle only).

2   Remove the pressure plate and clutch disc (see Chapter 8) (manual transaxle models). Now is a good time to check the clutch components.

3   Use a center-punch, or paint, to make alignment marks on the flywheel/driveplate and crankshaft to ensure correct alignment during reinstallation **(see illustration)**.

4   Remove the bolts that secure the flywheel/driveplate to the crankshaft. If the crankshaft turns, wedge a screwdriver in the ring gear teeth to jam the flywheel.

5   Remove the flywheel/driveplate from the crankshaft. Since the flywheel is fairly heavy, be sure to support it while removing the last bolt. Automatic transaxle equipped models have spacers on both sides of the driveplate **(see illustration)** to give added strength to the center where it mounts to the crankshaft.

6   Clean the flywheel to remove grease and oil. Inspect the surface

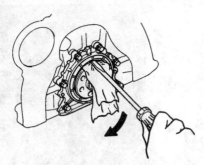

16.2 The quick (but not recommended) way to replace the rear main oil seal is to simply pry the old one out with a screwdriver, lubricate the crankshaft journal and the lip of the new seal with multi-purpose grease and push the new seal into place - the trouble is, the seal lip is stiff and can be easily damaged during installation if you're not careful

16.5 Remove one bolt and take off the rear end plate by pulling it off of the two alignment dowels

1   Alignment dowel locations
2   Bolt

for cracks, rivet grooves, burned areas and score marks. Light scoring can be removed with emery cloth. Check for cracked and broken ring gear teeth. Lay the flywheel on a flat surface and use a straightedge to check for warpage.

7   Clean and inspect the mating surfaces of the flywheel/driveplate and the crankshaft. If the crankshaft rear seal is leaking, replace it before reinstalling the flywheel/driveplate.

8   Position the flywheel/driveplate against the crankshaft. Be sure to align the marks made during removal. Note that some engines have an alignment dowel or staggered bolt holes to ensure correct installation. Before installing the bolts, apply thread locking compound to the threads.

9   Wedge a screwdriver in the ring gear teeth to keep the flywheel/driveplate from turning as you tighten the bolts to the torque listed in this Chapter's Specifications. Follow a criss-cross pattern and work up to the final torque in three or four steps.

10   The remainder of installation is the reverse of the removal procedure.

16   Rear main oil seal - replacement

Refer to illustrations 16.2, 16.5, 16.6, 16.7, 16.8 and 16.10

1   The transaxle must be removed from the vehicle for this procedure (see Chapter 7).

2   The seal can be replaced without dropping the oil pan or removing the seal retainer. However, this method is not recommended.

Access to the seal is very limited and the crankshaft can be damaged during removal. The lip of the seal is quite stiff and it's possible to cock the seal in the retainer bore or damage it during installation. If you want to take the chance, pry out the old seal with a screwdriver **(see illustration)**. Apply multi-purpose grease to the crankshaft seal journal and the lip of the new seal and carefully push the new seal into place. The lip is stiff so carefully work it onto the seal journal of the crankshaft with a smooth object like the end of an extension as you tap the seal into place. Don't rush it or you may damage the seal.

3   Remove the oil pan (see Section 13).

4   Remove the flywheel/driveplate (see Section 15).

5   Remove the rear end plate from the block **(see illustrations)**.

6   Remove the bolts, detach the seal retainer **(see illustration)** and clean off all the old gasket material on the seal retainer and cylinder block.

7   Position the seal and retainer assembly on a couple of wood blocks to evenly support the aluminum housing, then drive the old seal out from the back side with a hammer and punch **(see illustration)**. A screwdriver can also be used, being careful not to gouge or nick the housing during seal removal.

8   Place the new seal squarely on the retainer and drive it into the retainer with a block of wood **(see illustration)** or a section of pipe slightly smaller in diameter than the outside diameter of the seal.

9   Lubricate the crankshaft seal journal and the lip of the new seal with multi-purpose grease.

10   After the housing, and block, has been cleaned of all gasket material, apply a thin, uniform layer of RTV sealant to the seal retainer

2A

16.6 Remove the four remaining bolts (arrows) and separate the oil seal retainer from the block

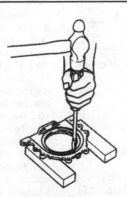

16.7 After removing the retainer from the block, support it on a couple of wood blocks and drive out the old seal with a screwdriver and hammer

16.8 Drive the new seal into the retainer with a wood block or a section of pipe, if you have one large enough - make sure that you don't cock the seal in the retainer bore

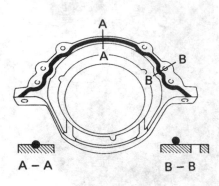

16.10 After the new seal has been installed, place a bead of RTV sealant on the retainer and bolt it to the block

17.9a To remove the right engine mount, remove the through bolt and the two nuts under the insulator

17.9b To remove the mount from the engine bracket, remove this bolt (arrow) . . .

17.9c . . . and these two nuts, which must be taken off from underneath the bracket

17.12 To disconnect the front engine mount from the body, remove the through bolt (arrow) . . .

17.13 . . . then remove the bolts (arrows) and detach the engine mount from the block

(see illustration).

11   Slowly and carefully push the seal onto the crankshaft. The seal lip is stiff, so work it onto the crankshaft with a smooth object such as the end of a socket extension as you push the retainer against the block.

12   Install and tighten the retainer bolts to the torque listed in this Chapter's Specifications. The bottom sealing flange of the retainer must not extend below the bottom sealing flange (oil pan rail) of the block.

13   The remaining steps are the reverse of removal.

17 Engine mounts - check and replacement

1   Engine mounts seldom require attention, but broken or deteriorated mounts should be replaced immediately or the added strain placed on the driveline components may cause damage or wear.

Check

2   During the check, the engine must be raised slightly to remove the weight from the mounts.

3   Raise the vehicle and support it securely on jackstands (see Chapter 1) and remove the splash shields.

4   Position a jack under the engine oil pan. Place a large block of wood between the jack head and the oil pan **(see illustration 7.9)**, then carefully raise the engine *just enough* to take the weight off the mounts. **Warning:** *DO NOT place any part of your body under the engine when it's supported only by a jack!*

5   Check the mounts to see if the rubber is cracked, hardened or separated from the metal plates. Sometimes the rubber will split right

down the center.

6   Check for relative movement between the mount plates and the engine or frame (use a large screwdriver or prybar to attempt to move the mounts). If movement is noted, lower the engine and tighten the mount fasteners.

7   Rubber preservative should be applied to the mounts to slow deterioration.

Replacement

Refer to illustrations 17.9a, 17.9b, 17.9c, 17.12 and 17.13

8   Disconnect the negative battery cable from the battery, then raise the vehicle and support it securely on jackstands (if not already done). Support the engine as described in Step 4. **Caution:** *If the stereo in your vehicle is equipped with an anti-theft system, make sure you have the correct activation code before disconnecting the battery.*

9   To remove the right engine mount, the timing belt end of the engine, remove the nut and withdraw the through-bolt from the frame bracket **(see illustrations)**.

10   Remove the mount-to-bracket nuts and detach the mount.

11   To remove the front engine mount, remove the splash shields (see Chapter 1).

12   Remove the engine mount through bolt **(see illustration)**.

13   Remove the engine block-to-mount bolts **(see illustration)** to remove the entire mount. **Note:** *There are two mounts attached to the transaxle. One at the rear, between the engine and firewall, and another at the left front corner of the engine compartment. See Chapter 7 for transaxle mount replacement.*

14   Installation is the reverse of removal. Use thread locking compound on the mount bolts/nuts and be sure to tighten them securely.

Chapter 2 Part B
General engine overhaul procedures

Contents

2B

Specifications

General

Displacement	91.5 cubic inches (1.5 liters)
Cylinder compression pressure	
Standard	184 psi
Minimum	142 psi
Difference between cylinders	14 psi
Oil pressure (engine warm)	
At idle	4.3 psi minimum
At 3000 rpm	36-to-71 psi

Valves and related components

Minimum valve margin width	
Intake and exhaust	0.031 inch
Valve seat width	0.047-to-0.063 inch
Valve face angle	44.5 degrees
Valve seat angles	
Intake	30 degrees/45 degrees (contact angle)/75 degrees
Exhaust	60 degrees
Valve length	
Standard	
Intake	
Main	3.6223 inches
Sub	3.6142 inches
Exhaust	3.6223 inches
Limit	
Intake	
Main	3.6126 inches minimum
Sub	3.5945 inches minimum
Exhaust	3.6126 inches minimum

Valves and related components (continued)

Stem diameter
    Intake .... 0.2350-to-0.2356 inch
    Exhaust.. 0.2348-to-0.2354 inch
Stem-to-guide clearance
    Standard
        Intake .... 0.0010-to-0.0024 inch
        Exhaust.. 0.0012-to-0.0026 inch
    Service limit
        Intake .... 0.0031 inch maximum
        Exhaust.. 0.0039 inch maximum
Valve spring
    Out-of-square limit .... 0.079 inch maximum
    Free length .... 1.6346 inches
    Installed height .... 1.3842 inches
    Pressure/length .... 35.1 lbs (at installed height)

Engine block

Cylinder head surface warpage limit .... 0.002 inch maximum
Cylinder bore diameter
    Standard
        Mark 1... 2.8740-to-2.8744 inches
        Mark 2... 2.8744-to-2.8748 inches
        Mark 3... 2.8748-to-2.8752 inches
    Service limit
        Standard piston .... 2.8831 inches maximum
        Oversized piston (0.50 inch) .... 2.9028 inches maximum

Crankshaft and connecting rods

Connecting rod journal
    Diameter
        Standard
            No. 1 .... 1.6923-to-1.6929 inches
            No. 2 .... 1.6923-to-1.6929 inches
            No. 3 .... 1.6923-to-1.6929 inches
            Undersized (0.25 inch) .... 1.6923-to-1.6929 inches
    Taper and out-of-round limits .... 0.0024 inch maximum
    Bearing oil clearance
        Standard .... 0.0006-to-0.0019 inch
        Service limit.. 0.0031 inch maximum
Connecting rod side clearance
    Standard... 0.0059-to-0.0138 inch
    Service limit.. 0.0177 inch maximum
Connecting rod twist.. 0.0020 inch maximum
Connecting rod bend.. 0.0012 inch maximum
Connecting rod bolt minimum diameter .... 0.2992 inch
Main bearing journal
    Diameter
        Mark 0 .... 1.9683-to-1.9685 inches
        Mark 1 .... 1.9681-to-1.9683 inches
        Mark 2 .... 1.9679-to-1.9681 inches
        Undersized (0.25 inch) .... 1.9585-to-1.9589 inches
    Taper and out-of-round limits .... 0.0008 inch maximum
    Runout limit... 0.0024 inch maximum
    Oil clearance
        Standard .... 0.0006-to-0.0014 inch
        Service limit.. 0.0031 inch maximum
Crankshaft endplay
    Standard... 0.0008-to-0.0079 inch
    Service limit.. 0.012 inch maximum
Thrust washer thickness
    Standard... 0.0957-to-0.0976 inch
    Oversized (0.125 inch)... 0.0981-to-0.1001 inch

Pistons and rings

Piston diameter
    1988 and earlier
        Standard .... 2.8709-to-2.8720 inches
        Oversized (0.050 inch) .... 2.8905-to-2.8917 inches

1989 and later
  Standard
    Mark 1 .... 2.8708-to-2.8712 inches
    Mark 2 .... 2.8712-to-2.8716 inches
    Mark 3 .... 2.8716-to-2.8720 inches
    Oversized (0.050 inch) .... 2.8905-to-2.8917 inches
Piston-to-bore clearance .... 0.0028-to-0.0035 inch maximum
Piston ring end gap
  1989 and earlier
    Standard
      No. 1 (top) .... 0.0102-to-0.0142 inch
      No. 2 (middle) .... 0.0118-to-0.0177 inch
      Oil ring .... 0.0059-to-0.0157 inch
    Service limit
      No. 1 (top) .... 0.0378 inch maximum
      No. 2 (middle) .... 0.0413 inch maximum
      Oil ring .... 0.0394 inch maximum
  1990 and later
    Standard
      No. 1 (top) .... 0.0102-to-0.0189 inch
      No. 2 (middle) .... 0.0118-to-0.0224 inch
      Oil ring .... 0.0059-to-0.0205 inch
    Service limit
      No. 1 (top) .... 0.0425 inch maximum
      No. 2 (middle) .... 0.0461 inch maximum
      Oil ring .... 0.0441 inch maximum
  Piston ring side clearance
    Top ring .... 0.0016-to-0.0031 inch maximum
    Middle ring .... 0.0012-to-0.0028 inch maximum

Torque specifications*

                                                                   Ft-lbs
Main bearing cap bolts 42
Connecting rod cap nuts 29
* **Note:** *Refer to Part A for additional torque specifications.*

1   General information

Refer to illustrations 1.3a, 1.3b and 1.3c

    Included in this portion of Chapter 2 are the general overhaul procedures for the cylinder head and internal engine components.

    The information ranges from advice concerning preparation for an overhaul and the purchase of replacement parts to detailed, step-by-step procedures covering removal and installation of internal engine components and the inspection of parts.

    The following Sections have been written based on the assumption that the engine has been removed from the vehicle **(see illustrations)**. For information concerning in-vehicle engine repair, as

well as removal and installation of the external components necessary for the overhaul, see Part A of this Chapter and Section 7 of this Part.

    The Specifications included in this Part are only those necessary for the inspection and overhaul procedures which follow. Refer to Part A for additional Specifications.

2   Engine overhaul - general information

Refer to illustration 2.4

    It's not always easy to determine when, or if, an engine should be completely overhauled, as a number of factors must be considered.

    High mileage is not necessarily an indication that an overhaul is

1.3a Left side view (front of engine compartment)

1.3b Right side view (rear of engine compartment)

1.3c Front view (right side of engine compartment)

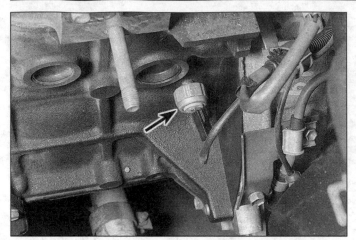

2.4 The oil pressure can be checked by removing the sending unit (arrow)

3.6 A compression gauge with a threaded fitting for the spark plug hole is preferred over the type that requires hand pressure to maintain the seal - be sure to open the throttle valve as far as possible during the compression check!

needed, while low mileage doesn't preclude the need for an overhaul. Frequency of servicing is probably the most important consideration. An engine that's had regular and frequent oil and filter changes, as well as other required maintenance, will most likely give many thousands of miles of reliable service. Conversely, a neglected engine may require an overhaul very early in its life.

Excessive oil consumption is an indication that piston rings, valve seals and/or valve guides are in need of attention. Make sure that oil leaks aren't responsible before deciding that the rings and/or guides are bad. Perform a cylinder compression check to determine the extent of the work required (see Section 3).

Check the oil pressure with a gauge installed in place of the oil pressure sending unit **(see illustration)** and compare it to the Specifications. If it's extremely low, the bearings and/or oil pump are probably worn out.

Loss of power, rough running, knocking or metallic engine noises, excessive valve train noise and high fuel consumption rates may also point to the need for an overhaul, especially if they're all present at the same time. If a complete tune-up doesn't remedy the situation, major mechanical work is the only solution.

An engine overhaul involves restoring the internal parts to the specifications of a new engine. During an overhaul, the piston rings are replaced and the cylinder walls are reconditioned (rebored and/or honed). If a rebore is done by an automotive machine shop, new oversize pistons will also be installed. The main bearings, connecting rod bearings and camshaft bearings are generally replaced with new ones and, if necessary, the crankshaft may be reground to restore the journals. Generally, the valves are serviced as well, since they're usually in less-than-perfect condition at this point. While the engine is being overhauled, other components, such as the distributor, starter and alternator, can be rebuilt as well. The end result should be a like new engine that will give many trouble free miles. **Note:** *Critical cooling system components such as the hoses, drivebelts, thermostat and water pump MUST be replaced with new parts when an engine is overhauled. The radiator should be checked carefully to ensure that it isn't clogged or leaking (see Chapter 3). Also, the oil pump parts may not be available to rebuild the pump. It's our recommendation that the oil pump always be replaced, as an assembly, when an engine is rebuilt.*

Before beginning the engine overhaul, read through the entire procedure to familiarize yourself with the scope and requirements of the job. Overhauling an engine isn't difficult, but it is time consuming. Plan on the vehicle being tied up for a minimum of two weeks, especially if parts must be taken to an automotive machine shop for repair or reconditioning. Check on availability of parts and make sure that any necessary special tools and equipment are obtained in advance. Most work can be done with typical hand tools, although a number of precision measuring tools are required for inspecting parts to determine if they must be replaced. Often an automotive machine

shop will handle the inspection of parts and offer advice concerning reconditioning and replacement. **Note:** *Always wait until the engine has been completely disassembled and all components, especially the engine block, have been inspected before deciding what service and repair operations must be performed by an automotive machine shop. Since the block's condition will be the major factor to consider when determining whether to overhaul the original engine or buy a rebuilt one, never purchase parts or have machine work done on other components until the block has been thoroughly inspected. As a general rule, time is the primary cost of an overhaul, so it doesn't pay to install worn or substandard parts.*

As a final note, to ensure maximum life and minimum trouble from a rebuilt engine, everything must be assembled with care in a spotlessly clean environment.

3   Compression check

Refer to illustration 3.6

1   A compression check will tell you what mechanical condition the upper end (pistons, rings, valves, head gasket) of your engine is in. Specifically, it can tell you if the compression is down due to leakage caused by worn piston rings, defective valves and seats or a blown head gasket. **Note:** *The engine must be at normal operating temperature and the battery must be fully charged for this check.*

2   Begin by cleaning the area around the spark plugs before you remove them (compressed air should be used, if available, otherwise a small brush or even a bicycle tire pump will work). The idea is to prevent dirt from getting into the cylinders as the compression check is being done.

3   Remove all of the spark plugs from the engine (see Chapter 1).

4   Block the throttle wide open.

5   If the vehicle is equipped with a separate ignition coil, detach the coil wire from the center of the distributor cap and ground it on the engine block. Use a jumper wire with alligator clips on each end to ensure a good ground. If the vehicle is equipped with the integral coil and distributor, disconnect the ignition primary wiring. On EFI-equipped models, the fuel pump circuit should also be disabled (see Chapter 5).

6   Install the compression gauge in the spark plug hole **(see illustration)**.

7   Crank the engine over at least seven compression strokes and watch the gauge. The compression should build up quickly in a healthy engine. Low compression on the first stroke, followed by gradually increasing pressure on successive strokes, indicates worn piston rings. A low compression reading on the first stroke, which doesn't

build up during successive strokes, indicates leaking valves or a blown head gasket (a cracked head could also be the cause). Deposits on the undersides of the valve heads can also cause low compression. Record the highest gauge reading obtained.

8   Repeat the procedure for the remaining cylinders and compare the results to the Specifications.

9   Add some engine oil (about three squirts from a plunger-type oil can) to each cylinder, through the spark plug hole, and repeat the test.

10   If the compression increases after the oil is added, the piston rings are definitely worn. If the compression doesn't increase significantly, the leakage is occurring at the valves or head gasket. Leakage past the valves may be caused by burned valve seats and/or faces or warped, cracked or bent valves.

11   If two adjacent cylinders have equally low compression, there's a strong possibility that the head gasket between them is blown. The appearance of coolant in the combustion chambers or the crankcase would verify this condition.

12   If one cylinder is 20-percent lower than the others, and the engine has a slightly rough idle, a worn exhaust lobe on the camshaft could be the cause.

13   If the compression is unusually high, the combustion chambers are probably coated with carbon deposits. If that's the case, the cylinder head(s) should be removed, and carbon deposits should be cleaned from the cylinder head combustion chamber and top surface of the piston. **Caution:** *Be certain to clean all pieces of carbon from the cylinder and head. Any small piece remaining could get wedged between the valve and seat or possibly go between the top ring landing and cylinder wall causing engine damage.*

14   If compression is way down or varies greatly between cylinders, it would be a good idea to have a leak-down test performed by an automotive repair shop. This test will pinpoint exactly where the leakage is occurring and how severe it is.

4   Vacuum gauge diagnostic checks

A vacuum gauge provides valuable information about what is going on in the engine at a low-cost. You can check for worn rings or cylinder walls, leaking head or intake manifold gaskets, incorrect carburetor adjustments, restricted exhaust, stuck or burned valves, weak valve springs, improper ignition or valve timing and ignition problems.

Unfortunately, vacuum gauge readings are easy to misinterpret, so they should be used in conjunction with other tests to confirm the diagnosis.

Both the absolute readings and the rate of needle movement are important for accurate interpretation. Most gauges measure vacuum in inches of mercury (in-Hg). As a point of reference, normal atmospheric pressure at sea level is about 30 in-Hg. As vacuum increases (or atmospheric pressure decreases), the reading will decrease. Also, for every 1,000 foot increase in elevation above sea level; the gauge readings will decrease about one inch of mercury.

Connect the vacuum gauge directly to intake manifold vacuum, not to ported (carburetor) vacuum. Be sure no hoses are left disconnected during the test or false readings will result.

Before you begin the test, allow the engine to warm up completely. Block the wheels and set the parking brake. With the transmission in neutral (or Park, on automatics), start the engine and allow it to run at normal idle speed. **Warning:** *Carefully inspect the fan blades for cracks or damage before starting the engine. Keep your hands and the vacuum tester clear of the fan and do not stand in front of the vehicle or in line with the fan when the engine is running.*

Read the vacuum gauge; an average, healthy engine should normally produce between 17 and 22 inches of vacuum with a fairly steady needle.

Refer to the following vacuum gauge readings and what they indicate about the engines condition:

1   A low steady reading usually indicates a leaking gasket between the intake manifold and carburetor or throttle body, a leaky vacuum

hose, late ignition timing or incorrect camshaft timing. Check ignition timing with a timing light and eliminate all other possible causes, utilizing the tests provided in this Chapter before you remove the timing chain cover to check the timing marks.

2   If the reading is three to eight inches below normal and it fluctuates at that low reading, suspect an intake manifold gasket leak at an intake port or a faulty injector (on port-injected models only).

3   If the needle has regular drops of about two to four inches at a steady rate the valves are probably leaking. Perform a compression or leak-down test to confirm this.

4   An irregular drop or down-flick of the needle can be caused by a sticking valve or an ignition misfire. Perform a compression or leak-down test and read the spark plugs.

5   A rapid vibration of about four in.-Hg vibration at idle combined with exhaust smoke indicates worn valve guides. Perform a leak-down test to confirm this. If the rapid vibration occurs with an increase in engine speed, check for a leaking intake manifold gasket or head gasket, weak valve springs, burned valves or ignition misfire.

6   A slight fluctuation, say one inch up and down, may mean ignition problems. Check all the usual tune-up items and, if necessary, run the engine on an ignition analyzer.

7   If there is a large fluctuation, perform a compression or leak-down test to look for a weak or dead cylinder or a blown head gasket.

8   If the needle moves slowly through a wide range, check for a clogged PCV system, incorrect idle fuel mixture, carburetor/throttle body or intake manifold gasket leaks.

9   Check for a slow return after revving the engine by quickly snapping the throttle open until the engine reaches about 2,500 rpm and let it shut. Normally the reading should drop to near zero, rise above normal idle reading (about 5 in.-Hg over) and then return to the previous idle reading. If the vacuum returns slowly and doesn't peak when the throttle is snapped shut, the rings may be worn. If there is a long delay, look for a restricted exhaust system (often the muffler or catalytic converter). An easy way to check this is to temporarily disconnect the exhaust ahead of the suspected part and redo the test.

5   Engine removal - methods and precautions

If you've decided that an engine must be removed for overhaul or major repair work, several preliminary steps should be taken.

Locating a suitable place to work is extremely important. Adequate work space, along with storage space for the vehicle, will be needed. If a shop or garage isn't available, at the very least a flat, level, clean work surface made of concrete or asphalt is required.

Cleaning the engine compartment and engine before beginning the removal procedure will help keep tools clean and organized.

An engine hoist or A-frame will also be necessary. Make sure the equipment is rated in excess of the combined weight of the engine and transaxle. Safety is of primary importance, considering the potential hazards involved in lifting the engine out of the vehicle.

If the engine is being removed by a novice, a helper should be available. Advice and aid from someone more experienced would also be helpful. There are many instances when one person cannot simultaneously perform all of the operations required when lifting the engine out of the vehicle.

Plan the operation ahead of time. Arrange for or obtain all of the tools and equipment you'll need prior to beginning the job. Some of the equipment necessary to perform engine removal and installation safely and with relative ease are (in addition to an engine hoist) a heavy duty floor jack, complete sets of wrenches and sockets as described in the front of this manual, wooden blocks and plenty of rags and cleaning solvent for mopping up spilled oil, coolant and gasoline. If the hoist must be rented, make sure that you arrange for it in advance and perform all of the operations possible without it beforehand. This will save you money and time.

Plan for the vehicle to be out of use for quite a while. A machine shop will be required to perform some of the work which the do-it-yourselfer can't accomplish without special equipment. These shops

2B

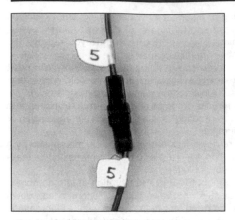

6.8 Label both ends of each wire before disconnecting it

6.12 Unbolt the air conditioning compressor and use wire or rope to tie it out of the way

6.15 Attach the engine hoist chain to the lifting fixtures (arrow) bolted to the engine

often have a busy schedule, so it would be a good idea to consult them before removing the engine in order to accurately estimate the amount of time required to rebuild or repair components that may need work.

Always be extremely careful when removing and installing the engine. Serious injury can result from careless actions. Plan ahead, take your time and a job of this nature, although major, can be accomplished successfully.

6   Engine - removal and installation

Refer to illustrations 6.8, 6.12, 6.15 and 6.20
Warning: *Gasoline is extremely flammable, so take extra precautions when disconnecting any part of the fuel system. Don't smoke or allow open flames or bare light bulbs in or near the work area and don't work in a garage where a natural gas appliance (such as a clothes dryer or water heater) is installed. If you spill gasoline on your skin, rinse it off immediately. Have a fire extinguisher rated for gasoline fires handy and know how to use it.*
Note: *Read through the entire Section before beginning this procedure. On automatic equipped vehicles, the engine can be removed separately from the automatic transaxle. While on vehicles with manual transaxle, the engine and transaxle are removed together and separated once out of the vehicle.*

Removal

1   Release the residual fuel pressure in the tank by removing the gas cap. Relieve the fuel system pressure (see Chapter 4), then undo the fuel lines connecting the engine to the chassis. Plug or cap all open fittings.
2   Remove the battery cable from the negative battery terminal.
Caution: *If the stereo in your vehicle is equipped with an anti-theft system, make sure you have the correct activation code before disconnecting the battery.*
3   Place protective covers on the fenders and cowl and remove the hood (see Chapter 11).
4   Raise the vehicle and support it securely on jackstands. Drain the cooling system and engine oil and remove the drivebelts (see Chapter 1).
5   Remove the air inlet hose and air cleaner assembly (see Chapter 4).
6   Disconnect the cruise control cable, electrical connector and actuator (if equipped), located at the left front strut tower in the engine compartment.
7   Disconnect the throttle linkage (and cruise control cable, if equipped) from the engine (see Chapter 4).
8   Clearly label, then disconnect all vacuum lines, coolant and emissions hoses, wiring harness connectors and ground straps.

6.20 Remove the transaxle-to-engine bolts and separate the engine from the transaxle (automatic only) and lift the engine from the vehicle

Masking tape and/or a touch up paint applicator work well for marking items **(see illustration)**. Take instant photos or sketch the locations of components and brackets.
9   Remove the evaporative emissions charcoal canister (see Chapter 6).
10   Remove the main cooling fan and radiator (see Chapter 3). **Note:** *The cooling fan can be removed together with the radiator.*
11   On power steering equipped vehicles, unbolt the power steering pump. If clearance allows, tie the pump aside without disconnecting the hoses. If necessary, remove the pump (see Chapter 10).
12   On air conditioning equipped vehicles, unbolt the compressor, without disconnecting refrigerant lines and hang it from the radiator core support **(see illustration)**.
13   Disconnect the front exhaust pipe from the exhaust manifold (see Chapter 4).
14   Remove the driveaxles (see Chapter 8) and clutch release cylinder (manual transaxle), wire harness, shift linkage and speedometer cable from the transaxle (see Chapter 7). It isn't necessary to disconnect the release cylinder hose.
15   Attach a lifting sling or chain, to the brackets on the engine **(see illustration)**. Position a hoist and connect the sling/chain to it. Take up the chain slack until there is slight tension on the hoist.
16   Recheck to be sure nothing except the mounts are still connected to the engine (automatic transaxle models) or engine/transaxle (manual transaxle models). Disconnect any necessary items.
17   On automatic transaxle equipped models. Remove the torque converter-to-driveplate fasteners (see Chapter 7) and push the

converter back slightly into the bellhousing.

18   Remove the engine-to-transaxle bolts and separate the engine from the transaxle (see Chapter 7). The torque converter should remain in the transaxle. **Note:** *On automatic transaxle equipped vehicles, the engine can be removed without removing the transaxle, as long as the transaxle is being supported properly. Vehicles equipped with a manual transaxle, require removing the transaxle with the engine because there isn't enough room in the engine compartment for the distance needed to pull the engine from the transaxle in order to disconnect it from the transaxle input shaft.*

19   Support the transaxle with a floor jack. Place a wood block on the jack head to prevent damage to the transaxle. Remove the through-bolts from the engine and/or transaxle mounts (on manual transaxle vehicles). **Warning:** *Do not place any part of your body under the engine/transaxle when it's supported only by a hoist or other lifting device.*

20   Slowly lift the engine or engine/transaxle out of the vehicle. It may be necessary to pry the mounts away from the frame brackets **(see illustration)**.

21   Move the engine/transaxle away from the vehicle and carefully lower the hoist until the transaxle is supported in a level position.

22   Place the engine on the floor or remove the flywheel or driveplate and mount the engine on an engine stand.

Installation

23   Check the engine/transaxle mounts. If they're worn or damaged, replace them (see Chapters 2A and/or Chapter 7).

24   On manual transaxle equipped models, inspect the clutch components (see Chapter 8) and, on automatic transaxle models, inspect the converter seal and bushing.

25   On automatic transaxle equipped models, apply a dab of grease to the nose of the torque converter and to the seal lips.

26   On manual transaxle models, carefully guide the transaxle into place, following the procedure outlined in Chapter 7. Install the engine-to-transaxle bolts and tighten them to the torque listed in Chapter 7 Specifications.

27   Attach the hoist to the engine and carefully lower the engine or engine/transaxle assembly into the engine compartment.

28   On automatic transaxle models, install the engine to transaxle bolts and tighten them to the torque listed in Chapter 7 Specifications. **Caution:** *Do not use the bolts to force the engine and transaxle into alignment. It may crack or damage major components.* Install the torque converter-to-driveplate fasteners and tighten them to the torque listed in Chapter 7 Specifications.

29   Install the mount bolts and tighten them securely.

30   Reinstall the remaining components and fasteners in the reverse order of removal.

31   Add coolant, oil, power steering and transmission fluids as needed (see Chapter 1).

32   Run the engine and check for proper operation and leaks. Shut off the engine and recheck the fluid levels.

7   Engine rebuilding alternatives

The do-it-yourselfer is faced with a number of options when performing an engine overhaul. The decision to replace the engine block, piston/connecting rod assemblies and crankshaft depends on a number of factors, with the number one consideration being the condition of the block. Other considerations are cost, access to machine shop facilities, parts availability, time required to complete the project and the extent of prior mechanical experience on the part of the do-it-yourselfer.

Some of the rebuilding alternatives include:

Individual parts - If the inspection procedures reveal that the engine block and most engine components are in reusable condition, purchasing individual parts may be the most economical alternative. The block, crankshaft and piston/connecting rod assemblies should all be inspected carefully. Even if the block shows little wear, the cylinder bores should be surface honed.

Short block - A short block consists of an engine block with a crankshaft and piston/connecting rod assemblies already installed. All new bearings are incorporated and all clearances will be correct. The existing camshaft, valve train components, cylinder head(s) and external parts can be bolted to the short block with little or no machine shop work necessary.

Long block - A long block consists of a short block plus an oil pump, oil pan, cylinder head, camshaft and valve train components, timing pulleys and belt. All components are installed with new bearings, seals and gaskets incorporated throughout. The installation of manifolds and external parts is all that's necessary.

Give careful thought to which alternative is best for you and discuss the situation with local automotive machine shops, auto parts dealers and experienced rebuilders before ordering or purchasing replacement parts.

8   Engine overhaul - disassembly sequence

Refer to illustration 8.5

1   It's much easier to disassemble and work on the engine if it's mounted on a portable engine stand. A stand can often be rented quite cheaply from an equipment rental yard. Before the engine is mounted on a stand, the flywheel/driveplate, rear end plate and rear oil seal retainer should be removed from the engine.

2   If a stand isn't available, it's possible to disassemble the engine with it blocked up on the floor. Be extra careful not to tip or drop the engine when working without a stand.

3   If you're going to obtain a rebuilt engine, all external components must come off first, to be transferred to the replacement engine, just as they will if you're doing a complete engine overhaul yourself. These include:

Alternator and brackets
Emissions control components
Distributor, spark plug wires and spark plugs
Thermostat and housing cover
Water pump
EFI or carburetor components (whichever vehicle is equipped with)
Intake/exhaust manifolds
Oil filter (always use a new filter)
Engine mounts
Clutch and flywheel/driveplate
Engine rear plate

Note: *When removing the external components from the engine, pay close attention to details that may be helpful or important during installation. Note the installed position of gaskets, seals, spacers, pins, brackets, washers, bolts and other small items. Make diagrams or take instant photos, to help in reassembly.*

4   If you're obtaining a short block, which consists of the engine block, crankshaft, pistons and connecting rods all assembled, then the cylinder head, oil pan and oil pump will have to be removed as well. See *Engine rebuilding alternatives* for additional information regarding the different possibilities to be considered.

5   If you're planning a complete overhaul, the engine must be disassembled and the internal components removed in the following order **(see illustration)**.

Valve cover
Intake and exhaust manifolds
Timing belt covers
Timing belt and pulleys
Camshaft and rocker arms
Cylinder head
Oil pan
Oil pump
Piston/connecting rod assemblies
Crankshaft rear oil seal retainer
Crankshaft and main bearings

2B

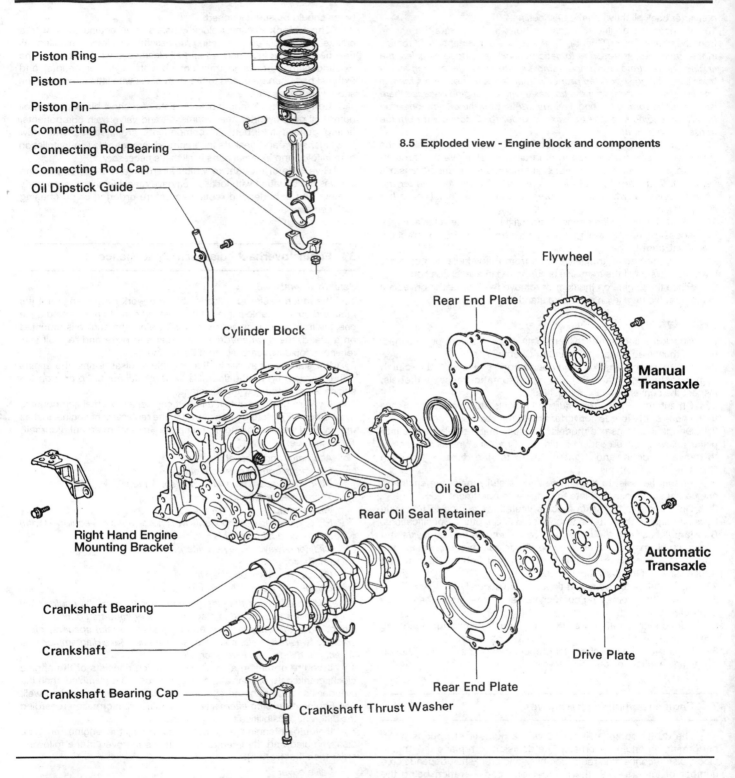

8.5 Exploded view - Engine block and components

Piston Ring

Piston

Piston Pin

Connecting Rod

Connecting Rod Bearing

Connecting Rod Cap

Oil Dipstick Guide

Cylinder Block

Flywheel

Rear End Plate

Manual Transaxle

Oil Seal

Rear Oil Seal Retainer

Right Hand Engine Mounting Bracket

Automatic Transaxle

Crankshaft Bearing

Crankshaft

Crankshaft Bearing Cap

Crankshaft Thrust Washer

Rear End Plate

Drive Plate

---

6   Before beginning the disassembly and overhaul procedures, make sure the following items are available. Also, refer to *Engine overhaul - reassembly sequence* for a list of tools and materials needed for engine reassembly.

Common hand tools
Small cardboard boxes or plastic bags for storing parts
Gasket scraper
Ridge reamer
Vibration damper puller
Micrometers

Telescoping gauges
Dial indicator set
Valve spring compressor
Cylinder surfacing hone
Piston ring groove cleaning tool
Electric drill motor
Tap and die set
Wire brushes
Oil gallery brushes
Cleaning solvent

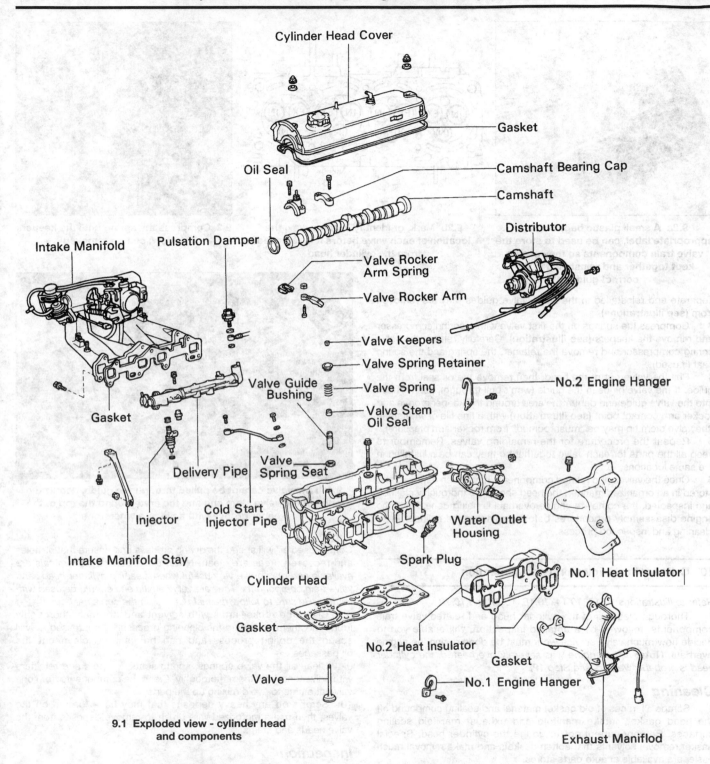

9.1 Exploded view - cylinder head
and components

2B

9 Cylinder head - disassembly

Refer to illustrations 9.1, 9.2a, 9.2b, 9.3 and 9.4
Note: *New and rebuilt cylinder heads are commonly available for most engines at dealerships and auto parts stores. Due to the fact that some specialized tools are necessary for the disassembly and inspection procedures, and replacement parts may not be readily available, it may be more practical and economical for the home mechanic to purchase*

a replacement head rather than taking the time to disassemble, inspect and recondition the original, or have it done by an automotive machine shop.

1   Cylinder head disassembly involves removal of the intake and exhaust valves and related components **(see illustration)**. It's assumed that valve cover, camshaft, rocker arms and rocker arm springs have already been removed (see Part A as needed).

2   Before the valves are removed, arrange to label and store each valve, along with their related components, so they can be kept

9.2a A small plastic bag, with an appropriate label, can be used to store the valve train components so they can be kept together and reinstalled in the correct guide

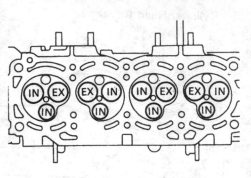

9.2b Mark, or identify in some way, the location of each valve before it is removed from the cylinder head

9.3 Compress the spring until the keepers (arrow) can be removed

separate and reinstalled in the same valve guides they are removed from **(see illustrations)**.

3   Compress the springs on the first valve with a spring compressor and remove the keepers **(see illustration)**. Carefully release the valve spring compressor and remove the retainer, the spring and the spring seat (if used).

4   Pull the valve out of the head, then remove the oil seal from the guide. If the valve binds in the guide (won't pull through), push it back into the valve guide and deburr the area around the keeper groove and rocker arm contact point **(see illustration)** with a fine file or whetstone (the valve stem tip may be "mushroomed" from rocker arm pressure).

5   Repeat the procedure for the remaining valves. Remember to keep all the parts for each valve together so they can be reinstalled in the same locations.

6   Once the valves and related components have been removed and stored in an organized manner, the head should be thoroughly cleaned and inspected. If a complete engine overhaul is being done, finish the engine disassembly procedures before beginning the cylinder head cleaning and inspection process.

9.4 If the valve cannot be pulled through the guide, deburr the edge of the valve stem end and the area around the top of the keeper groove with a file or a whetstone

10   Cylinder head - cleaning and inspection

Refer to illustrations 10.12, 10.14, 10.16, 10.17 and 10.18

1   Thorough cleaning of the cylinder head and related valve train components, followed by a detailed inspection, will enable you to decide how much valve service work must be done during the engine overhaul. **Note:** *If the engine was severely overheated, the cylinder head is probably warped (see Step 12).*

Cleaning

2   Scrape all traces of old gasket material and sealing compound off the head gasket, intake manifold and exhaust manifold sealing surfaces. Be very careful not to gouge the cylinder head. Special gasket removal solvents that soften gaskets and make removal much easier are available at auto parts stores.

3   Remove all built-up scale from the coolant passages.

4   Run a stiff wire brush through the various holes to remove deposits that may have formed in them.

5   Run an appropriate size tap into each of the threaded holes to remove corrosion and thread sealant that may be present. If compressed air is available, use it to clear the holes of debris produced by this operation. **Warning:** *Wear eye protection when using compressed air!*

6   Clean the exhaust and intake manifold stud threads with a wire brush. **Warning:** *Wear eye protection when using a wire brush to clean threads!*

7   Clean the cylinder head with solvent and dry it thoroughly.

Compressed air will speed the drying process and ensure that all holes and recessed areas are clean. **Note:** *Decarbonizing chemicals are available and may prove very useful when cleaning cylinder heads and valve train components. They are very caustic and should be used with caution. Be sure to follow the instructions on the container.*

8   Clean the rocker arms with solvent and dry them thoroughly (don't mix them up during the cleaning process). Compressed air will speed the drying process and can be used to clean out the oil passages.

9   Clean all the valve springs, spring seats, keepers and retainers with solvent and dry them thoroughly. Clean the components from one valve at a time to avoid mixing up the parts.

10   Scrape off any heavy deposits that may have formed on the valves, then use a motorized wire brush to remove deposits from the valve heads and stems.

Inspection

Note: *Be sure to perform all of the following inspection procedures before concluding that machine shop work is required. Make a list of the items that need attention. The inspection procedures for the and rocker arms and the camshaft, can be found in Part A.*

Cylinder head

11   Inspect the head very carefully for cracks, evidence of coolant leakage and other damage. If cracks are found, check with an automotive machine shop concerning repair. If repair isn't possible, a new cylinder head should be obtained.

12   Using a straightedge and feeler gauge, check the head gasket, intake and exhaust manifold surfaces for warpage **(see illustration)**. If

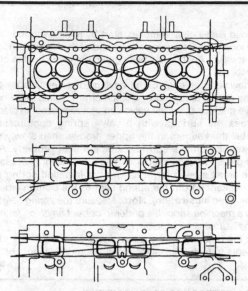

10.12 Check the cylinder head gasket surfaces (block, intake and exhaust manifolds) for warpage by trying to slip a feeler gauge under the precision straightedge (see the Specifications for the maximum warpage allowed and use a feeler gauge of that thickness)

the warpage exceeds the specified limit, it can be resurfaced at an automotive machine shop.

13   Examine the valve seats in each of the combustion chambers. If they're pitted, cracked or burned, the head will require valve service by an automotive machine shop or complete replacement.

14   Measure the valve guide inside diameter with a small hole gauge and micrometer **(see illustration)**, then measure the valve stem diameter and subtract it from the valve guide diameter to obtain the stem-to-guide clearance.

Valves

15   Carefully inspect each valve face for uneven wear, deformation, cracks, pits and burned areas. Check the valve stem for scuffing and galling and the neck for cracks. Rotate the valve and check for any obvious indication that it's bent. Look for pits and excessive wear on the end of the stem. The presence of any of these conditions indicates the need for valve service by an automotive machine shop.

16   Measure the margin width on each valve **(see illustration)**. Any valve with a margin narrower than specified will have to be replaced with a new one.

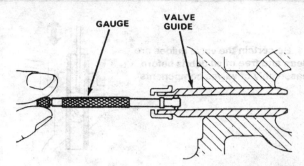

10.14 Use a small hole gauge to determine the inside diameter of the valve guides (the gauge is then measured with a micrometer)

Valve components

17   Check each valve spring for wear (on the ends) and pits. Measure the free length and compare it to the Specifications **(see illustration)**. Any springs that are shorter than specified have sagged and should not be reused. The tension of all springs should be checked with a special fixture before deciding that they're suitable for use in a rebuilt engine (take the springs to an automotive machine shop for this check). **Caution:** *Installed spring height and pressure are critical in properly reassembling the cylinder head. Poor performance or possible engine damage could result if done incorrectly.*

18   Stand each spring on a flat surface and check it for squareness **(see illustration)**. If any of the springs are distorted or sagged, replace all of them with new parts.

19   Check the spring retainers and keepers for obvious wear and cracks. Any questionable parts should be replaced with new ones, as extensive damage will occur if they fail during engine operation.

20   Any damaged or excessively worn parts must be replaced with new ones.

21   If the inspection process indicates that the valve components are in generally poor condition and worn beyond the limits specified, which is usually the case in an engine that's being overhauled, reassemble the valves in the cylinder head and refer to valve servicing recommendations (see Section 11).

11   Valves - servicing

1   Because of the complex nature of the job and the prohibitive cost of the special tools and equipment needed, servicing of the valves, the valve seats and the valve guides, commonly known as a valve job, is usually more easily, and inexpensively, done by a automotive

2B

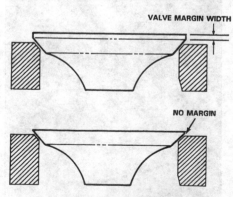

10.16 The margin width on each valve must be as specified (if the margin is below the minimum specification, the valve cannot be reused)

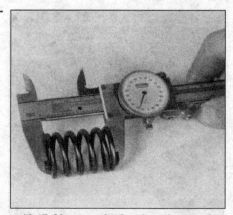

10.17 Measure the free length of each valve spring with a dial or vernier caliper

10.18 Check each valve spring for squareness

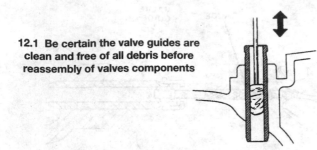

12.1 Be certain the valve guides are clean and free of all debris before reassembly of valves components

machine shop.

2   The home mechanic can remove and disassemble the head, do the initial cleaning and inspection, then reassemble and deliver it to a dealer service department or an automotive machine shop for the actual service work. Doing the inspection will enable you to see what condition the head and valve train components are in and will ensure that you know what work and new parts are required when dealing with an automotive machine shop.

3   The dealer service department, or automotive machine shop, will remove the valves and springs, recondition or replace the valves and valve seats, recondition or replace the valve guides, check and shim or replace the valve springs, spring retainers and keepers (as necessary), replace the valve seals with new ones, reassemble the valve components and make sure the installed spring height and pressure is correct. The cylinder head gasket surface will also be resurfaced if it's warped. **Note:** *It may be advisable to have the cylinder head pressure checked for internal coolant leaks, especially if the engine has been overheated.*

4   After the valve job has been performed, the head will be in like new condition. When the head is returned, be sure to clean it again before installation on the engine to remove any metal particles and abrasive grit that may still be present from the valve service or head resurfacing operations. Use compressed air, if available, to blow out all the oil holes and passages.

12   Cylinder head - reassembly

Refer to illustrations 12.1 and 12.7

1   Regardless of whether or not the head was sent to an automotive repair shop for valve servicing, make sure it's clean before beginning reassembly **(see illustration)**.

2   If the head was sent out for valve servicing, the valves and related components will already be in place and the head will be ready to bolt to the block.

3   If the head is still disassembled, start by reinstalling the valves in their correct locations. Beginning at one end of the head, lubricate and install the first valve. Apply moly-base grease or clean engine oil to the valve stem.

4   Install new seals on each of the valve guides (see Chapter 2A).

5   Drop the spring seat and/or shim(s) (if any shims were needed) over the valve guide and set the valve spring and retainer in place.

6   Compress the springs with a valve spring compressor and carefully install the keepers in the upper groove, then slowly release the compressor and make sure the keepers seat properly. Apply a small dab of grease to each keeper to hold it in place if necessary.

7   Using a small steel ruler, measure the installed spring height. Measure the distance from the spring seat to the bottom side of the spring retainer **(see illustration)**. **Note:** *Measure the spring height even if it did go to a machine shop. It's better to correct anything found now, rather than have it cause a problem later.*

8   Repeat the procedure for the remaining valves. Be sure to return the components to their original locations - don't mix them up!

13   Pistons/connecting rods - removal

Refer to illustrations 13.1, 13.3, 13.4a, 13.4b and 13.6

Note: *Prior to removing the piston/connecting rod assemblies, remove the cylinder head, the oil pan and the oil pump pick-up tube by referring to the appropriate Sections in Part A.*

1   Use your fingernail to feel if a ridge has formed at the upper limit of ring travel (about 1/4-inch down from the top of each cylinder). If carbon deposits or cylinder wear have produced ridges, they must be completely removed with a special tool, called a "ridge reamer", **(see illustration)**. Follow the manufacturer's instructions provided with the tool. Failure to remove the ridges before attempting to remove the piston/connecting rod assemblies may result in piston breakage.

2   After the cylinder ridges have been removed, turn the engine upside-down so the crankshaft is facing up.

3   Before the connecting rods are removed, check the side clearance with feeler gauges. Slide them between the first connecting rod and the crankshaft throw until the play is removed **(see illustration)**. The side clearance is equal to the thickness of the feeler gauge(s). If the side clearance exceeds the service limit, new connecting rods will be required. **Note:** *It is possible that the excessive connecting rod side clearance may be caused by the lack of a crankshaft journal radius. If this is the case the crankshaft will either have to be repaired, if possible, or replaced. If new rods (or a new crankshaft) are installed, the side clearance may fall under the specified minimum (if it does, the rods will have to be machined to restore clearance - consult an automotive machine shop for advice if*

12.7 Measure installed spring height by using a ruler placed between the spring shim/hardened washer and the spring retainer (arrows)

13.1 A ridge reamer is required to remove the ridge from the top of each cylinder - do this before removing the pistons!

13.3 Check the connecting rod side clearance with a feeler gauge as shown here

13.4a Don't mistake the numbering shown here as connecting rod identification, these numbers (and letters) are for bearing selection

13.4b The connecting rods and caps should be marked to indicate which cylinder they're installed in - if they aren't, mark them with a center-punch to avoid confusion during reassembly

13.6 To prevent damage to the crankshaft journals and cylinder walls, slip sections of hose over the rod bolts before removing the pistons

necessary). Repeat the procedure for the remaining connecting rods.

4   Check the connecting rods and caps for identification marks. If they aren't plainly marked, use a small center-punch, scribe or numbered punch (if available), to make the appropriate number of indentations on each rod and cap (1, 2, 3, etc., depending on the engine type and cylinder they're associated with) **(see illustrations)**.

5   Loosen each of the connecting rod cap nuts 1/2-turn at a time until they can be removed by hand. Remove the number one connecting rod cap and bearing insert. Don't drop the bearing insert out of the cap.

6   Slip a short length of plastic or rubber hose over each connecting rod cap bolt to protect the crankshaft journal and cylinder wall as the piston is removed **(see illustration)**.

7   Remove the bearing insert and push the connecting rod/piston assembly out through the top of the engine. Use a wooden hammer handle to push on the upper bearing surface in the connecting rod. If resistance is felt, double-check to make sure that all of the ridge was removed from the cylinder.

8   Repeat the procedure for the remaining cylinders.

9   After removal, reassemble the connecting rod caps and bearing inserts in their respective connecting rods and install the cap nuts finger tight. Leaving the old bearing inserts in place until reassembly will help prevent the connecting rod bearing surfaces from being accidentally nicked or gouged.

10   Don't separate the pistons from the connecting rods (see Section 18).

14 Crankshaft - removal

Refer to illustrations 14.1, 14.3 and 14.4

Note: *The crankshaft can be removed only after the engine has been removed from the vehicle. It's assumed that the flywheel or driveplate, vibration damper, timing belt, oil pan, oil pick-up tube, oil pump and piston/connecting rod assemblies have already been removed. The rear main oil seal retainer must be unbolted and separated from the block before proceeding with crankshaft removal.*

1   Before the crankshaft is removed, check the endplay. Mount a dial indicator with the stem in line with the crankshaft and just touching the crankshaft **(see illustration)**.

2   Push the crankshaft all the way to the rear and zero the dial indicator. Next, pry the crankshaft to the front as far as possible and check the reading on the dial indicator. The distance that it moves is the endplay. If it's greater than specified, check the crankshaft thrust surfaces for wear. If no wear is evident, new thrust washers should correct the endplay.

3   If a dial indicator isn't available feeler gauges can be used in the same way they were used to check connecting rod endplay. Gently pry or push the crankshaft all the way to the front of the engine. Slip feeler gauges between the crankshaft and the front face of the thrust main bearing to determine the clearance **(see illustration)**. The thrust bearing is number three (center).

14.1 Checking crankshaft endplay with a dial indicator

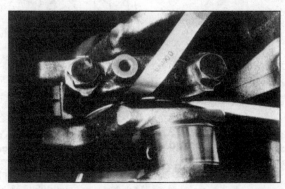

14.3 Checking crankshaft endplay with a feeler gauge

14.4 If the main bearing caps aren't already numbered (arrows), do so before removal

15.1a Use a hammer and a large punch to knock the core plugs sideways in their bores

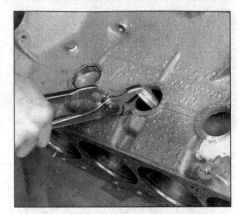

15.1b Pull the core plugs from the block with pliers

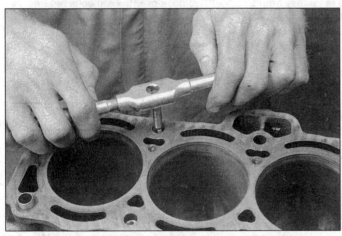

15.8 All bolt holes in the block - particularly the main bearing cap and head bolt holes - should be cleaned and restored with a tap (be sure to remove debris from the holes after this is done)

15.10 A large socket on an extension can be used to drive the new core plugs into the bores

4   Check the main bearing caps to see if they're marked to indicate their locations (see illustration). They should be numbered consecutively from the front of the engine to the rear. If they aren't, mark them with number stamping dies or a center-punch. Main bearing caps generally have a cast-in arrow, which points to the front of the engine.

5   Loosen the main bearing cap bolts 1/4-turn at a time each, starting with the front and rear caps and working toward the center, until they can be removed by hand. Note if any stud bolts are used and make sure they're returned to their original locations when the crankshaft is reinstalled.

6   Gently tap the caps with a soft-face hammer, then separate them from the engine block. If necessary, use the bolts as levers to remove

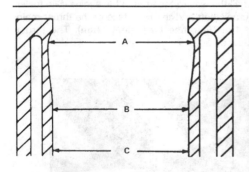

16.4a Measure the diameter of each cylinder just under the wear ridge (A), at the center (B) and at the bottom (C)

16.4b The ability to "feel" when the telescoping gauge is at the correct point will be developed over time, so work slowly and repeat the check until you're satisfied that the bore measurement is accurate

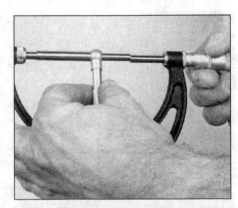

16.4c The gauge is then measured with a micrometer to determine the bore size

the caps. Do not drop the bearing inserts as the caps are removed.
7   Carefully lift the crankshaft out of the engine. It may be a good idea to have an assistant available, since the crankshaft is quite heavy. With the bearing inserts in place in the engine block and main bearing caps or cap assembly, return the caps to their respective locations on the engine block and tighten the bolts finger tight.

15   Engine block - cleaning

Refer to illustrations 15.1a, 15.1b, 15.8 and 15.10
1   Remove the core plugs from the engine. To do this, knock one side of the plug into the block with a hammer and a punch, then grasp the plug with a large pliers and pull it out **(see illustrations)**.
2   Using a gasket scraper, remove all traces of gasket material from the engine block. Be very careful not to nick or gouge the gasket sealing surfaces. **Note:** *A scouring pad, like ones used in the kitchen, work well in holes, or tight places, when cleaning surfaces before resealing.*
3   Remove the main bearing caps or cap assembly and separate the bearing inserts from the caps and the engine block. Tag the bearings, indicating which cylinder they were removed from and whether they were in the cap or the block, then set them aside.
4   Remove all of the threaded oil gallery plugs from the block. The plugs are usually very tight - they may have to be drilled out and the holes retapped. Use new plugs when the engine is reassembled.
5   If the engine is extremely dirty it should be taken to an automotive machine shop to be steam cleaned or hot tanked.
6   After the block is returned, clean all oil holes and oil galleries one more time. Brushes specifically designed for this purpose are available at most auto parts stores. Flush the passages with warm water until the water runs clear, dry the block thoroughly and wipe/spray all machined surfaces with a light, rust preventive oil. If you have access to compressed air, use it to speed the drying process and to blow out all the oil holes and galleries. **Warning:** *Wear eye protection when using compressed air!*
7   If the block isn't extremely dirty or sludged up, you can do an adequate cleaning job with hot soapy water and a stiff brush. Take plenty of time and do a thorough job. Regardless of the cleaning method used, be sure to clean all oil holes and galleries very thoroughly, dry the block completely and coat all machined surfaces with light oil.
8   The threaded holes in the block must be clean to ensure accurate torque readings during reassembly. Run the proper size tap into each of the holes to remove rust, corrosion, thread sealant or sludge and restore damaged threads **(see illustration)**. If possible, use compressed air to clear the holes of debris produced by this operation. Now is a good time to clean the threads on the head bolts and the main bearing cap bolts as well.
9   Reinstall the main bearing caps and tighten the bolts finger tight.
10   After coating the sealing surfaces of the new core plugs with Permatex no. 2 sealant, install them in the engine block **(see illustration)**. Make sure they're driven in straight and seated properly

or leakage could result. Special tools are available for this purpose, but a large socket, with an outside diameter that will just slip into the core plug, a 1/2-inch drive extension and a hammer will work just as well.
11   Apply non-hardening sealant (such as Permatex no. 2 or Teflon pipe sealant) to the new oil gallery plugs and thread them into the holes in the block. Make sure they're tightened securely.
12   If the engine isn't going to be reassembled right away, cover it with a large plastic trash bag to keep it clean.

16   Engine block - inspection

Refer to illustrations 16.4a, 16.4b, 16.4c, 16.12a and 16.12b
1   Before the block is inspected, it should be cleaned (see Section 15).
2   Visually check the block for cracks, rust and corrosion. Look for stripped threads in the threaded holes. It's also a good idea to have the block checked for hidden cracks by an automotive machine shop that has the special equipment to do this type of work. If defects are found, have the block repaired, if possible, or replaced.
3   Check the cylinder bores for scuffing and scoring.
4   Measure the diameter of each cylinder at the top (just under the ridge area), center and bottom of the cylinder bore, parallel to the crankshaft axis **(see illustrations)**.
5   Next, measure each cylinder's diameter at the same three locations across the crankshaft axis. Compare the results to the Specifications.
6   If the required precision measuring tools aren't available, the piston-to-cylinder clearances can be obtained, though not quite as accurately, using feeler gauge stock. Feeler gauge stock comes in 12-inch lengths and various thickness and is generally available at auto parts stores.
7   To check the clearance, select a feeler gauge and slip it into the cylinder along with the matching piston. The piston must be positioned exactly as it normally would be. The feeler gauge must be between the piston and cylinder on one of the thrust faces (90-degrees to the piston pin bore).
8   The piston should slip through the cylinder (with the feeler gauge in place) with moderate pressure.
9   If it falls through or slides through easily, the clearance is excessive and a new piston will be required. If the piston binds at the lower end of the cylinder and is loose toward the top, the cylinder is tapered. If tight spots are encountered as the piston/feeler gauge is rotated in the cylinder, the cylinder is out-of-round.
10   Repeat the procedure for the remaining pistons and cylinders.
11   If the cylinder walls are badly scuffed or scored, or if they're out-of-round or tapered beyond the limits given in the Specifications, have the engine block rebored and honed at an automotive machine shop. If a rebore is done, oversize pistons and rings will be required.
12   Using a precision straightedge and feeler gauge, check the block deck (the surface that mates with the cylinder head) for distortion **(see illustrations)**. If it's distorted beyond the specified limit, it can be resurfaced by an automotive machine shop.

2B

16.12a Check the block deck for distortion with a precision straightedge and feeler gauges

16.12b Lay the straightedge across the block, diagonally and from end-to-end when making the check

17.3a A "bottle brush" hone will produce better results if you have never honed cylinders before

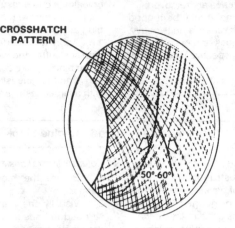

17.3b The cylinder hone should leave a smooth, crosshatch pattern with the lines intersecting at approximately a 60-degree angle

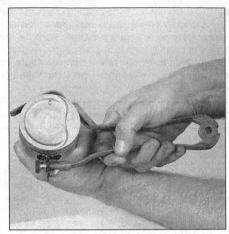

18.4a The piston ring grooves can be cleaned with a special tool, as shown here . . .

13   If the cylinders are in reasonably good condition and not worn to the outside of the limits, and if the piston-to-cylinder clearances can be maintained properly, then they don't have to be rebored. Honing is all that's necessary (see Section 17).

17   Cylinder honing

Refer to illustrations 17.3a and 17.3b

1   Prior to engine reassembly, the cylinder bores must be honed so the new piston rings will seat correctly and provide the best possible combustion chamber seal. **Note:** *If you don't have the tools or don't want to tackle the honing operation, most automotive machine shops will do it for a reasonable fee.*

2   Before honing the cylinders, install the main bearing caps (without bearing inserts) and tighten the bolts to the torque listed in this Chapter's Specifications.

3   Two types of cylinder hones are commonly available - the flex hone or "bottle brush" type and the more traditional surfacing hone with spring-loaded stones. Both will do the job, but for the less experienced mechanic the "bottle brush" hone will probably be easier to use. You'll also need some kerosene or honing oil, rags and an

electric drill motor. Proceed as follows:

a) *Mount the hone in the drill motor, compress the stones and slip it into the first cylinder (see illustration). Be sure to wear safety goggles or a face shield!*

b) *Lubricate the cylinder with plenty of honing oil, turn on the drill and move the hone up-and-down in the cylinder at a pace that will produce a fine crosshatch pattern on the cylinder walls. Ideally, the crosshatch lines should intersect at approximately a 60-degrees angle* **(see illustration).** *Be sure to use plenty of lubricant and don't take off any more material than is absolutely necessary to produce the desired finish.* **Note:** *Piston ring manufacturers may specify a smaller crosshatch angle than the traditional 60-degrees - read and follow any instructions included with the new rings.*

c) *Don't withdraw the hone from the cylinder while it's running. Instead, shut off the drill and continue moving the hone up-and-down in the cylinder until it comes to a complete stop, then compress the stones and withdraw the hone. If you're using a "bottle brush" type hone, stop the drill motor, then turn the chuck in the normal direction of rotation while withdrawing the hone from the cylinder.*

d) *Wipe the oil out of the cylinder and repeat the procedure for the remaining cylinders.*

18.4b . . . or a section of a broken ring

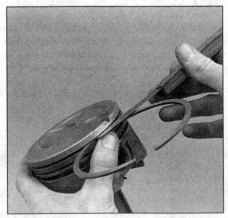

18.10 Check the ring side clearance with a feeler gauge at several points around the groove

18.11 Measure the piston diameter at a 90-degree angle to the piston pin - depending on the model, the pistons must be measured at a precise point:

4   After the honing job is complete, chamfer the top edges of the cylinder bores with a small file so the rings won't catch when the pistons are installed. Be very careful not to nick the cylinder walls with the end of the file.

5   The entire engine block must be washed again very thoroughly with warm, soapy water to remove all traces of the abrasive grit produced during the honing operation. **Note:** *The bores can be considered clean when a lint-free white cloth - dampened with clean engine oil - used to wipe them out doesn't pick-up any more honing residue, which will show up as gray areas on the cloth. Be sure to run a brush through all oil holes and galleries and flush them with running water.*

6   After rinsing, dry the block and apply a coat of light rust preventive oil to all machined surfaces. Wrap the block in a plastic trash bag to keep it clean and set it aside until reassembly.

18 Pistons/connecting rods - inspection

Refer to illustrations 18.4a, 18.4b, 18.10 and 18.11

1   Before the inspection process can be carried out, the piston/connecting rod assemblies must be cleaned and the original piston rings removed from the pistons. **Note:** *Always use new piston rings when the engine is reassembled.*

2   Using a piston ring installation tool, carefully remove the rings from the pistons. Be careful not to nick or gouge the pistons in the process.

3   Scrape all traces of carbon from the top of the piston. A hand-held wire brush or a piece of fine emery cloth can be used once the majority of the deposits have been scraped away. Do not, under any circumstances, use a wire brush mounted in a drill motor to remove deposits from the pistons. The piston material is soft and may be eroded away by the wire brush.

4   Use a piston ring groove cleaning tool to remove carbon deposits from the ring grooves. If a tool isn't available, a piece broken off the old ring will do the job. Be very careful to remove only the carbon deposits - don't remove any metal and do not nick or scratch the sides of the ring grooves **(see illustrations)**.

5   Once the deposits have been removed, clean the piston/rod assemblies with solvent and dry them with compressed air (if available). Make sure the oil return holes in the back sides of the ring grooves and the oil hole in the lower end of each rod are clear.

6   If the pistons and cylinder walls aren't damaged or worn excessively, and if the engine block is not rebored, new pistons won't be necessary. Normal piston wear appears as even vertical wear on the piston thrust surfaces and slight looseness of the top ring in its groove. New piston rings, however, should always be used when an engine is rebuilt.

7   Carefully inspect each piston for cracks around the skirt, at the pin bosses and at the ring lands.

8   Look for scoring and scuffing on the thrust faces of the skirt, holes in the piston crown and burned areas at the edge of the crown. If the skirt is scored or scuffed, the engine may have been suffering from overheating and/or abnormal combustion, which caused excessively high operating temperatures. The cooling and lubrication systems should be checked thoroughly. A hole in the piston crown is an indication that abnormal combustion (preignition) was occurring. Burned areas at the edge of the piston crown are usually evidence of spark knock (detonation). If any of the above problems exist, the causes must be corrected or the damage will occur again. The causes may include intake air leaks, incorrect fuel/air mixture, incorrect ignition timing and EGR system malfunctions.

9   Corrosion of the piston, in the form of small pits, indicates that coolant is leaking into the combustion chamber and/or the crankcase. Again, the cause must be corrected or the problem may persist in the rebuilt engine.

10   Measure the piston ring side clearance by laying a new piston ring in each ring groove and slipping a feeler gauge in beside it **(see illustration)**. Check the clearance at three or four locations around each groove. Be sure to use the correct ring for each groove - they are different. If the side clearance is greater than specified, new pistons will have to be used. **Note:** *Piston ring side clearance is only measured on the compression rings.*

11   Check the piston-to-bore clearance by measuring the bore (see Section 16) and the piston diameter. Make sure the pistons and bores are correctly matched. Measure the piston across the skirt, at a 90-degree angle to the piston pin **(see illustration)**. Subtract the piston diameter from the bore diameter to obtain the clearance. If it's greater than specified, the block will have to be rebored and new pistons and rings installed.

12   Check the piston-to-rod clearance by twisting the piston and rod in opposite directions. Any noticeable play indicates excessive wear, which must be corrected. The piston/connecting rod assemblies should be taken to an automotive machine shop to have the pistons and rods resized and new pins installed.

13   If the pistons must be removed from the connecting rods for any reason, they should be taken to an automotive machine shop. While they are there have the connecting rods checked for bend and twist, since automotive machine shops have special equipment for this purpose. **Note:** *Unless new pistons and/or connecting rods must be installed, do not disassemble the pistons and connecting rods.*

14   Check the connecting rods for cracks and other damage. Temporarily remove the rod caps, lift out the old bearing inserts, wipe the rod and cap bearing surfaces clean and inspect them for nicks, gouges and scratches. After checking the rods, replace the old bearings, slip the caps into place and tighten the nuts finger tight. **Note:** *If the engine is being rebuilt because of a connecting rod knock, be sure to install new rods.*

19 Crankshaft - inspection

Refer to illustrations 19.4 and 19.6

1   Remove any burrs from the crankshaft oil holes with a stone, file or scraper.

2   Clean the crankshaft with solvent and dry it with compressed air (if available). Be sure to clean the oil holes with a stiff brush and flush them with solvent.

3   Check the main and connecting rod bearing journals for uneven wear, scoring, pits and cracks.

4   Rub a penny across each journal several times **(see illustration)**. If a journal picks up copper from the penny, it's too rough and must be reground.

5   Check the rest of the crankshaft for cracks and other damage. It

19.4 Rubbing a penny lengthwise on each journal will reveal its condition - if copper rubs off and is embedded in the crankshaft the journals should be reground

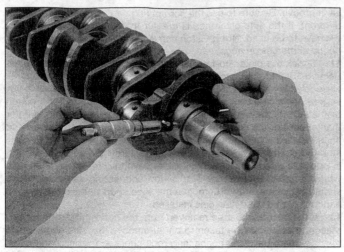

19.6 Measure the diameter of each crankshaft journal at several points to detect taper and out-of-round conditions

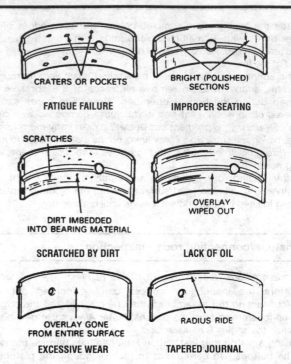

20.1 When inspecting the main and connecting rod bearings, look for these problems

should be magnafluxed to reveal hidden cracks - an automotive machine shop will handle the procedure.

6   Using a micrometer, measure the diameter of the main and connecting rod journals and compare the results to the Specifications **(see illustration)**. By measuring the diameter at a number of points around each journal's circumference, you'll be able to determine whether or not the journal is out-of-round. Take the measurement at each end of the journal, near the crank throws, to determine if the journal is tapered. Crankshaft runout should be checked also, but large V-blocks and a dial indicator are needed to do it correctly. If you don't have the equipment, have a machine shop check the runout.

7   If the crankshaft journals are damaged, tapered, out-of-round or worn beyond the limits given in the Specifications, have the crankshaft reground by an automotive machine shop. Be sure to use the correct size bearing inserts if the crankshaft is reconditioned. **Note:** *If the crankshaft is being reground, have the machine shop provided fitted bearings that are matched to that crankshaft.*

8   Check the oil seal journals at each end of the crankshaft for wear and damage. If the seal has worn a groove in the journal, or if it's nicked or scratched, the new seal may leak when the engine is reassembled. In some cases, an automotive machine shop may be able to repair the journal by pressing on a thin sleeve. If repair isn't feasible, a new or different crankshaft should be installed.

9   Examine the main and rod bearing inserts (see Section 20).

20   Main and connecting rod bearings - inspection and selection

Inspection

Refer to illustration 20.1

1   Even though the main and connecting rod bearings should be replaced with new ones during the engine overhaul, the old bearings should be retained for close examination, as they may reveal valuable information about the condition of the engine **(see illustration)**.

2   Bearing failure occurs because of lack of lubrication, the presence of dirt or other foreign particles, overloading the engine and corrosion. Regardless of the cause of bearing failure, it must be corrected before the engine is reassembled to prevent it from happening again.

3   When examining the bearings, remove them from the engine block, the main bearing caps, the connecting rods and the rod caps and lay them out on a clean surface in the same general position as their location in the engine. This will enable you to match any bearing problems with the corresponding crankshaft journal.

4   Dirt and other foreign particles get into the engine in a variety of

ways. It may be left in the engine during assembly, or it may pass through filters or the PCV system. It may get into the oil, and from there into the bearings. Metal chips from machining operations and normal engine wear are often present. Abrasives are sometimes left in engine components after reconditioning, especially when parts are not thoroughly cleaned using the proper cleaning methods. Whatever the source, these foreign objects often end up embedded in the soft bearing material and are easily recognized. Large particles will not embed in the bearing and will score or gouge the bearing and journal. The best prevention for this cause of bearing failure is to clean all parts thoroughly and keep everything spotlessly clean during engine assembly. Frequent and regular engine oil and filter changes are also recommended.

5   Lack of lubrication (or lubrication breakdown) has a number of interrelated causes. Excessive heat (which thins the oil), overloading (which squeezes the oil from the bearing face) and oil leakage or throw off (from excessive bearing clearances, worn oil pump or high engine speeds) all contribute to lubrication breakdown. Blocked oil passages, which usually are the result of misaligned oil holes in a bearing shell, will also oil starve a bearing and destroy it. When lack of lubrication is the cause of bearing failure, the bearing material is wiped or extruded from the steel backing of the bearing. Temperatures may increase to the point where the steel backing turns blue from overheating.

6   Driving habits can have a definite effect on bearing life. Full throttle, low speed operation (lugging the engine) puts very high loads on bearings, which tends to squeeze out the oil film. These loads cause the bearings to flex, which produces fine cracks in the bearing face (fatigue failure). Eventually the bearing material will loosen in pieces and tear away from the steel backing. Short trip driving leads to corrosion of bearings because insufficient engine heat is produced to drive off the condensed water and corrosive gases. These products collect in the engine oil, forming acid and sludge. As the oil is carried to the engine bearings, the acid attacks and corrodes the bearing material.

7   Incorrect bearing installation during engine assembly will lead to bearing failure as well. Tight fitting bearings leave insufficient bearing oil clearance and will result in oil starvation. Dirt or foreign particles trapped behind a bearing insert result in high spots on the bearing which lead to failure.

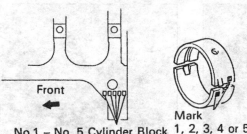

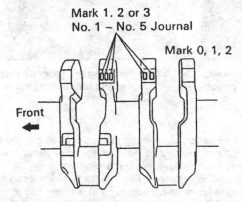

No.1 – No. 5 Cylinder Block Main Journal
Mark 1, 2, 3, 4 or 5

Mark 1. 2 or 3
No. 1 – No. 5 Journal
Mark 0, 1, 2

Front

20.9 Main journal grade numbers are stamped into the oil pan mating surface on the block - there are 5 journals, so there are 5 numbers

20.10 Engine main journal crankshaft grade numbers - most engines have the grade numbers on the edge of one of the crankshaft counter weights, as shown here

Cylinder Block	1	2	3	1	2	3	1	2	3
Crankshaft	0	0	0	1	1	1	2	2	2
Bearing	1	2	3	2	3	4	3	4	5

EXAMPLE: Cylinder block "2" + Crankshaft "1" =Total number (Use bearing "3")

20.11 Engine main bearing selection chart

Selection

Refer to illustrations 20.9, 20.10, 20.11 and 20.12

8   If the original bearings are worn or damaged, or if the oil clearances are incorrect (see Section 23 or 25), the following procedures should be used to select the correct new bearings for engine reassembly. However, if the crankshaft has been reground, new undersize bearings must be installed - the following procedure should not be used if undersize bearings are required! The automotive machine shop that reconditions the crankshaft will provide or help you select the correct size bearings. Regardless of how the bearing sizes are determined, use the oil clearance, measured with Plastigage, as a guide to ensure the bearings are the right size.

Main bearings

9   If you need to use a STANDARD size main bearing, install one that has the same number as the original bearing **(see illustration)**.
10   If the number on the original main bearing has been obscured, locate the main journal grade numbers stamped into the oil pan mating surface on the engine block and crankshaft **(see illustrations)**.
11   Use the accompanying chart to determine the correct bearings for each journal **(see illustrations)**.

Connecting rod bearings

12   If you need to use a STANDARD size rod bearing, install one that has the same number as the number stamped into the connecting rod cap **(see illustration)**.
13   Remember, the oil clearance is the final judge when selecting new bearing sizes. If you have any questions or are unsure which bearings to use, get help from a Toyota dealer parts or service department.

21 Engine overhaul - reassembly sequence

1   Before beginning engine reassembly, make sure you have all the necessary new parts, gaskets and seals as well as the following items on hand:

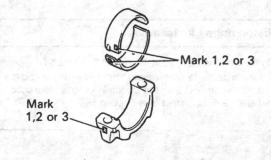

Mark 1,2 or 3

Mark 1,2 or 3

20.12 Connecting rod bearing cap mark location

Common hand tools
A torque wrench
Piston ring installation tool
Piston ring compressor
Short lengths of rubber or plastic hose to fit over connecting rod bolts
Plastigage
Feeler gauges
A fine-tooth file
New engine oil
Engine assembly lube or moly-base grease
Gasket sealant
Thread locking compound

2B

22.3 When checking piston ring end gap, the ring must be square in the cylinder bore (this is done by pushing the ring down with the top of a piston as shown)

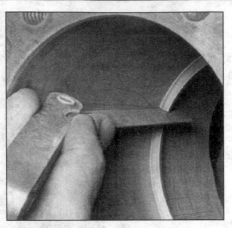

22.4 With the ring square in the cylinder, measure the end gap with a feeler gauge

22.9a Installing the spacer/expander in the oil control ring groove

2   In order to save time and avoid problems, engine reassembly must be done in the following general order: (Detailed information on component in Part A or B of Chapter 2).

Piston rings (Part B)
Crankshaft and main bearings (Part B)
Piston/connecting rod assemblies (Part B)
Rear main (crankshaft) oil seal (Part B)
Cylinder head (Part A)
Camshaft and rocker arms(Part A)
Oil pump (Part A)
Oil pick-up (Part A)
Oil pan (Part A)
Timing belt and pulleys (Part A)
Timing belt cover(s) (Part A)
Valve cover (Part A)
Intake and exhaust manifolds (Part A)
Flywheel/driveplate (Part A)

22   Piston rings - installation

Refer to illustrations 22.3, 22.4, 22.9a, 22.9b and 22.12

1   Before installing the new piston rings, the ring end gaps must be checked. It's assumed that the piston ring side clearance has been checked and verified correct (see Section 18).

2   Lay out the piston/connecting rod assemblies and the new ring sets so the ring sets will be matched with the same piston and cylinder during the end gap measurement and engine assembly.
3   Insert the top (number one) ring into the first cylinder and square it up with the cylinder walls by pushing it in with the top of the piston **(see illustration)**. The ring should be near the bottom of the cylinder, at the lower limit of ring travel.
4   To measure the end gap, slip feeler gauges between the ends of the ring until a gauge equal to the gap width is found **(see illustration)**. The feeler gauge should slide between the ring ends with a slight amount of drag. Compare the measurement to the Specifications. If the gap is larger or smaller than specified, double-check to make sure you have the correct rings before proceeding.
5   If the gap is too small, replace the rings - DO NOT file the ends to increase the clearance.
6   Excess end gap isn't critical unless it's greater than the specified limit. Again, double-check to make sure you have the correct rings for your engine.
7   Repeat the procedure for each ring that will be installed in the first cylinder and for each ring in the remaining cylinders. Remember to keep rings, pistons and cylinders matched up.
8   Once the ring end gaps have been checked/corrected, the rings can be installed on the pistons.
9   The oil control ring (lowest one on the piston) is usually installed first. It's composed of three separate components. Slip the spacer/expander into the groove **(see illustration)**. If an anti-rotation

22.9b DO NOT use a piston ring installation tool when installing the oil ring side rails

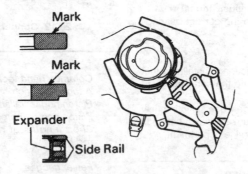

22.12 Install the compression rings with a ring expander - the mark must face up

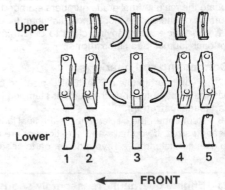

23.6 Disassembled view of the main bearings and caps - note the position of the thrust bearings in the number three position

tang is used, make sure it's inserted into the drilled hole in the ring groove. Next, install the lower side rail. Don't use a piston ring installation tool on the oil ring side rails, as they may be damaged. Instead, place one end of the side rail into the groove between the spacer/expander and the ring land, hold it firmly in place and slide a finger around the piston while pushing the rail into the groove **(see illustration)**. Next, install the upper side rail in the same manner.

10   After the three oil ring components have been installed, check to make sure that both the upper and lower side rails can be turned smoothly in the ring groove.

11   The number two (middle) ring is installed next. It's usually stamped with a mark which must face up, toward the top of the piston. **Note:** *Always follow the instructions printed on the ring package or box - different manufacturers may require different approaches. Do not mix up the top and middle rings, as they have different cross sections.*

12   Use a piston ring installation tool and make sure the identification mark is facing up, the top of the piston, then slip the ring into the number 2 compression ring position, middle groove, on the piston **(see illustration)**. Don't expand the ring any more than necessary to slide it over the piston.

13   Install the number one (top) ring in the same manner. Make sure the mark is facing up. Be careful not to confuse the number one and number two rings.

14   Repeat the procedure for the remaining pistons and rings.

---

23 Crankshaft - installation and main bearing oil clearance check

Refer to illustrations 23.6, 23.10, 23.12 and 23.14

1   Crankshaft installation is the first major step in engine reassembly. It's assumed at this point that the engine block and crankshaft have been cleaned, inspected and repaired or reconditioned.

2   Position the engine with the bottom facing up.

3   Remove the main bearing cap bolts and lift out the caps. Lay the caps out in the proper order to ensure correct installation.

4   If they're still in place, remove the old bearing inserts from the block and the main bearing caps. Wipe the main bearing surfaces of the block and caps with a clean, lint-free cloth. They must be kept spotlessly clean!

Main bearing oil clearance check

5   Clean the back sides of the new main bearing inserts and lay the bearing half with the oil groove in each main bearing saddle in the block. Lay the other bearing half from each bearing set in the corresponding main bearing cap. Make sure the tab on each bearing insert fits into the recess in the block or cap. Also, the oil holes in the block must line up with the oil holes in the bearing insert. **Caution:** *Do not hammer the bearings into place and don't nick or gouge the bearing faces. No lubrication should be used at this time.*

6   The thrust bearings (washers) must be installed in the number three (center) cap. On all engines, the bearings with oil holes (and

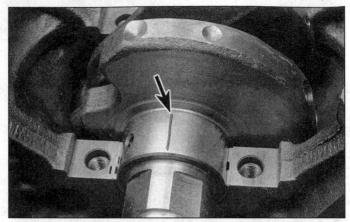

23.10 Lay the Plastigage strips (arrow) on the main bearing journals, parallel to the crankshaft centerline

many times a groove) go in the block and those without oil holes go in the caps **(see illustration)**.

7   Clean the faces of the bearings in the block and the crankshaft main bearing journals with a clean, lint-free cloth. Check or clean the oil holes in the crankshaft, as any dirt here can go only one way - straight through the new bearings.

8   Once you're certain the crankshaft is clean, carefully lay it in position in the main bearings.

9   Before the crankshaft can be permanently installed, the main bearing oil clearance must be checked.

10   Trim several pieces of the appropriate size Plastigage (they must be slightly shorter than the width of the main bearings) and place one piece on each crankshaft main bearing journal, parallel with the journal axis **(see illustration)**.

11   Clean the faces of the bearings in the caps and install the caps in their respective positions (don't mix them up). Don't disturb the Plastigage. Apply a light coat of oil to the bolt threads and the under sides of the bolt heads, then install them.

12   Following the recommended sequence **(see illustration)**, tighten the main bearing caps to the torque listed in this Chapter's Specifications. Don't rotate the crankshaft at any time during this operation!

13   Remove the bolts and carefully lift off the main bearing caps. Keep them in order. Don't disturb the Plastigage or rotate the crankshaft. If any of the main bearing caps are difficult to remove, tap them gently from side-to-side with a soft-face hammer to loosen them.

14   Compare the width of the crushed Plastigage on each journal to

23.12 Main bearing cap bolt tightening sequence

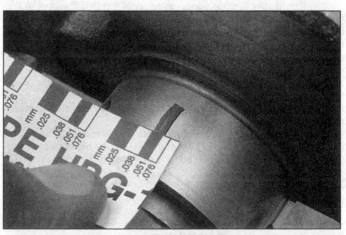

23.14 Compare the width of the crushed Plastigage to the scale on the envelope to determine the main bearing oil clearance (always take the measurement at the widest point of the Plastigage) - be sure to use the correct scale; standard and metric scales are included

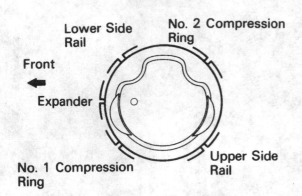

25.5 Stagger the ring end gaps around the piston, as shown, before installing the pistons

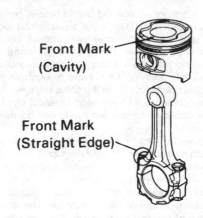

25.9 Both the mark on the piston and the mark on the connecting rod should face the timing belt end of the engine

the scale printed on the Plastigage envelope to obtain the main bearing oil clearance **(see illustration)**. Check the Specifications to make sure it's correct.

15   If the clearance is not as specified, the bearing inserts may be the wrong size which means different ones will be required (see Section 20). Before deciding that different inserts are needed, make sure that no dirt or oil was between the bearing inserts and the caps or block when the clearance was measured. If the Plastigage is noticeably wider at one end than the other, the journal may be tapered (see Section 19).

16   Carefully scrape all traces of the Plastigage material off the main bearing journals and/or the bearing faces. Don't nick or scratch the bearing faces.

Final crankshaft installation

17   Carefully lift the crankshaft out of the engine. Clean the bearing faces in the block, then apply a thin, uniform layer of clean moly-base grease or engine assembly lube to each of the bearing surfaces. Coat the thrust washers as well.

18   Lubricate the crankshaft surfaces that contact the oil seals with moly-base grease, engine assembly lube or clean engine oil.

19   Make sure the crankshaft journals are clean, then lay the crankshaft back in place in the block. Clean the faces of the bearings in the caps or cap assembly, then apply lubricant to them. Install the caps in their respective positions. **Note:** *Install the thrust washer in the number three cap with the oil grooves facing OUT.*

20   Apply a light coat of oil to the bolt threads and the under sides of the bolt heads, then install them. Following the recommended sequence **(see illustration 23.12)**, tighten the main bearing cap bolts, in three steps to the torque listed in this Chapter's Specifications. Tap the ends of the crankshaft forward and backward with a lead or brass hammer to seat the thrust washers.

21   Rotate the crankshaft a number of times by hand to check for any obvious binding.

22   Check the crankshaft endplay with a feeler gauge or a dial indicator (see Section 14). The endplay should be correct if the crankshaft thrust faces aren't worn or damaged and new thrust washers have been installed.

23   Install a new rear main oil seal, then bolt the retainer to the block (see Chapter 2, Part A).

24   Rear main oil seal installation

This procedure is the same for all model years and engines available. Refer to Chapter 2, Part A and follow the procedure and specifications outlined there.

25   Pistons/connecting rods - installation and rod bearing oil clearance check

Refer to illustrations 25.5, 25.9, 25.11, 25.13, 25.14 and 25.17

1   Before installing the piston/connecting rod assemblies, the cylinder walls must be perfectly clean, the top edge of each cylinder must be chamfered, and the crankshaft must be in place.

2   Remove the cap from the end of the number one connecting rod (refer to the marks made during removal). Remove the original bearing inserts and wipe the bearing surfaces of the connecting rod and cap with a clean, lint-free cloth. They must be kept spotlessly clean.

Connecting rod bearing oil clearance check

3   Clean the back side of the new upper bearing insert, then lay it in place in the connecting rod. Make sure the tab on the bearing fits into the recess in the rod so the oil holes line up. Don't hammer the bearing insert into place and be very careful not to nick or gouge the bearing face. Don't lubricate the bearing at this time.

4   Clean the back side of the other bearing insert and install it in the rod cap. Again, make sure the tab on the bearing fits into the recess in the cap, and don't apply any lubricant. It's critically important that the mating surfaces of the bearing and connecting rod are perfectly clean and oil free when they're assembled.

5   Position the piston ring gaps at staggered intervals around the piston **(see illustration)**. The ring end gaps should be in the positions shown.

6   Slip a section of plastic or rubber hose over each connecting rod cap bolt.

7   Lubricate the piston and rings with clean engine oil and attach a piston ring compressor to the piston. Leave the skirt protruding about 1/4-inch to guide the piston into the cylinder. The rings must be compressed until they're flush with the piston.

8   Rotate the crankshaft until the number one connecting rod journal is at BDC (bottom dead center) and apply a coat of engine oil to the cylinder walls.

9   With the dimple on top of the piston **(see illustration)** facing the front (timing belt end) of the engine, gently insert the piston/connecting rod assembly into the number one cylinder bore and rest the bottom edge of the ring compressor on the engine block. **Caution:** *Re-check and re-tighten the ring compressor. Any edge of a piston ring, no matter how little, that is outside the piston ring groove will cause the ring to be broken when tapping the piston into the cylinder.*

10   Tap the top edge of the ring compressor to make sure it's contacting the block around its entire circumference.

11   Gently tap on the top of the piston with the end of a wooden hammer handle **(see illustration)** while guiding the end of the connecting rod into place on the crankshaft journal. The piston rings

25.11 The piston can be driven gently into the cylinder bore with the end of a wooden or plastic hammer handle

25.13 Lay the Plastigage strips on each rod bearing journal, parallel to the crankshaft centerline

may try to pop out of the ring compressor just before entering the cylinder bore, so keep some pressure on the ring compressor. Work slowly, and if any resistance is felt as the piston enters the cylinder, stop immediately. Find out what's hanging up and fix it before proceeding. Do not, for any reason, force the piston into the cylinder - you might break a ring and/or the piston.

12   Once the piston/connecting rod assembly is installed, the connecting rod bearing oil clearance must be checked before the rod cap is permanently bolted in place.

13   Cut a piece of the appropriate size Plastigage slightly shorter than the width of the connecting rod bearing and lay it in place on the number one connecting rod journal, parallel with the journal axis **(see illustration)**.

14   Clean the connecting rod cap bearing face, remove the protective hoses from the connecting rod bolts and install the rod cap. Make sure the mating mark on the cap is on the same side as the mark on the connecting rod. Check the cap to make sure the front mark is facing the timing belt end of the engine **(see illustration)**.

15   Apply a light coat of oil to the under sides of the nuts, then install and tighten them to the torque listed in this Chapter's Specifications, working up to it in three steps. Use a thin-wall socket to avoid erroneous torque readings that can result if the socket is wedged between the rod cap and nut. If the socket tends to wedge itself between the nut and the cap, lift up on it slightly until it no longer

contacts the cap. Do not rotate the crankshaft at any time during this operation.

16   Remove the nuts and detach the rod cap, being very careful not to disturb the Plastigage.

17   Compare the width of the crushed Plastigage to the scale printed on the Plastigage envelope to obtain the oil clearance **(see illustration)**. Compare it to the Specifications to make sure the clearance is correct.

18   If the clearance is not as specified, the bearing inserts may be the wrong size (which means different ones will be required). Before deciding that different inserts are needed, make sure that no dirt or oil was between the bearing inserts and the connecting rod or cap when the clearance was measured. Also, recheck the journal diameter. If the Plastigage was wider at one end than the other, the journal may be tapered (see Section 19).

Final connecting rod installation

19   Carefully scrape all traces of the Plastigage material off the rod journal and/or bearing face. Be very careful not to scratch the bearing - use your fingernail or the edge of a credit card.

20   Make sure the bearing faces are perfectly clean, then apply a uniform layer of clean moly-base grease or engine assembly lube to

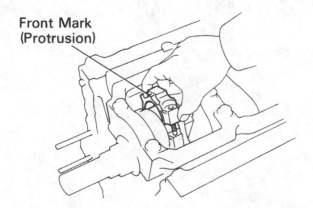

Front Mark (Protrusion)

25.14 Install the connecting rod caps with the front mark facing the timing belt end of the engine

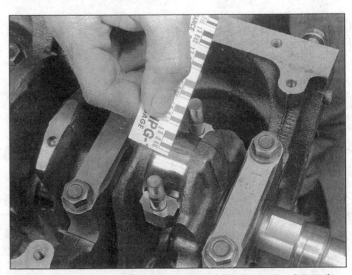

25.17 Measure the width of the crushed Plastigage to determine the rod bearing oil clearance (be sure to use the correct scale - standard and metric scales are included)

2B

both of them. You'll have to push the piston into the cylinder to expose the face of the bearing insert in the connecting rod - be sure to slip the protective hoses over the rod bolts first.

21   Slide the connecting rod back into place on the journal, remove the protective hoses from the rod cap bolts, install the rod cap and tighten the nuts to the torque listed in this Chapter's Specifications. Again, work up to the torque in three steps.

22   Repeat the entire procedure for the remaining pistons/connecting rods.

23   The important points to remember are:

a) *Keep the back sides of the bearing inserts and the insides of the connecting rods and caps perfectly clean when assembling them.*

b) *Make sure you have the correct piston/rod assembly for each cylinder.*

c) *The dimple on the piston must face the front (timing belt end) of the engine.*

d) *Lubricate the cylinder walls with clean oil.*

e) *Lubricate the bearing faces when installing the rod caps after the oil clearance has been checked.*

24   After all the piston/connecting rod assemblies have been properly installed, rotate the crankshaft a number of times by hand to check for any obvious binding.

25   As a final step, the connecting rod side clearance must be checked (see Section 13).

26   Compare the measured side clearance to the Specifications to make sure it's correct. If it was correct before disassembly and the original crankshaft and rods were reinstalled, it should still be right. If new rods or a new crankshaft were installed, the side clearance may be inadequate. If so, the rods will have to be removed and taken to an automotive machine shop for resizing.

26   Initial start-up and break-in after overhaul

Warning: *Have a fire extinguisher handy when starting the engine for the first time.*

1   Once the engine has been installed in the vehicle, double-check the engine oil and coolant levels.

2   With the spark plugs out of the engine and the ignition system disabled (see Section 3), crank the engine until oil pressure registers on the gauge or the light goes out.

3   Install the spark plugs, hook up the plug wires and restore the ignition system functions (see Section 3).

4   Start the engine. It may take a few moments for the fuel system to build up pressure, but the engine should start without a great deal of effort.

5   After the engine starts, it should be allowed to warm up to normal operating temperature. While the engine is warming up, make a thorough check for fuel, oil and coolant leaks.

6   Shut the engine off and recheck the engine oil and coolant levels.

7   Drive the vehicle to an area with minimum traffic, accelerate from 30 to 50 mph, then allow the vehicle to slow to 30 mph with the throttle closed. Repeat the procedure 10 or 12 times. This will load the piston rings and cause them to seat properly against the cylinder walls. Check again for oil and coolant leaks.

8   Drive the vehicle gently for the first 500 miles (no sustained high speeds) and keep a constant check on the oil level. It is not unusual for an engine to use oil during the break-in period.

9   At approximately 500 to 600 miles, change the oil and filter.

10   For the next few hundred miles, drive the vehicle normally. Do not pamper it or abuse it.

11   After 2000 miles, change the oil and filter again and consider the engine broken in.

Chapter 3
Cooling, heating and air conditioning systems

Contents

Specifications

General

Radiator cap pressure rating	8 to 15 psi
Cooling system test pressure	17.1 lbs
Thermostat rating (opening temperature)	176 to 183 degrees F
Cooling system capacity	See Chapter 1
Refrigerant type	
1993 and earlier	R-12
1994	R-134a
Refrigerant capacity	1.5 to 1.7 pounds

Torque specifications

	Ft-lbs (unless otherwise indicated)
Thermostat housing nuts	43 in-lbs
Water pump to engine block nuts/bolt	13
Water pump inlet pipe-to-engine block bolt	54 In-lbs

1 General information

Engine cooling system

Refer to illustrations 1.1a and 1.1b

All vehicles covered by this manual employ a pressurized engine cooling system with thermostatically controlled coolant circulation **(see illustrations)**. An impeller type water pump mounted on the drivebelt end of the block pumps coolant through the engine. The coolant flows around each cylinder and toward the transaxle end of the engine. Cast-in coolant passages direct coolant around the intake and exhaust ports, near the spark plug areas and in close proximity to the exhaust valve guides.

A wax pellet type thermostat is located in a housing near the transaxle end of the engine. During warm up, the closed thermostat prevents coolant from circulating through the radiator. As the engine nears normal operating temperature, the thermostat opens and allows hot coolant to travel through the radiator, where it's cooled before returning to the engine.

The cooling system is sealed by a pressure type radiator cap, which raises the boiling point of the coolant and increases the cooling efficiency of the radiator. If the system pressure exceeds the cap pressure relief value, the excess pressure in the system forces the spring-loaded valve inside the cap off its seat and allows the coolant to escape through the overflow tube into a coolant reservoir. When the system cools, the excess coolant is automatically drawn from the reservoir back into the radiator.

The coolant reservoir does double duty as both the point at which fresh coolant is added to the cooling system to maintain the proper fluid level and as a holding tank for overheated coolant.

This type of cooling system is known as a closed design because coolant that escapes past the pressure cap is saved and reused.

Heating system

The heating system consists of a blower fan and heater core located in the heater box, the hoses connecting the heater core to the engine cooling system and the heater/air conditioning control head on the dashboard. Hot engine coolant is circulated through the heater core. When the heater mode is activated, a flap door opens to expose the heater box to the passenger compartment. A fan switch on the control head activates the blower motor, which forces air through the core, heating the air.

Air conditioning system

The air conditioning system consists of a condenser mounted in front of the radiator, an evaporator mounted adjacent to the heater core, a compressor mounted on the engine, a filter-drier which contains a high pressure relief valve and the plumbing connecting all of the above components.

A blower fan forces the warmer air of the passenger compartment through the evaporator core (sort of a radiator-in-reverse), transferring the heat from the air to the refrigerant. The liquid refrigerant boils off into low pressure vapor, taking the heat with it when it leaves the evaporator.

The air conditioning systems on 1993 and earlier models use R-12 refrigerant. In 1994 the system was changed to use the new "environmentally friendly", R-134a refrigerant. Each system uses similar components and component locations but the components are NOT interchangeable.

2 Antifreeze/coolant - general information

Refer to illustration 2.5
Warning: *Do not allow antifreeze to come in contact with your skin or painted surfaces of the vehicle. Rinse off spills immediately with plenty of water. Antifreeze is highly toxic if ingested. Never leave antifreeze lying around in an open container or in puddles on the floor; children and pets are attracted by it's sweet smell and may drink it. Check with local authorities about disposing of used antifreeze. Many communities have collection centers which will see that antifreeze is disposed of safely.*

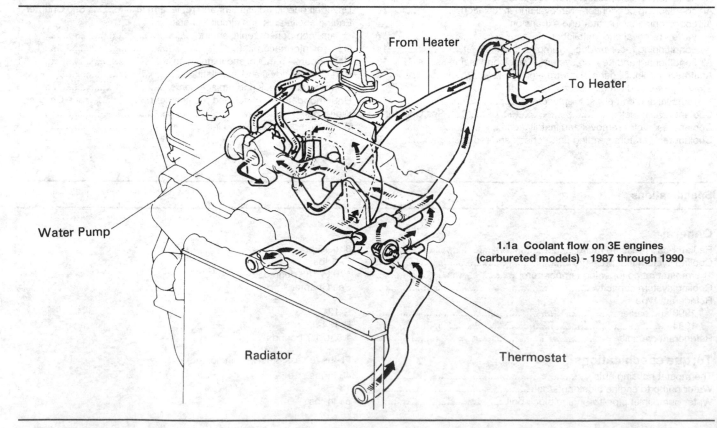

1.1a Coolant flow on 3E engines (carbureted models) - 1987 through 1990

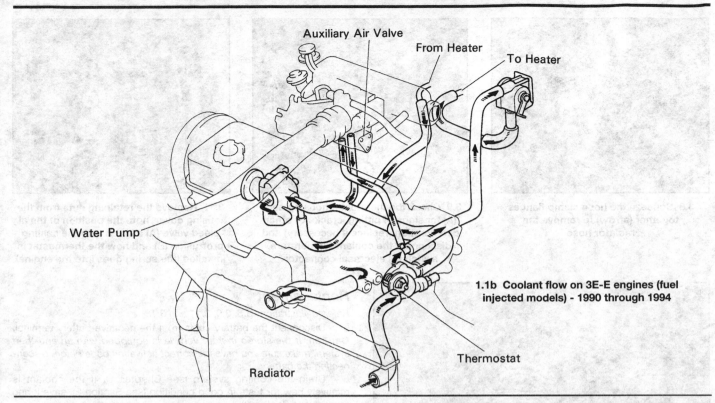

Auxiliary Air Valve

From Heater

To Heater

Water Pump

1.1b Coolant flow on 3E-E engines (fuel injected models) - 1990 through 1994

Thermostat

Radiator

The cooling system should be filled with a water/ethylene glycol based antifreeze solution, which will prevent freezing down to at least -20-degrees F, or lower if local climate requires it. It also provides protection against corrosion and increases the coolant boiling point.

The cooling system should be drained, flushed and refilled at the specified intervals (see Chapter 1). Old or contaminated antifreeze solutions are likely to cause damage and encourage the formation of corrosion and scale in the system. Use distilled water with the antifreeze.

Before adding antifreeze, check all hose connections, because antifreeze tends to leak through very minute openings. Engines don't normally consume coolant, so if the level goes down, find the cause and correct it.

The exact mixture of antifreeze to water which you should use depends on the relative weather conditions. The mixture should contain at least 50 percent antifreeze, but should never contain more

than 70 percent antifreeze. Consult the mixture ratio chart on the antifreeze container before adding coolant.

Antifreeze/coolant testing

Warning: *Do not remove the radiator cap to take a sample until the engine has cooled completely. The system is under pressure and extremely hot during and after running the engine, and will severely scald skin it comes in contact with.*

Hydrometers used to test the condition of the coolant are available at most auto parts stores. They are inexpensive and are very easy to use. To test coolant draw a small amount from the radiator, or coolant reservoir, with the hydrometer **(see illustration)** until all the balls, most have five small colored balls, are submerged (most of them will probably float). **Note:** *It is preferable to take the coolant sample from the radiator. The mixture in the coolant reservoir may be slightly diluted, if any water has recently been added.* The strength of the mixture is shown by the number of balls that are floating. Exact temperature protection indicated by the hydrometer is clearly described on the package instructions. Always use antifreeze which meets the vehicle manufacturer's specifications.

3 Thermostat - check and replacement

Warning: *Do not remove the radiator cap, drain the coolant or replace the thermostat until the engine has cooled completely.*

Check

1   Before assuming the thermostat is to blame for a cooling system problem, check the coolant level, drivebelt tension (see Chapter 1) and temperature gauge operation.
2   If the engine seems to be taking a long time to warm up (based on heater output or temperature gauge operation), the thermostat is probably stuck open. Replace the thermostat with a new one.
3   If the engine runs hot, use your hand to check the temperature of the lower radiator hose. If the hose isn't hot, but the engine is, the thermostat is probably stuck closed, preventing the coolant inside the engine from escaping to the radiator. Replace the thermostat.
Caution: *Don't drive the vehicle without a thermostat. The engine may*

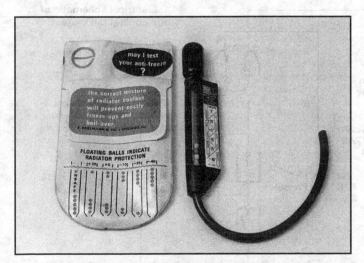

2.5 A typical, inexpensive coolant hydrometer that can be purchased at most auto parts stores

3

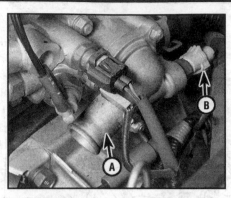

3.8 Squeeze the hose clamp flanges together (arrow) to remove the radiator hose

3.9 Check the thermostat housing neck (A) for signs of pitting, cracks or other deterioration (replace if necessary) and disconnect the coolant temperature switch (B) electrical connector

3.11 Remove the retaining nuts from the housing cover, note the position of the air bleed valve (A) aligned with the casting protrusion (B) and how the thermostat is installed (the spring goes into the engine)

3.13 The thermostat gasket fits over the edge of the thermostat

never reach the required temperature to allow the computer to go to closed loop operation. Performance, emissions and fuel economy will probably be poor.

4   If the lower radiator hose is hot, it means that the coolant is flowing and the thermostat is open. Consult the *Troubleshooting* section at the front of this manual for cooling system diagnosis.

Replacement

Refer to illustrations 3.8, 3.9, 3.11 and 3.13

5   Disconnect the battery cable from the negative battery terminal. **Caution:** *If the stereo in your vehicle is equipped with an anti-theft system, make sure you have the correct activation code before disconnecting the battery.*

6   Drain the cooling system (see Chapter 1). If the coolant is relatively new, or tests in good condition (see Section 2), save it and reuse it (see Section 2).

7   Follow the lower radiator hose to the engine to locate the thermostat housing.

8   Loosen the hose clamp and detach the hose from the fitting **(see illustration)**. If the hose is stuck, grasp it near the end with a pair of adjustable pliers and twist it to break the seal, then pull it off. If the hose is old or deteriorated, cut it off and install a new one.

9   If the outer surface of the large fitting on the thermostat housing, that mates with the hose **(see illustration)**, is deteriorated (corroded, pitted, etc.) it may be damaged further by hose removal. If it is, the thermostat housing cover will have to be replaced.

10   Disconnect the electrical connections at the thermostat housing cover.

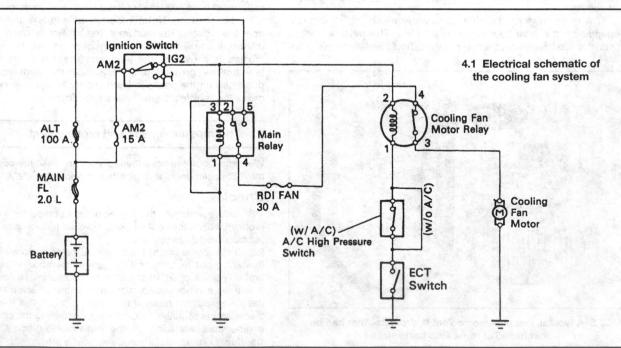

4.1 Electrical schematic of the cooling fan system

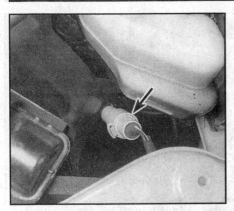

4.4a Disconnect the cooling fan electrical connector (arrow) . . .

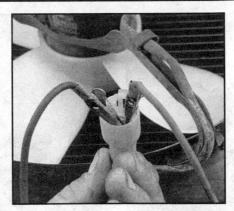

4.4b . . . and run jumper wires directly to the positive and negative terminals of the battery

4.12 Unbolt and remove the two bolts (arrows) at the top of the fan housing and the two additional bolts at the bottom of the fan housing

11 Remove the bolts/nuts and detach the housing cover **(see illustration)**. If the cover is stuck, tap it with a soft-face hammer to jar it loose. Be prepared for some coolant to spill as the gasket seal is broken.
12 Note the position of the air bleed valve **(see illustration 3.11)** and how the thermostat is installed.
13 Fit a new gasket over the thermostat **(see illustration)**.
14 Install the new thermostat in the housing. Make sure the air bleed faces up and the spring end is directed into the engine.
15 Install the cover and bolts. Tighten the bolts to the torque listed in this Chapter's Specifications.
16 Reattach the hose to the fitting and tighten the hose clamp securely. Reconnect the electrical connector for the cooling fan switch.
17 Refill the cooling system (see Chapter 1).
18 Start the engine and allow it to reach normal operating temperature, then check for leaks and proper thermostat operation (as described in Steps 2 through 4).

---

4   Engine cooling fan and circuit - check and component replacement

Cooling fan

Check

Refer to illustrations 4.1, 4.4a and 4.4b
1   The engine cooling fan is controlled by a temperature switch which is mounted on the thermostat cover **(see illustration 3.9)**. When the coolant reaches a predetermined temperature, the switch closes, completing the circuit to ground **(see illustration)**.

2   If the fan does not operate, first check the fuses (see Chapter 12).
3   Check the fusible link for continuity (see Chapter 12).
4   To test the fan motor, unplug the electrical connector and use fused jumper wires to connect the fan directly to the battery **(see illustrations)**. If the fan still does not work, replace the motor.
5   If the motor tested okay, the fault lies in the coolant temperature switch, the relays or the wiring harness.
6   Test the temperature switch by unplugging the connector, and with the ignition switch on, ground the connector. If the fan operates, the switch is probably bad.
7   If the fan does not operate, check the relay and wiring.

Replacement

Main cooling fan
Refer to illustrations 4.12, 4.13, 4.14 and 4.15
8   Disconnect the battery cable from the negative battery terminal.
Caution: *If the stereo in your vehicle is equipped with an anti-theft system, make sure you have the correct activation code before disconnecting the battery.*
9   Raise the front of the vehicle and support it securely on jackstands. Remove the left splash pan.
10   Unplug the cooling fan connector.
11   Remove the coolant reservoir bottle (see Section 6).
12   Unbolt the cooling fan assembly from the radiator **(see illustration)**.
13   Lift out the cooling fan assembly **(see illustration)**.
14   Remove the nut and detach the fan blade assembly from the motor shaft **(see illustration)**.
15   Remove the screws, retaining the fan motor to the mounting bracket, and detach the motor **(see illustration)**.

4.13 Lift the fan and housing out of the engine compartment

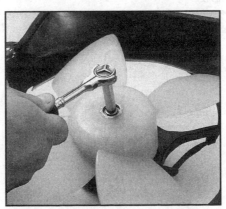

4.14 To replace the fan motor, remove the fan blade . . .

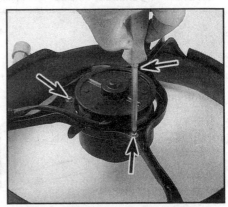

4.15 . . . remove the mounting screws (arrows) and remove the motor

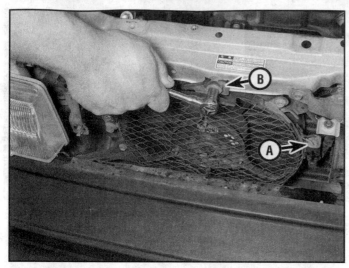

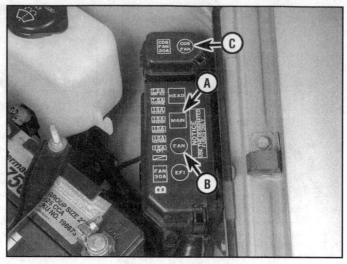

4.21 Remove the front grille, disconnect electrical connector (A) and remove the two attaching bolts(B), the other bolt is at the bottom of the fan similar to the upper bolt

4.23a Location of the cooling fan relays in the engine compartment relay box

A   Main relay
B   Cooling fan motor relay
C   Air conditioning condenser fan relay

16   Installation is the reverse of removal. Check the coolant level and the top radiator hose after reassembly (see Chapter 1).

Condenser fan (air conditioned models only)

Refer to illustration 4.21

17   Air conditioned models have an additional fan located in front of the condenser.
18   Disconnect the battery cable from the negative battery terminal. **Caution:** *If the stereo in your vehicle is equipped with an anti-theft system, make sure you have the correct activation code before disconnecting the battery.*
19   Remove the grill (see Chapter 11).
20   Unplug the electrical connector.
21   Remove the mounting bolts holding the fan assembly to the core support **(see illustration)** and remove the fan assembly.
22   Installation is the reverse of the removal procedure.

Main relay

Refer to illustrations 4.23a, 4.23b and 4.24

Continuity check

23   Locate the main relay **(see illustration)** and using an ohmmeter, inspect the relay for continuity at the indicated terminals **(see illustration).**

a) *Check for* **continuity** *between terminals 1 and 3.*

b) *Check for* **continuity** *between terminals 2 and 4.*
c) *There should be* **no continuity** *between terminals 4 and 5.*
If continuity isn't as specified, replace the relay.

Operation check

24   Inspect the relay operation as follows **(see illustration):**

a   *Using jumper wires, apply battery voltage to terminal numbers 1 and 3 of the relay.*
b) *Use an ohmmeter and check for* **continuity** *between terminals 4 and 5.*
c) *There should be* **no continuity** *between terminals 2 and 4.*
If continuity isn't as specified, replace the relay.

Cooling fan relay

Refer to illustrations 4.25 and 4.26

Continuity check

25   Locate the cooling fan relay **(see illustration 4.23a)** and using an ohmmeter inspect the relay for continuity at the indicated terminals **(see illustration).**

a) *Check for* **continuity** *between terminals 1 and 2.*
b) *Check for* **continuity** *between terminals 3 and 4.*
If continuity isn't as specified, replace the relay.

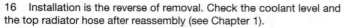

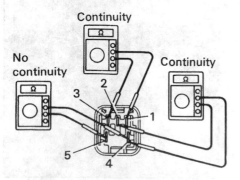

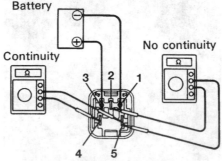

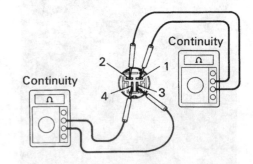

4.23b Main relay continuity check   **4.24 Main relay operation check**   **4.25 Cooling fan relay continuity check**

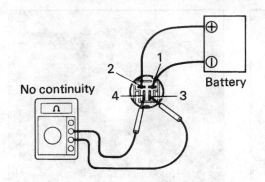

No continuity

Battery

4.26 Cooling fan relay operation check

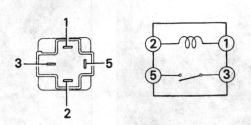

Condition	Tester connection to terminal number	Specified value
Constant	1 – 2	Continuity
Apply B+ between terminals 1 and 2.	3 – 5	Continuity

4.27 Air conditioning condenser fan relay continuity check

Operation check

26 Inspect the cooling fan relay operation as follows (see illustration):

a) Using jumper wires, apply battery voltage to terminal numbers 1 and 2 of the relay.
b) There should be **no continuity** between terminals 3 and 4.

If continuity isn't as specified, replace the relay.

Condenser fan relay

Refer to illustration 4.27

Check

27 Locate the condenser fan relay (see illustration 4.23a) and using an ohmmeter inspect the relay for continuity at the indicated terminals (see illustration). Note: *There are several different condenser fan relays used on various models. The relay shown is typical for most models.*

a) Check for **continuity** between terminals 1 and 2.
b) Using jumper wires, apply battery voltage to terminal numbers 1 and 2 of the relay, there should be **continuity** between terminals 3 and 5.

If continuity isn't as specified, replace the relay.

5   Radiator - removal and installation

Warning: *Do not start this procedure until the engine is completely cool.*

Removal

Refer to illustrations 5.5a, 5.5b, 5.6, 5.7a, 5.7b, 5.10a, 5.10b and 5.11

1   Disconnect the battery cable from the negative battery terminal. **Caution:** *If the stereo in your vehicle is equipped with an anti-theft system, make sure you have the correct activation code before disconnecting the battery.*

2   Raise the front of the vehicle and support it securely on jackstands. Remove the lower splash shields.

3   Drain the cooling system (see Chapter 1). If the coolant is relatively new, or tests in good condition, save it and reuse it (see Section 2).

4   On fuel injected models, remove the air intake duct.

5   Remove the bolt and upper radiator support (see illustrations) from each end of the radiator upper tank.

6   Disconnect the coolant reservoir hose from the radiator (see illustration).

7   Loosen the upper and lower hose clamps, then detach the radiator hoses from the fittings (see illustrations). If they're stuck,

3

5.5a Remove the bracket hold-down bolt from the support on each side of the radiator

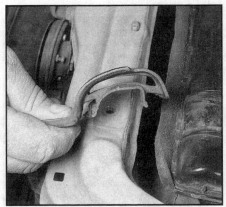

5.5b Inspect the rubber insulator for signs of damage or deterioration, replace if necessary

5.6 Disconnect the coolant reservoir tube at the radiator filler neck

5.7a Loosen the clamp and remove the upper radiator hose from the radiator

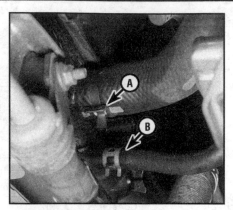

5.7b Disconnect the lower hose (A) and on automatic transmission models, disconnect the cooler lines (B), have a drain pan ready to catch the fluid

5.10 Carefully lift the radiator free, avoid scratching or spilling coolant on the vehicles paint work. The radiator can be removed with the cooling fan attached

grasp each hose near the end with a pair of adjustable pliers and twist it to break the seal, then pull it off - be careful not to damage the radiator fittings! If the hoses are old or deteriorated, cut them off and install new ones.

8   Disconnect the cooling fan connector **(see illustration 4.4a)**.

9   If the vehicle is equipped with an automatic transaxle, disconnect the cooler lines **(see illustration 5.7b)** and plug the lines and fittings.

10   Carefully lift out the radiator **(see illustration)**. Don't spill coolant on the vehicle or scratch the paint. Remove the bolts securing the cooling fan to the radiator and remove the fan assembly.

11   Inspect the lower radiator rubber supports **(see illustration)**. Replace them if they are deteriorated, split or broken.

12   With the radiator removed, it can be inspected for leaks and damage. If it needs repair, have a radiator shop or dealer service department perform the work as special techniques are required.

13   Bugs and dirt can be removed from the radiator with a garden hose or a soft brush. Don't bend the cooling fins as this is done.

Installation

14   Installation is the reverse of the removal procedure. Be sure the rubber radiator supports are seated properly.

15   After installation, fill the cooling system with the proper mixture of antifreeze and water (see Chapter 1).

16   Start the engine and check for leaks. Allow the engine to reach normal operating temperature, indicated by the upper radiator hose becoming hot. Recheck the coolant level and add more if required.

17   If you're working on an automatic transaxle equipped vehicle, check and add fluid as needed (see Chapter 1).

6   Coolant reservoir - removal and installation

Refer to illustrations 6.1 and 6.2

Warning: *Do not start this procedure until the engine is completely cool.*

1   Lift the cap off the coolant reservoir and withdraw the overflow hose **(see illustration)**.

2   Slide the coolant reservoir straight up to remove it **(see illustration)**.

3   Pour the coolant into a container. Wash out and inspect the reservoir for cracks and chafing. Replace if damaged.

4   Installation is the reverse of removal.

7   Water pump - check

Refer to illustrations 7.4 and 7.5

1   A failure in the water pump can cause serious engine damage due to overheating.

2   There are three ways to check the operation of the water pump while it's installed on the engine. If the pump is defective, it should be replaced with a new, or rebuilt unit.

3   With the engine running at normal operating temperature, squeeze the upper radiator hose. If the water pump is working properly, a pressure surge should be felt as the hose is released.

Warning: *Keep your hands away from the fan blades! The fan is computer operated and can come on at any time.*

5.11 Ensure that the rubber mountings are securely in place during radiator installation (viewed from below)

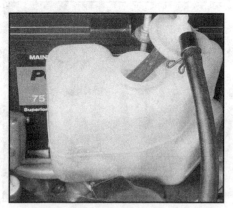

6.1 Remove the coolant reservoir cap and pull the overflow hose from the reservoir

6.2 Slide the reservoir bottle up and off the mounting bracket

7.4 If coolant is leaking from the weep hole (arrow) the water pump is defective

7.5 If there is play in the shaft (arrow), replace the water pump

4   Water pumps are equipped with weep or vent holes **(see illustration)**. If a failure occurs in the pump seal, coolant will leak from the hole. In most cases you'll need a flashlight to find the hole on the water pump from underneath to check for leaks.

5   If the water pump shaft bearings fail there may be a howling sound at the drivebelt end of the engine while it's running. Shaft wear can be felt if the water pump pulley is rocked up and down **(see illustration)**. Don't mistake drivebelt slippage, which causes a squealing sound, for water pump bearing failure.

6   Turn the pump shaft by hand and feel for roughness in the bearing. Replace the pump if roughness is felt.

8 Water pump - removal and installation

Warning: *Wait until the engine is completely cool before beginning this procedure.*

Removal

Refer to illustrations 8.6a, 8.6b, 8.9, and 8.12

1   Disconnect the battery cable from the negative battery terminal. **Caution:** *If the stereo in your vehicle is equipped with an anti-theft system, make sure you have the correct activation code before disconnecting the battery.*

2   Drain the cooling system (see Chapter 1). If the coolant is relatively new, or tests in good condition (see Section 2), save it and reuse it.

3   Remove the right hand splash shield (see Chapter 1).

4   Remove the High Altitude Compensator (HAC) valve (see Chapter 4) from bracket, if equipped (Federal and Canadian carbureted models only).

5   Remove the accessory drivebelt (see Chapter 1).

6   Remove the intake manifold brace **(see illustrations)**. **Note:** *On Federal and Canadian carbureted models, first remove the Air Suction (AS) valve (see Chapter 4) from the manifold brace.*

3

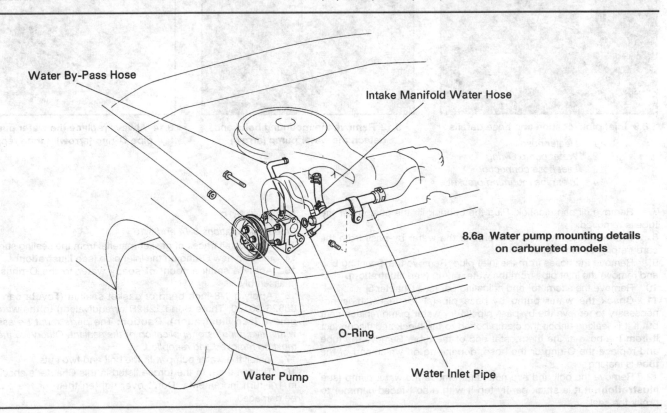

Water By-Pass Hose

Intake Manifold Water Hose

8.6a Water pump mounting details on carbureted models

O-Ring

Water Pump

Water Inlet Pipe

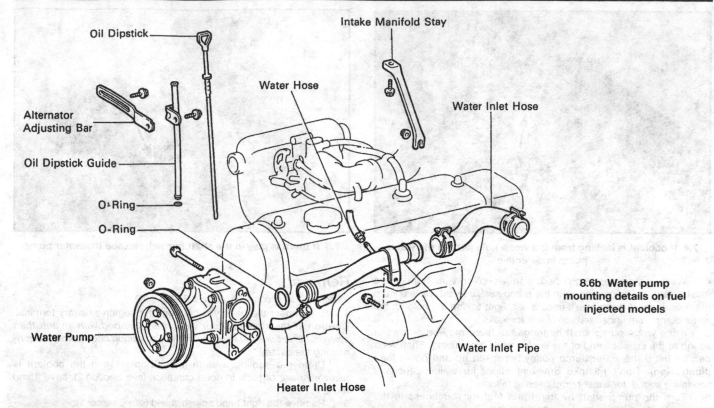

Oil Dipstick

Intake Manifold Stay

Water Hose

Water Inlet Hose

Alternator
Adjusting Bar

Oil Dipstick Guide

O-Ring

O-Ring

**8.6b Water pump
mounting details on fuel
injected models**

Water Pump

Water Inlet Pipe

Heater Inlet Hose

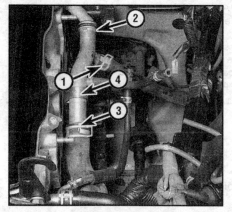

8.9 Inlet pipe location and hose details

1   Heater hose
2   Water pump O-ring
3   Inlet hose connection
4   Inlet pipe mounting bracket

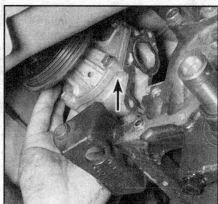

**8.12 Remove the mounting bolts and
detach the water pump (arrow)**

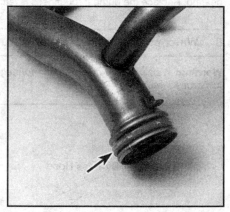

**8.14 Always replace the water pump inlet
pipe O-ring (arrow) during repairs**

7   Remove oil pan dipstick. Plug the opening in the pump after the tube is removed.

8   On carbureted models, disconnect the water by-pass from the carburetor **(see illustration 8.6a)**.

9   Remove the hoses from the inlet pipe. Remove the mounting bolt and remove the inlet pipe from the water pump **(see illustration)**.

10   Remove the alternator and adjusting bar (see Chapter 5).

11   Check the water pump by-pass pipe(s) for leaks. It is not necessary to remove the by-pass pipe(s) for water pump replacement but if it is leaking unbolt the clamp bolted to the block and disconnect it from the hose at the thermostat end of the tube. Remove the tube and replace the O-ring or the hose, depending on which end of the tube is leaking.

12   Remove the bolt and two nuts and remove the water pump **(see illustration)**. If it is stuck gently tap it with a soft faced hammer to break the seal.

Installation

Refer to illustrations 8.14 and 8.16

13   Remove all traces of gasket material from the sealing surfaces.

14   Install a new O-ring on the inlet pipe **(see illustration)**

15   Apply a small amount of soapy water to the O-rings to help in assembly.

16   Apply a 1/8-inch bead of gasket sealant (Toyota part number 08826-00100, Three Bond 1282B or equivalent) to the water pump groove **(see illustration)**. **Caution:** *The parts must be assembled within five minutes of application of the sealant. Otherwise the sealant must be removed and reapplied.*

17   Install the water pump with the bolt and two nuts.

18   Tighten them to the torque listed in this Chapter's specifications in 1/4-turn increments. Don't over tighten them or the pump may be damaged.

8.16 Apply sealant to the groove in the water pump housing (arrow)

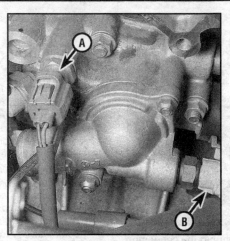

9.3 Location of the coolant temperature sending unit and cooling fan temperature switch

A   *Coolant temperature sending unit*
B   *Cooling fan temperature switch*

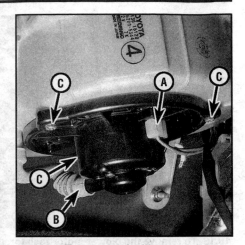

10.4 To remove the blower motor disconnect or remove the following

A   *Blower motor electrical connector*
B   *Air inlet*
C   *Retaining screws*

19   Reinstall all parts removed for access to the pump.
20   Refill the cooling system (see Chapter 1). Run the engine and check for leaks.

9   Coolant temperature sending unit - check and replacement

Refer to illustration 9.3
Warning: *The engine must be completely cool before removing the sending unit.*

Check

1   If the coolant temperature gauge is inoperative, check the fuses first (see Chapter 12).
2   If the temperature indicator shows excessive temperature after running awhile, see the *Troubleshooting* section in the front of the manual.
3   If the temperature gauge indicates Hot shortly after the engine is started cold, disconnect the wire at the coolant temperature sending unit **(see illustration)**. If the gauge reading drops, replace the sending unit. If the reading remains high, the wire to the gauge may be shorted to ground or the gauge is faulty.
4   If the coolant temperature gauge fails to indicate after the engine has been warmed up (approximately 10 minutes) and the fuses checked out okay, shut off the engine. Disconnect the wire at the sending unit and using a jumper wire, connect it to a clean ground on the engine. Turn on the ignition without starting the engine. If the gauge now indicates Hot, replace the sending unit.
5   If the gauge still does not work, the circuit may be open or the gauge may be faulty. See Chapter 12 for additional information.

Replacement

6   With the engine completely cool, remove the cap from the radiator to release any pressure, then reinstall the cap. This reduces coolant loss during sending unit replacement.
7   Disconnect the electrical connector from the sending unit.
8   Prepare the new sending unit for installation by applying a light coat of sealant to the threads.
9   Unscrew the sending unit from the engine and quickly install the new one to prevent coolant loss.
10   Tighten the sending unit securely and connect the wiring harness.
11   Refill the cooling system and run the engine. Check for leaks and proper gauge operation.

10   Blower motor and circuit - check, removal and component replacement

Blower motor

Check

Refer to illustration 10.4
1   If the blower motor speed does not correspond to the setting selected on the blower switch, or the blower motor does not operate at all, the problem could be a bad fuse, relay, switch, blower motor resistor, blower motor or blower motor circuit wiring.
2   Before checking the blower motor or circuit, always check the fuse and relay (if equipped) first (see Chapter 12).
3   Remove the glove compartment and dash trim (see Chapter 11) to gain access to the heater case and blower motor.
4   With the ignition key in the ON position, turn the blower switch to the faulty position(s) and, using a test light or voltmeter, check the voltage at the motor electrical connector **(see illustration)**. If the motor is receiving voltage but not operating, either the motor ground is bad (on these models, the blower switch and resistor are part of the ground circuit) or the motor itself is faulty or the fan is binding.
5   To check for a bad ground, disconnect the electrical connector from the blower motor, connect a jumper wire between the ground wire terminal on the blower motor and a good ground, then connect a fused jumper wire between the battery positive terminal and the positive terminal on the blower motor. If the motor now operates properly, the ground circuit is bad. If the motor does not operate, the fan is either binding or the motor is faulty.
6   If you suspect the blower motor fan is binding, remove the blower motor to check for free operation of the fan.

Replacement

7   Disconnect the battery cable from the negative battery terminal.
Caution: *If the stereo in your vehicle is equipped with an anti-theft system, make sure you have the correct activation code before disconnecting the battery.*
8   Unplug the electrical connection at the blower motor **(see illustration 10.4)**.
9   Disconnect the air inlet damper control cable from the blower motor.
10   Remove the three blower unit retaining screws **(see illustration 10.4)** and lower the unit from the housing.
11   If you are replacing the motor, detach the fan and transfer it to the new motor.

3

10.13 To remove the blower motor resistor, unplug the connector and remove the screw (arrow), then pull the resistor from the heater case

12 Installation is the reverse of removal. Run the blower and check for proper operation.

Blower motor resistor

Check

Refer to illustrations 10.13 and 10.15

13 Remove the passenger side interior trim panel, which includes the glovebox (see Chapter 11). Locate the electrical connector and wire for the heater blower motor resistor **(see illustration)**, usually attached to a heating/air conditioning duct or blower motor case.

14 Verify that the resistor is getting current from the blower motor:
a) *If the resistor is not getting current, check the wiring harness and the connectors between the resistor and the motor. Check for loose or corroded connections and damaged wires.*
b) *If the wires and connectors are good and the blower switch is getting current, verify current is flowing out of the blower speed control switch to ground. If it is not go to step 16.*

15 Check the blower resistor for continuity **(see illustration)** as shown. Replace the blower resistor if continuity isn't as specified.

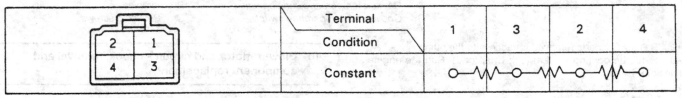

10.15 Heater blower motor resistor continuity check

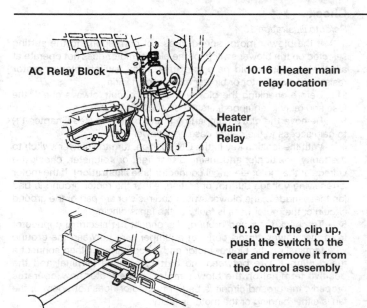

10.16 Heater main relay location

10.19 Pry the clip up, push the switch to the rear and remove it from the control assembly

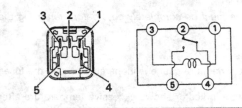

Terminal Condition	1	2	3	4	5
Constant	○—o○○○○—○				
		○————————○			
Apply battery positive voltage to terminals 1 and 3.				○———○	

10.17 Heater main relay continuity check

10.20 Blower speed control switch continuity check

Terminal Switch position	1	2	3	5	7	Illumination	
						6	8
OFF							
LO		○———○		○			
■	○	○———○		○		○—⊗—○	
■ ■			○———○	○			
HI		○———○	○	○			

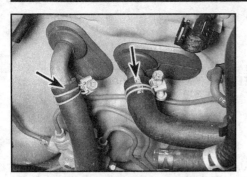

11.4 Disconnect the heater hoses (arrows) from the heater core tubes

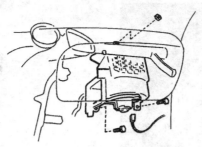

11.7 Blower unit installation details

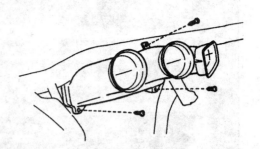

11.9 Remove the center duct

Heater main relay

Check

Refer to illustrations 10.16 and 10.17

16   Locate the heater main relay **(see illustration)**. It is mounted next to the blower motor in the air conditioning relay block.
17   Test the heater main relay for continuity **(see illustration)**:
  a) *Check for* **continuity** *between terminals 1 and 3.*
  b) *Check for* **continuity** *between terminals 2 and 4.*
  c) *Using jumper wires, apply battery voltage to terminal numbers 1 and 3, there should be* **continuity** *between terminals 4 and 5.*
18   If continuity isn't as specified, replace the relay.

Blower speed control switch

Refer to illustrations 10.19 and 10.20

Check

19   Remove the heater/air conditioning control assembly (see Section 12). Remove the blower switch from the heater/air conditioning control assembly by lightly prying the clip and pushing the switch out the rear of the assembly **(see illustration)**.
20   Unplug the electrical connector from the blower switch and with an ohmmeter, check the continuity across the indicated terminals **(see illustration)**.
21   If continuity isn't as specified, replace the switch.

11   Heater core - removal and installation

Warning: *The air conditioning system is under high pressure. Do not loosen any fittings or remove any components until after the system has been discharged. Air conditioning refrigerant should be properly discharged into an EPA-approved container at a dealer service department or an automotive air conditioning repair facility. Always wear eye protection when disconnecting air conditioning system fittings.*

Removal

Refer to illustrations 11.4, 11.7, 11.9, 11.10, 11.12 and 11.13

1   If equipped with air conditioning, have the refrigerant discharged at a dealer service department or an automotive air conditioning repair facility.
2   Disconnect the battery cable from the negative battery terminal.
Caution: *If the stereo in your vehicle is equipped with an anti-theft system, make sure you have the correct activation code before disconnecting the battery.*
3   Drain the cooling system (see Chapter 1).
4   Working in the engine compartment, disconnect the heater hoses where they enter the firewall **(see illustration)**.
4   Remove the rubber grommets where the heater core tubes go through the firewall.
5   Remove the heater/air conditioning control assembly (see Section 12). Be sure to mark the locations of the cable clamps on the cables to ensure correct adjustment upon reinstallation.
6   Remove the instrument panel dash pad, the lower trim panels and the glove box (see Chapter 11).
7   Remove heater blower unit **(see illustration)**.
8   If equipped with air conditioning, remove the cooling unit (see Section 17).
9   Remove the center duct **(see illustration)**.
10   Remove instrument panel reinforcement braces **(see illustration)**.
11   Label and detach the air ducts, wiring and ground straps and controls still attached to the heater housing.
12   Remove the heater unit **(see illustration)**.
13   Remove two screws and the two clamps securing the heater core to the case **(see illustration)**.
14   Remove the heater core from the heater case

Installation

17   Reassemble the heater unit and check the operation of the control flaps. If any parts bind, correct the problem before installation.
18   Reinstall the remaining parts in the reverse order of removal.
19   Refill the cooling system, reconnect the battery and run the engine. Check for leaks and proper system operation.

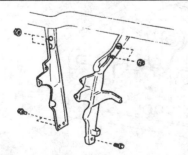

11.10 Remove the two center braces

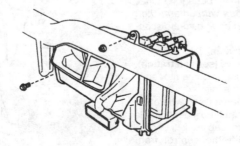

11.12 Heating unit installation details

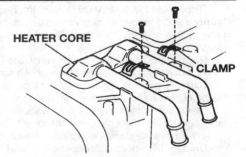

HEATER CORE **CLAMP**

11.13 Remove the two hold-down screws and clamps and lift the heater core from the case

12.3 Remove the control assembly retaining screws (arrows)

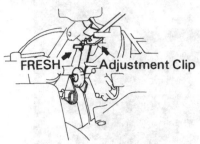

12.8a Set the air damper and control lever (on 1990 and earlier models) to the FRESH AIR intake position, install the control cable and lock the clamp

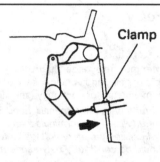

12.8b Set the air damper and control lever (on 1991 and later models) to the RECIRC position, install the control cable and lock the clamp

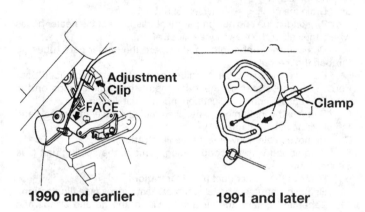

1990 and earlier   **1991 and later**

12.8c Set the mode selector and control lever to the FACE level position, install the control cable and lock the clamp

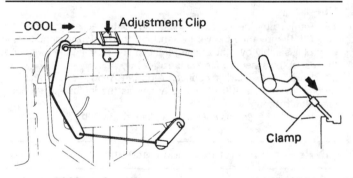

1990 and earlier   **1991 and later**

12.8d Set the air mix damper and control lever to the COOL position, install the control cable and lock the clamp

12 Air conditioner and heater control assembly - removal and installation

Refer to illustrations 12.3, 12.8a, 12.8b, 12.8c, 12.8d and 12.8e

1   Disconnect the battery cable from the negative battery terminal. **Caution:** *If the stereo in your vehicle is equipped with an anti-theft system, make sure you have the correct activation code before disconnecting the battery.*

2   Remove the center cluster trim panel (see Chapter 11).

3   Remove the control assembly mounting screws **(see illustration)**.

4   Carefully pull and tilt the unit out of the dash, on some models it may be necessary to loosen the trim pad to achieve this.

5   Check the outer sheath of the cables for indentations where the clamps grip them. Mark the cable sheath with paint if no indentation is visible. Remove the clamps and detach the control cables.

6   Unplug the electrical connectors and lift the control from the vehicle.

7   Installation is the reverse of removal.

8   Connect and/or adjust the heater control assembly cables as shown **(see illustrations)**.

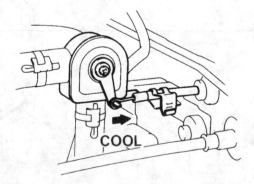

12.8e Set the water valve and control lever to the COOL position, hold in that position while clamping the cable in place

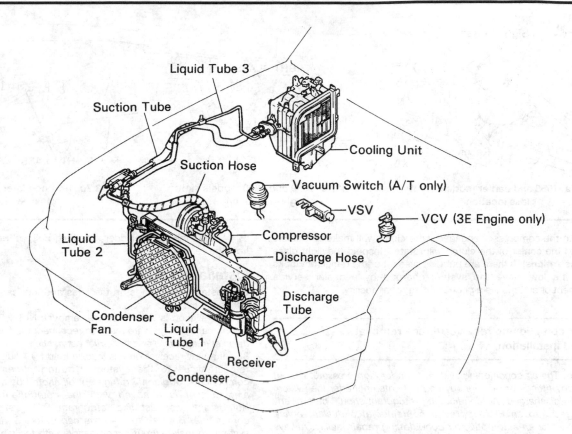

Liquid Tube 3

Suction Tube

Cooling Unit

Suction Hose

Vacuum Switch (A/T only)

VSV

VCV (3E Engine only)

Compressor

Liquid
Tube 2

Discharge Hose

Discharge
Tube

Condenser
Fan

Liquid
Tube 1

Receiver

Condenser

13.1a An overall view of the Air Conditioning system and components

3

13 Air conditioning and heating system - check and maintenance

Refer to illustrations 13.1a, 13.1b, 13.7a 13.7b and 13.7c

Check

1   The following maintenance checks should be performed on a regular basis to ensure that the air conditioning system continues to operate at peak efficiency **(see illustration)**.

a) *Check the compressor drivebelt. If it's worn or deteriorated, replace it (see Chapter 1).*
b) *Check the drivebelt tension and, if necessary, adjust it (see Chapter 1).*
c) *Check the system hoses. Look for cracks, bubbles, hard spots and deterioration. Inspect the hoses and all fittings for oil bubbles and seepage. If there's any evidence of wear, damage or leaks, replace the hose(s).*
d) *Inspect the condenser fins for leaves, bugs and other debris. Use a "fin comb" or compressed air to clean the condenser.*
e) *Make sure the system has the correct refrigerant charge.*
f) *Check the evaporator housing drain tube for blockage* **(see illustration)**.

2   It's a good idea to operate the system for about 10 minutes at least once a month, particularly during the winter. Long term non-use can cause hardening, and subsequent failure, of the seals.

3   Because of the complexity of the air conditioning system and the special equipment necessary to service it, in-depth troubleshooting and repairs are not included in this manual. However, simple checks and component replacement procedures are provided in this Chapter. For more complete information on the air conditioning system, refer to the Haynes Automotive Heating and Air Conditioning Manual.

4   The most common cause of poor cooling is simply a low system refrigerant charge. If a noticeable drop in cool air output occurs, one of the following quick checks will help you determine if the refrigerant level is low.

5   Warm the engine up to normal operating temperature.

6   Place the air conditioning temperature selector at the coldest setting and put the blower at the highest setting. Open the doors (to make sure the air conditioning system doesn't cycle off as soon as it cools the passenger compartment).

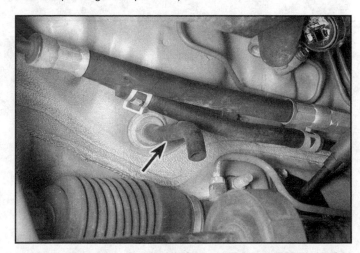

13.1b The drain tube is located above the right driveaxle boot (arrow), check that it is not blocked

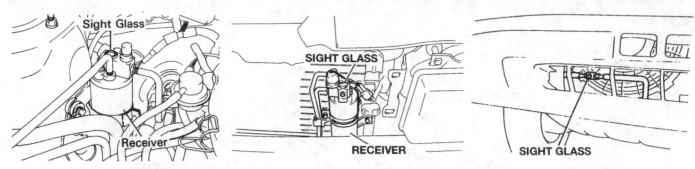

13.7a 1988 and earlier models sight glass location

13.7b 1989 and 1990 models sight glass location

13.7c 1991 and later models sight glass location

7   With the compressor engaged - the clutch will make an audible click and the center of the clutch will rotate - inspect the sight glass **(see illustrations)**. If there are bubbles present or the refrigerant looks foamy, it's low, have the system charged by a dealer service department or automotive air conditioning repair facility.

14 Air conditioning receiver/drier - removal and installation

Warning: *The air conditioning system is under high pressure. Do not loosen any fittings or remove any components until after the system has been discharged. Air conditioning refrigerant should be properly discharged into an EPA-approved container at a dealer service department or an automotive air conditioning repair facility. Always wear eye protection when disconnecting air conditioning system fittings.*

Removal

Refer to illustrations 14.3a and 14.3b

1   Have the refrigerant discharged at a dealer service department or an automotive air conditioning repair facility.
2   On 1989 and later models, remove the radiator grille (see Chapter 11).
3   Detach the refrigerant lines from the receiver/drier **(see illustrations)**. Disconnect the electrical connector to the pressure switch, if equipped.
4   Immediately cap the open fittings to prevent the entry of dirt and moisture.

5   Unbolt the receiver/drier mounting bolt, at the clamp, and lift it from the vehicle.

Installation

6   Install new O-rings on the lines and lubricate them with clean refrigerant oil.
7   Installation is the reverse of removal. **Note:** *Do not remove the sealing caps until you are ready to reconnect the lines. Do not mistake the inlet (marked IN) and the outlet connections.*
8   If a new receiver/drier is installed, add 0.7 fluid ounces (20 cc) of refrigerant oil to the system. **Caution:** *When replacing entire components, additional refrigerant oil should be added equal to the amount that is removed with the component being replaced. Refrigerant oils, just like refrigerant R-12 vs. R-134a, are not compatible. Be sure to read the can before adding any oil to the system, to make sure it is compatible with the type of system being repaired.*
9   Have the system evacuated, charged and leak tested by the shop that discharged it.

15 Air conditioning compressor - removal and installation

Warning: *The air conditioning system is under high pressure. Do not loosen any fittings or remove any components until after the system has been discharged. Air conditioning refrigerant should be properly discharged into an EPA-approved container at a dealer service department or an automotive air conditioning repair facility. Always wear eye protection when disconnecting air conditioning system fittings.*

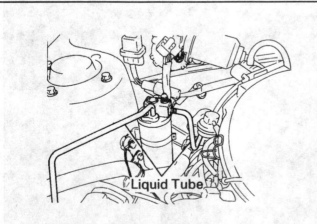

14.3a On 1988 and earlier models the receiver-drier is located on the right side of the engine compartment, next to the strut tower

14.3b On 1989 and later models, the receiver-drier is located at the left front corner of the condenser

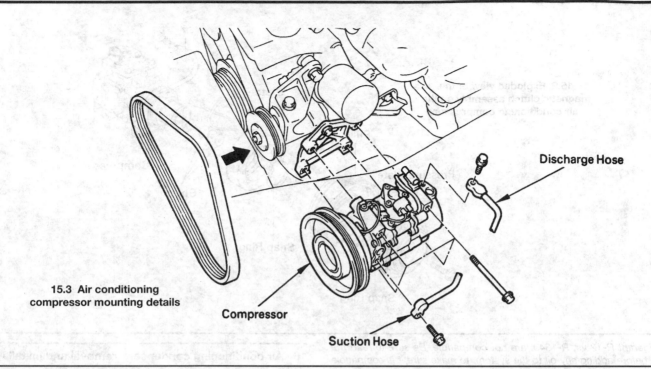

15.3 Air conditioning
compressor mounting details

Discharge Hose

Compressor

Suction Hose

Removal

Refer to illustrations 15.3, 15.4, and 15.6

1   Have the refrigerant discharged at a dealer service department or an automotive air conditioning repair facility.
2   Disconnect the battery cable from the negative battery terminal and remove the battery. **Caution:** *If the stereo in your vehicle is equipped with an anti-theft system, make sure you have the correct activation code before disconnecting the battery.*
3   Detach the refrigerant lines from the compressor **(see illustration)** and immediately cap the open fittings to prevent the entry of dirt and moisture.
4   Disconnect the clutch wire from the compressor **(see illustration)**.
5   Remove the accessory drivebelt (see Chapter 1).
6   Remove the compressor mounting bolts **(see illustration)** and remove the compressor from the engine compartment. **Note:** *Keep the compressor level during handling and storage. If the compressor seized or you find metal particles in the refrigerant lines, the system*

must be flushed out by an air conditioning repair facility or dealer service department and the receiver/drier must be replaced (see Section 14).

Installation

Refer to illustration 15.9

7   Prior to installation, turn the center of the clutch six times to disperse any oil that has collected in the head.
8   Install the compressor in the reverse order of removal.
9   If you are installing a new compressor, the cycling clutch assembly must be transferred to the new compressor **(see illustration)**. **Note:** *The removal of the clutch assembly will probably require the use of a special tool, to hold the clutch stationary while loosening the attaching bolt, to remove it from the old compressor.. Refer to the manufacturer's instructions for adding refrigerant oil to the system.* **Caution:** *When replacing entire components, additional refrigerant oil should be added equal to the amount that is removed with the component being replaced. Refrigerant oils, just like*

15.4 Disconnect the electrical connector (arrow) for the
magnetic clutch

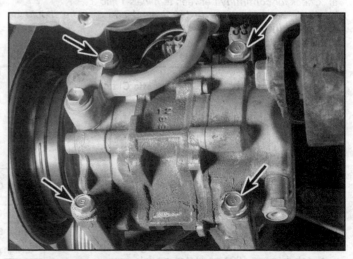

15.6 Once the refrigerant lines and electrical connections have
been separated from the compressor, remove the four mounting
bolts (arrows) and the compressor from the mounting bracket

3

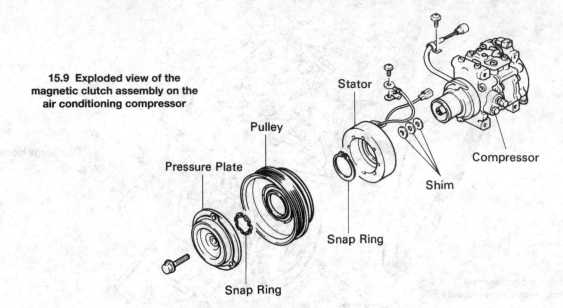

15.9 Exploded view of the magnetic clutch assembly on the air conditioning compressor

Pressure Plate

Pulley

Snap Ring

Stator

Shim

Compressor

Snap Ring

---

refrigerant R-12 vs. R-134a, are not compatible. Be sure to read the can before adding any oil to the system, to make sure it is compatible with the type of system being repaired.

10   Have the system evacuated, charged and leak tested by the shop that discharged it.

Air conditioning magnetic clutch relay

Refer to illustrations 15.11 and 15.12

11   If the compressor clutch fails to engage when the switch is activated, inspect the magnetic clutch relay. On 1990 and earlier models, the magnetic clutch relay is located in the relay center under the hood (see Chapter 12). On 1991 and later models, the magnetic clutch relay is located under the dash on the passenger side of the center control assembly **(see illustration)**. A trim panel will have to be removed to gain access to this relay (see Chapter 11). Remove the screw and disconnect the relay from the electrical connector.

Check

12   Using an ohmmeter, inspect the magnetic clutch relay for continuity at the indicated terminals **(see illustration)**.

  a) *Check for **continuity** between terminals 1 and 3.*
  b) *Apply battery voltage to terminals 1 and 3; there should be **continuity between terminals 2 and 4**.*

If continuity isn't as specified, replace the relay.

16   Air conditioning condenser - removal and installation

Warning: *The air conditioning system is under high pressure. Do not loosen any fittings or remove any components until after the system has been discharged. Air conditioning refrigerant should be properly discharged into an EPA-approved container at a dealer service department or an automotive air conditioning repair facility. Always wear eye protection when disconnecting air conditioning system fittings.*

Removal

Refer to illustration 16.3

1   Have the refrigerant discharged at a dealer service department or an automotive air conditioning repair facility.
2   Remove the grille (see Chapter 11) and the engine under covers.
3   Remove the hood latch, center brace and horns **(see illustration)**.
4   Remove the condenser fan (see Section 4).
5   Disconnect the refrigerant lines from the condenser. Be sure to use a back-up wrench to avoid twisting the lines (if equipped with two nuts).
6   Immediately cap the open fittings to prevent the entry of dirt and moisture.
7   Unbolt the condenser and lift it out of the vehicle. Store it upright to prevent oil loss.

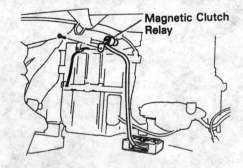

Magnetic Clutch Relay

15.11 Location of the air conditioning magnetic clutch relay on 1991 and later models - glove compartment and dash trim removed.

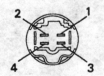

Condition	Tester connection to terminal number	Specified value
Constant	1 — 3	Continuity
Apply B+ between terminals 1 and 3.	2 — 4	Continuity

15.12 Air conditioning magnetic clutch relay continuity check

16.3 Removal of the following parts is necessary in order to remove the air conditioning condenser:

1	Horn	4	Hood lock assembly
2	Receiver-drier	5	Auxiliary cooling fan
3	Center brace	6	Condenser mounting bolts

Installation

8   Installation is the reverse of removal.
9   If a new condenser was installed, add 1.4 to 1.7 ounces (40 to 50 cc) of refrigerant oil to the system. **Caution:** *When replacing entire components, additional refrigerant oil should be added equal to the amount that is removed with the component being replaced. Refrigerant oils, just like refrigerant R-12 vs. R-134a, are not compatible. Be sure to read the can before adding any oil to the system, to make sure it is compatible with the type of system being repaired.*
10   Have the system evacuated, charged and leak tested by the shop that discharged it.

17 Air conditioning evaporator and expansion valve - removal and installation

Warning: *The air conditioning system is under high pressure. Do not loosen any fittings or remove any components until after the system*

17.6a Before removing the cooling unit (1), remove the amplifier (2) and the blower unit (3)

17.3 Disconnect the air conditioning refrigerant lines (arrows) from the evaporator

has been discharged. Air conditioning refrigerant should be properly discharged into an EPA-approved container at a dealer service department or an automotive air conditioning repair facility. Always wear eye protection when disconnecting air conditioning system fittings.

Removal

Refer to illustrations 17.3, 17.6a, 17.6b, 17.7a and 17.7b
1   Have the refrigerant discharged at a dealer service department or an automotive air conditioning repair facility.
2   Disconnect the battery cable from the negative battery terminal. **Caution:** *If the stereo in your vehicle is equipped with an anti-theft system, make sure you have the correct activation code before disconnecting the battery.*
3   Working in the engine compartment disconnect the refrigerant lines from the evaporator **(see illustration)**, use a back-up wrench to avoid twisting and damaging the lines.
4   Immediately cap the open fittings to prevent the entry of dirt and moisture and remove the inlet and outlet grommets.
5   Remove the glove box and lower trim panel (see Chapter 11).
6   Remove the blower unit and the air conditioning amplifier from the cooling unit **(see illustration)**. Disconnect all electrical connectors and tubing from the assembly. Remove the mounting nuts and bolts and pull the unit free **(see illustration)**.

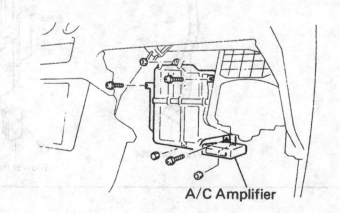

17.6b Cooling unit installation details

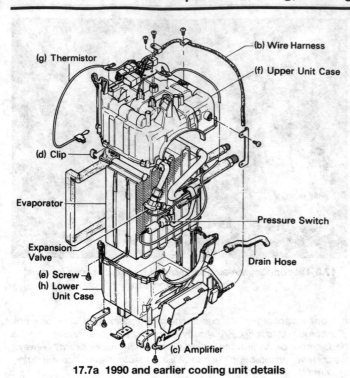

(g) Thermistor
(b) Wire Harness
(f) Upper Unit Case
(d) Clip
Evaporator
Pressure Switch
Expansion Valve
Drain Hose
(e) Screw
(h) Lower Unit Case
(c) Amplifier

17.7a 1990 and earlier cooling unit details

7   To remove the evaporator disconnect all connectors, unfasten the retaining clips and remove the retaining screws **(see illustrations)**.
8   Check the evaporator fins for blockage; if they are dirty clean them with compressed air - never use water for this purpose!
9   Check fittings for cracks and signs of wear; replace parts as necessary.

Installation

10   Installation is the reverse of the removal procedure. Be sure to replace all O-rings removed during disassembly with new ones.
11   If a new evaporator was installed, add 1.4 to 1.7 ounces (40 to 50 cc) of refrigerant oil to the system. **Caution:** *When replacing entire components, additional refrigerant oil should be added equal to the amount that is removed with the component being replaced. Refrigerant oils, just like refrigerant R-12 vs. R-134a, are not compatible. Be sure to read the can before adding any oil to the system, to make sure it is compatible with the type of system being repaired.*
12   Have the system evacuated, charged and leak tested by the shop that discharged it.

17.7b 1991 and later cooling unit details

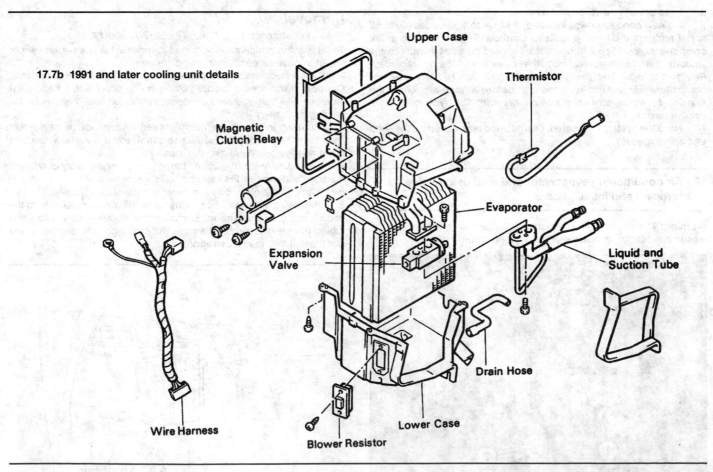

Upper Case
Thermistor
Magnetic Clutch Relay
Evaporator
Expansion Valve
Liquid and Suction Tube
Wire Harness
Blower Resistor
Lower Case
Drain Hose

Chapter 4
Fuel and exhaust systems

Contents

Specifications

Fuel pressure

Feedback carbureted systems	2 to 5 psi
Electronic fuel injection systems	
Terminals +B and Fp bridged (ignition ON, engine not running)	38 to 44 psi
Vacuum sensing hose detached (at idle)	38 to 44 psi
Vacuum sensing hose attached (at idle)	33 to 37 psi

Resistance values

Fuel injector	13.4 to 14.2 ohms
Cold start injector	2 to 4 ohms

Idle Speed

Automatic transmission	750 rpm
Manual transmission	700 rpm

Torque specifications

	Ft-lbs (unless otherwise indicated)
Throttle body mounting bolts	14
Fuel rail mounting bolts	14
Cold start injector mounting bolts	69 in-lbs
Cold start injector banjo bolt	14

1   General information

1987 through mid-year 1990 models are equipped with feedback carburetors. These systems use a mechanical fuel pump along with a sophisticated carburetor that incorporates a series of independent systems (oxygen sensor system, deceleration system, fuel control system etc.) that all contribute to the control of the fuel mixture at various operating conditions. Later models are equipped with an Electronic Fuel Injection system. This type of fuel system uses an electronic fuel pump along with the fuel injectors, fuel rail, TPS, oxygen sensor system etc. commonly designed for electronic fuel control.

Feedback carburetor systems

Feedback carburetors rely on an electronic signal which is generated by the oxygen sensor. Although the air/fuel mixture is controlled mechanically, many of the operating parameters are monitored by electronically controlled devices. For more information on the feedback carburetor systems, refer to Section 12.

Multi Point Fuel Injection (MPFI) system

Multi point fuel injection uses timed impulses to inject the fuel directly into the intake port of each cylinder. The injectors are controlled by the Electronic Control Module (ECM). The ECM monitors various engine parameters and delivers the exact amount of fuel into the intake ports, by controlling the injector "on" time, or duration. The throttle body serves only to control the amount of air passing into the system. Because each cylinder is equipped with an injector mounted directly behind the intake valve, much better control of the fuel/air mixture ratio is possible.

Fuel pump and lines

Fuel is circulated from the fuel tank to the fuel injection system, and back to the fuel tank, through a pair of metal lines running along the underside of the vehicle. An electric fuel pump is attached to the fuel level sending unit inside the fuel tank. A vapor return system routes all vapors and hot fuel back to the fuel tank through a separate return line.

The fuel pump will operate as long as the engine is cranking or running and the ECM is receiving ignition reference pulses from the electronic ignition system (see Chapter 5). If there are no reference pulses, the fuel pump will shut off after 2 or 3 seconds.

Exhaust system

The exhaust system includes an exhaust manifold fitted with an exhaust oxygen sensor, a catalytic converter, an exhaust pipe, and a muffler.

The catalytic converter is an emission control device added to the exhaust system to reduce pollutants. A single-bed converter is used in conjunction with a three-way (reduction) catalyst. Refer to Chapter 6 for more information regarding the catalytic converter.

2   Fuel pressure relief (fuel-injected models only)

Warning 1: *Gasoline is extremely flammable, so take extra precautions when you work on any part of the fuel system. Don't smoke or allow open flames or bare light bulbs near the work area, and don't work in a garage where a natural gas-type appliance (such as a water heater or a clothes dryer) with a pilot light is present. Since gasoline is carcinogenic, wear latex gloves when there's a possibility of being exposed to fuel, and, if you spill any fuel on your skin, rinse it off immediately with soap and water. Mop up any spills immediately and do not store fuel-soaked rags where they could ignite. The fuel system on fuel-injected models is under constant pressure, so, if any fuel lines are to be disconnected, the fuel pressure in the system must be relieved first. When you perform any kind of work on the fuel system, wear safety glasses and have a Class B type fire extinguisher on hand.*
Warning 2: *After the fuel pressure has been relieved, wrap shop towels around any fuel connection you'll be disconnecting. They'll absorb the residual fuel that may leak out, reducing the risk of fire and preventing contact with your skin.*

1   Before servicing any fuel system component, you must relieve the fuel pressure to minimize the risk of fire or personal injury.

2   Remove the fuel filler cap - this will relieve any pressure built up in the tank.

3   Remove the rear seat cushion (see Chapter 11) and unplug the electrical connector to fuel pump. **Note:** *1990 models have separate connectors for the fuel pump and the fuel level sending unit. Unplug both connectors if you're not sure which one is for the fuel pump.*

4   Start the engine and wait for it to stall, then turn OFF the ignition key.

5   The fuel system is now depressurized. Disconnect the cable from the negative terminal of the battery before beginning work. **Caution:** *If the vehicle is equipped with an anti-theft radio, make sure you have the correct activation code before disconnecting the battery.* **Note:** *Place a rag around the fuel line before removing any hose clamp or fitting to prevent any residual fuel from spilling onto the engine.*

3   Fuel pump/fuel pressure - check

Warning: *Gasoline is extremely flammable, so take extra precautions when you work on any part of the fuel system. Don't smoke or allow*

3.3 The fuel pump on carbureted engines is mounted on the left corner (driver's side) of the cylinder head

3.7 Bridge terminals FP and +B of the check connector using a jumper wire or paper clip. The check connector is located near the left shock tower

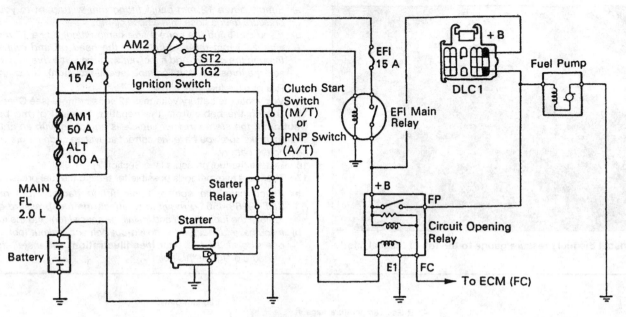

3.11 Typical fuel pump circuit

open flames or bare light bulbs near the work area, and don't work in a garage where a natural gas-type appliance (such as a water heater or a clothes dryer) with a pilot light is present. Since gasoline is carcinogenic, wear latex gloves when there's a possibility of being exposed to fuel, and, if you spill any fuel on your skin, rinse it off immediately with soap and water. Mop up any spills immediately and do not store fuel-soaked rags where they could ignite. The fuel system on fuel-injected models is under constant pressure, so, if any fuel lines are to be disconnected, the fuel pressure in the system must be relieved first (see Section 2). When you perform any kind of work on the fuel system, wear safety glasses and have a Class B type fire extinguisher on hand.

1   Check that there is adequate fuel in the fuel tank. If you doubt the reading on the gauge, insert a long wooden dowel into the fuel filler opening; it will serve as a dipstick.

Mechanical pump (carbureted engines)

Refer to illustration 3.3

2   Raise the vehicle and support it securely on jackstands. Examine all fuel lines between the fuel tank and fuel pump for leaks, loose connections, kinks or distortion of the rubber hoses. Air leaks

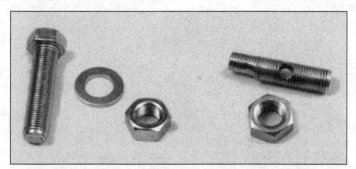

3.12 Cut the head off the bolt (12 mm diameter/1.25 thread pitch) and drill a hole directly through the center. Drill a vertical hole to allow system pressure to flow. It is important that the vertical hole is drilled in the correct location. The easiest method is to use the banjo bolt that was removed from the fuel filter and place it directly next to the tool for the correct alignment of the vertical passage for fuel flow. If necessary, grind the threads off one end so the hose from your fuel pressure gauge will fit.

upstream of the fuel pump can seriously affect the pump's output.

3   Start the engine and check the body of the pump for leaks (see illustration). Shut off the engine.

4   Remove the fuel filler cap to relieve the fuel tank pressure. Disconnect the fuel line at the carburetor. Disconnect the primary (low voltage) electrical connectors to the distributor so the engine can be cranked without it firing. Place an approved gasoline container at the end of the detached fuel line and have an assistant crank the engine for several seconds. There should be a strong spurt of gasoline from the line on every second revolution. If necessary, install a fuel pressure gauge and observe the pressure reading at idle. Refer to the Specifications listed in this Chapter.

5   If little or no gasoline emerges from the line during engine cranking, either the fuel line is clogged or the fuel pump is not working properly. Disconnect the fuel feed line from the pump and blow air through it to be sure that the line is clear. If the line is not clogged, the pump should be replaced with a new one.

Electric pump (fuel-injected engines)

Fuel pump operation check

Refer to illustrations 3.7 and 3.11

6   Turn ON the ignition switch (but do not start the engine).

7   Bridge terminals +B and Fp of the check connector with a jumper wire (see illustration). You should hear the fuel pump activate.

8   Listen for fuel return noises from the fuel pressure regulator and verify that there is pressure in the hose from the fuel filter.

9   Remove the jumper wire. Close the cap on the service electrical connector.

10   Turn the ignition switch OFF.

11   If there is no pressure, inspect the following electrical components: the EFI 15-amp fuse and the ignition 7.5-amp fuse (see Chapter 12) and/or the EFI main relay and the circuit opening relay, (see Steps 24 through 27), the fuel pump, the wiring (see illustration) and electrical connectors (see the wiring diagrams at the end of the book).

Fuel pressure check

Refer to illustrations 3.12 and 3.17

12   A fuel pressure gauge equipped with a banjo fitting on the end of the hose (factory tool SST 09268-45012) is required for the following procedure. There are a couple of alternatives to buying the special Toyota fuel pressure gauge setup:

3.17 Install the fuel pressure gauge to the top of the fuel filter

a) *Simply buy a 12 mm banjo fitting that will adapt to your fuel pressure gauge hose with a hose clamp.*

b) *If you can't find the correct size banjo fitting, buy a 12 mm bolt with 1.25 mm thread pitch, cut the head off and drill a hole through the center. Add a locknut with the same thread pitch and seal the threads with teflon tape* **(see illustration)**.

13 Remove the fuel tank cap.

14 Verify that the battery voltage is 12 volts or more (see Chapter 5).

15 Detach the cable from the negative terminal of the battery. **Caution:** *If the stereo in your vehicle is equipped with an anti-theft system, make sure you have the correct activation code before disconnecting the battery.*

16 Relieve the fuel pressure (see Section 2).

17 There are two methods possible for testing the fuel pressure.

a) *If you have the special banjo fitting (factory tool number SST 09268-45012) required to attach the fuel pressure gauge, remove the fuel rail bolt and install the special tool into the fuel rail.*

b) *If you have fabricated the drilled-out bolt and locknut tool, detach one side of the fuel filter* **(see illustration)** *and install the fuel pressure gauge at this point.*

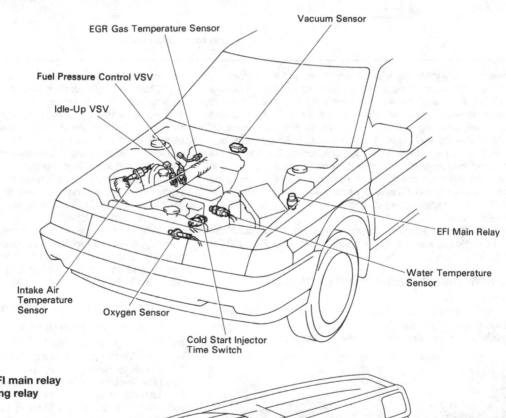

3.29a Locations of the EFI main relay and the circuit opening relay

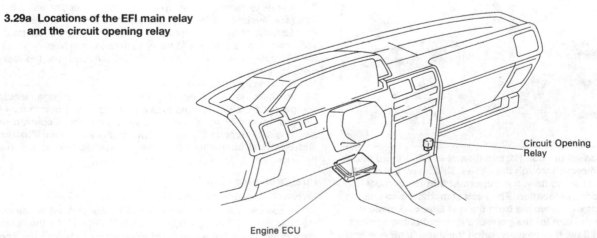

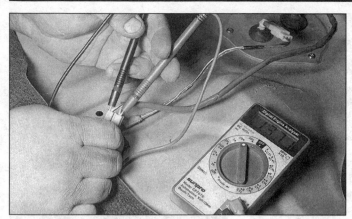

3.29b Remove the rear seat and check for battery voltage to the fuel pump (1990 model shown)

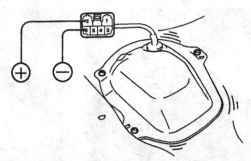

3.29c On 1991 through 1994 models, locate the terminals on the electrical connector (power side) that correspond to terminals 6 (-) and 2 (+) on the pump side and, using a voltmeter, check for battery voltage

18 To attach the fuel pressure gauge:

a) *If you are using the factory setup, use the special banjo fitting on the fuel rail to attach the fuel pressure gauge to the fuel rail. Be sure to use sealing washers on both sides of the banjo fitting.*

b) *If you are using a drilled out 12 mm bolt, working in the engine compartment, attach the bolt to the fuel filter, tighten the locknut and attach the fuel pressure gauge hose with a hose clamp (see illustration 3.17).*

19 Wipe off any gasoline that has leaked out of the fuel rail and attach the cable to the negative terminal of the battery.

20 Place the transmission in Neutral (manual) or Park (automatic) and apply the parking brake.

a) *Bridge terminals +B and Fp of the check connector (see illustration 3.7).*

b) *Turn the ignition to On (engine not running).*

21 Measure the fuel pressure and compare it to the fuel pressure listed in this Chapter's Specifications.

a) *If the pressure is high, check for a restricted fuel return line. If the line is clear, replace the pressure regulator.*

b) *If the pressure is low, pinch the fuel return line. If the pressure goes up, replace the fuel pressure regulator. If the pressure does not increase, check the fuel feed line, the fuel pump and the fuel filter.*

22 Remove the jumper wire from the check connector.

a) *Start the engine.*

b) *Detach the vacuum sensing hose from the fuel pressure regulator.*

c) *Measure the fuel pressure at idle and compare your reading to the fuel pressure listed in this Chapter's Specifications.*

d) *Reattach the vacuum sensing hose to the pressure regulator.*

e) *Measure the fuel pressure at idle and compare your reading to the fuel pressure listed in this Chapter's Specifications.*

f) *If the pressure is not as specified, check the vacuum sensing hose and fuel pressure regulator (see Steps 28 through 35).*

g) *Stop the engine. Verify that the fuel pressure remains at 21 psi or more for five minutes after the engine is turned off.*

23 Detach the cable from the negative terminal of the battery. **Caution:** *If the stereo in your vehicle is equipped with an anti-theft system, make sure you have the correct activation code before disconnecting the battery.*

24 Carefully remove the fuel pressure gauge. Be sure to cover the fitting with a rag before loosening it.

25 Using new sealing washers, reattach the banjo fitting to the fuel rail.

26 Be sure to wipe up any spilled gasoline.

27 Attach the cable to the negative terminal of the battery.

28 Start the engine and check for leaks.

Fuel pump electrical components

Refer to illustrations 3.29a, 3.29b, 3.29c, 3.30 and 3.31

29 There are two relays involved in the fuel pump circuit **(see illustration)**. First, test for battery voltage to the EFI main relay and then the circuit opening relay. **Note:** *Before testing the relays, it is a good idea to check for battery voltage back at the fuel pump* **(see illustrations)**.

30 Remove the EFI main relay from the electrical connector and, with the ignition key ON (engine not running), check for battery voltage at the blue/yellow wire **(see illustration)**.

31 If battery voltage is present, insert the relay back into the connector and check for battery voltage at the circuit opening relay **(see illustration)**.

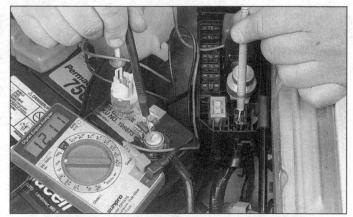

3.30 Check for battery voltage on the EFI main relay electrical connector

3.31 Check for battery voltage on the middle/bottom terminal of the circuit opening relay connector

4

3.33a Apply vacuum to the fuel pressure regulator and confirm that the fuel pressure decreases

3.33b Now release vacuum from the fuel pressure regulator and observe that the fuel pressure increases

3.34 Use a vacuum gauge and check for vacuum to the fuel pressure regulator

32   If battery voltage is present at the relay connectors, have the relays checked by a dealer service department or other qualified repair shop.

Fuel pressure regulator components

Refer to illustrations 3.33a, 3.33b and 3.34

33   Connect a vacuum pump to the fuel pressure regulator. Read the fuel pressure gauge with the vacuum applied to the fuel pressure regulator and also with no vacuum applied **(see illustrations)**. The fuel pressure should decrease as vacuum increases. Compare your readings with the values listed in this Chapter's Specifications.

34   Reconnect the vacuum hose to the regulator and check the fuel pressure at idle, comparing your reading with the value listed in this Chapter's Specifications. Disconnect the hose and watch the gauge - the pressure should jump up to the maximum specified pressure as soon as the hose is disconnected. If the pressure at idle was too high (with the hose disconnected), connect a vacuum gauge to the hose and check for vacuum **(see illustration)**. If there is no reading on the gauge, check the fuel pressure control system.

35   If the fuel pressure is LOW, pinch the fuel return line shut and watch the gauge. If the pressure doesn't rise, the fuel pump is defective or there is a restriction in the fuel feed line. If the pressure rises sharply, replace the fuel pressure regulator (see Section 13).

36   If the indicated fuel pressure is too high, disconnect the fuel return line and blow through it to check for blockage. If there is no blockage, replace the fuel pressure regulator (see Section 13).

37   If the fuel pressure does not fluctuate as described in Step 28, replace the fuel pressure regulator (see Section 13).

Fuel pressure control system

Refer to illustrations 3.39, 3.40 and 3.41

38   The fuel pressure control system controls the fuel pressure depending upon the running conditions of the engine; cold acceleration, cold idling, warm acceleration, air conditioning operation etc. This system consists of the coolant temperature sensor, vacuum switching valve(s), the ECM and the wiring harness. Be sure to test the condition of the coolant temperature sensor (see Chapter 6) before proceeding with the remaining checks.

39   Check the vacuum switching valve (VSV) resistance. Install the probes of an ohmmeter onto the harness connector **(see illustration)** and observe the resistance. It should be 33 to 39 ohms.

40   Make sure that air flows through inlet E and out P **(see illustration)** with no battery voltage applied.

41   Now, apply battery voltage to the VSV **(see illustration)** and observe that no air flows from P, but instead is released through outlet F.

42   If the VSV does not respond correctly, replace the VSV with a new part.

3.39 Use an ohmmeter and check the resistance of the VSV. It should be about 33 to 39 ohms

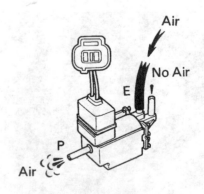

3.40 Apply air to the inlet (E) and observe that the air escapes through (P)

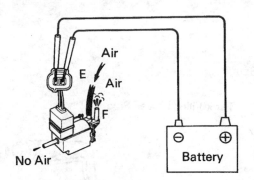

3.41 Now apply battery voltage to the VSV and observe that the air passes into port E but exits from port F instead of E

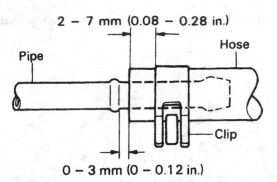

4.6 When attaching a section of rubber hose to a metal fuel line, be sure to overlap the hose as shown, secure it to the line with a new hose clamp of the proper type

4 Fuel lines and fittings - inspection and replacement

Warning: *Gasoline is extremely flammable, so take extra precautions when you work on any part of the fuel system. Don't smoke or allow open flames or bare light bulbs near the work area, and don't work in a garage where a natural gas-type appliance (such as a water heater or a clothes dryer) with a pilot light is present. Since gasoline is carcinogenic, wear latex gloves when there's a possibility of being exposed to fuel, and, if you spill any fuel on your skin, rinse it off immediately with soap and water. Mop up any spills immediately and do not store fuel-soaked rags where they could ignite. The fuel system on fuel-injected models is under constant pressure, so, if any fuel lines are to be disconnected, the fuel pressure in the system must be relieved first (see Section 2). When you perform any kind of work on the fuel system, wear safety glasses and have a Class B type fire extinguisher on hand.*

Inspection

1 Once in a while, you will have to raise the vehicle to service or replace some component (an exhaust pipe hanger, for example). Whenever you work under the vehicle, always inspect fuel lines and all fittings and connections for damage or deterioration.
2 Check all hoses and pipes for cracks, kinks, deformation or obstructions.
3 Make sure all hoses and pipe clips attach their associated hoses or pipes securely to the underside of the vehicle.
4 Verify all hose clamps attaching rubber hoses to metal fuel lines or pipes are snug enough to assure a tight fit between the hoses and pipes.

Replacement

Refer to illustration 4.6
5 If you must replace any damaged sections, use original equipment replacement hoses or pipes constructed from exactly the same material as the section you are replacing. Do not install substitutes constructed from inferior or inappropriate material or you could cause a fuel leak or a fire.
6 Always, before detaching or disassembling any part of the fuel line system, note the routing of all hoses and pipes and the orientation of all clamps and clips to assure that replacement sections are installed in exactly the same manner. When attaching hoses to metal lines, overlap them as shown **(see illustration)**.
7 Before detaching any part of the fuel system, be sure to relieve the fuel pressure (see Section 2) and disconnect the battery. Cover the fitting being disconnected with a rag to absorb any fuel that may spray out. **Caution:** *If the stereo in your vehicle is equipped with an anti-theft system, make sure you have the correct activation code before disconnecting the battery.*

8 While you're under the vehicle, it's a good idea to check the condition of the fuel filter - make sure that it's not damaged (see Chapter 1).

5 Fuel tank - removal and installation

Refer to illustrations 5.1a, 5.1b, 5.1c, 5.7a, 5.7b and 5.10
Warning: *Gasoline is extremely flammable, so take extra precautions when you work on any part of the fuel system. Don't smoke or allow open flames or bare light bulbs near the work area, and don't work in a garage where a natural gas-type appliance (such as a water heater or a clothes dryer) with a pilot light is present. Since gasoline is carcinogenic, wear latex gloves when there's a possibility of being exposed to fuel, and, if you spill any fuel on your skin, rinse it off immediately with soap and water. Mop up any spills immediately and do not store fuel-soaked rags where they could ignite. The fuel system on fuel-injected models is under constant pressure, so, if any fuel lines are to be disconnected, the fuel pressure in the system must be relieved first (see Section 2). When you perform any kind of work on the fuel system, wear safety glasses and have a Class B type fire extinguisher on hand.*
1 This procedure is much easier to perform if the fuel tank is empty. These models have a drain plug **(see illustrations)** for this purpose. If for some reason the drain plug can't be removed, postpone the job

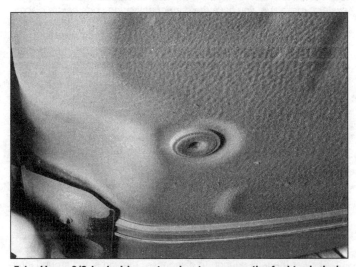

5.1a Use a 3/8-inch drive extension to remove the fuel tank drain plug. It may be necessary to chisel out some of the undercoating stuck inside the plug recess

4

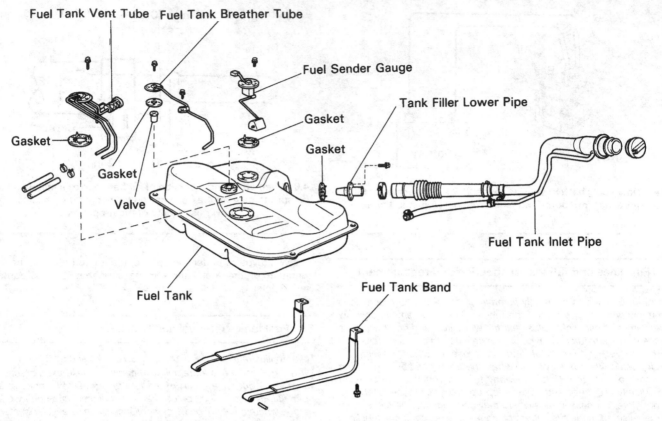

5.1b Exploded view of the fuel tank assembly on carbureted models

until the tank is empty or siphon the fuel into an approved container using a siphoning kit (available at most auto parts stores). **Warning:** *Do not start the siphoning action by mouth!*

2   Remove the fuel filler cap to relieve fuel tank pressure. If you're working on a fuel-injected model, relieve the fuel system pressure (see Section 2). If you're working on a 1990 model, also unplug the electrical connector for the fuel level sending unit.

3   Detach the cable from the negative terminal of the battery. **Caution:** *If the stereo in your vehicle is equipped with an anti-theft system, make sure you have the correct activation code before disconnecting the battery.*

4   If the tank is full or nearly full, drain the fuel into an approved container.

5   Raise the vehicle and place it securely on jackstands.

6   If you're working on a fuel-injected model, remove the fuel pump access cover from the floor. Push the grommet(s) and electrical connector(s) through the cover.

7   Disconnect the fuel lines, the vapor return line and the fuel filler pipe **(see illustrations). Note:** *The fuel feed and return lines and the vapor return line are different diameters, so reattachment is simplified. If you have any doubts, however, clearly label the three lines and their respective inlet or outlet pipes. Be sure to plug the hoses to prevent leakage and contamination of the fuel system.*

8   Support the fuel tank with a floor jack. Place a sturdy plank between the jack head and the fuel tank to protect the tank.

9   Detach the fuel line bracket and remove the fuel line or tank protectors.

10   Remove the bolts from the fuel tank support straps **(see illustration)**.

11   Lower the tank enough to disconnect the wires and ground strap from the fuel gauge sending unit, if you have not already done so.

12   Remove the tank from the vehicle.

13   Installation is the reverse of removal.

6   Fuel tank cleaning and repair - general information

1   Any repairs to the fuel tank or filler neck should be carried out by a professional who has experience in this critical and potentially dangerous work. Even after cleaning and flushing of the fuel system, explosive fumes can remain and ignite during repair of the tank.

2   If the fuel tank is removed from the vehicle, it should not be placed in an area where sparks or open flames could ignite the fumes coming out of the tank. Be especially careful inside garages where a natural gas-type appliance is located, because the pilot light could cause an explosion.

7   Fuel pump - removal and installation

Warning: *Gasoline is extremely flammable, so take extra precautions when you work on any part of the fuel system. Don't smoke or allow open flames or bare light bulbs near the work area, and don't work in a garage where a natural gas-type appliance (such as a water heater or a clothes dryer) with a pilot light is present. Since gasoline is carcinogenic, wear latex gloves when there's a possibility of being exposed to fuel, and, if you spill any fuel on your skin, rinse it off immediately with soap and water. Mop up any spills immediately and do not store fuel-soaked rags where they could ignite. The fuel system on fuel-injected models is under constant pressure, so, if any fuel lines are to be disconnected, the fuel pressure in the system must be relieved first (see Section 2). When you perform any kind of work on the fuel system, wear safety glasses and have a Class B type fire extinguisher on hand.*

1   Relieve the fuel system pressure (see Section 2).

2   Disconnect the cable from the negative terminal of the battery.

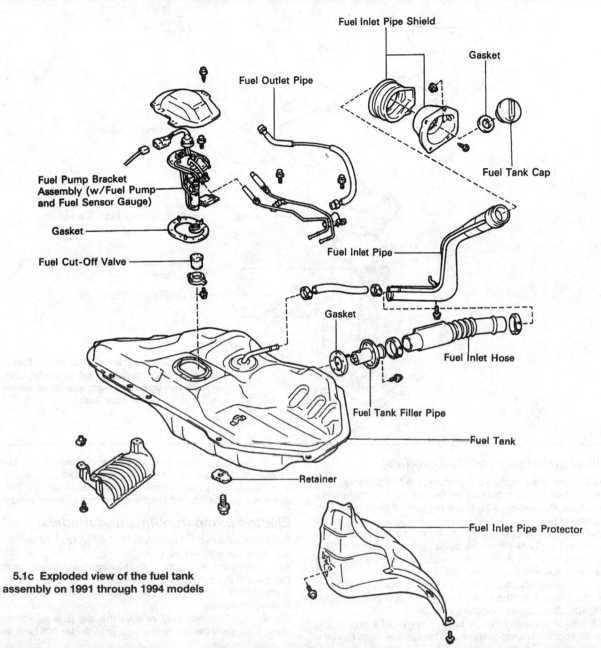

Fuel Inlet Pipe Shield

Gasket

Fuel Outlet Pipe

Fuel Tank Cap

Fuel Pump Bracket
Assembly (w/Fuel Pump
and Fuel Sensor Gauge)

Gasket

Fuel Cut-Off Valve

Fuel Inlet Pipe

Gasket

Fuel Inlet Hose

Fuel Tank Filler Pipe

Fuel Tank

Retainer

Fuel Inlet Pipe Protector

**5.1c Exploded view of the fuel tank
assembly on 1991 through 1994 models**

4

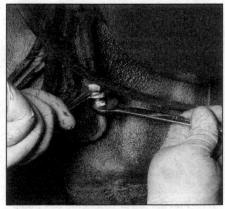

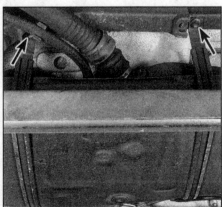

**5.7a Use a back-up wrench on the fuel
line to prevent the line from twisting**

**5.7b Remove the clamps (arrows) that
retain the fuel filler hose and the
vapor line**

**5.10 Remove the bolts (arrows) that retain
the straps to the body**

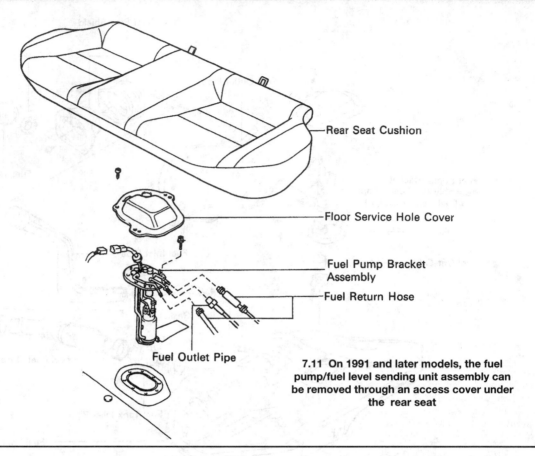

—Rear Seat Cushion

—Floor Service Hole Cover

—Fuel Pump Bracket Assembly

—Fuel Return Hose

Fuel Outlet Pipe

7.11 On 1991 and later models, the fuel pump/fuel level sending unit assembly can be removed through an access cover under the rear seat

Mechanical pump (carbureted models)

3   Relieve the fuel tank pressure by removing the fuel filler cap.

4   Locate the fuel pump mounted on the left rear corner of the cylinder head **(see illustration 3.3)**. Place rags underneath the pump to catch any spilled fuel.

5   Loosen hose clamps and slide them down the hoses, past the fittings. Disconnect the hoses from the pump, using a twisting motion as you pull them from the fittings. Immediately plug the hoses to prevent leakage of fuel and the entry of dirt.

6   Unscrew the fasteners that retain the pump to the cylinder head, then detach the pump from the head. Inspect the fuel pump arm for wear. Coat it with clean engine oil before installing it.

7   Using a gasket scraper or putty knife, remove all traces of old gasket material from the mating surfaces on the cylinder head (and the

fuel pump, if the same one will be reinstalled). While scraping, be careful not to gouge the soft aluminum surfaces.

8   Installation is the reverse of the removal procedure, but be sure to use a new gasket and tighten the mounting fasteners securely.

Electric pump (fuel-injected models)

Refer to illustrations 7.11, 7.12, 7.13, 7.14, 7.15, 7.16 and 7.20

9   Remove the fuel tank cap.

10   Disconnect the cable from the negative terminal of the battery. **Caution:** *If the stereo in your vehicle is equipped with an anti-theft system, make sure you have the correct activation code before disconnecting the battery.*

11   On 1990 models only, remove the fuel tank (see Section 5) and place it on a workbench or in a safe area. **Note:** *1991and later models*

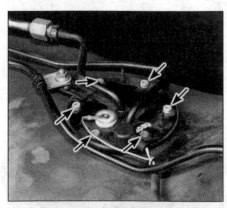

7.12 Remove the bolts (arrows) from the fuel pump cover (1990 model shown)

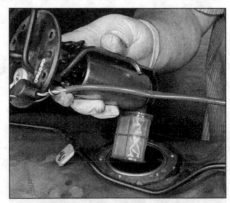

7.13 Simultaneously, lift and angle the assembly out of the fuel tank (1990 model shown)

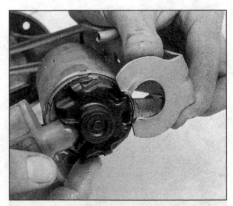

7.14 Pull the lower end of the fuel pump loose from the bracket and remove the rubber cushion that insulates the bottom of the pump

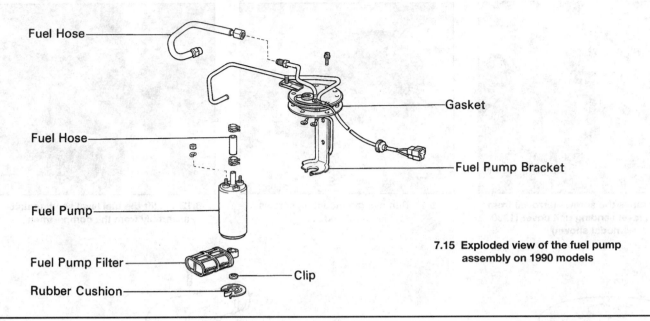

Fuel Hose

Fuel Hose

Gasket

Fuel Pump

Fuel Pump Bracket

Fuel Pump Filter

Clip

Rubber Cushion

7.15 Exploded view of the fuel pump assembly on 1990 models

are equipped with a fuel pump/fuel level sending unit assembly that is accessible through an access cover under the rear seat **(see illustration).**

12 Remove the fuel pump assembly retaining bolts **(see illustration)** from the top of the fuel tank.

13 Carefully withdraw the fuel pump assembly from the fuel tank **(see illustration).** On 1991 and later models, be careful not to bend the float arm of the fuel level sending unit.

14 Pull the lower end of the fuel pump loose from the bracket **(see illustration).**

15 Remove the rubber cushion from the lower end of the fuel pump **(see illustration).**

16 Remove the clip securing the filter to the pump **(see illustration).**

17 Pull out the filter and inspect it for contamination. If it is dirty, replace it.

18 If you are only replacing the fuel pump filter, install the new filter, the clip and the rubber cushion, push the lower end of the pump back into the bracket and install the pump/bracket assembly in the fuel tank.

19 If you are replacing the fuel pump, loosen the hose clamp at the upper end of the pump and disconnect the pump from the hose.

20 Disconnect the wires from the pump terminals and remove the pump **(see illustration).**

21 Installation is the reverse of removal.

8 Fuel level sending unit - check and replacement

Check

Refer to illustration 8.3

Note: *The fuel level sending unit can be benched tested to verify its operation. Although it will be more time consuming, the resistance readings are accurate.*

1 Before performing any tests on the fuel level sending unit, completely fill the tank with fuel.

2 Raise the vehicle and secure it with jackstands.

3 Disconnect the fuel level sending unit electrical connector **(see illustration)** located at the front of the fuel tank.

4 Position the ohmmeter probes onto the electrical connector terminals (light green/red wire and the green/yellow wire) and check for resistance. Use the 200 scale on the ohmmeter. **Note:** *Double-check the wiring diagram for your particular year and engine to ensure the correct terminal designations.*

5 With the fuel tank completely full, the resistance should be about 12.0 ohms.

6 Reconnect the electrical connector, lower the vehicle and drive it until the tank is nearly empty.

7.16 Pry off the clip that holds the filter to the fuel pump and pull the filter off - replace the clip if it is a loose fit

7.20 Disconnect the wires from the fuel pump terminals - be sure to get the polarity correct when installing the new pump (1990 model shown)

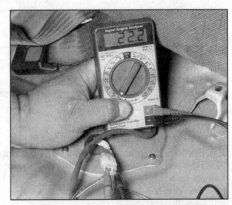

8.3 Position the probes of the ohmmeter onto the light green/red wire and the green/yellow wire of the fuel tank connector

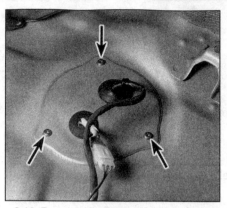

8.10 Remove the screws (arrows) from the fuel level sending unit cover (1990 model shown)

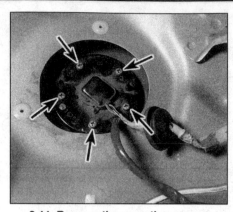

8.11 Remove the mounting screws (arrows) and . . .

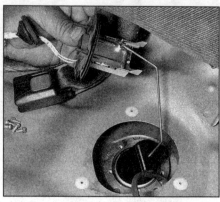

8.12 . . . lift the fuel level sending unit assembly from the compartment

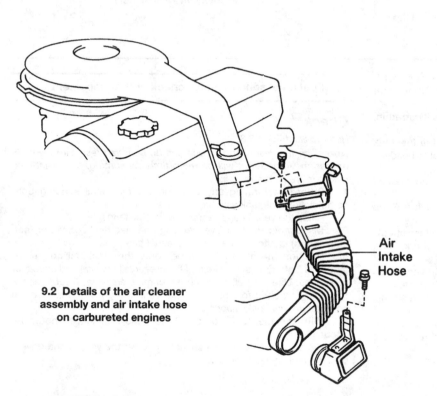

9.2 Details of the air cleaner assembly and air intake hose on carbureted engines

Air Intake Hose

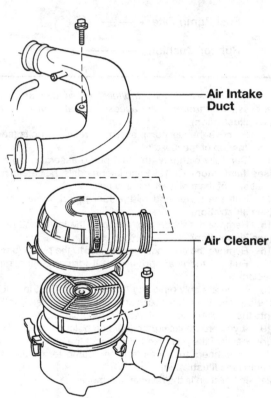

Air Intake Duct

Air Cleaner

9.6 Details of the air cleaner assembly on fuel-injected engines

7   Check the resistance. The resistance of the sending unit should be about 115 to 122 ohms.
8   If the readings are incorrect, replace the sending unit.

Replacement

Refer to illustrations 8.10, 8.11 and 8.12

9   Remove the rear seat cushion (see Chapter 11).
10   Remove the fuel level sending unit cover bolts **(see illustration)** the fuel tank.
11   Remove the screws that retain the cover to the fuel level sending unit **(see illustration)**.
12   Carefully angle the sending unit out of the opening without damaging the fuel level float located at the bottom of the assembly **(see illustration)**.

13   Remove the screw from the side of the sending unit bracket and separate the sending unit from the assembly.
14   Installation is the reverse of removal.

9   Air cleaner assembly - removal and installation

Refer to illustrations 9.2, 9.6, 9.7a and 9.7b

Carbureted engines

1   Remove the air filter from the air cleaner housing (see Chapter 1).
2   Disconnect and mark any hoses, vacuum lines, electrical connectors etc. from the air cleaner assembly **(see illustration)**.
3   Lift the air cleaner assembly from the engine.
4   Installation is the reverse of removal.

9.7a Remove the three bolts (arrows) from the air cleaner assembly and lift it from the engine compartment (1990 model shown)

9.7b Remove the three bolts (arrows) (1991 through 1994 models shown)

Fuel-injected engines

5   Detach the clips and remove the air filter/air intake sensor cover and the filter element (see Chapter 1).
6   Disconnect the air intake hose from the assembly **(see illustration)**.
7   Remove the three bolts and remove the air cleaner assembly from the engine compartment **(see illustrations)**.
8   Installation is the reverse of removal.

10   Accelerator cable - removal, installation and adjustment

Refer to illustrations 10.2a, 10.2b and 10.3

Removal

1   Detach the cable from the negative terminal of the battery. **Caution:** *If the stereo in your vehicle is equipped with an anti-theft system, make sure you have the correct activation code before disconnecting the battery.*
2   Loosen the locknut on the threaded portion of the accelerator cable at the throttle body **(see illustration)**, grasp the throttle lever arm and rotate it to put some slack in the cable, then slip the cable end out of its slot in the arm **(see illustration)**.
3   Detach the accelerator cable from the accelerator pedal **(see illustration)**.
4   From inside the vehicle, pull the cable through the cable casing.

Installation and adjustment

5   Installation is the reverse of removal.
6   To adjust the cable, fully depress the accelerator pedal and check that the throttle is fully opened.
7   If not fully opened, loosen the locknuts, depress accelerator pedal and adjust the cable.
8   Tighten the locknuts and recheck the adjustment. Make sure the throttle closes fully when the pedal isn't depressed.

11   Feedback carburetor - diagnosis and overhaul

Warning: *Gasoline is extremely flammable, so take extra precautions when you work on any part of the fuel system. Don't smoke or allow open flames or bare light bulbs near the work area, and don't work in a garage where a natural gas-type appliance (such as a water heater or a clothes dryer) with a pilot light is present. Since gasoline is carcinogenic, wear latex gloves when there's a possibility of being exposed to fuel, and, if you spill any fuel on your skin, rinse it off immediately with soap and water. Mop up any spills immediately and do not store fuel-soaked rags where they could ignite. The fuel system on fuel-injected models is under constant pressure, so, if any fuel lines are to be disconnected, the fuel pressure in the system must be relieved first (see Section 2). When you perform any kind of work on the fuel system, wear safety glasses and have a Class B type fire extinguisher on hand.*

4

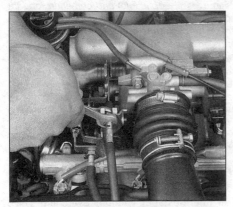

10.2a Use back-up wrenches to loosen the nuts on the accelerator cable

10.2b Rotate the throttle lever and remove the cable end from the slotted portion of the throttle lever

10.3 Pull the cable away from the accelerator pedal lever and pass it through the slot (arrow)

11.3 Component locations for the feedback carburetor system on 1988 through 1990 models

1	EGR valve (hidden from view under the air cleaner assembly)	3	Relay and fuse panel	5	Fuel pump
2	Check connector	4	AS bypass tube	6	Oxygen sensor
				7	PCV valve

General diagnosis

Refer to illustration 11.3

1   A thorough road test and check of carburetor adjustments should be done before any major carburetor service work. Specifications for some adjustments are listed on the Vehicle Emissions Control Information (VECI) label found in the engine compartment.

2   Carburetor problems usually show up as flooding, hard starting, stalling, severe backfiring and poor acceleration. A carburetor that's leaking fuel and/or covered with wet looking deposits definitely needs attention.

3   Some performance complaints directed at the carburetor are actually a result of loose, out-of-adjustment or malfunctioning engine or electrical components. Others develop when vacuum hoses leak, are disconnected or are incorrectly routed. The proper approach to analyzing carburetor problems should include the following items **(see illustration)**:

a) *Inspect all vacuum hoses and actuators for leaks and correct installation (see Chapters 1 and 6).*
b) *Tighten the intake manifold and carburetor mounting nuts/bolts evenly and securely.*
c) *Perform a cylinder compression test (see Chapter 2).*
d) *Clean or replace the spark plugs as necessary (see Chapter 1).*
e) *Check the spark plug wires (see Chapter 1).*
f) *Inspect the ignition primary wires.*
g) *Check the ignition timing (follow the instructions printed on the Emissions Control Information label).*
h) *Check the fuel pump (see Section 3).*
i) *Check the heat control valve in the air cleaner for proper operation (see Chapter 1).*
j) *Check/replace the air filter element (see Chapter 1).*
k) *Check the PCV system (see Chapters 1 and 6).*

l) *Check/replace the fuel filter (see Chapter 1). Also, the strainer in the tank could be restricted.*
m) *Check for a plugged exhaust system.*
n) *Check EGR valve operation (see Chapter 6).*
o) *Check the choke - it should be completely open at normal engine operating temperature (see Chapter 1).*
p) *Check for fuel leaks and kinked or dented fuel lines (see Chapters 1 and 4)*
q) *Check accelerator pump operation with the engine off (remove the air cleaner cover and operate the throttle as you look into the carburetor throat - you should see a stream of gasoline enter the carburetor).*
r) *Check for incorrect fuel or bad gasoline.*
s) *Check the valve clearances (if applicable) and camshaft lobe lift (see Chapters 1 and 2)*
t) *Have a dealer service department or repair shop check the electronic engine and carburetor controls.*

4   Diagnosing carburetor problems may require that the engine be started and run with the air cleaner off. While running the engine without the air cleaner, backfires are possible. This situation is likely to occur if the carburetor is malfunctioning, but just the removal of the air cleaner can lean the fuel/air mixture enough to produce an engine backfire. **Warning:** *Don't position any part of your body, especially your face, directly over the carburetor during inspection and servicing procedures. Wear eye protection!*

Feedback carburetor inspection

Refer to illustrations 11.5a, 11.5b and 11.6

5   Check the Bi-metal (thermostatic) Vacuum Switching Valve (BVSV) with a cold engine.

a) *The coolant temperature should be below 45-degrees Fahrenheit.*

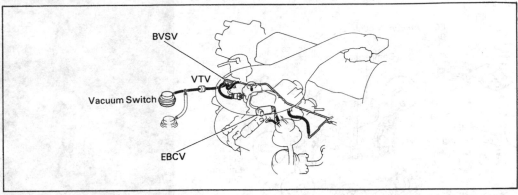

11.5a Vacuum schematic of the feedback carburetor system on 1988 through mid-year 1990 models

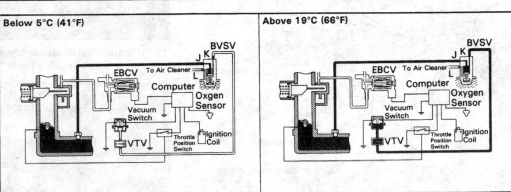

b) *Disconnect the vacuum hose from the vacuum switch* **(see illustrations)**.

c) *Start the engine and check that no vacuum is felt at the hose.*

d) *Reconnect the vacuum hose.*

6   Check the Electronic Air Bleed Control Valve (EBCV).

a) *Warm up the engine to normal operating temperature.*

b) *Disconnect the EBCV connector* **(see illustration)**.

c) *Maintain engine speed at 2,500 rpm.*

d) *Reconnect the EBCV connector and the engine rpm should drop about 300 rpm momentarily.*

e) *With the engine idling repeat steps (b) and (d).*

f) *Check that the engine speed does not change.*

g) *Disconnect the vacuum hose from the vacuum switch* **(see illustration 11.5a or 11.5b).**

h) *Repeat steps (b), (c) and (d). Check that the engine speed does not change.*

7   If no problems is found with this inspection the system is okay.

Any further check should be done by dealer service department or automotive repair shop.

Overhaul

Refer to illustration 11.10

8   Once it's determined that the carburetor needs an overhaul, several options are available. If you're going to attempt to overhaul the carburetor yourself, first obtain a good quality carburetor rebuild kit (which will include all necessary gaskets, internal parts, instructions and a parts list). You'll also need some special solvent and a means of blowing out the internal passages of the carburetor with air.

9   An alternative is to obtain a new or rebuilt carburetor. They're readily available from dealers and auto parts stores. Make absolutely sure the exchange carburetor is identical to the original. A tag is usually attached to the top of the carburetor or a number is stamped on the float bowl. It'll help determine the exact type of carburetor you have. When obtaining a rebuilt carburetor or a rebuild kit, make sure the kit

4

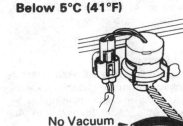

Below 5°C (41°F)

No Vacuum

11.5b Disconnect the hose from the vacuum switch as shown

Hot 2,500 rpm

Tachometer

2,500

rpm

Disconnect

11.6 Disconnect the electrical connector from the EBCV

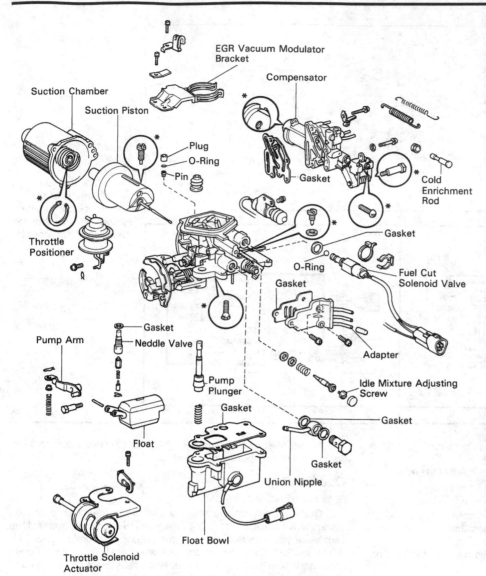

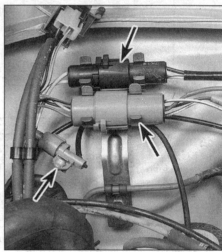

12.5 Clearly label all vacuum hoses before disconnecting them

12.7 Label and unplug the electrical connectors attached to the carburetor (arrows)

11.10 Exploded view of the feedback carburetor

or carburetor matches your application exactly. Seemingly insignificant differences can make a large difference in engine performance.

10   If you choose to overhaul your own carburetor **(see illustration)**, allow enough time to disassemble it carefully, soak the necessary parts in the cleaning solvent (usually for at least one-half day or according to the instructions listed on the carburetor cleaner) and reassemble it, which will usually take much longer than disassembly. When disassembling the carburetor, match each part with the illustration in the carburetor kit and lay the parts out in order on a clean work surface. Overhauls by inexperienced mechanics can result in an engine which runs poorly or not at all. To avoid this, use care and patience when disassembling the carburetor so you can reassemble it correctly.

11   Because carburetor designs are constantly modified by the manufacturer in order to meet increasingly more stringent emissions regulations, the overhaul procedures in this Chapter may not apply exactly to your vehicle. You'll receive a detailed, well illustrated set of instructions with any carburetor overhaul kit; they'll apply in a more specific manner to the carburetor on your vehicle.

12   Carburetor - removal and installation

Warning: *Gasoline is extremely flammable, so take extra precautions*

when you work on any part of the fuel system. Don't smoke or allow open flames or bare light bulbs near the work area, and don't work in a garage where a natural gas-type appliance (such as a water heater or a clothes dryer) with a pilot light is present. Since gasoline is carcinogenic, wear latex gloves when there's a possibility of being exposed to fuel, and, if you spill any fuel on your skin, rinse it off immediately with soap and water. Mop up any spills immediately and do not store fuel-soaked rags where they could ignite. When you perform any kind of work on the fuel system, wear safety glasses and have a Class B type fire extinguisher on hand.

Removal

Refer to illustrations 12.5 and 12.7

1   Remove the fuel tank cap to relieve the tank pressure.

2   Remove the air cleaner from the carburetor. Be sure to label all vacuum hoses attached to the air cleaner housing.

3   Disconnect the throttle cable from the throttle lever (see Section 10).

4   If the vehicle is equipped with an automatic transmission, disconnect the Throttle Valve (TV) cable from the throttle lever.

5   Clearly label all vacuum hoses and fittings, then disconnect the hoses **(see illustration)**.

6   Disconnect the fuel line from the carburetor.

13.1a Component locations for the EFI system on 1990 models

1	Intake air temperature sensor	7	Check connector
2	EGR valve	8	Relay and fuse panel
3	EGR vacuum modulator	9	TPS sensor
4	MAP sensor	10	PCV valve
5	Cold start injector (hidden from view under plenum)	11	Oxygen sensor
6	Purge control valve for the EVAP system	12	Fuel rail containing the fuel injectors

7   Label the wires and terminals, then unplug all electrical connectors **(see illustration)**.

8   Remove the mounting fasteners, remove the EGR modulator bracket out of the way and lift the carburetor from the intake manifold. Remove the carburetor mounting gasket. Do not remove the cold mixture heater. Stuff a shop rag into the intake manifold openings.

Installation

9   Use a gasket scraper to remove all traces of gasket material and sealant from the cold mixture heater, being careful not to damage the heater, (and the carburetor, if it's being reinstalled), then remove the shop rag from the manifold openings. Clean the mating surfaces with lacquer thinner or acetone.

10   Place a new gasket on the cold mixture heater.

11   Position the carburetor on the gasket, attach the EGR modulator bracket then install the mounting fasteners.

12   To prevent carburetor distortion or damage, tighten the fasteners, in a criss-cross pattern, 1/4-turn at a time.

13   The remaining installation steps are the reverse of removal.

14   Check and, if necessary, adjust the idle speed (see Chapter 1).

15   If the vehicle is equipped with an automatic transmission, refer to Chapter 7, Part B, for the TV cable adjustment procedure.

16   Start the engine and check carefully for fuel leaks.

13   Electronic Fuel Injection (EFI) system - general information

Refer to illustrations 13.1a and 13.1b

1   Mid-year 1990 through 1994 models are equipped with an Electronic Fuel Injection (EFI) system. The EFI system is composed of three basic sub systems: fuel system, air induction system and electronic control system **(see illustrations)**.

Fuel system

2   An electric fuel pump located inside the fuel tank supplies fuel under constant pressure to the fuel rail, which distributes fuel evenly to all injectors. From the fuel rail, fuel is injected into the intake ports, just above the intake valves, by four fuel injectors. The amount of fuel supplied by the injectors is precisely controlled by an Electronic Control Unit (ECU). On 1990 models an additional injector, known as the cold start injector, supplies extra fuel into the intake manifold for starting. A pressure regulator controls system pressure in relation to intake manifold vacuum. A fuel filter between the fuel pump and the fuel rail filters fuel to protect the components of the system.

Air induction system

3   The air system consists of an air filter housing, an airflow meter and a throttle body. The airflow meter is an information gathering device for the ECU. A potentiometer measures intake airflow and a temperature sensor measures intake air temperature. This information helps the ECU determine the amount (duration) of fuel to be injected by the injectors. The throttle plate inside the throttle body is controlled by the driver. As the throttle plate opens, the amount of air that can pass through the system increases, so the potentiometer opens further and the ECU signals the injectors to increase the amount of fuel delivered to the intake ports.

Electronic control system

4   The Computer Control System controls the EFI and other systems by means of an Electronic Control Unit (ECU), which employs a microcomputer. The ECU receives signals from a number of

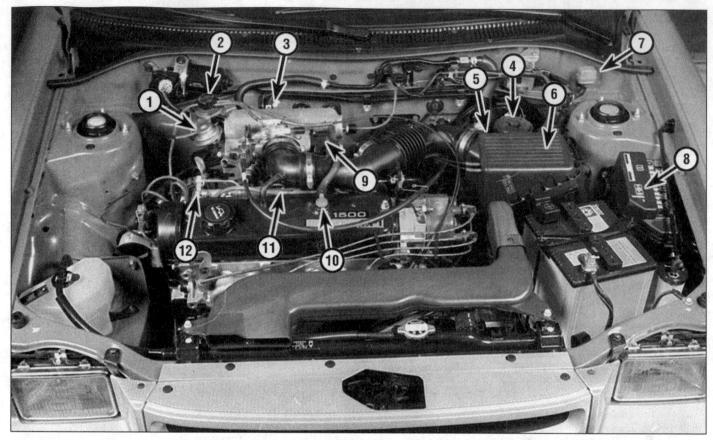

13.1b Component locations for the EFI system on 1991 and later models

1 *EGR valve*	7 *Check connector*
2 *EGR vacuum modulator*	8 *Relay and fuse panel*
3 *MAP sensor*	9 *TPS sensor*
4 *Charcoal canister for the EVAP system*	10 *PCV valve*
5 *Intake air temperature sensor*	11 *Fuel rail containing the fuel injectors*
6 *Air cleaner assembly*	12 *Fuel pressure regulator*

information sensors which monitor such variables as intake air volume, intake air temperature, coolant temperature, engine rpm, acceleration/deceleration and exhaust oxygen content. These signals help the ECU determine the injection duration necessary for the optimum air/fuel ratio. Some of these sensors and their corresponding ECU-controlled relays are not contained within EFI components, but are located throughout the engine compartment. For further information regarding the ECU and its relationship to the engine electrical and ignition system, see Chapter 6.

14 Electronic Fuel Injection (EFI) system - check

Refer to illustrations 14.6a, 14.6b, 14.7, 14.8 and 14.9
Warning: *Gasoline is extremely flammable, so take extra precautions when you work on any part of the fuel system. Don't smoke or allow open flames or bare light bulbs near the work area, and don't work in a garage where a natural gas-type appliance (such as a water heater or a clothes dryer) with a pilot light is present. Since gasoline is carcinogenic, wear latex gloves when there's a possibility of being exposed to fuel, and, if you spill any fuel on your skin, rinse it off immediately with soap and water. Mop up any spills immediately and do not store fuel-soaked rags where they could ignite. The fuel system on fuel-injected models is under constant pressure, so, if any fuel lines are to be disconnected, the fuel pressure in the system must be relieved first (see Section 2). When you perform any kind of work on the*

fuel system, wear safety glasses and have a Class B type fire extinguisher on hand.
1   Check the ground wire connections for tightness. Check all wiring and electrical connectors that are related to the system. Loose electrical connectors and poor grounds can cause many problems that resemble more serious malfunctions.
2   Check to see that the battery is fully charged, as the control unit and sensors depend on an accurate supply voltage in order to properly meter the fuel.
3   Check the air filter element - a dirty or partially blocked filter will severely impede performance and economy (see Chapter 1).
4   If a blown fuse is found, replace it and see if it blows again. If it does, search for a grounded wire in the harness related to the system.
5   Check the air intake duct from the airflow meter to the intake manifold for leaks, which will result in an excessively lean mixture. Also check the condition of the vacuum hoses connected to the intake manifold.
6   Remove the air intake duct from the throttle body and check for dirt, carbon or other residue build-up. If it's dirty, clean it with carburetor cleaner (make sure the can says it's safe for use with oxygen sensors and catalytic converters) and a toothbrush **(see illustrations)**.
7   With the engine running, place a stethoscope against each injector, one at a time, and listen for a clicking sound, indicating operation **(see illustration)**. If you don't have a stethoscope, place the tip of a long screwdriver against the body of the injector and listen through the handle.

14.6a This area inside the throttle body near the throttle plate (arrow) usually gets a lot of sludge build-up because of the PCV hose vents vapor from the crankcase here

14.6b With the engine off, use carburetor cleaner (make sure it is safe for use with catalytic converters and oxygen sensors) and a toothbrush to clean the throttle body - open the throttle plate so you can clean behind it

14.7 Use a stethoscope to determine if the injectors are working properly - they should make a steady clicking sound that rises and falls with engine speed changes

14.8 Install the "noid" light into the fuel injector electrical connector and check to see that it blinks when the engine is running

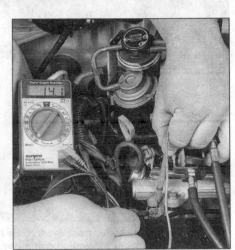

14.9 Using an ohmmeter, measure the resistance across the terminals of the injector

4

8   If there is a problem with an injector, purchase a special injector test light (sometimes called a "noid" light) and install it into the injector electrical connector **(see illustration)**. Start the engine and make sure that each injector connector flashes the noid light. This will test for the proper voltage signal to the injectors.

9   With the engine OFF and the fuel injector electrical connectors disconnected, measure the resistance of each injector **(see illustration)**. Each injector should measure about 13.4 to 14.2 ohms. If not, the injector is probably faulty.

10   The remainder of the system checks should be left to a Toyota service department or other qualified repair shop, as there is a chance that the control unit may be damaged if not performed properly.

15 Electronic Fuel Injection (EFI) system - component check and replacement

Warning: *Gasoline is extremely flammable, so take extra precautions when you work on any part of the fuel system. Don't smoke or allow* open flames or bare light bulbs near the work area, and don't work in a garage where a natural gas-type appliance (such as a water heater or a clothes dryer) with a pilot light is present. Since gasoline is carcinogenic, wear latex gloves when there's a possibility of being exposed to fuel, and, if you spill any fuel on your skin, rinse it off immediately with soap and water. Mop up any spills immediately and do not store fuel-soaked rags where they could ignite. The fuel system on fuel-injected models is under constant pressure, so, if any fuel lines are to be disconnected, the fuel pressure in the system must be relieved first (see Section 2). When you perform any kind of work on the fuel system, wear safety glasses and have a Class B type fire extinguisher on hand.

Throttle body

Refer to illustrations 15.2, 15.11a and 15.11b

Check

1   Verify that the throttle linkage operates smoothly.

2   Start the engine, detach each vacuum hose and, using your finger, check the vacuum at each port on the throttle body with the

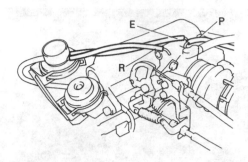

Port Name	At idling	Other than idling
P	No vacuum	Vacuum
E	No vacuum	Vacuum
R	No vacuum	No vacuum

15.2 The throttle body vacuum port guide (top) and vacuum table (bottom)

15.11b Detach the hoses from the throttle body and lift the unit from the engine compartment

15.11a Remove the throttle body bolts (arrows)

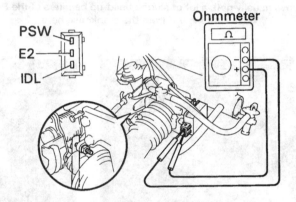

15.15 To check the throttle position sensor (TPS), insert a feeler gauge of the specified thickness between the throttle stop screw and the stop lever, then measure the resistance between the proper terminals (see illustration 15.16a) (1990 model shown)

engine at idle and above idle. Compare your observations with the vacuum table **(see illustration)**.

Replacement

3   Detach the cable from the negative terminal of the battery. **Caution:** *If the stereo in your vehicle is equipped with an anti-theft system, make sure you have the correct activation code before disconnecting the battery.*

4   Drain the radiator (see Chapter 1).

5   Loosen the hose clamps and remove the air intake duct.

6   Detach the accelerator cable from the throttle lever arm (see Section 10), then detach the throttle cable bracket and set it aside (it's not necessary to detach the throttle cable from the bracket).

7   If your vehicle is equipped with an automatic transmission, detach the throttle valve (TV) cable from the throttle linkage (see Chapter 7B), detach the TV cable brackets from the engine and set the cable and brackets aside.

8   Clearly label, then detach, all vacuum and coolant hoses from the throttle body.

9   Unplug the electrical connector from the Throttle Position Sensor (TPS).

10   Raise the vehicle and secure it on jackstands.

11   Remove the throttle body mounting bolts and detach the throttle body and gasket **(see illustrations)** from the intake manifold.

12   Using a soft brush and carburetor cleaner, thoroughly clean the throttle body casting, then blow out all passages with compressed air. **Caution:** *Do not clean the throttle position sensor with anything. Just wipe it off carefully with a clean soft cloth.*

13   Installation of the throttle body is the reverse of removal. Be sure to tighten the throttle body mounting bolts to the torque listed in the Specifications Section at the beginning of this Chapter.

Throttle Position Sensor (TPS)

Refer to illustrations 15.15, 15.16a, 15.16b, 15.17a, 15.17b and 15.17c

Check

14   Unplug the electrical connector from the throttle position sensor (TPS) and remove the throttle body from the engine compartment (see Steps 3 through 11).

15   Insert a feeler gauge of the specified thickness between the throttle stop screw and the stop lever **(see illustration)**.

16   Using an ohmmeter, check the continuity, or measure the resistance, between the indicated terminal pairs **(see illustrations)**.

17   If the resistance is not as specified, insert a 0.70 mm (0.0276 inch) feeler gauge between the throttle stop screw and lever, and connect the ohmmeter to terminals IDL and E2. Loosen the TPS mounting screws and slowly rotate the sensor clockwise until the ohmmeter reads infinity **(see illustrations)**.

18   Tighten the mounting screws, and using the proper feeler gauge, recheck the continuity between the specified terminals.

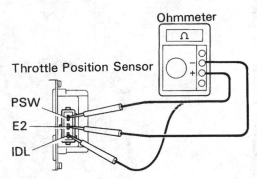

15.16a Use the terminal guide (top) and the continuity table (bottom) to check the TPS sensor (1990 model shown)

Clearance between lever and stop screw	Continuity between terminals		
	IDL – E2	PSW – E2	IDL – PSW
0.60 mm (0.0236 in.)	Continuity	No continuity	No continuity
0.80 mm (0.0315 in.)	No continuity	No continuity	No continuity
Throttle valve fully opened position	No continuity	Continuity	No continuity

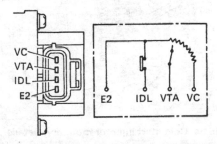

Clearance between lever and stop screw	Between terminals	Resistance
0 mm (0 in.)	VTA – E2	0.2 – 0.8 kΩ
0.50 mm (0.020 in.)	IDL – E2	2.3 kΩ or less
0.70 mm (0.028 in.)	IDL – E2	Infinity
throttle valve fully opened	VTA – E2	3.3 – 10 kΩ
–	VC – E2	3 – 7 kΩ

15.16b Terminal guide and continuity table for 1991 through 1994 models

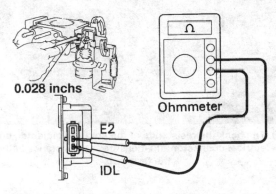

0.028 inchs

Ohmmeter

E2

IDL

5.17a To adjust the TPS, insert a feeler gauge and rotate the TPS clockwise until the needle deflects (to infinity) and tighten the screws at this point (1990 model shown)

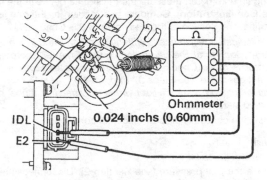

Ohmmeter

0.024 inchs (0.60mm)

IDL

E2

5.17b On 1991 through 1994 models, use a 0.024-inch feeler gauge to adjust the TPS

15.17c Location of the TPS adjustment screws (arrows)

15.25 Removing the fuel pressure regulator mounting bolts

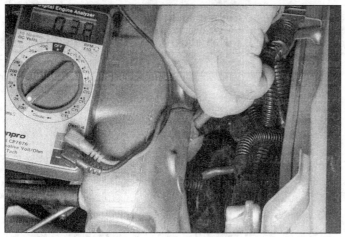

15.29 To check the resistance of the cold start injector, unplug the electrical connector and measure the resistance between the terminals

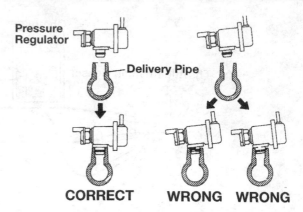

15.26 If the fuel pressure regulator is cocked during installation, it will not seal properly

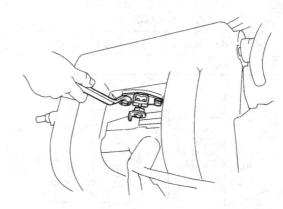

15.34 Cold start injector mounting details

and make sure that the pressure regulator is installed properly on the fuel rail **(see illustration)**.
27   The remainder of installation is the reverse of removal.

Cold start injector (1990 models only)

Note: *Be sure to check the operating condition of the cold start injector time switch along with the cold start injector. These components work in conjunction with each other.*

Check

Refer to illustration 15.29
28   Unplug the electrical connector from the cold start injector.
29   Using an ohmmeter, measure the resistance between the injector terminals **(see illustration)**. Compare this reading to the one listed in the Specifications Section at the beginning of this Chapter.

   a) *If the indicated resistance is within the range listed in the Specifications Section at the beginning of this Chapter, the cold start injector is okay. Check the cold start injector time switch for correct operation (see Steps 37 through 40).*
   b) *If the indicated resistance isn't within the specified range, replace the cold start injector.*

30   Plug in the cold start injector electrical connector.

Removal

Refer to illustration 15.34
31   Relieve the fuel pressure (see Section 2). Disconnect the cable from the negative terminal of the battery. **Caution:** *If the stereo in your vehicle is equipped with an anti-theft system, make sure you have the correct activation code before disconnecting the battery.*
32   Unplug the cold start injector electrical connector.

Replacement

19   If adjustment doesn't bring the sensor within specifications, unplug it, remove the screws and replace it with a new one, then adjust it as described.

Fuel pressure regulator

Check

20   Refer to the fuel pump/fuel pressure check procedure (see Section 3).

Removal

Refer to illustration 15.25
21   Relieve the fuel system pressure (see Section 2), then detach the cable from the negative terminal of the battery. **Caution:** *If the stereo in your vehicle is equipped with an anti-theft system, make sure you have the correct activation code before disconnecting the battery.*
22   Detach the vacuum sensing hose from the regulator.
23   Place a metal container or shop towel under the fuel return hose.
24   Slowly loosen the clamp screws, then remove it along with the fuel return hose.
25   Remove the pressure regulator mounting bolts **(see illustration)** and detach the pressure regulator from the fuel rail.

Installation

Refer to illustration 15.26
26   Installation is the reverse of removal. Be sure to use a new O-ring

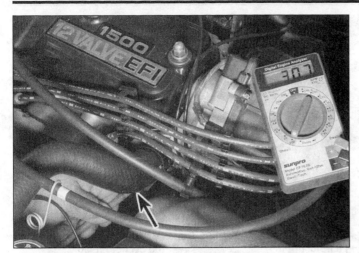

15.37 The cold start injector time switch (arrow) is located just below the upper radiator hose

33   Place a metal container or shop towel under the banjo fitting and remove the banjo bolt and sealing washers. Discard the washers.
34   Remove the cold start injector mounting bolts, the injector and the gasket **(see illustration)**.
35   The cold start injector can be bench tested (for spray pattern) but the test requires special equipment. If you have any doubt as to the condition of the cold start injector, take it to a dealer service department or other repair shop and have it tested.

Installation

36   Installation of the cold start injector is the reverse of removal. Be sure to use new sealing washers on each side of the banjo fitting. Also, tighten the mounting bolts and banjo bolt to the torque listed in this Chapter's Specifications.

Cold start injector time switch

Refer to illustration 15.37

Check

37   Disconnect the electrical connector from the cold start injector time switch **(see illustration)** and using an ohmmeter, check the resistance across the terminals.
38   First, check the resistance of the switch with the engine cold (below 86-degrees F). It should be 20 to 40 ohms resistance.
39   Next, warm up the engine (above 104-degrees F) and check the resistance of the switch. It should read 40 to 60 ohms resistance.
40   Check the resistance of terminal STA to ground. It should read 20 to 80 ohms.

Replacement

Warning: *The engine must be completely cool before beginning this procedure.*
41   Prepare the new switch for installation by wrapping the threads of the switch with Teflon sealing tape.
42   Use a deep socket and remove the switch from the engine. Be prepared for some coolant loss.
43   Install the new switch as quickly as possible to minimize coolant loss. After the switch has been installed, check the coolant level (see Chapter 1) and add coolant, if necessary, to bring it to the appropriate level.

Auxiliary air valve

Note: *The minimum idle speed is pre-set at the factory and should not require adjustment under normal operating conditions; however if the throttle body has been replaced or you suspect the minimum idle speed has been tampered with (for example, if the idle speed screw was removed from the throttle body) have the vehicle checked by a dealer service department or other qualified automotive repair shop.*

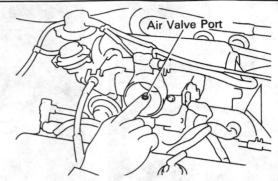

15.45 Place a finger over the air valve port and observe any changes in engine rpm during cold operation and then at normal operating temperature

Check

Refer to illustration 15.45

44   Install a tachometer to the manufacturer's specifications.
45   Start the engine and allow it to idle. With the engine coolant temperature below 176-degrees F, place the tip of your finger over the air valve port in the throttle body and confirm that the engine rpm drops **(see illustration)**.
46   Now, warm the engine up over 180-degrees F and confirm that the engine speed does not decrease more than 80 to 100 rpm.

Removal

Refer to illustration 15.48

47   Remove the throttle body (see Steps 3 through 11). **Note:** *The auxiliary air valve and assembly are difficult to reach, therefore it is recommended to remove the throttle body from the intake manifold first.*
48   Remove the mounting screws and detach the auxiliary air valve and gasket **(see illustration)**.

Installation

49   Installation of the auxiliary air valve is the reverse of removal for all models. Be sure to use a new gasket when installing the valve.

Fuel rail and fuel injectors

Check

50   Refer to Section 14 for the fuel injector checking procedure.

15.48 With the throttle body removed, remove the four screws (arrows) from the auxiliary air valve assembly and separate it from the throttle body

15.58 The fuel rail is secured by two bolts (arrows)

15.60 Lift the fuel injectors from the cylinder head, being careful not to damage the tip(s)

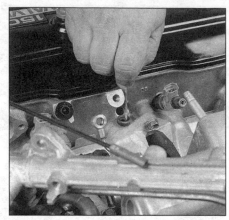

15.61 Remove the rubber grommets from the cylinder head

Replacement

Refer to illustrations 15.58, 15.60, 15.61, 15.63a and 15.63b

51   Relieve the fuel system pressure.

52   Detach the cable from the negative terminal of the battery. **Caution:** *If the stereo in your vehicle is equipped with an anti-theft system, make sure you have the correct activation code before disconnecting the battery.*

53   Remove the PCV hose from the cylinder head and intake manifold.

54   Unplug the electrical connectors from the fuel injectors and set the injector wire harness aside.

55   Disconnect the cold start injector fuel line from the fuel rail.

56   Detach the vacuum sensing hose from the fuel pressure regulator.

57   Disconnect the fuel lines from the fuel pressure regulator and the fuel rail.

58   Remove the fuel rail mounting bolts **(see illustration).**

59   Remove the fuel rail.

60   Remove the fuel injector(s) from the cylinder head **(see illustration).**

61   Remove the rubber grommets from the cylinder head and set them aside **(see illustration).**

62   If the injectors remain in the fuel rail, carefully remove them and set them aside in a clearly labeled storage container.

63   If you are replacing the injector(s), discard the old injector, the grommet and the O-ring. If you are simply replacing leaking injector O-rings and intend to re-use the same injectors, remove the old grommet and O-ring **(see illustrations)** and discard them.

64   Further testing of the injector(s) is beyond the scope of the home mechanic. If you are in doubt as to the status of any injector(s), it can

be bench tested for volume and leakage at a dealer service department.

65   Installation of the fuel injectors is the reverse of removal. Be sure to use new grommets and O-rings on the injector(s) and new crush washers on the fuel delivery pipe. Lubricate the O-rings with gasoline. Tighten the fuel rail mounting bolts to the torque listed in this Chapter's Specifications.

16 Exhaust system servicing - general information

Refer to illustrations 16.1a and 16.1b

Warning: *Inspection and repair of exhaust system components should be done only after enough time has elapsed after driving the vehicle to allow the system components to cool completely. Also, when working under the vehicle, make sure it is securely supported on jackstands.*

1   The exhaust system consists of the exhaust manifold, catalytic converter, the muffler, the tailpipe and all connecting pipes, brackets, hangers and clamps **(see illustrations).** The exhaust system is attached to the body with mounting brackets and rubber hangers. If any of these parts are damaged or deteriorated, excessive noise and vibration will be transmitted to the body.

2   Conducting regular inspections of the exhaust system will keep it safe and quiet. Look for any damaged or bent parts, open seams, holes, loose connections, excessive corrosion or other defects which could allow exhaust fumes to enter the vehicle. Deteriorated exhaust system components should not be repaired - they should be replaced with new parts.

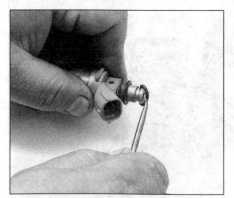

15.63a First, if you plan to reinstall the same injectors, be sure to remove and discard the old O-rings and replace them with new ones

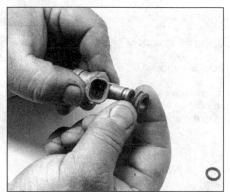

15.63b Also, remove and discard the old grommets and replace them with new ones

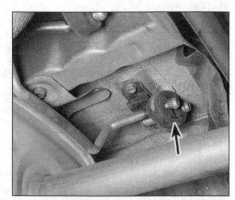

16.1a Typical exhaust system rubber hanger (arrow)

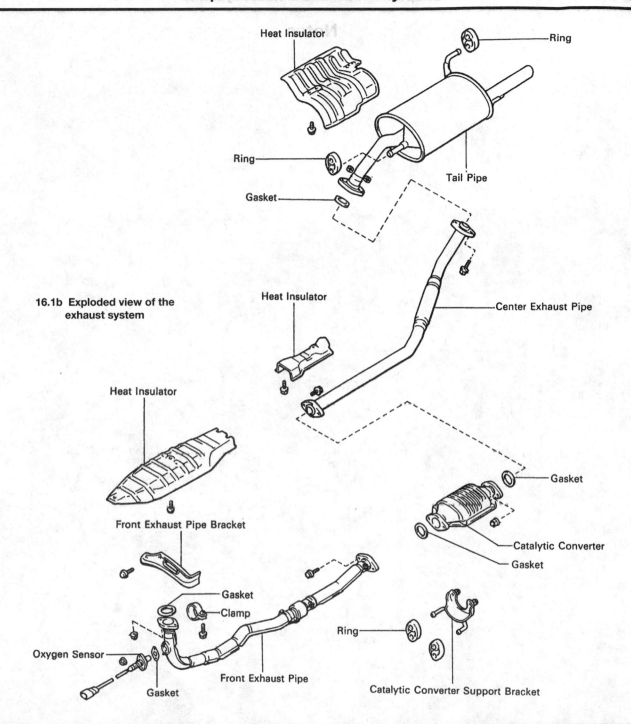

16.1b Exploded view of the exhaust system

3 If the exhaust system components are extremely corroded or rusted together, they will probably have to be cut from the exhaust system. The convenient way to accomplish this is to have a muffler repair shop remove the corroded sections with a cutting torch. If, however, you want to save money by doing it yourself and you don't have an oxy-acetylene welding outfit with a cutting torch), simply cut off the old components with a hack-saw. If you have compressed air, special pneumatic cutting chisels can also be used. If you do decide to tackle the job at home, be sure to wear eye protection to protect your eyes from metal chips and work gloves to protect your hands.

4 Here are some simple guidelines to apply when repairing the exhaust system:

a) *Work from the back to the front when removing exhaust system components.*

b) *Apply penetrating oil to the exhaust system component fasteners to make them easier to remove.*

c) *Use new gaskets, hangers and clamps when installing exhaust system components.*

d) *Apply anti-seize compound to the threads of all exhaust system fasteners during reassembly.*

e) *Be sure to allow sufficient clearance between newly installed parts and all points on the underbody to avoid overheating the floor pan and possibly damaging the interior carpet and insulation. Pay particularly close attention to the catalytic converter and its heat shield.* **Warning:** *The catalytic converter operates at very high temperatures and takes a long time to cool. Wait until it's completely cool before attempting to remove the converter. Failure to do so could result in serious burns.*

Notes

Chapter 5
Engine electrical systems

Contents

Specifications

Ignition timing (all models)
Carbureted models
Without vacuum advance hose connected	3 degrees BTDC
With vacuum advance hose connected	12 to 18 degrees BTDC

1990 through 1993 fuel-injected models
With test terminals T and E1 grounded	10 degrees BTDC
Without test terminals T and E1 grounded	timing fluctuates between 7 and 17 degrees BTDC

1994 fuel-injected models
With test terminals TE1 and E1 grounded	10 degrees BTDC
Without test terminals TE1 and E1 grounded	timing fluctuates between 7 and 17 degrees BTDC

Ignition coil
Primary resistance	0.3 to 0.6 ohms
Secondary resistance	9.0 to 15K ohms

Distributor
Air gap (all models)	0.008 to 0.016 inch

Pick-up coil resistance
Carbureted engines	140 to 180 ohms

1990 fuel-injected engines only
Ne+ to Ne- terminals	140 to 180 ohms
G+ to G- terminals	140 to 180 ohms
1991 and later models	370 to 530 ohms

Charging system

Charging voltage .... 13.9 to 15.1 volts
Standard amperage
    All lights and accessories turned off .... less than 10 amps
    Headlights (hi-beam) and heater blower motor turned on .... 30 amps or more
Alternator brush length
    Standard.. 0.413 inch
    Minimum... 0.059 inch

---

1   General information

Warning: *Some later models are equipped with airbags. The airbag is armed and can deploy (inflate) any time the battery is connected. To prevent accidental deployment (and possible injury), disconnect the negative battery cable whenever working near airbag components. After the battery is disconnected, wait at least 90 seconds before beginning work (the system has a back-up capacitor that must fully discharge). See chapter 12 for more information.*

The engine electrical systems include all ignition, charging and starting components. Because of their engine-related functions, these components are discussed separately from chassis electrical devices such as the lights, the instruments, etc. (which are included in Chapter 12).

Always observe the following precautions when working on the electrical systems:

a) *Be extremely careful when servicing engine electrical components. They are easily damaged if checked, connected or handled improperly.*

b) *Never leave the ignition switch on for long periods of time (10 minutes maximum) with the engine off.*

c) *Don't disconnect the battery cables while the engine is running.*

d) *Maintain correct polarity when connecting a battery cable from another vehicle during jump starting.*

e) *Always disconnect the negative cable first and hook it up last or the battery may be shorted by the tool being used to loosen the cable clamps.*

It's also a good idea to review the safety-related information regarding the engine electrical systems located in the *Safety first* section near the front of this manual before beginning any operation included in this Chapter.

2   Battery - removal and installation

Refer to illustration 2.2

1   Starting with the negative battery terminal, disconnect both cables from the battery terminals. **Caution:** *If the stereo in your vehicle is equipped with an anti-theft system, make sure you have the correct activation code before disconnecting the battery.*

2   Remove the battery hold-down clamp **(see illustration)**.

3   Lift out the battery. Be careful - it's heavy.

4   While the battery is out, inspect the carrier (tray) for corrosion.

5   If you are replacing the battery, make sure to get one that's identical, with the same dimensions, amperage rating, cold cranking rating, etc.

6   Installation is the reverse of removal.

3   Battery - emergency jump starting

Refer to the *Booster battery (jump) starting procedure* at the front of this manual.

4   Battery cables - check and replacement

1   Periodically inspect the entire length of each battery cable for damage, cracked or burned insulation and corrosion. Poor battery cable connections can cause starting problems and decreased engine performance.

2   Check the cable-to-terminal connections at the ends of the cables for cracks, loose wire strands and corrosion. The presence of white, fluffy deposits under the insulation at the cable terminal connection is a sign that the cable is corroded and should be replaced. Check the terminals for distortion, missing mounting bolts and corrosion.

3   When removing the cables, always disconnect the negative cable first and hook it up last or the battery may be shorted by the tool used to loosen the cable clamps. **Caution:** *If the stereo in your vehicle is equipped with an anti-theft system, make sure you have the correct activation code before disconnecting the battery. Even if only the positive cable is being replaced, be sure to disconnect the negative cable from the battery first (see Chapter 1 for further information regarding battery cable removal).*

4   Disconnect the old cables from the battery, then trace each of them to their opposite ends and detach them from the starter solenoid and ground terminals. Note the routing of each cable to ensure correct installation.

5   If you are replacing either or both of the old cables, take them with you when buying new cables. It is vitally important that you replace the cables with identical parts. Cables have characteristics that make them easy to identify: positive cables are usually red, larger in cross-section and have a larger diameter battery post clamp; ground cables are usually black, smaller in cross-section and have a slightly smaller diameter clamp for the negative post.

6   Clean the threads of the solenoid or ground connection with a wire brush to remove rust and corrosion. Apply a light coat of battery

2.2 To remove the battery, detach the negative (first) and positive (last) cables, remove the hold-down strap nuts (arrows) and hold-down strap, then carefully lift the battery out

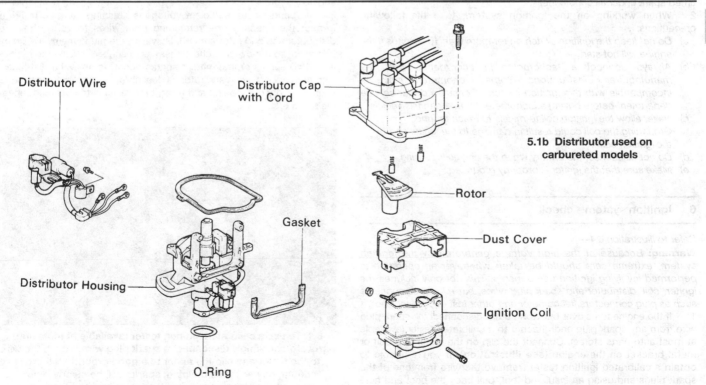

5.1a Schematic of the electronic ignition system on a fuel-injected model. The ignition systems on models with feedback carburetors are identical except the for the design of the distributors

terminal corrosion inhibitor, or petroleum jelly, to the threads to prevent future corrosion.

7   Attach the cable to the solenoid or ground connection and tighten the mounting nut/bolt securely.

8   Before connecting a new cable to the battery, make sure that it reaches the battery post without having to be stretched.

9   Connect the positive cable first, followed by the negative cable.

5   Ignition system - general information and precautions

Refer to illustrations 5.1a, 5.1b and 5.1c

1   The ignition system **(see illustration)** includes the ignition switch, the battery, the igniter, the coil, the primary (low voltage) and secondary (high voltage) wiring circuits, the distributor and the spark plugs **(see illustrations)**. The ignition system is controlled by the

5

5.1b Distributor used on carbureted models

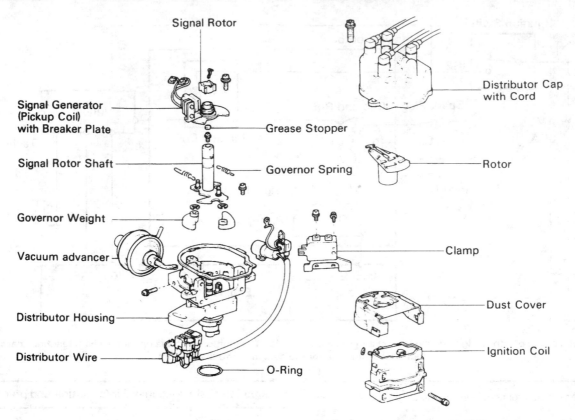

Signal Rotor

Signal Generator (Pickup Coil) with Breaker Plate

Grease Stopper

Signal Rotor Shaft

Governor Spring

Governor Weight

Vacuum advancer

Distributor Housing

Distributor Wire

O-Ring

Distributor Cap with Cord

Rotor

Clamp

Dust Cover

Ignition Coil

5.1c Distributor used on fuel-injected models

Electronic Control Unit (ECM). Using data provided by information sensors which monitor various engine functions (such as rpm, intake air volume, engine temperature, etc.), the ECM ensures a perfectly timed spark under all conditions.

2   When working on the ignition system, take the following precautions:

   a) Do not keep the ignition switch on for more than 10 seconds if the engine will not start.

   b) Always connect a tachometer in accordance with the manufacturer's instructions. Some tachometers may be incompatible with this ignition system. Consult a dealer service department before buying a tachometer for use with this vehicle.

   c) Never allow the ignition coil terminals to touch ground. Grounding the coil could result in damage to the igniter and/or the ignition coil.

   d) Do not disconnect the battery when the engine is running.

   e) Make sure that the igniter is properly grounded.

6   Ignition system - check

Refer to illustration 6.1

Warning: *Because of the high voltage generated by the ignition system, extreme care should be taken whenever an operation is performed involving ignition components. This not only includes the igniter, coil, distributor and spark plug wires, but related components such as plug connectors, tachometer and other test equipment also.*

1   If the engine turns over but won't start, disconnect the spark plug wire from any spark plug and attach it to a calibrated tester (available at most auto parts stores). Connect the clip on the tester to a bolt or metal bracket on the engine **(see illustration)**. If you're unable to obtain a calibrated ignition tester, remove the wire from one of the spark plugs and using an insulated tool, pull back the boot and hold the end of the wire about 1/4-inch from a good ground.

2   Crank the engine and watch the end of the tester or spark plug wire to see if bright blue, well-defined sparks occur.

If you're not using a calibrated tester, have an assistant crank the engine for you.

3   If sparks occur, sufficient voltage is reaching the plug to fire it (repeat the check at the remaining plug wires to verify that the distributor cap and rotor are OK). However, the plugs themselves may be fouled, so remove and check them as described in Chapter 1.

4   If no sparks or intermittent sparks occur, remove the distributor cap and check the cap and rotor as described in Chapter 1. If moisture is present, dry out the cap and rotor, then reinstall the cap and repeat the spark test.

6.1 To use a calibrated ignition tester (available at most auto parts stores), simply disconnect a spark plug wire, attach the wire to the tester and clip the tester to a good ground - if there is enough power to fire the plug, sparks will be clearly visible between the electrode tip and the tester body as the engine is turned over

7.2a Remove the screws (arrows) and . . .

7.2b . . . separate the heat shield from the coil (distributor removed for clarity) (fuel-injected 3E-E engine shown in following sequence)

7.3 Remove the nuts from the coil terminals (arrows)

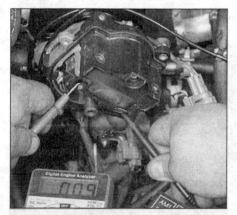
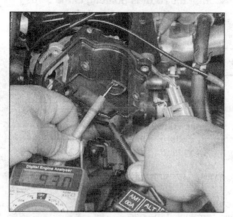

7.4a To check the primary resistance of the coil, measure the resistance between the positive and the negative terminals

7.4b To check the secondary resistance of the coil, measure the resistance between the positive terminal and the high tension terminal

7.9a Remove the retaining screws (arrows) . . .

5   If there's still no spark, detach the coil secondary wire from the distributor cap and hook it up to the tester (reattach the plug wire to the spark plug), then repeat the spark check. Again, if you don't have a tester, hold the end of the wire about 1/4-inch from a good ground.

6   If sparks now occur, the distributor cap, rotor or plug wire(s) may be defective.

7   If no sparks occur, check the primary wire connections at the coil to make sure they're clean and tight. Check for voltage to the coil. Check the coil (see Section 7). Make any necessary repairs, then repeat the check again.

8   If there's still no spark, the coil-to-cap wire may be bad (check the resistance with an ohmmeter and compare it to the spark plug wire resistance Specifications found in Chapter 1). If a known good wire doesn't make any difference in the test results, the igniter may be defective.

7   Ignition coil - check and replacement

Check

Refer to illustrations 7.2a, 7.2b, 7.3, 7.4a and 7.4b

1   Detach the cable from the negative terminal of the battery. **Caution:** *If the stereo in your vehicle is equipped with an anti-theft system, make sure you have the correct activation code before disconnecting the battery.*

2   Raise the vehicle and secure it on jackstands. Remove the heat

shield from the coil **(see illustrations)**.

3   Remove the mounting bolts from the coil electrical connectors **(see illustration)**.

4   Using an ohmmeter, check the coil:

a) *Measure the resistance between the positive and negative terminals* **(see illustration)**. *Compare your reading with the coil primary resistance listed in the Specifications Section at the beginning of this Chapter.*

b) *Measure the resistance between the positive terminal and the high tension terminal* **(see illustration)**. *Compare your reading with the coil secondary resistance listed in the Specifications Section at the beginning of this Chapter.*

5   If either of the above tests yield resistance values outside the specified amount, replace the coil.

Replacement

Refer to illustrations 7.9a and 7.9b

6   Detach the cable from the negative terminal of the battery. **Caution:** *If the stereo in your vehicle is equipped with an anti-theft system, make sure you have the correct activation code before disconnecting the battery.*

7   Remove the heat shield from the coil **(see illustration 7.2a and 7.2b)**.

8   Label and disconnect the wires from the coil terminals.

9   Remove the coil mounting screws **(see illustrations)** and separate the coil from the distributor.

10   Installation is the reverse of removal.

7.9b . . . and lift the coil from the distributor housing (distributor removed for clarity)

8.5a Paint or scribe a mark (arrow) on the edge of the distributor housing immediately below the rotor tip to ensure that the rotor is pointing in the same direction when the distributor is reinstalled

8.5b Paint or scribe another mark across the cylinder head and the distributor body (arrows) to ensure that the distributor is aligned correctly when it is reinstalled

8   Distributor - removal and installation

Removal

Refer to illustrations 8.5a, 8.5b and 8.7

1   Detach the cable from the negative battery terminal. **Caution:** *If the stereo in your vehicle is equipped with an anti-theft system, make sure you have the correct activation code before disconnecting the battery.*

2   Raise the vehicle and secure it on jackstands. Unplug the electrical connectors from the distributor.

3   Look for a raised "1" on the distributor cap. This marks the location for the number one cylinder spark plug wire terminal. If the cap does not have a mark for the number one terminal, locate the number one spark plug and trace the wire back to the terminal on the cap.

4   Remove the distributor cap (see Chapter 1) and turn the engine over until the rotor is pointing toward the number one spark plug terminal (see locating TDC procedure in Chapter 2A).

5   Make a mark on the edge of the distributor base directly below the rotor tip and in line with it. Also, mark the distributor base and the cylinder head to ensure that the distributor is installed correctly **(see illustrations)**.

6   Loosen but do not remove the two bolts in the distributor collar. This will give the distributor shaft clearance.

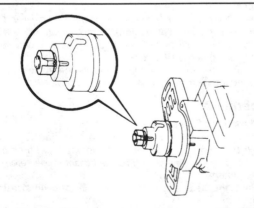

8.8 If you've set the engine at TDC compression for number one cylinder, align the grooved tang of the coupling with the protrusion in the distributor housing

8.7 Remove the hold-down bolt from the distributor body and pull the distributor straight out

7   Remove the distributor hold-down bolt **(see illustration)**, then pull the distributor straight out to remove it. **Caution:** *DO NOT turn the crankshaft while the distributor is out of the engine, or the alignment marks will be useless.*

Installation

If crankshaft has been turned

Refer to illustration 8.8

8   If the crankshaft has been moved while the distributor is out, locate Top Dead Center (TDC) for the number one piston (see Chapter 2A), then align the grooved tang of the coupling with the protrusion on the housing **(see illustration)**. Proceed to Step 11.

If crankshaft has not been turned

9   Insert the distributor into the cylinder head in exactly the same relationship to the cylinder head that it was in when removed.

10   If the distributor does not seat completely, recheck the alignment marks between the distributor base and the block to verify that the distributor is in the same position it was in before removal. Also check the rotor to see if it's aligned with the mark you made on the edge of the distributor base.

11   Loosely install the distributor hold-down bolt(s).

12   The remainder of installation is the reverse of removal.

13   Check the ignition timing (see Section 9) and tighten the distributor hold-down bolt securely.

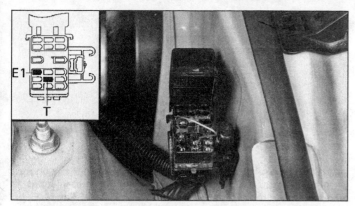

9.2 Install a jumper wire into terminals T and E1 in the check connector in the corner of the engine compartment

9.4 Point the timing light at the timing marks with the engine at idle and set the timing to the correct mark

9   Ignition timing - check and adjustment

Refer to illustrations 9.2 and 9.4

Note: *The following ignition timing procedure should apply to all vehicles covered by this manual. However, if the procedure specified on the VECI label of your vehicle differs from this one, use the one contained on the VECI label.*

1   Connect a tachometer according to the manufacturer's specifications (see Chapter 1).

2   On models equipped with fuel-injected engines, locate the diagnostic electrical connector and insert a jumper wire between terminals E1 and T **(see illustration)**. On carbureted models, disconnect the vacuum hose from the vacuum advance unit and plug the hose.

3   Locate the timing marks on the timing cover and the crankshaft pulley.

4   Start the engine and allow it to warm up to normal operating temperature (upper radiator hose hot). Verify that the engine idle is correct (refer to the Specifications listed in Chapter 1 or to the VECI label). Aim the timing light at the timing scale on the front cover **(see illustration)**. The mark (notch) on the crankshaft pulley should line up with the correct timing mark on the scale. If necessary, loosen the distributor hold-down bolt and slowly rotate the distributor until the timing marks align. Tighten the hold-down bolt and recheck the timing.

5   On fuel-injected engines, remove the jumper wire from the diagnostic connector and confirm the ignition timing fluctuates between 7 and 17 degrees BTDC. On feedback carbureted engines, reconnect the vacuum hose to the vacuum advance unit.

6   Turn the engine off and remove the tachometer and the timing light.

10   Igniter - replacement

Refer to illustration 10.3

1   Detach the cable from the negative terminal of the battery.
Caution: *If the stereo in your vehicle is equipped with an anti-theft system, make sure you have the correct activation code before disconnecting the battery.*

2   Disconnect the electrical connector from the igniter.

3   Remove the screws and detach the igniter from the bracket **(see illustration)**.

4   Installation is the reverse of removal.

11   Air gap - check

Refer to illustration 11.3

1   Detach the cable from the negative terminal of the battery.
Caution: *If the stereo in your vehicle is equipped with an anti-theft system, make sure you have the correct activation code before disconnecting the battery.*

2   Remove the distributor from the engine (see Section 8).

3   Using a brass feeler gauge, measure the gap between the signal rotor and the pick-up coil projection **(see illustration)**. Compare your measurement to the air gap listed in this Chapter's Specifications. If the air gap is not as specified, replace the distributor (the air gap is not adjustable).

5

10.3 Remove the bolts (arrows) that retain the igniter assembly to the firewall in the engine compartment

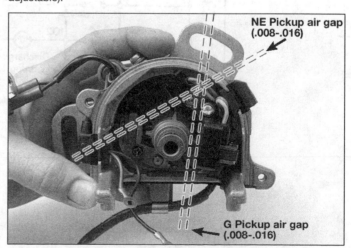

11.3 Measure the air gap between the signal rotor (G pick-up) and the coil projection - if the gap is not within specification, replace the distributor (fuel-injected engine shown). Note that on fuel-injected engines, be sure to check the air gap on the NE pick-up coil, too

12   Pick-up coil - check

Refer to illustrations 12.1

1   Using an ohmmeter, measure the resistance between the pick-up coil terminals **(see illustration)**.

2   Compare the measurements to those listed in the Specifications Section at the beginning of this Chapter. If the resistance is not as specified, replace the distributor.

13   Charging system - general information and precautions

Refer to illustration 13.1

   The charging system includes the alternator, an internal voltage regulator, a charge indicator, the battery, a fusible link and the wiring between all the components. The charging system **(see illustration)** supplies electrical power for the ignition system, the lights, the radio, etc. The alternator is driven by a drivebelt.

   The purpose of the voltage regulator is to limit the alternator's voltage to a preset value. This prevents power surges, circuit overloads, etc., during peak voltage output.

   The fusible link is a short length of insulated wire integral with the engine compartment wiring harness. The link is several wire gauges smaller in diameter than the circuit it protects. Production fusible links and their identification flags are identified by the flag color. See Chapter 12 for additional information regarding fusible links.

   The charging system doesn't ordinarily require periodic maintenance. However, the drivebelt, battery and wires and connections should be inspected at the intervals outlined in Chapter 1.

   The dashboard warning light should come on when the ignition key is turned to Start, then should go off immediately. If it remains on, there is a malfunction in the charging system (see Section 14). Some vehicles are also equipped with a voltage gauge. If the voltage gauge indicates abnormally high or low voltage, check the charging system (see Section 14).

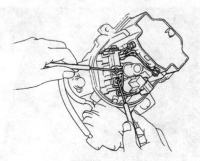

12.1 On carbureted engines, probe the terminals directly on top of the pick-up coil to check the resistance. On fuel-injected engines, check the resistance between terminals NE+ and NE- on the pick-up coil. Follow the terminal designations and the resistance values for the remaining terminals listed in this Chapter's Specifications. On 1990 fuel-injected models, be sure to also check the resistance between G+ and G-

   Be very careful when making electrical circuit connections to a vehicle equipped with an alternator and note the following:

a) *When reconnecting wires to the alternator from the battery, be sure to note the polarity.*

b) *Before using arc welding equipment to repair any part of the vehicle, disconnect the wires from the alternator and the battery terminals.*

c) *Never start the engine with a battery charger connected.*

d) *Always disconnect both battery cables before using a battery charger.*

e) *The alternator is driven by an engine drivebelt which could cause serious injury if your hand, hair or clothes become entangled in it with the engine running.*

f) *Because the alternator is connected directly to the battery, it could arc or cause a fire if overloaded or shorted out.*

g) *Wrap a plastic bag over the alternator and secure it with rubber bands before steam cleaning the engine.*

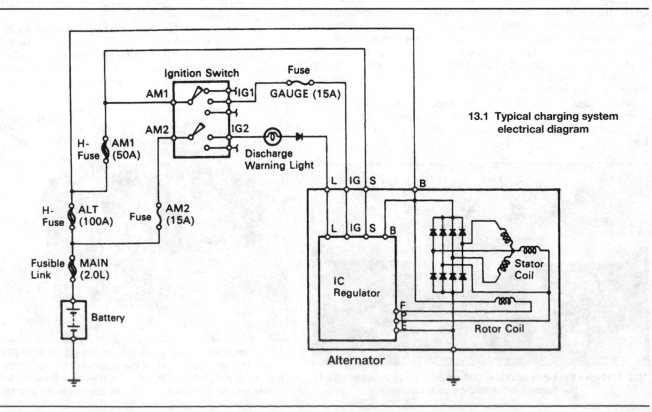

13.1 Typical charging system electrical diagram

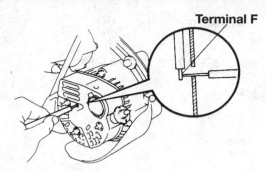

14.7 If the alternator is putting out less than standard voltage, ground terminal F, start the engine and check the voltage at terminal B - if the reading is greater than standard voltage, replace the regulator; if the reading is less than standard, check the alternator or have it checked by a dealer

14 Charging system - check

Refer to illustrations 14.7 and 14.8

1   If a malfunction occurs in the charging circuit, don't automatically assume that the alternator is causing the problem. First check the following items:

a) *Check the drivebelt tension and its condition. Replace it if worn or deteriorated.*

b) *Make sure the alternator mounting and adjustment bolts are tight.*

c) *Inspect the alternator wiring harness and the electrical connectors at the alternator and voltage regulator. They must be in good condition and tight.*

d) *Check the fusible link (if equipped) located between the starter solenoid and the alternator or the large main fuses in the engine compartment. If it's burned, determine the cause, repair the circuit and replace the link or fuse (the vehicle won't start and/or the accessories won't work if the fusible link or fuse blows).*

e) *Start the engine and check the alternator for abnormal noises (a shrieking or squealing sound indicates a bad bushing).*

f) *Check the specific gravity of the battery electrolyte. If it's low, charge the battery (doesn't apply to maintenance free batteries).*

g) *Make sure that the battery is fully charged (one bad cell in a battery can cause overcharging by the alternator).*

h) *Disconnect the battery cables (negative first, then positive).* **Caution:** *If the stereo in your vehicle is equipped with an anti-theft system, make sure you have the correct activation code before disconnecting the battery. Inspect the battery posts and the cable clamps for corrosion. Clean them thoroughly if necessary (see Section 4 and Chapter 1). Reconnect the cable to the positive terminal.*

i) *With the key off, insert a test light between the negative battery post and the disconnected negative cable clamp.*

  1) *If the test light does not come on, reattach the clamp and proceed to the next step.*

  2) *If the test light comes on, there is a short in the electrical system of the vehicle. The short must be repaired before the charging system can be checked.*

  3) *Disconnect the alternator wiring harness.*

    a) *If the light goes out, the alternator is bad.*

    b) *If the light stays on, pull each fuse until the light goes out (this will tell you which component is shorted).*

2   Using a voltmeter, check the battery voltage with the engine off. It should be approximately 12-volts.

3   Start the engine and check the battery voltage again. It should now be approximately 13.5 to 15.1-volts.

4   Turn on the headlights. The voltage should drop and then come back up, if the charging system is working properly.

5   If the voltage reading is greater than the specified charging voltage, replace the voltage regulator (see Section 16).

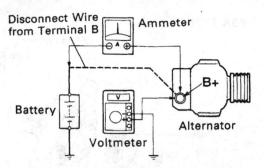

14.8 Hook up an ammeter as shown to check alternator output

6   If the voltmeter reading is less than standard voltage, check the regulator and alternator as follows.

7   Remove the rear cover from the alternator. Ground terminal F, start the engine, check the voltage at terminal B **(see illustration)** and compare your reading to the standard voltage.

a) *If the voltmeter reading is greater than standard voltage, replace the regulator.*

b) *If the voltmeter reading is less than standard voltage, check the alternator (or have it checked by a dealer service department if you do not have an ammeter).*

8   If you have an ammeter, hook it up to the charging system as shown **(see illustration)**. If you don't have a professional ammeter, you can also use an inductive-type current indicator. This device is inexpensive, readily available at auto parts stores and accurate enough to perform simple amperage checks like the following test.

9   With the engine running at 2000 rpm, check the reading on the ammeter with all accessories and lights off, then again with the high-beam headlights on and the heater blower switch turned to the HI position. Compare your readings to the standard amperage listed in this Chapter's Specifications.

10   If the ammeter reading is less than standard amperage, repair or replace the alternator.

15 Alternator - removal and installation

Refer to illustration 15.3

1   Detach the cable from the negative terminal of the battery. **Caution:** *If the stereo in your vehicle is equipped with an anti-theft system, make sure you have the correct activation code before disconnecting the battery.*

2   Detach the electrical connectors from the alternator.

3   Loosen the alternator adjustment and pivot bolts **(see illustration)** and detach the drivebelt.

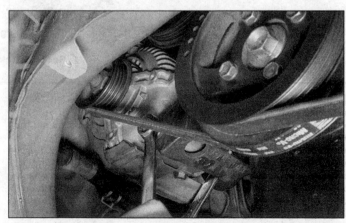

15.3 First loosen the pivot bolt, then turn out the adjustment bolt using a wrench to release the tension on the drivebelt

5

50A TYPE

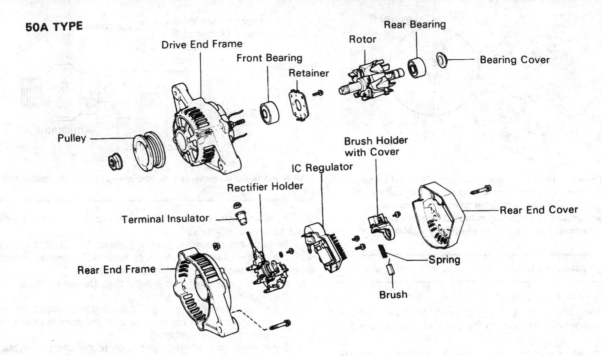

55A, 60A TYPE

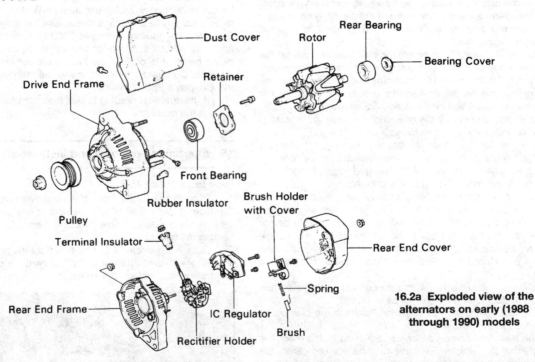

16.2a Exploded view of the alternators on early (1988 through 1990) models

4　Remove the adjustment and pivot bolts from the alternator adjustment bracket.

5　Remove the two bracket-to-water pump bolts and separate the alternator and bracket from the engine.

6　If you are replacing the alternator, take the old alternator with you when purchasing a replacement unit. Make sure that the new/rebuilt unit is identical to the old alternator. Look at the terminals - they should be the same in number, size and locations as the terminals on the old alternator. Finally, look at the identification markings - they will be stamped in the housing or printed on a tag or plaque affixed to the housing. Make sure that these numbers are the same on both alternators.

7　Many new/rebuilt alternators do not have a pulley installed, so you may have to switch the pulley from the old unit to the new/rebuilt one. When buying an alternator, find out the shop's policy regarding installation of pulleys - some shops will perform this service free of charge.

8　Be sure the ground strap makes a strong and clean connection to the body of the alternator as well as the engine block.

9　Installation is the reverse of removal.

10　After the alternator is installed, adjust the drivebelt tension (see Chapter 1).

11　Check the charging voltage to verify proper operation of the alternator (see Section 14).

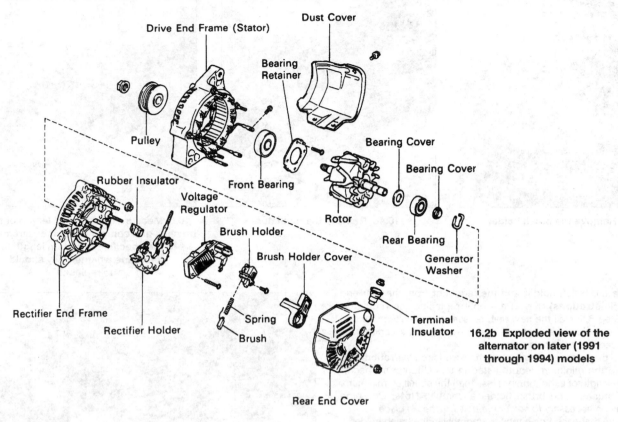

16.2b Exploded view of the alternator on later (1991 through 1994) models

Drive End Frame (Stator)
Dust Cover
Bearing Retainer
Bearing Cover
Bearing Cover
Pulley
Front Bearing
Rotor
Rear Bearing
Generator Washer
Rubber Insulator
Voltage Regulator
Brush Holder
Brush Holder Cover
Rectifier End Frame
Rectifier Holder
Spring
Brush
Terminal Insulator
Rear End Cover

16 Voltage regulator and alternator brushes - replacement

Refer to illustrations 16.2a, 16.2b, 16.2c, 16.2d, 16.3, 16.4a, 16.4b, 16.5 and 16.7

1   Remove the alternator (see Section 15) and place it on a clean workbench.

2   Remove the three rear cover nuts, the nut and terminal insulator and the rear cover **(see illustrations)**.

3   Remove the five voltage regulator and brush holder mounting screws **(see illustration)**.

16.2c Remove the three nuts from the rear cover

16.2d Take the nut, washer and insulator off terminal B and remove the alternator end cover

16.3 Once the rear cover is removed, remove the five screws (arrows) that retain the voltage regulator and the brush holder

5

16.4a Remove the brush holder

16.4b Remove the regulator

16.5 Measure the exposed length of the brushes and compare your measurements to the specified minimum length to determine whether they should be replaced

4   Remove the brush holder and the regulator from the rear end frame **(see illustrations)**. If you are only replacing the regulator, proceed to Step 8, install the new unit, reassemble the alternator and install it on the engine (see Section 15). If you are going to replace the brushes, proceed with the next Step.

5   Measure the exposed length of each brush **(see illustration)** and compare it to the minimum length listed in this Chapter's Specifications. If the length of either brush is less than the specified minimum, replace the brushes and brush holder assembly. **Note:** *On some models it may be necessary to solder the new brushes in place.*

6   Make sure that each brush moves smoothly in the brush holder.

7   Install the brush holder by depressing each brush with a small screwdriver to clear the shaft **(see illustration)**.

8   Install the voltage regulator and brush holder screws into the rear frame.

9   Install the rear cover and tighten the three nuts securely.

10   Install the terminal insulator and tighten it with the nut.

11   Install the alternator (see Section 15).

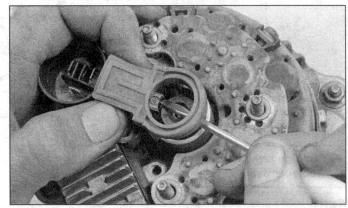

16.7 To install the brush holder, depress each brush with a small screwdriver to clear the shaft

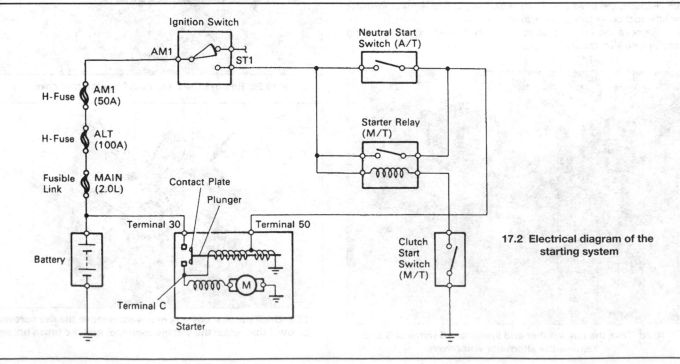

17.2 Electrical diagram of the starting system

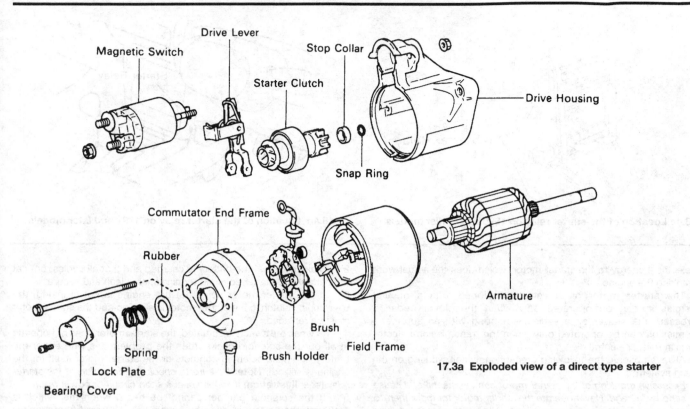

17.3a **Exploded view of a direct type starter**

17 Starting system - general information and precautions

Refer to Illustrations 17.2, 17.3a and 17.3b

The sole function of the starting system is to turn over the engine quickly enough to allow it to start.

The starting system consists of the battery, the starter motor, the starter solenoid and the wires connecting them **(see illustration)**. The

solenoid is mounted directly on the starter motor.

The solenoid/starter motor assembly **(see illustrations)** is Installed on the upper part of the engine, next to the transmission bellhousing.

When the ignition key is turned to the Start position, the starter solenoid is actuated through the starter control circuit. The starter solenoid then connects the battery to the starter. The battery supplies

5

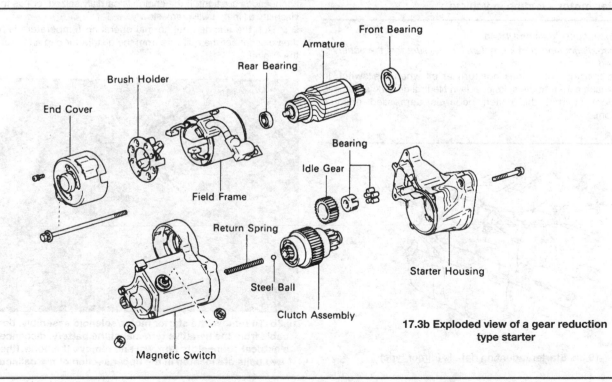

17.3b **Exploded view of a gear reduction type starter**

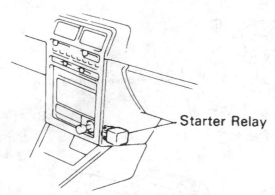

18.4a Location of the starter relay on 1990 and earlier models

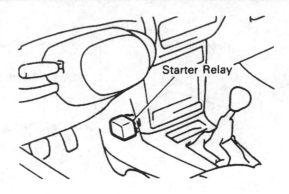

18.4b Location of the starter relay on 1991 and later models

the electrical energy to the starter motor, which does the actual work of cranking the engine.

The starter motor on a vehicle equipped with a manual transmission can be operated only when the clutch pedal is depressed; the starter on a vehicle equipped with an automatic transmission can be operated only when the transmission selector lever is in Park or Neutral.

Always observe the following precautions when working on the starting system:

a) *Excessive cranking of the starter motor can overheat it and cause serious damage. Never operate the starter motor for more than 15 seconds at a time without pausing to allow it to cool for at least two minutes.*

b) *The starter is connected directly to the battery and could arc or cause a fire if mishandled, overloaded or shorted out.*

c) *Always detach the cable from the negative terminal of the battery before working on the starting system.* **Caution:** *If the stereo in your vehicle is equipped with an anti-theft system, make sure you have the correct activation code before disconnecting the battery.*

18 Starter motor - testing in vehicle

Refer to illustrations 18.4a and 18.4b
Note: *Before diagnosing starter problems, make sure that the battery is fully charged.*

1   If the starter motor does not turn at all when the switch is operated, make sure that the shift lever is in Neutral or Park (automatic transmission) or that the clutch pedal is depressed (manual transmission).

2   Make sure that the battery is charged and that all cables, both at the battery and starter solenoid terminals, are clean and secure.
3   If the starter motor spins but the engine is not cranking, the overrunning clutch in the starter motor is slipping and the starter motor must be replaced.
4   If, when the switch is actuated, the starter motor does not operate at all but the solenoid clicks, then the problem lies with either the battery, the main solenoid contacts or the starter motor itself (or the engine is seized). **Note:** *Be sure to check the operation of the starter relay* **(see illustration)** *if you suspect a short circuit or power failure.*
5   If the solenoid plunger cannot be heard when the switch is actuated, the battery is bad, the fusible link is burned (the circuit is open) or the solenoid itself is defective.
6   To check the solenoid, connect a jumper lead between the battery (+) and the ignition switch terminal (the small terminal) on the solenoid. If the starter motor now operates, the solenoid is OK and the problem is in the ignition switch, Neutral start switch or in the wiring.
7   If the starter motor still does not operate, remove the starter/solenoid assembly for disassembly, testing and repair.
8   If the starter motor cranks the engine at an abnormally slow speed, first make sure that the battery is charged and that all terminal connections are tight. If the engine is partially seized, or has the wrong viscosity oil in it, it will crank slowly.
9   Run the engine until normal operating temperature is reached, then disconnect the coil wire from the distributor cap and ground it on the engine.

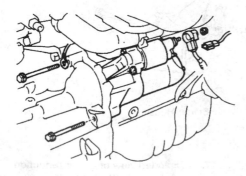

19.3a Starter mounting details (direct type)

19.3b To remove the starter motor/solenoid assembly, detach the cable from the negative terminal of the battery, disconnect the electrical connectors (arrows) and remove the bolts (the other two bolts are located in the upper section of the bellhousing)

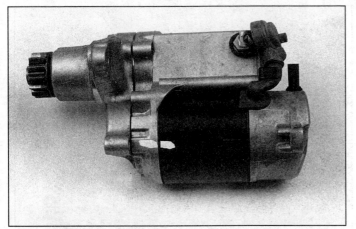

20.2 Before disassembling the starter motor, solenoid and gear reduction assembly, scribe or paint an alignment mark across the starter motor and the gear reduction assembly

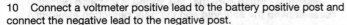

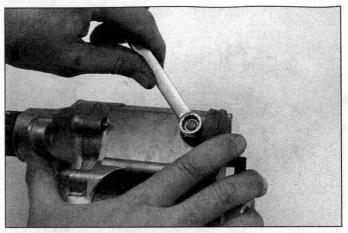

20.3 To disconnect the strap that connects the starter to the solenoid, remove this nut

10   Connect a voltmeter positive lead to the battery positive post and connect the negative lead to the negative post.

11   Crank the engine and take the voltmeter readings as soon as a steady figure is indicated. Do not allow the starter motor to turn for more than 15 seconds at a time. A reading of nine volts or more, with the starter motor turning at normal cranking speed, is normal. If the reading is nine volts or more but the cranking speed is slow, the motor is faulty. If the reading is less than nine volts and the cranking speed is slow, the solenoid contacts are probably burned, the starter motor is bad, the battery is discharged or there is a bad connection.

19 Starter motor - removal and installation

Refer to illustrations 19.3a and 19.3b

1   Detach the cable from the negative terminal of the battery. **Caution:** *If the stereo in your vehicle is equipped with an anti-theft system, make sure you have the correct activation code before disconnecting the battery.*

2   Detach the electrical connectors from the starter/solenoid assembly.

3   Remove the starter motor mounting bolts **(see illustrations)**. **Note:** *If equipped with a manual transmission, it may be necessary to remove the clutch release cylinder. Remove the mounting bolts (see Chapter 8) and move the cylinder aside, but DO NOT disconnect the hydraulic line.*

4   Remove the bracket from the upper section of the starter/solenoid assembly. **Note:** *It is necessary to loosen one or two of the bracket bolts to allow the starter/solenoid assembly to partially drop down to gain access to the remaining bracket assembly bolts and hardware.*

5   Installation is the reverse of removal.

20 Starter solenoid - removal and installation

1   Remove the starter motor (see Section 19).

Gear reduction type

Refer to illustrations 20.2, 20.3, 20.4, 20.5, 20.6a and 20.6b

2   Scribe or paint a mark across the starter motor and gear reduction assembly **(see illustration)**.

3   Disconnect the strap from the solenoid to the starter motor terminal **(see illustration)**.

4   Remove the screws **(see illustration)** which secure the gear reduction assembly to the solenoid.

5   Remove the through-bolts **(see illustration)** which secure the

20.4 To detach the solenoid from the starter motor, remove the screws (arrows) which secure the gear reduction assembly to the solenoid . . .

20.5 . . . then remove the through-bolts (arrows) which secure the starter motor to the gear reduction assembly

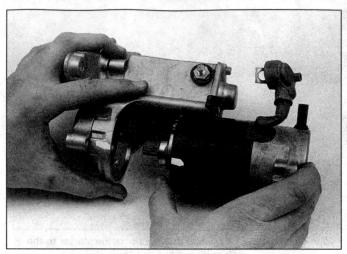

20.6a   Separate the starter from the gear reduction assembly . . .

20.6b   . . . then separate the solenoid from the gear reduction assembly (note the return spring protruding from the solenoid assembly - make sure that this spring is installed before reassembling the solenoid and the gear reduction assembly)

starter motor to the gear reduction assembly.

6   Separate the motor from the gear reduction and solenoid assembly then remove the solenoid from the gear reduction assembly **(see illustrations)**.

7   Installation is the reverse of removal. Be sure to align the paint or scribe mark.

Direct type

Refer to illustration 20.9

8   Remove the nut and disconnect the lead wire from the solenoid electrical terminal.

9   Remove the two bolts from the solenoid and separate the solenoid from the starter assembly **(see illustration)**.

10   Installation is the reverse of removal.

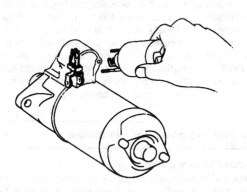

20.9   Carefully unhook the solenoid and remove it from the starter assembly

Chapter 6
Emissions and engine control systems

Contents

Specifications

EGR gas temperature sensor resistance	
122-degrees F	69 to 89K ohms
212-degrees F	11 to 15K ohms
302-degrees F	2 to 4K ohms

1   General information

Refer to illustrations 1.1a through 1.1d

To minimize pollution of the atmosphere from incompletely burned and evaporating gases and to maintain good driveability and fuel economy, a number of emission control systems are used on these vehicles **(see illustrations)**. They include the:

Positive Crankcase Ventilation (PCV) system
Evaporative Emission Control (EVAP) system
Exhaust Gas Recirculation (EGR) system
Three-way catalytic converter (TWC) system
Electronic Fuel Injection (EFI) system
Feedback carburetor system
Air suction (AS) system
Spark control (SC) system
Throttle positioner (TP) system
High Altitude Compensation (HAC) system
Auxiliary systems:
Hot Air Intake (HAI)
Hot idle compensation (HIC)
Number 1 cold enrichment breaker system
Number 2 cold enrichment breaker system
Deceleration fuel cut system
Cold mixture heater (CMH) and fuel heater system

The sections in this chapter include general descriptions, checking procedures within the scope of the home mechanic and component replacement procedures (when possible) for each of the systems listed above.

Before assuming an emissions control system is malfunctioning, check the fuel and ignition systems carefully (see Chapters 4 and 5). The diagnosis of some emission control devices requires specialized tools, equipment and training. If checking and servicing become too difficult or if a procedure is beyond the scope of your skills, consult your dealer service department or other repair shop.

This doesn't mean, however, that emission control systems are particularly difficult to maintain and repair. You can quickly and easily perform many checks and do most of the regular maintenance at home with common tune-up and hand tools. **Note:** *The most frequent cause of emissions problems is simply a loose or broken electrical connector or vacuum hose, so always check the electrical connectors and vacuum hoses first.*

Pay close attention to any special precautions outlined in this chapter. It should be noted that the illustrations of the various systems may not exactly match the system installed on your vehicle because of changes made by the manufacturer during production or from year-to-year.

The Vehicle Emissions Control Information (VECI) label and a vacuum hose diagram are located on the underside of the hood. These contain important emissions specifications and setting procedures, and a vacuum hose schematic with emissions components identified. When servicing the engine or emissions systems, the VECI label in your particular vehicle should always be checked for up-to-date information.

2   Electronic control system - general information and ECU removal and installation

TCCS general information

1   The Toyota Computer Control System (TCCS) controls the fuel injection system by means of a microcomputer known as the Engine Control Unit (ECU) **(see illustration 3.29 in Chapter 4)**.

2   The ECU receives signals from various sensors which monitor changing engine operating conditions such as intake air volume, intake air temperature, coolant temperature, engine rpm, acceleration/deceleration, exhaust oxygen content, etc. These signals are utilized by the ECU to determine the correct injection duration.

3   The system is analogous to the central nervous system in the human body: The sensors (nerve endings) constantly relay signals to the ECU (brain), which processes the data and, if necessary, sends out a command to change the operating parameters of the engine (body).

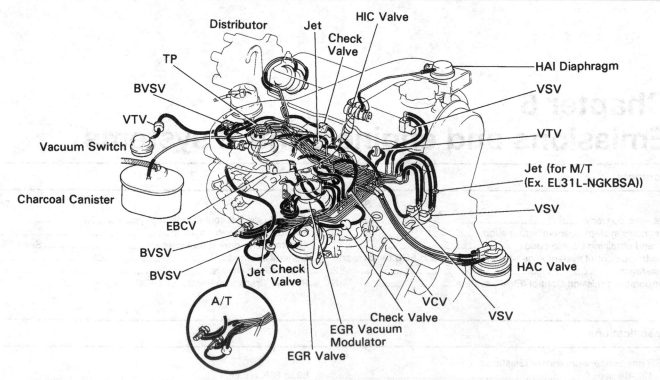

1.1a Emission control components and locations for feedback carburetor systems (1990 and earlier Federal and Canada models)

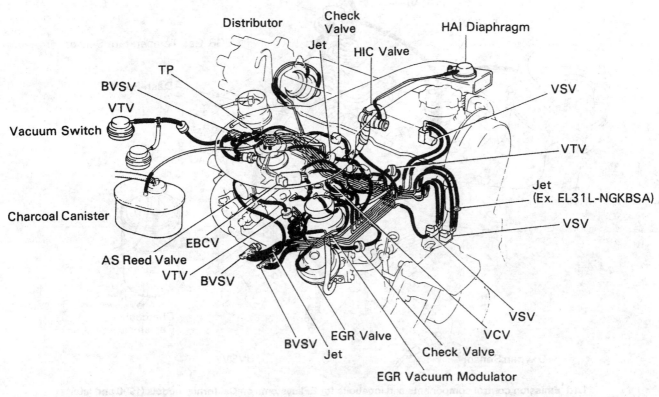

1.1b Emission control components and locations for feedback carburetor systems on California models (1990 and earlier)

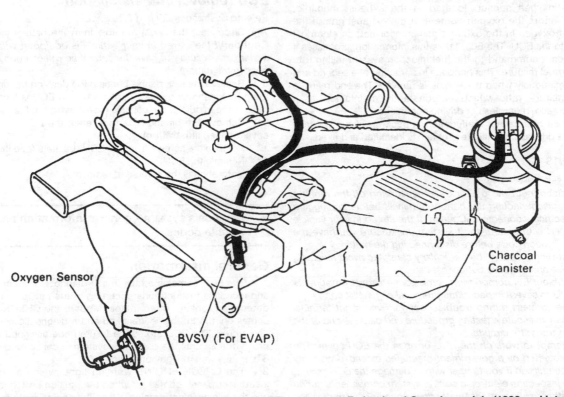

1.1c Emission control components and locations for EFI systems on Federal and Canada models (1990 and later)

6

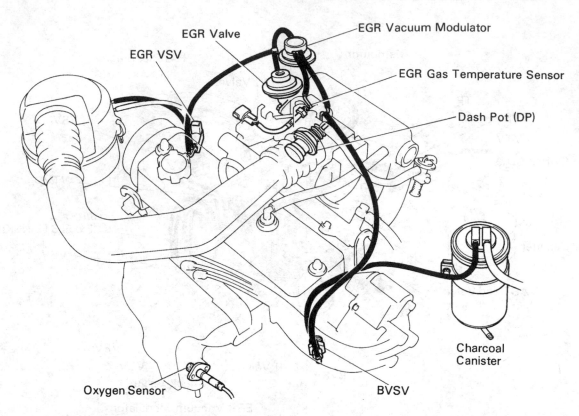

1.1d Emission control components and locations for EFI systems on California models (1990 and later)

4   Here's a specific example of how one portion of this system operates: An oxygen sensor, located in the exhaust manifold, constantly monitors the oxygen content of the exhaust gas. If the percentage of oxygen in the exhaust gas is incorrect, an electrical signal is sent to the ECU. The ECU takes this information, processes it and then sends a command to the fuel injection system telling it to change the air/fuel mixture. This happens in a fraction of a second and it goes on continuously when the engine is running. The end result is an air/fuel mixture ratio which is constantly maintained at a predetermined ratio, regardless of driving conditions.

5   In the event of a sensor malfunction, a back-up circuit will take over to provide driveability until the problem is identified and fixed.

Precautions

6   Follow these steps:

a) *Always disconnect the power by either turning off the ignition switch or disconnecting the battery terminals before unplugging TCCS electrical connectors. Caution: If the stereo in your vehicle is equipped with an anti-theft system, make sure you have the correct activation code before disconnecting the battery.*

b) *When installing a battery, be particularly careful to avoid reversing the positive and negative battery cables.*

c) *Do not subject EFI components, emissions-related components or the ECU to severe impact during removal or installation.*

d) *Do not be careless during troubleshooting. Even slight terminal contact can invalidate a testing procedure and damage one of the numerous transistor circuits.*

e) *Never attempt to work on the ECU or open the ECU cover. The ECU is protected by a government-mandated extended warranty that will be nullified if you tamper with or damage the ECU.*

f) *If you are inspecting electronic control system components during rainy weather, make sure that water does not enter any part. When washing the engine compartment, do not spray these parts or their electrical connectors with water.*

ECU removal and installation

Refer to illustrations 2.9 and 2.10

7   Disconnect the negative cable from the battery (see Chapter 5). **Caution:** *If the stereo in your vehicle is equipped with an anti-theft system, make sure you have the correct activation code before disconnecting the battery.*

8   Remove the kick panels beneath the dash on the driver's side and the passenger's side (see Chapter 11). The ECU is located under the radio in the middle of the console **(see illustration 3.29a in Chapter 4).**

9   Remove the plastic nuts that retain the ECU cover and lift the cover off **(see illustration).**

10   Remove the screws from the ECU brackets **(see illustration).**

11   Remove the ECU.

12   Installation is the reverse of removal.

---

3   Diagnosis system - general information and obtaining trouble codes

---

General information

1   The ECU contains a built-in self-diagnosis system which detects and identifies malfunctions occurring in the network. When the ECU detects a problem, three things happen: the CHECK ENGINE light comes on, the trouble is identified and a diagnostic code is recorded and stored. The ECU stores the failure code assigned to the specific problem area until the diagnosis system is canceled by removing the STOP fuse with the ignition switch off.

2   The CHECK ENGINE warning light, which is located on the instrument panel, comes on when the ignition switch is turned to On and the engine is not running. When the engine is started, the warning light should go out. If the light remains on, the diagnosis system has detected a malfunction in the system.

2.9 First, remove the plastic nuts (arrow) from the plastic cover and remove the cover . . .

2.10 . . . then remove the mounting screws (arrows) from the ECU bracket

Obtaining diagnosis code output

Refer to illustration 3.5

3   To obtain an output of diagnostic codes, verify first that the battery voltage is above 11 volts, the throttle is fully closed, the transaxle is in Neutral, the accessory switches are off and the engine is at normal operating temperature.

4   Turn the ignition switch to On. Do not start the engine.

5   Use a jumper wire to bridge terminals T and E1 of the check connector under the hood **(see illustration)**.

6   Read the diagnosis code as indicated by the number of flashes of the CHECK ENGINE light on the dash. Normal system operation is indicated by Code No. 1 (no malfunctions) for all models. The CHECK ENGINE light displays a Code No. 1 by blinking once every 1/4-second.

7   If there are any malfunctions in the system, their corresponding trouble codes are stored in computer memory and the light will blink the requisite number of times for the indicated trouble codes. If there's more than one trouble code in the memory, they'll be displayed in numerical order (from lowest to highest) with a pause between each one. After the code with the largest number of flashes has been displayed, there will be another pause and then the sequence will begin all over again. **Note:** *On 1991 and later models, the diagnostic trouble codes 25, 26 and 71 apply to California models only and use a special diagnostic capability called "two trip detection logic". With this system, when a malfunction is first detected, it is temporarily stored into the ECU on the first test drive or "trip." The engine must be turned OFF and the*

vehicle taken on another test drive "trip" to allow the malfunction to be stored permanently in the ECU. This will distinguish a true problem from a false alarm on vehicles with these particular codes entered into the ECU. Normally the self diagnosis system will detect the malfunctions, but in the event the home mechanic wants to double-check the diagnosis by canceling the codes and rechecking, then it will be necessary to go on two test drives to determine any malfunctions with these particular codes.

8   To ensure correct interpretation of the blinking CHECK ENGINE light, watch carefully for the interval between the end of one code and the beginning of the next; otherwise, you will become confused by the apparent number of blinks and misinterpret the display (the length of this interval varies with the model year).

Canceling a diagnostic code

Refer to illustration 3.9

9   After the malfunctioning component has been repaired/replaced, the trouble code(s) stored in computer memory must be canceled. To accomplish this, simply remove the 15A EFI fuse on fuel injected models **(see illustration 2.3a in Chapter 4)** or the 15A RADIO fuse **(see illustration)** on carbureted models for at least 30 seconds with the ignition switch off (the lower the temperature, the longer the fuse must be left out).

10   A stored code can also be canceled by removing the cable from the battery negative terminal, but other memory systems (such as the clock and radio preset stations) will also be canceled. **Caution:** *If the stereo in your vehicle is equipped with an anti-theft system, make sure you have the correct activation code before disconnecting the battery.*

11   If the diagnosis code is not canceled, it will be stored by the ECU and appear with any new codes in the event of future trouble.

12   Should it become necessary to work on engine components requiring removal of the battery terminal, always check to see if a diagnostic code has been recorded before disconnecting the battery.

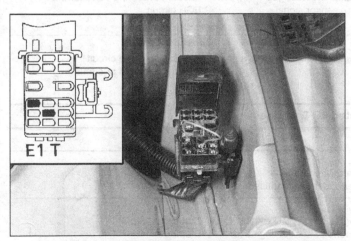

3.5 To access the self-diagnosis system, locate the check connector on the left side of the engine compartment and, using a jumper wire or paper clip, bridge terminals T and E1

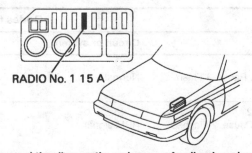

RADIO No. 1 15 A

3.9 To cancel the diagnostic codes on a feedback carburetor model, remove the 15A RADIO fuse from the panel

6

Codes for carbureted 3-E engines

Code	Circuit or system	Diagnosis	Trouble area
Code 1 1 Flash, Pause, 1 Flash	Normal	This appears when none of the other codes are identified	
Code 12 1 Flash, Pause, 2 Flashes	RPM signal	No "Ne" signal to the ECU within several seconds after the engine is cranked.	* Distributor circuit * Distributor * Starter circuit * ECU
Code 21 2 Flashes, Pause, 1 Flash	Oxygen sensor	Problem in the oxygen sensor circuit	* Main oxygen sensor circuit * ECU
Code 22 2 Flashes, Pause, 2 Flashes	Coolant temperature sensor(s)	Open or short in the coolant temperature sensor circuit	* Number 1 or 2 temperature sensor circuit(s) * Number 1 or 2 temperature sensor(s) * ECU
Code 25 2 Flashes, Pause, 5 Flashes	Air/fuel ratio lean malfunction	Open circuit in the oxygen sensor signal EBCV always open	* Oxygen sensor or circuit * ECU * Air leak * Air intake system
Code 26 2 Flashes, Pause, 6 Flashes	Air/fuel ratio rich malfunction	EBCV always closed or a possible clogged hose Open or short circuit in the oxygen sensor	* Coolant temperature sensor or circuit * Oxygen sensor or circuit * ECU * Carburetor
Code 31 3 Flashes, Pause, 1 Flash	Vacuum switch signal	Open or short circuit detected in vacuum switches	* Number 1 or number 2 vacuum switches signal * Number 1 or number 2 vacuum switches defective
Code 41 4 Flashes, Pause, 1 Flash	Throttle position sensor	Open or short in the throttle position sensor circuit	* Throttle position sensor or circuit * ECU
Code 71 7 Flashes, Pause, 1 Flash	EGR system	EGR valve normally closed or a clogged vacuum line Open circuit in the EGR gas temperature sensor signal	* EGR system (EGR valve, hoses, etc.) * EGR gas temperature sensor or circuit * Vacuum switching valve for the * EGR circuit * ECU
Code 72 7 Flashes, Pause, 2 Flashes	Fuel cut solenoid	Open circuit in fuel cut solenoid signal	* Fuel cut solenoid circuit * Fuel cut solenoid or circuit * ECU

Codes for fuel-injected 3E-E engines

Code	Circuit or system	Diagnosis	Trouble area
Code 1 1 Flash, Pause, 1 Flash	Normal	This appears when none of the other codes are identified	
Code 12 Flash, Pause, 2 Flashes	RPM signal	No "Ne" signal to the ECU within several seconds after the engine is cranked.	* Distributor circuit * Distributor * Starter circuit * ECU

Codes for fuel-injected 3E-E engines

Code	Circuit or system	Diagnosis	Trouble area
Code 13 1 Flash, Pause, 3 Flashes	RPM signal	No "Ne" signal to the ECU engine speed is above 1,000 rpm	* Distributor circuit * Distributor * ECU
Code 14 1 Flash, Pause, 4 Flashes	Ignition signal	No "IGF" signal to the ECU 4 times in succession	* Igniter circuit * Igniter * ECU
Code 21 2 Flashes, Pause, 1 Flash	Main oxygen sensor (two-trip detection logic on 1991 and later models)	Problem in the oxygen sensor circuit	* Oxygen sensor circuit * ECU
Code 22 2 Flashes, Pause, 2 Flashes	Coolant temperature sensor	Open or short in the coolant temperature sensor circuit	* Coolant temperature sensor circuit * Coolant temperature sensor * ECU
Code 24 2 Flashes, Pause, 4 Flashes	Intake air temperature sensor	Open or short in the intake air sensor sensor circuit	* Intake air temperature sensor * Intake air temperature * ECU
Code 25 2 Flashes, Pause, 5 Flashes	Air/fuel ratio lean malfunction (two-trip detection logic on 1991 and later models)	The air/fuel ratio feedback correction value or adaptive control value continues at the upper (lean) or lower (rich) limit for a certain period of time	* Injector or injector circuit * Oxygen sensor or circuit * ECU * Fuel line pressure (injector blockage or leakage) * Coolant temperature sensor or circuit * Air temperature sensor or circuit * Air leak * Airflow meter * Air intake system * Ignition system
Code 26 2 Flashes, Pause, 6 Flashes	Air/fuel ratio rich malfunction (California models only) (two-trip detection logic on 1991 and later models)	The air/fuel ratio is overly rich. Open or short circuit in the oxygen sensor	* Injector or injector circuit * Coolant temperature sensor or circuit * Air temperature sensor or circuit * Airflow meter * Oxygen sensor or circuit * Cold start injector * ECU
Code 31 3 Flashes, Pause, 1 Flash	MAP (Manifold Absolute Pressure) sensor	Open or short circuit detected continuously for 0.5 seconds or more in MAP sensor circuit	* Open or shorted circuit in MAP sensor system
Code 41 4 Flashes, Pause, 1 Flash	Throttle position sensor	Open or short in the throttle position sensor circuit	* Throttle position sensor or circuit * ECU
Code 42 4 Flashes, Pause, 2 Flashes	Vehicle speed sensor	No "SPD" signal for 8 seconds when the engine speed is above 2000 rpm	* Vehicle speed sensor or circuit * ECU
Code 43 4 Flashes, Pause, 3 Flashes	Starter signal	No "STA" signal to the ECU until engine speed reaches 800 rpm with the vehicle not moving	* Starter signal circuit * Ignition switch * Main relay switch * ECU

6

Codes for fuel-injected 3E-E engines

Code	Circuit or system	Diagnosis	Trouble area
Code 51 5 Flashes, Pause, 1 Flash	Switch condition signal	No IDL signal or no NSW signal or A/C signal to the ECU when the test connector E1 and T are connected	* A/C switch or circuit * A/C amplifier * Neutral start switch (A/T) * Throttle position sensor * ECU
Code 71 7 Flashes, Pause, 1 Flash	EGR system (California models only) (two-trip detection logic on 1991 and later models)	EGR gas temperature signal is too low	* EGR system (EGR valve, hoses, etc.) * EGR gas temperature sensor or circuit * Vacuum switching valve for the * EGR circuit * ECU

4   Information sensors

Caution: *The following tests must be performed with a high-impedance digital multi-meter.*
Note 1: *Most of the components described in this section are protected by a Federally mandated extended warranty. See your dealer for the details regarding your vehicle. It therefore makes little sense to either check or replace any of these parts yourself as long as they are still under warranty. However, once the warranty has expired, you may wish to perform some of the component checks and/or replacement procedures in this Chapter to save money.*
Note 2: *Refer to Chapters 4 and 5 for additional information on the location and the diagnostics of the information sensors that are not directly covered in this section.*

Coolant temperature sensor

General description
Refer to illustrations 4.2 and 4.3

1   The coolant temperature sensor is a thermistor (a resistor which varies the value of its voltage output in accordance with temperature changes). The change in the resistance values will directly affect the voltage signal from the sensor. As the sensor temperature DECREASES, the resistance values will INCREASE. As the sensor temperature INCREASES, the resistance values will DECREASE. A failure in this sensor circuit should set a Code 22. This code indicates a failure in the water thermosensor circuit, so in most cases the appropriate solution to the problem will be either repair of a connector or wire, or replacement of the sensor.

Check

2   To check the sensor, measure its resistance value **(see illustration)** while it is completely cold (50 to 80-degrees F = 2,200 to 2,700 ohms). Next, start the engine and warm it up until it reaches operating temperature. The resistance should be lower (180 to 200-degrees F = 280 to 350 ohms). **Note:** *Limited access to the coolant temperature sensor makes it difficult to position electrical probes on the terminals. If necessary, remove the sensor and perform the tests in a pan of heated water to simulate the conditions. Compare the resistance values with the accompanying graph.* **Note:** *you'll need a cooking thermometer to monitor the water temperature.*
3   If the resistance values of the coolant temperature sensor are correct, check the circuit for the proper signal voltage. Turn the ignition key ON (engine not running) and check for signal voltage **(see illustration)**. It should be approximately 5 volts.

Replacement

Warning: *The engine must be completely cool before beginning this procedure.*
4   Before installing the new sensor, wrap the threads with Teflon sealing tape to prevent leakage and thread corrosion.
5   To remove the sensor, depress the locking tabs, unplug the electrical connector, then carefully unscrew the sensor. Be prepared for coolant loss. **Caution:** *Handle the coolant sensor with care. Damage to this sensor will affect the operation of the entire fuel injection system.*
6   Install the new sensor as quickly as possible to minimize coolant loss. Check the coolant level and add some, if necessary (see Chapter 1).

4.2 To check the coolant temperature sensor, use an ohmmeter to measure the resistance between the two sensor terminals (arrow)

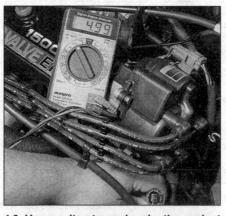

4.3 Use a voltmeter and probe the coolant temperature sensor electrical connector terminal for reference voltage with the ignition key ON (engine not running)

4.13 Backprobe the oxygen sensor harness connector using a pin, check for voltage output. There should be 0.1 to 0.4 volts at idle and 0.5 to 1.0 volts at high rpm

Oxygen sensor
General description

7   The oxygen sensor, which is located in the exhaust manifold, monitors the oxygen content of the exhaust gas stream. The oxygen content in the exhaust reacts with the oxygen sensor to produce a voltage output which varies from 0.1-volt (high oxygen, lean mixture) to 0.9-volts (low oxygen, rich mixture). The ECU constantly monitors this variable voltage output to determine the ratio of oxygen to fuel in the mixture. The ECU alters the air/fuel mixture ratio by controlling the pulse width (open time) of the fuel injectors. A mixture ratio of 14.7 parts air to 1 part fuel is the ideal mixture ratio for minimizing exhaust emissions, thus allowing the catalytic converter to operate at maximum efficiency. It is this ratio of 14.7 to 1 which the ECU and the oxygen sensor attempt to maintain at all times.

8   The oxygen sensor produces no voltage when it is below its normal operating temperature of about 600-degrees F. During this initial period before warm-up, the ECU operates in open loop mode.

9   If the engine reaches normal operating temperature and/or has been running for two or more minutes, and if the oxygen sensor is producing a steady signal voltage below 0.45-volts at 1,500 or more rpm, the ECU will set a Code 21.

10   When there is a problem with the oxygen sensor or its circuit, the ECU operates in the open loop mode - that is, it controls fuel delivery in accordance with a programmed default value instead of feedback information from the oxygen sensor.

11   The proper operation of the oxygen sensor depends on four conditions:

a)   *Electrical - The low voltages generated by the sensor depend upon good, clean connections which should be checked whenever a malfunction of the sensor is suspected or indicated.*

b)   *Outside air supply - The sensor is designed to allow air circulation to the internal portion of the sensor. Whenever the sensor is removed and installed or replaced, make sure the air passages are not restricted.*

c)   *Proper operating temperature - The ECU will not react to the sensor signal until the sensor reaches approximately 600-degrees F. This factor must be taken into consideration when evaluating the performance of the sensor.*

d)   *Unleaded fuel - The use of unleaded fuel is essential for proper operation of the sensor. Make sure the fuel you are using is of this type.*

12   In addition to observing the above conditions, special care must be taken whenever the sensor is serviced.

a)   *The oxygen sensor has a permanently attached pigtail and electrical connector which should not be removed from the sensor. Damage to or removal of the pigtail or electrical connector can adversely affect operation of the sensor.*

b)   *Grease, dirt and other contaminants should be kept away from the electrical connector and the louvered end of the sensor.*

c)   *Do not use cleaning solvents of any kind on the oxygen sensor.*

d)   *Do not drop or roughly handle the sensor.*

e)   *The silicone boot must be installed in the correct position to prevent the boot from being melted and to allow the sensor to operate properly.*

Check

Refer to illustrations 4.13, 4.16a and 4.16b

13   Warm up the engine and let it run at idle. Disconnect the oxygen sensor electrical connector and connect the positive probe of a voltmeter to the blue wire terminal of the oxygen sensor connector **(see illustration)** and the negative probe to ground.

14   Increase, then decrease, the engine speed and monitor the voltage.

15   When the speed is increased, the voltage should increase to 0.5 to 1.0 volts. When the speed is decreased, the voltage should decrease to about 0.1 to 0.4 volts.

16   Inspect the feedback voltage. On EFI engines, with the engine completely warmed up and the oxygen sensor connected, connect a voltmeter to the check connector VF and E1 **(see illustration)**. **Note:** *Connect the positive probe (+) of the voltmeter to VF and connect the*

negative probe (—) to E1 on the SST test connector. **Note:** *Use only an analog type voltmeter because it will be necessary to watch the needle fluctuations.* On feedback carbureted engines, connect a voltmeter to the SST test connector Ox and E1 **(see illustration)**. **Note:** *Connect the positive probe (+) of the voltmeter to Ox and connect the negative probe (—) to E1 on the SST test connector.*

17   Run the engine at 2,500 rpm and then jump terminals T and E1 **(see illustration 3.5)**.

18   Check the number of times the needle fluctuates in 10 seconds. It should fluctuate six times or more. If it does not, warm the engine up again and repeat the test.

19   If the voltmeter still does not fluctuate six times or more, remove the jumper wire from terminals T and E1 of the SST test connector. Maintain engine speed at 2,500 rpm and measure the voltage between terminals VF and E1. If the voltage reading is more than 0 volts, then replace the oxygen sensor with a new part. If the voltage reading is 0 volts, access the self diagnostic codes (see Section 3) and check for any malfunctions.

20   If codes 21, 25 or 26 are obtained, then remove the PCV hose from the valve cover (see Section 7) and measure the voltage between VF and E1. If the voltage is 0 volts, replace the oxygen sensor. If the voltage reading is more than 0 volts, repair the over-rich running condition.

21   If codes other than 21, 25 or 26 are obtained, repair the particular sensor or circuit.

Replacement

Note: *Because it is installed in the exhaust manifold or pipe, which contracts when cool, the oxygen sensor may be very difficult to loosen when the engine is cold. Rather than risk damage to the sensor (assuming you are planning to re-use it in another manifold or pipe), start and run the engine for a minute or two, then shut it off. Be careful not to burn yourself during the following procedure.*

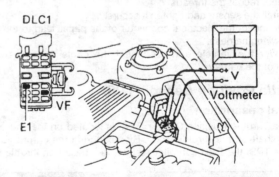

4.16a Connect the probes of the voltmeter to terminals VF and E1, raise the rpm to 2,500 and jump terminals T and E1 with a jumper wire or paper clip (EFI engines only)

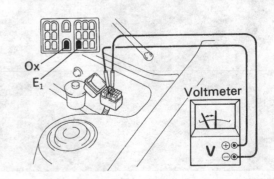

4.16b On carbureted models, probe terminals Ox and E1 on the check connector

6

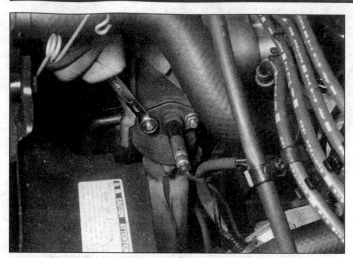

4.25 Removing the nuts from the oxygen sensor

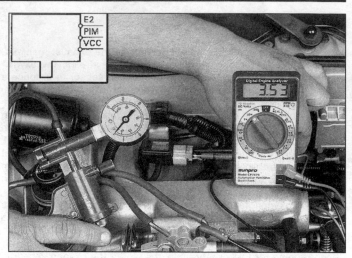

4.32 Connect the probes of the voltmeter to terminals PIM and E2 of the MAP sensor electrical connector and observe the voltage with the ignition key ON (engine not running)

Refer to illustration 4.25

22   Disconnect the cable from the negative terminal of the battery.
23   Raise the vehicle and place it securely on jackstands.
24   Carefully disconnect the electrical connector from the sensor pigtail lead.
25   Remove the nuts that secure the oxygen sensor to the exhaust system **(see illustration)**. **Caution:** *Excessive force may damage the threads.*
26   Anti-seize compound must be used on the threads of the sensor to facilitate future removal. The threads of new sensors will already be coated with this compound, but if an old sensor is removed and reinstalled, recoat the threads.
27   Install the sensor and tighten it securely.
28   Reconnect the electrical connector of the pigtail lead to the main engine wiring harness.
29   Lower the vehicle and reconnect the cable to the negative terminal of the battery.

Throttle Position Sensor (TPS)

General description

30   The Throttle Position Sensor (TPS) is located on the end of the throttle shaft on the throttle body. By monitoring the output voltage from the TPS, the ECU can alter fuel delivery based on throttle valve angle (driver demand). A broken or loose TPS can cause intermittent bursts of fuel from the injector and an unstable idle because the ECU thinks the throttle is moving. All the checks and replacement procedures are covered in Chapter 4.

MAP sensor

General description

31   The Manifold Absolute Pressure (MAP) sensor monitors the intake manifold pressure changes resulting from changes in engine load and speed and converts the information into a voltage output. The ECU uses the MAP sensor to control fuel delivery. The ECU will receive information as a voltage signal that will vary from 1.0 to 1.5 volts at closed throttle (high vacuum) to 4.0 to 4.5 volts at wide open throttle (low vacuum). A failure in the MAP sensor will set code 31.

Check

Refer to illustrations 4.32 and 4.34

32   With the ignition key ON (engine not running), backprobe terminals PIM and E2 **(see illustration)** of the MAP electrical connector.
33   Without vacuum applied to the MAP sensor (idle condition) the voltmeter should register high (3.5 to 4.5 volts).

4.34 With vacuum applied to the MAP sensor (wide open throttle conditions) the voltage should decrease to approximately 1.0 to 2.0 volts

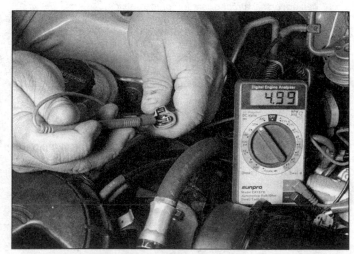

4.39 Check for the reference voltage from the computer to the IAT sensor with the ignition key ON (engine not running). It should be about 5.0 volts

4.42 The IAT sensor resistance should decrease when the air temperature is high

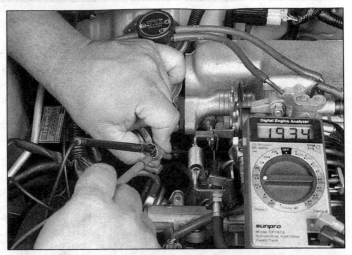

4.46a Measuring the resistance of the EGR gas temperature sensor

34   Using a hand-held vacuum pump, apply approximately 20 inches hg (wide open throttle) to the MAP sensor **(see illustration)** and observe the voltage. It should decrease to 1.0 to 2.0 volts.
35   If the measurements are incorrect, replace the MAP sensor with a new part.

Replacement

36   Disconnect the harness electrical connector from the MAP sensor.
37   Remove the mounting bolts and lift the MAP sensor from the engine compartment.

Intake Air Temperature

General description

38   The Intake Air Temperature (IAT) sensor is located in the airflow meter assembly. This sensor acts as a resistor which changes values according to the temperature of the air entering the engine. Low temperatures produce a high resistance value (for example, at 68 degrees F the resistance is about 3,000 ohms) while high temperatures produce low resistance values (at 140-degrees F the resistance is 700 ohms). The voltage will change according to the temperature of the incoming air. The IAT sensor is incorporated into the air cleaner assembly.

Check

Refer to illustrations 4.39 and 4.42

39   Disconnect the harness electrical connector from the IAT sensor and with the ignition key ON (engine not running), check for a reference signal from the computer **(see illustration)**.
40   Measure the voltage. It should be approximately 5.0 volts.
41   If the reference voltage is incorrect, have the ECU tested by a dealer service department.
42   Measure the resistance of the sensor **(see illustration)**. The resistance should be high when the temperature is low.
43   Warm the engine up until normal operating temperature is attained. The resistance should be low when the air temperature is high.
44   Installation is the reverse of removal.

EGR gas temperature sensor (California models only)

General Description

45   All California models are equipped with an EGR gas temperature sensor mounted near the EGR valve, installed into the EGR tube. This sensor detects the temperature of the exhaust as it moves through the EGR valve. The information is sent to the ECU and in turn the EGR on/off time is regulated precisely and more efficiently. Any malfunction with the EGR gas temperature sensor will set a code 71.

4.46b If the resistance values of the EGR gas temperature sensor are correct, check for a reference voltage signal from the computer. It should be about 5.0 volts with the ignition key ON (engine not running)

Check

Refer to illustrations 4.46a and 4.46b

46   Disconnect the harness connector for the EGR gas temperature sensor and measure the resistance of the sensor at the various temperatures **(see illustration)**. Refer to the Specifications listed in this Chapter for a list of the temperatures and the resistance. Also check the reference voltage to the sensor **(see illustration)**.

Removal and installation

47   Disconnect the electrical connector for the EGR gas temperature sensor and using an open-end wrench, remove the sensor from the intake manifold.
48   Installation is the reverse of removal.

Vehicle speed sensor

General description

49   The Vehicle Speed Sensor (VSS) is located on the tail-section of the transmission (see Chapter 7B). The sensor is electronically controlled and sends a pulsing voltage signal to the ECU, which the ECU converts to miles per hour.
50   Any problems with the VSS and its circuit will set a code 42. Have the vehicle speed sensor, circuit and the ECU diagnosed by a dealership service department or other qualified repair shop.

6

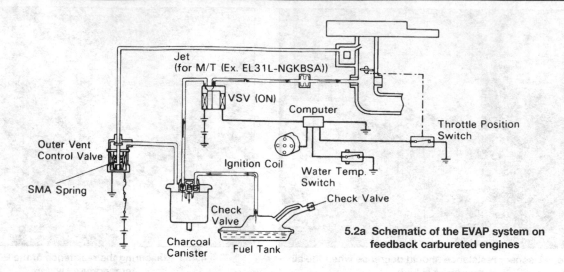

5.2a Schematic of the EVAP system on feedback carbureted engines

5 Evaporative Emission Control (EVAP) system

General description

Refer to illustrations 5.2a, 5.2b, 5.4a and 5.4b

1   This system is designed to trap and store fuel that evaporates from the fuel tank, throttle body and intake manifold that would normally enter the atmosphere in the form of hydrocarbon (HC) emissions.

2   The Evaporative Emission Control (EVAP) system consists of a charcoal-filled canister, the lines connecting the canister to the fuel tank and a check valve **(see illustrations)**.

3   Fuel vapors are transferred from the fuel tank and throttle body to a canister where they're stored when the engine isn't running. When the engine is running, the fuel vapors are purged from the canister by intake airflow and consumed in the normal combustion process.

4   The charcoal canister is equipped with a check valve that incorporates three check balls. Depending upon the running conditions and the pressure in the fuel tank, the check balls open and close the passageways to the throttle body and fuel tank **(see illustrations)**.

Check

5   Poor idle, stalling and poor driveability can be caused by an inoperative check valve, a damaged canister, split or cracked hoses or hoses connected to the wrong fittings. Check the fuel filler cap for a damaged or deformed gasket (see Chapter 1).

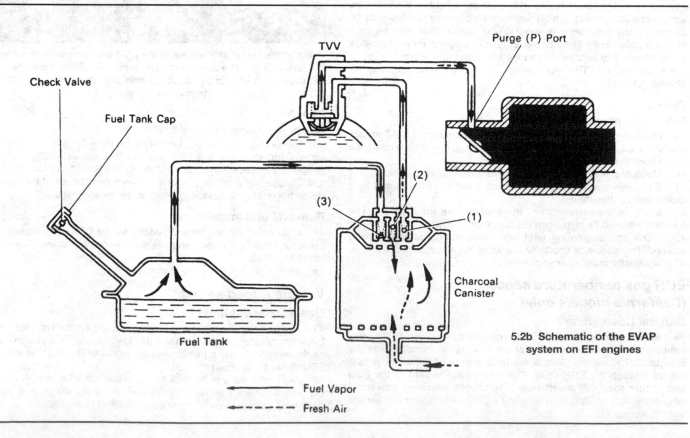

5.2b Schematic of the EVAP system on EFI engines

To reduce HC emission, evaporated fuel from the fuel tank and float chamber is routed through the charcoal canister to the intake manifold for combustion in the cylinders.

IG SW	SMA Temp.	Outer Vent Control Valve	Coolant Temp.	Water Temp. SW	Engine RPM	Throttle Position SW	VSV	Canister Check Valve (1)	Canister Check Valve (2)	Check Valve in Fuel Tank Cap	Evaporation Fuel (HC)
OFF	Below 46°C (115°F)	CLOSED	–	–	–	–	–	–	–	–	HC from tank is absorbed into the canister.
OFF	Above 60°C (140°F)	OPEN	–	–	–	–	–	–	–	–	HC from tank and float chamber is absorbed into the canister.
ON	–	CLOSED	Below 48°C (118°F)	ON	–	–	OFF	–	–	–	HC from tank is absorbed into the canister.
ON	–	CLOSED	Above 60°C (140°F)	OFF	Cranking	–	OFF	–	–	–	HC from tank is absorbed into the canister.
ON	–	CLOSED	Above 60°C (140°F)	OFF	Below 1,200 rpm	–	OFF	–	–	–	HC from tank is absorbed into the canister.
ON	–	CLOSED	Above 60°C (140°F)	OFF	Between 1,300 – 1,500 rpm	–	ON	–	–	–	HC from canister is led into the intake manifold.
ON	–	CLOSED	Above 60°C (140°F)	OFF	Between 1,300 – 1,500 rpm	ON	ON	–	–	–	HC from canister is led into the intake manifold.
ON	–	CLOSED	Above 60°C (140°F)	OFF	Above 2,310 rpm	OFF	OFF	–	–	–	HC from tank is absorbed into the canister.
High pressure in tank			–	–	–	–	–	OPEN	CLOSED	CLOSED	HC from tank is absorbed into the canister.
High vacuum in tank			–	–	–	–	–	CLOSED	OPEN	OPEN	Air is led into the tank.

Remarks: • When the deceleration fuel cut system is on, however, the computer turns the VSV off and HC is not led into the intake manifold (See page EC-51).

5.4a This is the EVAP system operational chart for feedback carbureted engines. The check valve on the charcoal canister allows the fuel vapors to pass into the charcoal canister depending upon the conditions in the fuel tank and throttle body (running conditions).

To reduce HC emission, evaporated fuel from the fuel tank is routed through the charcoal canister to the intake manifold for combustion in the cylinders.

Engine Coolant Temp.	TVV	Throttle Valve Opening	Canister Check Valve in Canister (1)	Canister Check Valve in Canister (2)	Canister Check Valve in Canister (3)	Check Valve in Cap	Evaporated Fuel (HC)
Below 35°C (95°F)	CLOSED	–	–	–	–	–	HC from tank is absorbed into canister.
Above 54°C (129°F)	OPEN	Positioned below P port	CLOSED	–	–	–	HC from tank is absorbed into canister.
Above 54°C (129°F)	OPEN	Positioned above P port	OPEN	–	–	–	HC from canister is led into air intake chamber.
High pressure in tank	–	–	–	OPEN	CLOSED	CLOSED	HC from tank is absorbed into the canister.
High vacuum in tank	–	–	–	CLOSED	OPEN	OPEN	Air is led into the fuel tank.

5.4b Operational chart for the EVAP system on EFI engines

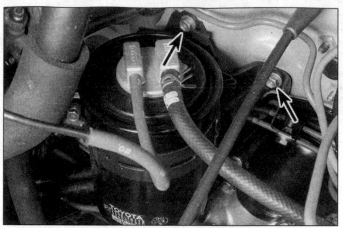

5.12 Remove the bolts (arrows) from the charcoal canister bracket and lift the canister from the engine compartment

6   Evidence of fuel loss or fuel odor can be caused by liquid fuel leaking from fuel lines, a cracked or damaged canister, an inoperative check valve, disconnected, misrouted, kinked, deteriorated or damaged vapor or control hoses.

7   Inspect each hose attached to the canister for kinks, leaks and cracks along its entire length. Repair or replace as necessary.

8   Look for fuel leaking from the bottom of the canister. If fuel is leaking, replace the canister and check the hoses and hose routing.

9   Inspect the canister. If it's cracked or damaged, replace it.

10   Check for a clogged filter or a stuck check valve. Using low pressure compressed air, blow into the canister tank pipe. Air should flow freely from the other pipes. If a problem is found, replace the canister.

Charcoal canister replacement

Refer to illustration 5.12

11   Clearly label, then detach the vacuum hoses from the canister.

12   Remove the mounting clamp bolts **(see illustration)**, lower the canister with the bracket, disconnect the hoses from the check valve and remove it from the vehicle.

13   Installation is the reverse of removal.

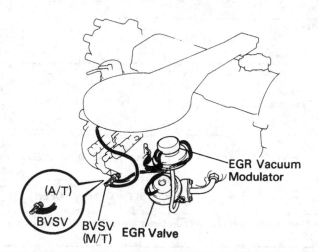

6.2a Operational chart of the EGR system on feedback carbureted engines

To reduce NOx emission, part of the exhaust gases are recirculated through the EGR valve to the intake manifold to lower the maximum combustion temperature.							
Coolant Temp.	**BVSV**	**Throttle Valve Opening Angle**	**Pressure in the EGR Valve Pressure Chamber**		**EGR Vacuum Modulator**	**EGR Valve**	**Exhaust Gas**
Below 40°C (104°F)	OPEN	–	–		–	CLOSED	Not recirculated
Above 54°C (129°F)	CLOSED	Positioned below EGR P port	–		–	CLOSED	Not recirculated
		Positioned between EGR P port and EGR R port	(1) LOW	*Pressure constantly alternating between low and high	OPENS passage to atmosphere	CLOSED	Not recirculated
			(2) HIGH		CLOSES passage to atmosphere	OPEN	Recirculated
		Positioned above EGR R port	(3) HIGH	**	CLOSES passage to atmosphere	OPEN	Recirculated (increase)

Remarks: * Pressure increases ──→ Modulator closes ──→ EGR valve opens ──→ Pressure drops
                              ↑ ──────── EGR valve closes ←── Modulator opens ←──────────┘

        ** When the throttle valve is positioned above the EGR R port, the EGR vacuum modulator will close the atmosphere passage and open the EGR valve to increase the EGR gas, even if the exhaust pressure is insufficiently low.

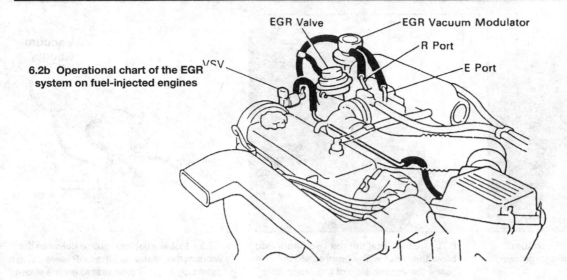

EGR Valve

EGR Vacuum Modulator

R Port

E Port

6.2b Operational chart of the EGR VSV system on fuel-injected engines

To reduce NOx emission, part of the exhaust gases is recirculated through the EGR valve to the intake manifold to lower the maximum combination temperature.								
Engine coolant temp.	Engine RPM	Intake Air Volume	VSV	Throttle Valve Opening	Pressure in the EGR Valve Pressure Chamber	EGR Vacuum Modulator	EGR Valve	Exhaust Gas
Below 47°C (117°F)	–	–	(4) ON	–	–	–	CLOSED	Not recirculated
Above 53°C (127°F)	Above 4,000 rpm	–	ON	–	–	–	CLOSED	Not recirculated
	Below 4,000 rpm	LOW	ON	–	–	–	CLOSED	Not recirculated
		HIGH	OFF	Positioned below E port	–	–	CLOSED	Not recirculated
				Positioned between E port and R port	(1) LOW	• Pressure constantly alternating between low and high	OPENS passage to atmosphere	CLOSED	Not recirculated
					(2) HIGH		CLOSES passage to atmosphere	OPEN	Recirculated
				Positioned above E port	(3) HIGH	••	CLOSES passage to atmosphere	OPEN	Recirculated (increase)

* Pressure increases → Modulator closes → EGR valve opens → Pressure drops →
  EGR valve closes ← Modulator opens ←

** When the throttle valve is positioned above the R port, the EGR vacuum modulator will close the atmosphere passage and open the EGR valve to increase the EGR gas, even if the exhaust pressure is insufficiently low.

6 Exhaust Gas Recirculation (EGR) system

General description

Refer to illustrations 6.2a and 6.2b

1   To reduce oxides of nitrogen (NOx) emissions, some of the exhaust gases are recirculated through the EGR valve to the intake manifold to lower combustion temperatures.

2   The EGR system consists of the EGR valve, the EGR modulator, vacuum switching valve, the Engine Control Unit (ECU) and the EGR gas temperature sensor (California models only) **(see illustrations)**.

Check

EGR valve

Refer to illustration 6.4

3   Start the engine and allow it to idle.

4   Detach the vacuum hose from the EGR valve and attach a hand-held vacuum pump in its place **(see illustration)**.

5   Apply vacuum to the EGR valve. Vacuum should remain steady and the engine should run poorly.

6.4 Apply vacuum to the EGR valve and make sure it holds vacuum - the engine should also run rough or even stall (fuel-injected engine shown)

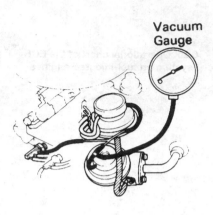

6.7a To remove the EGR vacuum modulator filters for cleaning, remove the cap . . .

6.7b . . . then pull out the two filters and blow them out with compressed air - be sure the coarse side of the outer filter faces the atmosphere (out) when reinstalling the filters

6.9a Install a vacuum gauge between the vacuum modulator and the EGR valve using a three way adapter (carbureted engine shown)

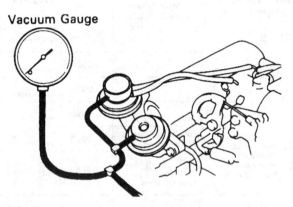

6.9b This is how the vacuum gauge should be connected to the EGR system on fuel-injected engines

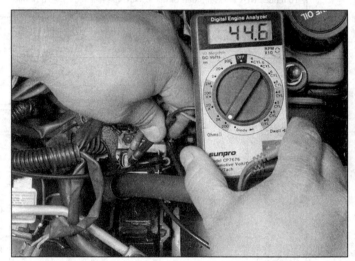

6.10a On EFI engines, use an ohmmeter and check the resistance of the EGR VSV. It should be between 35 and 45 ohms

a) *If the vacuum doesn't remain steady and the engine doesn't run poorly, replace the EGR valve and re-check it.*
b) *If the vacuum remains steady but the engine doesn't run poorly, remove the EGR valve and check the valve and the intake manifold for blockage. Clean or replace parts as necessary and recheck.*

EGR vacuum modulator valve
Refer to illustrations 6.7a and 6.7b
6   Remove the valve (see Step 13 below).
7   Pull the cover off and check the filters **(see illustrations).**
8   Clean them with compressed air, reinstall the cover and the modulator.

EGR system
Refer to illustrations 6.9a, 6.9b, 6.10a, 6.10b and 6.10c
9   Disconnect the hose from the EGR valve and install a three-way union between the EGR valve and the EGR vacuum modulator **(see illustrations)** with a vacuum gauge attached.
10   Check the bi-metal vacuum switching valve (BVSV) on feedback carburetors or the thermal vacuum switching valve (VSV) **(see illustration)** on fuel injected engines for the correct operation. **Note:** *On feedback carburetors, the BVSV can be removed and tested as a*

separate component in the event the following tests have not clearly demonstrated the operating conditions of the valve.
a) *With the coolant temperature below 99 degrees F (cold), verify that the vacuum gauge indicates zero (no vacuum) at 2,500 rpm.*
b) *With the engine warm, verify that the vacuum gauge indicates low vacuum at 2,500 rpm.*
c) *Disconnect the vacuum hose from the R port of the EGR vacuum modulator (see illustration) and connect the R port directly to the intake manifold using an extension. Raise the rpm to 2,500 and observe the vacuum gauge indicate high vacuum.*
d) *If the tests are incorrect, replace the BVSV (feedback carburetors) or the TVV (fuel injected engines) with a new part.*

Component replacement
EGR valve
Refer to illustration 6.11
11   Detach the vacuum hose, disconnect the threaded fitting that attaches the EGR pipe to the EGR valve, remove the two EGR valve mounting bolts **(see illustration)**, remove the EGR valve from the intake manifold and check it for sticking and heavy carbon deposits. If the valve is sticking or clogged with deposits, clean or replace it.
12   Installation is the reverse of removal.

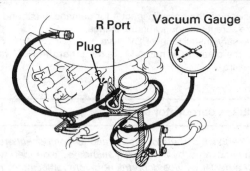

6.10b Disconnect the vacuum hose from the R port and install a piece of vacuum line directly to the intake manifold. This will bypass the VSV and check for a blocked vacuum modulator (feedback carbureted engine shown)

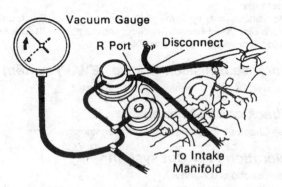

6.10c Location of the R port on fuel injected engines

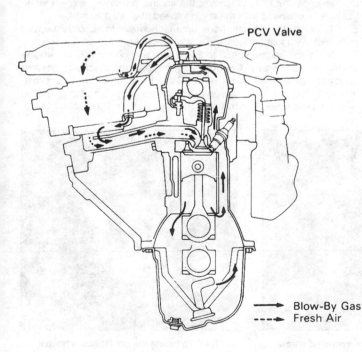

7.1a Diagram of the PCV system on a feedback carbureted engine

6.11 Remove the mounting bolts from the EGR valve and separate it from the intake manifold

EGR vacuum modulator valve

13   Label and disconnect the vacuum hoses and remove the EGR vacuum modulator from it's bracket.
14   Installation is the reverse of removal.

7   Positive Crankcase Ventilation (PCV) system

Refer to illustrations 7.1a, 7.1b and 7.5

General information

1   The Positive Crankcase Ventilation (PCV) system reduces hydrocarbon emissions by scavenging crankcase vapors. It does this by circulating fresh air from the air cleaner through the crankcase, where it mixes with blow-by gases and is then re-routed through a PCV valve to the intake manifold **(see illustrations)**.
2   The main components of the PCV system are the PCV valve, a fresh air intake and the vacuum hoses connecting these components with the engine (valve cover).

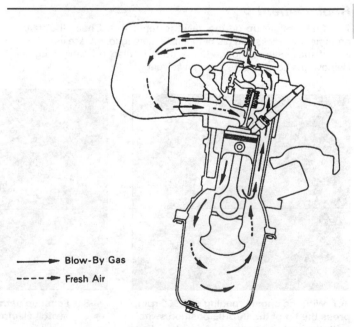

7.1b Diagram of the PCV system on a fuel-injected engine

7.5 Pull the PCV valve and hose straight up and out of the grommet in the valve cover

3   To maintain idle quality, the PCV valve restricts the flow when the intake manifold vacuum is high. If abnormal operating conditions (such as piston ring problems) arise, the system is designed to allow excessive amounts of blow-by gases to flow back through the crankcase vent tube into the air cleaner to be consumed by normal combustion.

4   This system directs the blow-by into the throttle body which, over time, can cause an oily residue build up in the area near the throttle plate. Consequently, it's a good idea to periodically clean this residue from the throttle body. Refer to Chapter 4 for this cleaning procedure.

Check

5   To check the valve, first pull it out of the grommet in the valve cover **(see illustration)** and shake the valve. It should rattle, indicating that it's not clogged with deposits. If the valve does not rattle, replace it with a new one.

6   Start the engine and allow it to idle, then place your finger over the valve opening. If vacuum is felt, the PCV valve is working properly. If no vacuum is felt, the PCV valve may be bad or the hose may be plugged. Also, check for vacuum leaks at the valve, oil filler cap and all the hoses.

Replacement

7   Pull straight up on the valve to remove it. Check the rubber grommet for cracks and distortion. If it's damaged, replace it.

8   If the valve is clogged, the hose is also probably plugged. Remove the hose and clean it with solvent.

9   After cleaning the hose, inspect it for damage, wear and deterioration. Make sure it fits snugly on the fittings.

10   If necessary, install a new PCV valve.

11   Install the clean PCV hose. Make sure that the PCV valve and hose are secure.

---

8   Feedback carburetor system

Note: *The feedback carburetor system and all components related to the system is covered by a Federally mandated extended warranty. Check with a dealer service department before replacing or repairing the system components at your own expense.*

1   The feedback carburetor (FBC) system maintains the air/fuel ratio at the desired 14.7-to-1 during normal operation. The system is designed to operate somewhat richer than desired. This sets up the rich limit of the system operation. When a more lean operation is desired, the Electronic Control Unit (ECU) commands air to be bled into the carburetor's main metering system and into the carburetor primary bore. A lean operating condition is therefore easily obtained.

2   The various sub-systems and components of the feedback system are discussed below. Checking and component replacement information is provided, where possible.

Evaporative Emission Control (EVAP) system

3   See Section 5 for information on this system.

Feedback control system

4   See Chapter 4 for information on this system.

Deceleration Fuel Cut system

Refer to illustrations 8.7 and 8.8

5   During deceleration, this system cuts off part of the fuel flow in the idle circuit of the carburetor to prevent overheating and afterburning in the exhaust system. The fuel cut solenoid is kept energized by the ECU whenever the engine is running, except when the throttle is closed with the engine speed above 2,190 rpm.

6   To check the system, hook up a tachometer in accordance with manufacturer's instructions and start the engine.

7   Raise the engine speed to 2,200 rpm and check that the engine speed remains steady. **Caution:** *Perform this step quickly to prevent overheating the catalytic converter.* Raise the engine rpm to approximately 2,900 and use a screwdriver or press the tip of the throttle position switch **(see illustration)**. The engine should hesitate.

8.7 With the engine running at 2,900 rpm, press the tip of the throttle position switch with the end of a screwdriver and confirm that the engine hesitates

8.8 Location of the throttle position switch electrical connector

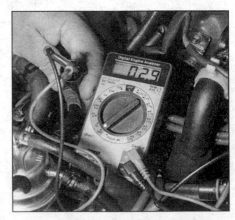

8.11 To locate the cold mixture heater electrical connector, follow the harness all the way down under the carburetor to the base of the heater which is positioned between the carburetor and the intake manifold

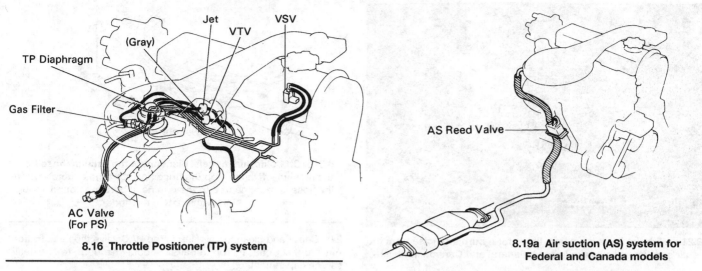

8.16 Throttle Positioner (TP) system

8.19a Air suction (AS) system for Federal and Canada models

8 Release the accelerator, disconnect the throttle position switch connector **(see illustration)**, and observe the idle condition becomes rough and inconsistent.
9 If no problems are found, the system is okay. Any further checks or repairs should be left to a dealer service department or other qualified repair shop.

Cold Mixture Heater (CMH) system

Refer to illustration 8.11

10 The Cold Mixture Heater (CMH) system reduces cold engine emissions and improves driveability during engine warm up. The intake manifold is heated during cold engine operation to accelerate vaporization of the liquid fuel. The ECU will turn the CMH on and off according to engine coolant temperature.
11 To check the cold mixture heater, locate the connector, unplug it and, using an ohmmeter, measure the resistance between the terminals **(see illustration)**. It should be between 0.5 and 2.2 ohms at 68-degrees F. If the readings are not within specification, replace the heater. Any further checks should be done by a dealer service department or other repair shop.
12 To replace the cold mixture heater, first remove the carburetor (see Chapter 4).
13 Unplug the cold mixture heater connector, remove the PCV hose and lift the heater from the intake manifold.
14 Installation is the reverse of removal.

Positive Crankcase Ventilation (PCV) system

15 See Section 7 for information on this system.

Throttle Positioner (TP)

Refer to illustration 8.16

16 To reduce HC and CO emissions, the throttle positioner opens the throttle valve slightly when decelerating **(see illustration)**. This keeps the air/fuel ratio from becoming excessively rich when the throttle valve is quickly closed. The TP is also used to increase idle speed when power steering fluid pressure exceeds a pre-set value and when a large electrical load is placed on the electrical system. Any checks or repairs should be left to a dealer service department or other repair shop.

Exhaust Gas Recirculation (EGR) system

17 See Section 6 for information on this system.

Catalytic Converter

18 See Section 9 for further information on the catalytic converter.

Air Suction (AS) system

Refer to illustrations 8.19a, 8.19b, 8.21a and 8.21b

19 Additional oxygen is needed to aid the oxidation of HC and CO in the catalytic converter. The air suction valve is a simple reed-type valve that opens when vacuum is present in the exhaust system. When open, oxygen-rich air is drawn into the exhaust to aid the converter with the oxidation process **(see illustrations)**.
20 To check the system, first check the hoses and fittings for cracks, kinks, damage or loose connections.

6

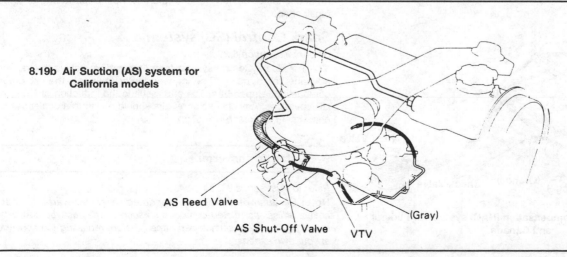

8.19b Air Suction (AS) system for California models

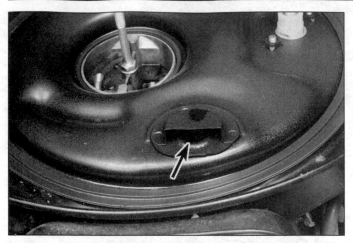

8.21a With the engine running, listen for a burbling noise from the air suction valve intake (arrow) (Federal and Canada models)

21   Remove the air cleaner top cover.
  a) *On Federal and Canadian models, with the engine idling, check that a burbling noise is heard from the air suction valve inlet* **(see illustration)**. *Any further checks or repairs should be left to a dealer service department.*
  b) *On California models, disconnect and plug the shut-off valve vacuum hose* **(see illustration)**. *Start the engine, unplug and reconnect the hose and listen for a burbling noise from the air suction valve inlet. It should occur within two to six seconds. Any further checks or repairs should be left to a dealer service department.*

High Altitude Compensation (HAC) system (Federal and Canada models only)

Refer to illustrations 8.22 and 8.24

22   As altitude increases, air density decreases causing the air/fuel mixture to become richer. The High Altitude Compensation (HAC) system insures proper air/fuel mixture by supplying additional air to the primary and high-speed circuit of the carburetor. The system also advances the ignition timing to improve driveability at high altitudes **(see illustration)**.
23   To check the system, first inspect all hoses for cracks, kinks, damage or loose connections.

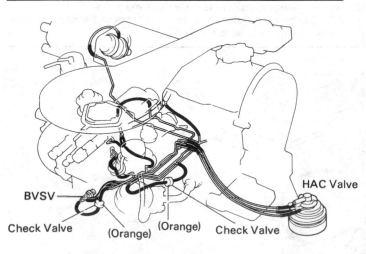

BVSV

Check Valve   (Orange)   (Orange)   Check Valve

HAC Valve

8.22 High Altitude Compensation (HAC) system for Federal and Canada

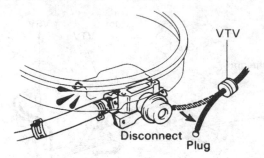

8.21b On California models, disconnect the vacuum hose from the air shut-off valve, cap the hose and start the engine - when the hose is reconnected to the engine, a burbling sound should start within 2 to 6 seconds

24   Check and clean the air filter in the HAC valve **(see illustration)**. Any further checks or repairs should be left to a dealer service department.

Thermostatic Air Cleaner (TAC) system

25   This system directs hot air to the carburetor in cold weather to improve driveability and to prevent carburetor icing in extremely cold weather.
26   See Chapter 1 for the TAC system check.

Hot Idle Compensation (HIC) system

Refer to illustrations 8.27, 8.28 and 8.29

27   The Hot Idle Compensation (HIC) system allows additional air to enter the intake manifold to maintain proper air/fuel mixture during high temperatures at idle **(see illustration)**.
28   To check the system, remove the HIC valve from the air cleaner housing **(see illustration)**.
29   With the temperature above 72-degrees F, check the operation of the valve by placing a finger over the atmospheric port and blowing into the port for the HIC diaphragm (2) **(see illustration)**. Air should flow from the port normally connected to the carburetor (1).
30   At temperatures below 72-degrees F, carry out a similar airflow test. Place a finger over the port normally connected to the carburetor. Blow through the port for the HIC diaphragm and make sure that air does not pass out of the atmospheric port.

Automatic choke

31   The automatic choke system temporarily supplies a rich air/fuel mixture to the engine by closing the choke valve when the engine is cold. It automatically opens the choke as the engine warms up. See Chapter 1 for the choke check procedure. Any further checks or repairs should be left to a dealer service department or other repair shop.

Spark Control (SC) system

Refer to illustration 8.32

32   The Spark Control system **(see illustration)** delays the vacuum advance for a given time consequently lowering the maximum combustion temperature. The end result is the reduction of NOx and HC emissions. Any checks or repairs should be left to a dealer service department or other repair shop.

---

9   Catalytic converter

Refer to illustrations 9.2 and 9.4

Note: *Because of a federally-mandated extended warranty which covers emissions-related components such as the catalytic converter, check with a dealer service department before replacing the converter at your own expense.*

8.24 Remove the HAC cover and peel the filter out, clean it with compressed air, inspect it and, if necessary, replace it

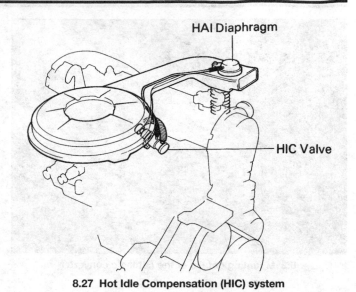

8.27 Hot Idle Compensation (HIC) system

8.28 Label and detach the vacuum hoses from the HIC valve, then remove the mounting screws (arrows)

8.29 A typical HIC valve

1   Carburetor port
2   Hot air Intake diaphragm port
3   Atmospheric port

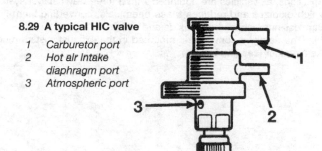

8.32 Spark Control (SC) system

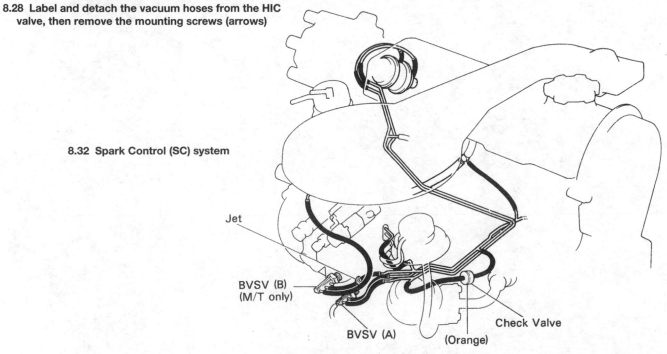

6

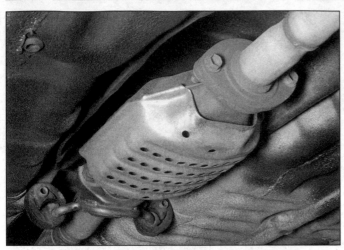

9.2 Mounting details of the catalytic converter

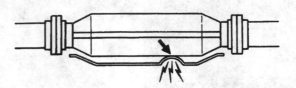

9.4 Periodically inspect the shield for dents and other damage - if a dent is deep enough to touch the surface of the converter, replace the shield

General description

1   To reduce hydrocarbon, carbon monoxide and oxides of nitrogen emissions, all vehicles are equipped with a three-way catalyst system which oxidizes and reduces these chemicals, converting them into harmless nitrogen, carbon dioxide and water.

2   The catalytic converter is mounted in the exhaust system much like a muffler **(see illustration)**.

Checking

3   Periodically inspect the catalytic converter-to-exhaust pipe mating flanges and bolts. Make sure that there are no loose bolts and no leaks between the flanges.

4   Look for dents in or damage to the catalytic converter protector **(see illustration)**. If any part of the protector is damaged or dented enough to touch the converter, repair or replace it.

5   Inspect the heat insulator for damage. Make sure that there is adequate clearance between the heat insulator and the catalytic converter.

Replacement

6   To replace the catalytic converter, refer to Chapter 4.

Chapter 7 Part A
Manual transaxle

Contents

Specifications

Torque specifications

Ft-lbs (unless otherwise indicated)

Back-up light switch	30
Engine-to-transaxle bolts	
A bolts	47
B bolts	34
C bolts	65 in-lbs

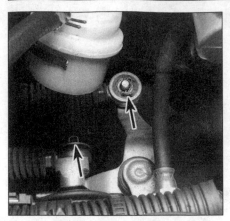

2.1 To disconnect the shift cables from the transaxle linkage, remove these two clips and washers (arrows)

2.2 To detach the shift cable assembly from the cable bracket, remove these two retainers (arrows) with a pair of pliers

2.5 To disconnect the shift cables from the shift lever, remove these clips and washers (arrow)

1   General information

The vehicles covered by this manual are equipped with either a 4-speed (C-140 or C-141) or a 5-speed (C-150) manual transaxle, or a 3-speed automatic transaxle. Information on the manual transaxle is included in this Part of Chapter 7. Service procedures for the automatic transaxle are contained in Chapter 7, Part B.

The manual transaxle is a compact, two-piece, lightweight aluminum alloy housing containing both the transmission and differential assemblies.

Because of the complexity, unavailability of replacement parts and special tools necessary, internal repair procedures for the manual transaxle are beyond the scope of this manual. For readers who wish to tackle a transaxle rebuild, exploded views and a brief *Manual transaxle overhaul - general information* Section are provided. The bulk of information in this Chapter is devoted to removal and installation procedures.

2   Shift cables - removal and installation

Refer to illustrations 2.1, 2.2 and 2.5

1   In the engine compartment, remove the retaining clips and washers and disconnect the shift cables from the selecting bellcrank **(see illustration)**.

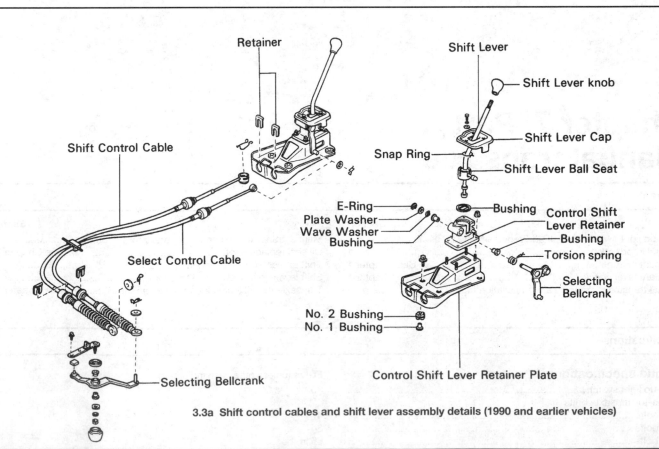

3.3a Shift control cables and shift lever assembly details (1990 and earlier vehicles)

2   Remove the cable retainers from the cable bracket **(see illustration)**.
3   Inside the vehicle, remove the floor console (see Chapter 11).
4   Remove the cable retainers from the shift lever base **(see illustrations 3.3a, 3.3b and 3.3c)**.
5   Remove the retaining clips and washers from the cable ends **(see illustration)** and disconnect the cables from the shift lever assembly.
6   Trace the cable assembly to the firewall and remove the weatherproofing grommet. Pull the cable assembly through the firewall.
7   Installation is the reverse of removal.

3   Shift lever - removal and installation

Refer to illustrations 3.3a, 3.3b and 3.3c
1   Remove the center console (see Chapter 11).
2   Remove the shift cable retainers and disconnect both cables from the shift lever (see Section 2).
3   Remove the retaining bolts from the shift lever base **(see illustrations)** and detach the shift lever from the vehicle. **Note:** *If you're replacing the shift lever assembly on a 1991 or later vehicle, it*

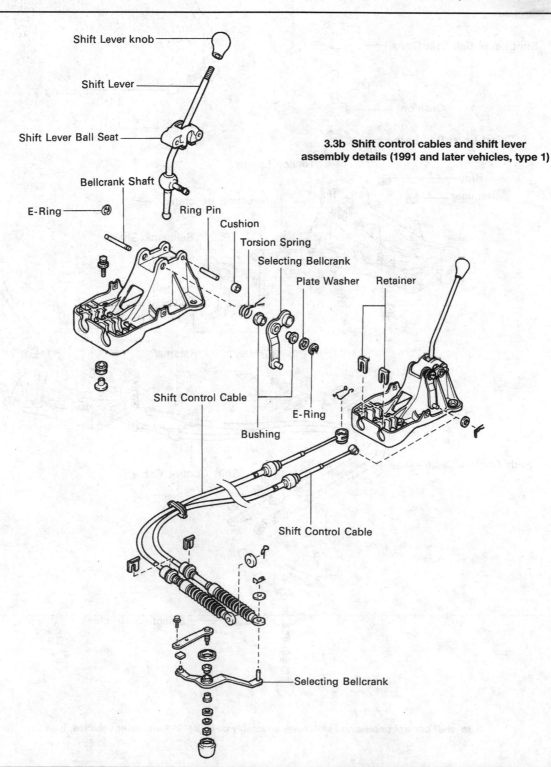

3.3b Shift control cables and shift lever assembly details (1991 and later vehicles, type 1)

Shift Lever knob
Shift Lever
Shift Lever Ball Seat
Bellcrank Shaft
E-Ring
Ring Pin
Cushion
Torsion Spring
Selecting Bellcrank
Plate Washer
Retainer
Shift Control Cable
E-Ring
Bushing
Shift Control Cable
Selecting Bellcrank

7A

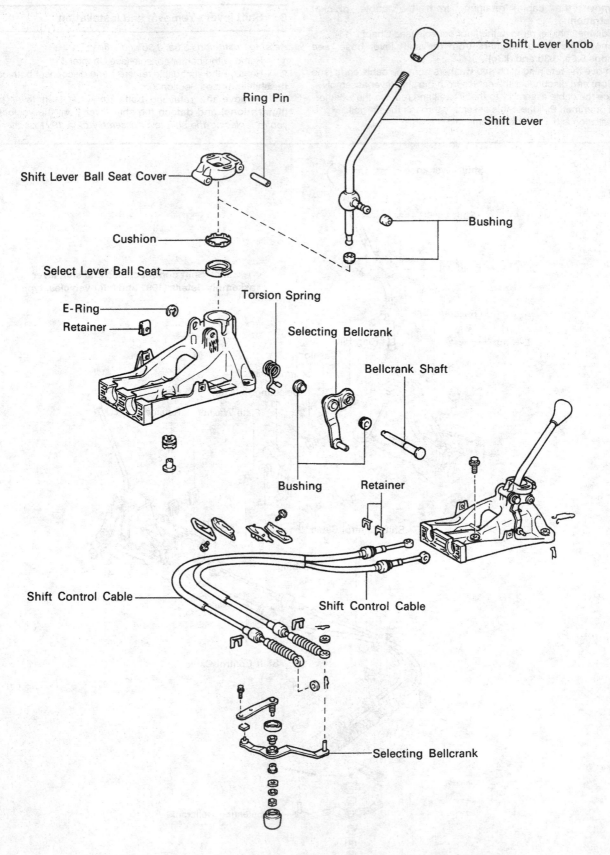

3.3c shift control cables and shift lever assembly details (1991 and later vehicles, type 2)

4.8 Disconnect the connector to the back-up light switch (arrow)

5.7 To detach the connecting bellcrank and bracket from the transaxle housing on 1990 and earlier vehicles, remove these two bolts (arrows)

could use either the shift lever shown in illustration 3.3b or the one shown in illustration 3.3c. It's a good idea to take the shift lever assembly with you when purchasing a replacement unit to, ensure that you get the right unit for your vehicle.

4   Installation is the reverse of removal.

4   Back-up light switch - check and replacement

Check

1   The back-up light switch is located on top of the transaxle.
2   Turn the ignition key to the On position and move the shift lever to the Reverse position. The switch should turn on the back-up lights.
3   If it doesn't, check the back-up light fuse (see Chapter 12).
4   If the fuse is okay, verify that there's voltage available on the battery side of the switch (with the ignition turned to On).
5   If there's no voltage on the battery side of the switch, check the wire between the fuse and the switch; if there is voltage, put the shift lever in reverse and see if there's voltage on the ground side of the switch.
6   If there's no voltage on the ground side of the switch, replace the switch (see below); if there is voltage, note whether only one or both back-up lights are out.
7   If only one bulb is out, replace it; if they're both out, the bulbs could be the problem, but it's more likely that the wire between the switch and the bulbs has an open somewhere.

Replacement

Refer to illustration 4.8

8   Disconnect the electrical connector from the back-up light switch **(see illustration).**

9   Unscrew the switch.
10   Screw in the new switch and tighten it securely.
11   Connect the electrical connector.
12   Check the switch to ensure it's working properly.

5   Manual transaxle - removal and installation

Removal

Refer to illustrations 5.7, 5.8, 5.9a, 5.9b, 5.13, 5.16, 5.18, 5.20, 5.21a and 5.21b

1   Disconnect the negative cable from the battery. **Caution:** *If the stereo in your vehicle is equipped with an anti-theft system, make sure you have the correct activation code before disconnecting the battery.*
2   On 1990 and earlier vehicles with cruise control, remove the battery (see Chapter 5) and the cruise control actuator.
3   On 1991 and later vehicles, remove the air cleaner assembly (see Chapter 4).
4   Remove the clutch release cylinder and the clutch hydraulic line (see Chapter 8).
5   Disconnect the electrical connector for the back-up light switch.
6   Disconnect the shift cables from the transaxle (see Section 2).
7   On 1990 and earlier vehicles, remove the selecting bellcrank and bracket from the transaxle housing **(see illustration).**
8   On 1991 and later vehicles, remove the clutch release cylinder bracket and ground cable **(see illustration).**
9   Remove the upper transaxle-to-engine mounting bolts **(see illustrations).** Note the location of any ground connectors or brackets, so that they may be installed in their original location.
10   Loosen the wheel lug nuts. Raise the vehicle and support it securely on jackstands. Remove the wheels.

7A

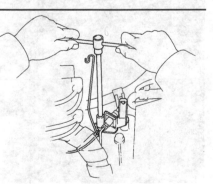

5.8 On 1991 and later vehicles, remove the clutch release cylinder bracket and ground cable

5.9a Remove the upper transaxle-to-engine bolt (arrow) located behind the clutch release cylinder . . .

5.9b . . . and the bolt (arrow) located under the thermostat housing

5.13 Remove the hold-down bolt (arrow) and strap, then disconnect the speedometer cable from the transaxle housing

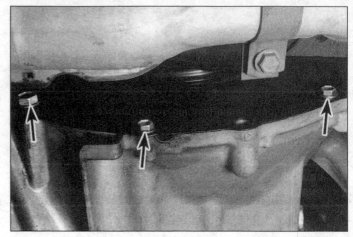

5.16 Remove the flywheel/clutch access cover bolts (arrows) and remove the cover

11   Remove the splash shields (see Chapter 2).
12   Drain the transaxle fluid (see Chapter 1).
13   Disconnect the speedometer cable **(see illustration)**.
14   Remove the driveaxles (see Chapter 8).
15   Remove the starter motor (see Chapter 5).
16   Remove the flywheel/clutch access cover **(see illustration)**.
17   Support the engine. This can be done from above by using an engine hoist, or by placing a jack (with a block of wood as an insulator) under the engine oil pan. The engine should remain supported at all times while the transaxle is out of the vehicle.
18   On 1990 and earlier vehicles, remove the front engine mount (see Chapter 2) and the rear engine mount **(see illustration)**. On 1991 and later vehicles, remove the rear engine mounting bracket.
19   Support the transaxle with a jack (preferably a special jack made for this purpose). If you're using a floor jack, be sure to place a block of wood between the lifting pad and the transaxle to protect the cast aluminum housing. Safety chains will help steady the transaxle on the jack.
20   Raise the engine and transaxle slightly and disconnect the left transaxle mount **(see illustration)**.
21   Remove the rest of the bolts securing the transaxle to the engine **(see illustrations)**.
22   Make a final check that all wires and hoses have been disconnected from the transaxle.
23   Lower the left (driver's) end of the engine, then roll the transaxle and jack toward the side of the vehicle. Once the input shaft is clear of

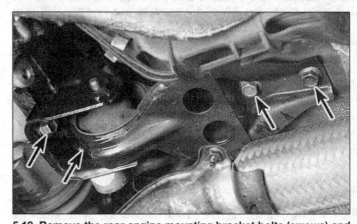

5.18 Remove the rear engine mounting bracket bolts (arrows) and remove the brackets

the splines in the clutch hub, lower the transaxle and remove it from under the vehicle. Try to keep the transaxle as level as possible. **Caution:** Do not depress the clutch pedal while the transaxle is removed from the vehicle.
24   The clutch components can now be inspected (see Chapter 8). In most cases, new clutch components should be routinely installed whenever the transaxle is removed.

5.20 Remove the left transaxle mount bolts (arrows) and remove the mount

5.21a Remove the lower engine-to-transaxle bolt (arrow) located near the starter motor . . .

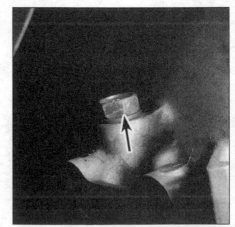

5.21b . . .and this lower transaxle-to-engine bolt located on the firewall side of the bellhousing

Installation

Refer to illustration 5.27

25   If removed, install the clutch components (see Chapter 8).

26   With the transaxle secured to the jack as on removal, raise it into position and then carefully slide it forward, engaging the input shaft with the splines in the clutch hub. Do not use excessive force to install the transaxle - if the input shaft does not slide into place, readjust the angle of the transaxle so it is level and/or turn the input shaft so the splines engage properly with the clutch.

27   Install the transaxle-to-engine bolts **(see illustration)**. Tighten the bolts to the torque listed in this Chapter's Specifications.

28   Install the transaxle mount nuts and bolts. Tighten all nuts and bolts securely.

29   Install the chassis and suspension components which were removed. Tighten all nuts and bolts securely.

30   Remove the jacks supporting the transaxle and the engine.

31   Install the various items removed previously. Refer to Chapter 8

for the installation of the driveaxles and Chapter 4 for information regarding the exhaust system components.

32   Make a final check that all wires, hoses and the speedometer cable have been connected and that the transaxle has been filled with the specified lubricant to the proper level (see Chapter 1). Lower the vehicle.

33   Connect the shift cables (see Section 3).

34   Connect the negative battery cable. Road test the vehicle to check for proper transaxle operation and check for leakage.

6   Manual transaxle overhaul - general information

Refer to illustrations 6.4a, 6.4b and 6.4c

1   Overhauling a manual transaxle is a difficult job for the do-it-yourselfer. It involves the disassembly and reassembly of many small parts. Numerous clearances must be precisely measured and, if

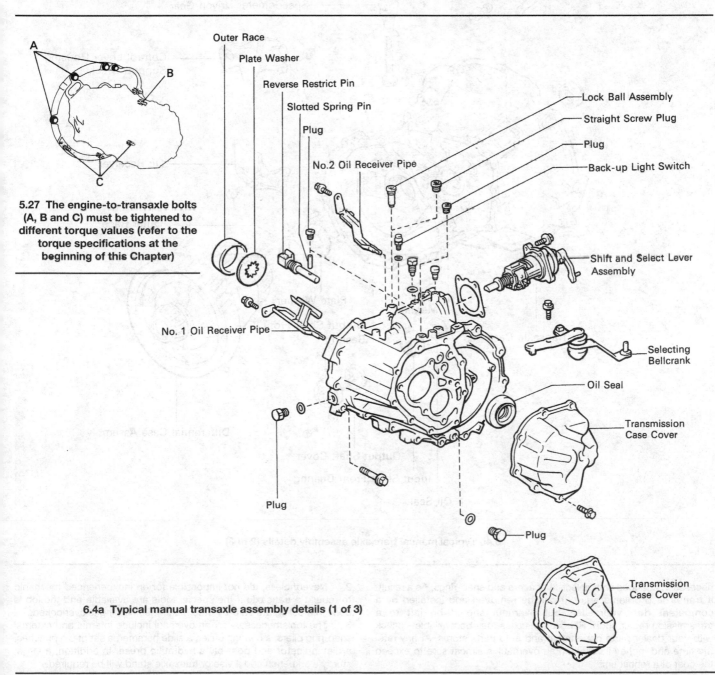

5.27 The engine-to-transaxle bolts (A, B and C) must be tightened to different torque values (refer to the torque specifications at the beginning of this Chapter)

6.4a Typical manual transaxle assembly details (1 of 3)

7A

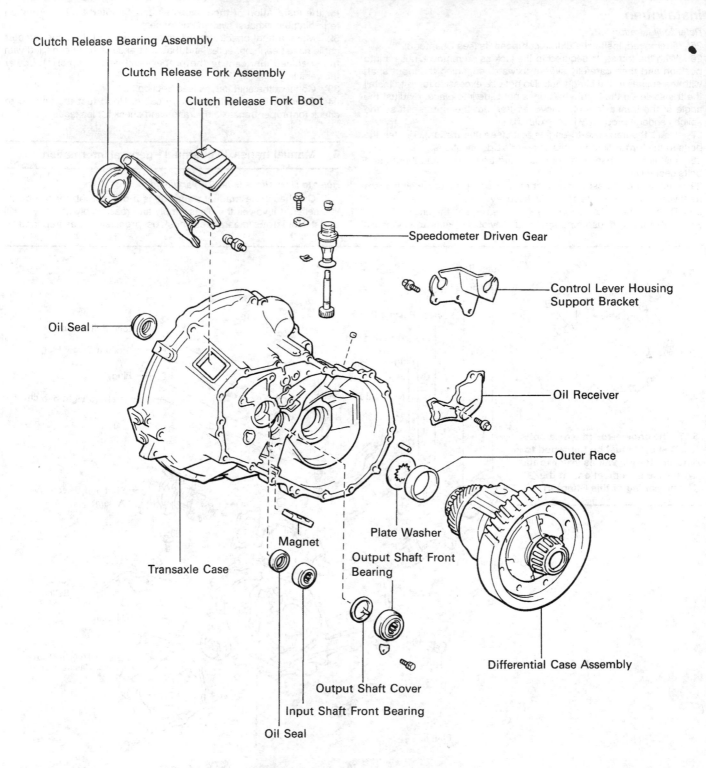

Clutch Release Bearing Assembly

Clutch Release Fork Assembly

Clutch Release Fork Boot

Speedometer Driven Gear

Control Lever Housing
Support Bracket

Oil Seal

Oil Receiver

Outer Race

Transaxle Case

Plate Washer

Magnet

Output Shaft Front
Bearing

Differential Case Assembly

Output Shaft Cover

Input Shaft Front Bearing

Oil Seal

6.4b Typical manual transaxle assembly details (2 of 3)

necessary, changed with select-fit spacers and snap-rings. As a result, if transaxle problems arise, it can be removed and installed by a competent do-it-yourselfer, but overhaul should be left to a transmission repair shop. Rebuilt transaxles may be available - check with your dealer parts department and auto parts stores. At any rate, the time and money involved in an overhaul is almost sure to exceed the cost of a rebuilt unit.

2   Nevertheless, it's not impossible for an inexperienced mechanic to rebuild a transaxle if the special tools are available and the job is done in a deliberate step-by-step manner so nothing is overlooked.

3   The tools necessary for an overhaul include internal and external snap-ring pliers, a bearing puller, a slide hammer, a set of pin punches, a dial indicator and possibly a hydraulic press. In addition, a large, sturdy workbench and a vise or transaxle stand will be required.

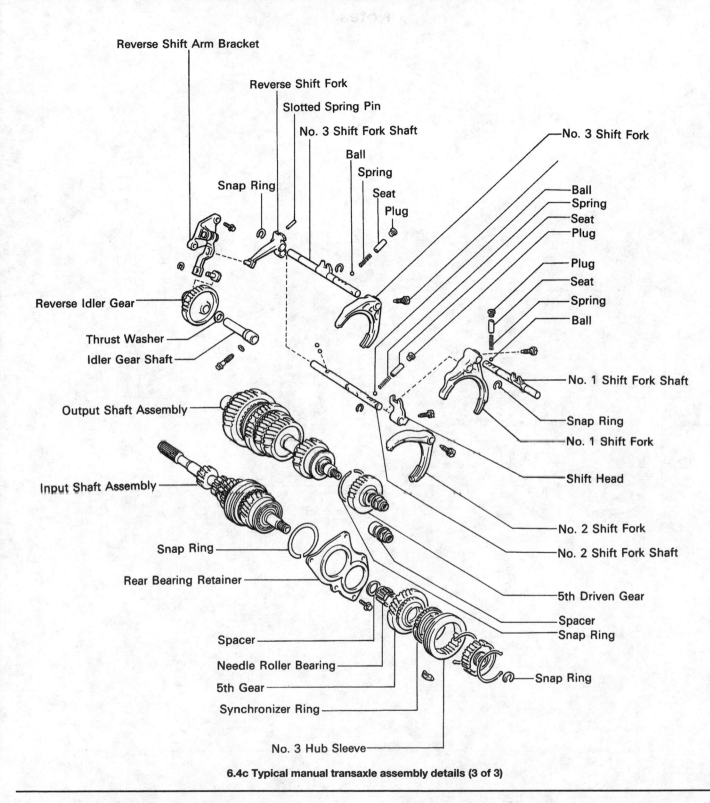

6.4c Typical manual transaxle assembly details (3 of 3)

7A

4   During disassembly of the transaxle, make careful notes of how each piece comes off, where it fits in relation to other pieces and what holds it in place. Exploded views are included **(see illustrations)** to show where the parts go - but actually noting how they are installed when you remove the parts will make it much easier to get the transaxle back together.

5   Before taking the transaxle apart for repair, it will help if you have some idea what area of the transaxle is malfunctioning. Certain problems can be closely tied to specific areas in the transaxle, which can make component examination and replacement easier. Refer to the *Troubleshooting* section at the front of this manual for information regarding possible sources of trouble.

Notes

Chapter 7 Part B
Automatic transaxle

Contents

Specifications

Shift lock system

Shift lock solenoid
1990	21 to 27 ohms
1991 on	30 to 35 ohms
Key interlock solenoid	12.5 to 16.5 ohms

Torque specifications

Ft-lbs (unless otherwise indicated)

Neutral start switch	48 in-lbs
Torque converter-to-driveplate bolts	156 in-lbs
Transaxle-to-engine bolts	47

1   General information

All vehicles covered in this manual come equipped with either a 4- or 5-speed manual transaxle or a 3-speed automatic transaxle. All information on the automatic transaxle is included in this Part of Chapter 7. Information for the manual transaxle can be found in Part A of this Chapter.

Because of the complexity of the automatic transaxles and the specialized equipment necessary to perform most service operations, this Chapter contains only those procedures related to general diagnosis, routine maintenance, adjustment and removal and installation.

If the transaxle requires major repair work, it should be left to a dealer service department or an automotive or transmission repair shop. You can, however, remove and install the transaxle yourself and save the expense, even if the repair work is done by a transmission shop.

2   Diagnosis - general

Note: *Automatic transaxle malfunctions may be caused by five general conditions: poor engine performance, improper adjustments, hydraulic malfunctions, mechanical malfunctions or malfunctions in the computer or its signal network. Diagnosis of these problems should always begin with a check of the easily repaired items: fluid level and condition (see Chapter 1), shift linkage adjustment and throttle linkage adjustment. Next, perform a road test to determine if the problem has been corrected or if more diagnosis is necessary. If the problem persists after the preliminary tests and corrections are completed, additional diagnosis should be done by a dealer service department or transmission repair shop. Refer to the Troubleshooting section at the front of this manual for information on symptoms of transaxle problems.*

Preliminary checks

1   Drive the vehicle to warm the transaxle to normal operating temperature.

2   Check the fluid level as described in Chapter 1:

a) *If the fluid level is unusually low, add enough fluid to bring the level within the designated area of the dipstick, then check for external leaks (see below).*

b) *If the fluid level is abnormally high, drain off the excess, then check the drained fluid for contamination by coolant. The presence of engine coolant in the automatic transmission fluid indicates that a failure has occurred in the internal radiator walls that separate the coolant from the transmission fluid (see Chapter 3).*

c) *If the fluid is foaming, drain it and refill the transaxle, then check for coolant in the fluid, or a high fluid level.*

3   Check the engine idle speed. **Note:** *If the engine is malfunctioning, do not proceed with the preliminary checks until it has been repaired and runs normally.*

4   Check the throttle valve cable for freedom of movement. Adjust it if necessary (see Section 4). **Note:** *The throttle cable may function properly when the engine is shut off and cold, but it may malfunction once the engine is hot. Check it cold and at normal engine operating temperature.*

5   Inspect the shift control linkage (see Section 5). Make sure that it's properly adjusted and that the linkage operates smoothly.

Fluid leak diagnosis

6   Most fluid leaks are easy to locate visually. Repair usually consists of replacing a seal or gasket. If a leak is difficult to find, the following procedure may help.

7   Identify the fluid. Make sure it's transmission fluid and not engine oil or brake fluid (automatic transmission fluid is a deep red color).

8   Try to pinpoint the source of the leak. Drive the vehicle several miles, then park it over a large sheet of cardboard. After a minute or two, you should be able to locate the leak by determining the source of the fluid dripping onto the cardboard.

9   Make a careful visual inspection of the suspected component and the area immediately around it. Pay particular attention to gasket mating surfaces. A mirror is often helpful for finding leaks in areas that are hard to see.

10   If the leak still cannot be found, clean the suspected area thoroughly with a degreaser or solvent, then dry it.

11   Drive the vehicle for several miles at normal operating temperature and varying speeds. After driving the vehicle, visually inspect the suspected component again.

12   Once the leak has been located, the cause must be determined before it can be properly repaired. If a gasket is replaced but the sealing flange is bent, the new gasket will not stop the leak. The bent flange must be straightened.

13   Before attempting to repair a leak, check to make sure that the following conditions are corrected or they may cause another leak. **Note:** *Some of the following conditions cannot be fixed without highly specialized tools and expertise. Such problems must be referred to a transmission shop or a dealer service department.*

Gasket leaks

14   Check the pan periodically. Make sure the bolts are tight, no bolts are missing, the gasket is in good condition and the pan is flat (dents in the pan may indicate damage to the valve body inside).

15   If the pan gasket is leaking, the fluid level or the fluid pressure may be too high, the vent may be plugged, the pan bolts may be too tight, the pan sealing flange may be warped, the sealing surface of the transaxle housing may be damaged, the gasket may be damaged or the transaxle casting may be cracked or porous. If sealant instead of gasket material has been used to form a seal between the pan and the transaxle housing, it may be the wrong sealant.

Seal leaks

16   If a transaxle seal is leaking, the fluid level or pressure may be too high, the vent may be plugged, the seal bore may be damaged, the seal itself may be damaged or improperly installed, the surface of the shaft protruding through the seal may be damaged or a loose bearing may be causing excessive shaft movement.

17   Make sure the dipstick tube seal is in good condition and the tube is properly seated. Periodically check the area around the speedometer gear or sensor for leakage. If transmission fluid is evident, check the O-ring for damage.

Case leaks

18   If the case itself appears to be leaking, the casting is porous and will have to be repaired or replaced.

19   Make sure the oil cooler hose fittings are tight and in good condition.

Fluid comes out vent pipe or fill tube

20   If this condition occurs, the transaxle is overfilled, there is coolant in the fluid, the case is porous, the dipstick is incorrect, the vent is plugged or the drain-back holes are plugged.

3   Oil seal replacement

Refer to illustrations 3.4, 3.6, 3.9 and 3.10

1   Oil leaks frequently occur due to wear of the driveaxle oil seals and/or the speedometer drive gear oil seal and O-rings. Replacement of these seals is relatively easy, since the repairs can usually be performed without removing the transaxle from the vehicle.

Driveaxle oil seals

2   The driveaxle oil seals are located on the sides of the transaxle, where the inner ends of the driveaxles are splined into the differential side gears. If you suspect that a driveaxle oil seal is leaking, raise the

3.4 Carefully pry out the driveaxle oil seal with a seal removal tool or a screwdriver; make sure you don't damage the seal bore or the new seal may leak

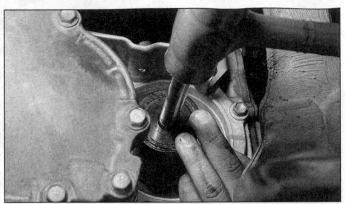

3.6 Use a seal installer, a large socket or a piece of pipe to install the new seal

3.9 Disconnect the speedometer cable, remove the bolt (arrow) and pull the speedometer driven gear straight out of the transaxle

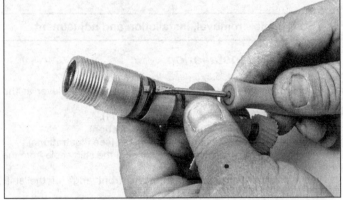

3.10 Remove the oil seal O-ring from the speedometer driven gear with a small screwdriver

vehicle and support it securely on jackstands. If the seal is leaking, you'll see lubricant on the side of the transaxle, below the seal.

3   Remove the driveaxle (see Chapter 8).

4   Using a screwdriver or pry bar, carefully pry the oil seal out of the transaxle bore **(see illustration)**.

5   If the oil seal cannot be removed with a screwdriver or pry bar, a special oil seal removal tool (available at auto parts stores) will be required.

6   Using a large section of pipe or a large deep socket as a drift, install the new oil seal. Drive it into the bore squarely and make sure that it is completely seated **(see illustration)**. Lubricate the lip of the new seal with multi-purpose grease.

7   Install the driveaxle(s). Be careful not to damage the lip of the new seal.

Speedometer gear O-ring

8   The speedometer cable and driven gear housing is located on the transaxle housing. Look for lubricant around the cable housing to determine if the seal and O-ring are leaking.

9   Disconnect the speedometer cable and remove the speedometer gear from the transaxle **(see illustration)**.

10   Using a scribe or a small screwdriver, remove the O-ring seal **(see illustration)**.

11   Install a new O-ring on the driven gear housing.

12   Installation is the reverse of removal.

---

4   Throttle valve (TV) cable - check and adjustment

Refer to illustration 4.3

1   If the vehicle is carbureted, remove the air cleaner; if it's fuel-

injected, remove the duct between the air cleaner and the throttle body (see Chapter 5).

2   Have an assistant press the accelerator pedal all the way to the floor and hold it while you measure the distance between the end of the boot and the stopper on the cable.

3   If the measurement taken is out-of range, have the assistant continue to hold the pedal down while you loosen the adjusting nuts and adjust the cable housing so that the distance between the end of the boot and the stopper on the cable is within the range shown **(see illustration)**.

4   Tighten the adjusting nuts securely, recheck the clearance and make sure the throttle valve opens all the way when the throttle is depressed.

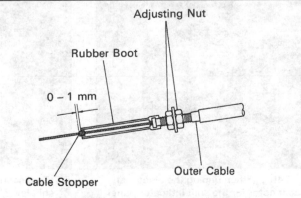

4.3 Throttle cable adjustment details

7B

5.1 To disconnect the shift cable from the manual shift lever at the transaxle, remove this nut (arrow)

5.3 To remove the shift lever handle, remove the two screws - one in front, one in back - from the shift lever and pull the handle straight up

5.4a To remove the gear position indicator panel, remove these four screws (arrows) . . .

5   Shift cable - removal, installation and adjustment

Removal and installation

Refer to illustrations 5.1, 5.3, 5.4a, 5.4b, 5.5 and 5.8

1   Disconnect the shift cable from the manual shift lever at the transaxle **(see illustration)**.
2   Remove the center console (see Chapter 11).
3   Remove the shift lever handle **(see illustration)**.
4   Remove the gear-position indicator panel **(see illustrations)**.
5   Remove the retaining clip and disconnect the shift cable from the shift lever **(see illustration)**.
6   Remove the retaining clip from the front edge of the shift lever base.
7   Pull the cable through the grommet in the firewall.
8   Installation is the reverse of removal. Make sure the shift lock override is properly engaged **(see illustration)**.
9   When you're done, adjust the shift cable.

Adjustment

10   Loosen the nut on the manual shift lever at the transaxle **(see illustration 5.1)**.
11   Push the lever toward the right side of the vehicle until it stops, then return it two notches to the Neutral position.
12   Move the shift lever inside the vehicle to the Neutral position.
13   While holding the lever with a slight pressure toward the Reverse position, tighten the nut securely.
14   Check the operation of the transaxle in each shift lever position

(try to start the engine in each gear - the starter should operate in the Park and Neutral positions only).

6   Neutral start switch - check, adjustment and replacement

Adjustment

Refer to illustrations 6.4 and 6.5

1   If the engine will start with the shift lever in any position other than Park or Neutral, adjust the neutral start switch.
2   Raise the front of the vehicle and place it securely on jackstands.
3   There are two ways to adjust the Neutral start switch. First, check the continuity of the switch with an ohmmeter. Unplug the electrical connector from the switch and loosen the switch retaining bolts.
4   Touch the ohmmeter leads to the switch terminals inside the electrical connector and rotate the switch until there is continuity between the terminals, indicating that it's now in the Neutral position **(see illustration)**. Tighten the bolts securely.
5   Here's the other way to adjust the switch: Rotate the switch until the neutral basic line on the switch housing is lined up with the groove in the shift shaft, hold the switch in this position and tighten the bolts securely **(see illustration)**.

Replacement

6   Disconnect the negative cable from the battery. **Caution:** *If the stereo in your vehicle is equipped with an anti-theft system, make sure you have the correct activation code before disconnecting the battery.*

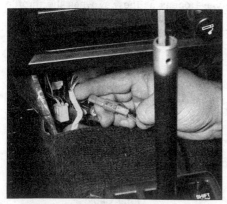

5.4b . . . then unplug the electrical connector for the shift indicator panel light and remove the panel

5.5 To disconnect the shift cable from the shift lever, pull out the retaining clip (arrow) and disengage the cable from the shift lever

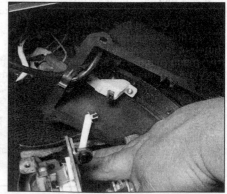

5.8 When installing the gear position indicator panel, make sure the shift lock override mechanism is properly engaged

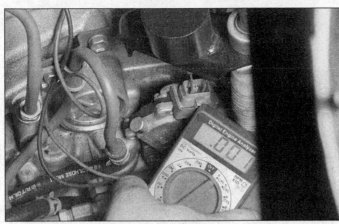

6.4 With the transaxle in Neutral, check continuity with an ohmmeter as shown: Loosen the switch retaining bolts, touch the leads of the ohmmeter to the switch terminals inside the electrical connector and rotate the switch until the meter indicates zero resistance

7   Shift the transaxle into Neutral.
8   Remove the nut and lift off the shift lever.
9   Unplug the electrical connector.
10   Remove the retaining bolts and lift the switch off the shift shaft.
11   To install, line up the flats on the shift shaft with the flats in the switch and push the switch onto the shaft.
12   Install the bolts, but leave them loose and follow the adjustment procedure above. The remainder of installation is the reverse of removal.

7   Shift lock system - description, check and component replacement

Description

Refer to illustration 7.1

1   The shift lock system **(see illustration)** prevents the shift lever

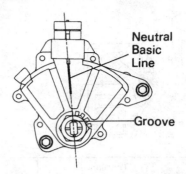

6.5 Rotate the switch until the neutral basic line aligns with the groove and tighten the bolts

from being shifted out of Park or Neutral until the brake pedal is applied.

Key interlock solenoid

Refer to illustration 7.4

2   Remove the steering column covers (see Chapter 11).
3   Unplug the electrical connector for the key interlock solenoid.
4   Using an ohmmeter, measure the resistance between the indicated terminals **(see illustration)**.
5   Apply battery voltage between the same two terminals. Verify that the solenoid makes an audible "click" when energized.
6   If the key interlock solenoid fails either of these tests, replace it.
7   Install the steering column covers.

Shift lock solenoid

Refer to illustration 7.10

8   Remove the floor console (see Chapter 11).
9   Unplug the shift lock solenoid connector.
10   Using an ohmmeter, measure the resistance between the indicated terminals **(see illustration)**, and compare your measurement with the resistance listed in this Chapter's Specifications.
11   Apply battery voltage to the same two terminals and verify that there's an audible "click" from the solenoid.
12   If the shift lock solenoid fails either of these tests, replace it.

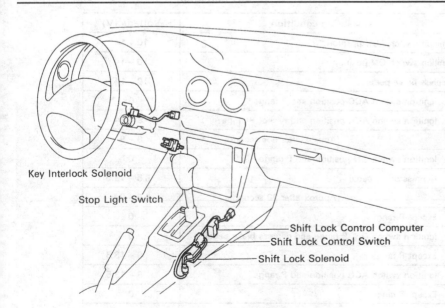

Key Interlock Solenoid

Stop Light Switch

Shift Lock Control Computer
Shift Lock Control Switch
Shift Lock Solenoid

7.1 Typical shift lock system

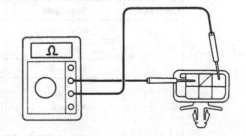

7.4 Terminal guide, key interlock solenoid

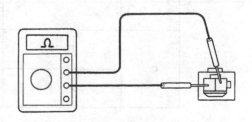

7.10 Terminal guide, shift lock solenoid

7B

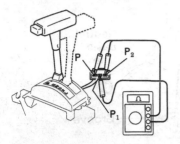

○—○ : Continuity

Terminal Shift Position	P	P₁	P₂
P range (Release button is not pushed)	○—○		
R, N, D, 2, L range	○—	—○	

7.13a Terminal guide and continuity table, shift lock control switch (1990 models)

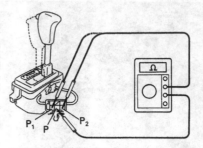

Shift position	Tester condition to terminal number	Specified value
P position (Release button is not pushed)	P − P₁	Continuity
R position (Release button is pushed)	P − P₁ P − P₂	Continuity
R, N, D, 2, L position	P − P₂	Continuity

7.13b Terminal guide and continuity table, shift lock control switch (1991 and later models)

Shift lock control switch

Refer to illustrations 7.13a and 7.13b

13   Verify that there's continuity between the indicated terminals in each shift lever position **(see illustrations)**.

14   If the shift lock control switch fails any of these tests, replace it.

Shift lock control computer

Refer to illustration 7.15

15   Using a voltmeter, measure the voltage at the indicated terminals **(see illustration)** and compare your measurements with the voltage values specified in the accompanying illustrations. **Note:** *Do NOT*

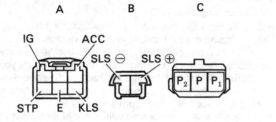

1990

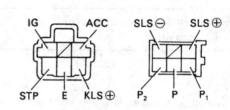

1991 and later

Connector	Terminal	Measuring condition	Voltage (V)
A	ACC − E	Ignition switch ACC position	10 – 14
	IG − E	Ignition switch ON position	10 – 14
	STP − E	Depress brake pedal	10 – 14
	KLS − E	① Ignition switch ACC position and P range	0
		② Ignition switch ACC position and except P range	8 – 14
		③ (Approx-after one second)	6 – 9
B	SLS ⊕ − SLS ⊖	① Ignition switch ON position and P range	0
		② Depress brake pedal	8.5 – 13.5
		③ (Approx-after 20 seconds)	5.5 – 9.5
		④ Except P range	0
C	P₁ − P	① Ignition switch ON, P range and depress brake pedal	0
		② Except P range	9 – 13.5
	P₂ − P₁	③ Ignition switch ACC position and P range	9 – 13.5
		④ Except P range	0

7.15 Terminal guide and voltage table, shift lock control computer

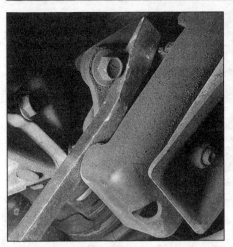

8.1 To check the transaxle mount, insert a large screwdriver or prybar between the rubber insulator and the bracket as shown, and try to lever the transaxle up and down

9.2 Remove this bolt (arrow) and detach the wiring harness clamp from the transaxle

9.4 To disconnect the throttle valve (TV) cable from the throttle link, loosen the locknuts (right arrow) at the bracket, then pull the cable toward the firewall and disengage the plug on the end (left arrow) from the throttle lever

unplug the computer connector; instead, "backprobe" it (go in through the back, the wiring harness side of the connector, with a small T-head needle, which you can obtain at any fabric store).

16   If the shift lock control computer fails any of these tests, replace it.

17   Install the floor console (see Chapter 11).

8   Transaxle mount - check and replacement

Refer to illustration 8.1

1   Insert a large screwdriver or prybar between the mount and the transaxle and pry up **(see illustration)**.

2   The transaxle should not move excessively away from the mount. If it does, replace the mount.

3   To replace a mount, support the transaxle with a jack, remove the nuts and bolts and remove the mount. It may be necessary to raise the transaxle slightly to provide enough clearance to remove the mount.

4   Installation is the reverse of removal.

9   Automatic transaxle - removal and installation

Removal

Refer to illustrations 9.2, 9.4, 9.6, 9.9, 9.13, 9.14, 9.18, 9.19 and 9.20

1   Detach the cable from the negative battery terminal. **Caution:** *If the stereo in your vehicle is equipped with an anti-theft system, make sure you have the correct activation code before disconnecting the battery.* On 1991 and later vehicles, remove the battery (see Chapter 5).

2   Unplug the neutral start switch electrical connector (see Section 6) and detach the wiring harness clamp **(see illustration)**.

3   Disconnect the speedometer cable.

4   Disconnect the throttle cable from the throttle link **(see illustration)**.

5   Remove the starter (see Chapter 5).

6   Remove the upper transaxle-to-engine bolts **(see illustration)**.

7   Raise the vehicle and support it securely on jackstands.

8   Drain the transmission fluid and the differential fluid (see Chapter 1).

9   Disconnect the oil cooler hoses **(see illustration)**.

10   Remove the engine splash shields (see Chapter 1).

11   Disconnect the shift cable from the transaxle (see Section 5).

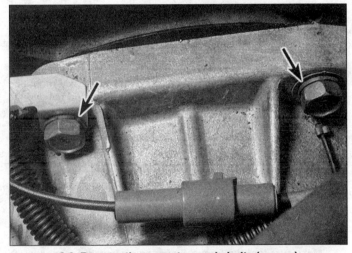

9.6 Remove the upper transaxle bolts (arrows)

9.9 Disconnect the oil cooler hoses from the transaxle

7B

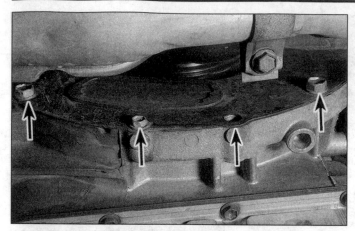

9.13 Remove the torque converter access plate bolts (arrows) and remove the cover

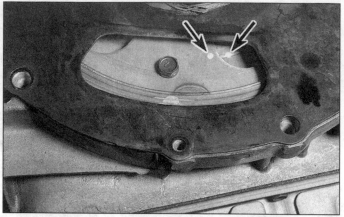

9.14 Mark the relationship of the torque converter to the driveplate (arrows) to ensure proper dynamic balance when it's reattached, then remove all six torque converter bolts by rotating the crankshaft to bring each bolt to the bottom, where you can get at it

12   Remove the driveaxles (see Chapter 8).
13   Remove the torque converter cover (see illustration).
14   Mark the relationship of the torque converter to the driveplate so they can be installed in the same position (see illustration).
15   Remove the six torque converter mounting bolts. Turn the crankshaft for access to each one in turn.
16   Support the engine using a hoist from above, or a jack and a wood block under the oil pan to spread the load.
17   Support the transaxle with a jack - preferably a special jack made for this purpose. Safety chains will help steady the transaxle on the jack.
18   Remove the mounting bolts from the left transaxle mounting bracket, detach the ground cable from the bracket and remove the bracket (see illustration).
19   Remove the rear engine mounting bracket (see illustration).
20   Remove the lower engine-to-transaxle bolts (see illustration).
21   Lower the transaxle slightly and disconnect and plug the transaxle cooler lines.
22   Move the transaxle to the side to disengage it from the engine block dowel pins and make sure the torque converter is detached from the driveplate. Secure the torque converter to the transaxle so that it will not fall out during removal. Lower the transaxle from the vehicle.

Installation

23   Make sure that the torque converter is securely engaged in the transaxle prior to installation.
24   With the transaxle secured to the jack, raise it into position. Be sure to keep it level so the torque converter does not slide forward. Connect the cooler lines.

25   Move the transaxle carefully into place until the dowel pins are engaged and the torque converter is engaged.
26   Turn the torque converter to line up the bolt holes with the holes in the driveplate. The match marks on the torque converter and driveplate, made during step 5, must line up.
27   Install the transaxle-to-engine bolts and nuts. Tighten them to the torque listed in this Chapter's Specifications.
28   Install the torque converter-to-driveplate bolts. Tighten them to the torque listed in this Chapter's Specifications.
29   Install the transaxle and any suspension and chassis components which were removed. Tighten the bolts and nuts to the torque values listed in the Chapter 10 Specifications section.
30   Remove the jacks supporting the transaxle and the engine.
31   Install the fluid filler tube.
32   Install the starter.
33   Connect the vacuum hose(s) (if equipped).
34   Connect the shift and throttle valve linkage.
35   Plug in the transaxle electrical connectors.
36   Install the torque converter cover.
37   Connect the driveaxles to the transaxle (see Chapter 8).
38   Connect the speedometer.
39   Adjust the shift linkage (see Section 5).
40   Install any exhaust system components which were removed.
41   Lower the vehicle.
42   Fill the transaxle with the proper type and amount of fluid (see Chapter 1). Run the vehicle and check for fluid leaks.

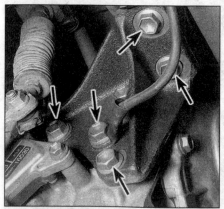

9.18 Remove the bolts (arrows), the ground strap and the left transaxle mounting bracket

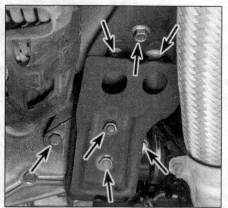

9.19 Remove the bolts and nuts (arrows) and remove the rear engine mounting bracket

9.20 Remove the lower transaxle-to-engine bolts (arrow)

Chapter 8
Clutch and driveaxles

Contents

Specifications

Clutch

Fluid type	See Chapter 1
Pedal freeplay	See Chapter 1
Clutch start switch clearance	Greater than 0.04 inch
Driveaxle standard length	
Left driveaxle	21-13/16 ± 3/16 inches
Right driveaxle	30-7/8 ± 3/16 inches

Torque specifications

Ft-lbs (unless otherwise indicated)

Clutch master cylinder mounting nuts	9
Clutch pressure plate-to-flywheel bolts	14
Clutch release cylinder mounting bolts	9
Control arm-to-lower balljoint bolt and nuts	59
Driveaxle/hub nut	
1991 and earlier	137
1992 and 1993	166
1994	159
Wheel lug nuts	See Chapter 1

8

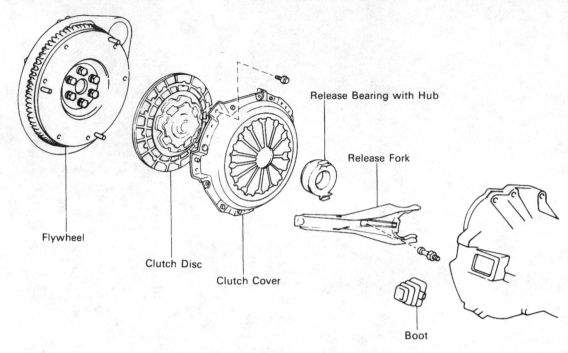

2.1 Typical clutch assembly details

1   General information

The information in this Chapter deals with the components from the rear of the engine to the front wheels, except for the transaxle, which is dealt with in Chapter 7A and 7B. For the purposes of this Chapter, these components are grouped into two categories: Clutch and driveaxles. Separate Sections within this Chapter offer general descriptions and checking procedures for both groups.

Since nearly all the procedures covered in this Chapter involve working under the vehicle, make sure it's securely supported on sturdy jackstands or a hoist where the vehicle can be easily raised and lowered.

2   Clutch - description and check

Refer to illustration 2.1

1   All vehicles with a manual transaxle use a single dry plate, diaphragm spring type clutch **(see illustration)**. The clutch disc has a splined hub which allows it to slide along the splines of the transaxle input shaft. The clutch and pressure plate are held in contact by spring pressure exerted by the diaphragm in the pressure plate.

2   The clutch release system is operated by hydraulic pressure. The hydraulic release system consists of the clutch pedal, a master cylinder and fluid reservoir, the hydraulic line, a slave cylinder which actuates the clutch release lever and the clutch release (or throw-out) bearing.

3   When pressure is applied to the clutch pedal to release the clutch, hydraulic pressure is exerted against the outer end of the clutch release lever. As the lever pivots, the shaft fingers push against the release bearing. The bearing pushes against the fingers of the diaphragm spring of the pressure plate assembly, which in turn releases the clutch plate.

4   Terminology can be a problem regarding the clutch components because common names have in some cases changed from that used by the manufacturer. For example, the driven plate is also called the clutch plate or disc, the pressure plate assembly is sometimes referred

to as the clutch cover, the clutch release bearing is sometimes called a throw-out bearing, and the release cylinder is sometimes called the operating or slave cylinder.

5   Other than replacing components that have obvious damage, some preliminary checks should be performed to diagnose a clutch system failure.

a)   *The first check should be of the fluid level in the clutch master cylinder (see Chapter 1). If the fluid level is low, add fluid as necessary and inspect the hydraulic clutch system for leaks. If the master cylinder reservoir has run dry, bleed the system (see Section 7) and retest the clutch operation.*

b)   *To check "clutch spin down time," run the engine at normal idle speed with the transaxle in Neutral (clutch pedal up - engaged). Disengage the clutch (pedal down), wait several seconds and shift the transaxle into Reverse. No grinding noise should be heard. A grinding noise would most likely indicate a problem in the pressure plate or the clutch disc.*

c)   *To check for complete clutch release, run the engine (with the parking brake applied to prevent movement) and hold the clutch pedal approximately 1/2-inch from the floor. Shift the transaxle between 1st gear and Reverse several times. If the shift is not smooth, component failure is indicated. Check the release cylinder pushrod travel. With the clutch pedal depressed completely the release cylinder pushrod should extend substantially. If it doesn't, check the fluid level in the clutch master cylinder.*

d)   *Visually inspect the clutch pedal bushing at the top of the clutch pedal to make sure there is no sticking or excessive wear.*

e)   *Under the vehicle, check that the clutch release lever is solidly mounted on the ball stud.*

3   Clutch components - removal, inspection and installation

Warning: *Dust produced by clutch wear and deposited on clutch components may contain asbestos, which is hazardous to your health. DO NOT blow it out with compressed air and DO NOT inhale it. DO*

3.6 Mark the relationship of the pressure plate to the flywheel (in case you're going to reuse the same pressure plate)

3.10 Examine the clutch disc for evidence of excessive wear, such as smeared friction material, chewed-up rivets, worn hub splines and distorted damper cushions or springs

NOT use gasoline or petroleum based solvents to remove the dust. Brake system cleaner should be used to flush the dust into a drain pan. After the clutch components are wiped clean with a rag, dispose of the contaminated rags and cleaner in a labeled, covered container.

Removal

Refer to illustration 3.6

1   Access to the clutch components is normally accomplished by removing the transaxle, leaving the engine in the vehicle. If, of course, the engine is being removed for major overhaul, then the opportunity should always be taken to check the clutch for wear and replace worn components as necessary. However, the relatively low cost of the clutch components compared to the time and labor involved in gaining access to them warrants their replacement any time the engine or transaxle is removed, unless they are new or in near-perfect condition. The following procedures assume that the engine will stay in place.

2   Remove the release cylinder (see Section 6). Hang it out of the way with a piece of wire - it's not necessary to disconnect the hose.

3   Remove the transaxle from the vehicle (see Chapter 7A). Support the engine while the transaxle is out. Preferably, an engine hoist should be used to support it from above. However, if a jack is used underneath the engine, make sure a piece of wood is used between the jack and oil pan to spread the load. **Caution:** *The pick-up for the oil pump is very close to the bottom of the oil pan. If the pan is bent or distorted in any way, engine oil starvation could occur.*

4   The release fork and release bearing can remain attached to the transaxle for the time being.

5   To support the clutch disc during removal, install a clutch alignment tool through the clutch disc hub.

6   Carefully inspect the flywheel and pressure plate for indexing marks. The marks are usually an X, an O or a white letter. If they cannot be found, scribe marks yourself so the pressure plate and the flywheel will be in the same alignment during installation **(see illustration)**.

7   Slowly loosen the pressure plate-to-flywheel bolts. Work in a diagonal pattern and loosen each bolt a little at a time until all spring pressure is relieved. Then hold the pressure plate securely and completely remove the bolts, followed by the pressure plate and clutch disc.

Inspection

Refer to illustrations 3.10, 3.12a and 3.12b

8   Ordinarily, when a problem occurs in the clutch, it can be attributed to wear of the clutch driven plate assembly (clutch disc). However, all components should be inspected at this time.

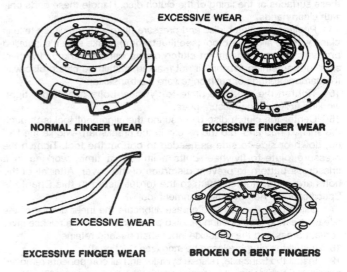

3.12a Replace the pressure plate if any of these conditions are noted

EXCESSIVE WEAR

NORMAL FINGER WEAR   EXCESSIVE FINGER WEAR

EXCESSIVE WEAR

EXCESSIVE FINGER WEAR   BROKEN OR BENT FINGERS

9   Inspect the flywheel for cracks, heat checking, score marks and other damage. If the imperfections are slight, a machine shop can resurface it to make it flat and smooth. Refer to Chapter 2 for the flywheel removal procedure.

10   Inspect the lining on the clutch disc. There should be at least 1/16-inch of lining above the rivet heads. Check for loose rivets, distortion, cracks, broken springs and other obvious damage **(see illustration)**. As mentioned above, ordinarily the clutch disc is replaced as a matter of course, so if in doubt about the condition, replace it with a new one.

11   The release bearing should be replaced along with the clutch disc (see Section 4).

12   Check the machined surface and the diaphragm spring fingers of the pressure plate **(see illustrations)**. If the surface is grooved or otherwise damaged, replace the pressure plate assembly. Also check for obvious damage, distortion, cracking, etc. Light glazing can be removed with emery cloth or sandpaper. If a new pressure plate is indicated, new or factory rebuilt units are available.

8

3.12b Examine the pressure plate friction surface for score marks, cracks and evidence of overheating (blue spots)

3.14 Center the clutch disc in the pressure plate with a clutch alignment tool

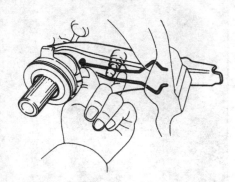

4.3 Reach behind the release lever and disengage the lever from the ball stud by pulling on the retention spring, then remove the lever and bearing

Installation

Refer to illustration 3.14

13   Before installation, carefully wipe the flywheel and pressure plate machined surfaces clean. It's important that no oil or grease is on these surfaces or the lining of the clutch disc. Handle these parts only with clean hands.

14   Position the clutch disc and pressure plate with the clutch held in place with an alignment tool **(see illustration)**. Make sure it's installed properly (most replacement clutch plates will be marked "flywheel side" or something similar - if not marked, install the clutch disc with the damper springs or cushion toward the transaxle).

15   Tighten the pressure plate-to-flywheel bolts only finger tight, working around the pressure plate.

16   Center the clutch disc by ensuring the alignment tool is through the splined hub and into the recess in the crankshaft. Wiggle the tool up, down or side-to-side as needed to bottom the tool. Tighten the pressure plate-to-flywheel bolts a little at a time, working in a crisscross pattern to prevent distortion of the cover. After all of the bolts are snug, tighten them to the torque listed in this Chapter's Specifications. Remove the alignment tool.

17   Using high-temperature grease, lubricate the inner groove of the release bearing (see Section 4). Also place grease on the release lever contact areas and the transaxle input shaft bearing retainer.

18   Install the clutch release bearing (see Section 4).

19   Install the transaxle, release cylinder and all components removed previously, tightening all fasteners to the proper torque specifications.

4.4 To check the operation of the bearing, hold it by the outer race and rotate the inner race while applying pressure - the bearing should turn smoothly - if it doesn't, replace it

4   Clutch release bearing and lever - removal, inspection and installation

Warning: *Dust produced by clutch wear and deposited on clutch components may contain asbestos, which is hazardous to your health. DO NOT blow it out with compressed air and DO NOT inhale it. DO NOT use gasoline or petroleum-based solvents to remove the dust. Brake system cleaner should be used to flush it into a drain pan. After the clutch components are wiped clean with a rag, dispose of the contaminated rags and cleaner in a labeled, covered container.*

Removal

Refer to illustration 4.3

1   Disconnect the negative cable from the battery. **Caution:** *If the stereo in your vehicle is equipped with an anti-theft system, make sure you have the correct activation code before disconnecting the battery.*

2   Remove the transaxle (see Chapter 7).

3   Remove the clutch release lever from the ball stud, then remove the bearing from the lever **(see illustration)**.

Inspection

Refer to illustration 4.4

4   Hold the bearing by the outer race and rotate the inner race while applying pressure **(see illustration)**. If the bearing doesn't turn smoothly or if it's noisy, replace the bearing/hub assembly with a new one. Wipe the bearing with a clean rag and inspect it for damage, wear and cracks. Don't immerse the bearing in solvent - it's sealed for life and to do so would ruin it. Also check the release lever for cracks and bends.

Installation

Refer to illustrations 4.5 and 4.6

5   Fill the inner groove of the release bearing with high-temperature

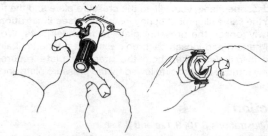

4.5 Apply a light coat of high-temperature grease to the transaxle bearing retainer and also fill the release bearing groove

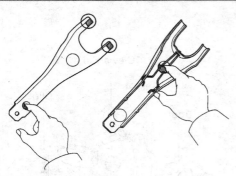

4.6 Apply high temperature grease to the release lever in the areas indicated

5.2 To release the clutch pushrod from the clutch pedal, remove this clip (arrow), the wave washer (if equipped) and the clevis pin

grease. Also apply a light coat of the same grease to the transaxle input shaft splines and the front bearing retainer **(see illustration)**.

6   Lubricate the release lever ball socket, lever ends and release cylinder pushrod socket with high-temperature grease **(see illustration)**.

7   Attach the release bearing to the release lever.

8   Slide the release bearing onto the transaxle input shaft front bearing retainer while passing the end of the release lever through the opening in the clutch housing. Push the clutch release lever onto the ball stud until it's firmly seated.

9   Apply a light coat of high-temperature grease to the face of the release bearing where it contacts the pressure plate diaphragm fingers.

10   The remainder of installation is the reverse of the removal procedure.

5   Clutch master cylinder - removal, overhaul and installation

Note: *Before beginning this procedure, contact local parts stores and dealer service departments concerning the purchase of a rebuild kit or a new master cylinder. Availability and cost of the necessary parts may dictate whether the cylinder is rebuilt or replaced with a new one. If it's decided to rebuild the cylinder, inspect the bore as described in Step 12 before purchasing parts.*

Removal

Refer to illustration 5.2

1   Disconnect the negative cable from the battery. **Caution:** *If the stereo in your vehicle is equipped with an anti-theft system, make sure you have the correct activation code before disconnecting the battery.*

2   Under the dashboard, disconnect the pushrod from the top of the clutch pedal. It's held in place with a clevis pin. To remove the clevis pin, remove the clip **(see illustration)**. On 1989 and earlier vehicles, there's also a wave washer.

3   Disconnect the hydraulic line at the clutch master cylinder. If available, use a flare-nut wrench on the fitting, to protect the fitting from being rounded off. Have rags handy as some fluid will be lost as the line is removed. **Caution:** *Don't allow brake fluid to come into contact with paint, as it will damage the finish.*

4   From under the dash, remove the nuts which attach the master cylinder to the firewall. Remove the master cylinder, again being careful not to spill any of the fluid.

Overhaul

Refer to illustrations 5.5a, 5.5b, 5.6 and 5.8

5   Remove the reservoir cap and drain all fluid from the master cylinder. On 1990 and earlier vehicles, loosen the hose clamp and

8

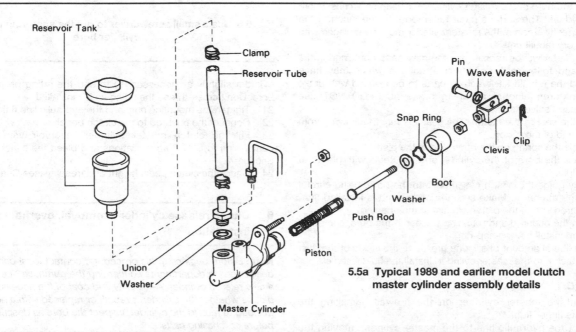

5.5a Typical 1989 and earlier model clutch master cylinder assembly details

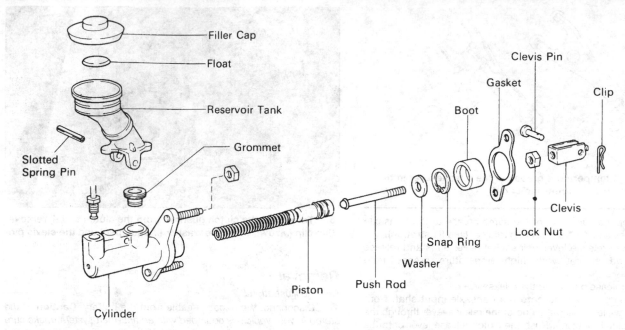

5.5b Typical 1990 and later model clutch master cylinder assembly details

separate the remote reservoir from the reservoir-to-master cylinder hose. On 1991 and later vehicles, drive out the spring pin with a hammer and punch, then carefully pry the reservoir off **(see illustration)**.

6   Pull back the dust cover on the pushrod and remove the snap-ring **(see illustration)**. On 1989 and earlier vehicles, you can pry out the snap-ring with a small screwdriver. On 1990 and later vehicles, you'll need to use snap-ring pliers with the right size tips.

7   Remove the retaining washer and the pushrod from the cylinder.

8   Tap the master cylinder on a block of wood to eject the piston assembly from inside the bore **(see illustration)**. **Note:** *If the rebuild kit supplies a complete piston assembly, ignore the Steps which don't apply.*

9   Separate the spring from the piston.

10   Carefully remove the seal from the piston.

11   Inspect the bore of the master cylinder for deep scratches, score marks and ridges. The surface must be smooth to the touch. If the bore isn't perfectly smooth, the master cylinder must be replaced with a new or factory rebuilt unit.

12   If the cylinder will be rebuilt, use the new parts contained in the rebuild kit and follow any specific instructions which may have accompanied the rebuild kit. Wash all parts to be re-used with brake cleaner, denatured alcohol or clean brake fluid. DO NOT use petroleum-based solvents.

13   Attach the seal to the piston. The seal lips must face away from the pushrod end of the piston.

14   Assemble the spring on the other end of the piston.

15   Lubricate the bore of the cylinder and the seals with plenty of fresh brake fluid.

16   Carefully guide the piston assembly into the bore, being careful not to damage the seals. Make sure the spring end is installed first, with the pushrod end of the piston closest to the opening.

17   Position the pushrod and retaining washer in the bore, compress the spring and install a new snap-ring.

18   Apply a liberal amount of silicone grease to the inside of the dust cover and attach it to the master cylinder. Install the fluid reservoir

Installation

19   Position the master cylinder on the firewall, installing the mounting nuts finger-tight.

20   Connect the hydraulic line to the master cylinder, moving the

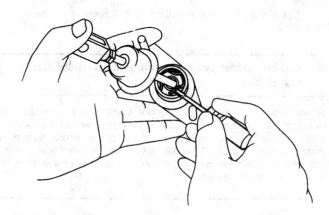

5.6 Use a small screwdriver to pry the snap-ring from the cylinder bore

cylinder slightly as necessary to thread the fitting properly into the bore. Don't cross-thread the fitting as it's installed.

21   Tighten the mounting nuts and the hydraulic line fitting securely.

22   Connect the pushrod to the clutch pedal.

23   Fill the clutch master cylinder reservoir with brake fluid conforming to DOT 3 specifications and bleed the clutch system (see Section 7).

24   Check the clutch pedal height and freeplay (see Chapter 1).

6   Clutch release cylinder - removal, overhaul and installation

Note: *Before beginning this procedure, contact local parts stores and dealer service departments concerning the purchase of a rebuild kit or a new release cylinder. Availability and cost of the necessary parts may dictate whether the cylinder is rebuilt or replaced with a new one. If it's decided to rebuild the cylinder, inspect the bore as described in Step 8 before purchasing parts.*

5.8 Invert the cylinder and tap it against a block of wood to eject the piston

6.3 Use a flare-nut wrench when disconnecting the hydraulic line fitting (arrow) to prevent rounding off the corners of the tubing nut, then remove the two mounting bolts (arrows)

Removal

Refer to illustration 6.3

1   Disconnect the negative cable from the battery. **Caution:** *If the stereo in your vehicle is equipped with an anti-theft system, make sure you have the correct activation code before disconnecting the battery.*
2   Raise the vehicle and support it securely on jackstands.
3   Disconnect the hydraulic line at the release cylinder. If available, use a flare-nut wrench on the fitting, which will prevent the fitting from being rounded off **(see illustration)**. Have a small can and rags handy, as some fluid will be spilled as the line is removed.
4   Remove the release cylinder mounting bolts.
5   Remove the release cylinder.

Overhaul

Refer to illustration 6.6

6   Remove the pushrod and the boot **(see illustration)**.
7   Tap the cylinder on a block of wood to eject the piston and seal.

Remove the spring from inside the cylinder.
8   Carefully inspect the bore of the cylinder. Check for deep scratches, score marks and ridges. The bore must be smooth to the touch. If any imperfections are found, the release cylinder must be replaced with a new one.
9   Using the new parts in the rebuild kit, assemble the components using plenty of fresh brake fluid for lubrication. Note the installed direction of the spring and the seal.

Installation

10   Install the release cylinder on the clutch housing. Make sure the pushrod is seated in the release fork pocket.
11   Connect the hydraulic line to the release cylinder. Tighten the connection.
12   Fill the clutch master cylinder with brake fluid (conforming to DOT 3 specifications).
13   Bleed the system (see Section 7).
14   Lower the vehicle and connect the negative battery cable.

8

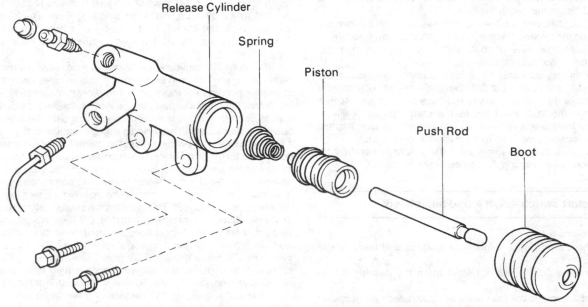

Release Cylinder

Spring

Piston

Push Rod

Boot

6.6 Typical clutch release cylinder assembly details

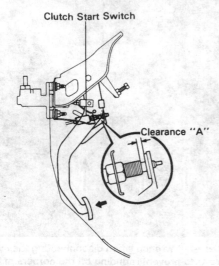

Clutch Start Switch

Clearance "A"

8.4 To check the clutch start switch adjustment on 1990 and earlier vehicles, depress the clutch pedal, measure clearance "A" and compare your measurement to the dimension listed in this Chapter's Specifications

7   Clutch hydraulic system - bleeding

1   The hydraulic system should be bled of all air whenever any part of the system has been removed or if the fluid level has been allowed to fall so low that air has been drawn into the master cylinder. The procedure is very similar to bleeding a brake system.

2   Fill the master cylinder with new brake fluid conforming to DOT 3 specifications. **Caution:** *Do not re-use any of the fluid coming from the system during the bleeding operation or use fluid which has been inside an open container for an extended period of time.*

3   Raise the vehicle and place it securely on jackstands to gain access to the release cylinder, which is located on the left side of the clutch housing.

4   Remove the dust cap which fits over the bleeder valve and push a length of plastic hose over the valve. Place the other end of the hose into a clear container with about two inches of brake fluid in it. The hose end must be submerged in the fluid.

5   Have an assistant depress the clutch pedal and hold it. Open the bleeder valve on the release cylinder, allowing fluid to flow through the hose. Close the bleeder valve when fluid stops flowing from the hose. Once closed, have your assistant release the pedal.

6   Continue this process until all air is evacuated from the system, indicated by a full, solid stream of fluid being ejected from the bleeder valve each time and no air bubbles in the hose or container. Keep a close watch on the fluid level inside the clutch master cylinder reservoir; if the level drops too low, air will be sucked back into the system and the process will have to be started all over again.

7   Install the dust cap and lower the vehicle. Check carefully for proper operation before placing the vehicle in normal service.

8   Clutch start switch - check and adjustment

Refer to illustrations 8.4 and 8.5

1   Check the clutch pedal height and freeplay and the pushrod freeplay (see Chapter 1).

2   Verify that the engine will not start when the clutch pedal is released.

3   Verify that the engine will start when the clutch pedal is depressed all the way.

4   On 1990 and earlier vehicles, measure clearance "A" **(see illustration)** with the clutch pedal depressed, and compare your

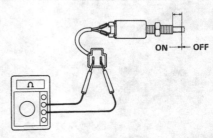

ON ⟶ OFF

8.5 Using an ohmmeter, check the continuity of the clutch start switch - there should be continuity when the switch is On (pushed) and no continuity when it's Off (released)

measurement with the clearance listed in this Chapter's Specifications. If the indicated clearance isn't as specified, adjust clutch start switch. On 1991 and later vehicles, this clearance is self-adjusting.

5   Verify that there is continuity between the clutch start switch terminals when the switch is On **(see illustration).**

6   Verify that no continuity exists between the switch terminals when the switch is Off.

7   If the switch fails either of the tests, replace it: Remove the nut nearest the plunger end of the switch and unscrew the switch. Unplug the wire harness. Installation is the reverse of removal.

8   To adjust the clutch start switch on 1990 and earlier vehicles, depress the clutch pedal completely and turn the switch in or out to achieve the distance shown in illustration 8.4. Again, 1991 and later vehicles have a self-adjusting switch.

9   Verify again that the engine doesn't start when the clutch pedal is released.

9   Driveaxles - general information and inspection

1   Power is transmitted from the transaxle to the wheels through a pair of driveaxles. The inner end of each driveaxle is splined into the differential side gears. The outer ends of the driveaxles are splined to the axle hubs and locked in place by a large nut.

2   The inner ends of the driveaxles are equipped with sliding constant velocity joints, which are capable of both angular and axial motion. Each inner joint assembly consists of a tripod bearing and a joint housing (outer race) in which the joint is free to slide in and out as the driveaxle moves up and down with the wheel. The joints can be disassembled and cleaned in the event of a boot failure (see Section 11), but if any parts are damaged, the joints must be replaced as a unit.

3   The outer CV joints are the "Rzeppa" type, which consists of ball bearings running between an inner race and an outer cage, is capable of angular but not axial movement. The outer joints should be cleaned, inspected and repacked, but they cannot be disassembled. If an outer joint is damaged, it must be replaced along with the axleshaft (the outer joint and axleshaft are sold as a single component).

4   The boots should be inspected periodically for damage and leaking lubricant. Torn CV joint boots must be replaced immediately or the joints can be damaged. Boot replacement involves removal of the driveaxle (see Section 10). **Note:** *Some auto parts stores carry "split" type replacement boots, which can be installed without removing the driveaxle from the vehicle. This is a convenient alternative; however, the driveaxle should be removed and the CV joint disassembled and cleaned to ensure the joint is free from contaminants such as moisture and dirt which will accelerate CV joint wear.* The most common symptom of worn or damaged CV joints, besides lubricant leaks, is a clicking noise in turns, a clunk when accelerating after coasting and vibration at highway speeds. To check for wear in the CV joints and driveaxle shafts, grasp each axle (one at a time) and rotate it in both directions while holding the CV joint housings, feeling for play indicating worn splines or sloppy CV joints. Also check the driveaxle shafts for cracks, dents and distortion.

10.4a Remove the cotter pin . . .

10.4b . . . and the nut lock

10.5 Use a large prybar to immobilize the hub while loosening the driveaxle hub nut

10 Driveaxle - removal and installation

Removal

Refer to illustrations 10.4a, 10.4b, 10.5, 10.6, 10.9 and 10.10

1   Disconnect the cable from the negative terminal of the battery. **Caution:** *If the stereo in your vehicle is equipped with an anti-theft system, make sure you have the correct activation code before disconnecting the battery.*

2   Set the parking brake.

3   Loosen the front wheel lug nuts, raise the vehicle and support it securely on jackstands. Remove the wheel.

4   Remove the cotter pin and the bearing nut lock from the driveaxle hub nut **(see illustrations)**.

5   Remove the driveaxle hub nut and washer. To prevent the hub from turning, wedge a prybar between two of the wheel studs and allow the prybar to rest against the ground or the floorpan of the vehicle **(see illustration)**.

6   To loosen the driveaxle from the hub splines, tap the end of the driveaxle with a soft-faced hammer or a hammer and a brass punch **(see illustration)**. If the driveaxle is stuck in the hub splines and won't move, it may be necessary to remove the brake disc (see Chapter 9) and push it from the hub with a two-jaw puller.

7   Remove the engine splash shields (see Chapter 1). Place a drain pan underneath the transaxle to catch the lubricant that will spill out when the driveaxles are removed.

8   Remove the nuts and bolt securing the balljoint to the control arm, then pry the control arm down to separate the components (see Chapter 10)

9   Pull out on the steering knuckle and detach the driveaxle from the hub **(see illustration)**.

10   Carefully pry the inner CV joint out of the transaxle **(see illustration)**.

11   Refer to Chapter 7 for the driveaxle oil seal replacement procedure.

Installation

12   Installation is the reverse of the removal procedure, but with the following additional points:

a) *When installing the left driveaxle, push the driveaxle sharply inward to seat the retaining ring on the inner CV joint in the groove in the differential side gear.*

b) *Tighten the driveaxle hub nut to the torque listed in this Chapter's Specifications, then install the nut lock and a new cotter pin.*

c) *Install the wheel and lug nuts, lower the vehicle and tighten the lug nuts to the torque listed in the Chapter 1 Specifications.*

d) *Check the transaxle or differential lubricant and add, if necessary, to bring it to the proper level (see Chapter 1).*

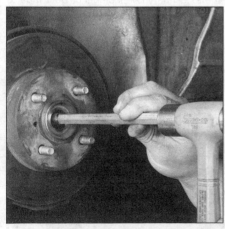

10.6 Using a brass punch, strike the end of the driveaxle sharply with a hammer; when it breaks free, it will move noticeably

10.9 Pull the steering knuckle out and slide the end of the driveaxle out of the hub

10.10 To separate the inner end of the driveaxle from the transaxle, pry on the CV joint housing like this with a large screwdriver or prybar, you may need to give the prybar a sharp rap with a brass hammer

8

11.3 Lift the tabs on all the the boot clamps with a screwdriver, then open the clamps

11.4 Remove the boot from the inner CV joint and slide the tripod from the joint housing

11.6 Remove the snap-ring with a pair of snap-ring pliers

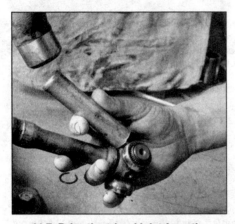

11.7 Drive the tripod joint from the driveaxle with a brass punch and hammer; be careful not to damage the bearing surfaces or the splines on the shaft

11.8 Wrap the splined area of the axleshaft with tape to prevent damage to the boots when removing or installing them

11.10a Install the tripod with the recessed portion of the splines facing the axleshaft

11 Driveaxle boot replacement and CV joint overhaul

Note: *If the CV joints must be overhauled (usually due to torn boots), explore all options before beginning the job. Complete rebuilt driveaxles are available on an exchange basis, which eliminates much time and work. Whichever route you choose to take, check on the cost and availability of parts before disassembling the vehicle.*

1   Remove the driveaxle (see Section 10).

Disassembly

Refer to illustrations 11.3, 11.4, 11.6, 11.7 and 11.8

2   Mount the driveaxle in a vice with wood lined jaws (to prevent damage to the axleshaft). Check the CV joint for excessive play in the radial direction, which indicates worn parts. Check for smooth operation throughout the full range of motion for each CV joint. If a boot is torn, disassemble the joint, clean the components and inspect for damage due to loss of lubrication and possible contamination by foreign matter.

3   Using a small screwdriver, pry the retaining tabs of the clamps up to loosen them and slide them off **(see illustration)**.

4   Using a screwdriver, carefully pry up on the edge of the outer boot and push it away from the CV joint. Old and worn boots can be cut off. Pull the inner CV joint boot back from the housing and slide the housing from the tripod **(see illustration)**.

5   Mark the tripod and axleshaft to ensure that they are reassembled properly.

6   Remove the tripod joint snap-ring with a pair of snap-ring pliers

(see illustration).

7   Use a hammer and a brass punch to drive the tripod joint from the driveaxle **(see illustration)**.

8   If you haven't already cut them off, remove both boots. Wrap the splines on the inner end the axleshaft with electrical or duct tape to protect the boots from the sharp edges of the splines **(see illustration)**.

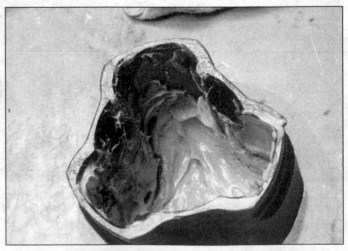

11.10b Place grease at the bottom of the CV joint housing

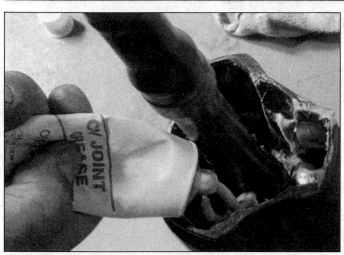

11.10c Install the boot and clamps onto the axleshaft, then insert the tripod into the housing, followed by the rest of the grease

11.12a Equalize the pressure inside the boot by inserting a small, dull screwdriver between the boot and the outer race

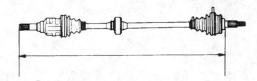

11.11 The driveaxle standard length should be set to the dimension listed in this Chapter's Specifications before the boot clamps are tightened

Check

9   Thoroughly clean all components, including the outer CV joint assembly, with solvent until the old CV joint grease is completely removed. Inspect the bearing surfaces of the inner tripods and housings for cracks, pitting, scoring and other signs of wear. It's not possible to inspect the bearing surfaces of the inner and outer races of the outer CV joint, but you can at least check the surfaces of the ball bearings themselves. If they're in good shape, so are the races; if they're not, neither are the races. If the inner CV joint is worn, you can buy a new inner CV joint and install it on the old axleshaft; if the outer CV joint is worn, you'll have to purchase a new outer CV joint *and* axleshaft (they're sold preassembled).

Reassembly

Refer to illustrations 11.10a, 11.10b, 11.10c, 11.11, 11.12a, 11.12b and 11.12c

10   Slide the clamps and boot onto the axleshaft, then place the tripod on the shaft. Apply grease to the tripod assembly and inside the housing. Insert the tripod into the housing and pack the remainder of the grease around the tripod. **(see illustrations)**.
11   Slide the boot into place, making sure both ends seat in their grooves. Adjust the length of the driveaxle to the dimension listed in this Chapter's Specifications **(see illustration)**.
12   Equalize the pressure in the boot, then tighten and secure the boot clamps **(see illustrations)**.

11.12b To install the new clamps, bend the tang down . . .

8

11.12c . . . then tap the tabs over to hold it in place

Notes

Chapter 9 Brakes

Contents

Specifications

General

Brake fluid type	See Chapter 1
Brake pedal height	
1990 and earlier	5-51/64 to 6-3/16 inches
1991 and later	
Four-speed manual transaxle	5-5/8 to 6 inches
All others	5-29/64 to 5-27/32 inches
Brake pedal freeplay	
1992 and earlier	1/8 to 1/4 inch
1993 and later	3/64 to 1/4 inch
Brake pedal reserve distance	
1990 and earlier	More than 2-13/64 inches
1991 and later	More than 1-31/32 inches
Brake light switch-to-pedal clearance	1/64 to 3/32 inch
Power brake booster pushrod-to-master cylinder piston clearance	0.0 inch

Disc brakes

Minimum brake pad thickness	See Chapter 1
Disc thickness*	
1990 and earlier	
Standard	0.433 inch
Minimum	0.394 inch
1991 and later	
Standard	0.709 inch
Minimum	0.669 inch
Disc runout limit	
1990 and earlier	0.0059 inch
1991 and later	0.0035 inch

Drum brakes

Drum inside diameter*	
Standard	7.087 inches
Maximum	7.126 inches

Note: *If different specifications are cast into the disc or drum, they supersede information printed here.*

9

Parking brake

Parking brake lever travel
    1990 and earlier.. 7 to 9 clicks
    1991 and later .... 4 to 7 clicks

Torque specifications

                                                Ft-lbs (unless otherwise indicated)
Brake hose to brake line fittings .... 132 in-lbs
Brake hose-to-caliper banjo fitting bolts 22
Caliper mounting bolts 18
Caliper torque plate bolts 65
Master cylinder-to-brake booster nuts .... 108 in-lbs
Power brake booster mounting nuts .... 108 in-lbs
Wheel cylinder mounting bolts .... 84 in-lbs
Wheel lug nuts .... See Chapter 1

1   General information

The vehicles covered by this manual are equipped with hydraulically operated front and rear brake systems. The front brakes are disc type and the rear brakes are drum type. Both the front and rear brakes are self adjusting. The disc brakes automatically compensate for pad wear, while the drum brakes incorporate an adjustment mechanism which is activated as the parking brake is applied.

Hydraulic system

The hydraulic system consists of two separate circuits. The master cylinder has separate reservoirs for the two circuits, and, in the event of a leak or failure in one hydraulic circuit, the other circuit will remain operative. A dual proportioning valve on the firewall provides brake balance between the front and rear brakes.

Power brake booster

The power brake booster, utilizing engine manifold vacuum and atmospheric pressure to provide assistance to the hydraulically operated brakes, is mounted on the firewall in the engine compartment.

Parking brake

The parking brake operates the rear brakes only, through cable

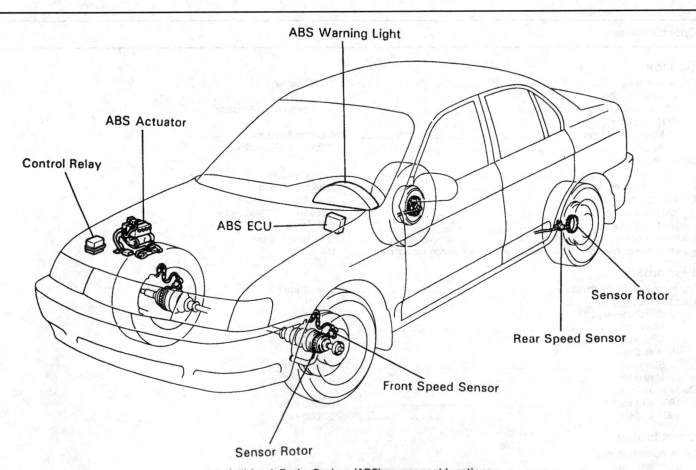

2.1 Anti-Lock Brake System (ABS) component locations

Service

After completing any operation involving disassembly of any part of the brake system, always test drive the vehicle to check for proper braking performance before resuming normal driving. When testing the brakes, perform the tests on a clean, dry, flat surface. Conditions other than these can lead to inaccurate test results.

Test the brakes at various speeds with both light and heavy pedal pressure. The vehicle should stop evenly without pulling to one side or the other. Avoid locking the brakes, because this slides the tires and diminishes braking efficiency and control of the vehicle.

Tires, vehicle load and wheel alignment are factors which also affect braking performance.

2 Anti-lock Brake System (ABS) - general information

Refer to illustration 2.1

1   The anti-lock brake system (ABS) **(see illustration)**, which was introduced in 1993, is designed to maintain vehicle steerability, directional stability and optimum deceleration under severe braking conditions and on most road surfaces. It does so by monitoring the rotational speed of each wheel and controlling the brake line pressure to each wheel during braking. This prevents the wheel from locking up.

Components

Actuator assembly

2   The actuator assembly consists of an electric hydraulic pump and four solenoid valves. The electric pump provides hydraulic pressure to charge the reservoirs in the actuator, which supplies pressure to the braking system. The pump and reservoirs are housed in the actuator assembly. The solenoid valves modulate brake line pressure during ABS operation. The body contains four valves - one for each wheel.

Speed sensors

Refer to illustrations 2.4 and 2.5

3   The speed sensors, which are located at each wheel, generate small electrical pulsations when the toothed sensor rotors are turning, sending a variable voltage signal to the ABS electronic control unit (ECU) indicating wheel rotational speed.

4   The front speed sensors **(see illustration)** are mounted on the front backing plates in close relationship to the toothed sensor rotors, which are integral with the outer constant velocity (CV) joints.

5   The rear wheel sensors are bolted to the brake backing plates or axle carriers **(see illustration)**. The sensor rotors are integral with the rear brake drum assemblies.

ABS computer

6   The ABS electronic control unit (ECU), which is mounted under the dashboard, is the "brain" of the ABS system. The function of the ECU is to accept and process information received from the wheel speed sensors to control the hydraulic line pressure, avoiding wheel lock up. The ECU also constantly monitors the system, even under normal driving conditions, to find faults within the system.

7   If a problem develops within the system, an "ABS" light will glow on the dashboard. A diagnostic code will also be stored in the ECU, which, when retrieved by a service technician, will indicate the problem area or component.

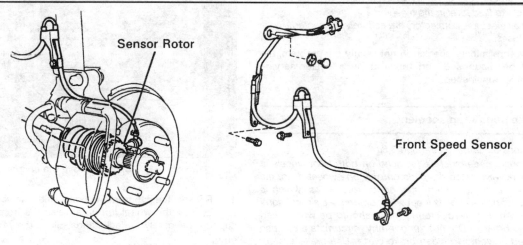

2.4 ABS front wheel speed sensor and sensor rotor

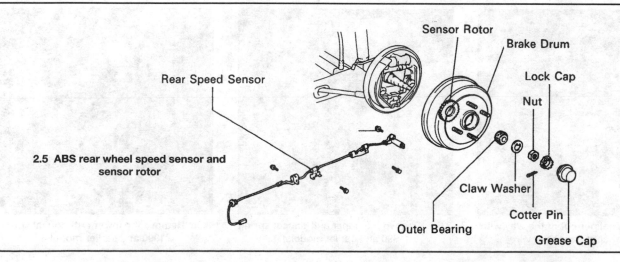

2.5 ABS rear wheel speed sensor and sensor rotor

9

3.5 Use a C-clamp to depress the piston into the caliper before removing the caliper and pads

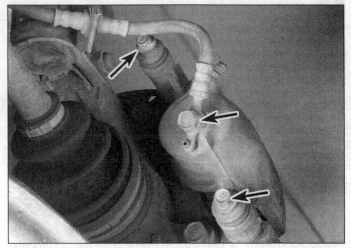

3.6a Remove these two bolts (upper and lower arrows) to detach the caliper from the torque plate; the middle arrow points to the brake hose banjo bolt

Diagnosis and repair

8   If a dashboard warning light comes on and stays on while the vehicle is in operation, the ABS system requires attention. Although a special electronic ABS diagnostic tester is necessary to properly diagnose the system, the home mechanic can perform a few preliminary checks before taking the vehicle to a dealer service department or other repair shop which is equipped with a tester.

a) *Check the brake fluid level in the reservoir.*
b) *Check that all electrical connectors are securely connected.*
c) *Check the fuses.*

9   If the above preliminary checks do not rectify the problem, the vehicle should be diagnosed and repaired by a dealer service department or other repair shop.

3.6b Remove the caliper

---

3   Disc brake pads - replacement

Refer to illustrations 3.5 and 3.6a through 3.6u
Warning: *Disc brake pads must be replaced on both front wheels at the same time - never replace the pads on only one wheel. Also, the dust created by the brake system may contain asbestos, which is harmful to your health. Never blow it out with compressed air and don't inhale any of it. An approved filtering mask should be worn when working on the brakes. Do not, under any circumstances, use petroleum-based solvents to clean brake parts. Use brake system cleaner only!*

1   Remove the cap from the brake fluid reservoir.
2   Loosen the wheel lug nuts, raise the front of the vehicle and support it securely on jackstands. Block the wheels at the opposite end.
3   Remove the wheels. Work on one brake assembly at a time, using

3.6c Hang the caliper out of the way with a piece of coat hanger or wire

3.6d Remove the upper anti-squeal spring (1990 and earlier models)

3.6e Remove the lower anti-squeal spring (1990 and earlier models)

3.6f Remove the outer brake pad shim

3.6g Remove the outer brake pad

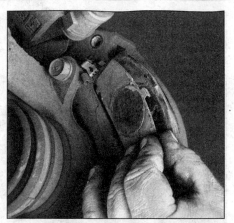

3.6h Remove the inner brake pad shim

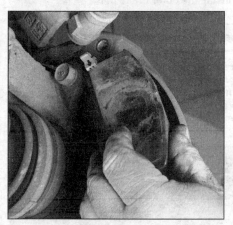

3.6i Remove the inner brake pad

3.6j Remove the dust boots and the
sliding bushings

3.6k Clean off the sliding bushings and
examine them for scoring and excessive
wear; if they're damaged or worn,
replace them

the assembled brake for reference if necessary.

4   Inspect the brake disc carefully as outlined in Section 5. If machining is necessary, follow the information in that Section to remove the disc, at which time the pads can be removed as well.

5   Push the piston back into its bore to provide room for the new brake pads. A C-clamp can be used to accomplish this (see illustration). As the piston is depressed to the bottom of the caliper bore, the fluid in the master cylinder will rise. Make sure that it doesn't overflow. If necessary, siphon off some of the fluid.

6   Follow the accompanying photos (illustrations 3.6a through 3.6u), for the actual pad replacement procedure. Be sure to stay in order and read the caption under each illustration.

7   When reinstalling the caliper, be sure to tighten the mounting bolts to the torque listed in this Chapter's Specifications. After the job has been completed, firmly depress the brake pedal a few times to bring the pads into contact with the disc. Check the level of the brake fluid, adding some if necessary. Check the operation of the brakes carefully before placing the vehicle into normal service.

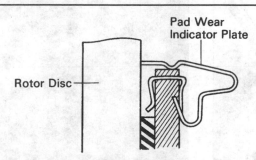

3.6l Cross-sectional view showing proper installation of
upper pad wear indicator (lower pad wear indicator
installation is identical)

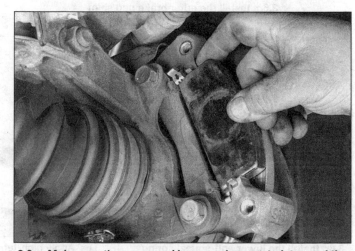

3.6m Make sure the upper and lower pad support plates and the
wear indicators are in place, then install
the inner brake pad

9

3.6n **Install the inner brake pad shim**

3.6o **Install the outer brake pad**

4　Disc brake caliper - removal, overhaul and installation

Warning: *Dust created by the brake system may contain asbestos, which is harmful to your health. Never blow it out with compressed air and don't inhale any of it. An approved filtering mask should be worn when working on the brakes. Do not, under any circumstances, use petroleum-based solvents to clean brake parts. Use brake system cleaner.*

3.6p **Install the outer brake pad shim**

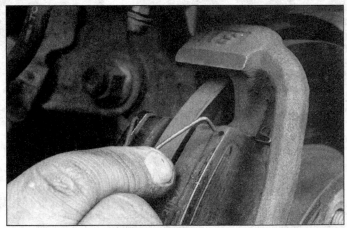

3.6q **Install the upper anti-squeal spring (1990 and earlier models)**

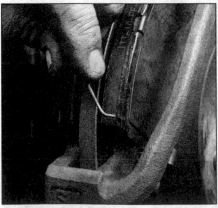

3.6r **Install the lower anti-squeal spring (1990 and earlier models)**

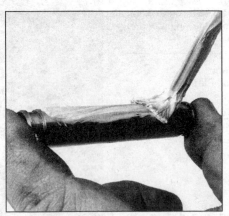

3.6s **Apply high-temperature grease to the sliding bushings**

3.6t **Install the sliding bushings into the caliper ears, then install the caliper and tighten the caliper bolts to the torque listed in this Chapter's Specifications**

3.6u If you have difficulty installing the caliper over the new pads, use a C-clamp to bottom the piston in its bore, then try again - it should now slip over the pads

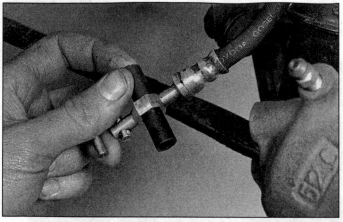

4.2 Using a piece of rubber hose of the appropriate size, plug the brake line

Note: *If an overhaul is indicated (usually because of fluid leakage), explore all options before beginning the job. New and factory rebuilt calipers are available on an exchange basis, which makes this job quite easy. If it's decided to rebuild the calipers, make sure a rebuild kit is available before proceeding. Always rebuild the calipers in pairs - never rebuild just one of them.*

Removal

Refer to illustration 4.2

1   Loosen the front wheel lug nuts, raise the front of the vehicle and place it securely on jackstands. Remove the wheel.
2   Remove the bolt and disconnect the brake hose from the caliper

(see illustration 3.6a). Plug the brake hose to keep contaminants out of the brake system and to prevent losing any more brake fluid than is necessary **(see illustration).**
3   Refer to Section 3 for the caliper removal procedure (it's part of the brake pad replacement procedure).

Overhaul

Refer to illustrations 4.4a, 4.4b, 4.5, 4.7 and 4.8

4   To overhaul the caliper, remove the boot set ring and the boot **(see illustrations).** Before you remove the piston, place a wood block between the piston and caliper to prevent damage as it is removed.
5   To remove the piston from the caliper, apply compressed air to

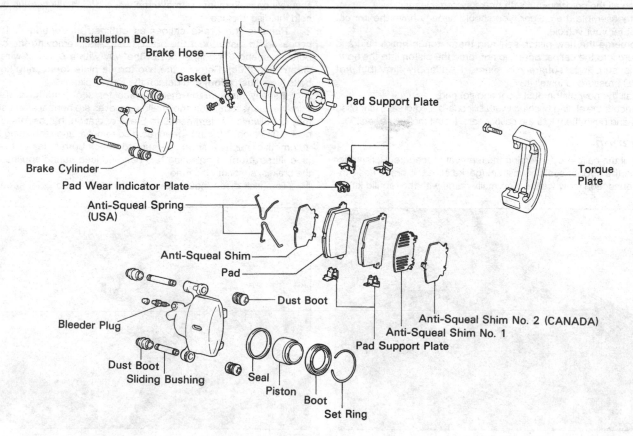

4.4a An exploded view of a typical brake caliper assembly (anti-squeal springs are used only on 1990 and earlier models)

Installation Bolt

Brake Hose

Gasket

Pad Support Plate

Brake Cylinder

Pad Wear Indicator Plate

Anti-Squeal Spring (USA)

Anti-Squeal Shim

Pad

Dust Boot

Bleeder Plug

Dust Boot
Sliding Bushing

Seal

Piston

Boot

Set Ring

Pad Support Plate

Anti-Squeal Shim No. 1

Anti-Squeal Shim No. 2 (CANADA)

Torque Plate

9

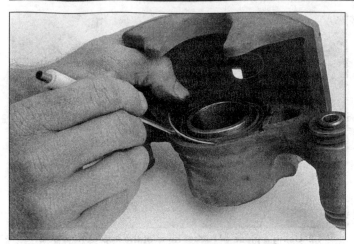

4.4b Using a screwdriver, remove the cylinder boot set ring

4.5 With the caliper padded to catch the piston, use compressed air to force the piston out of its bore - make sure your hands or fingers are not between the piston and caliper

the brake fluid hose connection on the caliper body **(see illustration)**. Use only enough pressure to ease the piston out of its bore. **Warning:** *Be careful not to place your fingers between the piston and the caliper, as the piston may come out with some force.*

6   Inspect the mating surfaces of the piston and caliper bore wall. If there is any scoring, rust, pitting or bright areas, replace the complete caliper unit with a new one.

7   If these components are in good condition, remove the piston seal from the caliper bore using a wooden or plastic tool **(see illustration)**. Metal tools may damage the cylinder bore.

8   Push the sliding bushings out of the caliper ears **(see illustration)** and remove the dust boots from both ends.

9   Wash all the components with brake system cleaner.

10   To reassemble the caliper, you should already have the correct rebuild kit for your vehicle.

11   Submerge the new piston seal and the piston in brake fluid and install them into the caliper bore. Do not force the piston into the bore, but make sure it is squarely in place, then apply firm (but not excessive) pressure to install it.

12   Install the new piston dust boot and set ring.

13   Lubricate the sliding bushings with silicone-based grease (supplied in the kit) and push them into the caliper ears. Install the dust boots.

Installation

14   Install the caliper by reversing the removal procedure. Remember to replace the copper sealing washers (gaskets) at the brake hose-to-caliper connection (new washers normally come with the rebuild kit).

15   Bleed the brake circuit according to the procedure in Section 10. Make sure there are no leaks from the hose connections. Test the brakes carefully before returning the vehicle to normal service.

---

5   Brake disc - inspection, removal and installation

Inspection

Refer to illustrations 5.2, 5.3, 5.4a, 5.4b, 5.5a and 5.5b

1   Loosen the wheel lug nuts, raise the vehicle and support it securely on jackstands. Remove the wheel and install two lug nuts to hold the disc in place.

2   Remove the brake caliper as outlined in Section 4. It isn't necessary to disconnect the brake hose. After removing the caliper bolts, suspend the caliper out of the way with a piece of wire **(see illustration 3.6c)**. Remove the two torque plate-to-steering knuckle bolts **(see illustration)** and detach the torque plate.

3   Visually inspect the disc surface for score marks and other damage. Light scratches and shallow grooves are normal after use and may not always be detrimental to brake operation, but deep scoring - over 0.039-inch (1.0 mm) - requires disc removal and refinishing by an automotive machine shop. Be sure to check both sides of the disc **(see illustration)**. If pulsating has been noticed during application of the brakes, suspect disc runout.

4   To check disc runout, place a dial indicator at a point about 1/2-

4.7 To remove the seal from the caliper bore, use a plastic or wooden tool, such as a pencil

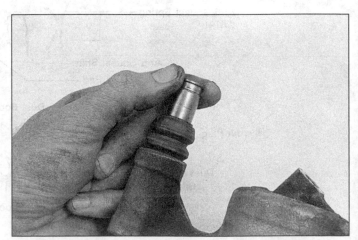

4.8 Push the sliding bushing on each side of the caliper up through the boot and pull it free, then remove the dust boots

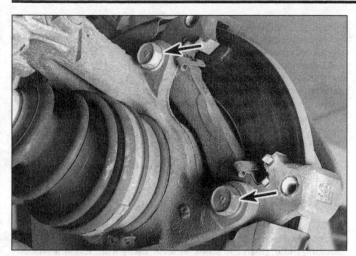

5.2 To remove the torque plate, remove these two bolts (arrows); the pad support plates and pad wear indicators might fall off while the torque plate is removed, so it's a good idea to note how they're installed before removing the torque plate)

5.3 The brake pads on this vehicle were obviously neglected, as they wore down to the rivets and cut deep grooves into the disc - wear this severe means the disc must be replaced

inch from the outer edge of the disc **(see illustration)**. Set the indicator to zero and turn the disc. The indicator reading should not exceed the specified allowable runout limit. If it does, the disc should be refinished by an automotive machine shop. **Note:** *The discs should be resurfaced regardless of the dial indicator reading, as this will impart a smooth finish and ensure a perfectly flat surface, eliminating any brake pedal pulsation or other undesirable symptoms related to questionable discs. At the very least, if you elect not to have the discs resurfaced, remove the glaze from the surface with emery cloth using a swirling motion* **(see illustration)**.

5   It's absolutely critical that the disc not be machined to a thickness under the specified minimum allowable disc refinish thickness. The minimum wear (or discard) thickness is cast into the inside of the disc **(see illustration)**. The disc thickness can be checked with a micrometer **(see illustration)**.

Removal

6   Remove the lug nuts which were installed to hold the disc in place and remove the disc from the hub.

Installation

7   Place the disc in position over the threaded studs.
8   Install the torque plate and caliper assembly over the disc and position it on the steering knuckle. Tighten the torque plate bolts to the torque listed in this Chapter's Specifications.
9   Install the wheel, then lower the vehicle to the ground. Tighten the

5.4a To check disc runout, mount a dial indicator as shown and rotate the disc

lug nuts to the torque listed in the Chapter 1 Specifications. Depress the brake pedal a few times to bring the brake pads into contact with the disc. Bleeding won't be necessary unless the brake hose was disconnected from the caliper. Check the operation of the brakes carefully before driving the vehicle.

9

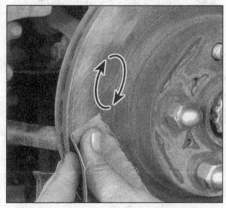

5.4b Using a swirling motion, remove the glaze from the disc surface with sandpaper or emery cloth

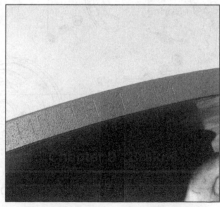

5.5a The minimum wear dimension is stamped into the edge of the disc

5.5b Use a micrometer to measure disc thickness

6.4a Mark the relationship of the drum to the hub, so the drum will retain its dynamic balance after reassembly

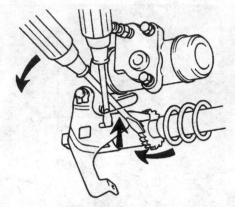

6.4b If the brake drum is hanging up on the shoes because of excessive wear, insert two screwdrivers through the hole in the backing plate, push the adjuster lever away from the star wheel and turn the star wheel to retract the brake shoes

6   Drum brake shoes - replacement

Refer to illustrations 6.4a through 6.4ee and 6.5

Warning: *Drum brake shoes must be replaced on both wheels at the same time - never replace the shoes on only one wheel. Also, the dust created by the brake system may contain asbestos, which is harmful to your health. Never blow it out with compressed air and don't inhale any of it. An approved filtering mask should be worn when working on the brakes. Do not, under any circumstances, use petroleum-based solvents to clean brake parts. Use brake system cleaner only!*

Caution: *Whenever the brake shoes are replaced, the return and*

hold-down springs should also be replaced. Due to the continuous heating/cooling cycle the springs are subjected to, they lose tension over a period of time and may allow the shoes to drag on the drum and wear at a much faster rate than normal.

1   Loosen the wheel lug nuts, raise the rear of the vehicle and support it securely on jackstands. Block the front wheels to keep the vehicle from rolling.

2   Release the parking brake.

3   Remove the wheel. **Note:** *All four rear brake shoes must be replaced at the same time, but to avoid mixing up parts, work on only one brake assembly at a time.*

4   Follow the accompanying illustrations for the brake shoe

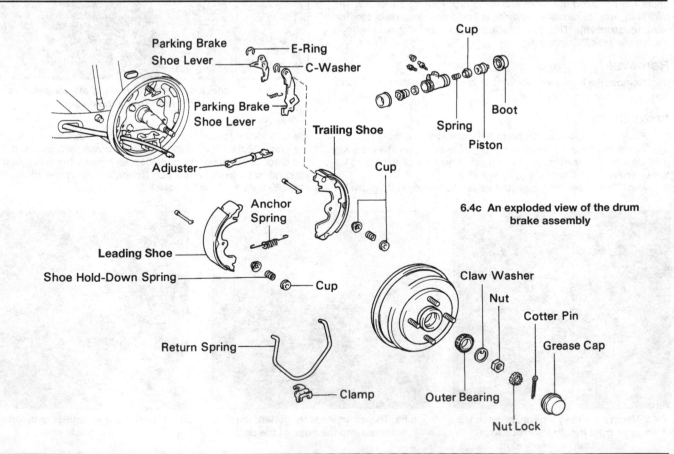

6.4c An exploded view of the drum brake assembly

6.4d Pull the upper end of the return spring out of its hole in the front shoe, then pull the other upper end out of the hole in the rear shoe

6.4e Remove the return spring

6.4f Remove the front hold-down spring (the tool shown here is available at most auto parts stores and makes this task much easier)

replacement procedure **(see illustrations 6.4a through 6.4ee)**. Be sure to stay in order and read the caption under each illustration. **Note:** *If the brake drum cannot be easily pulled off the axle and shoe assembly, make sure the parking brake is completely released. If the drum still cannot be pulled off, the brake shoes will have to be retracted.* This is done by first removing the plug from the backing plate. With the plug removed, push the lever off the adjuster star wheel with a narrow screwdriver while turning the adjuster wheel with another

screwdriver, moving the shoes away from the drum **(see illustration 6.4b)**. The drum should now come off.

5   Before reinstalling the drum, it should be checked for cracks, score marks, deep scratches and hard spots, which will appear as small discolored areas. If the hard spots cannot be removed with fine emery cloth or if any of the other conditions listed above exist, the drum must be taken to an automotive machine shop to have it turned. **Note:** *Professionals recommend resurfacing the drums each time a*

6.4g Remove the rear hold-down spring

6.4h Remove the leading brake shoe

6.4i Disconnect the leading shoe from the anchor spring

6.4j Remove the anchor spring

6.4k Remove the adjuster and star wheel

6.4l Remove the adjusting lever spring

9

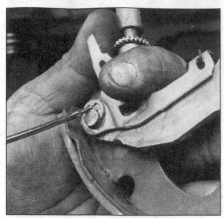

6.4m Remove the C-clip that retains the automatic adjusting lever

6.4n Remove the automatic adjusting lever and the adjuster from the trailing brake shoe

6.4o Pull back the spring and disconnect the parking brake cable from the parking brake lever

6.4p Remove the C-clip that retains the parking brake lever to the trailing shoe and remove the lever

6.4q Attach the parking brake lever to the new trailing brake shoe with the C-clip

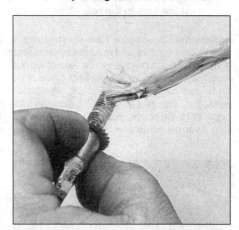

6.4r Coat the threads of the adjuster with high-temperature grease

6.4s Coat the friction surfaces of the backing plate with high-temperature grease

6.4t Attach the parking brake cable to the parking brake lever

6.4u Attach the automatic adjusting lever to the trailing shoe with the C-clip

brake job is done. Resurfacing will eliminate the possibility of out-of-round drums. If the drums are worn so much that they can't be resurfaced without exceeding the maximum allowable diameter (stamped into the drum), then new ones will be required **(see illustration)**. At the very least, if you elect not to have the drums resurfaced, remove the glaze from the surface with emery cloth using a swirling motion.

6   Install the brake drum on the axle flange.

7   Mount the wheel, install the lug nuts, then lower the vehicle.

8   Make a number of forward and reverse stops and operate the parking brake to adjust the brakes until satisfactory pedal action is obtained.

9   Check the operation of the brakes carefully before driving the vehicle.

6.4v Place the trailing shoe, parking brake lever and automatic adjusting lever in position and attach the adjusting lever spring

6.4w Make sure the rear tangs on the adjuster are properly engaged with the automatic adjusting lever and the trailing shoe

6.4x Insert the hold-down pin (arrow) through the holes in the backing plate and trailing shoe as shown

6.4y Install the hold-down spring seat, spring and retainer cup, compress them with a brake hold-down tool and rotate the cup a quarter turn to lock it into place

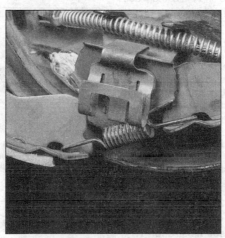

6.4z Attach the anchor spring to the leading and trailing shoes

6.4aa Insert the hold-down pin through the holes in the backing plate and leading shoe as shown

6.4bb Install the hold-down spring seat, spring and retainer cup, compress them with the brake hold-down tool and lock them into place by turning the cup one-quarter turn

6.4cc Place the return spring in position

9

7   Wheel cylinder - removal, overhaul and installation

Note: *If an overhaul is indicated (usually because of fluid leaks or sticky operation), explore all options before beginning the job. New wheel cylinders are available, which makes this job quite easy. If it's decided to rebuild the wheel cylinder, make sure a rebuild kit is available before proceeding. Never overhaul only one wheel cylinder - always rebuild both of them at the same time.*

Removal

Refer to illustration 7.4

1   Raise the rear of the vehicle and support it securely on jackstands. Block the front wheels to keep the vehicle from rolling.
2   Remove the brake shoe assembly (see Section 6).
3   Remove all dirt and foreign material from around the wheel cylinder.
4   Disconnect the brake line **(see illustration)** with a flare-nut wrench, if available. Don't pull the brake line away from the wheel cylinder.
5   Remove the wheel cylinder mounting bolts.
6   Detach the wheel cylinder from the brake backing plate and place it on a clean workbench. Immediately plug the brake line to prevent fluid loss and contamination.

Overhaul

Refer to illustration 7.7

7   Remove the bleeder screw, cups, pistons, boots and spring assembly from the wheel cylinder body **(see illustration)**.
8   Clean the wheel cylinder with brake fluid, denatured alcohol or brake system cleaner. **Warning:** *Do not, under any circumstances, use petroleum-based solvents to clean brake parts!*
9   Use compressed air to dry the wheel cylinder and blow out the passages.
10   Check the bore for corrosion and score marks. Crocus cloth can be used to remove light corrosion and stains, but the cylinder must be replaced with a new one if the defects cannot be removed easily, or if the bore is scored.
11   Lubricate the new cups with brake fluid.
12   Assemble the brake cylinder components **(see illustration 7.7)**. Make sure the cup lips face in.

Installation

13   Place the wheel cylinder in position and install the bolts finger tight. Connect the brake line to the cylinder, being careful not to cross-thread the fitting. Tighten the wheel cylinder bolts to the torque listed in this Chapter's Specifications.
14   Tighten the brake line and install the brake shoe assembly.

6.4dd Make sure the front tangs of the adjuster are properly engaged with the leading shoe, then insert the front end of the return spring into its hole in the leading shoe

6.4ee Insert the rear end of the return spring into its hole in the trailing shoe and you're done! Make sure the brake looks as shown; if something's amiss, go back and do it over - don't install the drum until the brake is properly reassembled

15   Bleed the brakes (see Section 10).
16   Check the operation of the brakes carefully before driving the vehicle.

6.5 The maximum drum diameter is cast into the drum

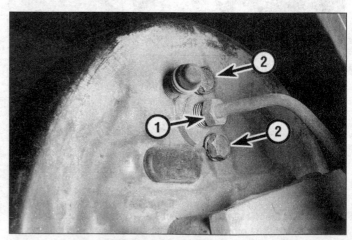

7.4 Disconnect the brake line fitting (1), then remove the two wheel cylinder bolts (2)

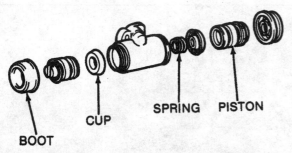

7.7 An exploded view of the wheel cylinder

BOOT CUP SPRING PISTON

8.2 To locate the electrical connector for the fluid level warning switch, follow the lead from the reservoir

8.4 Loosen the brake line fittings (arrows) with a flare-nut wrench and remove the master cylinder mounting nuts (arrow, left nut not visible in this photo)

Removal

Refer to illustrations 8.2, 8.4 and 8.6

1   On 1991 and later models, remove the air cleaner assembly (see Chapter 5).

2   Unplug the electrical connector for the fluid level warning switch **(see illustration)**.

3   Remove as much fluid as possible from the reservoir with a syringe.

4   Place rags under the fittings and prepare caps or plastic bags to cover the ends of the lines once they're disconnected. **Caution:** *Brake fluid will damage paint. Cover all body parts and be careful not to spill fluid during this procedure.* Loosen the fittings at the ends of the brake lines where they enter the master cylinder **(see illustration)**. To prevent rounding off the flats, use a flare-nut wrench, which wraps around the fitting hex.

5   Pull the brake lines away from the master cylinder and plug the ends to prevent contamination.

6   Remove the nuts attaching the master cylinder to the power booster **(see illustration)**. Pull the master cylinder off the studs to remove it. Again, be careful not to spill the fluid as this is done. Remove and discard the old gasket between the master cylinder and the power brake booster.

8   Master cylinder - removal, overhaul and installation

Note: *Before deciding to overhaul the master cylinder, check on the availability and cost of a new or factory rebuilt unit and also the availability of a rebuild kit.*

8.6 Master cylinder mounting details

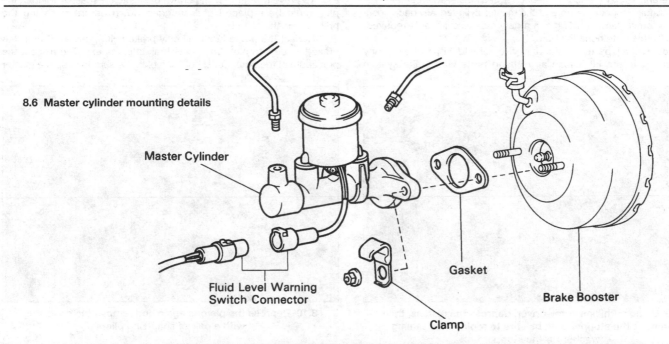

Master Cylinder

Fluid Level Warning Switch Connector

Clamp

Gasket

Brake Booster

9

8.8a The brake fluid reservoir is retained by a screw

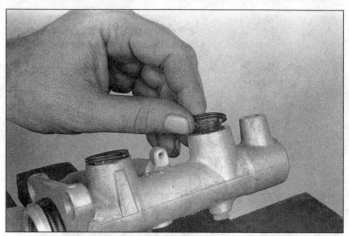

8.8b After the reservoir has been removed, pull the grommets from the master cylinder body; if they're hard, cracked or damaged, or have been leaking, replace them

Overhaul

Refer to illustrations 8.8a, 8.8b, 8.9, 8.10, 8.11a, 8.11b and 8.11c

7   Before attempting the overhaul of the master cylinder, obtain the proper rebuild kit, which will contain the necessary replacement parts and also any instructions which may be specific to your model.

8   Remove the reservoir retaining screw, pull off the reservoir and remove the grommets **(see illustrations)**. **Note:** *On 1990 and earlier units the reservoir retaining screw is on the left (driver's) side of the master cylinder; on 1991 and later units it's on the right (passenger) side.*

9   Place the cylinder in a vise and use a punch or Phillips screwdriver to depress the pistons until they bottom against the other end of the master cylinder. Hold the pistons in this position and remove the stopper bolt from the master cylinder **(see illustration)**. **Note:** *On 1990 and earlier units the stopper bolt is on the right (passenger) side of the master cylinder; on 1991 and later models it's on the left (driver's) side.*

10   Carefully remove the snap-ring at the end of the master cylinder **(see illustration)**.

11   The internal components can now be removed from the bore **(see illustrations)**. Make a note of the proper order of the components so they can be returned to their original locations. **Note:** *The two springs are different, so pay particular attention to their installed order.*

12   Carefully inspect the bore of the master cylinder. Any deep score marks or other damage will mean a new master cylinder is required. DO NOT attempt to hone the bore.

13   Replace all parts included in the rebuild kit, following any instructions in the kit. Clean all re-used parts with brake system cleaner. **Warning:** *Do not use any petroleum-based solvents. During reassembly, lubricate all parts liberally with clean brake fluid.*

14   Push the assembled components into the bore, bottoming them against the end of the master cylinder, then install the stopper bolt.

15   Install the new snap-ring, making sure it's seated properly in the groove.

16   Install the reservoir grommets, reservoir and screw.

17   Before installing the master cylinder, it should be bench bled. Since you'll have to apply pressure to the master cylinder piston and, at the same time, control flow from the brake line outlets, the master cylinder should be mounted in a vise, with the jaws of the vise clamping on the mounting flange.

18   Insert threaded plugs into the brake line outlet holes and snug them down so no air will leak past them, but not so tight that they can't be easily loosened.

19   Fill the reservoir with brake fluid of the recommended type (see Chapter 1).

20   Remove one plug and push the piston assembly into the bore to expel the air from the master cylinder. A large Phillips screwdriver can be used to push on the piston assembly.

21   To prevent air from being drawn back into the master cylinder, the plug must be replaced and snugged down before releasing the pressure on the piston.

22   Repeat the procedure until only brake fluid is expelled from the brake line outlet hole. When only brake fluid is expelled, repeat the procedure at the other outlet hole and plug. Be sure to keep the master

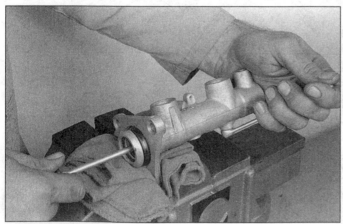

8.9 Using a Phillips screwdriver, depress the pistons, then remove the stopper bolt; be sure to replace the sealing washer for the stopper bolt

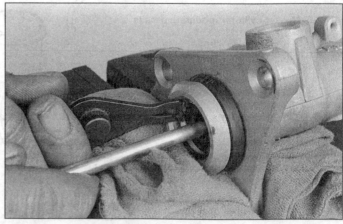

8.10 Depress the pistons again and remove the snap-ring with a pair of snap-ring pliers

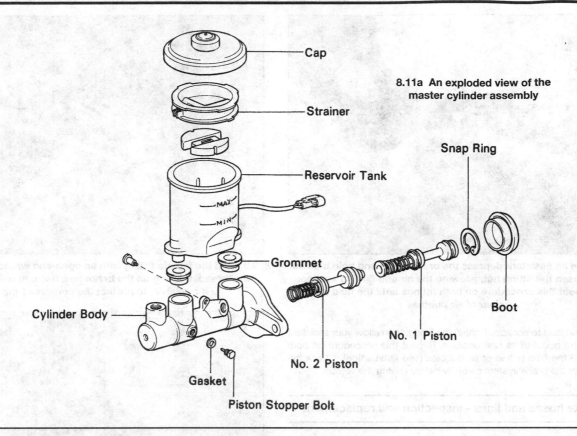

Cap

Strainer

8.11a An exploded view of the master cylinder assembly

Snap Ring

Reservoir Tank

Boot

Grommet

No. 1 Piston

Cylinder Body

No. 2 Piston

Gasket

Piston Stopper Bolt

oylinder reservoir filled with brake fluid to prevent the introduction of air into the system.

23 Since high pressure isn't involved in the bench bleeding procedure, an alternative to the removal and replacement of the plugs with each stroke of the piston assembly is available. Before pushing in on the piston assembly, remove the plug as described in Step 20. Before releasing the piston, however, instead of replacing the plug, simply put your finger tightly over the hole to keep air from being drawn back into the master cylinder. Wait several seconds for brake fluid to be drawn from the reservoir into the bore, then depress the piston again, removing your finger as brake fluid is expelled. Be sure to put your finger back over the hole each time before releasing the piston, and when the bleeding procedure is complete for that outlet, replace the plug and tighten it before going on to the other port.

Installation

Refer to illustration 8.27

24 Install the master cylinder over the studs on the power brake booster and tighten the nuts only finger-tight at this time. Don't forget to use a new gasket.

25 Thread the brake line fittings into the master cylinder. Since the master cylinder is still a bit loose, it can be moved slightly so the fittings thread in easily. Don't strip the threads as the fittings are tightened.

26 Tighten the mounting nuts and the brake line fittings.

27 Fill the master cylinder reservoir with fluid, then bleed the master cylinder (only if hasn't been bench bled) and the brake system (see Section 10). To bleed the master cylinder on the vehicle, have an assistant depress the brake pedal and hold it down. Loosen the fitting to

8.11b After the snap-ring has been removed, the primary (No. 1) piston assembly can be removed

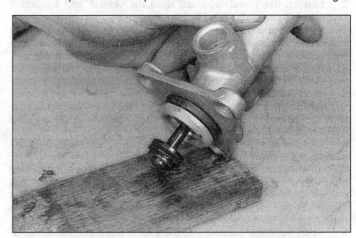

8.11c Remove the cylinder from the vise and tap it against a block of wood until the secondary (No. 2) piston is exposed. Pull the piston assembly STRAIGHT OUT - if it becomes even slightly cocked, the bore may be damaged

9

8.27 Have an assistant depress the brake pedal and hold it down, then loosen the fitting nut, allowing the air and fluid to escape; repeat this procedure on both fittings until the fluid is clear of air bubbles

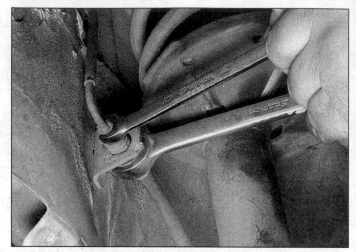

9.3 Hold the female fitting with an open-end wrench and loosen the threaded fitting on the brake line; use a flare-nut wrench, if available, to protect the corners of the nut

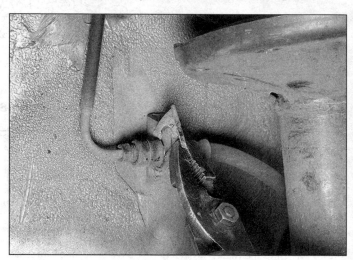

9.4 Pull off the U-clip with a pair of pliers

allow air and fluid to escape. Tighten the fitting, then allow your assistant to return the pedal to its rest position. Repeat this procedure on both fittings until the fluid is free of air bubbles **(see illustration)**. Check the operation of the brake system carefully before driving the vehicle.

9 Brake hoses and lines - inspection and replacement

Inspection

1   About every six months, with the vehicle raised and supported securely on jackstands, the rubber hoses which connect the steel brake lines with the front and rear brake assemblies should be inspected for cracks, chafing of the outer cover, leaks, blisters and other damage. These are important and vulnerable parts of the brake system and inspection should be complete. A light and mirror will be helpful for a thorough check. If a hose exhibits any of the above conditions, replace it with a new one.

Replacement

Front brake hose

Refer to illustrations 9.3 and 9.4

2   Loosen the wheel lug nuts, raise the vehicle and support it securely on jackstands. Remove the wheel.
3   At the frame bracket, hold the hose fitting with an open-end wrench and unscrew the brake line fitting from the hose **(see illustration)**. Use a flare-nut wrench to prevent rounding off the corners.
4   Remove the U-clip from the female fitting at the bracket with a pair of pliers **(see illustration)**, then pass the hose through the bracket.
5   At the caliper end of the hose, remove the banjo fitting bolt, then separate the hose from the caliper. Note that there are two copper sealing washers on either side of the fitting - they should be replaced with new ones during installation.
6   Remove the U-clip from the strut bracket, then feed the hose through the bracket.
7   To install the hose, pass the caliper fitting end through the strut bracket, then connect the fitting to the caliper with the banjo bolt and copper washers. Make sure the locating lug on the fitting is engaged with the hole in the caliper, then tighten the bolt to the torque listed in this Chapter's Specifications.
8   Push the metal support into the strut bracket and install the U-clip. Make sure the hose isn't twisted between the caliper and the strut bracket.
9   Route the hose into the frame bracket, again making sure it isn't twisted, then connect the brake line fitting, starting the threads by

hand. Install the U-clip, then tighten the fitting securely.
10   Bleed the caliper (see Section 10).
11   Install the wheel and lug nuts, lower the vehicle and tighten the lug nuts to the torque specified in Chapter 1.

Rear brake hose

12   The rear brake hose serves as the flexible connection between two rigid metal lines, one on the body and the other on the axle. Both ends of the hose are attached to these metal lines with threaded fittings and U-clips. Refer to Steps 2, 3 and 4 above. Be sure to bleed the wheel cylinder when you're done (see Section 10).

Metal brake lines

13   When replacing brake lines, be sure to use the correct parts. Don't use copper tubing for any brake system components. Purchase steel brake lines from a dealer or auto parts store.
14   Prefabricated brake line, with the tube ends already flared and fittings installed, is available at auto parts stores and dealer parts departments. These lines are also bent to the proper shapes.
15   When installing the new line, make sure it's securely supported in the brackets and has plenty of clearance between moving or hot components.
16   After installation, check the master cylinder fluid level and add fluid as necessary. Bleed the brake system (see Section 10) and test the brakes carefully before driving the vehicle in traffic.

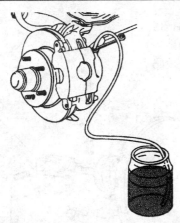

10.8 When bleeding the brakes, a hose is connected to the bleed screw at the caliper or wheel cylinder and then submerged in brake fluid - air will be seen as bubbles in the tube and container (all air must be expelled before moving to the next wheel)

10 Brake hydraulic system - bleeding

Refer to illustration 10.8

Warning: *Wear eye protection when bleeding the brake system. If the fluid comes in contact with your eyes, immediately rinse them with water and seek medical attention.*

Note: *Bleeding the hydraulic system is necessary to remove any air that manages to find its way into the system when it's been opened during removal and installation of a hose, line, caliper or master cylinder.*

1   You'll probably have to bleed the system at all four brakes if air has entered it due to low fluid level, or if the brake lines have been disconnected at the master cylinder.

2   If a brake line was disconnected only at a wheel, then only that caliper or wheel cylinder must be bled.

3   If a brake line is disconnected at a fitting located between the master cylinder and any of the brakes, that part of the system served by the disconnected line must be bled.

4   Remove any residual vacuum from the brake power booster by applying the brake several times with the engine off.

5   Remove the master cylinder reservoir cover and fill the reservoir with brake fluid. Reinstall the cover. **Note:** *Check the fluid level often during the bleeding operation and add fluid as necessary to prevent the fluid level from falling low enough to allow air bubbles into the master cylinder.*

6   Have an assistant on hand, as well as a supply of new brake fluid, a clear plastic container partially filled with clean brake fluid, a length of 3/16-inch plastic, rubber or vinyl tubing to fit over the bleeder valve and a wrench to open and close the bleeder valve.

7   Beginning at the right rear wheel, loosen the bleeder valve slightly, then tighten it to a point where it's snug but can still be loosened quickly and easily.

8   Place one end of the tubing over the bleeder valve and submerge the other end in brake fluid in the container **(see illustration)**.

9   Have the assistant pump the brakes slowly a few times to get pressure in the system, then hold the pedal down firmly.

10   While the pedal is held down, open the bleeder valve just enough to allow a flow of fluid to leave the valve. Watch for air bubbles to exit the submerged end of the tube. When the fluid flow slows after a couple of seconds, close the valve and have your assistant release the pedal.

11   Repeat Steps 9 and 10 until no more air is seen leaving the tube, then tighten the bleeder valve and proceed to the left front wheel, the left rear wheel and the right front wheel, in that order, and perform the same procedure. Be sure to check the fluid in the master cylinder reservoir frequently.

12   Never use old brake fluid. It contains moisture which will deteriorate the brake system components.

13   Refill the master cylinder with fluid at the end of the operation.

11.7 To disconnect the power brake booster pushrod from the brake pedal, remove the retaining clip and clevis pin (arrow); to detach the booster from the firewall, remove the four mounting nuts (arrows, two right nuts not visible in this photo)

14   Check the operation of the brakes. The pedal should feel solid when depressed, with no sponginess. If necessary, repeat the entire process. **Warning:** *Do not operate the vehicle if you're in doubt about the effectiveness of the brake system.*

11 Power brake booster - check, removal and Installation

Operating check

1   Depress the brake pedal several times with the engine off and make sure there's no change in the pedal reserve distance.

2   Depress the pedal and start the engine. If the pedal goes down slightly, operation is normal.

Airtightness check

3   Start the engine and turn it off after one or two minutes. Depress the brake pedal slowly several times. If the pedal depresses less each time, the booster is airtight.

4   Depress the brake pedal while the engine is running, then stop the engine with the pedal depressed. If there's no change in the pedal reserve travel after holding the pedal for 30 seconds, the booster is airtight.

Removal

Refer to illustration 11.7

5   Power brake booster units shouldn't be disassembled. They require special tools not normally found in most automotive repair stations or shops. They're fairly complex and, because of their critical relationship to brake performance, should be replaced with a new or rebuilt one.

6   To remove the booster, first remove the brake master cylinder (see Section 8).

7   Remove the steering column lower finish panel. Locate the pushrod clevis connecting the booster to the brake pedal **(see illustration)**. It's accessible from inside the vehicle, under the dash on the driver's side.

8   Remove the clevis pin retaining clip with pliers and pull out the pin.

9   Holding the clevis with pliers, unscrew the locknut with a wrench. The clevis is now loose.

10   Disconnect the hose leading from the engine to the booster. Be careful not to damage the hose when removing it from the booster fitting.

11   Remove the four nuts and washers holding the brake booster to the firewall **(see illustration 11.7)**; you may need a light to see them.

12   Slide the booster straight out from the firewall until the studs clear the holes.

9

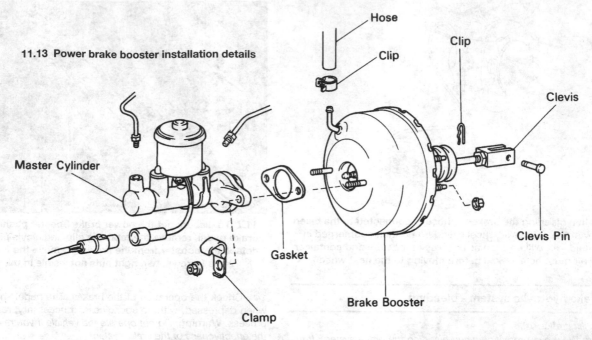

11.13 Power brake booster installation details

Hose

Clip

Clip

Clevis

Master Cylinder

Gasket

Clevis Pin

Clamp

Brake Booster

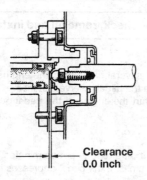

Clearance
0.0 inch

11.14a There should be no clearance between the booster pushrod and the master cylinder pushrod, but no interference either; if there is interference between the two, the brakes may drag; if there is clearance, there will be excessive brake pedal travel

11.14b To adjust the length of the booster pushrod, hold the serrated portion of the rod with a pair of pliers and turn the adjusting screw in or out, as necessary, to achieve the desired setting

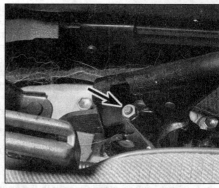

12.3 Loosen the locknut, then turn the adjusting nut until the desired handle travel is obtained

Installation

Refer to illustrations 11.13, 11.14a and 11.14b

13   Installation procedures are basically the reverse of removal. Tighten the clevis locknut securely and the booster mounting nuts to the torque listed in this Chapter's Specifications (see illustration).

14   If the power booster unit is being replaced, the clearance between the master cylinder piston and the pushrod in the vacuum booster must be measured and, if necessary, adjusted. Using a depth micrometer or vernier calipers, measure the distance from the seat (recessed area) in the master cylinder to the master cylinder mounting flange. Next, measure the distance from the end of the vacuum booster pushrod to the mounting face of the booster (including gasket) where the master cylinder mounting flange seats. The measurements should be the same (see illustration). If not, turn the adjusting screw on the end of the power booster pushrod until the clearance is within the specified limit (see illustration).

15   After the final installation of the master cylinder and brake hoses and lines, the brake pedal height and freeplay must be adjusted and the system must be bled. See the appropriate Sections of this Chapter for the procedures.

12   Parking brake - adjustment

Refer to illustration 12.3

1   The parking brake lever, when properly adjusted, should travel seven to nine clicks on 1990 and earlier models or four to seven clicks on 1991 and later models, when a moderate pulling force is applied. If it travels less than the specified minimum number of clicks, there's a chance the parking brake might not be releasing completely and might be dragging on the drum. If the lever can be pulled up more than the specified maximum number of clicks, the parking brake may not hold adequately on an incline, allowing the car to roll.

2   To gain access to the parking brake cable adjuster, remove the center console (see Chapter 11).

3   Loosen the locknut (the upper nut) while holding the adjusting nut (lower nut) with a wrench (see illustration). Tighten the adjusting nut until the desired travel is attained. Tighten the locknut.

4   Install the console.

13.4a Pinch the cable housing together with a pair of pliers as shown . . .

13.4b . . . and pull the cable through the brake backing plate

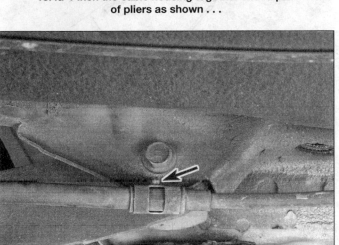

13.5 Remove this nut (arrow) and detach this cable bracket from the frame near the forward end of the axle beam (the large bolt right above the bracket is the pivot bolt for the axle beam trailing arm)

13.6 Remove this bolt (arrow) and detach this cable bracket from the frame near the exhaust pipe

13 Parking brake cables - replacement

Equalizer-to-parking brake cable

Refer to illustrations 13.4a, 13.4b, 13.5, 13.6 and 13.8

1   Loosen the rear wheel lug nuts, raise the rear of the vehicle and support it securely on jackstands. Block the front wheels. Remove the wheel.

2   Make sure the parking brake is completely released, then remove the brake drum.

3   Remove the brake shoes and disconnect the cable from the parking brake lever (see Section 6).

4   Pinch the cable casing with a pair of pliers as shown and pull it through the backing plate **(see illustrations)**.

5   Unbolt the cable bracket from the frame at the forward end of the axle beam **(see illustration)**.

6   Unbolt the cable bracket from the frame near the exhaust pipe **(see illustration)**.

7   Remove the exhaust pipe and catalytic converter heat shields (see Chapter 5).

8   Remove the bracket retaining bolt **(see illustration)** and disconnect the cable from the equalizer.

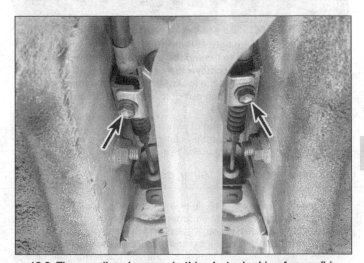

13.8 The equalizer (as seen in this photo, looking forward) is located between the exhaust pipe/catalytic converter heat shields and the floorpan; to disconnect either rear parking brake cable, remove the bracket retaining bolt (arrow), back off the adjustment nut next to the parking brake lever between the seats and disengage the forward end of the cable from the equalizer

9

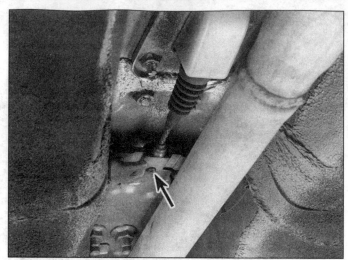

13.15 To remove the equalizer-to-brake lever cable, back off the adjustment nut at the parking brake lever, disengage the rear end of the cable (arrow) from the equalizer and pull the cable up through the floorpan (this view of the equalizer is as seen from the front, looking toward the rear)

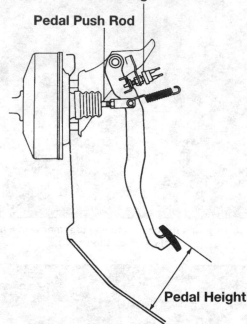

14.1 Brake pedal height is the distance between the pedal and the firewall when the pedal is released (1990 and earlier brake light switch shown)

14.11 Typical brake light switch (1990 and earlier unit shown, later units similar); to loosen the switch, simply back off the locknuts (arrows); to remove the switch, unplug the electrical connector, remove the locknuts and pull the threaded part of the switch out of its mounting bracket

9   Installation is the reverse of removal. Apply a light coat of grease to the portion of the cable end that engages with the equalizer.
10   Adjust the parking brake when you're done (see Section 12).

Equalizer-to-brake lever cable

Refer to illustration 13.15
11   Remove the center console (see Chapter 11).
12   With the lever in the down (off) position, remove the locknut and the adjusting nut (see Section 12) and detach the cable from the lever.
13   Raise the rear of the vehicle and place it securely on jackstands.
14   Remove the exhaust pipe and catalytic converter heat shields (see Chapter 5).
15   Disconnect the cable from the equalizer **(see illustration)**.
16   Pull the cable through the hole in the floorpan.
17   Installation is the reverse of removal. Apply a light coat of grease to the portion of the cable end that engages with the equalizer.
18   Adjust the parking brake lever when you're done (see Section 12).

14 Brake pedal - check and adjustment

Pedal height

Refer to illustration 14.1
1   Measure the pedal height **(see illustration)** and compare your measurement to the pedal height listed in this Chapter's Specifications. If the pedal height is incorrect, adjust it as follows:

1990 and earlier models

2   Remove the steering column lower finish panel and air duct.
3   Loosen the brake light switch.
4   Loosen the pushrod locknut.
5   Adjust the pedal height by turning the pedal pushrod.
6   Adjust the brake light switch locknuts until the switch just touches the pedal stopper.
7   Tighten the brake light switch locknuts.
8   Verify that the brake lights come on when the brake pedal is depressed, and go off when the brake pedal is released.
9   Adjust the pedal freeplay (see below).

1991 and later models

Refer to illustrations 14.11 and 14.17
10   Unplug the electrical connector from the brake light switch.
11   Loosen the brake light switch locknuts **(see illustration)** and remove the brake light switch.
12   Loosen the pushrod locknut.
13   Adjust the pedal height by turning the pedal pushrod.
14   Tighten the pushrod locknut.
15   Install the brake light switch and turn it until it lightly contacts the pedal stopper.
16   Back off the brake light switch one turn.
17   Measure the distance (clearance "A") between the brake light switch and the pedal **(see illustration)** and compare your measurement to the clearance listed in this Chapter's Specifications. If the clearance is not as specified, repeat the previous two steps and try again.

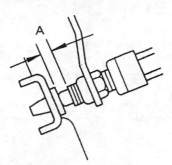

14.17 Clearance "A" is the distance between the brake light switch and the pedal arm

18 Tighten the brake light switch locknuts.
19 Plug in the brake light switch electrical connector.
20 Verify that brake lights come on when the brake pedal is depressed, and go off when the brake pedal is released.
21 Check the pedal freeplay (see below).

Pedal freeplay

Refer to illustrations 14.23

22 Stop the engine, if it's running, and depress the brake pedal several times until there's no more vacuum left in the booster.
23 Push in the pedal until you feel some resistance, then measure the distance between the release pedal and this point at which you can feel resistance **(see illustration)**. Compare your measurement with the pedal freeplay listed in this Chapter's Specifications. If the pedal freeplay is incorrect, adjust it as follows:

1990 and earlier models

24 Start the engine and verify that there is some pedal freeplay.
25 Adjust the pedal freeplay by turning the pedal pushrod.
26 After adjusting the pedal freeplay, check the pedal height (see above).
27 Install the air duct and steering column lower finish panel.

1991 and later models

28 Check the brake light switch clearance. If the brake light switch clearance is okay, troubleshoot the brake system.

Pedal reserve

29 Start the engine, depress the brake pedal a few times, then press down hard and hold it.
30 Pedal reserve travel is measured from the floor to the top of the pedal while it's being depressed. Compare your measurement to the pedal reserve listed in this Chapter's Specifications.
31 If the pedal reserve is less than specified, check the adjustment of the rear brake shoes and/or the power brake booster pushrod-to-master cylinder piston clearance. If the brake pedal feels spongy, bleed the brake system (see Section 10).

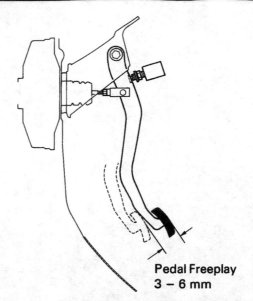

**Pedal Freeplay
3 – 6 mm**

14.23 Brake pedal freeplay is the distance between the pedal when it's released and the point at which some resistance is first felt when the pedal is depressed

15 Brake light switch - check and replacement

Check

1 The brake light switch is located on a bracket at the top of the brake pedal **(see illustration 14.1)**. The switch activates the brake lights at the rear of the vehicle when the pedal is depressed.
2 To check the brake light switch, simply note whether the brake lights come on when the pedal is depressed and go off when the pedal is released. If they don't, adjust the switch as described in Section 14 (adjusting the switch is part of brake pedal adjustment).
3 If the switch still doesn't work properly, either it's not getting voltage, or the switch itself is defective.
4 Use a voltmeter to verify that there's voltage at the switch connector. If there's voltage present, replace the switch. If there's no voltage present, follow the hot wire back to the main harness until you find an open or a short (see the Wiring Diagrams at the end of Chapter 12).

Replacement

5 Disconnect the negative battery cable from the battery.
6 Unplug the electrical connector for the brake light switch.
7 Loosen the locknuts **(see illustration 14.11)** and unscrew the switch from the pedal bracket.
8 Installation is the reverse of removal.
9 Adjust the brake pedal and brake light switch (see Section 14).

9

Notes

Chapter 10
Suspension and steering systems

Contents

Specifications

Torque specifications

Ft-lbs (unless otherwise indicated)

Front suspension

Balljoint-to-control arm bolt/nuts	59
Balljoint-to-steering knuckle nut	72
Control arm	
Front pivot bolt	
1990 and earlier	108
1991 and later	105
Rear bracket bolts	
1993 and earlier	94
1994	55
Strut suspension support-to-piston rod nut	34
Strut-to-steering knuckle bolts/nuts	
1991 and earlier	166
1992 and later	181
Strut upper mounting nuts	
1990 and earlier	23
1991 and later	29

Rear suspension

Axle beam trailing arm pivot bolt	105
Lateral rod-to-axle beam nut	
1990 and earlier	47
1991 and later	43
Lateral rod-to-upper bracket bolt/nut	83
Shock absorber suspension support-to-piston rod nut	40
Shock absorber-to-axle beam bolt/nut	
1990 and earlier	47
1991 and later	50
Shock absorber upper mounting nuts	
1990 and earlier	23
1991 and later	29

10

Torque specifications (continued)

Ft-lbs (unless otherwise indicated)

Steering

Power steering pressure line

    Pressure line-to-power steering pump fitting (1990 and earlier)........ 18

    Pressure line-to-power steering pump banjo bolt

        1991 36

        1992 and later 40

Steering gear bracket bolts

    1990 and earlier.. 32

    1991 and later 43

Steering wheel horn pad screws (airbag-equipped vehicles).................. 48 in-lbs

Steering wheel nut

    1993 and earlier.. 25

    1994 26

Tie-rod ends

    Tie-rod end-to-steering knuckle.. 36

    Tie-rod end locknut

        1990 and earlier 41

        1991 and later 35

Universal joint-to-pinion shaft pinch bolt

    1990 and earlier.. 26

    1991 and later 21

1.1 Typical front suspension components

  1   *Shock absorber and coil spring assembly*   *5*   *Rack-and-pinion steering assembly*

  2   *Control arm*   *6*   *Axleshaft assembly*

  3   *Control arm bushing clamp*   *7*   *CV joint*

  4   *Balljoint-to-control arm bolt and nuts*

1   General information

Refer to illustrations 1.1 and 1.2

The front suspension is a Macpherson strut design. The upper end of each strut is attached to the vehicle's body strut support. The lower end of the strut is connected to the upper end of the steering knuckle. The steering knuckle is attached to a balljoint mounted on the outer end of the suspension control arm **(see illustration)**.

The rear suspension utilizes integral shock absorber/coil spring assemblies. The upper end of each shock is attached to the vehicle body. The lower end of each shock is attached to the axle beam. The axle beam is located by a pair of suspension arms on each side, and a diagonally-mounted lateral control rod between an upper bracket welded to the body and a stud on the front side of the axle beam **(see illustration)**.

The rack-and-pinion steering gear is located behind the engine/transaxle assembly on the firewall and actuates the tie-rods, which are attached to the steering knuckles. The inner ends of the tie-rods are protected by rubber boots which should be inspected periodically for secure attachment, tears and leaking lubricant.

The power assist system consists of a belt-driven pump and associated lines and hoses. The fluid level in the power steering pump reservoir should be checked periodically (see Chapter 1).

The steering wheel operates the steering shaft, which actuates the steering gear through universal joints. Looseness in the steering can be caused by wear in the steering shaft universal joints, the steering gear, the tie-rod ends and loose retaining bolts.

Frequently, when working on the suspension or steering system components, you may come across fasteners which seem impossible to loosen. These fasteners on the underside of the vehicle are continually subjected to water, road grime, mud, etc., and can become rusted or "frozen," making them extremely difficult to remove. In order to unscrew these stubborn fasteners without damaging them (or other components), be sure to use lots of penetrating oil and allow it to soak in for a while. Using a wire brush to clean exposed threads will also ease removal of the nut or bolt and prevent damage to the threads. Sometimes a sharp blow with a hammer and punch will break the bond between a nut and bolt threads, but care must be taken to prevent the punch from slipping off the fastener and ruining the threads. Heating the stuck fastener and surrounding area with a torch sometimes helps too, but isn't recommended because of the obvious dangers associated with fire. Long breaker bars and extension, or "cheater," pipes will increase leverage, but never use an extension pipe on a ratchet - the ratcheting mechanism could be damaged. Sometimes tightening the nut or bolt first will help to break it loose. Fasteners that require drastic measures to remove should always be replaced with new ones.

Since most of the procedures dealt with in this Chapter involve jacking up the vehicle and working underneath it, a good pair of jackstands will be needed. A hydraulic floor jack is the preferred type

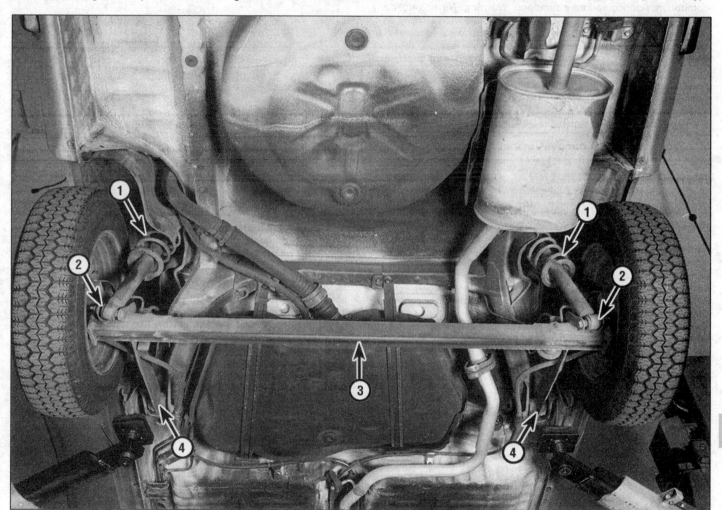

1.2 Typical rear suspension components

1 Shock absorber and coil spring assembly	*3 Axle beam*
2 Shock absorber-to-axle beam mounting bolt	*4 Axle beam-to-frame mounting bolt*

10

2.3 To detach the strut assembly from the steering knuckle, remove the two nuts (arrows), then knock out the bolts with a hammer and punch

2.5 To detach the upper end of the strut assembly from the body, remove the upper mounting nuts (arrows)

of jack to lift the vehicle, and it can also be used to support certain components during various operations. **Warning:** *Never, under any circumstances, rely on a jack to support the vehicle while working on it. Whenever any of the suspension or steering fasteners are loosened or removed they must be inspected and, if necessary, replaced with new ones of the same part number or of original equipment quality and design. Torque specifications must be followed for proper reassembly and component retention. Never attempt to heat or straighten any suspension or steering components. Instead, replace any bent or damaged part with a new one.*

2   Strut assembly - removal, inspection and installation

Removal

Refer to illustrations 2.3 and 2.5

1   Loosen the wheel lug nuts, raise the vehicle and support it securely on jackstands. Remove the wheel.
2   Unbolt the brake hose from the caliper (see Chapter 9). Have some rags and a container handy to catch the brake fluid. Unclip the hose from the strut bracket (see Chapter 9) and push it through. If the vehicle is equipped with ABS, detach the speed sensor wiring harness from the strut by removing the clamp bracket bolt.
3   Remove the strut-to-knuckle nuts **(see illustration)** and knock the bolts out with a hammer and punch.
4   Separate the strut from the steering knuckle. Be careful not to overextend the inner CV joint.
5   Support the strut and spring assembly with one hand and remove the three (1990 and earlier) or four (1991 and later) strut-to-shock tower nuts **(see illustration)**. Remove the assembly out from the fenderwell.

Inspection

6   Check the strut body for leaking fluid, dents, cracks and other obvious damage which would warrant repair or replacement.
7   Check the coil spring for chips or cracks in the spring coating (this will cause premature spring failure due to corrosion). Inspect the spring seat for cuts, hardness and general deterioration.
8   If any undesirable conditions exist, proceed to the strut disassembly procedure (see Section 3).

Installation

9   Guide the strut assembly up into the fenderwell and insert the upper mounting studs through the holes in the shock tower. Once the studs protrude from the shock tower, install the nuts so the strut won't

3.3 Install the spring compressor according to the tool manufacturer's instructions and compress the spring until all pressure is relieved from the upper spring seat

fall back through. This is most easily accomplished with the help of an assistant, as the strut is quite heavy and awkward.
10   Slide the steering knuckle into the strut flange and insert the two bolts. Install the nuts and tighten them to the torque listed in this Chapter's Specifications.
11   Guide the brake hose through its bracket in the strut, reconnect it to the brake caliper. Tighten the banjo bolt to the torque listed in the Chapter 9 Specifications Section and bleed the brakes (see Chapter 9). If the vehicle is equipped with ABS, install the speed sensor wiring harness bracket.
12   Install the wheel and lug nuts, then lower the vehicle and tighten the lug nuts to the torque listed in the Chapter 1 Specifications.
13   Tighten the upper mounting nuts to the torque listed in this Chapter's Specifications.
14   Drive the vehicle to an alignment shop to have the front end alignment checked, and if necessary, adjusted.

3   Strut/spring assembly - replacement

1   If the struts or coil springs exhibit the telltale signs of wear (leaking fluid, loss of damping capability, chipped, sagging or cracked coil springs) explore all options before beginning any work. The

3.4 **Remove the damper shaft nut**

3.5 **Lift the suspension support off the damper shaft**

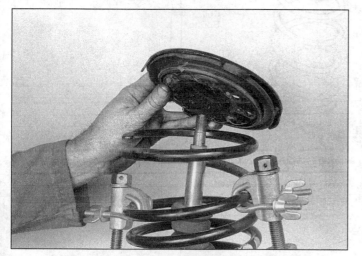
3.6 **Remove the spring seat from the damper shaft**

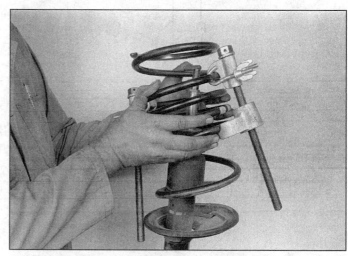
3.7 **Remove the compressed spring assembly - keep the ends of the spring pointed away from your body**

strut/shock absorber assemblies are not serviceable and must be replaced if a problem develops. However, strut assemblies complete with springs may be available on an exchange basis, which eliminates much time and work. Whichever route you choose to take, check on the cost and availability of parts before disassembling your vehicle. **Warning:** *Disassembling a strut assembly is a potentially dangerous undertaking and utmost attention must be directed to the job at hand, or serious bodily injury may result. Use only a high quality spring compressor and carefully follow the manufacturer's instructions furnished with the tool. After removing the coil spring from the strut assembly, set it aside in a safe, isolated area (a steel cabinet is preferred).*

Disassembly

Refer to illustrations 3.3, 3.4, 3.5, 3.6 and 3.7

2   Remove the strut and spring assembly following the procedure described in the previous Section. Mount the strut assembly in a vise. Line the vise jaws with wood or rags to prevent damage to the unit and don't tighten the vise excessively.

3   Following the tool manufacturer's instructions, install the spring compressor (which can be obtained at most auto parts stores or equipment yards on a daily rental basis) on the spring and compress it sufficiently to relieve all pressure from the upper spring seat **(see illustration)**. This can be verified by wiggling the spring.

4   Loosen the damper shaft nut with a socket wrench **(see illustration)**.

5   Remove the nut and suspension support **(see illustration)**. Inspect the bearing in the suspension support for smooth operation. If it doesn't turn smoothly, replace the suspension support. Check the rubber portion of the suspension support for cracking and general deterioration. If there is any separation of the rubber, replace it.

6   Lift the spring seat and upper insulator from the damper shaft **(see illustration)**. Check the rubber spring seat for cracking and hardness, replacing it if necessary.

7   Carefully lift the compressed spring from the assembly **(see illustration)** and set it in a safe place, such as a steel cabinet. **Warning:** *Never place your head near the end of the spring!*

8   Slide the rubber bumper off the damper shaft.

9   Check the lower insulator (if equipped) for wear, cracking and hardness and replace it if necessary.

Reassembly

Refer to illustrations 3.10, 3.11 and 3.12

10   If the lower insulator is being replaced, set it into position with the dropped portion seated in the lowest part of the seat. Extend the damper rod to its full length and install the rubber bumper **(see illustration)**.

10

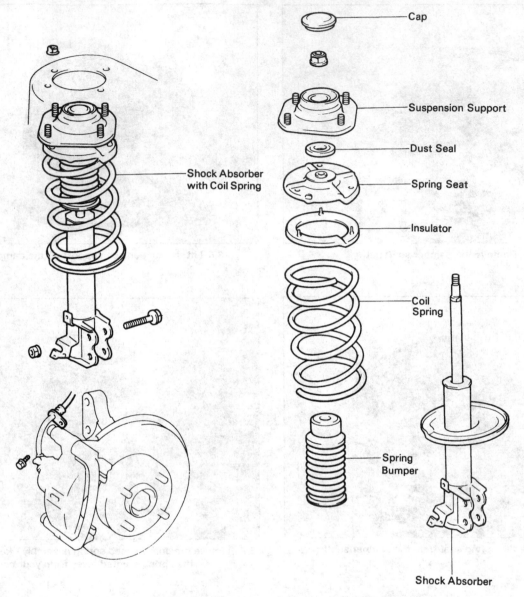

- Cap
- Suspension Support
- Dust Seal
- Spring Seat
- Insulator
- Coil Spring
- Shock Absorber with Coil Spring
- Spring Bumper
- Shock Absorber

3.10 Typical strut and coil spring assembly details

11 Carefully place the coil spring onto the lower insulator, with the end of the spring resting in the lowest part of the insulator **(see illustration)**.

12 Install the upper insulator and spring seat, making sure that the flats in the hole in the seat match up with the flats on the damper shaft **(see illustration)**.

13 Install the dust seal and suspension support to the damper shaft.

14 Install the nut and tighten it to the torque listed in this Chapter's Specifications.

15 Install the strut/shock absorber and coil spring assembly following the procedure outlined previously (see Section 2).

4 Control arm - removal, inspection and installation

Removal

Refer to illustrations 4.2a, 4.2b, 4.3 and 4.4

1 Loosen the wheel lug nuts on the side to be dismantled, raise the front of the vehicle, support it securely on jackstands and remove the wheel.

2 Remove the bolt and two nuts holding the control arm to the steering knuckle. Use a prybar to disconnect the control arm from the steering knuckle **(see illustrations)**.

3 Remove the control arm pivot bolt **(see illustration)**.

4 Remove the two bolts at the rear of the control arm bracket **(see illustration)**.

5 Remove the control arm.

Inspection

6 Check the control arm for distortion and the bushings for wear, replacing parts as necessary. Do not attempt to straighten a bent control arm.

Installation

Refer to illustration 4.7

7 Installation is the reverse of removal **(see illustration)**. Tighten all of the fasteners to the torque values listed in this Chapter's Specifications.

8 Install the wheel and lug nuts, lower the vehicle and tighten the lug nuts to the torque listed in the Chapter 1 Specifications.

9 It's a good idea to have the front wheel alignment checked, and if necessary, adjusted after this job has been performed.

3.11 When installing the spring, make sure the end fits into the recessed portion of the lower seat (arrow)

3.12 The flats on the damper shaft (arrow) must match up with the flats in the spring seat

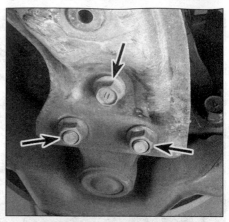

4.2a To detach the control arm from the steering knuckle balljoint, remove the bolt and nuts (arrows) . . .

4.2b . . . and pry the control arm and balljoint apart with a large prybar or screwdriver

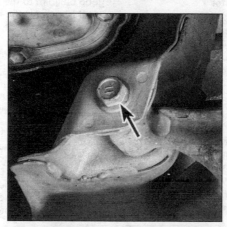

4.3 To detach the front of the control arm from the frame, remove the pivot bolt (arrow)

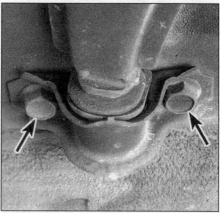

4.4 To detach the rear end of the control arm from the frame, remove these two bracket bolts (arrows) and the bracket

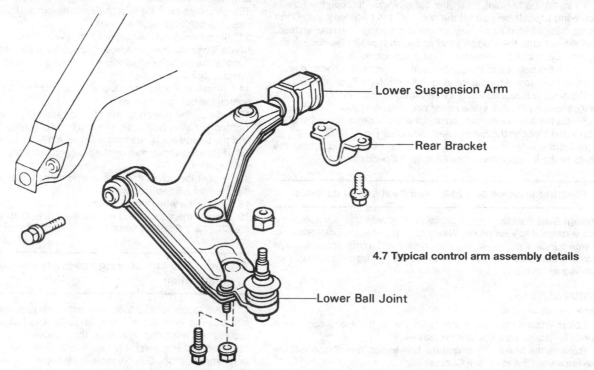

Lower Suspension Arm

Rear Bracket

Lower Ball Joint

4.7 Typical control arm assembly details

10

5.3 Separate the balljoint from the steering knuckle with a picklefork-type balljoint separator

6.8 If you're replacing the steering knuckle, and want to swap a good balljoint to the new steering knuckle, use a balljoint removal tool to remove the balljoint; using a pickle fork can damage the balljoint boot, rendering it useless for further service

5   Balljoints - replacement

Refer to illustration 5.3

1   Loosen the wheel lug nuts, raise the vehicle and support it securely on jackstands. Remove the wheel.

2   Remove the cotter pin (if equipped) from the balljoint stud and loosen the nut (but don't remove it yet).

3   Separate the balljoint from the steering knuckle with a picklefork-type balljoint separator **(see illustration)**. Lubricate the rubber boot with grease and work carefully, so as not to tear the boot. Remove the balljoint stud nut. The clearance between the balljoint stud and the CV joint is very tight. To remove the stud nut, you'll have to alternately back off the nut a turn or two, pull down the stud, turn the nut another turn or two, etc. until the nut is off.

4   Remove the bolt and nuts securing the balljoint to the control arm. Separate the balljoint from the control arm with a prybar **(see illustration 4.2b)**.

5   To install the balljoint, insert the balljoint stud through the hole in the steering knuckle and install the nut, but don't tighten it yet. Don't push the balljoint stud all the way up into and through the hole; instead, thread the nut onto the stud as soon as the stud protrudes through the hole, then turn the nut to draw the stud up through the hole.

6   Attach the balljoint to the control arm and install the bolt and nuts, tightening them to the torque listed in this Chapter's Specifications.

7   Tighten the balljoint stud nut to the torque listed in this Chapter's Specifications and install a new cotter pin. If the cotter pin hole doesn't line up with the slots on the nut, tighten the nut additionally until it does line up - don't loosen the nut to insert the cotter pin.

8   Install the wheel and lug nuts. Lower the vehicle and tighten the lug nuts to the torque listed in the Chapter 1 Specifications.

6   Steering knuckle and hub - removal and installation

Warning: *Dust created by the brake system may contain asbestos, which is harmful to your health. Never blow it out with compressed air and don't inhale any of it. Do not, under any circumstances, use petroleum-based solvents to clean brake parts. Use brake cleaner or denatured alcohol only.*

Removal

Refer to illustration 6.8

1   Loosen the wheel lug nuts, raise the vehicle and support it securely on jackstands. Remove the wheel.

2   Remove the brake caliper and the brake disc, and disconnect the brake hose from the strut (see Chapter 9).

3   If the vehicle is equipped with ABS, disconnect and remove the wheel speed sensor.

4   Loosen, but don't remove the strut-to-steering knuckle nuts and bolts (see Section 2).

5   Separate the tie-rod from the steering knuckle arm (see Section 12).

6   Remove the balljoint-to-lower arm bolt and nuts **(see illustrations 4.2a and 4.2b)**.

7   Push the driveaxle from the hub as described in Chapter 8. Support the end of the driveaxle with a piece of wire.

8   Using a balljoint removal tool **(see illustration)** or a small puller, remove the balljoint. Don't use a pickle fork! Unless, of course, you're planning to install a new balljoint on the new knuckle.

9   The strut-to-knuckle bolts can now be removed.

10   Carefully separate the steering knuckle from the strut.

Installation

11   Guide the knuckle and hub assembly into position, inserting the driveaxle into the hub.

12   Push the knuckle into the strut flange and install the bolts and nuts, but don't tighten them yet.

13   If you removed the balljoint from the old knuckle, and are planning to use it with the new knuckle, connect the balljoint to the knuckle and tighten the balljoint stud nut to the torque listed in this Chapter's Specifications.

14   Attach the balljoint to the control arm (see Section 4), but don't tighten the bolt and nuts yet.

15   Attach the tie-rod to the steering knuckle arm (see Section 12). Tighten the strut bolt nuts, the balljoint-to-control arm bolt and nuts and the tie-rod nut to the torque listed in this Chapter's Specifications.

16   Place the brake disc on the hub and install the caliper as outlined in Chapter 9.

17   Install the driveaxle/hub nut and tighten it to the torque listed in the Chapter 8 Specifications.

18   Install the wheel and lug nuts.

19   Lower the vehicle and tighten the lug nuts to the torque listed in the Chapter 1 Specifications.

7   Front hub and bearing assembly - removal and installation

Due to the special tools and expertise required to press the hub and bearing from the steering knuckle, this job should be left to a professional mechanic. However, the steering knuckle and hub may be removed and the assembly taken to a dealer service department or other repair shop. See Section 7 for the steering knuckle and hub removal procedure.

8.3 To detach the lower end of the shock absorber/coil spring assembly from the axle beam, remove this nut and bolt (arrow)

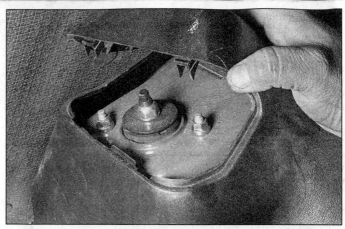

8.4 To gain access to the upper shock absorber mounting nuts on liftback models, remove this access cover

8 Shock absorber and coil spring - removal, inspection and installation

Removal

Refer to illustrations 8.3, 8.4 and 8.5

1   Loosen the rear wheel lug nuts, raise the rear of the vehicle and support it securely on jackstands. Remove the wheels.
2   Support the axle beam with a floor jack. Place a block of wood between the axle and the jack head to protect the axle.
3   Remove the shock-to-axle bolt and nut **(see illustration)**.
4   To access the upper mounting nuts on liftback models, raise the hatch and remove the access cover **(see illustration)**. The upper mounting nuts on 1990 and earlier sedan models are accessed through the luggage compartment. On 1991 and later models, remove the rear seat (see Chapter 11) for access.
5   Remove the upper mounting nuts **(see illustration)** while an assistant supports the shock so it doesn't fall. Guide the shock out of the fenderwell.

Inspection

6   Follow the inspection procedures described in Section 2. If you determine that the shock assembly must be disassembled for replacement of the shock or coil spring, refer to Section 3.

Installation

7   Maneuver the shock and coil spring assembly up into the fenderwell and insert the mounting studs through the holes in the body. Install the nuts, but don't tighten them yet.

8   Position the lower end of the shock between the two mounting brackets on the axle beam, install the bolt and nut, and tighten them to the torque listed in this Chapter's Specifications.
9   Install the wheel and lug nuts, lower the vehicle and tighten the lug nuts to the torque listed in the Chapter 1 Specifications.
10   Tighten the shock upper mounting nuts to the torque listed in this Chapter's Specifications.

9 Lateral control rod - removal and installation

Refer to illustrations 9.3 and 9.4

Note: *On 1990 and earlier vehicles, the lower end of the lateral rod is attached to the left (driver's) end of the axle beam and the upper end is attached to the frame bracket on the right (passenger's) side of the vehicle. On 1991 and later vehicles, it's reversed, i.e. the lower end is attached to the right end of the axle beam and the upper end is attached to a bracket on the left. The removal and installation procedure, however, is identical for both types.*

1   Loosen the rear wheel lug nuts, raise the rear of the vehicle and support it securely on jackstands. Remove the wheels.
2   Support the axle beam with a floor jack. Place a block of wood between the axle and the jack head to protect the axle.
3   Remove the nut that attaches the lower end of the lateral rod to the stud on the axle beam **(see illustration)**. Note that the larger washer goes on the same side as the nut; the smaller washer goes between the lateral rod and the axle beam.
4   Remove the bolt and nut that attach the upper end of the rod to the frame bracket **(see illustration)**.
5   Remove the lateral rod.

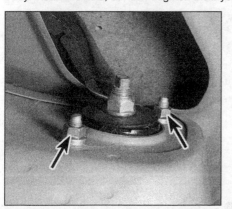

8.5 To detach the upper end of the shock absorber from the body, remove the upper mounting nuts (arrows)

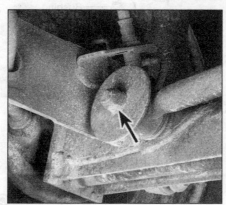

9.3 To detach the lower end of the lateral rod from the axle beam, remove this nut (arrow) from the stud on the axle beam

9.4 To detach the upper end of the lateral rod from the frame bracket, remove this nut (arrow) and bolt

10

6   Inspect the bushings in both ends of the rod. If they're torn, cracked or damaged, take the rod to an automotive machine shop and have new ones installed or replace the rod.

7   Installation is the reverse of removal. Be sure to tighten the upper and lower bolts and nuts to the torque listed in this Chapter's Specifications.

8   After lower the vehicle to the ground, tighten the lug nuts to the torque listed in the Chapter 1 Specifications.

10 Rear axle beam - removal, inspection and installation

Warning: *Dust created by the brake system may contain asbestos, which is harmful to your health. Never blow it out with compressed air*

10.4 To remove the brake backing plates from the axle beam assembly, remove the brake assemblies, then remove these four bolts (arrows)

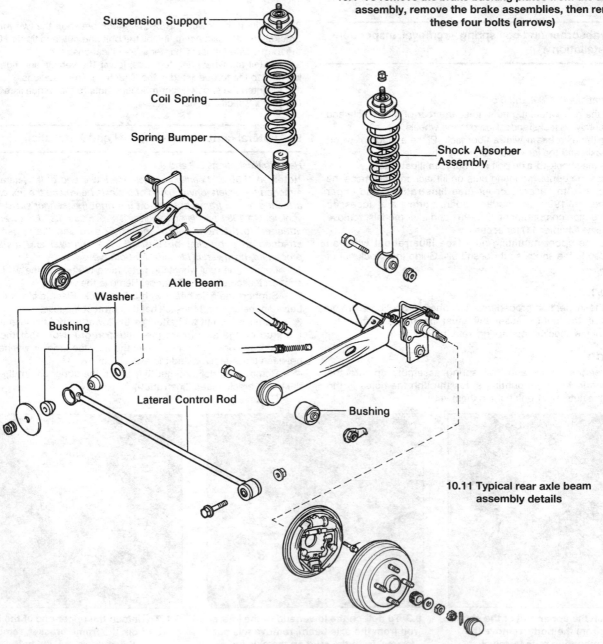

Retainer

Suspension Support

Coil Spring

Spring Bumper

Shock Absorber Assembly

Axle Beam

Washer

Bushing

Lateral Control Rod

Bushing

10.11 Typical rear axle beam assembly details

11.2a To access the horn pad retaining clip or retaining screw, find this hole in the backside of each steering wheel spoke

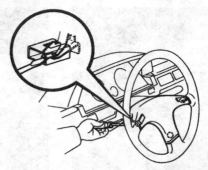

11.2b On 1990 and earlier non DX-models with a beige, brown or blue steering wheel, insert a screwdriver through the hole in the backside of each of the three steering wheel spokes, release the claw of the wheel pad and disengage the pad

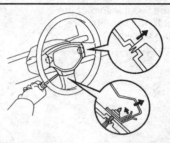

11.2d On 1990 and earlier DX models, the horn pad is retained by three screws, one in the backside of each steering wheel spoke

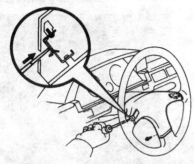

11.2c On 1990 and earlier non-DX models with a black steering wheel, insert a screwdriver through the hole in the backside of each of the two horizontal steering wheel spokes, release the claw of the wheel pad and disengage the pad, then remove the retaining screw from the vertical spoke and remove the pad

wear. If they're damaged or worn out, take the axle beam assembly to a dealer service department or an automotive machine shop to have the old ones pressed out and new ones pressed in.

Installation

Refer to Illustration 10.11

11   Installation is the reverse of removal **(see Illustration)**. Be sure to tighten all fasteners to the torque listed in this Chapter's Specifications.

12   Lower the vehicle and tighten the lug nuts to the torque listed in the Chapter 1 Specifications.

13   Bleed the brakes (see Chapter 9).

11   Steering wheel - removal and installation

Non-airbag vehicles

Refer to illustrations 11.2a, 11.2b, 11.2c, 11.2d, 11.3 and 11.4

Removal

1   Disconnect the cable from the negative terminal of the battery. **Caution:** *If the stereo in your vehicle is equipped with an anti-theft system, make sure you have the correct activation code before disconnecting the battery.*

2   On 1990 and earlier USA vehicles, the horn pad is attached to the steering wheel with various combinations of clips and/or screws, depending on the model and steering wheel color. On non-DX models with a beige, brown or blue steering wheel, insert a small screwdriver into the hole **(see illustration)** in the backside of each spoke, push the claw of the wheel pad **(see illustration)** and disengage the pad. Non-DX models with a black steering wheel also use this setup on the two horizontal spokes, but they use a screw in the center, or vertical, spoke **(see illustration)**. DX models also use a screw in the center spoke, and you can release the clips in the other two spokes simply by pulling the pad straight off **(see illustration)**. To remove the horn pad on later vehicles and early Canadian vehicles, simply pull it straight off.

3   Remove the steering wheel retaining nut, then mark the

and don't inhale any of it. Do not, under any circumstances, use petroleum-based solvents to clean brake parts. Use brake cleaner or denatured alcohol only.

Removal

Refer to illustration 10.4

1   Loosen the wheel lug nuts, raise the rear of the vehicle and place it securely on jackstands. Block the front wheels and remove the rear wheels.

2   Remove the rear brake drums and the brake assemblies (see Chapter 9).

3   Disconnect the brake lines from the wheel cylinders and disconnect the brake hoses from the brake lines (see Chapter 9). Plug the brake lines to prevent moisture and contamination from entering the brake system.

4   Detach the backing plates **(see illustration)** from the axle beam and suspend them from the coil springs with pieces of wire. It isn't necessary to remove the parking brake cable from the backing plate.

5   Support the axle beam with a floor jack. Place a block of wood between the axle and the jack head to protect the axle.

6   Disconnect the lower ends of the shock absorbers from the axle beam (see Section 8).

7   Disconnect the lower end of the lateral control rod from the axle beam (see Section 9).

8   Remove the pivot bolts from the forward ends of the axle beam trailing arms **(see illustration 13.5 in Chapter 9)**.

9   Remove the axle beam assembly.

Inspection

10   Inspect the trailing arm bushings for cracks, deformation and

 10

11.3 Remove the steering wheel retaining nut, then mark the relationship of the steering wheel to the shaft before removing the wheel

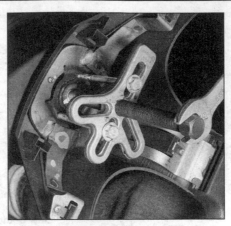

11.4 If the steering wheel is difficult to remove from the shaft, use a steering wheel puller to remove it

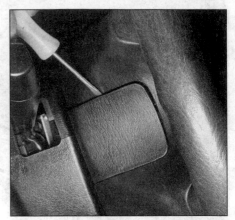

11.10a To remove the horn pad from an airbag-equipped steering wheel, remove these two small covers from each side of the steering wheel . . .

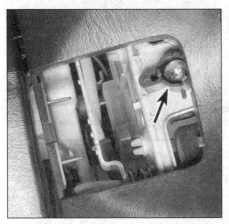

11.10b . . . and loosen the Torx-head screws (arrow) until the groove around the circumference of each screw catches on the screw case

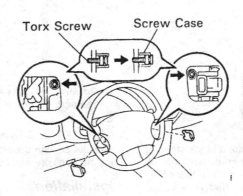

11.10c Once each Torx screw is backed out, it will continue to turn freely, but it won't come out - don't try to actually *remove* either screw

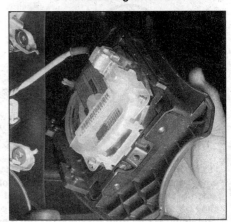

11.11a Pull the horn pad off the steering wheel . . .

relationship of the steering shaft to the hub (if marks don't already exist or don't line up) to simplify installation and ensure steering wheel alignment **(see illustration)**.
4   Use a puller to disconnect the steering wheel from the shaft **(see illustration)**.

Installation

5   To install the wheel, align the mark on the steering wheel hub with the mark on the shaft and slip the wheel onto the shaft. Install the nut and tighten it to the torque listed in this Chapter's Specifications.
6   Connect the horn wire and install the horn pad.
7   Connect the negative battery cable.

Airbag-equipped vehicles

Refer to illustrations 11.10a, 11.10b, 11.10c, 11,11a, 11.11b, 11.13 and 11.14
Warning: *The airbag is armed and can deploy (inflate) anytime the battery is connected. To prevent accidental deployment (and possible injury), disconnect the negative battery cable whenever working near airbag components. After the battery is disconnected, wait at least 90 seconds before beginning work (the system has a back-up capacitor that must fully discharge). For more information see Chapter 12.*

Removal

8   Disconnect the cable from the negative battery terminal. **Caution:** *If the stereo in your vehicle is equipped with an anti-theft system, make sure you have the correct activation code before disconnecting the*

battery.
9   Turn the steering wheel so that the front wheels are pointing straight ahead.
10   Remove the small covers from each side of the steering wheel **(see illustration)** and loosen the Torx-head screws **(see illustration)** behind them. You'll need a T30 Torx bit. Loosen the Torx screws until the groove around the circumference of each screw catches on the screw case **(see illustration)**.
11   Pull the horn pad off the steering wheel and unplug the airbag electrical connector **(see illustrations)**. **Warning:** *Handle the airbag module with care and store it in a safe location. See precautions in Chapter 12.*
12   The remainder of steering wheel removal is identical with a non-airbag steering wheel (refer to Steps 3 and 4 above). **Warning:** *Do not turn the steering wheel shaft while the steering wheel is removed.*

Installation

13   Verify that the front wheels are pointing straight ahead, then turn the spiral cable counterclockwise by hand until it becomes hard to turn the cable, then rotate the spiral cable clockwise about three turns and align the red marks **(see illustration)**. (The spiral cable will rotate about three turns to the left or the right of center).
14   The remainder of installation is the reverse of removal. When installing the horn pad, make sure that no wiring interferes with or is pinched between other parts **(see illustration)**. Be sure to tighten the steering wheel retaining nut and the horn pad screws to the torque listed in this Chapter's Specifications.

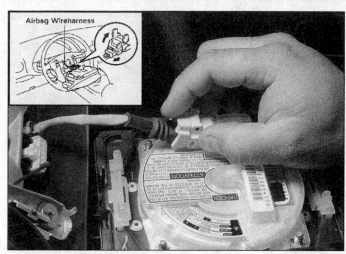

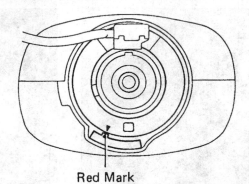

11.11b ... flip open the lock on the airbag electrical connector and unplug the connector. Warning: *Make sure you don't pull on the harness itself. And don't attempt to disassemble the airbag assembly.*

12 Tie-rod ends - removal and installation

Removal

Refer to illustrations 12.2a, 12.2b and 12.4

1   Loosen the wheel lug nuts. Raise the front of the vehicle, support it securely on jackstands, block the rear wheels and set the parking brake. Remove the front wheel.
2   Loosen the jam nut enough to mark the position of the tie-rod end in relation to the threads **(see illustrations)**.
3   Remove the cotter pin and loosen the nut on the tie-rod end stud.
4   Disconnect the tie-rod from the steering knuckle arm with a puller **(see illustration)**. Remove the nut and separate the tie-rod.
5   Unscrew the tie-rod end from the tie-rod.

Installation

6   Thread the tie-rod end on to the marked position and insert the tie-rod stud into the steering knuckle arm. Tighten the jam nut securely.
7   Install the castellated nut on the stud and tighten it to the torque listed in this Chapter's Specifications. Install a new cotter pin.
8   Install the wheel and lug nuts. Lower the vehicle and tighten the lug nuts to the torque listed in the Chapter 1 Specifications.
9   Have the alignment checked by a dealer service department or an alignment shop.

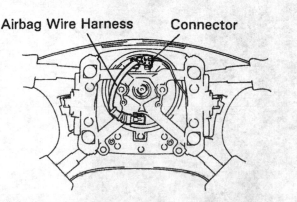

Red Mark

11.13 Verify that the front wheels are pointing straight ahead, then turn the spiral cable counterclockwise by hand until it becomes hard to turn the cable, then rotate the spiral cable clockwise about three turns and align the red marks (the spiral cable will rotate about three turns to the left or the right of center)

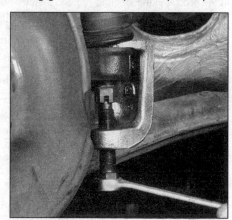

Airbag Wire Harness   Connector

11.14 When installing the horn pad, make sure that no wiring interferes with, or is pinched between, other parts; if you route the airbag wire harness as shown, it should be fine

13 Steering gear boots - replacement

Refer to illustrations 13.3a and 13.3b

1   Loosen the lug nuts, raise the vehicle and support it securely on jackstands. Remove the wheel.
2   Remove the tie-rod end and jam nut (see Section 12).
3   Remove the outer steering gear boot clamp with a pair of pliers

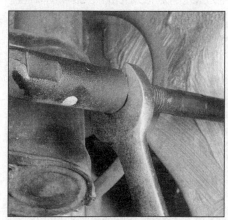

12.2a Loosen the jam nut . . .

12.2b . . . then mark the position of the tie-rod end in relation to the threads

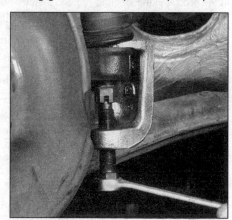

12.4 Disconnect the tie-rod from the steering knuckle arm with a puller

10

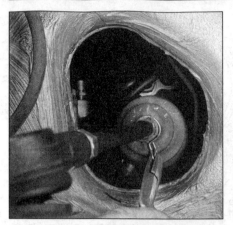  

13.3a The outer ends of the steering gear boots are secured by wire-type retaining rings

13.3b The inner ends of the steering gear boots are retained by boot clamps which must be cut off and discarded

14.2 Disconnect the power steering line fittings (arrows)

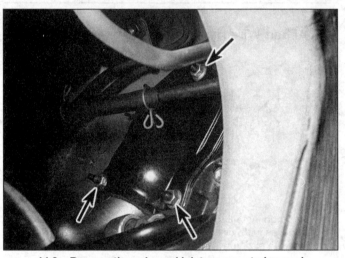 

14.3a Remove the universal joint cover nuts (arrows) and remove the cover

14.3b Mark the relationship of the universal joint to the steering gear input shaft and loosen the U-joint pinch bolt (arrow)

(see illustration). Cut off the inner boot clamp with a pair of diagonal cutters **(see illustration)**. Slide the boot off.

4   Before installing the new boot, wrap the threads and serration's on the end of the steering rod with a layer of tape so the small end of the new boot isn't damaged.

5   Slide the new boot into position on the steering gear until it seats in the groove in the steering rod and install new clamps.

6   Remove the tape and install the tie-rod end (see Section 12).

7   Install the wheel and lug nuts. Lower the vehicle and tighten the lug nuts to the torque listed in the Chapter 1 Specifications.

14   Steering gear - removal and installation

Removal

Refer to illustrations 14.2, 14.3a, 14.3b, 14.5a and 14.5b

1   Loosen the front wheel lug nuts, raise the front of the vehicle and support it securely on jackstands. Apply the parking brake and remove the wheels. Remove the engine splash shields (see Chapter 1).

2   If equipped with power steering, place a drain pan under the steering gear. Detach the power steering pressure and return lines **(see illustration)** and cap the ends to prevent excessive fluid loss and contamination.

3   Remove the universal joint cover **(see illustration)**. Mark the relationship of the lower universal joint to the steering gear input shaft

(see illustration). Remove the lower intermediate shaft pinch bolt.

4   Separate the tie-rod ends from the steering knuckle arms (see Section 12).

5   Support the steering gear and remove the steering gear bracket-to-firewall mounting bolts **(see illustrations)**. Separate the intermediate shaft from the steering gear input shaft and remove the steering gear assembly. **Warning:** *Do NOT turn the steering wheel, while the steering gear is removed, on vehicles equipped with an airbag. If the steering wheel is inadvertently turned, remove the steering wheel and center the spiral cable (see Section 11).*

6   Check the steering gear mounting grommets for excessive wear or deterioration, replacing them if necessary.

Installation

7   Raise the steering gear into position and connect the U-joint, aligning the marks.

8   Install the mounting brackets and bolts and tighten them to the torque listed in this Chapter's Specifications.

9   Connect the tie-rod ends to the steering knuckle arms (see Section 12).

10   Install the U-joint pinch bolt and tighten it to the torque listed in this Chapter's Specifications.

11   If equipped with power steering, connect the power steering pressure and return hoses to the steering gear and fill the power steering pump reservoir with the recommended fluid (see Chapter 1).

12   Lower the vehicle and bleed the steering system (see Section 16).

14.5a Remove the lower bolt (arrow) and the upper nut (not visible in this photo) from the left steering gear bracket

14.5b Remove the lower bolt (arrow) and the upper nut (arrow) from the right steering gear bracket

15.3 Remove the fluid return hose (arrow) and the pressure line (arrow) from the power steering pump

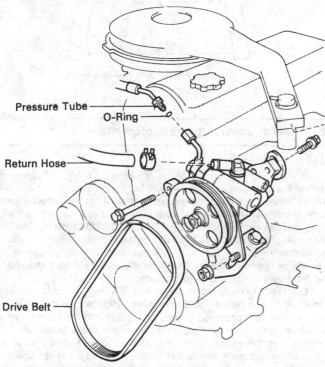

15.5a Typical 1989 and earlier power steering pump assembly details

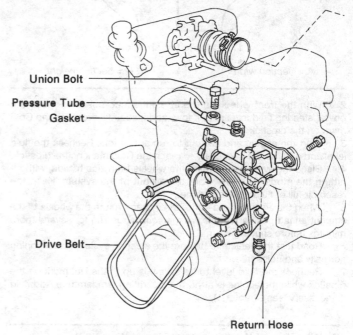

15.5b Typical 1990 and later power steering pump assembly details

15 Power steering pump - removal and installation

Removal

Refer to illustrations 15.3, 15.5a and 15.5b

1   Disconnect the cable from the negative battery terminal. **Caution:** *If the stereo in your vehicle is equipped with an anti-theft system, make sure you have the correct activation code before disconnecting the battery.*

2   Using a large syringe or suction gun, suck as much fluid out of the power steering fluid reservoir as possible. Place a drain pan under the vehicle to catch any fluid that spills out when the hoses are disconnected.

3   Loosen the clamp and disconnect the fluid return hose from the pump **(see illustration)**.

4   Remove the pressure line-to-pump fitting or banjo bolt, then

detach the line from the pump. Remove and discard the copper sealing washers. They must be replaced when installing the pump.

5   Loosen the pivot and adjuster bolt and remove the drivebelt (see Chapter 1). Remove the pivot, adjuster and mounting bolts **(see illustrations)**, then remove the pump from the vehicle.

Installation

6   Installation is the reverse of removal. Be sure to tighten the pressure line fitting or banjo bolt to the torque listed in this Chapter's Specifications. Adjust the drivebelt tension following the procedure described in Chapter 1.

7   Top up the fluid level in the reservoir (see Chapter 1) and bleed the system (see Section 16).

16 Power steering system - bleeding

1   Following any operation in which the power steering fluid lines have been disconnected, the power steering system must be bled to remove all air and obtain proper steering performance.

10

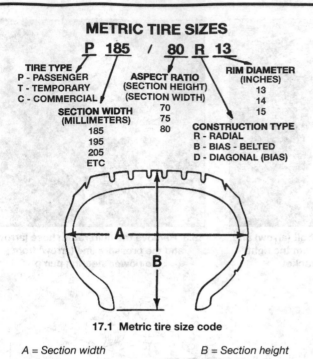

METRIC TIRE SIZES

P   185 / 80 R 13

TIRE TYPE
P - PASSENGER
T - TEMPORARY
C - COMMERCIAL

SECTION WIDTH
(MILLIMETERS)
185
195
205
ETC

ASPECT RATIO
(SECTION HEIGHT)
(SECTION WIDTH)
70
75
80

RIM DIAMETER
(INCHES)
13
14
15

CONSTRUCTION TYPE
R - RADIAL
B - BIAS - BELTED
D - DIAGONAL (BIAS)

17.1 Metric tire size code

A = Section width   B = Section height

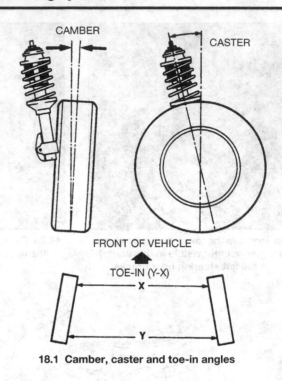

18.1 Camber, caster and toe-in angles

2   With the front wheels in the straight ahead position, check the power steering fluid level and, if low, add fluid until it reaches the Cold mark on the dipstick.
3   Start the engine and allow it to run at fast idle. Recheck the fluid level and add more if necessary to reach the Cold mark on the dipstick.
4   Bleed the system by turning the wheels from side to side, without hitting the stops. This will work the air out of the system. Keep the reservoir full of fluid as this is done.
5   When the air is worked out of the system, return the wheels to the straight ahead position and leave the vehicle running for several more minutes before shutting it off.
6   Road test the vehicle to be sure the steering system is functioning normally and noise free.
7   Recheck the fluid level to be sure it is up to the Hot mark on the dipstick while the engine is at normal operating temperature. Add fluid if necessary (see Chapter 1).

17   Wheels and tires - general information

Refer to illustration 17.1
1   All vehicles covered by this manual are equipped with metric-sized fiberglass or steel belted radial tires **(see illustration)**. Use of other size or type of tires may affect the ride and handling of the vehicle. Don't mix different types of tires, such as radials and bias belted, on the same vehicle as handling may be seriously affected. It's recommended that tires be replaced in pairs on the same axle, but if only one tire is being replaced, be sure it's the same size, structure and tread design as the other.
2   Because tire pressure has a substantial effect on handling and wear, the pressure on all tires should be checked at least once a month or before any extended trips (see Chapter 1).
3   Wheels must be replaced if they are bent, dented, leak air, have elongated bolt holes, are heavily rusted, out of vertical symmetry or if the lug nuts won't stay tight. Wheel repairs that use welding or peening are not recommended.
4   Tire and wheel balance is important in the overall handling, braking and performance of the vehicle. Unbalanced wheels can adversely affect handling and ride characteristics as well as tire life. Whenever a tire is installed on a wheel, the tire and wheel should be balanced by a shop with the proper equipment.

18   Wheel alignment - general information

Refer to illustration 18.1
A wheel alignment refers to the adjustments made to the wheels so they are in proper angular relationship to the suspension and the ground. Wheels that are out of proper alignment not only affect vehicle control, but also increase tire wear. The front end angles normally measured are camber, caster and toe-in **(see illustration)**. Camber and toe-in are adjustable on 1989 and earlier models. Toe-in is the only adjustable angle on 1990 and later models. The only adjustment possible on the rear is toe-in. The other angles should be measured to check for bent or worn suspension parts.
Getting the proper wheel alignment is a very exacting process, one in which complicated and expensive machines are necessary to perform the job properly. Because of this, you should have a technician with the proper equipment perform these tasks. We will, however, use this space to give you a basic idea of what is involved with a wheel alignment so you can better understand the process and deal intelligently with the shop that does the work.
Toe-in is the turning in of the wheels. The purpose of a toe specification is to ensure parallel rolling of the wheels. In a vehicle with zero toe-in, the distance between the front edges of the wheels will be the same as the distance between the rear edges of the wheels. The actual amount of toe-in is normally only a fraction of an inch. On the front end, toe-in is controlled by the tie-rod end position on the tie-rod. On the rear end, it's controlled by a cam on the inner end of the rear (number two) suspension arm. Incorrect toe-in will cause the tires to wear improperly by making them scrub against the road surface.
Camber is the tilting of the wheels from vertical when viewed from one end of the vehicle. When the wheels tilt out at the top, the camber is said to be positive (+). When the wheels tilt in at the top the camber is negative (-). The amount of tilt is measured in degrees from vertical and this measurement is called the camber angle. This angle affects the amount of tire tread which contacts the road and compensates for changes in the suspension geometry when the vehicle is cornering or traveling over an undulating surface.
Caster is the tilting of the front steering axis from the vertical. A tilt toward the rear is positive caster and a tilt toward the front is negative caster.

Chapter 11 Body

Contents

1 General information

These models feature a "unibody" construction, using a floor pan with front and rear frame side rails which support the body components, front and rear suspension systems and other mechanical components. Certain components are particularly vulnerable to accident damage and can be unbolted and repaired or replaced. Among these parts are the body moldings, bumpers, hood and trunk lids and all glass.

Only general body maintenance practices and body panel repair procedures within the scope of the do-it-yourselfer are included in this Chapter.

2 Body - maintenance

1   The condition of your vehicle's body is very important, because the resale value depends a great deal on it. It's much more difficult to repair a neglected or damaged body than it is to repair mechanical components. The hidden areas of the body, such as the wheel wells, the frame and the engine compartment, are equally important, although they don't require as frequent attention as the rest of the body.

2   Once a year, or every 12,000 miles, it's a good idea to have the underside of the body steam cleaned. All traces of dirt and oil will be removed and the area can then be inspected carefully for rust, damaged brake lines, frayed electrical wires, damaged cables and other problems. The front suspension components should be greased after completion of this job.

3   At the same time, clean the engine and the engine compartment with a steam cleaner or water soluble degreaser.

4   The wheel wells should be given close attention, since undercoating can peel away and stones and dirt thrown up by the tires can cause the paint to chip and flake, allowing rust to set in. If rust is found, clean down to the bare metal and apply an anti-rust paint.

5   The body should be washed about once a week. Wet the vehicle thoroughly to soften the dirt, then wash it down with a soft sponge and plenty of clean soapy water. If the surplus dirt is not washed off very carefully, it can wear down the paint.

6   Spots of tar or asphalt thrown up from the road should be removed with a cloth soaked in solvent.

7   Once every six months, wax the body and chrome trim. If a chrome cleaner is used to remove rust from any of the vehicle's plated parts, remember that the cleaner also removes part of the chrome, so use it sparingly.

11

3   Vinyl trim - maintenance

Don't clean vinyl trim with detergents, caustic soap or petroleum-based cleaners. Plain soap and water works just fine, with a soft brush to clean dirt that may be ingrained. Wash the vinyl as frequently as the rest of the vehicle.

After cleaning, application of a high quality rubber and vinyl protectant will help prevent oxidation and cracks. The protectant can also be applied to weather-stripping, vacuum lines and rubber hoses, which often fail as a result of chemical degradation, and to the tires.

4   Upholstery and carpets - maintenance

1   Every three months remove the carpets or mats and clean the interior of the vehicle (more frequently if necessary). Vacuum the upholstery and carpets to remove loose dirt and dust.
2   Leather upholstery requires special care. Stains should be removed with warm water and a very mild soap solution. Use a clean, damp cloth to remove the soap, then wipe again with a dry cloth. Never use alcohol, gasoline, nail polish remover or thinner to clean leather upholstery.
3   After cleaning, regularly treat leather upholstery with a leather wax. Never use car wax on leather upholstery.
4   In areas where the interior of the vehicle is subject to bright sunlight, cover leather seats with a sheet if the vehicle is to be left out for any length of time.

5   Body repair - minor damage

See photo sequence

Repair of minor scratches

1   If the scratch is superficial and does not penetrate to the metal of the body, repair is very simple. Lightly rub the scratched area with a fine rubbing compound to remove loose paint and built-up wax. Rinse the area with clean water.
2   Apply touch-up paint to the scratch, using a small brush. Continue to apply thin layers of paint until the surface of the paint in the scratch is level with the surrounding paint. Allow the new paint at least two weeks to harden, then blend it into the surrounding paint by rubbing with a very fine rubbing compound. Finally, apply a coat of wax to the scratch area.
3   If the scratch has penetrated the paint and exposed the metal of the body, causing the metal to rust, a different repair technique is required. Remove all loose rust from the bottom of the scratch with a pocket knife, then apply rust inhibiting paint to prevent the formation of rust in the future. Using a rubber or nylon applicator, coat the scratched area with glaze-type filler. If required, the filler can be mixed with thinner to provide a very thin paste, which is ideal for filling narrow scratches. Before the glaze filler in the scratch hardens, wrap a piece of smooth cotton cloth around the tip of a finger. Dip the cloth in thinner and then quickly wipe it along the surface of the scratch. This will ensure that the surface of the filler is slightly hollow. The scratch can now be painted over as described earlier in this section.

Repair of dents

4   When repairing dents, the first job is to pull the dent out until the affected area is as close as possible to its original shape. There is no point in trying to restore the original shape completely as the metal in the damaged area will have stretched on impact and cannot be restored to its original contours. It is better to bring the level of the dent up to a point which is about 1/8-inch below the level of the surrounding metal. In cases where the dent is very shallow, it is not worth trying to pull it out at all.
5   If the back side of the dent is accessible, it can be hammered out gently from behind using a soft-face hammer. While doing this, hold a block of wood firmly against the opposite side of the metal to absorb the hammer blows and prevent the metal from being stretched.
6   If the dent is in a section of the body which has double layers, or some other factor makes it inaccessible from behind, a different technique is required. Drill several small holes through the metal inside the damaged area, particularly in the deeper sections. Screw long, self-tapping screws into the holes just enough for them to get a good grip in the metal. Now the dent can be pulled out by pulling on the protruding heads of the screws with locking pliers.
7   The next stage of repair is the removal of paint from the damaged area and from an inch or so of the surrounding metal. This is done with a wire brush or sanding disk in a drill motor, although it can be done just as effectively by hand with sandpaper. To complete the preparation for filling, score the surface of the bare metal with a screwdriver or the tang of a file, or drill small holes in the affected area. This will provide a good grip for the filler material. To complete the repair, see the subsection on filling and painting later in this Section.

Repair of rust holes or gashes

8   Remove all paint from the affected area and from an inch or so of the surrounding metal using a sanding disk or wire brush mounted in a drill motor. If these are not available, a few sheets of sandpaper will do the job just as effectively.
9   With the paint removed, you will be able to determine the severity of the corrosion and decide whether to replace the whole panel, if possible, or repair the affected area. New body panels are not as expensive as most people think and it is often quicker to install a new panel than to repair large areas of rust.
10   Remove all trim pieces from the affected area except those which will act as a guide to the original shape of the damaged body, such as headlight shells, etc. Using metal snips or a hacksaw blade, remove all loose metal and any other metal that is badly affected by rust. Hammer the edges of the hole in to create a slight depression for the filler material.
11   Wire brush the affected area to remove the powdery rust from the surface of the metal. If the back of the rusted area is accessible, treat it with rust inhibiting paint.
12   Before filling is done, block the hole in some way. This can be done with sheet metal riveted or screwed into place, or by stuffing the hole with wire mesh.
13   Once the hole is blocked off, the affected area can be filled and painted. See the following subsection on filling and painting.

Filling and painting

14   Many types of body fillers are available, but generally speaking, body repair kits which contain filler paste and a tube of resin hardener are best for this type of repair work. A wide, flexible plastic or nylon applicator will be necessary for imparting a smooth and contoured finish to the surface of the filler material. Mix up a small amount of filler on a clean piece of wood or cardboard (use the hardener sparingly). Follow the manufacturer's instructions on the package, otherwise the filler will set incorrectly.
15   Using the applicator, apply the filler paste to the prepared area. Draw the applicator across the surface of the filler to achieve the desired contour and to level the filler surface. As soon as a contour that approximates the original one is achieved, stop working the paste. If you continue, the paste will begin to stick to the applicator. Continue to add thin layers of paste at 20-minute intervals until the level of the filler is just above the surrounding metal.
16   Once the filler has hardened, the excess can be removed with a body file. From then on, progressively finer grades of sandpaper should be used, starting with a 180-grit paper and finishing with 600-grit wet-or-dry paper. Always wrap the sandpaper around a flat rubber or wooden block, otherwise the surface of the filler will not be completely flat. During the sanding of the filler surface, the wet-or-dry paper should be periodically rinsed in water. This will ensure that a very smooth finish is produced in the final stage.
17   At this point, the repair area should be surrounded by a ring of bare metal, which in turn should be encircled by the finely feathered edge of good paint. Rinse the repair area with clean water until all of

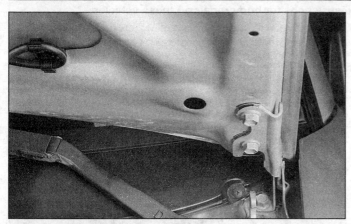

9.1 Before removing the hood, make marks around the hinge plate

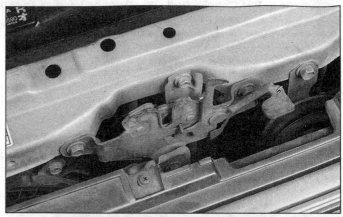

9.10 Loosen the hood latch bolts, move the latch and retighten bolts, then close the hood to check the fit - repeat the procedure until the hood is flush with the fenders

the dust produced by the sanding operation is gone.

18   Spray the entire area with a light coat of primer. This will reveal any imperfections in the surface of the filler. Repair the imperfections with fresh filler paste or glaze filler and once more smooth the surface with sandpaper. Repeat this spray-and-repair procedure until you are satisfied that the surface of the filler and the feathered edge of the paint are perfect. Rinse the area with clean water and allow it to dry completely.

19   The repair area is now ready for painting. Spray painting must be carried out in a warm, dry, windless and dust free atmosphere. These conditions can be created if you have access to a large indoor work area, but if you are forced to work in the open, you will have to pick the day very carefully. If you are working indoors, dousing the floor in the work area with water will help settle the dust which would otherwise be in the air. If the repair area is confined to one body panel, mask off the surrounding panels. This will help minimize the effects of a slight mismatch in paint color. Trim pieces such as chrome strips, door handles, etc., will also need to be masked off or removed. Use masking tape and several thickness of newspaper for the masking operations.

20   Before spraying, shake the paint can thoroughly, then spray a test area until the spray painting technique is mastered. Cover the repair area with a thick coat of primer. The thickness should be built up using several thin layers of primer rather than one thick one. Using 600-grit wet-or-dry sandpaper, rub down the surface of the primer until it is very smooth. While doing this, the work area should be thoroughly rinsed with water and the wet-or-dry sandpaper periodically rinsed as well. Allow the primer to dry before spraying additional coats.

21   Spray on the top coat, again building up the thickness by using several thin layers of paint. Begin spraying in the center of the repair area and then, using a circular motion, work out until the whole repair area and about two inches of the surrounding original paint is covered. Remove all masking material 10 to 15 minutes after spraying on the final coat of paint. Allow the new paint at least two weeks to harden, then use a very fine rubbing compound to blend the edges of the new paint into the existing paint. Finally, apply a coat of wax.

6   Body repair - major damage

1   Major damage must be repaired by an auto body shop specifically equipped to perform unibody repairs. These shops have the specialized equipment required to do the job properly.

2   If the damage is extensive, the body must be checked for proper alignment or the vehicle's handling characteristics may be adversely affected and other components may wear at an accelerated rate.

3   Due to the fact that all of the major body components (hood, fenders, etc.) are separate and replaceable units, any seriously damaged components should be replaced rather than repaired. Sometimes the components can be found in a wrecking yard that

specializes in used vehicle components, often at considerable savings over the cost of new parts.

7   Hinges and locks - maintenance

Once every 3000 miles, or every three months, the hinges and latch assemblies on the doors, hood and trunk should be given a few drops of light oil or lock lubricant. The door latch strikers should also be lubricated with a thin coat of grease to reduce wear and ensure free movement. Lubricate the door and trunk locks with spray-on graphite lubricant.

8   Windshield and fixed glass - replacement

Replacement of the windshield and fixed glass requires the use of special fast-setting adhesive/caulk materials and some specialized tools. It is recommended that these operations be left to a dealer or a shop specializing in glass work.

9   Hood - removal, installation and adjustment

Refer to illustrations 9.1, 9.10 and 9.11
Note: *The hood is heavy and somewhat awkward to remove and install - at least two people should perform this procedure.*

Removal and installation

1   Make marks around the bolt heads to ensure proper alignment during installation **(see illustration)**.

2   Use blankets or pads to cover the cowl area of the body and fenders. This will protect the body and paint as the hood is lifted off.

3   Disconnect any cables or wires that will interfere with removal.

4   Have an assistant support the hood. Remove the hinge-to-hood screws or bolts.

5   Lift off the hood.

6   Installation is the reverse of removal.

Adjustment

7   Fore-and-aft and side-to-side adjustment of the hood is done by moving the hinge plate slot after loosening the bolts or nuts.

8   Scribe a line around the entire hinge plate so you can judge the amount of movement **(see illustration 9.1)**

9   Loosen the bolts or nuts and move the hood into correct alignment. Move it only a little at a time. Tighten the hinge bolts and carefully lower the hood to check the position.

10   If necessary after installation, the entire hood latch assembly can

11

These photos illustrate a method of repairing simple dents. They are intended to supplement *Body repair - minor damage* in this Chapter and should not be used as the sole instructions for body repair on these vehicles.

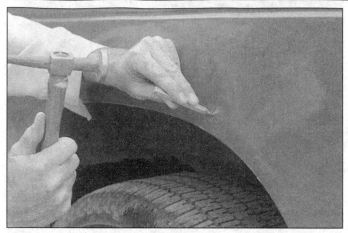

1   If you can't access the backside of the body panel to hammer out the dent, pull it out with a slide-hammer-type dent puller. In the deepest portion of the dent or along the crease line, drill or punch hole(s) at least one inch apart . . .

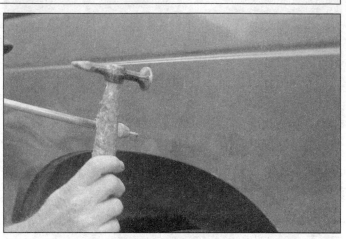

2   . . . then screw the slide-hammer into the hole and operate it. Tap with a hammer near the edge of the dent to help 'pop' the metal back to its original shape. When you're finished, the dent area should be close to its original contour and about 1/8-inch below the surface of the surrounding metal

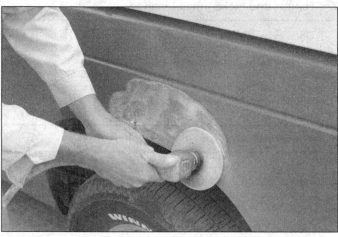

3   Using coarse-grit sandpaper, remove the paint down to the bare metal. Hand sanding works fine, but the disc sander shown here makes the job faster. Use finer (about 320-grit) sandpaper to feather-edge the paint at least one inch around the dent area

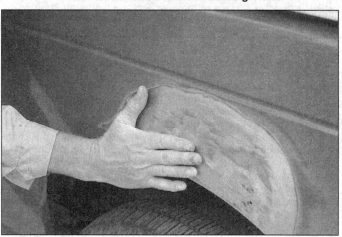

4   When the paint is removed, touch will probably be more helpful than sight for telling if the metal is straight. Hammer down the high spots or raise the low spots as necessary. Clean the repair area with wax/silicone remover

5   Following label instructions, mix up a batch of plastic filler and hardener. The ratio of filler to hardener is critical, and, if you mix it incorrectly, it will either not cure properly or cure too quickly (you won't have time to file and sand it into shape)

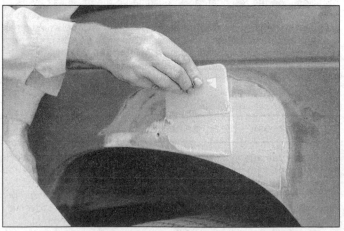

6   Working quickly so the filler doesn't harden, use a plastic applicator to press the body filler firmly into the metal, assuring it bonds completely. Work the filler until it matches the original contour and is slightly above the surrounding metal

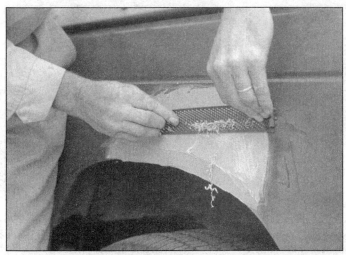

7   Let the filler harden until you can just dent it with your fingernail. Use a body file or Surform tool (shown here) to rough-shape the filler

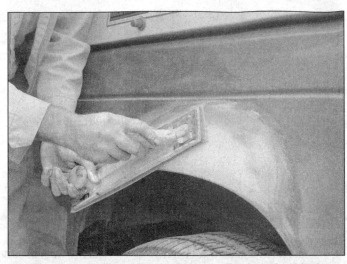

8   Use coarse-grit sandpaper and a sanding board or block to work the filler down until it's smooth and even. Work down to finer grits of sandpaper - always using a board or block - ending up with 360 or 400 grit

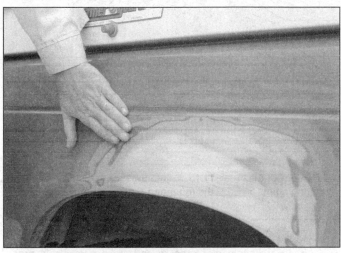

9   You shouldn't be able to feel any ridge at the transition from the filler to the bare metal or from the bare metal to the old paint. As soon as the repair is flat and uniform, remove the dust and mask off the adjacent panels or trim pieces

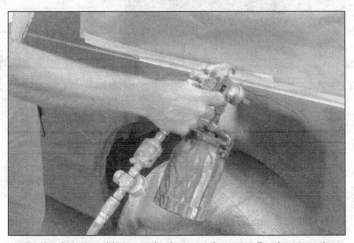

10   Apply several layers of primer to the area. Don't spray the primer on too heavy, so it sags or runs, and make sure each coat is dry before you spray on the next one. A professional-type spray gun is being used here, but aerosol spray primer is available inexpensively from auto parts stores

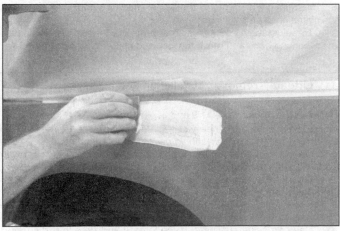

11   The primer will help reveal imperfections or scratches. Fill these with glazing compound. Follow the label instructions and sand it with 360 or 400-grit sandpaper until it's smooth. Repeat the glazing, sanding and respraying until the primer reveals a perfectly smooth surface

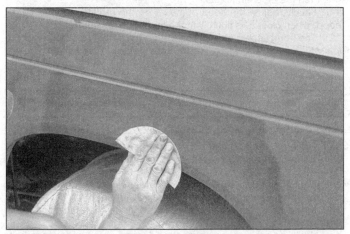

12   Finish sand the primer with very fine sandpaper (400 or 600-grit) to remove the primer overspray. Clean the area with water and allow it to dry. Use a tack rag to remove any dust, then apply the finish coat. Don't attempt to rub out or wax the repair area until the paint has dried completely (at least two weeks)

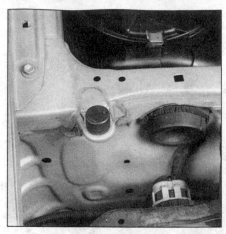

9.11 Adjust the hood closing by screwing the hood bumpers in-or-out

10.3 Scribe a mark around the bolt heads to help with lid realignment on installation

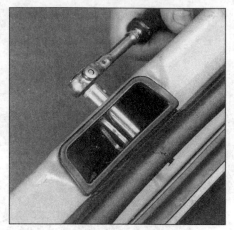

10.9 Loosen the bolts, then adjust the latch and striker position

11.3 Draw a line around the hinge plate on the liftgate before removing the bolts

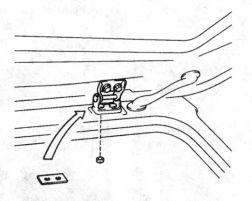

11.9 Adjust the vertical alignment of the liftgate by adding or removing shims

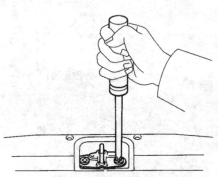

11.10 Adjust the lock striker by loosening the mounting screws slightly and tapping the striker with a soft-faced hammer

be adjusted up-and-down as well as from side-to-side on the radiator support so the hood closes securely, flush with the fenders. To make the adjustment, scribe a line around the hood latch mounting bolts to provide a reference point, then loosen them and reposition the latch assembly, as necessary **(see illustration)**. Following adjustment, retighten the mounting bolts.

11   Finally, adjust the hood bumpers on the radiator support so the hood, when closed, is flush with the fenders **(see illustration)**.

12   The hood latch assembly, as well as the hinges, should be periodically lubricated with white, lithium-base grease to prevent binding and wear.

10   Trunk lid - removal, installation and adjustment

Refer to illustrations 10.3 and 10.9

1   Open the trunk lid and cover the edges of the trunk compartment with pads or cloths to protect the painted surfaces when the lid is removed.

2   Disconnect any cables or wire harness connectors attached to the trunk lid that would interfere with removal.

3   Make alignment marks around the hinge mounting bolts **(see illustration)**.

4   While an assistant supports the lid, remove the lid-to-hinge bolts on both sides and lift it off.

5   Installation is the reverse of removal. **Note:** *When reinstalling the trunk lid, align the lid-to-hinge bolts with the marks made*

during removal.

6   After installation, close the lid and make sure it's in proper alignment with the surrounding panels.

7   Forward-and-backward and side-to-side adjustments are made by loosening the hinge-to-lid bolts and gently moving the lid into correct alignment.

8   Vertical adjustments to the lid are made by adding or removing the shims used on the hinge.

9   To adjust the lid so it is flush with the body when closed, loosen the mounting bolts and move the lock and striker **(see illustration)**.

11   Liftgate - removal, installation and adjustment

Refer to illustrations 11.3, 11.9 and 11.10

Note: *The rear liftgate is heavy and somewhat awkward to remove and install - at least two people should perform this procedure.*

1   Open the liftgate and cover the edges of the compartment with pads or cloths to protect the painted surfaces when the lid is removed.

2   Disconnect any cables or wire harness connectors attached to the liftgate that would interfere with removal.

3   Use a marking pen to make alignment marks around the hinge mounting flanges **(see illustration)**.

4   Have an assistant support the liftgate and detach the support struts (see Section 12).

5   While an assistant supports the liftgate, remove the lid-to-hinge bolts on both sides and lift it off.

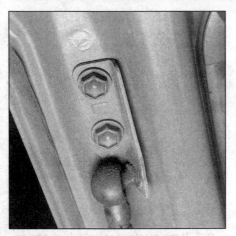

12.1 After supporting the liftgate, remove the bolts at each end and detach the support strut

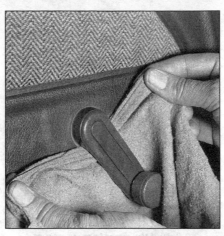

13.2a Work a cloth up behind the regulator handle and move it back-and-forth . . .

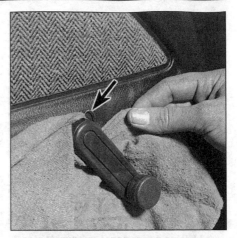

13.2b . . . until the retainer (arrow) is pushed up so you can remove it

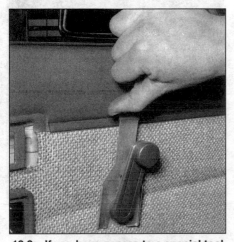

13.2c If you have access to a special tool like this one, use it to disengage the retainer

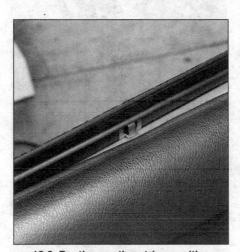

13.3 Pry the weatherstrip up with a screwdriver until the clips are disengaged, then lift it off

13.4 Some screws are located in out-of-the-way places

6   Installation is the reverse of removal. **Note:** *When reinstalling the liftgate, align the hinges with the marks made during removal.*

7   After installation, close the liftgate and make sure it's in proper alignment with the surrounding panels.

8   Forward-and-backward and side-to-side adjustments are made by loosening the hinge to liftgate bolts and gently moving the liftgate into correct alignment.

9   Vertical adjust of the liftgate is made by detaching the headliner, removing the hinge nuts and removing or adding shims between the hinge and body **(see illustration)**.

10   The liftgate latch position can be adjusted by loosening the adjusting bolts and moving the latch. The latch striker can be adjusted by loosening the mounting screws and gently tapping it into position with a plastic hammer **(see illustration)**.

12 Liftgate support strut - replacement

Refer to illustration 12.1

Warning: *The support strut is filled with pressurized gas - do not disassemble this component. If it is faulty replace it with a new one.*

Note: *The trunk lid/rear liftgate is heavy and somewhat awkward to hold securely while replacing the struts - at least two people should perform this procedure.*

1   Remove the bolts at the ends and detach the strut from the liftgate **(see illustration)**.

2   Installation is the reverse of the removal procedure.

13 Door trim panel - removal and installation

Refer to illustrations 13.2a, 13.2b, 13.2c, 13.3, 13.4, 13.5, 13.6 and 13.7

1   Disconnect the negative cable from the battery. **Caution:** *If the stereo in your vehicle is equipped with an anti-theft system, make sure you have the correct activation code before disconnecting the battery.*

2   On manual window regulator equipped models, remove the window crank by working a cloth back-and-forth behind the handle to dislodge the retainer **(see illustrations)**. A special tool is available for this purpose **(see illustration)** but it's not essential. With the retainer removed, pull off the handle.

3   Use a screwdriver to pry up on the weathershield at the top of the door and detach the clips, then lift it out **(see illustration)**. Remove the outside mirror trim cover (see Section 19).

4   Remove the inside door handle (see Section 15) and any door trim panel retaining screws and door pull/armrest assemblies **(see illustration)**.

5   Insert a wide putty knife, a thin screwdriver or a special trim panel

11

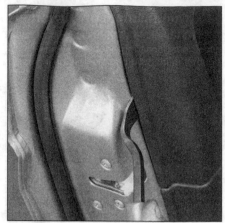

13.5 Use a trim panel removal tool to detach the trim panel retaining clips

13.6 Pull the door trim up and out to remove it

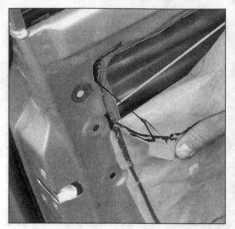

13.7 If the plastic watershield is peeled off carefully it can be reused

14.2 Use two jackstands padded with rags (to protect the paint) to support the door during the removal and installation procedures

14.3 Gently tap the pin (arrow) free of the stop strut

14.4 Before loosening or removing them, mark the door bolt locations

removal tool between the trim panel and door to disengage the retaining clips **(see illustration)**. Work around the outer edge until the panel is free.

6 Once all of the clips are disengaged, detach the trim panel, unplug any electrical connectors and remove the trim panel from the vehicle by gently pulling it up and out **(see illustration)**.

7 For access to the inner door remove the plastic watershield. Peel back the plastic cover, taking care not to tear it **(see illustration)**. Remove the plastic grommets, if necessary. To install the trim panel, first press the watershield back into place. If necessary, add more sealant to hold it in place.

8 Prior to installation of the door panel, be sure to reinstall any clips in the panel which may have come out during the removal procedure and stayed in the door.

9 Plug in any electrical connectors and place the panel in position. Press it into place until the clips are seated and install any retaining screws and armrest/door pulls. Install the manual regulator window crank or power switch assembly.

14 Door - removal, installation and adjustment

Removal and installation

Refer to illustrations 14.2, 14.3 and 14.4

1 Remove the door trim panel (see Section 13) and disconnect any electrical connectors and push them through the door opening so they won't interfere with removal.

2 Position a jack or jackstands under the door or have an assistant on hand to support the door when the hinge bolts are removed **(see illustration)**. **Note:** *If a jack or stand is used, place a rag between it and the door to protect the door's paint.*

3 Remove the door stop strut center pin **(see illustration)**.

4 Scribe around the door bolts **(see illustration)**.

5 Remove the hinge-to-door bolts and carefully detach the door. Installation is the reverse of removal.

Adjustment

Refer to illustrations 14.6a, 14.6b and 14.6c

6 Following installation, make sure the door is aligned properly. Adjust it if necessary as follows:

a) *Up-and-down and forward-and-backward adjustments are made by loosening the hinge-to-body bolts and moving the door, as necessary. A special offset tool may be required to reach some of the bolts* **(see illustration)**.

b) *In-and-out and up-and-down adjustments are made by loosening the door side hinge bolts and moving the door, as necessary. A special offset tool may be required to reach some of the bolts* **(see illustration)**.

c) *The door lock striker can also be adjusted both up-and-down and sideways to provide a positive engagement with the locking mechanism. This is done by loosening the screws and moving the striker, as necessary* **(see illustration)**.

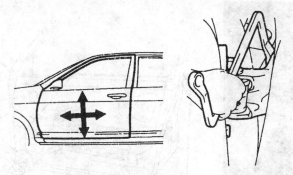

14.6a When adjusting the door up-and-down or forward-and-backward a special cranked wrench such as this one will make the job easier

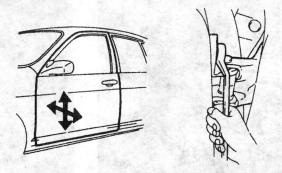

14.6b Adjust the door up-and-down or in-and-out after loosening the hinge to door bolts

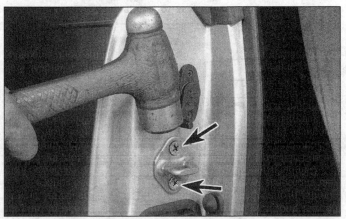

14.6c Adjust the door lock striker by loosening the mounting screws (arrows) and gently tapping the striker in the desired direction

15 Door latch, lock cylinder and handle - removal and installation

1 Remove the door trim panel and the plastic watershield (Section 13).

Door latch

Refer to illustration 15.3

2 Reach behind inside the door panel and disconnect the control links from the latch.

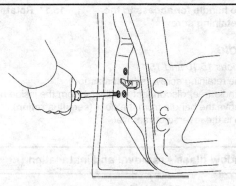

15.3 Remove the latch screws from the end of the door

3 If so equipped, disconnect the power door connectors and their bolt. Remove the latch retaining screws from the end of the door **(see illustration)**.
4 Detach the door latch and (if equipped) the door lock solenoid.
5 Installation is the reverse of removal.

Lock cylinder and outside handle

Refer to illustrations 15.7a, 15.7b and 15.8

6 Disconnect the control link and electrical connector (if equipped) from the lock cylinder and outside handle.
7 Remove the outside handle retention nut/bolts and pull the handle and lock cylinder from the door **(see illustrations)**.
8 Use a screwdriver to pry the retaining clip off and remove the lock cylinder from the door **(see illustration)**.
9 Installation is the reverse of removal.

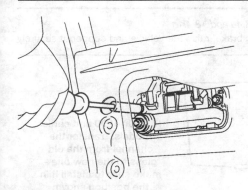

15.7a The outside handle retention bolts can be reached through access holes in the door frame

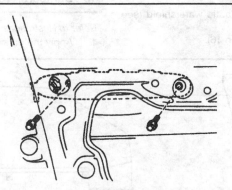

15.7b Later model outside handle mounting details

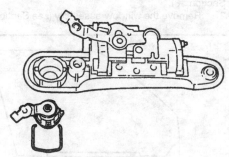

15.8 To separate the lock cylinder from the handle, pry the retaining clip off

11

15.10 Lift the handle for access to the retaining screw

15.11 Rotate the handle out, then detach the control link

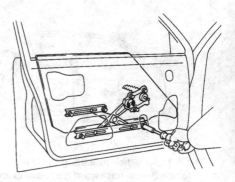

16.4a Typical early model glass-to-regulator mounting details

Inside handle

Refer to illustrations 15.10 and 15.11

10   Remove the retaining screw **(see illustration)**.
11   Pull the handle free, disconnect the link(s) from the inside handle control and remove the handle from the door **(see illustration)**.
12   Installation is the reverse of removal.

16   Door window glass - removal and installation

Refer to illustrations 16.4a, 16.4b and 16.6

1   Remove the door trim panel and the plastic watershield (Section 13).
2   Lower the window glass.
3   Carefully pry the inner weather-strip out of the door window opening.
4   Place a rag inside the door panel to help prevent scratching the glass and remove the two glass mounting nuts/bolts **(see illustrations)**.
5   Remove the glass by pulling it up.
6   When replacing a broken window on 1990 and earlier models, pry the channel off and install it on the new glass in the position shown **(see illustration)**. The job will be made easier by applying soapy water to the channel, then tapping it in place with a plastic hammer.
7   Installation is the reverse of the removal procedure.

17   Window regulator - removal and installation

Refer to illustrations 17.4a and 17.4b

1   Remove the door trim panel and the plastic watershield (see Section 13).
2   Remove the window assembly (see Section 16).

16.4b Later model window glass details - remove the two mounting bolts and lift the glass free - place a rag over the glass to help prevent scratching it

3   If so equipped, unclip the power window control connector from the panel and disconnect it.
4   Remove the equalizer arm bracket mounting bolts and the regulator mounting bolts **(see illustrations)**.
5   Pull the regulator through the service hole to remove it.
6   Installation is the reverse of removal.

18   Bumpers - removal and installation

Refer to illustrations 18.4a and 18.4b

1   Apply the parking brake, raise the vehicle and support it securely

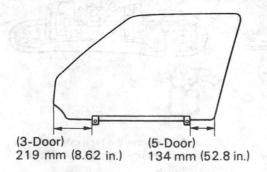

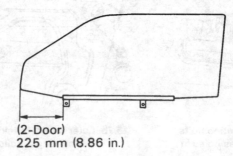

(3-Door)
219 mm (8.62 in.)

(5-Door)
134 mm (52.8 in.)

(2-Door)
225 mm (8.86 in.)

16.6 On 1990 and earlier models, transfer the channel from the old glass to the new one - make sure to install it in the position shown

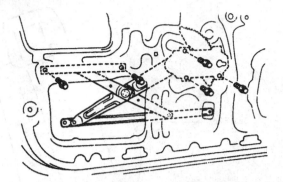

17.4a Early model regulator mounting details

17.4b Later model regulator mounting details

18.4a Early model bumper retention bolt (viewed from below)

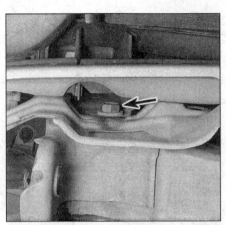

18.4b Typical bumper bracket bolt location (arrow)

19.1a Remove the screw and detach the control handle

on jackstands.

2   Disconnect the cable from the negative battery terminal and disconnect any wiring that would interfere with bumper removal.

3   Remove the bumper cover if equipped, taking care to avoid damaging the cover and the fender.

4   Working under the vehicle remove the bumper retention bolts **(see illustrations)**.

5   Pull the bumper assembly from the vehicle.

6   Installation is the reverse of the removal procedure.

19   Outside mirror - removal and installation

Refer to illustrations 19.1a, 19.1b and 19.2

1   On manually operated mirrors, remove the control handle **(see illustration)**. Grasp the mirror cover and detach it **(see illustration)**.

2   Remove the three retaining nuts and detach the mirror **(see illustration)**.

3   Installation is the reverse of removal.

19.1b Detach the cover and lift it out

19.2 Remove the three nuts securing the outside mirror to the door

11

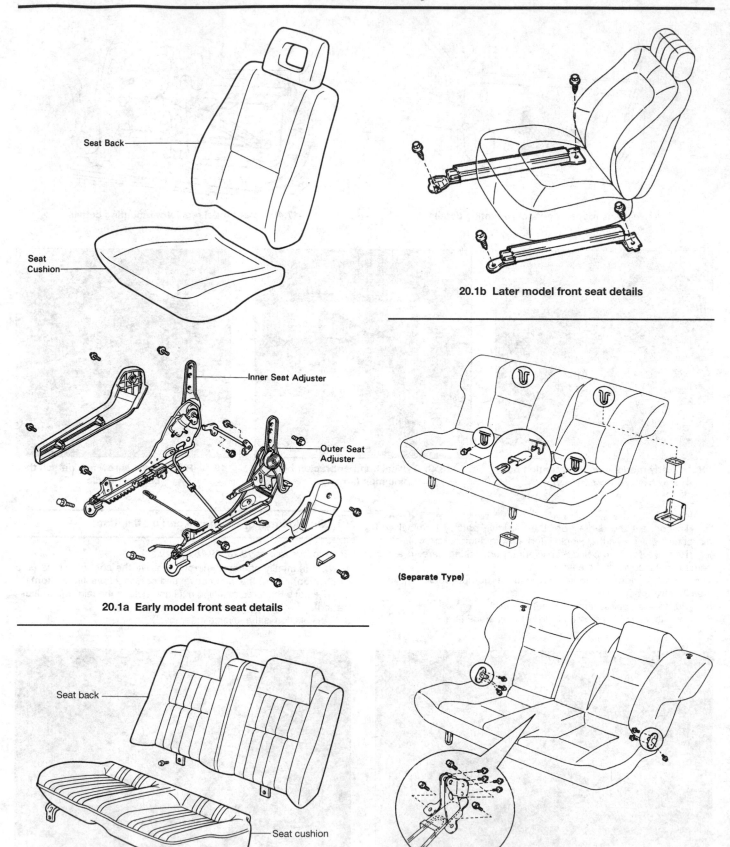

Seat Back

Seat Cushion

20.1b   Later model front seat details

Inner Seat Adjuster

Outer Seat Adjuster

20.1a   Early model front seat details

(Separate Type)

Seat back

Seat cushion

20.3a   Early model rear seat details

20.3b   Later model rear seat details

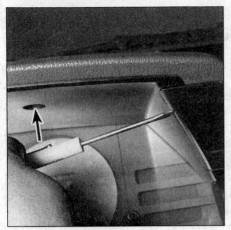

21.2a On early models, remove the upper bezel screw (there are two) and use a small screwdriver to pry off the covers at each end

21.2b Remove the screws at each end of the bezel (arrow)

21.3 Detach the bezel and lift it off

20 Seats - removal and installation

Front seats

Refer to illustrations 20.1a and 20.1b

1 Remove the retaining bolts, unplug any electrical connectors and lift the seats from the vehicle **(see illustrations)**.
2 Installation is the reverse of removal.

Rear seats

Refer to illustrations 20.3a and 20.3b

3 Remove the retaining bolts at the base of the seat cushion, then detach the cushion for access to the seat back bolts **(see illustrations)**.
4 Remove the seat back retaining bolts, then lift up on the back to release the seat back from the body.
5 Installation is the reverse of removal.

21 Instrument cluster bezel - removal and installation

Refer to illustrations 21.2a, 21.2b, 21.3 and 21.5

Warning: *Some later models are equipped with airbags. The airbag is armed and can deploy (inflate) anytime the battery is connected. To prevent accidental deployment (and possible injury), disconnect the negative battery cable whenever working near airbag components. After the battery is disconnected, wait at least 90 seconds before beginning work (the system has a back-up capacitor that must fully discharge). For more information see Chapter 12.*

1 Disconnect the cable from the negative battery terminal. **Caution:** *If the stereo in your vehicle is equipped with an anti-theft system, make sure you have the correct activation code before disconnecting the battery.*

1990 and earlier models

2 Remove the two screws along the top of the bezel, then pry out the cover for access to the screws at each end **(see illustrations)**.
3 Grasp the bezel securely and detach it **(see illustration)**.
4 Installation is the reverse of the removal procedure.

1991 and later models

5 Remove the two screws, grasp the bezel securely and pull straight back to detach the three clips, then remove the bezel **(see illustration)**.
6 Installation is the reverse of the removal procedure.

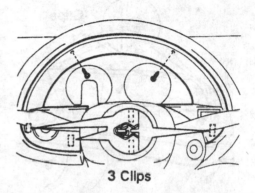

3 Clips

21.5 On later models, remove the two screws, detach the clips and remove the bezel

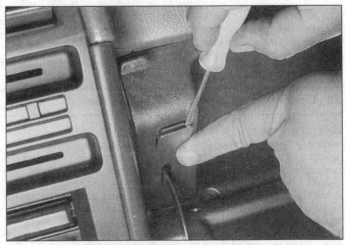

22.1a Pry off the covers for access to the screws

22 Glovebox - removal and installation

Refer to illustrations 22.1a, 22.1b, 22.1c and 22.2

1 On early models, remove the screw covers, remove the screws, then detach the glovebox and pull it out of the instrument panel **(see illustrations)**.

11

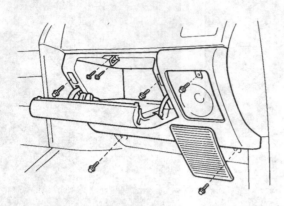

22.1b Early model glove box installation details

22.1c Pull the glove box straight back and lift it out of the instrument panel

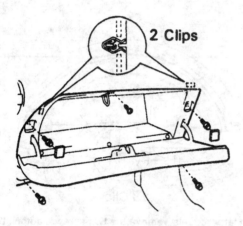

22.2 Later model glove box installation details

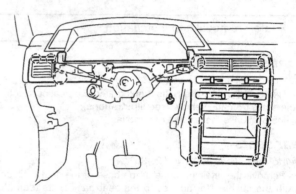

23.2 On early models, remove the bolt, then grasp the center panel securely and detach it from the clips, working from the left side

2   On later models remove the five screws, then grasp the glovebox securely and detach the clips to remove it **(see illustration)**.
3   Installation is the reverse of removal.

23   Center trim panel - removal and installation

Refer to illustrations 23.2 and 23.3
Warning: *Some later models are equipped with airbags. The airbag is armed and can deploy (inflate) anytime the battery is connected. To prevent accidental deployment (and possible injury), disconnect the negative battery cable whenever working near airbag components. After the battery is disconnected, wait at least 90 seconds before beginning work (the system has a back-up capacitor that must fully discharge). For more information see Chapter 12.*
1   Disconnect the cable from the negative battery terminal. **Caution:** *If the stereo in your vehicle is equipped with an anti-theft system, make sure you have the correct activation code before disconnecting the battery.*
2   On early models, remove the steering column lower finish panel (see Section 25). Remove the retaining screws, grasp the center trim panel and working from the left end, detach the clips and remove it from the vehicle **(see illustration)**.
3   On later models, detach the panel by pulling out sharply to release the clips, then unplug the electrical connector and remove the panel from the vehicle **(see illustration)**.
4   Installation is the reverse of the removal procedure.

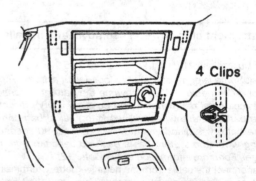

23.3 Later models use clips to retain the cover

24   Steering column cover - removal and installation

Refer to illustration 24.1
Warning: *Some later models are equipped with airbags. The airbag is armed and can deploy (inflate) anytime the battery is connected. To prevent accidental deployment (and possible injury), disconnect the negative battery cable whenever working near airbag components. After the battery is disconnected, wait at least 90 seconds before beginning work (the system has a back-up capacitor that must fully discharge). For more information see Chapter 12.*
1   Remove the steering column cover screws **(see illustration)**.

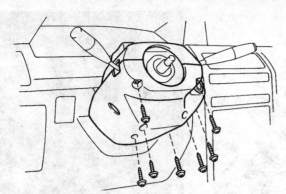

24.1 Remove the screws and separate the steering column cover halves

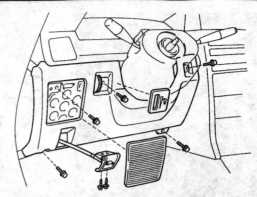

25.1 Remove the panel screws and the two hood release latch screws, then detach the finish panel

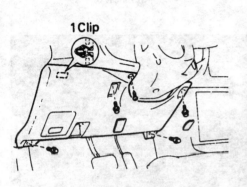

25.3 On later models remove the bolts and detach the clips

26.3a Lift up the carpet piece inside the console for access to the retaining screw

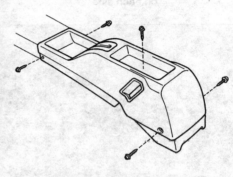

26.3b Early model rear console mounting details

2   Separate the cover halves and detach them from the steering column.
3   Disconnect any electrical connections and the covers.
4   Installation is the reverse of the removal procedure.

25 Steering column lower finish panel - removal and installation

Refer to illustrations 25.1 and 25.3
Warning: *Some later models are equipped with airbags. The airbag is armed and can deploy (inflate) anytime the battery is connected. To prevent accidental deployment (and possible injury), disconnect the negative battery cable whenever working near airbag components. After the battery is disconnected, wait at least 90 seconds before beginning work (the system has a back-up capacitor that must fully discharge). For more information see Chapter 12.*
1   On early models, remove the hood release handle and light control rheostat **(see illustration)**.
2   Remove the retaining bolts, disconnect any electrical connections and pull the panel off.
3   On later models, remove the retaining bolts, pull the panel out sharply to detach the clip and lower the panel from the dash **(see illustration)**.
4   Installation is the reverse of the removal procedure.

26 Console - removal and installation

Refer to illustrations 26.3a, 26.3b, 26.3c 26.4a, 26.4b and 26.5
Warning: *Some later models are equipped with airbags. The airbag is*

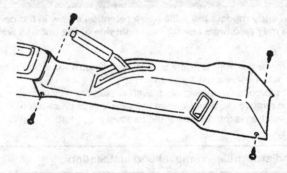

26.3c Later model rear console mounting details

armed and can deploy (inflate) anytime the battery is connected. To prevent accidental deployment (and possible injury), disconnect the negative battery cable whenever working near airbag components. After the battery is disconnected, wait at least 90 seconds before beginning work (the system has a back-up capacitor that must fully discharge). For more information see Chapter 12.
1   Disconnect the cable from the negative battery terminal. **Caution:** *If the stereo in your vehicle is equipped with an anti-theft system, make sure you have the correct activation code before disconnecting the battery.*
2   Pull the hand brake on.
3   Remove retaining screws and lift out the rear console **(see illustrations)**.

11

26.4a On early models, the front console is held in place by two screws (arrow), one on each side

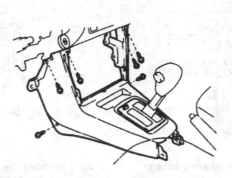

26.4b Later model front console installation details

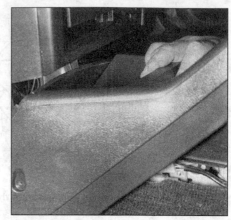

26.5 Rotate the console forward and lift it out

27.1 On early models the grille has a retention screw in the center (some may also have one on the underside of the grille as well)

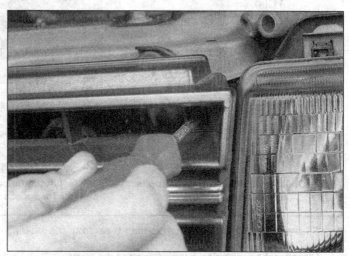

27.2a Use a screwdriver to detach the four clips

4   Remove the front console screws (see illustrations). On manual shift models, unscrew the shift knob.
5   Lift the console up over shift lever, unplug any electrical connections and remove the console from the vehicle (see illustration).
6   Installation is the reverse of the removal procedure.

27   Radiator grille - removal and installation

Refer to illustrations 27.1, 27.2a, 27.2b, 27.3 and 27.4
Warning: Some later models are equipped with airbags. The airbag is armed and can deploy (inflate) anytime the battery is connected. To prevent accidental deployment (and possible injury), disconnect the negative battery cable whenever working near airbag components. After the battery is disconnected, wait at least 90 seconds before beginning work (the system has a back-up capacitor that must fully discharge). For more information see Chapter 12.

1990 and earlier models

1   Remove screws at the top and bottom center of the grille (see illustration).
2   Disengage the four grille retaining clips with a screwdriver (see illustrations).
3   Once all of the retaining clips are disengaged, pull the grille out and remove it (see illustration).

27.2b Lift up on the clip to release it (grille removed for clarity)

1991 and later models

4   Remove the five screws across the top of the grille (see illustration).
5   Detach the grille and lift if from the vehicle.
6   Installation is the reverse of removal.

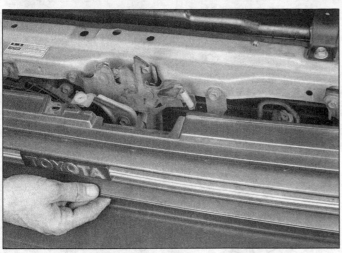

27.3 Pull the grille straight out to detach it

27.4 Later model grille details

28 Seat belts - check

Refer to illustrations 28.4a and 28.4b

1   Check the seat belts, buckles, latch plates and guide loops for any obvious damage or signs of wear.
2   Make sure the seat belt reminder light comes on when the key is turned on.

3   The seat belts are designed to lock up during a sudden stop or impact, yet allow free movement during normal driving. The retractors should hold the belt against your chest while driving and rewind the belt when the buckle is unlatched.
4   If any of the above checks reveal problems with the seat-belt system, replace parts as necessary (see illustrations).

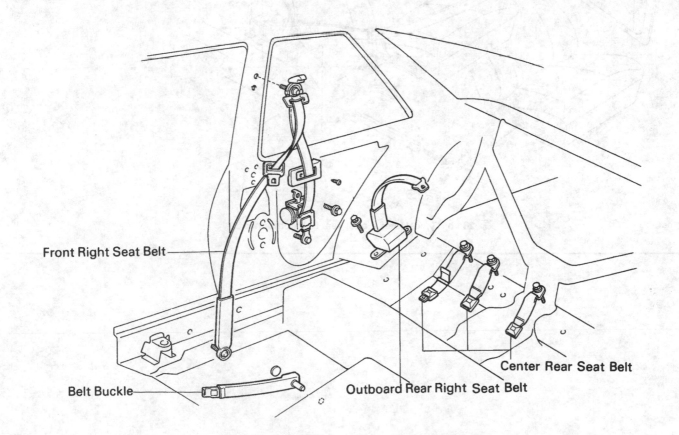

Front Right Seat Belt

Belt Buckle

Outboard Rear Right Seat Belt

Center Rear Seat Belt

28.4a Typical early model seat belt components

11

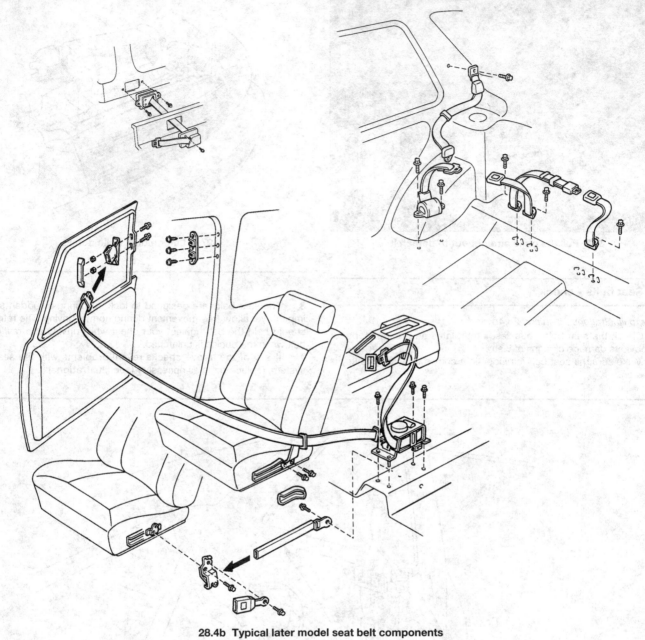

28.4b Typical later model seat belt components

Chapter 12
Chassis electrical system

Contents

1   General information

The electrical system is a 12-volt, negative ground type. Power for the lights and all electrical accessories is supplied by a lead/acid-type battery which is charged by the alternator.

This Chapter covers repair and service procedures for the various electrical components not associated with the engine. Information on the battery, alternator, distributor and starter motor can be found in Chapter 5.

It should be noted that when portions of the electrical system are serviced, the cable should be disconnected from the negative battery terminal to prevent electrical shorts and/or fires. **Caution:** *If the stereo in your vehicle is equipped with an anti-theft system, make sure you have the correct activation code before disconnecting the battery.*

12

3.1a The main fuse block is located in the driver's side kick panel, under a cover

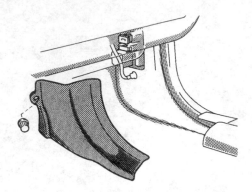

3.1b A smaller fuse and relay block is found under the passenger's side kick panel

2   Electrical troubleshooting - general information

A typical electrical circuit consists of an electrical component, any switches, relays, motors, fuses, fusible links or circuit breakers related to that component and the wiring and electrical connectors that link the component to both the battery and the chassis. To help you pinpoint an electrical circuit problem, wiring diagrams are included at the end of this book.

Before tackling any troublesome electrical circuit, first study the appropriate wiring diagrams to get a complete understanding of what makes up that individual circuit. Trouble spots, for instance, can often be narrowed down by noting if other components related to the circuit are operating properly. If several components or circuits fail at one time, chances are the problem is in a fuse or ground connection, because several circuits are often routed through the same fuse and ground connections.

Electrical problems usually stem from simple causes, such as loose or corroded connections, a blown fuse, a melted fusible link or a bad relay. Visually inspect the condition of all fuses, wires and connections in a problem circuit before troubleshooting it.

If testing instruments are going to be utilized, use the diagrams to plan ahead of time where you will make the necessary connections in order to accurately pinpoint the trouble spot.

The basic tools needed for electrical troubleshooting include a circuit tester or voltmeter (a 12-volt bulb with a set of test leads can

also be used), a continuity tester, which includes a bulb, battery and set of test leads, and a jumper wire, preferably with a circuit breaker incorporated, which can be used to bypass electrical components. Before attempting to locate a problem with test instruments, use the wiring diagram(s) to decide where to make the connections.

Voltage checks

Voltage checks should be performed if a circuit is not functioning properly. Connect one lead of a circuit tester to either the negative battery terminal or a known good ground. Connect the other lead to a electrical connector in the circuit being tested, preferably nearest to the battery or fuse. If the bulb of the tester lights, voltage is present, which means that the part of the circuit between the electrical connector and the battery is problem free. Continue checking the rest of the circuit in the same fashion. When you reach a point at which no voltage is present, the problem lies between that point and the last test point with voltage. Most of the time the problem can be traced to a loose connection. **Note:** *Keep in mind that some circuits receive voltage only when the ignition key is in the Accessory or Run position.*

Finding a short

One method of finding shorts in a circuit is to remove the fuse and connect a test light or voltmeter in its place to the fuse terminals. There should be no voltage present in the circuit. Move the wiring harness from side to side while watching the test light. If the bulb goes on, there is a short to ground somewhere in that area, probably where the insulation has rubbed through. The same test can be performed on each component in the circuit, even a switch.

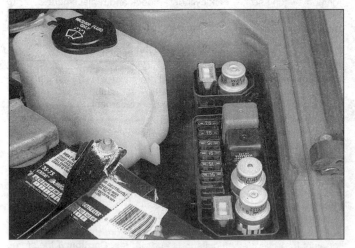

3.1c A third fuse and relay block is located in the engine compartment next to the battery

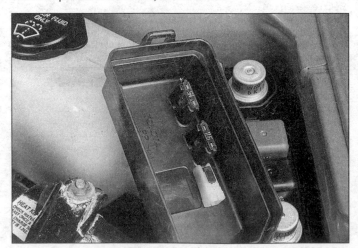

3.1d The engine compartment fuse block cover contains spare fuses and a fuse puller

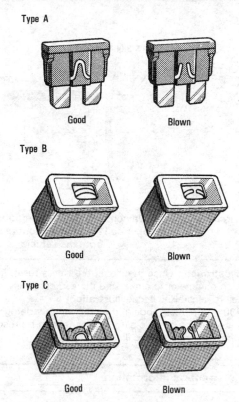

Type A

Good   Blown

Type B

Good   Blown

Type C

Good   Blown

3.3 Three types of fuses are used on these models - all can be visually checked

Ground check

Perform a ground test to check whether a component is properly grounded. Disconnect the battery and connect one lead of a self-powered test light, known as a continuity tester, to a known good ground. Connect the other lead to the wire or ground connection being tested. If the bulb goes on, the ground is good. If the bulb does not go on, the ground is not good.

Continuity check

A continuity check is done to determine if there are any breaks in a circuit - if it is passing electricity properly. With the circuit off (no power in the circuit), a self-powered continuity tester can be used to check the circuit. Connect the test leads to both ends of the circuit (or to the "power" end and a good ground), and if the test light comes on the circuit is passing current properly. If the light doesn't come on, there is a break somewhere in the circuit. The same procedure can be used to test a switch, by connecting the continuity tester to the power in and power out sides of the switch. With the switch turned On, the test light should come on.

Finding an open circuit

When diagnosing for possible open circuits, it is often difficult to locate them by sight because oxidation or terminal misalignment are hidden by the electrical connectors. Merely wiggling an electrical connector on a sensor or in the wiring harness may correct the open circuit condition. Remember this when an open circuit is indicated when troubleshooting a circuit. Intermittent problems may also be caused by oxidized or loose connections.

Electrical troubleshooting is simple if you keep in mind that all electrical circuits are basically electricity running from the battery, through the wires, switches, relays, fuses and fusible links to each electrical component (light bulb, motor, etc.) and to ground, from which it is passed back to the battery. Any electrical problem is an interruption in the flow of electricity to and from the battery.

3 Fuses - general information

Refer to illustrations 3.1a, 3.1b, 3.1c, 3,1d and 3.3

The electrical circuits of the vehicle are protected by a combination of fuses, circuit breakers and fusible links. The fuse blocks are located under the instrument panel on the left and right sides of the dashboard, and in the engine compartment next to the battery (see illustrations).

Each of the fuses is designed to protect a specific circuit, and the various circuits are identified on the fuse panel itself.

Three types of miniaturized fuses are employed in the fuse block. These compact fuses, with blade terminal design, allow fingertip removal and replacement. If an electrical component fails, always check the fuse first. A blown fuse is easily identified through the clear plastic body. Visually inspect the element for evidence of damage (see illustration). If a continuity check is called for on the type A fuse, the blade terminal tips are exposed in the fuse body.

Be sure to replace blown fuses with the correct type. Fuses of different ratings are physically interchangeable, but only fuses of the proper rating should be used. Replacing a fuse with one of a higher or lower value than specified is not recommended. Each electrical circuit needs a specific amount of protection. The amperage value of each fuse is molded into the fuse body.

If the replacement fuse immediately fails, don't replace it again until the cause of the problem is isolated and corrected. In most cases, this will be a short circuit in the wiring caused by a broken or deteriorated wire.

4 Fusible links - general information

Refer to illustration 4.2

Some circuits are protected by fusible links. The links are used in circuits which are not ordinarily fused, such as the ignition circuit.

The fusible links on these models are similar to fuses in that they can be visually checked to determine if they are melted (see illustration).

To replace a fusible link, first disconnect the negative cable from the battery. **Caution:** *If the stereo in your vehicle is equipped with an anti-theft system, make sure you have the correct activation code before disconnecting the battery.* Unplug the burned-out link and replace it with a new one (available from your dealer or auto parts store). Always determine the cause for the overload which melted the fusible link before installing a new one.

4.2 The fusible links are next to the battery under a cover and can be checked visually to determine if they're melted

12

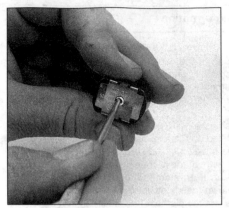

5.3a Insert a pin or paper clip into the circuit breaker reset hole and push it in to reset it

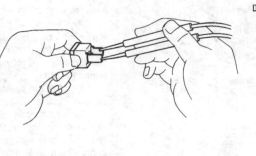

5.3b After resetting, check the circuit breaker for continuity

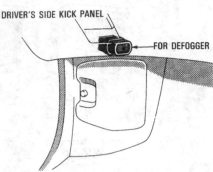

5.4 On some models the defogger circuit breaker can be reset without removing it from the vehicle

5   Circuit breakers - general information

Refer to illustrations 5.3a, 5.3b and 5.4

On early models circuit breakers protect components such as power windows, power door locks and headlights. Some circuit breakers are located in the fuse boxes.

Because on some models the circuit breaker resets itself automatically, an electrical overload in a circuit breaker protected system will cause the circuit to fail momentarily, then come back on. If the circuit does not come back on, check it immediately. Note, however, that some circuit breakers must be reset manually. Once the condition is corrected, the circuit breaker will resume its normal function.

To reset a manual circuit breaker, first disconnect the cable from the negative battery terminal. **Caution:** *If the stereo in your vehicle is equipped with an anti-theft system, make sure you have the correct activation code before disconnecting the battery.* Remove the circuit breaker, insert a pin into the reset hole and push in until you hear a click **(see illustration)**. Once the circuit breaker is reset, it's a good idea to use an ohmmeter to make sure there is continuity across the terminals before reinstalling it **(see illustration)**.

On 1990 and earlier models, the rear window defogger circuit breaker located in the driver's side kick panel can be reset without removing it from the vehicle **(see illustration)**.

6   Relays - general information

Refer to illustrations 6.2a and 6.2b

Several electrical accessories in the vehicle use relays to transmit the electrical signal to the component. If the relay is defective, that component will not operate properly.

The various relays are mounted in several locations throughout the vehicle **(see illustrations)**.

If a faulty relay is suspected, it can be removed and tested by a dealer or other qualified shop. Defective relays must be replaced as a unit.

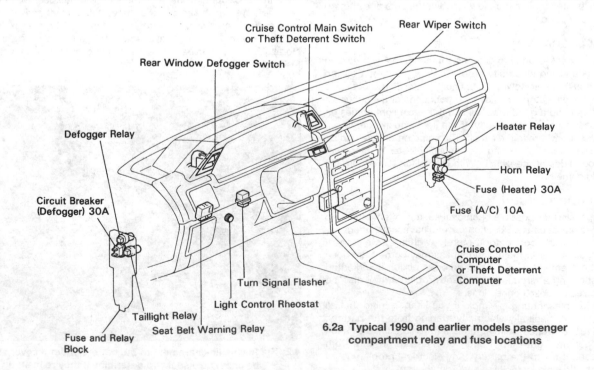

6.2a Typical 1990 and earlier models passenger compartment relay and fuse locations

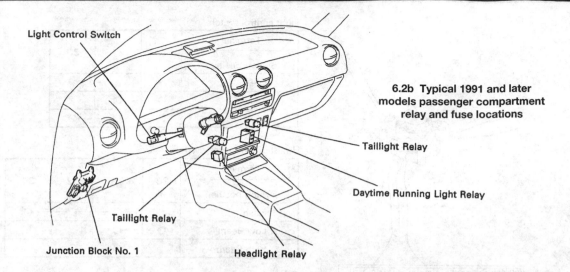

6.2b Typical 1991 and later models passenger compartment relay and fuse locations

Light Control Switch

Taillight Relay

Daytime Running Light Relay

Taillight Relay

Junction Block No. 1

Headlight Relay

7 Turn signal/hazard flashers - check and replacement

Warning: *Some later models are equipped with airbags. The airbag is armed and can deploy (inflate) anytime the battery is connected. To prevent accidental deployment (and possible injury), disconnect the negative battery cable whenever working near airbag components. After the battery is disconnected, wait at least 90 seconds before beginning work (the system has a back-up capacitor that must fully discharge). For more information see Section 22.*

1   The turn signal/hazard flasher, a small canister shaped unit located under the dash flashes the turn signals **(see illustration 6.2b)**.

2   When the flasher unit is functioning properly, an audible click can be heard during its operation. If the turn signals fail on one side or the other and the flasher unit does not make its characteristic clicking sound, a faulty turn signal bulb is indicated.

3   If both turn signals fail to blink, the problem may be due to a blown fuse, a faulty flasher unit, a broken switch or a loose or open connection. If a quick check of the fuse box indicates that the turn signal fuse has blown, check the wiring for a short before installing a new fuse.

4   To replace the flasher, simply pull it out of the fuse block or wiring harness.

5   Make sure that the replacement unit is identical to the original. Compare the old one to the new one before installing it.

6   Installation is the reverse of removal.

8 Combination switch - removal and installation

Refer to illustrations 8.4 and 8.5

Warning: *Some later models are equipped with airbags. The airbag is armed and can deploy (inflate) anytime the battery is connected. To prevent accidental deployment (and possible injury), disconnect the negative battery cable whenever working near airbag components. After the battery is disconnected, wait at least 90 seconds before beginning work (the system has a back-up capacitor that must fully discharge). For more information see Section 22.*

1   Disconnect the negative cable at the battery. **Caution:** *If the stereo in your vehicle is equipped with an anti-theft system, make sure you have the correct activation code before disconnecting the battery.*

2   Remove the steering wheel (see Chapter 10).

3   Remove the cluster finish lower panel and steering column cover (see Chapter 11).

4   Remove the combination switch retaining screws **(see illustration)**.

5   Trace the wiring harness down the steering column to the connector. Release the wiring retainer clamps, if equipped, unplug the connector and slide the switch up off the column **(see illustration)**.

6   Installation is the reverse of removal. If equipped with an airbag, refer to Chapter 10 and center the spiral cable before installing the steering wheel.

8.4 Remove the four combination switch mounting screws (arrows)

8.5 Unplug the connector and slip the combination switch off the steering column

12

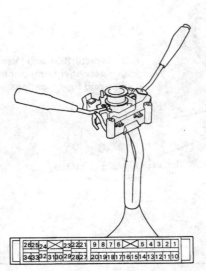

9.4a 1990 and earlier model light control switch, headlight dimmer switch, turn signal and hazard warning switch continuity charts

Light control switch

Terminal / Switch position	22	31	33
OFF			
TAIL	O—————O		
HEAD	O—————O—————O		

Headlight dimmer switch

Terminal / Switch position	23	29	32	34
Flash		O—————O—————O		
Low Beam	O—————O			
High Beam		O—————O		

Turn signal and Hazard warning switch

Terminal / Switch position		25	21	28	26	24	27
Turn signal	L	O—————O			O—————O		
Turn signal	N				O—————O		
Turn signal	R		O—————O		O—————O		
Hazard	ON	O—————O				O—————O	

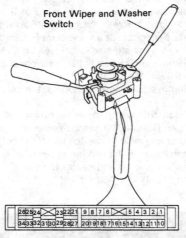

Front Wiper and Washer Switch

9.4b 1990 and earlier model front wiper and washer switch continuity charts

FRONT WIPER AND WASHER SWITCH

Switch	Terminal / Switch position	18	13	7	4	16	8
Wiper	MIST	O—————————O				
Wiper	OFF			O—————O		
Wiper	INT			O—————O		
Wiper	LO	O—————————O				
Wiper	HI	O—————O				
Washer	OFF					
Washer	ON					O—————O

9   Steering column switches - check and replacement

Refer to illustrations 9.4a, 9.4b, 9.4c, 9.4d, 9.7a, 9.7b and 9.9

Warning: *Some later models are equipped with airbags. The airbag is armed and can deploy (inflate) anytime the battery is connected. To prevent accidental deployment (and possible injury), disconnect the negative battery cable whenever working near airbag components. After the battery is disconnected, wait at least 90 seconds before beginning work (the system has a back-up capacitor that must fully discharge). For more information see Section 22.*

1   Disconnect the negative cable at the battery. **Caution:** *If the stereo in your vehicle is equipped with an anti-theft system, make sure you have the correct activation code before disconnecting the battery.*

2   Remove the cluster finish lower panel and steering column cover (see Chapter 11).

3   On early models, trace the wiring harness down the steering column to the large electrical connector. On later models, trace the wiring harness from the component to be checked to the harness connector.

Check

4   Unplug the electrical connector and using an ohmmeter, check for continuity between the indicated terminals with the various switches in each of the indicated positions **(see illustrations)**.

5   If the continuity is not as specified, replace the defective switch.

Replacement

6   Remove the combination switch (see Section 8). If equipped with an airbag, remove the four screws retaining the spiral cable and remove the spiral cable from the combination switch.

LIGHT CONTROL SWITCH CONTINUITY

Terminal / Switch position		1	5	6	7	8	9
Light control SW	Dimmer SW						
OFF	Low beam						
OFF	High beam						
OFF	Flash	o—o					
TAIL	Low beam					o—o	
TAIL	High beam					o—o	
TAIL	Flash	o—o				o—o	
HEAD	Low beam			o		o—o	
HEAD	Low beam	o			o		
HEAD	High beam	o—o		o		o—o	
HEAD	Flash	o—o		o		o—o	

TURN SIGNAL SWITCH CONTINUITY

Terminal / Switch position	2	3	4
Left turn	o	o	
Neutral			
Right turn		o	o

9.4c 1991 and later model light control switch and turn signal switch continuity charts

WIPER AND WASHER SWITCH CONTINUITY

w/ Mist Wiper

w/ Mist Wiper Switch

Terminal / Switch position		1	2	5	6	3	4
Wiper	MIST	o		o			
Wiper	OFF	o			o		
Wiper	LO	o		o			
Wiper	HI		o	o			
Washer	OFF						
Washer	ON					o	o

w/ Intermittent Wiper

w/ Intermittent Wiper Switch

Terminal / Switch position		1	2	5	6	3	4
Wiper	OFF	o			o		
Wiper	INT	o		o	o		
Wiper	LO	o			o		
Wiper	HI		o	o			
Washer	OFF						
Washer	ON					o	o

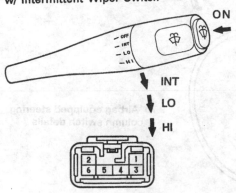

9.4d 1991 and later model wiper and washer switch continuity charts

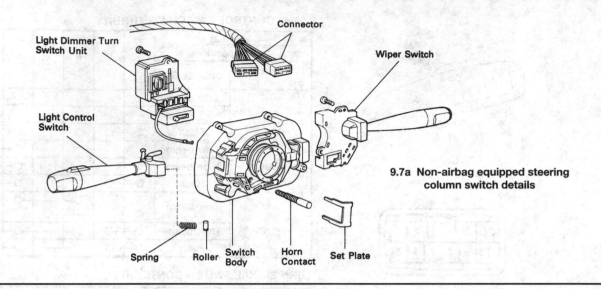

Light Dimmer Turn Switch Unit

Connector

Wiper Switch

Light Control Switch

Spring   Roller   Switch Body   Horn Contact   Set Plate

9.7a Non-airbag equipped steering column switch details

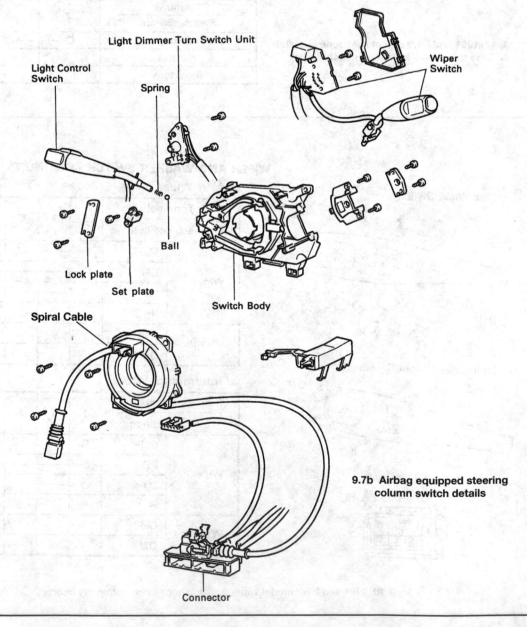

Light Dimmer Turn Switch Unit

Light Control Switch

Spring

Wiper Switch

Ball

Lock plate

Set plate

Switch Body

Spiral Cable

9.7b Airbag equipped steering column switch details

Connector

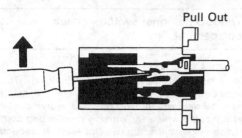

Pull Out

9.9 To remove a terminal from the connector, pry down on the locking lug and pull the terminal out from the rear

7   Remove the retaining screws from the switch being replaced and remove the defective switch from the switch body **(see illustrations)**.

8   Separate the wiring harness of the switch being replaced from the main wiring harness and remove the terminals from the connector.

9   Release the tabs from the terminal cover at the rear of the connector. From the front of the connector, insert a small screwdriver or pick, pry down on the locking lug and remove the terminal from the rear **(see illustration)**.

10   Insert the terminals from the new switch into the connector, pushing in until they are securely locked in place.

11   The remainder or installation is the reverse of removal. If equipped with an airbag, refer to Chapter 10 and center the spiral cable before installing the steering wheel.

10   Ignition switch and key lock cylinder - check and replacement

Warning: *Some later models are equipped with airbags. The airbag is armed and can deploy (inflate) anytime the battery is connected. To prevent accidental deployment (and possible injury), disconnect the negative battery cable whenever working near airbag components. After the battery is disconnected, wait at least 90 seconds before beginning work (the system has a back-up capacitor that must fully discharge). For more information see Section 22.*

Ignition switch

1   Disconnect the negative cable at the battery. **Caution:** *If the stereo in your vehicle is equipped with an anti-theft system, make sure you have the correct activation code before disconnecting the battery.*

2   Remove the steering wheel (see Chapter 10).

3   Remove the steering column cover and lower finish panel (see Chapter 11).

Check

Refer to illustrations 10.5a and 10.5b

4   Trace the wire from the switch to the connector and unplug the connector.

5   Use an ohmmeter to check for continuity at the indicated terminals with the switch in each indicated position **(see illustrations)**.

6   Replace the switch if continuity is not as specified.

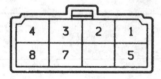

Ignition switch

Terminal / Switch position	4	3	2	1	8	7	5
LOCK							
ACC	o—o						
ON	o—o—o				o—o		
START	o		o—o		o—o—o		

Unlock warning switch

Terminal / Switch pin position	9	10
Released (Remove ignition switch)		
Pushed in (Set ignition switch)	o—o	

10.5a 1990 and earlier model ignition switch continuity chart

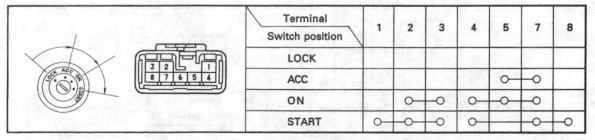

Terminal / Switch position	1	2	3	4	5	7	8
LOCK							
ACC					o—o		
ON	o—o		o—o—o				
START	o—o—o			o	o—o		

If continuity is not as specified, replace the switch.

10.5b 1991 and later model ignition switch continuity chart

12

10.9 With the key in the ACC position. push in on the release button and pull the lock cylinder straight out

Replacement

7   Remove the screw(s) retaining the switch to the rear of the lock cylinder housing and remove the switch.

8   Installation is the reverse of removal. If equipped with an airbag, refer to Chapter 10 and center the spiral cable before installing the steering wheel.

Key lock cylinder

Refer to illustration 10.9

9   With the key in the Accessory position, insert a small screwdriver or punch in the hole in the casting and press the release button while pulling the lock cylinder straight out, then remove it from the steering column **(see illustration)**.

10   Installation is the reverse of removal. If equipped with an airbag, refer to Chapter 10 and center the spiral cable before installing the steering wheel.

11   Rear window defogger switch - check and replacement

Refer to illustrations 11.4a and 11.4b

Warning: *Some later models are equipped with airbags. The airbag is armed and can deploy (inflate) anytime the battery is connected. To prevent accidental deployment (and possible injury), disconnect the negative battery cable whenever working near airbag components. After the battery is disconnected, wait at least 90 seconds before beginning work (the system has a back-up capacitor that must fully discharge). For more information see Section 22.*

1   Detach the cable from the negative battery terminal. **Caution:** *If the stereo in your vehicle is equipped with an anti-theft system, make sure you have the correct activation code before disconnecting the battery.*

2   Use a small screwdriver to detach the switch and pull it gently free.

3   Pull the defogger switch out and unplug the connector.

4   Use an ohmmeter to check for continuity at the indicated terminals with the switch in the indicated position **(see illustrations)**.

5   Replace the switch if the continuity is not as specified.

12   Rear window defogger - check and repair

Refer to illustrations 12.4, 12.5 and 12.7

1   The rear window defogger consists of a number of horizontal elements baked onto the glass surface.

2   Small breaks in the element can be repaired without removing the rear window.

Check

3   Turn the ignition switch and defogger system switches to On.

4   When measuring voltage during the next two tests, wrap a piece of aluminum foil around the tip of the voltmeter negative probe and press the foil against the wire with your finger **(see illustration)**.

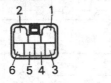

Terminal				Illumination	
Switch position	4	3	1	6	5
OFF		○─▶◀─○		○─▶◀─○	
ON	○──○─▶◀─○			○─▶◀─○	

11.4a 1990 and earlier model defogger switch continuity chart

11.4b 1991 and later model defogger switch continuity chart

Condition	Tester connection to terminal number	Specified value
Switch OFF	−	No continuity
Switch ON	2 − 4 − 6	Continuity
Illumination circuit	1 − 3	Continuity

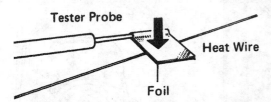

12.4 When measuring the voltage at the rear window defogger grid, wrap a piece of aluminum foil around the negative probe of the voltmeter and press the foil against the wire with your finger

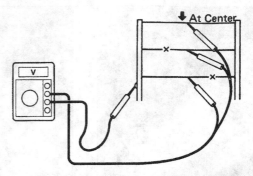

12.5 To determine if a wire has broken, check the voltage at the *center* of each wire - if the voltage is 5-volts, the wire is unbroken; if the voltage is 10-volts, the wire is broken between the center of the wire and the positive end; if the voltage is 0-volts, the wire is broken between the center of the wire and ground

11   Use masking tape to mask off the area being repaired.
12   Thoroughly mix the epoxy, following the instructions provided with the repair kit.
13   Apply the epoxy material to the slit in the masking tape, overlapping the undamaged area about 3/4-inch on either end.
14   Allow the repair to cure for 24 hours before removing the tape and using the system.

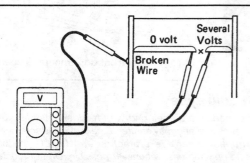

12.7 To find the break, place the voltmeter positive lead against the defogger positive terminal, place the voltmeter negative lead with the foil strip against the heat wire at the positive terminal end and slide it toward the negative terminal end - the point at which the voltmeter deflects from zero to several volts is the point at which the wire is broken

5   Check the voltage at the center of each heat wire **(see illustration)**. If the voltage is 5-volts, the wire is okay (there is no break). If the voltage is 10-volts, the wire is broken between the center of the element and the positive end. If the voltage is 0-volts the wire is broken between the center of the element and ground.
6   Connect the negative lead to a good body ground. The reading should stay the same.
7   To find the break, place the voltmeter positive lead against the defogger positive terminal. Place the voltmeter negative lead with the foil strip against the heat wire at the positive terminal end and slide it toward the negative terminal end. The point at which the voltmeter deflects from zero to several volts is the point at which the heat element is broken **(see illustration)**. **Note:** *If the heat element is not broken, the voltmeter will indicate no voltage at the positive end of the heat element but gradually increase to about 12-volts.*

Repair

8   Repair the break in the element using a repair kit specifically recommended for this purpose, such as Dupont paste No. 4817 (or equivalent). Included in this kit is plastic conductive epoxy.
9   Prior to repairing a break, turn off the system and allow it to cool off for a few minutes.
10   Lightly buff the element area with fine steel wool, then clean it thoroughly with rubbing alcohol.

13   Radio and speakers - removal and installation

Warning: *Some later models are equipped with airbags. The airbag is armed and can deploy (inflate) anytime the battery is connected. To prevent accidental deployment (and possible injury), disconnect the negative battery cable whenever working near airbag components. After the battery is disconnected, wait at least 90 seconds before beginning work (the system has a back-up capacitor that must fully discharge). For more information see Section 22.*
1   Disconnect the negative cable at the battery. **Caution:** *If the stereo in your vehicle is equipped with an anti-theft system, make sure you have the correct activation code before disconnecting the battery.*

Radio

Refer to illustrations 13.3a, 13.3b, 13.4a and 13.4b
2   Remove the center trim panel (see Chapter 11).
3   Remove the mounting screws or bolts and pull the housing out of the dash **(see illustrations)**.

13.3b ... and pull the radio/bracket unit out

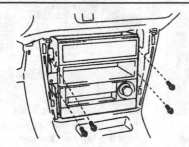

13.3a Remove the mounting screws ...

12

13.4a Unplug the power connector . . .

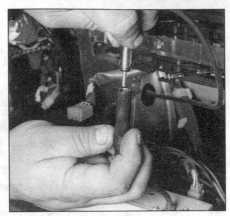

13.4b . . . and disconnect the antenna cable

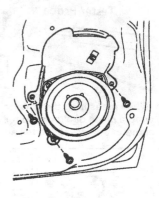

13.7a Typical front door mounted speaker

4   Remove the screws or nuts, pull the radio out, then unplug the electrical connector and the antenna lead and lift the radio out **(see illustrations)**.
5   Installation is the reverse of removal.

Speakers

Refer to illustrations 13.7a and 13.7b
6   Remove the front door trim panel (see Chapter 11).
7   Remove the speaker retaining screws/nuts. Unplug the electrical connector and remove the speaker **(see illustration)**.
8   Installation is the reverse of removal.

14 Headlights - replacement

Refer to illustrations 14.2, 14.3, 14.7, 14.8 and 14.9

Sealed beam-type

1   Remove the radiator grille (see Chapter 11) and turn signal light housing (see illustrations 17.1a, 17.1b and 17.1c).
2   Detach the headlight bezel, using a small screwdriver to lift up on the four clips at each corner while pulling out on the bezel **(see illustration)**.
3   Remove the screws holding the headlight retainer in place then remove the retainer **(see illustration)**. Don't disturb the adjustment screws.
4   Pull the headlight out, unplug the electrical connector and remove the headlight assembly.
5   Installation is the reverse of removal.

Composite bulb-type

Warning: *Some models are equipped with halogen gas-filled bulbs which are under pressure and may shatter if the surface is scratched or the bulb is dropped. Wear eye protection and handle the bulbs carefully, grasping only the base whenever possible. Do not touch the surface of the bulb with your fingers because the oil from your skin could cause it to overheat and fail prematurely. If you do touch the bulb surface, clean it with rubbing alcohol.*
6   Open the hood and locate the bulb retainer on the back of the headlight housing.
7   Rotate the headlight retaining ring counterclockwise (viewed from the rear) **(see illustration)**.
8   Withdraw the bulb assembly from the headlight housing **(see illustration)**.
9   Squeeze the clips and unplug the bulb holder from the electrical connector **(see illustration)**.
10   Without touching the glass with your bare fingers, insert the new bulb assembly into the headlight housing, install and tighten the retaining ring.
11   Plug in the electrical connector. Test headlight operation, then close the hood.

15 Headlights - adjustment

Refer to illustrations 15.1 and 15.2
Note: *It is important that the headlights are aimed correctly. If adjusted incorrectly they could blind the driver of an oncoming vehicle and*

13.7b Some speakers are mounted on the back side of the panel which must first be removed for access to the connector and retaining nuts

14.2 Lift up on the clips with a screwdriver to detach the bezel (bezel removed for clarity)

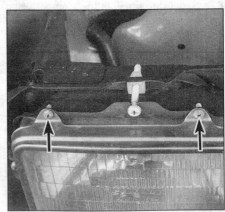

14.3 Remove the screws (arrows) located on the top and bottom of the headlight retainer - do not touch the adjustment screws

14.7 Unscrew the retaining ring by turning it counterclockwise (when viewed from behind)

14.8 Pull the bulb assembly out of the housing

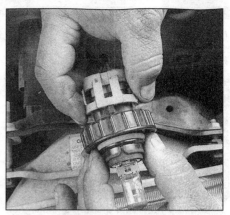

14.9 Disconnect the electrical connector and remove the bulb

cause a serious accident or seriously reduce your ability to see the road. The headlights should be checked for proper aim every 12 months and any time a new headlight is installed or front end body work is performed. It should be emphasized that the following procedure is only an interim step which will provide temporary adjustment until the headlights can be adjusted by a properly equipped shop.

1   Sealed beam-type headlights have an adjusting screw on the top controlling up-and-down movement and one on the side controlling left-and-right movement **(see illustration)**.

2   Late models equipped with composite headlights also have two adjustment screws, one to the side controlling left-and-right movement and one below the light for up-and-down movement that are accessible from behind the headlight housing **(see illustration)**.

3   There are several methods of adjusting the headlights. The simplest method requires a blank wall 25 feet in front of the vehicle and a level floor.

4   Position masking tape vertically on the wall in reference to the vehicle centerline and the centerlines of both headlights.

5   Position a horizontal tape line in reference to the centerline of all the headlights. **Note:** It may be easier to position the tape on the wall with the vehicle parked only a few inches away.

6   Adjustment should be made with the vehicle sitting level, the gas tank half-full and no unusually heavy load in the vehicle.

7   Starting with the low beam adjustment, position the high intensity zone so it is two inches below the horizontal line and two inches to the right of the headlight vertical line. Twist the adjustment screws until the

desired level has been achieved.

8   With the high beams on, the high intensity zone should be vertically centered with the exact center just below the horizontal line. **Note:** It may not be possible to position the headlight aim exactly for both high and low beams. If a compromise must be made, keep in mind that the low beams are the most used and have the greatest effect on driver safety.

9   Have the headlights adjusted by a dealer service department at the earliest opportunity.

16   Composite headlight housing - removal and installation

Refer to illustrations 16.5a and 16.5b

1   Disconnect the cable from the negative battery terminal. **Caution:** *If the stereo in your vehicle is equipped with an anti-theft system, make sure you have the correct activation code before disconnecting the battery.*

2   Remove the headlight bulb (Section 14).

3   Remove the radiator grille (Chapter 11).

4   Remove the parking light housing (Section 17).

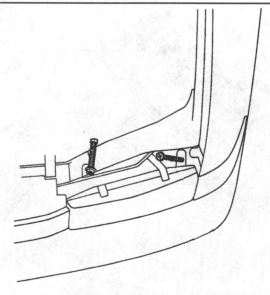

15.2 On composite bulb-type headlights, the adjustment screws are reached from the back side of the housing

15.1 Sealed beam-type headlight adjustment screws (arrows)

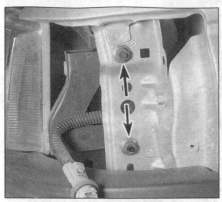

16.5a After removing the turn signal light assembly, the two side retaining bolts (arrows) are accessible

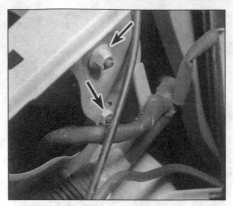

16.5b The right side retaining nuts (arrows) are accessible from the engine compartment

17.1a On 1990 and earlier models, remove the retaining screw and push the lens housing forward to detach it . . .

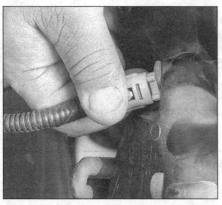

17.1b . . . then rotate the bulb holder to remove it from the housing

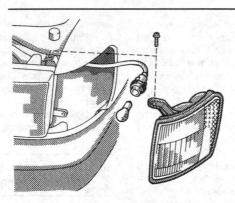

17.1c 1991 and later model parking, side marker and turn signal light housing details

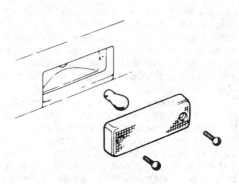

17.2 1990 and earlier model front turn signal light details

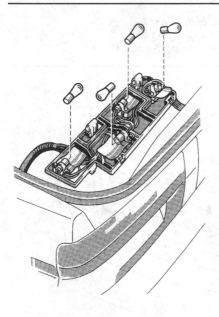

17.3a 1990 and earlier sedan model rear tail light housing details

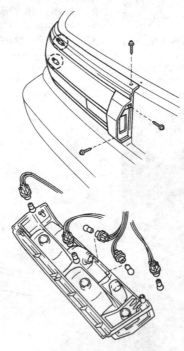

17.3b 1990 and earlier liftback model rear tail light housing details

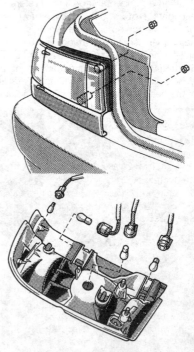

17.4 1991 and later model rear tail light housing details

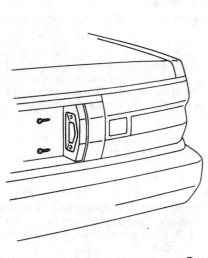

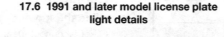

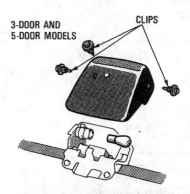

17.6 1991 and later model license plate light details

17.7a Typical 1990 and earlier model high mounted brake light details

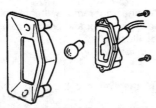

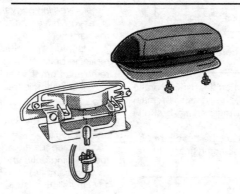

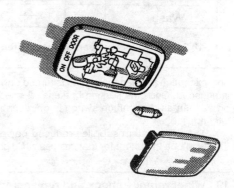

17.5 1990 and earlier sedan model license plate light details

17.7b 1991 and later model high mounted brake light details

17.8 Typical interior light details

5   Remove the retaining nuts, detach the housing and withdraw it from the vehicle (**see illustrations**).
6   Installation is the reverse of removal.

17   Bulb replacement

Front parking, side marker and turn signal lights

Refer to illustrations 17.1a, 17.1b, 17.1c and 17.2

1   Remove the lens housing from the fender. The bulb holder can then be removed from the backside and the bulb replaced (**see illustrations**).
2   On 1990 and earlier models the turn signal is mounted in the front bumper. Remove the two screws retaining the lens and replace the bulb (**see illustration**).

Rear side marker, turn signal, brake, tail and back-up lights

Refer to illustrations 17.3a, 17.3b and 17.4

3   On 1990 and earlier sedan models, remove the backside of the light housing from inside the luggage compartment. On liftback models, remove the screws retaining the housing to the rear panel. Remove the bulb holders from the housing and replace the bulbs (**see illustrations**).
4   On 1991 and later models, from inside the luggage compartment, remove the trim (if necessary). Remove the nuts retaining the housing, remove the housing and replace the bulbs (**see illustration**).

License plate light

Refer to illustrations 17.5 and 17.6

5   On 1990 and earlier sedan models, remove the screws retaining the housing, pull the housing out and replace the bulb (**see illustration**). On liftback models, the license plate light is located in the tail light housing (**see illustration 17.3b**).
6   On 1991 and later models, pry the housing over and down. Pull the housing out and replace the bulb (**see illustration**).

High mounted brake light

Refer to illustrations 17.7a and 17.7b

7   The brake light covers are retained by plastic clips. Pull the centers of the clips out and remove all of the clips. Remove the cover and replace the bulb (**see illustrations**).

Interior lights

Refer to illustration 17.8

8   Remove the cover and replace the bulb (**see illustration**).

Instrument cluster illumination

9   To gain access to the instrument cluster illumination lights, the instrument cluster will have to be removed (see Section 20). The bulbs can then be removed and replaced from the rear of the cluster.

18   Daytime Running Lights (DRL) - general information

The Daytime Running Lights (DRL) system, used on Canadian models, turns the headlights on whenever the engine is started. The

12

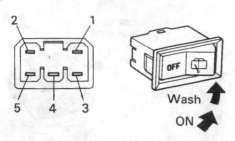

Terminal Switch position	3	4	5	2	1
OFF	o—o				
ON		o—o			
Wash		o—o		o—o	

19.3 Rear window wiper/washer switch continuity chart

only exception is when the engine is turned on when the parking brake is engaged. Once the parking brake is released, the lights will remain on as long as the ignition switch is on, even if the parking brake is later applied.

The DRL system supplies reduced power to the headlights so they won't be too bright for daytime use while prolonging headlight life.

19 Wiper motor - check and replacement

Refer to illustrations 19.3 and 19.7
Warning: *Some later models are equipped with airbags. The airbag is armed and can deploy (inflate) anytime the battery is connected. To prevent accidental deployment (and possible injury), disconnect the negative battery cable whenever working near airbag components. After the battery is disconnected, wait at least 90 seconds before beginning work (the system has a back-up capacitor that must fully discharge). For more information see Section 22.*
1   Disconnect the cable from the negative battery terminal. **Caution:** *If the stereo in your vehicle is equipped with an anti-theft system, make sure you have the correct activation code before disconnecting the battery.* The windshield wiper motor is located on the right (passenger) side of the underhood compartment and the rear wiper motor (some 1990 and earlier models) is mounted in the liftgate.

19.7 Unplug the wiper motor connector (A), remove the bolts (arrows) and detach the motor

Check

Windshield washer/wiper switch
2   Refer to Section 9 for the wiper and washer switch check procedure.

Rear wiper switch
3   Use a small screwdriver to pry the switch out of the dash, then unplug it and check for continuity between the indicated terminals with the switch in each of the indicated positions (**see illustration**).
4   If the continuity is not as specified, replace the switch.

Wiper motor
5   If a motor doesn't work or doesn't park properly and the switch checks out okay, the relay or the motor must be replaced.

Replacement

Windshield wiper motor
6   Disconnect the cable from the negative battery terminal. **Caution:** *If the stereo in your vehicle is equipped with an anti-theft system, make sure you have the correct activation code before disconnecting the battery.*
7   Unplug the electrical connector, remove the motor bracket retaining bolts, then lower the wiper motor and bracket assembly and remove it from the vehicle (**see illustration**).
8   Installation is the reverse of removal.

Rear wiper motor
9   Remove the wiper arm, then remove the shaft spindle nuts and washers.
10   Unplug the electrical connector, detach the wiper linkage, remove the retaining bolts and lower the motor through the liftgate access hole as an assembly.
11   Installation is the reverse of removal.

20 Instrument cluster - removal and installation

Refer to illustrations 20.3 and 20.4
Warning: *Some later models are equipped with airbags. The airbag is armed and can deploy (inflate) anytime the battery is connected. To prevent accidental deployment (and possible injury), disconnect the negative battery cable whenever working near airbag components. After the battery is disconnected, wait at least 90 seconds before beginning work (the system has a back-up capacitor that must fully discharge). For more information see Section 22.*
1   Disconnect the cable from the negative battery terminal. **Caution:** *If the stereo in your vehicle is equipped with an anti-theft system, make sure you have the correct activation code before disconnecting the battery.*
2   Remove the instrument cluster bezel (see Chapter 11).
3   Remove the retaining screws and pull the cluster forward (**see illustration**).

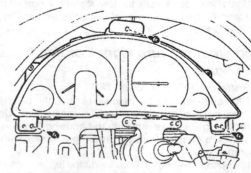

20.3 Typical instrument cluster mounting details

4   Reach behind the cluster and disconnect the speedometer cable **(see illustration)**. It may be necessary to disconnect the speedometer cable at the transaxle to provide slack in the cable so the cluster can be pulled out.

5   Installation is the reverse of the removal procedure.

21 Cruise control system - description and check

The cruise control system maintains vehicle speed by means of a vacuum actuated servo motor located in the engine compartment which is connected to the throttle linkage by a cable. The system consists of the servo motor, clutch switch, stoplight switch, control switches, a relay and associated vacuum hoses.

Because of the complexity of the cruise control system and the special tools and techniques required for diagnosis and repair, this should be left to a dealer or properly equipped shop. However, it is possible for the home mechanic to make simple checks of the wiring and vacuum connections for minor faults which can be easily repaired. These include:

a) *Inspecting the cruise control actuating switches and wiring for broken wires or loose connections.*
b) *Checking the cruise control fuse.*
c) *Checking the hoses in the engine compartment for tight connections, cracked hoses and obvious vacuum leaks. The cruise control system is operated by a vacuum so it is critical that all vacuum switches, hoses and connections be secure.*

22 Supplemental Restraint System - general information

Refer to illustrations 22.1

Later models are equipped with a Supplemental Restraint System

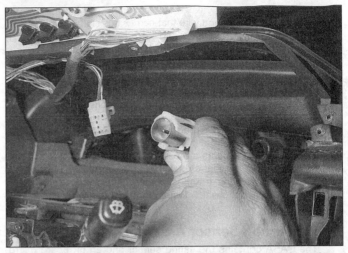

20.4 Press on the cable connector clips to release it from the cluster (cluster removed for clarity)

(SRS), more commonly known as an airbag. This system is designed to protect the driver from serious injury in the event of a head-on or frontal collision. It consists of an airbag module in the center of the steering wheel, two crash sensors mounted at the front of the vehicle and a diagnostic module which also contains a crash sensor located inside the passenger compartment **(see illustration)**.

Airbag module

The airbag module contains a housing incorporating the cushion (airbag) and inflator unit. The inflator assembly is mounted on the back of the housing over a hole through which gas is expelled, inflating the

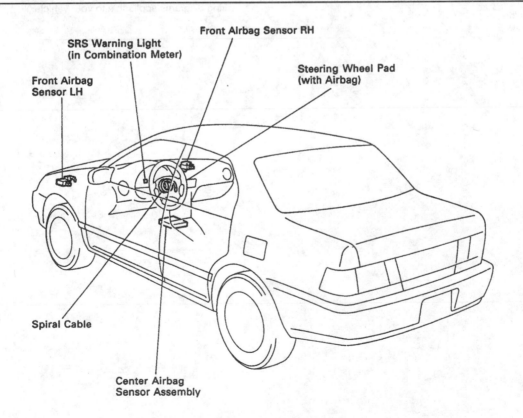

Front Airbag Sensor RH

SRS Warning Light
(in Combination Meter)

Steering Wheel Pad
(with Airbag)

Front Airbag
Sensor LH

Spiral Cable

Center Airbag
Sensor Assembly

22.1 Airbag system component layout

bag almost instantaneously when an electrical signal is sent from the system. The specially wound wire that carries this signal to the module is called a spiral cable. The spiral cable is a flat, ribbon-like electrically conductive tape which is wound many times so that it can transmit an electrical signal regardless of steering wheel position.

Sensors

The system has three sensors: two crash sensors at the front of the vehicle behind the bumper and above the wheel arches and a safing sensor in the center airbag sensor assembly located under the instrument panel, just in front of the center console.

The front crash sensors are basically pressure sensitive switches that complete an electrical circuit during an impact of sufficient G force. The electrical signal from the crash sensors is sent to the center airbag sensor assembly, which then completes the circuit and inflates the airbag.

Center Airbag Sensor Assembly (CASA)

The CASA contains the safing sensor and an on-board microprocessor which monitors the operation of the system. It checks this system every time the vehicle is started, causing the "AIRBAG" light to go on then off, if the system is operating properly. If there is a fault in the system, the light will go on and stay on and the CASA will store fault codes indicating the nature of the fault. If the AIRBAG light goes on and stays on, the vehicle should be taken to your dealer immediately for service.

Precautions and disarming

Warning: *Failure to follow these precautions could result in accidental deployment of the airbag and personal injury.*

Whenever working in the vicinity of the steering wheel, steering column or any of the other SRS system components, the system must be disarmed. To disarm the system:

a) *Point the wheels straight ahead and turn the key to the Lock position.*

b) *Disconnect the cable from the negative battery terminal.*
c) *Wait at least 90 seconds for the back-up power supply to be depleted*

Whenever handling an airbag module, always keep the airbag opening pointed away from your body. Never place the airbag module on a bench of other surface with the airbag opening facing the surface. Always place the airbag module in a safe location with the airbag opening facing up.

Never measure the resistance of any SRS component. An ohmmeter has a built-in battery supply that could accidentally deploy the airbag.

Never use electrical welding equipment on a vehicle equipped with an airbag without first disconnecting the yellow airbag connector, located under the steering column near the combination switch connector.

Never dispose of a live airbag module. Return it to your dealer for safe deployment, using special equipment, and disposal.

23   Wiring diagrams - general information

Refer to illustration 23.4

Since it isn't possible to include all wiring diagrams for every year covered by this manual, the following diagrams are those that are typical and most commonly needed.

Prior to troubleshooting any circuits, check the fuse and circuit breakers (if equipped) to make sure they are in good condition. Make sure the battery is properly charged and has clean, tight cable connections (see Chapter 1).

When checking the wiring system, make sure that all electrical connectors are clean, with no broken or loose pins. When unplugging an electrical connector, do not pull on the wires, only on the connector housings themselves.

Refer to the accompanying illustration for an explanation of the wiring diagrams applicable to your vehicle.

ELECTRICAL CONNECTORS

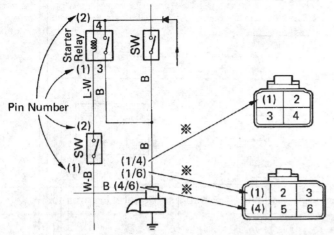

Pin Number

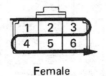

Numbered in order from upper left to lower right

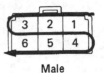

Numbered in order from upper right to lower left

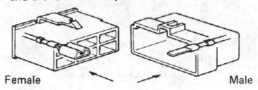

Female   Male

Male & female connectors distinguished by shape of their internal pins.
● All connectors are shown from the open end, and the lock is on top.

Female   Male

※ When connectors with different numbers of terminals are used with the same parts, the pin number and the numbers of terminals are specified.
e.g. (1/4) = No. 1 pin/4 terminals connector

JUNCTION BLOCK OR RELAY BLOCK

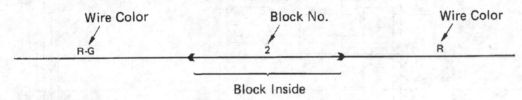

Wire Color   Block No.   Wire Color

R-G   2   R

Block Inside

WIRE COLOR

Wire colors are indicated by an alphabetical code.

B = Black	BR = Brown	G = Green	GR = Gray	L = Blue
LG = Light Green	O = Orange	P = Pink	R = Red	V = Violet
W = White	Y = Yellow			

The 1st letter indicates the basic wire color and the 2nd indicates the stripe color.

Example: R-G indicates a Red wire with a Green stripe.

ABBREVIATION

The following abbreviations are used in this wiring diagram.

A/C	= Air Conditioner	LH	= Left-hand
A/T	= Automatic Transaxle	M/T	= Manual Transaxle
CB	= Circuit Breaker	OX	= Oxygen
CMH	= Cold Mixture Heater	RH	= Right-hand
COMB.	= Combination	SW	= Switch
EBCV	= Electronic Air Bleed Control Valve	TP	= Throttle Positioner
EGR	= Exhaust Gas Recirculation	VSV	= Vacuum Switching Valve
FL	= Fusible Link	w/	= With
IIA	= Integrated Ignition Assembly	w/o	= Without
INT	= Intermittent		

12

23.4 How to read electrical wiring diagrams

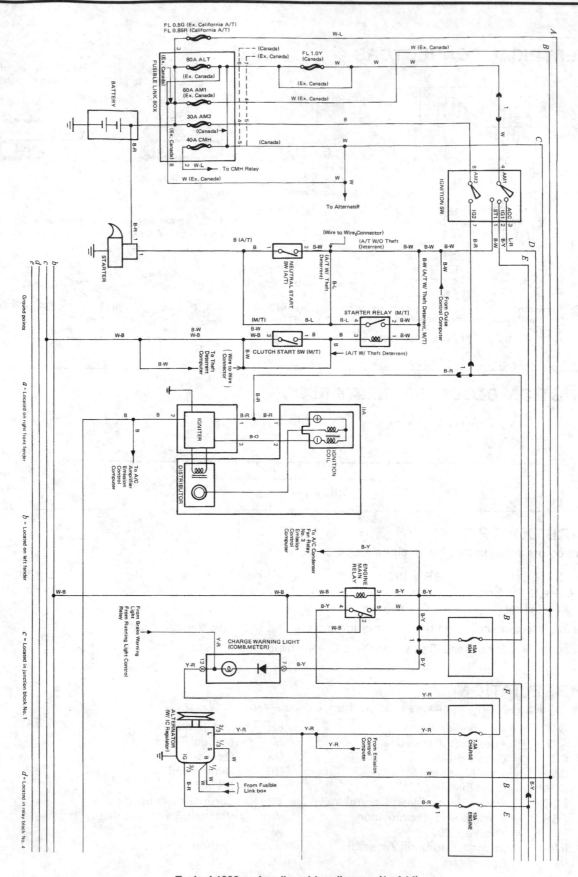

Typical 1990 and earlier wiring diagram (1 of 14)

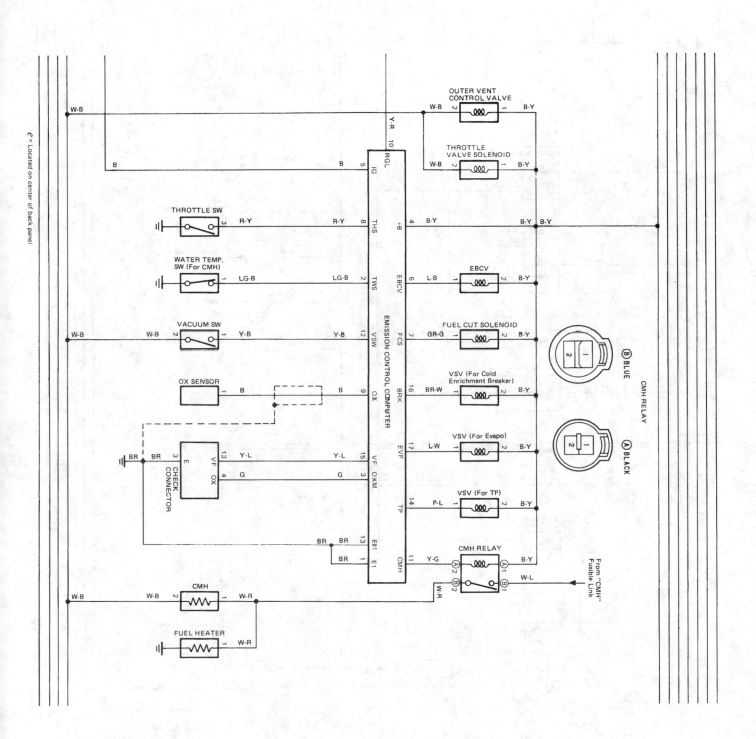

Typical 1990 and earlier wiring diagram (2 of 14)

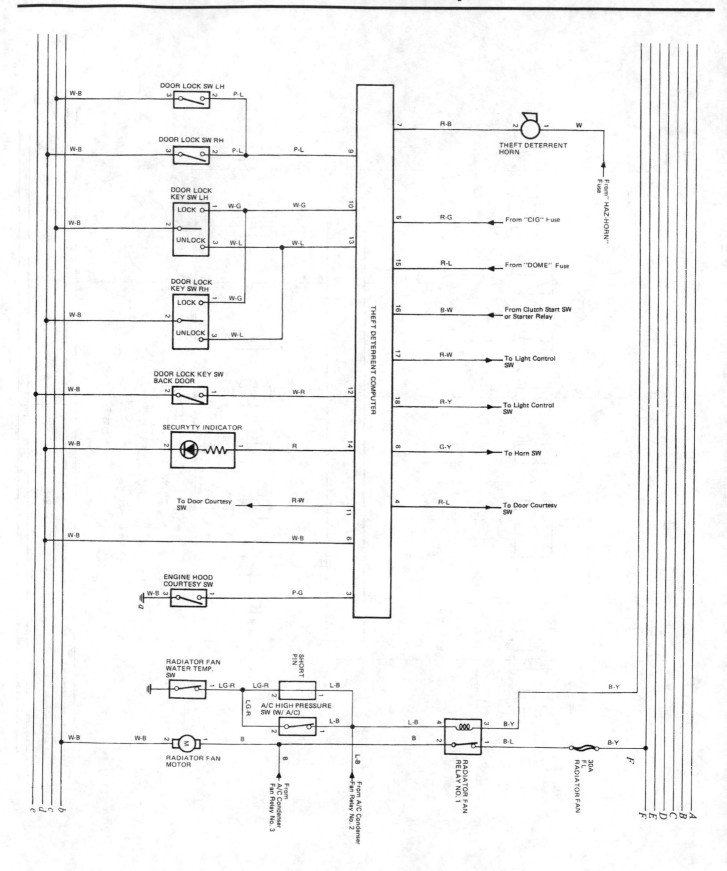

Typical 1990 and earlier wiring diagram (3 of 14)

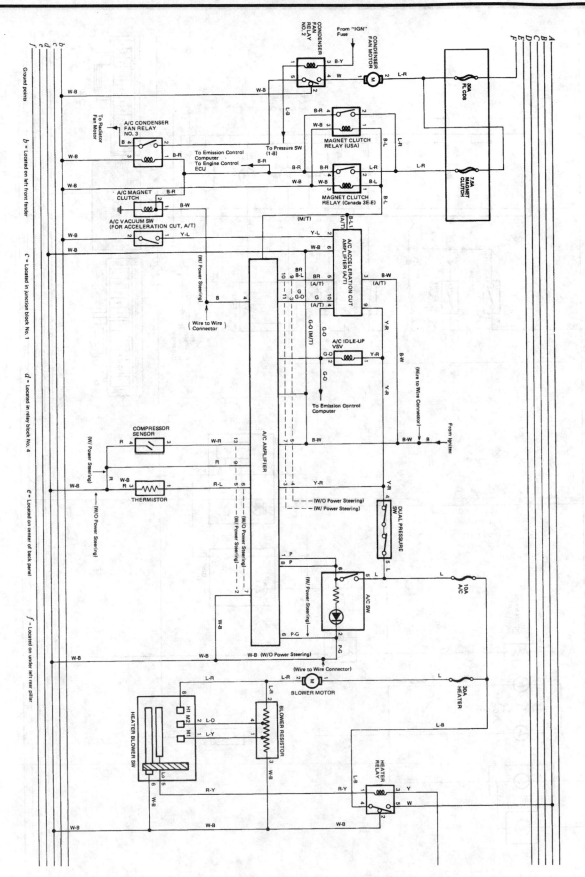

Typical 1990 and earlier wiring diagram (4 of 14)

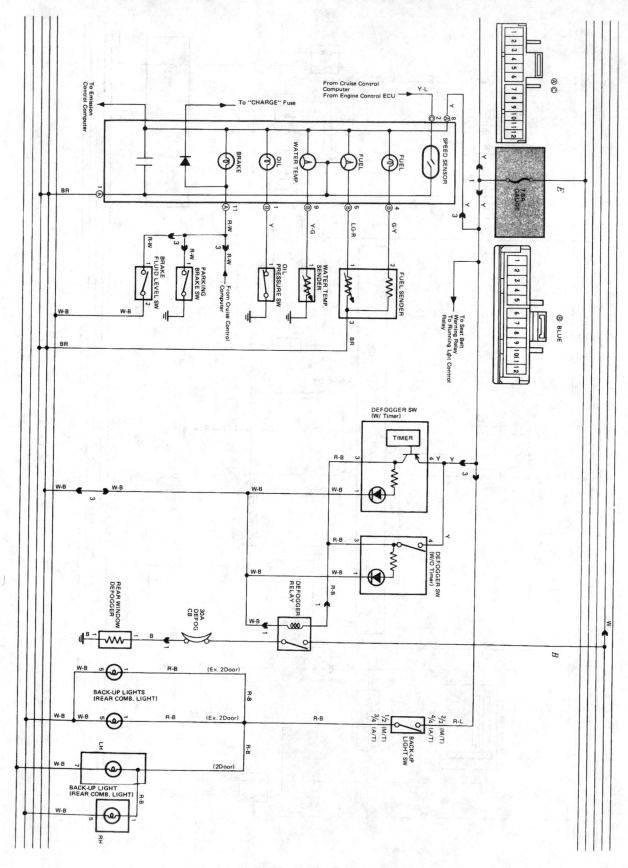

Typical 1990 and earlier wiring diagram (5 of 14)

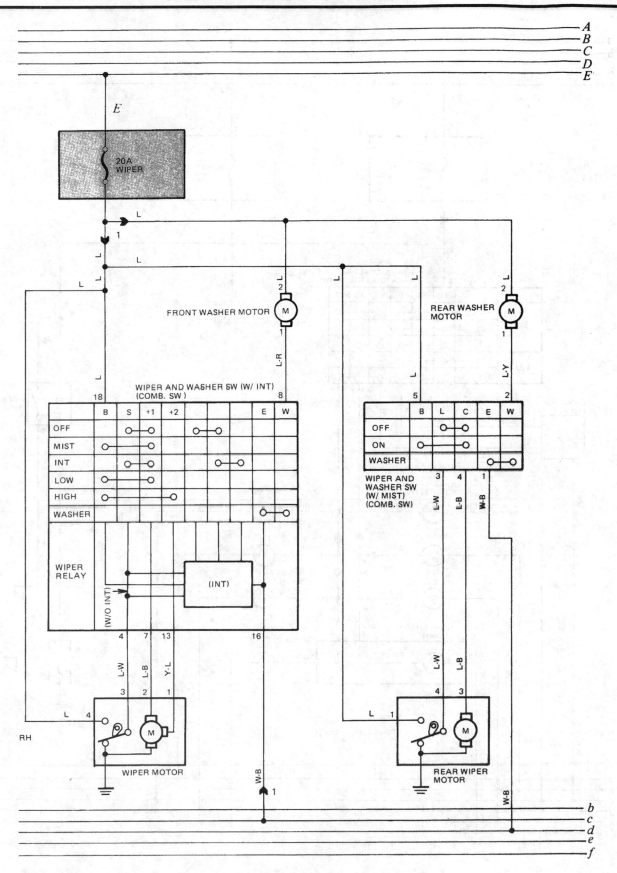

Typical 1990 and earlier wiring diagram (6 of 14)

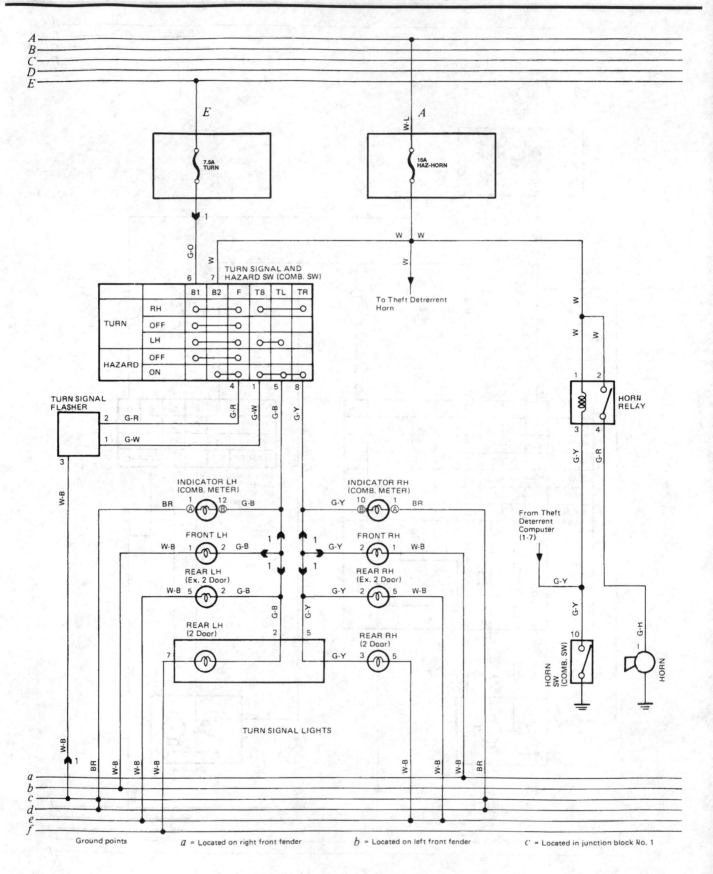

Ground points a = Located on right front fender b = Located on left front fender c = Located in junction block No. 1

Typical 1990 and earlier wiring diagram (7 of 14)

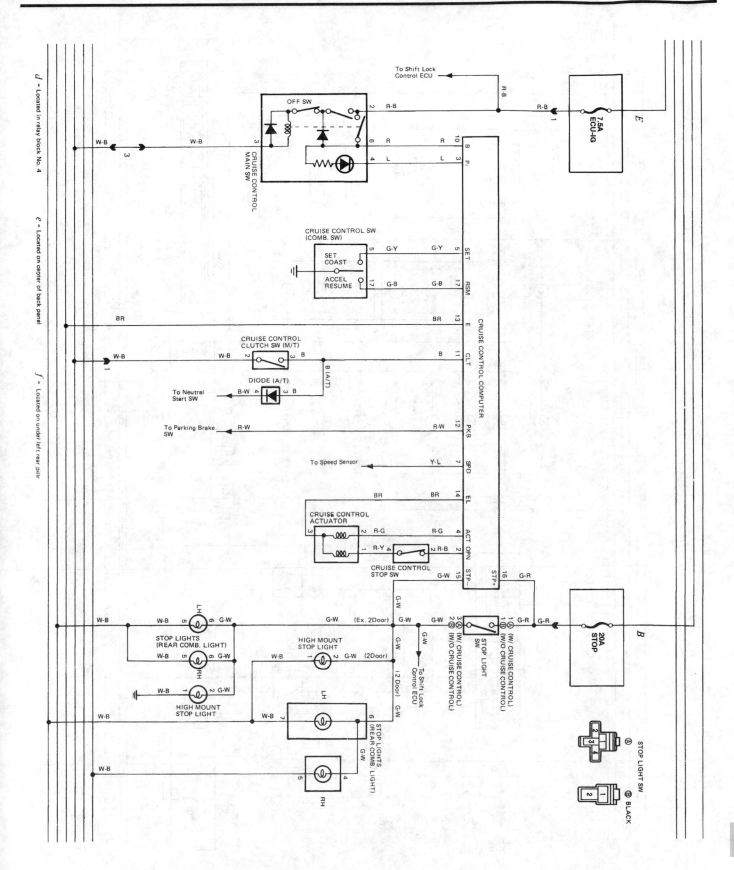

Typical 1990 and earlier wiring diagram (8 of 14)

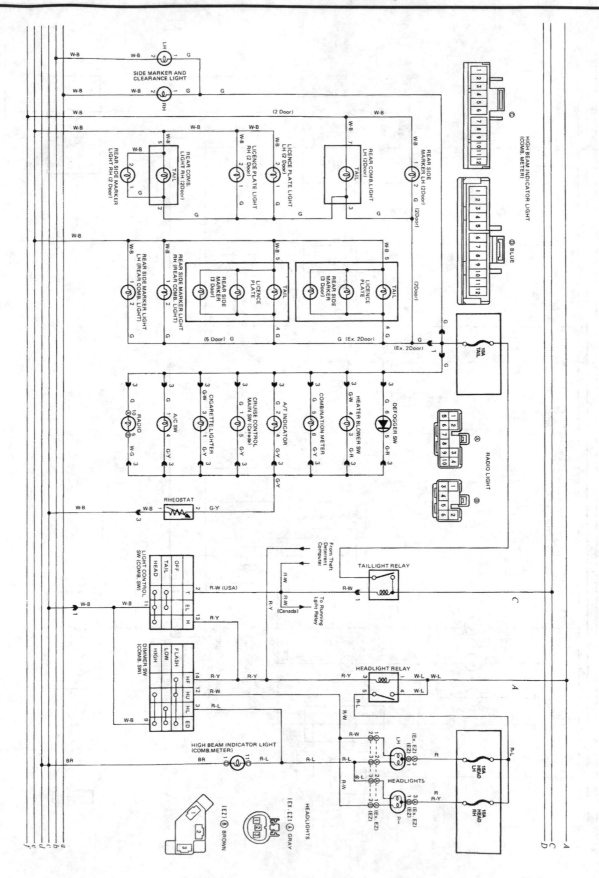

Typical 1990 and earlier wiring diagram (9 of x14)

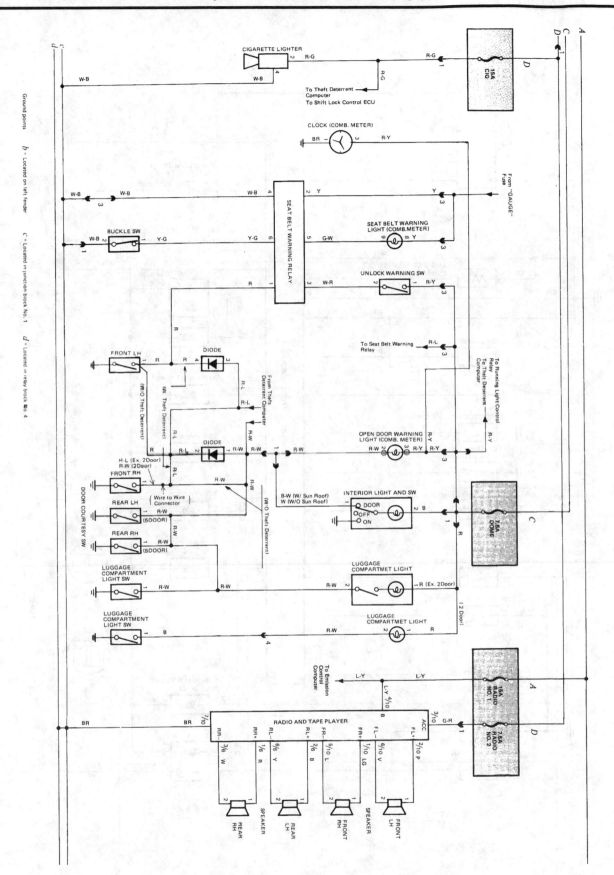

Typical 1990 and earlier wiring diagram (10 of 14)

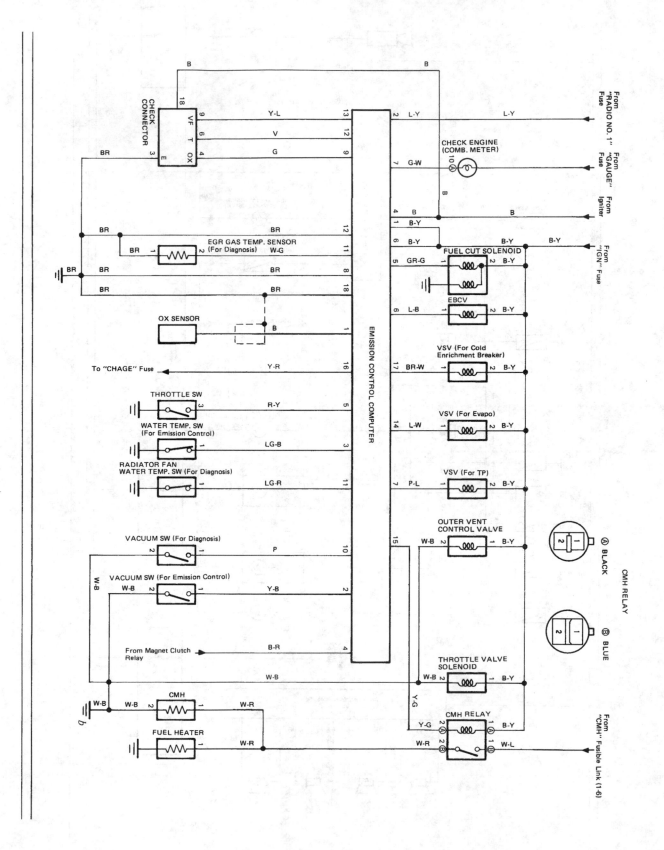

Typical 1990 and earlier wiring diagram (11 of 14)

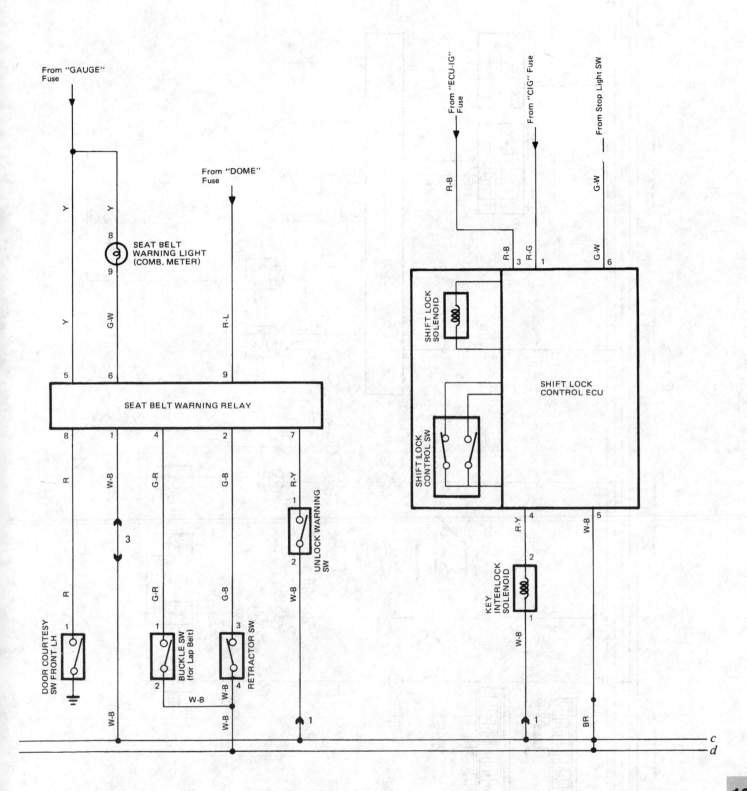

Typical 1990 and earlier wiring diagram (12 of 14)

12

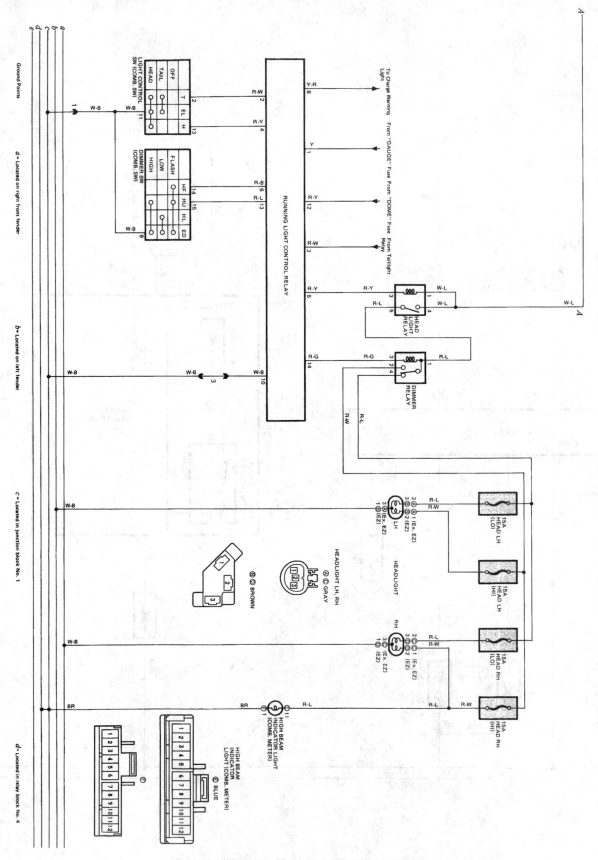

Typical 1990 and earlier wiring diagram (13 of 14)

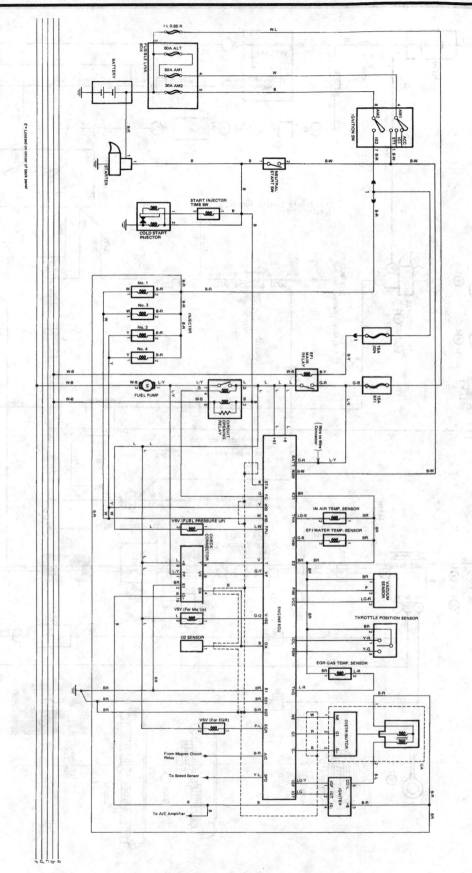

Typical 1990 and earlier wiring diagram (14 of 14)

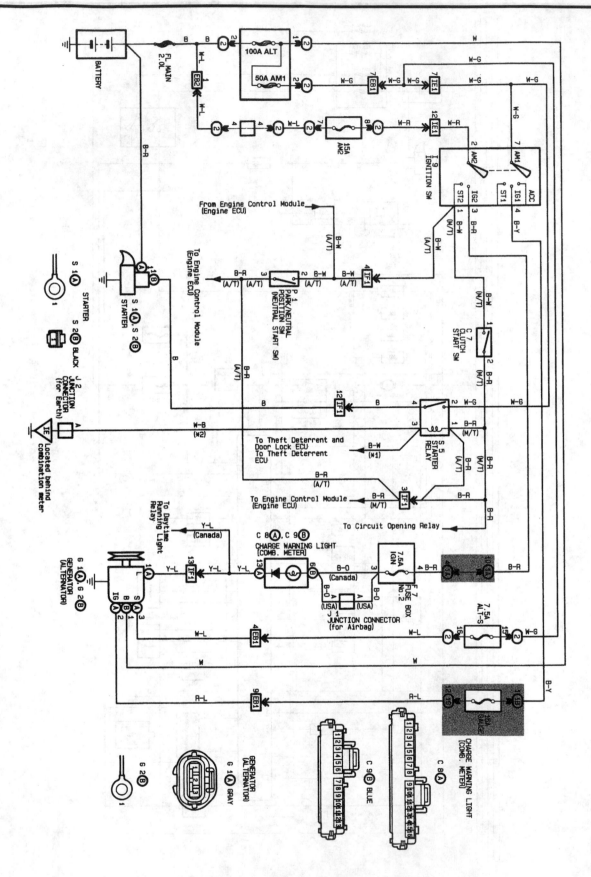

Typical 1991 and later wiring diagram (1 of 10)

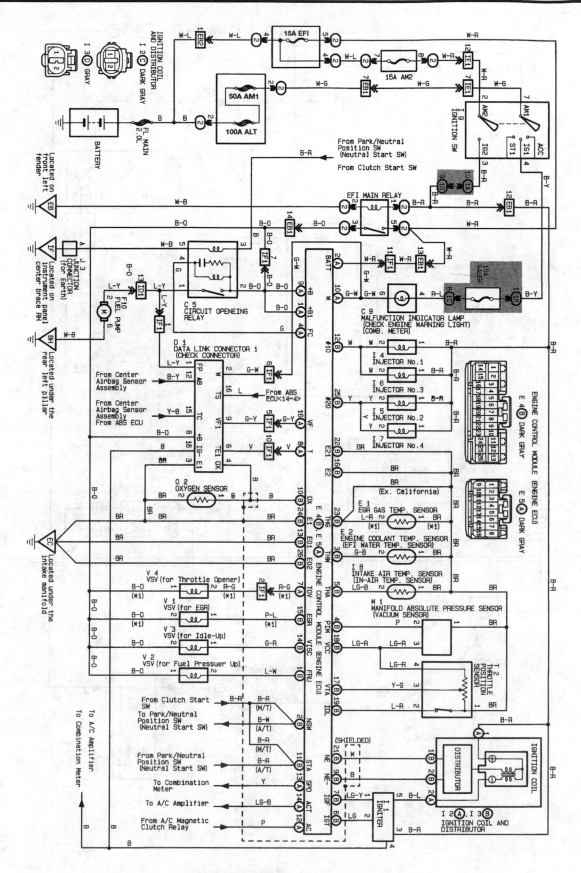

Typical 1991 and later wiring diagram (2 of 10)

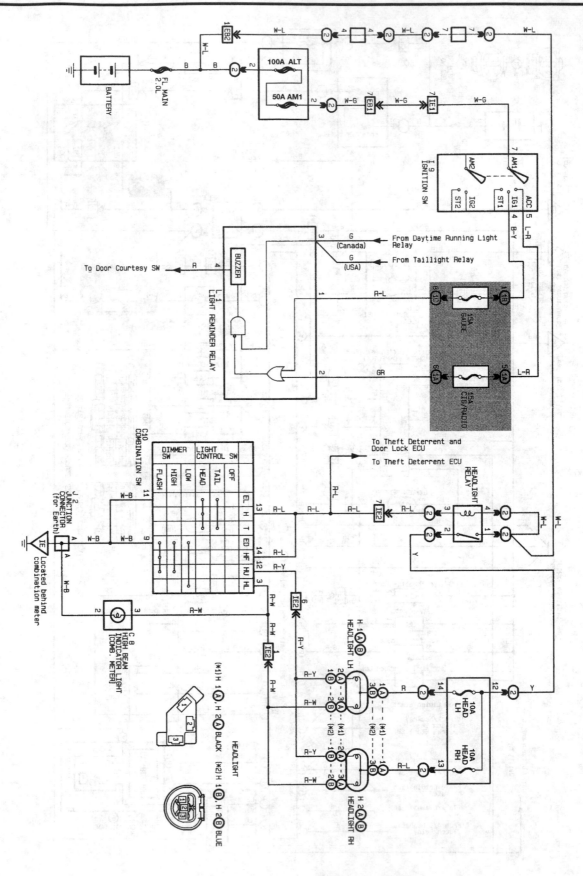

Typical 1991 and later wiring diagram (3 of x10)

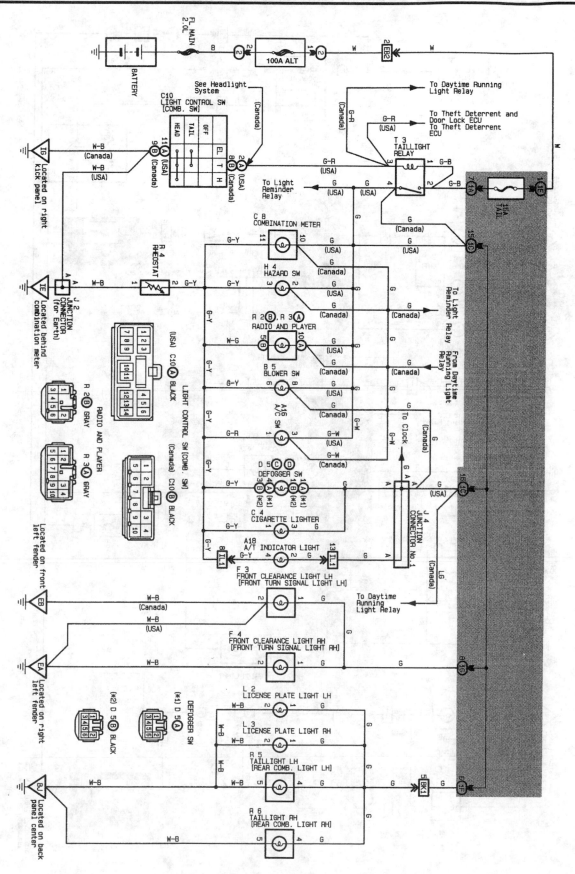

Typical 1991 and later wiring diagram (4 of 10)

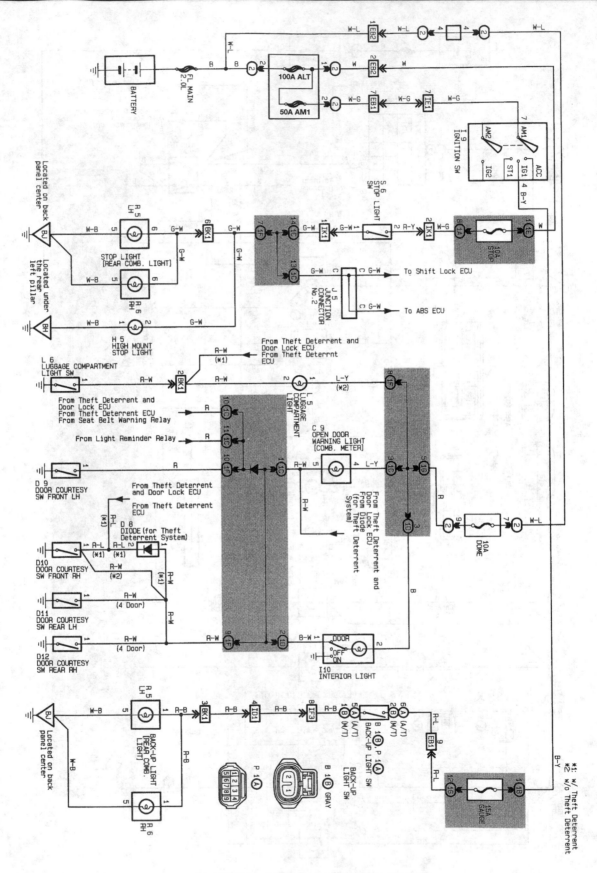

Typical 1991 and later wiring diagram (5 of 10)

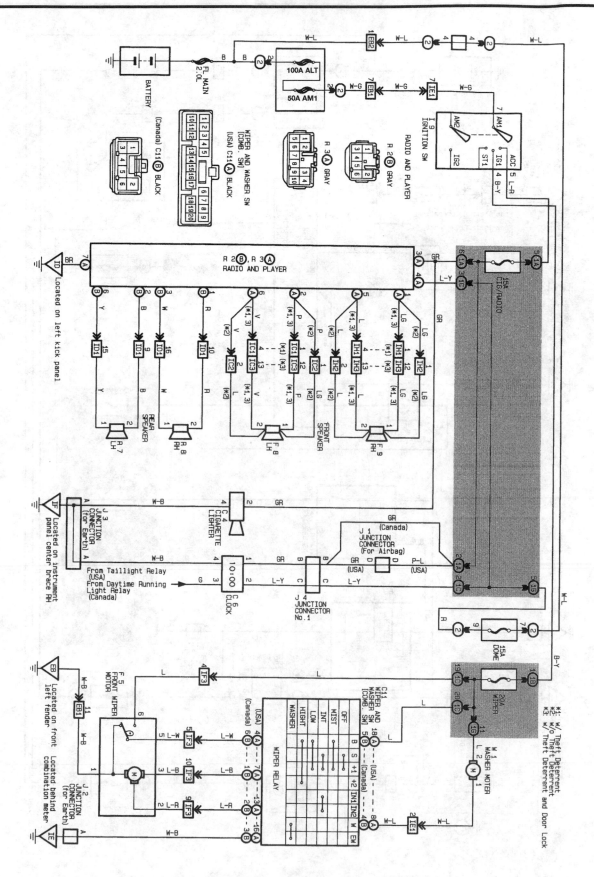

Typical 1991 and later wiring diagram (6 of 10)

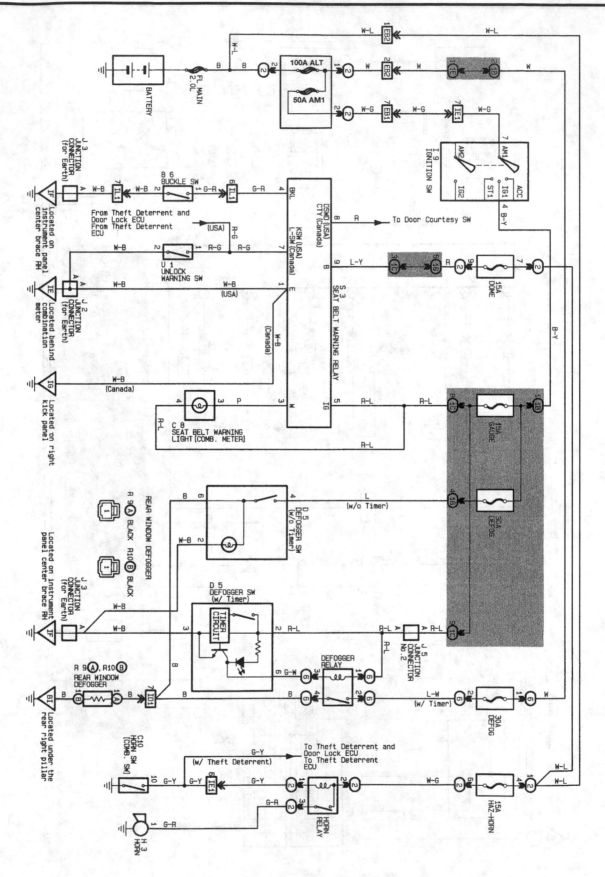

Typical 1991 and later wiring diagram (7 of 10)

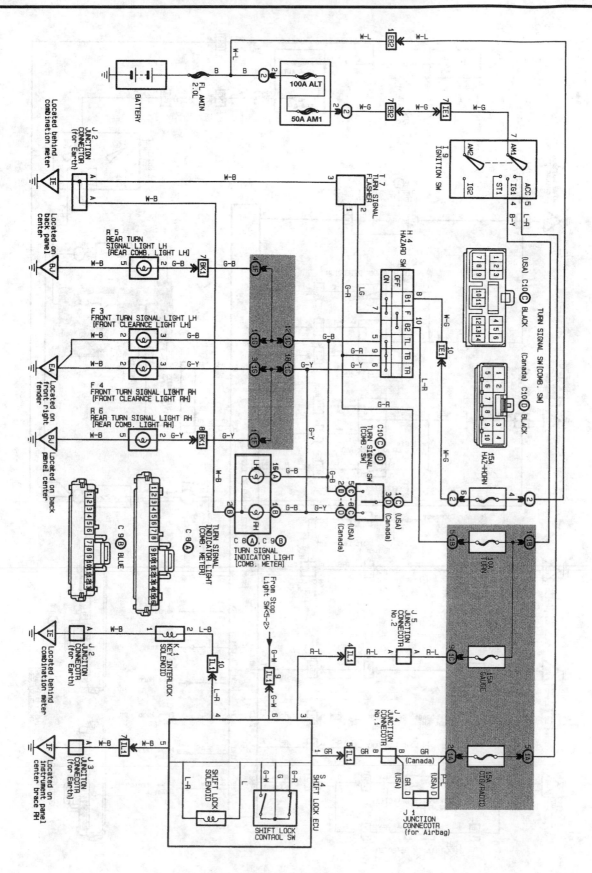

Typical 1991 and later wiring diagram (8 of 10)

12

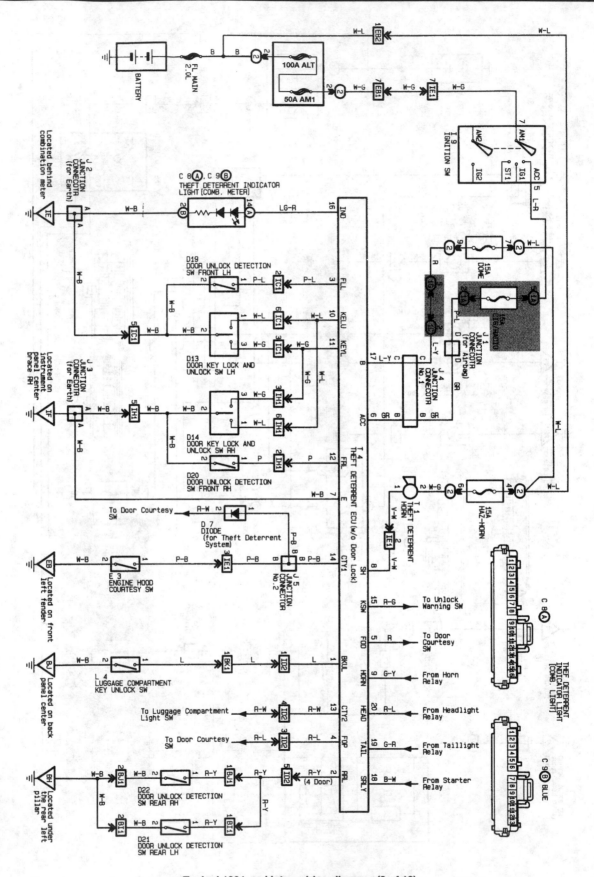

Typical 1991 and later wiring diagram (9 of 10)

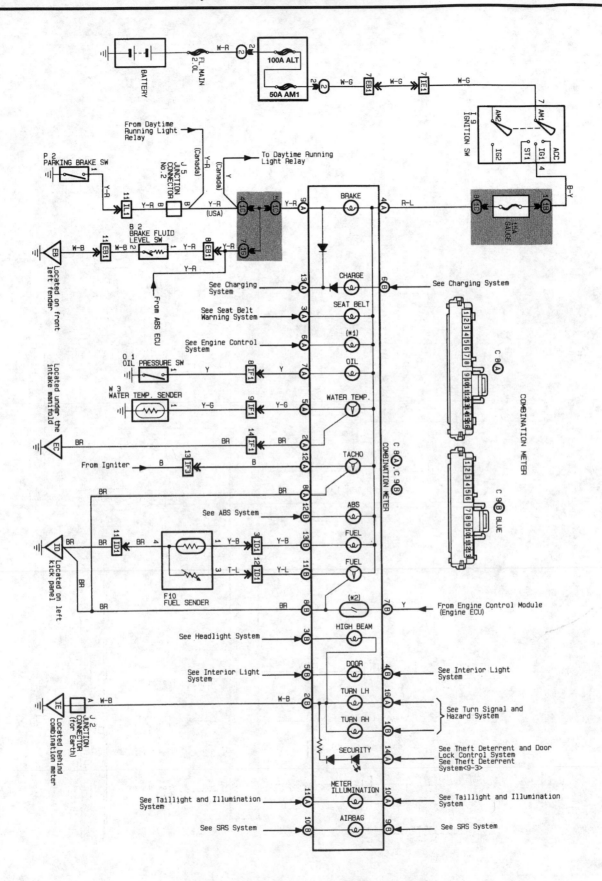

Typical 1991 and later wiring diagram (10 of 10)

Index

Haynes Automotive Manuals

NOTE: New manuals are added to this list on a periodic basis. If you do not see a listing for your vehicle, consult your local Haynes dealer for the latest product information.

ACURA
*12020 Integra '86 thru '89 & Legend '86 thru '90

AMC
Jeep CJ - see JEEP (50020)
14020 Concord/Hornet/Gremlin/Spirit '70 thru '83
14025 (Renault) Alliance & Encore '83 thru '87

AUDI
15020 4000 all models '80 thru '87
15025 5000 all models '77 thru '83
15026 5000 all models '84 thru '88

AUSTIN
Healey Sprite - see MG Midget (66015)

BMW
*18020 3/5 Series '82 thru '92
*18021 3 Series except 325iX models '92 thru '97
18025 320i all 4 cyl models '75 thru '83
18035 528i & 530i all models '75 thru '80
18050 1500 thru 2002 except Turbo '59 thru '77

BUICK
Century (FWD) - see GM (38005)
*19020 Buick, Oldsmobile & Pontiac Full-size (Front wheel drive) '85 thru '98
Buick Electra, LeSabre and Park Avenue; Oldsmobile Delta 88 Royale, Ninety Eight and Regency; Pontiac Bonneville
19025 Buick Oldsmobile & Pontiac Full-size (Rear wheel drive) '70 thru '90
Buick Estate '70 thru '90, Electra'70 thru '84, LeSabre '70 thru '85, Limited '74 thru '79
Oldsmobile Custom Cruiser '70 thru '90, Delta 88 '70 thru '85,Ninety-eight '70 thru '84
Pontiac Bonneville '70 thru '81, Catalina '70 thru '81, Grandville '70 thru '75, Parisienne '83 thru '86
19030 Mid-size Regal & Century '74 thru '87
Regal - see GENERAL MOTORS (38010)
Skyhawk - see GM (38030)
Skylark - see GM (38020, 38025)
Somerset - see GENERAL MOTORS (38025)

CADILLAC
*21030 Cadillac Rear Wheel Drive '70 thru '93
Cimarron, Eldorado & Seville - see GM (38015, 38030)

CHEVROLET
10305 Chevrolet Engine Overhaul Manual
*24010 Astro & GMC Safari Mini-vans '85 thru '93
24015 Camaro V8 all models '70 thru '81
24016 Camaro all models '82 thru '92
Cavalier - see GM (38015)
Celebrity - see GM (38005)
24017 Camaro & Firebird '93 thru '97
24020 Chevelle, Malibu, El Camino '69 thru '87
24024 Chevette & Pontiac T1000 '76 thru '87
Citation - see GENERAL MOTORS (38020)
*24032 Corsica/Beretta all models '87 thru '96
24040 Corvette all V8 models '68 thru '82
*24041 Corvette all models '84 thru '96
24045 Full-size Sedans Caprice, Impala, Biscayne, Bel Air & Wagons '69 thru '90
24046 Impala SS & Caprice and Buick Roadmaster '91 thru '96
Lumina '90 thru '94 - see GM (38010)
24048 Lumina & Monte Carlo '95 thru '98
Lumina APV - see GM (38038)
24050 Luv Pick-up all 2WD & 4WD '72 thru '82
24055 Monte Carlo all models '70 thru '88
Monte Carlo '95 thru '98 - see LUMINA
24059 Nova all V8 models '69 thru '79
*24060 Nova/Geo Prizm '85 thru '92
24064 Pick-ups '67 thru '87 - Chevrolet & GMC, all V8 & in-line 6 cyl, 2WD & 4WD '67 thru '87; Suburbans, Blazers & Jimmys '67 thru '91
*24065 Pick-ups '88 thru '98 - Chevrolet & GMC, all full-size models '88 thru '98; Blazer & Jimmy '92 thru '94; Suburban '92 thru '98; Tahoe & Yukon '95 thru '98
*24070 S-10 & GMC S-15 Pick-ups '82 thru '93
24071 S-10, GMC S-15 & Jimmy '94 thru '96
*24075 Sprint & Geo Metro '85 thru '94
24080 Vans - Chevrolet & GMC '68 thru '96

CHRYSLER
10310 Chrysler Engine Overhaul Manual
*25015 Chrysler Cirrus, Dodge Stratus, Plymouth Breeze, '95 thru '97
*25020 Full-size Front-Wheel Drive '88 thru '93
K-Cars - see DODGE Aries (30008)
Laser - see DODGE Daytona (30030)
25025 Chrysler LHS, Concorde & New Yorker, Dodge Intrepid, Eagle Vision, '93 thru '97
*25030 Chrysler/Plym. Mid-size '82 thru '95
Rear-wheel Drive - see DODGE (30050)

DATSUN
28005 200SX all models '80 thru '83
28007 B-210 all models '73 thru '78
28009 210 all models '78 thru '82
28012 240Z, 260Z & 280Z Coupe '70 thru '78
28014 280ZX Coupe & 2+2 '79 thru '83
300ZX - see NISSAN (72010)
28016 310 all models '78 thru '82
28018 510 & PL521 Pick-up '68 thru '73
28020 510 all models '78 thru '81
28022 620 Series Pick-up all models '73 thru '79
720 Series Pick-up - NISSAN (72030)
28025 810/Maxima all gas models, '77 thru '84

DODGE
400 & 600 - see CHRYSLER (25030)
*30008 Aries & Plymouth Reliant '81 thru '89
30010 Caravan & Ply. Voyager '84 thru '95
*30011 Caravan & Ply. Voyager '96 thru '98
30012 Challenger/Plymouth Saporro '78 thru '83
Challenger '67-'76 - see DART (30025)
30016 Colt/Plymouth Champ '78 thru '87
*30020 Dakota Pick-ups all models '87 thru '96
30025 Dart, Challenger/Plymouth Barracuda & Valiant 6 cyl models '67 thru '76
*30030 Daytona & Chrysler Laser '84 thru '89
Intrepid - see Chrysler (25025)
*30034 Dodge & Plymouth Neon '95 thru '97
*30035 Omni & Plymouth Horizon '78 thru '90
30040 Pick-ups all full-size models '74 thru '93
30041 Pick-ups all full-size models '94 thru '96
*30045 Ram 50/D50 Pick-ups & Raider and Plymouth Arrow Pick-ups '79 thru '93
30050 Dodge/Ply./Chrysler RWD '71 thru '89
*30055 Shadow/Plymouth Sundance '87 thru '94
*30060 Spirit & Plymouth Acclaim '89 thru '95
*30065 Vans - Dodge & Plymouth '71 thru '96

EAGLE
Talon - see MITSUBISHI Eclipse (68030)
Vision - see CHRYSLER (25025)

FIAT
34010 124 Sport Coupe & Spider '68 thru '78
34025 X1/9 all models '74 thru '80

FORD
10355 Ford Automatic Transmission Overhaul
10320 Ford Engine Overhaul Manual
*36004 Aerostar Mini-vans '86 thru '96
Aspire - see FORD Festiva (36030)
*36006 Contour/Mercury Mystique '95 thru '98
36008 Courier Pick-up all models '72 thru '82
36012 Crown Victoria & Mercury Grand Marquis '88 thru '96
*36016 Escort/Mercury Lynx '81 thru '90
*36020 Escort/Mercury Tracer '91 thru '96
*36022 Expedition - see FORD Pick-up (36059)
*36024 Explorer & Mazda Navajo '91 thru '95
*36028 Fairmont & Mercury Zephyr '78 thru '83
36030 Festiva & Aspire '88 thru '97
36032 Fiesta all models '77 thru '80
36036 Ford & Mercury Full-size, Ford LTD & Mercury Marquis ('75 thru '82); Ford Custom 500,Country Squire, Crown Victoria & Mercury Colony Park ('75 thru '87); Ford LTD Crown Victoria & Mercury Gran Marquis ('83 thru '87)
36040 Granada & Mercury Monarch '75 thru '80
36044 Ford & Mercury Mid-size, Ford Thunderbird & Mercury Cougar ('75 thru '82); Ford LTD & Mercury Marquis ('83 thru '86); Ford Torino,Gran Torino, Elite, Ranchero pick-up, LTD II, Mercury Montego, Comet, XR-7 & Lincoln Versailles ('75 thru '86)
36048 Mustang V8 all models '64-1/2 thru '73
36049 Mustang II 4 cyl, V6 & V8 '74 thru '78
36050 Mustang & Mercury Capri incl. Turbo Mustang, '79 thru '93; Capri, '79 thru '86
*36051 Mustang all models '94 thru '97
36054 Pick-ups and Bronco '73 thru '79
36058 Pick-ups and Bronco '80 thru '96
*36059 Pick-ups, Expedition & Lincoln Navigator '97 thru '98
36062 Pinto & Mercury Bobcat '75 thru '80
*36066 Probe all models '89 thru '92
*36070 Ranger/Bronco II gas models '83 thru '92
*36071 Ford Ranger '93 thru '97 & Mazda Pick-ups '94 thru '97
*36074 Taurus & Mercury Sable '86 thru '95
*36075 Taurus & Mercury Sable '96 thru '98
*36078 Tempo & Mercury Topaz '84 thru '94
36082 Thunderbird/Mercury Cougar '83 thru '88
*36086 Thunderbird/Mercury Cougar '89 and '97
36090 Vans all V8 Econoline models '69 thru '91
*36094 Vans full size '92 thru '95
*36097 Windstar Mini-van '95 thru '98

GENERAL MOTORS
*10360 GM Automatic Transmission Overhaul
*38005 Buick Century, Chevrolet Celebrity, Olds Cutlass Ciera & Pontiac 6000 all models '82 thru '96
*38010 Buick Regal, Chevrolet Lumina, Oldsmobile Cutlass Supreme & Pontiac Grand Prix front wheel drive '88 thru '95
*38015 Buick Skyhawk, Cadillac Cimarron, Chevrolet Cavalier, Oldsmobile Firenza Pontiac J-2000 & Sunbird '82 thru '94
*38016 Chevrolet Cavalier & Pontiac Sunfire '95 thru '98
38020 Buick Skylark, Chevrolet Citation, Olds Omega, Pontiac Phoenix '80 thru '85
38025 Buick Skylark & Somerset, Olds Achieva, Calais & Pontiac Grand Am '85 thru '95
38030 Cadillac Eldorado & Oldsmobile Toronado '71 thru '85, Seville '80 thru '85, Buick Riviera '79 thru '85
*38035 Chevrolet Lumina APV, Oldsmobile Silhouette & Pontiac Trans Sport '90 thru '95
General Motors Full-size Rear-wheel drive - see BUICK (19025)

GEO
Metro - see CHEVROLET Sprint (24075)
Prizm - see CHEVROLET (24060) or TOYOTA (92036)
*40030 Storm all models '90 thru '93
Tracker - see SUZUKI Samurai (90010)

GMC
Safari - see CHEVROLET ASTRO (24010)
Vans & Pick-ups - see CHEVROLET

HONDA
42010 Accord CVCC all models '76 thru '83
42011 Accord all models '84 thru '89
42012 Accord all models '90 thru '93
*42013 Accord all models '94 thru '95
42020 Civic 1200 all models '73 thru '79
42021 Civic 1300 & 1500 CVCC '80 thru '83
42022 Civic 1500 CVCC all models '75 thru '79
42023 Civic all models '84 thru '91
42024 Civic & del Sol '92 thru '95
Passport - see ISUZU Rodeo (47017)
*42040 Prelude CVCC all models '79 thru '89

HYUNDAI
*43015 Excel all models '86 thru '94

ISUZU
Hombre - see CHEVROLET S-10 (24071)
*47017 Rodeo '91 thru '97, Amigo '89 thru '94, Honda Passport '95 thru '97
*47020 Trooper '84 thru '91, Pick-up '81 thru '93

JAGUAR
*49010 XJ6 all 6 cyl models '68 thru '86
*49011 XJ6 all models '88 thru '94
*49015 XJ12 & XJS all 12 cyl models '72 thru '85

JEEP
*50010 Cherokee, Comanche & Wagoneer Limited all models '84 thru '96
50020 CJ all models '49 thru '86
*50025 Grand Cherokee all models '93 thru '98
*50029 Grand Wagoneer & Pick-up '72 thru '91
*50030 Wrangler all models '87 thru '95

LINCOLN
Navigator - see FORD Pick-up (36059)
59010 Rear Wheel Drive all models '70 thru '96

MAZDA
61010 GLC (rear wheel drive) '77 thru '83
61011 GLC (front wheel drive) '81 thru '85
*61015 323 & Protegé '90 thru '97
*61016 MX-5 Miata '90 thru '97
*61020 MPV all models '89 thru '94
Navajo - see FORD Explorer (36024)
61030 Pick-ups '72 thru '93
Pick-ups '94 on - see Ford (36071)
61035 RX-7 all models '79 thru '85
*61036 RX-7 all models '86 thru '91
61040 626 (rear wheel drive) '79 thru '82
*61041 626 & MX-6 (front wheel drive) '83 thru '91

MERCEDES-BENZ
63012 123 Series Diesel '76 thru '85
*63015 190 Series 4-cyl gas models, '84 thru '88
63020 230, 250 & 280 6 cyl sohc '68 thru '72
63025 280 123 Series gas models '77 thru '81
63030 350 & 450 all models '71 thru '80

MERCURY
See FORD Listing

MG
66010 MGB Roadster & GT Coupe '62 thru '80
66015 MG Midget & Austin Healey Sprite Roadster '58 thru '80

MITSUBISHI
*68020 Cordia, Tredia, Galant, Precis & Mirage '83 thru '93
*68030 Eclipse, Eagle Talon & Plymouth Laser '90 thru '94
*68040 Pick-up '83 thru '96, Montero '83 thru '93

NISSAN
72010 300ZX all models incl. Turbo '84 thru '89
*72015 Altima all models '93 thru '97
*72020 Maxima all models '85 thru '91
*72030 Pick-ups '80 thru '96, Pathfinder '87 thru '95
72040 Pulsar all models '83 thru '86
72050 Sentra all models '82 thru '94
*72051 Sentra & 200SX all models '95 thru '98
72060 Stanza all models '82 thru '90

OLDSMOBILE
*73015 Cutlass '74 thru '88
For other OLDSMOBILE titles, see BUICK, CHEVROLET or GENERAL MOTORS listing.

PLYMOUTH
For PLYMOUTH titles, see DODGE.

PONTIAC
79008 Fiero all models '84 thru '88
79018 Firebird V8 models except Turbo '70 thru '81
79019 Firebird all models '82 thru '92
For other PONTIAC titles, see BUICK, CHEVROLET or GENERAL MOTORS listing.

PORSCHE
*80020 911 Coupe & Targa models '65 thru '89
80025 914 all 4 cyl models '69 thru '76
80030 924 all models incl. Turbo '76 thru '82
*80035 944 all models incl. Turbo '83 thru '89

RENAULT
Alliance, Encore - see AMC (14020)

SAAB
*84010 900 including Turbo '79 thru '88

SATURN
*87010 Saturn all models '91 thru '96

SUBARU
89002 1100, 1300, 1400 & 1600 '71 thru '79
*89003 1600 & 1800 2WD & 4WD '80 thru '94

SUZUKI
*90010 Samurai/Sidekick/Geo Tracker '86 thru '96

TOYOTA
92005 Camry all models '83 thru '91
*92006 Camry all models '92 thru '96
92015 Celica Rear Wheel Drive '71 thru '85
*92020 Celica Front Wheel Drive '86 thru '93
92025 Celica Supra all models '79 thru '92
92030 Corolla all models '75 thru '79
92032 Corolla rear wheel drive models '80 thru '87
*92035 Corolla front wheel drive models '84 thru '92
*92036 Corolla & Geo Prizm '93 thru '97
92040 Corolla Tercel all models '80 thru '82
92045 Corona all models '74 thru '82
92050 Cressida all models '78 thru '82
92055 Land Cruiser Series FJ40, 43, 45 & 55 '68 thru '82
*92056 Land Cruiser Series FJ60, 62, 80 & FZJ80 '68 thru '82
92065 MR2 all models '85 thru '87
92070 Pick-up all models '69 thru '78
*92075 Pick-up all models '79 thru '95
*92076 Tacoma '95 thru '98, 4Runner '96 thru '98, T100 '93 thru '98
*92080 Previa all models '91 thru '95
92085 Tercel all models '87 thru '94

TRIUMPH
94007 Spitfire all models '62 thru '81
94010 TR7 all models '75 thru '81

VW
96008 Beetle & Karmann Ghia '54 thru '79
96012 Dasher all gasoline models '74 thru '81
*96016 Rabbit, Jetta, Scirocco, & Pick-up gas models '74 thru '91 & Convertible '80 thru '92
*96017 Golf & Jetta '93 thru '97
96020 Rabbit, Jetta, Pick-up diesel '77 thru '84
96030 Transporter 1600 all models '68 thru '79
96035 Transporter 1700, 1800, 2000 '72 thru '79
96040 Type 3 1500 & 1600 '63 thru '73
96045 Vanagon air-cooled models '80 thru '83

VOLVO
97010 120, 130 Series & 1800 Sports '61 thru '73
97015 140 Series all models '66 thru '74
*97020 240 Series all models '76 thru '93
97025 260 Series all models '75 thru '82
*97040 740 & 760 Series all models '82 thru '88

TECHBOOK MANUALS
10205 Automotive Computer Codes
10210 Automotive Emissions Control Manual
10215 Fuel Injection Manual, 1978 thru 1985
10220 Fuel Injection Manual, 1986 thru 1996
10225 Holley Carburetor Manual
10230 Rochester Carburetor Manual
10240 Weber/Zenith/Stromberg/SU Carburetor
10305 Chevrolet Engine Overhaul Manual
10310 Chrysler Engine Overhaul Manual
10320 Ford Engine Overhaul Manual
10330 GM and Ford Diesel Engine Repair
10340 Small Engine Repair Manual
10345 Suspension, Steering & Driveline
10355 Ford Automatic Transmission Overhaul
10360 GM Automatic Transmission Overhaul
10405 Automotive Body Repair & Painting
10410 Automotive Brake Manual
10415 Automotive Detailing Manual
10420 Automotive Eelectrical Manual
10425 Automotive Heating & Air Conditioning
10430 Automotive Reference Dictionary
10435 Automotive Tools Manual
10440 Used Car Buying Guide
10445 Welding Manual
10450 ATV Basics

SPANISH MANUALS
98903 Reparación de Carrocería & Pintura
98905 Códigos Automotrices de la Computadora
98910 Frenos Automotriz
98915 Inyección de Combustible 1986 al 1994
99040 Chevrolet & GMC Camionetas '67 al '87
99041 Chevrolet & GMC Camionetas '88 al '95
99042 Chevrolet Camionetas Cerradas '68 al '95
99055 Dodge Caravan/Ply. Voyager '84 al '95
99075 Ford Camionetas y Bronco '80 al '94
99077 Ford Camionetas Cerradas '69 al '91
99083 Ford Modelos de Tamaño Grande '75 al '87
99088 Ford Modelos de Tamaño Mediano '75 al '86
99091 Ford Taurus & Mercury Sable '75 al '86
99095 GM Modelos de Tamaño Grande '70 al '90
99100 GM Modelos de Tamaño Mediano '70 al '88
99110 Nissan Camionetas '80 al '96, Pathfinder '87 al '95
99118 Nissan Sentra '82 al '94
99125 Toyota Camionetas y 4-Runner '79 al '95

Nearly 100 Haynes motorcycle manuals also available

5-98

Listings shown with an asterisk (*) indicate model coverage as of this printing. These titles will be periodically updated to include later model years - consult your Haynes dealer for more information.

Haynes North America, Inc., 861 Lawrence Drive, Newbury Park, CA 91320 • (805) 498-6703